ORGANIZATIONAL BEHAVIOR

The Challenges of the New Millennium

Meshack M. Sagini

D0107769

University Press of America,® Inc.
Lanham · New York · Oxford

Copyright © 2001 by
University Press of America,® Inc.
4720 Boston Way
Lanham, Maryland 20706

12 Hid's Copse Rd.
Cumnor Hill, Oxford OX2 9JJ

Library of Congress Cataloging-in-Publication Data

Sagini, Meshack M.
Organizational behavior : the challenges of the
new millennium / Meshack M. Sagini.
p.   cm
Includes bibliographical references and index.
1. Organizational behavior. 2. Management. I. Title.
HD58.7 .S234 2001   658.4'06—dc21   2001034771 CIP

ISBN 0-7618-2075-2 (cloth : alk. paper)
ISBN 0-7618-2076-0 (pbk. : alk. paper)

This scholarly work is dedicated to Rachel M. Nyabate, my wife, and our four children – Paul, Dennis, Eileen, and Kathy.

Contents

Section One: Theoretical Base of Organization

List of Figures

List of Tables

Abbreviations

A&M   Agricultural and Mechanical
ABC   Atanasoff-Berry Computer
ACE   Automatic Computer Engine
ABCD See Appendix
ACLU   American Civil Liberties Union
ACPs   African, Caribbean, and Pacific Countries
ADVAC Electronic Digital Computer
APEC   Asian Pacific Economic Cooperation
ARPANET Advanced Research Projects Agency Network
CAD   Computer-Aided Design
CAM   Computer-Aided Manufacturing System
CCM   Chama cha Mapinduzi, i.e., Revolutionary Political Party of Tanzania
CDA   Communications Decency Act
COBOL Common Business-Oriented Language
DEC   Digital Equipment Corporation
DRC   Democratic Republic of Congo
DSS   Decision Support Systems
ENIAC Electronic Numerical Integration and Computer
EU   European Union
FDI   Direct Foreign Investment
FDR   Franklin Delano Roosevelt
GATT   General Agreement on Trade and Tariffs (WTO)

HBCU	Historically Black Colleges and Universities
IBM	International Business Machines
IDL	International Division of Labor
IMF	International Monetary Fund
IR	International Relations
KGB	Russian counterpart for CIA, i.e., Central Intelligence Agency
MBO	Management By Objectives
MIT	Massachusetts Institute of Technology
MITI	Ministry of International Trade and Industry
MITS	Micro Instrumentation Telemetry Systems
MPA	Masters of Public Administration
NAFTA	North American Free Trade Agreement
NAPS	Network Access Points
NASA	National Aeronautics and Space Administration
NASPAA	National Association of Schools of Public Affairs Administration
NATO	North Atlantic Treaty Organization
NGOs	Non-Governmental Organizations
NIDL	New International Division of Labor
NPR	National Performance Review
NTG	Normal Group Technique
NWIO	New World Information Order
OCR	Reading Optical Characters
OECD	Organization for Economic Cooperation and Development
OPEC	Organization of Petroleum Exporting Countries
OSU	Oklahoma State University
PACs	Political Action Committees
PCs	Personal Computers
PET	Position Emission Tomography
POSDCORB	Planning, Organizing, Staffing, Directing, Coordinating, Reporting, and Budgeting
PTA	Parents Teachers Association
RAND	Research and Development
RSFSR	Russian Soviet Federated Socialist Republic
SRB	Solid Rocket Booster
TCP	Transmission Control Protocol
MIS	Management Information System
TQM	Total Quality Management
TVA	Tennessee Valley Authority
UK	United Kingdom

UNCTAD United Nations Cultural, Trade, and Development
UNESCO United Nations Educational, Scientific, and Cultural
      Organization
UNIVAC Universal Automatic Computer
UNO   United Nations Organization
USA   United States of America
USSR   Union of Soviet Socialist Republics
VDL   Vertical Dyad Linkage
VRML Virtual Reality Modeling Language
WTO   World Trade Organization
YMCA Young Men Christian Association

Foreword

The academic disciplines of organizational theory and organizational behavior define the study and practice of management. Professor Sagini has marvelously defined both fields of the organization in a single book. The book will prove invaluable to students (new and old) of management in four important ways.

First, the book is an excellent example of academic scholarship; it is thoroughly researched and grounded in literature. The literature reviewed and cited is exhaustive. Professor Sagini draws from a rich variety of theoretical models and intellectual traditions. Moreover, unlike most current organizational theory/behavior books, the discussion is placed in a historical and comparative context. The historical perspective adds depth and insight to the study of organizations. The comparative perspective adds breadth to the analysis and moves us beyond the confines of the U.S. management model.

Second, the book is comprehensive in nature. All of the traditional topics associated with organizational structure and organizational processes, such as bureaucracy, open systems analysis, communications, and decision making, are covered. In addition, the "new" theories and management models are introduced and explained. For example, Professor Sagini discusses contemporary topics such as organizational diversity, organizational culture, and organizational technology. This discussion places the study of management in a dynamic, synergistic, and fluid environment. An environment in which organizations are constantly being "reinvented" and "reengineered."

Third, the book is unique in its scope and examples used to illustrate key theoretical themes and concepts. For example, to illustrate concepts associated with organizational goals, Professor Sagini discusses the mission of Langston University, his home academic institution. The chapter brings life to the narrative discussion presented in previous chapters and allows students to capture the "real world" of management. The book is also unique in that it systematically and comprehensively analyzes the section on political economy and organizational behavior. The three chapters devoted to this topic are among the most interesting in the book and allow the reader to truly understand the concepts of open systems analysis and the "new globalism" so often discussed in the popular media.

Finally, in the last chapter of the book, Professor Sagini offers an insightful comparative and deconstructive critique of the traditional management paradigm. This chapter moves beyond the traditional concluding summary found in most books and literally forces the reader to understand more fully what will be required for organizations in the third millennium to be successful—greater organizational humanism.

For you who want to better understand organizational theory and behavior—whether as a student, a teacher, or a practitioner in the public sector or corporate sector—this book is for you. Professor Sagini, thank you for your hard work and excellent product.

Robert E. England
Department of Political Science
Oklahoma State University

Preface

Organization behavior is a unified collection of philosophical and empirical ideas or body of thinking and literary knowledge about how to productively organize by using theories, processes, structures, principles and people as resources in a given setting. Data generation for the construction of this book originated with the ideas of eminent and scholarly social and behavioral scientists and management scholars whose inquiry, thoughts, and practice have inspired the discipline. These scholars affirm that organization behavior is the study of the evolutionary theory, structure, processes and behavioral paradigms. Historically, organization behavior is as old as the evolution of ancient social organizations. Throughout history, the evolutionary development and adaptation of the organization has been influenced by the increasingly ceaseless growth of knowledge in technology, leadership theory, communication, strategy, motivation, cultural diversity and decision making and control.

In spite of its rich heterogeneity in terms of the contributions of political scientists, psychologists, economists, philosophers, historians, sociologists, educationists, and management theorists and practitioners, the science of organization behavior has recently been animated by the bourgeois spirit inherent in the synergistic evolution of the professional, social, humanistic, and management disciplines. The scholarly and scientific theorists have collected information on organizational behavior and distilled theories concerning how organizations function, the roles of managers, employees, workers, and the strategic importance of managing these organizations. Their work has essentially been theoretical because they have tried to discover and "invent" certain generalizations that are applicable to organizations in general and how these organizations evolve, differ, and change. Above all, these old assumptions and theories have influenced and will continue to influence unique and specific organizations, common organizations and adaptively redesigned organizations.

This book is immensely valuable because it paradigmatically speaks about the traditional functionalist approach to organizational behavior by radically proposing a new paradigm. The functionalist paradigm is comparatively assessed in the light of the new ecocentric paradigm of organization theory and practice. Syncretically, the comparative and interpretive analysis of both paradigms which guide and will guide organizational practice will hopefully and deconstructively evolve a postmodern organization perspective reflective of the social, ethnic, and global representativeness, inclusiveness, and uniqueness which are mandatorily required in the race for ecologically ecocentric and global sustainability. Finally, the interdisciplinary character of the book shows how and why traditional, functionalistic and mechanistic organizational theory is increasingly becoming less and less competitive in its application in the face of synergistically projected ecocentric, global and humanistic postmodernism. In other words, the "archaic antiquity" of mechanistic and functionalistic organizational paradigms should either be abandoned for better models or synergistically adapted to new conditions and circumstances that will enable it to become the base for dynamic organizational change. Such a form of dynamic organizational change will fill the vacuum for its competitive and more rational scientific claim.

In addition, since a book of this kind of ambitious and theoretical analysis of the discipline hardly exists in the academic market place, its production will fill the current vacuum in global organizational theory. This thinking, it is hoped, will animate and guide organizational behavior and practice of the twenty-first century and beyond. The other major characteristic of this work is its historical and comparative deep-rootedness of organizational theory whose recency in emancipatory and evolutionary development of the global community compliments organizational behavior.

Organization of the Book

This theoretical and multidisciplinary book has been designed to meet the unique needs of literate citizens, students, scholars, policymakers, trainers, and consultants in all societies. It has a global bias which makes it more analytically and theoretically inclusive, interesting and appealing. Such a multicentric theoretical design will, hopefully, make it an excellent current and special resource for the twenty-first century and beyond. The book has 18 chapters, excluding the main conclusion. As an incentive element of its creativity, six constructed case studies, seventeen figures and seven tables have been included for illustrative reasons.

Section One consists of three major chapter perspectives which are organizational paradigms. These three paradigmatic models are the rational, behavioral, and open systems theories. The models are rich theoretical explanation and analytical comparisons from which coherent traditions of research and praxis are advanced and referenced. In this section, the three models are viewed as a form of intellectual consciousness which give organizations their morphology, evolution, and esoteric and living conscience.

Section Two concerns organizational structure. The chapters of this section include organizational goals, organizational structure, organizational diversity, and organizational culture. In its entirety, organizational structure views the organization as logically constructed elements of physical, structural, normative, and ecological hierarchy that is purposed to effectively accomplish its mission. The section is also seen as the base upon which the ecosystem symbiotically interacts to enhance ecological balance, creative productivity, and universal sustainability.

Section Three is about organizational processes. The major organizational processes the book addresses are seven, namely organizational leadership, organizational communication, organizational decision making, organizational technology, organizational work motivation, organizational control, and organizational change. Organizational processes are forward looking, sequentially organized and step by step procedures, ways, techniques, and hierarchically constructed belief systems and activities that are collectively activated to serve as the "engine" of productivity and performance.

Section Four views the organization as a political economy rather than an insular construct. This section has three chapters that discuss political economy and its effects on nations and organizations, African political economy and its global context and organizational development and forces of migration in Africa and elsewhere. This section shows that political economy is hierarchically stratified and universally hegemonic system of international dependence. The system is held together by exchange contracts between legally independent property owners. The property owners have rights that are constitutionally enshrined. Theoretically, political economy can be explained in the light classical, radical, and neoclassical economic theories of the state. Above all, political economy is the regulation of the dialectical relationships between and among independent property owners of whom organizational owners, managers, and employees are a replica.

Finally, the last chapter is chapter 19. The chapter is a metaphoric summary of the entire text. The chapter underscores the traditional management paradigm because it is less humanistic, less competitive, and a more risky operation. At the backdrop of the traditional management paradigm, this author has tried to advance the more humanistic, competitive, and less risky but elegant theory which is economically sustainable, humanistically postmodern, globally appealing and universally relevant, interesting and inclusive.

Acknowledgments

A work of this magnitude could not have come to fruition without tremendous personal indebtedness to others who sacrificed their time, energy and intellect for its accomplishment. First, Dr. D. Chongo Mundende, Director of the Policy Research and Analysis Center at Langston University assisted in the typing of the manuscript, making it camera ready. Second, Dr. Bob England, Professor of Political Science at Oklahoma State University, critiqued the document constructively by offering instrumental and literary suggestions. He also graciously agreed to write the foreword for the book. Third, Dr. Thomas E. Patterson, Bradlee Professor of Government and the Press and Chair of the John F. Kennedy School of Government at Harvard University, provided constructive and scholarly critique by appraising the manuscript. Fourth, Langston University which allowed me to use Title III funds for faculty improvement whenever Dr. Darlene Abram, Dean of the School of Education and Behavioral Sciences, Dr. Clyde Montgomery, Dean of the School of Arts and Sciences and Associate Vice President for Academic Affairs, and Dr. Jean Bell Manning, Vice President for Academic Affairs, who authorized the issuance of resources for attending professional conferences at which some of the chapters were initially presented.

Meshack M. Sagini
December 2000

Chapter 1

What Is Organization Theory as Behavior?

A theory is a system of ideas and concepts designed to set forth and interrelate concepts and facts in such a way that they summarize existing knowledge used for further observations within an organization, discipline, or elsewhere. If theory is scientific, the function of such a theory is to validate, predict, control, or explain human behavior in a scientific or natural way (Coon, 1989). Such a scientific and organizational or social theory could be falsifiable (Popper, 1957). The falsifiability of a scientific theory is reflective of its ability to be used to examine trends as opposed to laws. Scientific theory is canonized by the use of scientific instrumentation (methods of data collection). These methods or techniques, are forms of scientific and philosophical rationality.

Organizations use scientific theory to bring about change. For instance, a few systematic efforts have been used in different scientific specialties to demonstrate how change takes place in organizations.

> Such specialties are viewed here as organizations in which workers deal with various degrees of task uncertainty and mutual dependence. The sociological theory of change suggests that scientific change is generally triggered by competition, but that various types of change depend on the

social organization and status of scientific groups. Some fields change through permanent discoveries, some through specialization and cumulation, yet others change through cognitive fragmentation (Fuchs, 1993, p. 933), and others love the status quo.

Given this reality, organizations change or develop, or advance when some of their brightest minds make discoveries or inventions that are used to empower these organizations. To invent or make great discoveries requires the maximum use of efforts of professional specialists and cumulative expertise in a variety of disciplines. In one way then, organizations are definable as resource pools (Buchanan, 1977). They evolve when individuals place the resources in them, which evolutionary organizations use. These resources include technology, skills, money, prestige, central control or management, and time.

Organizations use rules that are based on either autocratic-hierarchical principle or on cooperative-democratic approaches. In the first, one person assumes the role of being a central coordinator in the management of distribution of rewards and punishments, in decision making, and in designing and structuring organizational operations. In the second, all members participate equally to coordinate tasks and distribute time for decision making. Thirdly, most organizations fall somewhere between these two extremes.

Rules are formalized and enforced for the purpose of assigning tasks to jobs. They specify how tasks will be done. They determine the decisions a jobholder is allowed to make and to whom he is allowed to give orders. The rules control the process of recruitment, training, hiring, promotion, tenure, renumeration, production, and dismissal. All formalized organizational rules consist of the organizational structure of values, beliefs, and practices which dictate the ways in which individual skills and technology are used to realize organizational goals.

Scientific theory has been used in social organizations from time immemorial. The first organization theory was written by an Egyptian, Ptah-hotep who "wrote the first known guide on running an organization on papyrus in 2700 BC." With the emergence of modern industrialization, professional practitioners have tried to encapsulate effective organizational solutions. Effective organizational solutions have enhanced good business practice in these organizations. Some of the modern classical leaders who designed organizational principles were Ure and Babbage in England (1835), Fayol and Taylor of the United States (1903 and 1911). Taylor wrote and applied scientific management theory which applied experimental engineering methods to such problems as assigning tasks to jobs, standardization of work, optimizing work tools and work flows and selecting workers. Though Taylor's theory of scientific management is still basically used, the functionalistic and logically exploitative aspects of this theory have made it less emancipatory, less humanistic, less postmodern and less competitive because work (production) in itself, which this theory emphasized, failed to motivate the worker unless other incentives like motivation, benefits, and privileges were employed.

Theoretically, design problems such as choosing between functional, divisional, or matrix organizational structures for determining the number of departments or selecting coordination systems continue to defy attempts to quantify and optimize. The type of decision support which management can expect to use for the solution of organizational problems requires that they use the decision alternatives by empirically weighing the pros and cons of the relevant case studies (Nystrom and Starbuck, 1981). Organizational theory studies are more profoundly analyzed in the field of organizational sociology which includes administration, bureaucracy, cartels, trade associations, cooperatives, interest groups, international organizations, labor unions, medical care, political parties, penology, social movements, voluntary associations, and industrial organizations (Sills, 1968). Distinguished academics of this field (organizational sociology) include Banard, Mayo, Michels, Max, and Weber.

Both social sciences and behavioral sciences can be used to study organizational theory especially organizational behavior. The social science disciplines, according to the Ford Foundation definition, consists of anthropology, economics, political science, sociology, most of psychology, history, and statistics. Likewise, the disciplines of behavioral sciences include sociology, anthropology without archeology, technical linguistics, physical anthropology, psychology without its physiological counterpart, behavioral biology, economics, geography, law, psychiatry, and political science. Extensions of social and behavioral sciences can be found in other disciplines of the academy. With the funding from Ford Foundation, these disciplines were analytically structured and systematized to mean "behavioral sciences" during the early 1950s. The main purpose for their structural systematization was to programmatically construct a credible intellectual and theoretical reservoir for "the establishment of peace, the strengthening of democracy, the strengthening of the economy" and "education in a democratic society, and individual behavior and human relations" (Sills, 1968, p. 42). Through the study of both the social sciences and the behavioral sciences, theories of organizations can be constructed and rationalized. Evidently, human relations theory has not been, for sometime, and for obvious reasons, part and parcel of the behavioral sciences movement. In such organizations, it can be hypothesized that the unavailability/availability of particular technologies influences the way organizations can pursue new opportunities for solving problems and reaching goals. The same technologies may breed risk, uncertainty, control and destabilization within interorganizational relations (Nelson and Cooperman, 1998). Therefore, although the traditional industrial organizational paradigm is being replaced by the postmodern and postindustrial organizational paradigm, the latter is not without same serious risks either. The new paradigm, as discussed in the conclusion, could be a portrayal of technologically based and differentially and inherently crisis-prone organizational exceptionalism.

Major Organizational Theories

An organization exists when procedures are laid down in order to coordinate the activities of a group whose interest is to achieve specific goals and objectives. The collective efforts of people get formally organized because the people have some common interests or because a leading subgroup has furnished inducements to the rest to work on behalf of its interest. For instance, factory workers organize themselves into unions to bargain collectively with management. Alternatively, management organizes workers' tasks for the purpose of producing marketable products for service or profit. Some of the formal organizations we know of include unions, factories, churches, government bureaus, political parties, armies, hospitals, and academia. In capitalist societies communities and individuals that belong to the formally established organizations do compete. Individuals and communities that support these organizations enter into competitive exchange relations and use their resources to establish social structures whose members acquire power to control others.

The social structures are deliberately established to achieve certain objectives. The observable regularities of these structures tend and strife to achieve certain objectives for which the former are designed. According to Sumner, such social systems which are formed through formally crescive and enacted procedures, rather than merely emergent forces, are called organizations. Analytically, crescive and enacted forces interact to have effect on social systems. The crescivity and enactment of organizations distinguish them from other social collectivities. What makes the organizational collectivities of scientific interest is their evolutionary social structures which do not coincide with their pre-established forms.

Organizations are collectivities, quasi-markets, political economies, and products of ecological populations (Scott, 1981). They are also, in spite of their complexity and diversity, open, rational, and natural systems. A rational system is theoretically grounded on classical, traditional, the scientific management, and Weberian or bureaucratic presuppositions. In an esoteric sense, rationality is a technical and functional proposition. It refers to a series of actions that are organized in such a way as to result in predetermined goals with maximum efficiency.

Efficiency is the amount of resources (in terms of minimum cost) used to reach goals on time. Other than goal specificity, a rational system is formalized or officially structured to function and succeed. Each person or substructure performs prescribed roles that are culturally definable as duties, rights, or obligations. While a formalized, rational, and open system tend to objectify structure, so that roles and relationships can be viewed objectively and "external to the participating actors" (p. 61), the informal aspect of this structure tends to socially restructure the same functions and actions sociometrically. The sociometric structure of the formal informality facilitates effective ties among participants. In such a setting, tensions, hostilities, and anxieties are reduced. Friendships are enhanced, relationships are harmonized, and differences are psychologically ironed out because participants see themselves as an ideologically and functionally collective entity working for specific goals. Given this collective realization by the group and its leaders, potentially conflicting or potentially disruptive, or potentially dysfunctional organizational forces are identified, orchestrated, and suppressed or creatively controlled to enhance productivity. Affirmatively, group cohesion and organizational goals are harmonized to enhance individual creativity and organizational innovation. In doing so, the competition of hostile and conflicting interests is professionally managed in such a way that major future problems are eliminated for the realization of the organizational mission.

Rationally, the behavior of the organization is seen as actions performed purposefully and coordinatedly by its agents. Linguistically, the rational system employs terms like "information, efficiency, optimization, implementation and design" (p. 58). Cognitively, rationality is limited in terms of capability to make sound decisions that influence the organizational context. Such limitations are inherently common in organizations and hence – "constraints, authority, rules, directives, jurisdiction performance, programs, coordination" (p. 258). There are three major classical and mechanistic schools through which organizational theory of rationality is articulated. These schools include Taylorism, (scientific management), Administrative behavior, and Weberian bureaucratic theory. Each school will be discussed individually. Further details on these schools will be explained in later chapters. These three schools represent the first of the four major theoretical and classical perspectives of organizational theory.

The first perspective is the rational system which comprises of the classical, the traditional, the scientific management and Weberian blueprints. The second perspective is the natural or behavioral perspective which includes the human relations and organizational humanism. The third major perspective includes open and general systems theories and design, environmental approaches (strategic planning) and contingency theories. The fourth and most recent postmodern and post-structural perspective is the multicultural organization whose global and cultural imperatives tend to be appealing in sociotechnical, ecological and universalistic ways. In their evolutionary development, they may have eclectically and synergistically been responsible for the future fifth theory which will try to explain and rationalize high technology and the imperative for its "futuristicism."

From the beginning, Americans were and remained stateless (Stillman, 1991) for a considerable period. The absence of the state, or rather, the relatively weak state in American public administration was a reflection that American political and public officials did not want to emulate the rigid, compartmentalized, efficient and bloated Eurocentric bureaucratic traditions. The absence of the state during the era of settlement (17th century) and the subsequent statelessness at federal level during the era of the Articles of Confederation's constitutionalism helped to establish a historical and political legacy of statelessness in American public administration circles. Absence of the state in the constitution made politics and administration the same rather than different fields in theory and practice. The first attempt to introduce a radical departure from this malaise was 1887 when Wilson, the Ph.D. scholar from Princeton had his first essay on public administration published. Wilson believed that politics and public administration needed to be separated in order to run an efficient administration, which exercised economy, autonomy, accountability and reason.

Like Wilson, Taylor introduced the scientific management theory of economy and efficiency in 1880s. He believed that efficiency promoted productivity rather than profit. The purpose of a public administrator is to make efficient decisions which enable the government and the bureaus in particular to run their respective agencies effectively. Mosher supported Taylor and Wilson.

The Wilsonian and Taylorist models of administration were classical because the men were pioneers. They were rigid and rationally mechanistic because they dealt with structures rather than processes of bureaucratic millieux. At that time, mechanistic rationality was the only one best way used in both public and private organizations. Other "best" ways were irrelevant, unthinkable and at least for some decades, undesignable.

During the 1920s and 1930s, Gulick constructed POSDCORB, an acronym for Planning, Organizing, Staffing, Directing, Coordinating, Reporting, and Budgeting. White and the Brownlow Commission supported Gulick's model. The purpose of constructing it was not only to improve public administration during the progressive era, when votes were exchanged for citizenship and when the upper middle classes were initiating reforms, but it was also the New Deal Age when FDR's search for new models to improve economic and political management was at stake. The Great Depression was severe. Both laissez-faire and Keynesianism complemented POSTCORD in the struggle to eliminate poverty, hopelessness, and inefficiency by increasing accountability, administrative efficiency and responsibility of bureaus.

The emergence of new models that were created by Simon and ratified by Waldo and Appleby was a historic and revolutionary break away from Wilsonian and Taylorist orthodoxy. Simon created and introduced the new school of thought called the open systems theory. He argued that efficient and effective public administration should not rely on "one best" way but on many because the supranational system is characterized by complexity. Bounded rationality or heterodoxy in decision making is better than the one best way. Decisions are made rationally by using the logical positivist tradition. This tradition is based on scientific observation. Scientific methods are used to collect data and facts rather than values. Data are analyzed to get the best ideas and information from various groups, structures and organizations. Simon's approach is not only multicephalous, morphogenetic, morphostatic, but also equifinal. This behaviorist and informal approach to problem solving in organizations was the impetus for the evolution of more models like those which evolved in the 1960s, 1970s and 1980s. For instance, McGregor's Theory X and Y contrast each other in terms how people behave at work. Theory X indicates that they work because they are unmotivated. Theory Y means that people are motivated to work and are not necessarily supervised. They are self-directed.

Theory Z is a 1981 Japanese cultural model of Ouchi that places emphasis in teamwork and participatory management. The pillars of Theory Z of which the Japanese use techroculture to be managerially competitive and productively superior are trust, subtlety, and intimacy.

Other theories that have evolved from Simon's open systems theory are the Darwinian theory which sees overall populations as an organization, Maslow's emancipatory and humanistic theory of needs which indicates that basic needs have to be satisfied first before higher level ones are in order for the person or system to self-actualize. The human relations theory of Mayo which predates Simon's open systems helps the informal organization to understand human nature, feelings, attitudes, and emotions in order to effectively manage them for the productivity of the organization.

Open systems theory emphasizes interdependence between the bureaus and the environment which is governed by legislative, judicial and executive authority. Interdependence allows the effective flow of resources, energy and information to be used as inputs that can be transformed into outputs in terms of goods, services and wastes.

In spite of the apparent "statelessness" of the American public administration system, the evolutionary and historic management techniques have enabled the system to function imperfectly but dynamically. The current power of the state rests on the strength of the trinity of globalism, technology and technocracy (Stillman, 1991).

What is an organization which theory rationalizes? An organization is a social, contextual and cultural reproduction of the larger society – the social system. It exists as a means that receives and intellectually integrates human needs while transforming the values, norms and traditions of the past. Organizations may dangerously articulate stricture rather than structure. Unlike institutions which are more abstract, organizations are more concrete structural entities which regulate the social system(s). During periods of uncertainty, institutional and organizational resources can be harnessed in search of their interdependent relationship with the larger social system(s). Unlike organizations, institutions do not change quickly or regularly. At times, social forces which pressure institutions to change end up making them to have "a hard institutional core, a rigidity, as a defense against conflicting ideas" (Alfonso, Firth, and Neville, 1981 [1975], p. 55). Social institutions are products of tradition. Whenever change occurs, it does occur in organizations which constitute institutional values at large. Therefore, as "institutional commitments change, organizational goals, structures and procedures are vulnerable and subject to pressures for change" (p. 55).

According to Dubin's (1965) anthropological observation, the relationship between cultural order and organizational productivity is concrete. This concreteness or deterministic reality places emphasis on cultural determinism of working and productive behaviors by its attention to "the kinds of pursuits that engage human energies for the production of goods and services, and…the particular working behaviors that produce the goods and services. Working behaviors in a society are determined by the culture which characterizes that society" (Alfonso, Firth, and Neville, 1981, p. 55)

Though Dubin's explanation is rooted in cultural anthropology and Darwinian evolutionism, it could have embraced humanistic instincts as a force of production and productivity too. For many centuries of the evolutionary development of society, the major difficulty of any science has been the inability to identify the sources of change. The recency of the social sciences in the constellation of the academic disciplines and the intellectual limitations of the human species have been a great barrier to human knowledgeability about the sources of change. Traditional academic intellectuals thought that the sources of change were also the sources of power – i.e.,

> the personal will of kings, lawgivers, and prophets, those who governed states, drafted laws, and established or reinforced religious beliefs … gradually did men realize that behind these visible sets of acts were such intangible nets as customs, institutions, and cultures which subtly constrained and set the boundaries of social action. At the same time … social forces which generated change, whether they be impersonal processes such as demographic pressures, technology, and science, or conscious striving such as the demands of disadvantaged groups for equality or social mobility (Bell, 1964, p. 846).

In brief, if change is what is important in the organization, then the nature of the organization's management system will be determined by both the larger sociocultural system and the organization's production technology. Historically speaking, some of the prominent organizational philosophical scholars who caused change were "Aristotle, Ibn-Khaldun, Thucydides, Caesar, Marsilius, Aquinas, and Bentham" (March, 1965, p. ix) and Jesus. Three modern organizational scholars (Talcott Parsons, Etzioni and Gross) have given respective scholarly definitions of the term organization. The Parsonian conceptual definition indicates that:

An organization is a system which, as the attainment of its goal 'produces' an identifiable something which can be utilized in some way by another system; that is, the output of the organization with economic primacy, this output may be a class of goods or services which are either consumable or serve as instruments for a further phase of the production process by other organizations. In the case of a government agency the output may be a class of regulatory decisions; in that of an educational organization it may be a certain type of 'trained capacity' on the part of the students who have been subjected to its influence (Parsons, 1965, pp. 63-85).

In other words, an organization is ecologically, functionally and normatively interdependent with other organizations in the social system in terms of means – ends continuum or process, input, and output and substantive value. To be more specific, and as Barnard correctly hypothesized, an organization is a cooperative system that is characterized by complex "physical, biological, personal, and social components which are in a specific systematic relationship by reason of the cooperation of two or more persons for at least one definite end" (Barnard, 1938, p. 65). Gaus (1936) commented that an organization is a structure which facilitates and accomplishes a predetermined purpose through the utilization of functions and responsibilities.

Amitai Etzioni's definition of an organization is normative, exclusionary and reconstructively constructive. Specifically, Etzioni said that

> Organizations are social units (or human groupings) deliberately constructed and reconstructed to seek specific goals. Corporations, armies, schools, hospitals, churches, and prisons are included; tribes, classes, ethnic groups, friendship groups, and families are excluded. Organizations are characterized by: (a) divisions of labor, power, and communication responsibilities, divisions which are not random or traditionally patterned, but deliberately planned to enhance the realization of specific goals; (b) the presence of one or more power centers which control the concerned efforts of the organization and direct them toward its goals; these power centers also must review continuously the organization's performance and repattern its structure, where necessary, to increase its efficiency; (c) substitution of personnel, i.e., unsatisfactory persons can be removed and others assigned their tasks. The organization can also recombine its personnel through transfer and promotion (Etzioni, 1964, p. 3).

Etzioni's exclusion of classes and groups is grounded on the extent of their membership which is organized in terms of structure, management, and restructuration of their subsystem. In other words, Etzioni's definition articulates the attributes of the formal rather than the informal organization because the formal organization is more conscious of its nature, destiny and challenges.

The formal organization which Etzioni dealt with is consciously coordinated in such a way that its productivity, which is a product of its activities, results in identifiable goals. In this organization, individual behavior and contributions are elements of empowerment of both the smaller (organization) and larger (society) system. Above all, the real state for organization should reflect or portray the synergistic wholism of purpose, knowledge, skill, production requirements e.g., equipment and technology, and emotional and psychological commitment.

According to Gross (1964) who has written about organizations from a positivist perspective, formal organizations are group, or teamwork, or cooperative subsystems. These subsystems are characterized by an accepted scheme of purposes, a sense of belonging and identification, regular and continuous interaction of members, differential differentiation of functions (roles) and conscious but spontaneous integration of organizational members.

In terms of cognitive psychology and scientific philosophy of mind, the term organization, like any other words, is a concept. Concepts, their meanings, and lexical representations are basic constituents of thought and belief. The centrality of concepts in the intelligible world is rooted in 'cognitive economy' (Rosch, 1978) of classes that decreases or that inductively influence the volume of information which we should or must "perceive, learn, remember, communicate, and reason about" (Smith, 1989, p. 501).

Public Agencies (Bureaus)

This chapter is largely about organizational theory in public rather than private organizations. The chapter as well as the text it introduces is couched in interdisciplinary and multidisciplinary perspectives (Gortner, et al., 1997). This interdisciplinary multiplicity is multitheoretical. The multitheoreticalism places emphasis concerning the utilization of public agencies or bureaus, on the "demands of constituencies and clients rather than on markets, suppliers and customers" (p. 1) which relate to private agencies. Such theoretical understanding of public organizations creates avenues for "designing organizational structures, communication networks, control systems"

(p. 1) and legal requirements whose public mission influences how power, authority and leadership are to be behavioristically exercised. Above all, the sources of organizational ethos, commitment, and motivation affect intelligent and decision-making systems of bureaus. What is an organization? An organization is a government agency or private firm. Regardless of its size and interrelatedness, this collectivity uses specialization to create interdependency for accomplishing its major goals-the mission. For the organization to survive, the activities of its members are personalized rather than codified or descriptively ascribed. It uses specialization which is division of labor whose end result is efficiency. Efficient and effective coordination of organizational activities yield high productivity.

With the end of the Cold War, Industrial Revolution, and the "on set" of the high-technology revolution, organizations are changing from their bureaucratic age into the post-bureaucratic age" (p. 2) because the "information age organization, the participative democratic organization, or the learning organization" (p. 2) has emerged. The authors paraphrase Wilson by saying that a person's identity and rank are nurtured by the organization. This person is also affected by biological, social, and educational influences. These people, as Simon (1976) interactively and intercommunicatively argues, are affected by knowledge, beliefs, attention, hopes, wishes, fears and emphatic propositions. While it is important to understand how organizations evolve, their images and ideas help to rationalize their bureaucratic essence in terms of structure, resources, processes, procedures and goals. Public organizations are government agencies whose main purpose is to administer the law. Unlike private organizations which are accountable to owners and boards of directors, bureaus or nonprofit third sector organizations are charged with public oversight and accountability.

Bureaucracy

The term bureaucracy is identified with an organizational structure which it also derides by criticizing it. The German sociologist Max Weber (1947) is the leading exponent of bureaucratic theory. Weber depicted several unique characteristics of "organizational structure and personnel policy that set the bureaucratic institution apart from all others, less neutral, stable, and expert means of administering the law and coordination of the intricate activities of vast numbers of people in a predictable and efficient manner" (p. 4). According to Weber, the bureaucracy is characterized by "the specialization of function; the requirement that the hiring and promotion of officials be based solely on expertise; that authority be exercised through a centralized, hierarchical chain of command; and the development of an intricate system of rules to cover all possible actions and to minimize discretion" (p. 4).

The purpose and motivation of bureaus is not efficiency but greater recognition and support from those who finance them. Because bureaus are marketless, their "existence, growth, motivation, communications, control systems, leadership styles, ... Decision making" demand public approval and accountability (pp. 4-5). Hummel (1994) argues like Weber by saying that the "bureaucracy destroys spontaneity" (p. 5) and thereby becomes a danger to personality development in terms of elimination of human freedom. Since bureaucratic personality is oriented to efficiency, its rationality enhances a mechanistic rather than humanistic orientation to decision making. The "rationalistic expert is incapable of emotion and devoid of will" (p. 5). In addition, Burrell and Morgan (1979) and Denhardt (1981, 1993) have been cited by Gortner and asserted that bureaus are "complex linguistic games," as cultural constructions rather than the objective realities we assume we perceive or as "Psychic Prisons" or instruments of class domination (p. 5).

As it was emphasized earlier, organization theory is theoretical multiplicity and interdisciplinary orientation of a particular field of study including political science and public administration. In other words, organization theory is not the theoretical "unisingularity" of a multitheoretical and interdisciplinary field of study. The "themes, questions, methods, and explanatory modes" (Gortner et al., 1997, p. 5) of the organizational discipline are very diverse. Dwight Waldo (1978) has commented that organization theory is characterized by "vogues, heterogeneity, and claims and counter claims" (Gortner, 1997, p. 5) reflective of the issues, concepts and variables of the social sciences whose theoretical interdisciplinarity define organization theory.

Varieties of Organization Theory

One approach to understanding organization theory is to conceptually view it through three levels. First, varieties of organization theory differ in subject matter or content. Second, their explanatory forms differ as systems analysis, political economy or some other theoretical explanation. Third, as tools of analysis, theories are purposively able to differentiate and are differentiating (Gortner, 1997). In terms of subject matter, organization research and theory can be typologized in terms of theories of individual and group behavior, process (e.g., decision making) and global or overall theories of the organization. The mutual use of these theories makes organizations to function synergistically. In terms of individuals, research on motivation informs that people's "inborn needs, attitudes and perceptions" determine their productivity as the end result of "organizational outputs" (p. 9).In other words, genetics and socialization patterns contribute to human performance.

Research on groups and intergroup relations articulates such topics as "dynamics and effectiveness of work groups or decision-making groups, conflict management, and leadership" (p. 9). At the organization's overall or global level, use of research and speculative theory issues concerning the "reigning values of the organization, relations with outside clients or constituents, motivation, coordination and leadership" (p. 9) are paramount. Concepts of total quality (Walton, 1990), excellent organizations (Peters and Waterman, 1982), theory Z (Ouchi, 1981) and the dialectical organization (White, 1969) are classic theoretical underpinnings of the global organization.

Structurally, research informs the "organization's hierarchy, centralization and decentralization" that "shape the organization chart and its lines of authority, the formation of organization subdivisions, and the coordination of those subdivisions" (Gortner, et al, 1997, p. 9). Finally, organizational processes comprise of basic activities of the organization of which "decision making and policy development, control and communication (key processes in policy making and analysis), budgeting, evaluation, and program implementation" (p. 9) are compellingly significant. All these theories vary in typology and purpose.

A variety of theories are used in the discipline of organizational theory. The major theories that are involved include "systems theory, theories of political economy, public choice theory, theories of group politics and influence, theories of personality and attitude formation, theories of psychological humanism, theories of culture interpretation, and theories of social change" (p. 9) and artificial intelligence or information theory.

Though the selected theories of organization theory are diverse in explanatory power, content and topical focus, these theories shape basic assumptions about the nature of organizations and the purpose of organization theory ... the mainstream theories are empirical diverse, and based on quantitative and qualitative observations. In spite of the lack of "scientific objectivity" (p. 10) of most of these theories, they are effectively used to help organizations uncover reality, predict and control that reality in order to improve organizational functions. How organizations function is the primary interest of organizational owners (administrative professionals, the public, policymakers and practitioners). Given the fact that organizations, particularly the bureaucratic ones, are conceptualizations of phenomenology, which is to say "the divided need for 'high tech and high touch' (Naisbitt, 1982), they tend to be "intentionalist" (p. 11). While some organizations escape bureaucratic systems in search of "charismatic guidance" (p. 11), the intentionalistic organization concentrates on the "intentions and beliefs of workers, and on the perceptions and language that link one human being to another" (p. 11). Public choice is the capitalist economic theory of the market in which theoreticians tend to stress individual self-interest rather than group goals and intentions. For instance;

> The appeal to an internalized sense of public trust may work partially or temporarily, but human egoism will eventually challenge the pattern of strict accountability that the machine model of bureaucracy implies. Bureaucratic actors have interests of their own to advance. Inevitably, these interests will come into conflict, at least to some degree, with the goals of the organization. The temptation of a conflicted employee to sacrifice the group goal for the personal one is likely to be irresistible. Thus, ... if subordinates have any latitude for discretion, they will sooner or later abuse it (Garvey, 1993, p. 29; and Gortner, et al, 1997, p. 11).

Private versus Public Organizations

The rest of this chapter will discuss the differences between public and private organizations and their evolutionary typologies. The chapter uses a comprehensive synthesis in showing how the differences influence the evolution of public organization theory. Blau and Meyer (1993) have shown that private and public organizations are theoretically interdependent and bureaucratically the same. In spite of the more complex differences in their "purposes, structures, ways of doing things, and methods for coordinating activities ... the variations largely (but not exclusively) reflect an organization's adaptation to its environment. Organizations are 'open systems' that are influenced by and have an impact on the world around them" (Shafritz and Ott, 1996).

Organizations and People

In relation to human lives, we are born in, marry in, and die in organizations. The organizations document our history, educate us, employ us, compensate or pay us. They process our foods, manufacture and sell our clothes. They entertain us, defend us in peace and in wartime. These complex creatures are intertwined into our social, economic, political, legal and spiritual fabric. The effective management of organizations (business, academia, hospitals, and political, or military organizations) require that they remain, as open or closed systems, accountable, empowered and malleable (Gortner, 1997).

Literary theory, particularly the work of Rainey, Backoff, and Levine (1976) has been used to summarize a list of propositions about public organizations in comparison with private ones. The comparative analysis of the differences articulates environmental factors of the organization, the environmental transactions of the organizations and the internal structures and processes of the same organizations.

As far as environmental factors are concerned, public organizations are exposed to incentive cost reduction, operating efficiency, and effective performance than private organizations. The tendency for their being less exposed to the market as indicated makes public organizations to experience lower allocation efficiency (reflection of consumer preferences) and proportioning supply to demand. In addition, less market exposure of the public organizations results in lower availability of market indicators and information concerning price, profits, etc. (Gortner, 1997).

The legal, legislative, and bureaucratic machinery of public organizations create mechanisms for administrative efficiency and accountability which may be viewed as "constraints" (p. 20) on procedures and the use of autonomy. However, public organizations are credited and sometimes criticized for the proliferation of many specifications and controls. These agencies are characterized by the availability of more "external sources of formal influence and greater fragmentation" of them (p. 20). The bureaus are politically amenable to diverse and intense external informal influences that seek power to make decisions, bargaining, public opinion, and a variety of interest groups. Since these public agencies serve a variety of client groups from their political constituencies, the bureaus display a greater need for sympathetic understanding and vice versa from formal authorities.

In terms of the organization environment transactions, government agencies are intentionally coercive, and monopolistic due to the fact that they finance and consume mandatory services. In doing so, the public interest (p. 20) is symbolically and widely expressed or articulated, or enhanced. As these agencies are scrutinized for accountability and productivity, officials and the actions they take should affirm them as responsible. Such unique public expectations require that the bureaucracy display "fairness, responsiveness, accountability and honesty" (p. 21).

Internally, the structures and processes of bureaus have complex evaluation and decision making criteria. The aim of the criteria possess a multiplicity of diverse "objectives (p. 21) whose goals are, at times, vague, intangible, and conflicting. In terms of roles of the administrators, they have less autonomy and flexibility in decision making and "weaker, more fragmented authority over subordinates" (p. 21) and other lower ranks of the bureaucratic pyramid. Subordinates can bypass supervisors by appealing to other authorities without the system. Thus, the merit system of bureaus has many constraints as compared to private firms and organizations.

In addition, bureaucrats are reluctant to delegate authority for fear of accountability. They go through a lot of programmatic reviews and a greater variety of formal regulations related to supervisory and delegation of responsibility. Bureaucrats are more politically exposed to interaction mechanisms with top officials or managers. In terms of agency performance, bureaucrats exercise or experience more caution and rigidity but less innovativeness than their counterparts in the private sector. Public officials experience more frequent turnover of top leaders because elections and political appointments tend to disrupt the implementation of plans, strategies, and goals.

The bureaus have complex structures and processes which cause greater difficulty, as compared to the private sector, particularly "in devising incentives for effective and efficient performance" (p. 21). Their employees are not motivated by money than by meritorious service. Because bureaus work in a climate of conformity and legal constraints, employees can be depersonalized and depersonalizable. They are depersonalized because they exercise less freedom, cannot exercise full dominance, flexibility or reach maximum potential" at their own disposal. As a result, bureaucratic employees have "lower work satisfaction and lower organizational commitment" (p. 22) than corporate employees.

Economic Difference: Nature of Bureau's Role and the Market

Since firms exist in a theoretically free market environment, they seek economic opportunity and enhancement. Their objective is to maximize profits through "voluntary exchange transactions" (p. 26). The government plays a supplementary or complementary and regulatory role only. However, if the market (private sector) fails as an allocative device, then this kind of market inefficiency will dictate governmental or political intervention for corrective measures. Although classical market theory indicates that "public and private spheres are not categories of nature, they are categories of history, culture, and law" (Waldo, 1980, p. 164) by which they are ethically and morally sanctioned and constrained.

The line between "public and private" agencies "is not immutable" (Gortner, 1997, p. 27). Since the role of government is not determined only by economic matters, "but by cultural and political" forces also, bureaus are charged with promoting and protecting both cultural and economic values" (p. 27). Because the market is free and competitive, "our governments' economic activities conform, to a large extent, to the role prescribed by market theory" of free and fair competition (p. 27). As a result, economic policies are not adopted due to their desirability as economic theory, "but because of political acceptability, demand, and expediency" (p. 27). In essence, "economic policy is adopted primarily as a means to achieve politically sanctioned ends" (p. 27) of the larger and more complex social system.

Economic versus Political Markets

Bureaus and firms have radical differences in terms of their markets and in terms of their relationship to them. According to Downs (1967), every "producer engages in voluntary transactions with buyers who exchange money for the producers' output. Anthony Downs points out the effects of output markets and shows that those which do not have them are affected. First, output markets provide a built in tool for evaluating "producer can sell his outputs for more than his inputs cost ... his product is valuable to its buyers" (Downs, 1967, p. 29). If the market price does not cover the cost of producing the product, organizationally the output is not valuable enough. Second, output markets are a means of allocating resources among organizations. Also, the third "function of the market is that of producing a standard for evaluating the individual performance of members of organizations" (Gortner, 1997, p. 27).

Bureaus do not have economic output markets. Consequently, "they cannot evaluate the costs of producing their output or its value on the external basis" (p. 28). The bureau's income is not directly related to the services it provides. Hence, the bureau's ability to obtain income in a market cannot serve as an objective guide to the appropriateness of the level of current expenditures. Nor can it aid the bureau in determining how to use the resources it controls, or in appraising the performance of individual bureaucrats. In other words, the standards for decision making used by private firms are unavailable to those who run or manage bureaus. On the other hand, the yardstick for bureau productivity and performance is different from that of firms. They use goals, purposes, and functions to ascertain the productivity, effectiveness, and efficiency of their bureaucratic operations.

Administration, Subordinate to Law

Private sector managers can, in general terms, take any action, establish any policy, or use any means of operation which is not legally prohibited. On the contrary public managers may not exercise such authority without permission. "Private organizations can act unless proscribed or forbidden; public ones may act only if authority is granted" (p. 25). Because of legal constraints, policy implementation is often difficult particularly when managers lack "control over budget and personnel resources" (p. 25). In addition to the other limitations on "taxes, budgets, and personnel created by state constitutions, state and local governments are told what they must do by higher level of government" (p. 25). For instance, unfunded mandates, i.e., "programs created by law but with no concomitant financial support—often limit the alternatives of state and local officials" (p. 25). Such constraints are the province of bureaus. Contrary to public managerial arena,

> Private executives have the flexibility to adopt various courses of action with little external Kibitzing. Procedures may be changed and the organization redesigned: projects may be reduced, canceled, expedited, or enlarged, new markets may be entered. Resources may be shifted from one purpose to others, workers laid off or additional ones hired. Legal requirements or prohibitions are sometimes placed on private organizations, for example, affirmative action policies. The role of law for most private organizations, however, is relatively peripheral, and in no way is it central and pervasive to the private firm's management as to the bureau (Gortner, Mahler, and Nicholson, 1997, p. 25).

Bureaus differ from firms in many ways. Because of the role they play, and since these roles affect politically ambitious members of the electorate who represent them, public bureau managers are inevitably drown into the game of politics. Because of this form of involvement, administrative agencies have close links with legislators and executives. Such interconnectedness and interdependence of control of bureaus by the public officials has no precedent in the private sector. Such external control produces conflict among "overseers, creates a climate of uncertainty, hostility, and risk" (p. 39). Such circumstances make bureaus to play political roles that make them to look like "passive defensive reactors, or active influence pursuers" (p. 39). While public bureaus function in a climate of "open systems theory," the private sectors enjoy a "closed" one. The closed system promotes the "value of stability, rationality, and efficiency" while the open one promotes instability, power, conflict that is characterized by "uncertainty, hostility and risk" (p. 39). Though they do not make profits as the private sector does, bureaus, like many organizations, are a form of political economy. Lasswell (1958) has defined politics as the study of "who gets what, when, and how." On the other hand, Easton (1965) described politics as the process of society's "authoritative allocation of values." Who gets what, when and how and the authoritative allocation of values including the allocative device of the market, whether that market is economic, political, or professional evokes the notion of political economy with which the discipline of organization theory is enriched. While bureaus exist to formulate, implement, or enforce public policy, their relationship with firms radically differs in the light of "clientele, interest groups, goal-setting, goal ambiguity and diversity and the role of the manager in all these" (Gortner, 1997, p. 34).

Organization theory is not the theories of the organization, though they may be associated with it, it is not an organizational philosophy or goals, though these are major elements of it, it is not the organizational participants and the roles they are expected to play in it either. Probably, organization theory is an elusive and inclusive paradigm. The inclusive elusiveness of this paradigmatic theory is complex because of its interdisciplinarity and synergistic multitheoreticalness. In addition, the complex differences and similarities of the private and public domains of organizational theory tend to enhance the dialectical elusiveness of the paradigm in question.

Organizational Typologies

Organizational typologies are classifactory and comparative entities of social groups that make organizations or from which organizations are made. According to Scott (1981), organizational typologies may be based on goals, social and normative structure, behavioral structure, technology, participants and the environment. Organizational typologies may be derivatively and theoretically rooted in conceptual, empirical, deductive or inductive propositions. Though typologies can be used to promote many ways in which organizations can be analyzed, they may obscure causal connections and particularistically relevant variables. This makes them to be relatively "weak and nonproductive...because by their nature, social organizations are open systems—highly permeated by and interdependent with their environments and comprised of loosely linked and semiautonomous component systems" (p. 54).

During the 20th century, organizations and organizational typologies have benefited from their "close integration into corporate and other hierarchies" (Lipartito and Miranti, 1998, p. 301). Professional organizations and their professionals exchange knowledge and resources for their own empowerment. They use task structures which vary with technology. These complex organizations use technology for control and coordination within three levels of management. In turn, social structure is related to technology and task structure. The utilization of technology in this way "avoids many problems found in other schemes utilizing structure, function and goals as the basis for comparison" (Perrow, 1998, p. 194).

Diamond's (1997) *Guns, Germs and Steel: The Fates of Human Societies* was constructed with the use of interdisciplinary theories of anthropology, archaeology, linguistics and sociology. Economics was not among the disciplines used. By summoning geography, biology, immunology and genetics, the former disciplines were integratively used with the latter ones to explain the deterministic role of geography in Caucasoid rather than Negroid evolutionary advancement throughout history. Diamond's ignorance of studies in paleoanthropology (Caspari and Wolpoff, 1998) makes his assertions inexcusable. Diamond argues that Paleolithic humankind used superior tools rather than intelligence to cause not only the Neolithic revolution in agriculture, but this form of agricultural innovations became the base for population increase and expansion (from East to West and vice versa rather than from North to South or South to North). Secondly, this revolution of 8,000 B.C. did not only result in the production of new products, new productive processes, and new and more advanced technology, but such technology was instrumental to the enhancement of political and other organizations which evolved in urban and maritime centers of the civilizations of historical antiquity.

As writing, political organization and religion (Karl Marx) became more complex with these ancient civilizations, their many peninsulas, islands, and mountains rather than intelligence, desertification, culture, and religion enabled them to construct vessels that were used to navigate the seas, search for new lands and raw materials for conversion into wealth. Africans and African Americans still have their Paleolithic past in them because they neither became competitive nor learned to borrow from their Caucasoid and Asian counterparts except during East-West diffusion of science and culture. Their Neolithic past is viewed as a handicap by people who colonized, branded, whipped, sodomized, bartered and enslaved them using their culturally biased standards and theories to suppress their evolutionary development. Because unscientific and culturally biased standards and theories that were used particularly in IQ tests and medical experimentation, they have influenced Diamond not to use intelligence as one of the elements in the evolutionary development of the Caucasoid or European social structure. Throughout human history, science and technology have been used to create tension which is necessary for change in all societies.

Between the Neolithic period and the 14th century A.D., scientific and technological advancements were used to view human organizations and their progress in organismic terms. Every living thing including humankind was viewed as an organism. Knowledge, life, science and technology were dominated by religious orthodoxy, dogmatic and authoritarian regimes and the practice and emulation of tradition rather than innovation. Organizational forms and institutional life were antiquated, prescientific and archaic.

With the dawn of the 15th century, elements of modernity emerged. The modern period spans to the 19th century. This period was enlightened by the mathematical and scientific and economic works of Isaac Newton, Rene Discartes, Karl Marx, Adam Smith, Lenin, and Charles Darwin. Their scientific ideas became popular in mathematics, economics, physics, chemistry, biology and industrial technology. Knowledge, religion and culture were not only influenced and theoretically and empirically empowered with these scientific breakthroughs, but the scientific knowledge became the intellectual property that was instrumental for the evolution of modern industrial and professional organizations. Mechanistic Taylorism, rationality, and sociological functionalism were the dominant theoretical paradigms of the age.

The 20th century was enlightened by the scientific theories of quantum physics and the theory of relativity. These theories view organizational and institutional life to be dynamic and interrelated experience in which there are no absolutes. Since there are no absolutes, postmodern human relations, organizational humanism, diversity and organizational culture are bounded by rationality in decision making and organizational operations. Existing problems can be solved through experimentation, research and development, and consulting and counseling services of experts and specialists. The solutions to problems require organizations to be managed in terms of participatory management, use of networks and high technology to process information, theories and assumptions in order to discover and solve existing and systemic problems of the post-structural, postmodern, and post-industrial world. Synoptically, Table 1.1 portrays the past, present and future in the evolutionary development of organizational forms.

References

Alfonso, Firth, and Neville. 1981. *Instructional Supervision: A Behavior System.* Boston: Allyn and Bacon, Inc.

Bell, D. 1964. Twelve models of prediction – A preliminary sorting of approaches in social sciences. *Journal of American Academy of Arts and Sciences,* Boston: 846

Blau, P.M., and M.W. Meyer. 1993. *Bureaucracy in Modern Society.* New York: McGraw-Hill.

Buchanan, J.M. 1977. *Freedom in Constitutional Contract: Perspective of a Political Economist.* London: McMillan Publishers.

Burrell, G., and G. Morgan. 1979. *Sociological Paradigms and Organizational Analysis.* London: Heinemann.

Caspari, R., and M. Wolpoff. 1998. Race and human evolution. Ann Arbor: LSA Magazine, College of Literature, Science and the Arts, University of Michigan.

Coon, D. 1989. *An Introduction to Psychology: Exploration and Application.* St. Paul: West Publishing Company.

Denhardt, R.B. 1993. *Theories of Public Organization.* Belmont, CA: Wadsworth.

Denhardt, R.B. 1981. *In the Shadow of Organization.* Lawrence, KS: Regents Press of Kansas.

Diamond, J. 1997. Guns, germs and steel: The fate of human societies. *Journal of Interdisciplinary History* XXVIII, 3: 405-415

Downs, A. 1967. *Inside Bureaucracy.* Boston: Little Brown. (Reissued, Prospect Heights, III: Waveland Press, 1994).

Dubin, R., et al. 1965. *Leadership and Productivity.* San Francisco: Chandler Publishing Co.: 7.

Fuchs, S. 1993. A sociological theory of scientific change. *Social Forces* 71, 4: 933-953.

Garvey, G. 1993. *Facing the Bureaucracy: Living and Dying in a Public Agency.* San Francisco: Jossey-Bass.

Gaus, J.M. 1936. A theory of organization in public administration. *The Frontier of Public Administration*, Chicago: University of Chicago Press: 66.

Gortner, H.F., et al. 1997. *Organization Theory: A Public Perspective.* Fort Worth: Harcourt Brace College Publishers.

Gross, B.M. 1968. *The Managing of Organization.* New York and London: Free Press of Glencoe, Inc.; Collier Macmillan Ltd.

Hummel, R.P. 1994. *The Bureaucratic Experience.* New York: St. Martins Press.

Lipartito, K.J., and P.J. Miranti. 1998. Professions and organizations in twentieth century America. *Social Science Quarterly* 79, 2: 301-320.

March, J.G. 1965. *Handbook of Organizations.* Chicago: Rand McNally and Co.: ix.

Naisbitt, J. 1982. *Megatrends: Ten New Directions Transforming Our Lives.* New York: Warner Books.

Nystrom, P.C., and W.H. Starbuck, eds. 1981. *Handbook of Organizational Design.* 2, Oxford: Oxford University Press.

Oster, S.M. 1995. Strategic management for nonprofit organizations: Theory and cases. New York: Oxford University Press.

Ouchi, W.G. 1981. *Theory Z: How American Business Can Meet the Japanese Challenge.* New York: Avon Books.

Parsons, T. 1965. Suggestions for a sociological approach to the theory of organizations. *Administrative Science Quarterly* 1: 63-85.

Perrow, C. 1998. A Framework for the comparative analysis of organizations. *American Sociological Review:* 194-207.

Peters, T.P., and R.H. Waterman. 1982. *In Search of Excellence.* New York: Warner Books.

Popper, K.R. 1957. *The Poverty of Historicism.* New York: Harper and Row.

Rainey, H.G., et al. 1976. Comparing public and private organizations. *Public Administration Review* 36: 233-244.

Rosch, E. 1978. Principles of categorization. In *Cognition and Categorization,* eds. E. Rosch and B.B. Lloyd, Hillsdale, N.J.: Erlbaum.

Scott, W.R. 1981. *Organizations: Rational, Natural, and Open Systems.* Englewood Cliffs, N.J.: Prentice Hall.

Shafritz, J.M., and J.S. Ott. 1996. *Classics of Organization Theory.* Belmont, CA: Wadsworth.

Sills, D.L. ed. 1968. *International Encyclopedia of Social Sciences* Vol. II. New York: Macmillan Company and the Free Press.

Simon, H.A. 1976. *Administrative Behavior.* New York: Free Press.

Smith, E.E. 1989. Concepts and induction. In *Foundations of Cognitive Science,* ed. Michael I. Posner, 501. Cambridge, MA: The MIT Press.

Stillman, R.J. II. 1991. *Preface to Public Administration: A Search for Themes and Direction.* New York: St. Martins Press.

Waldo, D. 1980. *The Enterprise of Public Administration.* Navato, CA: Chandler and Sharp Publishers.

Waldo, D. (1978). Organization Theory: Revisiting the Elephant. *Public Administration Review* 589-597.

Walton, M. 1990. *Deming Management at Work.* New York: G.P. Putnam's Sons.

Weber, M. 1947. *Theory of Social and Economic Organization.* The Free Press.

White, O. 1969. The dialectical organization: An alternative to bureaucracy. *Public Administration Review* 29: 32-42.

Section One: Theoretical Base of Organization

Section One consists of three paramount perspectives or paradigmatic models from which analytical comparisons can be drawn and on which coherent traditions of research and praxis can be advanced and referenced. As theoretical and methodologically constructed paradigms, they provide a framework of assumptions and axioms for scientific rationality and scholarly exploration. The Table below shows author, system (open-closed), perspectives and order or type of perspective respectively. These perspectives are "rational, natural" (behavioral) and "open" (Scott, 1981, p. 132). Since the perspectives are triangulatively rationalized by many theories, the former are preparadigms.

Author	System	Model	Type
Taylor (1911)	Closed	Rational	I
Weber (1947)	Closed	Rational	I
Fayol (1949)	Closed	Rational	I
Gulij and Urwick (1937)	Closed	Rational	I
Roethlisberger and Dickson (1939)	Closed	Natural	II
Mayor (1941?)	Closed	Natural	II
Katz, et al. (1951)	Closed	Natural	II
Roy (1952)	Closed	Natural	II
Dalton (1959)	Closed	Natural	II
McGregor (1960)	Closed	Natural	II

Organizational Behavior

Udy (1959)	Open	Rational	III
Woodward (1965)	Open	Rational	III
Thompson (1967)	Open	Rational	III
Perrow and (1967)	Open	Rational	III
Pugh et al (1969)	Open	Rational	III
Blau (1970)	Open	Rational	III
Galbraith (1973)	Open	Rational	III
Hickson et al. (1971)	Open	Natural	IV
March and Olsen (1976)	Open	Natural	IV
Meyer and Rowen	Open	Natural	IV
Pfeffer and Salancik (1978)	Open	Natural	IV

Chapter 2

The Organization as a Rational Structure

The Western Tradition

Weber's model is used to describe organizations that establish structures that enable them to achieve their aims. These aims are carried forward through the regularization of allocation, coordination, and supervision of activities. The modern structured society is governed by bureaucratic authority whose specialization is based on immense technical efficiency. Bureaucratic authority is a legal administrative staff (Weber, 1947). Their effectiveness depends on their mutual interdependence in terms of:

1. rational norms and values that demand expediency and obedience,
2. abstract principles that are rationally and legally used as rules for the pursuit of the corporate group interest,
3. people with authority who have offices, power, and status that give them legitimacy to issue commands to their subordinates who are also, just like their superiors, governed by the impersonal rules of the bureaucracy,
4. bureaucrats or members obey authority because they belong to a corporate group that obeys the law of the association, organization, commune, church, or state, and

5. in respect to number three above, members obey the delimited impersonal rational order or authority rather than individuals or organizations per se.

The rational legal authority of which the bureaucratic order is an example is a system of values whose official duties are grounded on law. The bureaucrats have competence which enables them to exercise expert authority in specialization or division of labor. Because the competent bureaucrats are specialized, they have power and authority to make decisions, enforce the law, and supervise organizational functions. The supervision of organizational functions is an administrative, coordinating, and allocative responsibility which private and public organizations deal with and promote. Bureaucratic organizational offices are patterned on the principle of hierarchy. This means that subordinate offices are controlled and supervised by superior offices. In other words, the authority of offices and officials is rank ordered on the basis of a descending scale of subordinate relationships. The conduct of each office is regulated by a plethora of technical rules or norms. In Weberian view, rules that are technical are used to "prescribe a course of action which is dedicated primarily on grounds touching efficiency of the performance of the immediate functions" (p. 18). Also, by "norms he probably means rules which limit conduct on grounds other than those of efficiency" (p. 18). The office holders have fixed salaries, they are pensionable and can be demoted, dismissed or resign if they do wrong. Their superiors promote them on the basis of seniority and achievement. In essence, rules and norms are prescriptively used for maintaining conduct and conformity in problematic organizational settings.

The bureaucratic organization is a rational and formal organization whose disciplined officials, employees, and workers do not own and are not expected to own the organization's "non-human means of production and administration" (p. 18). They are provided with the non-human resources which are accounted for. They may use their own private property in the offices or premises but are not allowed to live there. Their fulfillment of these expectations will protect them from conflicts of interest in order to enhance efficiency and accountability. Given this reality, the incumbent (judge or official) cannot appropriate his/her official position. Definitively, he/she cannot make a public office or use it for personal gain. Office in this context is the institutionally defined status of a person or work premises that is called bureau.

Given the demands for accountability, which is a legal supervisory requirement, "administrative acts, decisions, and rules are formulated and recorded in writing" (p. 19). Mandatory oral discussions and rules, and proposals, discussions and decisions and orders need to be recorded in writing.

Rational Types of Legitimate Authority

Rationally, there are three types of legitimate authority that is bureaucratizable. First, the legal-rational type is the basis for bureaucracy particularly common in the Western society. This typical Western bureaucratic system is characterized by the presence of laws that are legislatively enacted and implemented to ensure accountability and administrative efficiency of the bureaus. The second rational type of legitimate authority is traditional leadership which exercises personal rule. Examples of these include hereditary monarchs, papal personages and in some ways, patriarchal caliphs and chiefs (see next paragraph on rationality in Islam). Since the procedures for their social mobility are either hereditary or reflections of well established religious and traditional orthodoxy their ability and character are not well testable or tested before they rise to power. Third, the charismatic leadership is so magnetic and inspiring that his/her personal qualities contribute to regime instability and failure. Hitler's Nazi Germany and Musolini's fascist Italy are classic examples of regimes which had charismatic leaders. Of these three types of authority the charismatic and the traditional leaderships are more monocratic or autocratic systems whose authoritarian regimes lack formulas for democratic efficacy. The monocratic variety of the bureaucracies "is so technical and efficient that it develops the capability for "attaining the highest degree of efficiency and is in this sense formally the most rational known means of carrying out imperative control over human beings. It is superior to any other form in precision, in stability, in the stringency of its discipline and its reliability" (Weber, 1947, p. 24). The evolution of modern corporate organizations are offshoot reflections of bureaucratic machinery. Churches, states, armies, political parties, economic organizations, associations and clubs, etc. trace their normative ad structural morphology in bureaucratic systems. These bureaucratic organizations do not exactly look like the "bureaucracies" of the academy, parliamentary or congressional committees, Soviets in former USSR, honorary officers and lay judges. Relative to these latter bodies, the bureaucratic administration is a formal, technical and rational type whose indispensability and massification are essentially paramount. Both the capitalistic and socialistic economic systems have structured, rational and technical bureaucracies.

Weber argued that "When those subject to bureaucratic control seek to escape the influence of the existing bureaucratic apparatus, this is normally possible only by creating an organization of their own which is equally subject to the process of bureaucratization. Similarly the "existing bureaucratic apparatus is driven to continue functioning by the most powerful interests which are material and objective, but also in character" (p. 25). Without the use of bureaucracy, Western, Eastern, and Southern societies would not function. The societies would experience entropy and falter. Under normal circumstances, Third World permanent secretaries who have experience, technical knowledge and social clout are better able to control the bureaucratic machinery than the nominal and politically elected ministers who may be less informed than their counterparts. Though both capitalism and bureaucracy are dichotomous and concomitant systems, the roots of their evolutionary and historical development are radically different. The former is a product of medieval feudalism and the Protestant Ethic. The latter is a byproduct of the state, empire, and public and private administration.

As a rational machinery, the bureaucracy is very "stable, strict, intensive and calculable administration" (p. 25). It is a central and crucial element of any large-scale administration. Its political, religious, and economic elements have been improved by the historical development of the capitalist and socialist systems. The radical contradictions between the two systems whose ideological and philosophical orientations are perpetually antagonistic to each other. Though bureaucratic administration, has in the recent past, relied on the services of railway, telephone, and telegraph for transportation and communication, postmodern society has started to rely on these same services and the new ones provided by the use of the computer, fax and automobile, and aircraft. These services are not only massively consumed, but their consumption is associated with bureaucratic evolution and advancement in terms of their technocratic technostructure. Within the socialist camp, and due to lack of discipline and creative innovation, absence of historic precedent and moral rational philosophical consciousness, the Soviet bureaucracy lost the vitality of its essence – the rationality of its irrationality. With the massive presence of its ideological bankruptcy, the Soviet bureaucratic machinery lost its important theological rhetoric for power that was used for organizing the social fabric for action. Though the economic, political, military, and technological weaknesses of the Soviet Empire

Table 1.1. McKelvey's Improved Typology of Evolutionary Organizational Forms

Chronology	Era	Main Environmental Features	Technology Innovation	Organizational Form
1. Future	Intergalactic and Space Technology	Large Modules for Moving Variety	Ballistic and Supersonic Speed	Intergalactic Space and Ecocentric Societies
2. 1985-Now	Information	High-tech, High-touch	Computer	Internet
3. 1980-1990s	Diversity	Cultural Diversity	Globalism	Networks
4. 1970-1980	Participation	Culture	Theory Z	Teams
5. 1940-1970	R&D Product Oriented Organization	Technical Change, Product Innovation and Diversity	Organic Form, Grid and Matrix Forms	Organics, Matrices
6. 1900-1940	Assembly Line	Workplace Interdependence	Sequential Coordination	Sequentials
7. 1700-1900	Steam Engine	Large workplaces, Many Operations	Workplace Coordination	Factories
8. 1500-1700	Textile Revolution	Combining Many Family Units into Cottage Industry	Coordination of Many Units under the Same Roof	Textiles
9. 2100-1750 BC	Pre-Babylonian Dynasties	Dynastic Influences	Mediating Interdependency; Utilitarian Legitimacy	Commercials
10. 2900-2100 BC	Earliest Dynasties in Mesopotamia and Egypt	Threats of Intercity Warfare	Mediating Interdependency; Coercive Legitimacy	Palaces and Temples

contributed to its collapse, the bankruptcy of its ideological theology, which was initially, when it was strong, used to create it, was responsible for its collapse. The bureaucracy lost its religious zeal for creating new, dynamic and universal zealots who could have extended and strengthened, through management, the mission and value, the glorious, and universal beauty and contributions of the empire. This collapse shows how formal or instrumental and substantive rationality could be conflictual. Apart from Weber who has descriptively prescribed rational procedures and structures, Taylor, Gulick, Urwick and other great thinkers have ratified the rational theory of scientific management and scientific administration (Gortner, 1997). These minds argue that all modern organizations must and should seek to use rationality. Rationality is the "quality or state of having or being based on reason" (p. 61). Rationality is "central to all organizations in our modern, technological, interdependent world" (p. 61).

There are two levels of rationality. The first level is substantive rationality which is concerned with goals or ends that an organization wants to achieve. The second level is instrumental rationality which is concerned with means or how (processes) organizations strife to achieve established goals or ends. Though both levels are imperative, the logic and analytic tools involving the use of each are radically different.

According to Paul Diesing (1962), the five types of rationality that exist in modern society include the "technical, economic, social, legal, and political" (Gortner, 1997, p. 61). The bureaucracy is superior in technological and global interdependence, superior in stability because it is predictable, superior in discipline because it is strict, superior in calculation because it is knowledgeable, technical, and legal, and superior in efficiency because the bureaucracy gets things down on time with a sense of accountability. When a rational bureaucracy is superior in predictability, discipline, technostructure, interdependence, and calculable lawfulness, the consequences of its performance are instrumental – hence instrumental rationality (Weber, 1947). The classical Weberian and Taylorist school of thought assumed that such bureaucratic and rationalized instrumental superiority with respect to the use of rationality was the "only one best way" (Gortner, 1997, p. 61; Scott 1981; and Pugh, 1987).

The rational bureaucracy's weaknesses may include waste, incompetence, red-tape, and mediocrity (McKenna, 1994). Its meritocracy enables it to establish and maintain high standards of performance. For example, the bureaucracy has ability to make decisions and control abstract, concrete and "official secrets" (Pugh,

1981, p. 26). There are three consequences of bureaucratic control. These include:

1. The general tendency to hire or recruit on the basis of technical competence.
2. The bureaucracy is a Plutocracy (government by wealthy people only) that has technical training (30 years).
3. The bureaucracy is dominated by the spirit of "formalistic impersonality, sine ira et studio which has neither hatred nor passion, which lacks affection and enthusiasm." Its norms are "duty and formal equality of treatment" (p. 27).

These characteristics produce an ideal official who is capable of managing his/her office. The leveling of social classes in the capitalistic world is suitable for the evolutionary development of the bureaucracy. Such form of societal leveling creates a favorable climate conducive to the elimination of its class privileges of which "the appropriation of means of administration and the appropriation of authority as well as the occupation of offices on an honorary basis or as an avocation by virtue of wealth. This combination everywhere inevitably foreshadows the development of mass democracy" (Pugh, 1987, p. 27). In terms of how it operates, the rational bureaucracy is formalistic because it is interested in its own "personal" security and survival. Contrary to its formalism, the bureaucracy substantively function in a utilitarian way in order to articulate the interest and welfare of those they serve. This is a form of substantive rationality that is supportive of democracy.

In the private sector, rationality and efficiency can be determined by observing "how successful the organization is achieving the goals of profit, size and growth" (Gortner, 1997, p. 62). The strategic success of the whole market is assessed in the context of long term business cycles and in terms of TQM. Both in private and public administrative management, substantive rationality dominates the planning and operational stages of the organizations. In other words, "procedural efficiency and rationality are the goals of TQM" (p. 63) though most of the goals are not, for obvious reasons, implementable in the public sector.

Rago (1994) argues that unlike the business world, successful public agencies pay the price without expanding their revenue base. For instance,

many companies in the industrial sector undertake TQM to improve their bottom lines by increasing the market share by improving quality.

Increased market share means new customers and new revenues. Conceivably, increased revenue enables companies to hire employees and purchase equipment as necessary to ensure that supply keeps up with demand. In many government service organizations, the order of business is opposite that of industry. That is, the more customers the organization has the less money is available to provide the service.

As the government service organization gains efficiency in the delivery of services as a result of TQM, it expands its customer base by providing services to those citizens who needed services but who were too far down on the waiting list to obtain them typically, this expansion occurs without a correlated expansion in revenue (pp. 63-64, and Gortner, 1997, p. 63).

According to Gortner et al. (1997) "TQM assumes top management support but political officials operate under a different concept of rationality than do business officials...TQM focuses ultimately, on economic factors – in the long term, businesses increase profits or gain a larger segment of the market. Public officials focus on the short term – next election" (p. 63). They must be reelected. If not, their closest supports must be elected. Public officials have fewer incentives for management. For example, the fact that a mayor, a governor, a senator or minister, or president has been elected and has been successful during his/her first tenure does not automatically translate into a guaranteed possibility for his/her reelection.

Second, substantive rationality (efficiency) is different from instrumental rationality. As normally it is the case, total quality management looks for "efficiency in procedures and uses scientific methods to achieve the one current best way of production. Other theorists such as Weber, Taylor, Gulick, and others value only the instrumental level of rationality. They definitely theorize that rationality and efficiency are identical. They argue that "efficient achievement of a single goal is technical rationality" (Taylor, 1911 and Gortner, 1997, p. 64). The maximum achievement of many goals is economic rationality (Gulick and Urwick, 1937, and Weber, 1947). Gulick and Urwick argue that rationality, which is efficiency, is an effective principle of departmentalization and departmentalism which is comparable to, in the eyes of the alchemists, "the philosopher's stone" (Gulick and Urwick, 1937, p. 31). Like Weber, they assert that all formal organizations have structural commonalities or similarities with which they are characterized. In other words, administrative and Taylorist principles of management are characteristically affinal.

In the context of rationality or efficiency, substantive rationality could be irrelevant since the goals with which it is associated are externally constructed. In Taylorist perspective, technical rationality was intended to increase "output for the same amount of input; that equals efficiency" (Gortner, p. 64). Because Gulick and Urwick were interested in efficient, scientific administrative organizational structures that maximized managerial functions, they were convinced that good organizational or bureaucratic management "guaranteed efficiency in operation and maximum return for tax dollars spent" (p. 64). Weber interchangeably uses technical efficiency to mean rationality. Rationality is "the major benefit to be gained from bureaucracy and the reason that bureaucracy developed in the first place" (p. 64).

In accordance with Flew's (1979) perspective, rationality is the opposite of irrationality or non-rationality or arationality. Humans are both rational and irrational. Taylor and his management contemporaries may have been influenced by Descartes, Spinoza and Leibnitz who were 17th and 18th centuries philosophers from the school of rationalism. The rationalist intellectual tradition was and is characterized by three logical assumptions: (a) "the belief that it is possible to obtain by reason alone a knowledge of the nature of what exists; (b) the view that knowledge forms a single system, which (c) is deductive in character; and (d) the belief that everything is explicable, that is, that everything can in principle be brought under the single system" (p. 299). The rationalist school of thought rejects religious belief for being irrational and unscientific. Also, because it is committed to using reason and reason alone, it is analytically antagonistic to faith, prejudice, habit and all sources of irrationality. In other words, contemporary intellectual analysts agree that communism, as opposed to capitalism and democracy, came to an end in the former USSR because the foundations upon which it rested were more irrational and religious than the foundations of its capitalistic counterpart.

In general, in his interest for the study of organizations, Weber, unlike other scholars, was able to "(1) identify the characteristics of an entity he labelled bureaucracy; (2) to describe its growth and the reasons for its growth; (3) to isolate the concomitant social changes; (4) to discover the consequences of bureaucratic organization for the achievement of bureaucratic goals" (March and Simon, 1958, pp. 36, 47) which fundamentally are the goals of political authority. Unlike other scholars, Weber intends to show to what degree the bureaucracy as an organization, is a rational solution to complex modern problems. Specifically, Weber wants to show that the bureaucratic organization can solve decision making problems, some of which are computational, by overcoming individual limitations with alternative forms of the organization in terms of labor. Though Weber's bureaucratic model is similar to that of Urwick and Gulick, it differs radically from the mechanistic and other models. Details related to these differences will be dealt with later. Weber's model is more complex and elaborate because he analyzes the relationship between the official and the office. He views the bureaucracy to be an adaptive or strategic device whose specialization is instrumental to the solution of organizational problems in spite of human limitations.

Merton's Model

More recent students of the bureaucracy – particularly Merton (1940), Selznick (1949) and Gouldner (1954) agree with Weber that bureaucracies are more efficient with respect to the operationalization of goals of bureaucratic (formal) hierarchy than alternative forms of organization. The major contributions of these organizational scholars is their recognition that the bureaucratic organization is characterized by important dysfunctional consequences. Together, they theoretically agree that there are anticipated and unanticipated consequences that leaders think result from the treatment of human beings as machines. When the machine model of human behavior is used for control, this usage encourages not only the continued use of the machine model, but, the resulting consequences strengthen the tendency to use the control device. The unanticipated consequences are undesired by the organization. Merton assertively concludes that "changes in the personality of individual members of the organization stem from factors in the organizational structure" (Pugh, 1987, p. 29). The term personality refers to an externally observed consistent and persisting behavioral phenomenon which individuals display.

Merton elaborates that the system demands control to be the prerogative of the top leaders of the organizational hierarchy. The demand is characterized with an "increased emphasis on the reliability of behavior" (p. 30) in the organization. In the light of the organizational echelons, reliability of behavior reinforces the need for accountability and predictability. Strict adherence to these behaviors results in the "machine model of human behavior" (p. 30). The three consequences resulting from mechanistic human behavior include but are not limited to: (1) a reduction in the amount of personalized instrumental or expressive relationship; (2) internalization of the rules of the organization by the participants is increased for instrumental purposes in spite of their unanticipated consequences of which goal displacement is one; overspecialization and internalization of subgoals leads to goal displacement because specialists cannot communicate with people outside their speciality. (3) Increased use of categorization as a decision-making strategy decreases the search for usable alternatives by making use of the first ones.

The reduction in personalized relationships, the increased internalization of rules, and the decreased search for alternatives combine to make the behavior of members of the organization highly predictable; i.e. they result in an increase in the rigidity of behavior of participants. At the same time, the reduction in personalized relations (p. 31), including those of a competitive nature, helps to facilitate the development of an esprit de corps, i.e. increases the degree with which goals are shared with group members. Such sharing of common purpose, goals, and interest "increases the propensity of organization members to defend each other against outside pressures" (p. 31). While such behavior intensely solidifies rigidity, such behavior is reminiscent of innovativeless "group think."

Rigidity of behavior is characterized by three main consequences. First, rigid behavior satisfies the initial demand for reliability, maintenance need of the system, and strengthening of in-group identification. Second, it increases the defensibility of individual action at all levels of the bureaucratic pyramid. Finally, "the rigidity of behavior increases the amount of difficulty with clients of the organization and complicates the achievement of client satisfaction – a near-universal organizational goal" (p. 31). Subordinate and defensive in-group members like to subject clients to the "trappings of authority" (p. 31). Also, rigidity of behavior which needfully has the tendency to increase defensibility of individual action, prevents discrimination by resolving the conflict between service and impartiality related to the implementation of public organizational goals. Figure 2.1 illustrates Merton's theory of dysfunctional organizational learning in the structure of organizations.

Selznick's Model

Merton's model puts emphasis on rules as a response to the demand for control. Selznick's (1949) model stresses delegation of authority. Like Merton and unlike no one else, Selznick wants to show how delegation as (a control technique) is responsible for provoking a variety of unanticipated consequences. In addition, and unlike Merton as well, Selznick points out that the consequences emanate from the

Figure 2.1. The Structure of Organizations

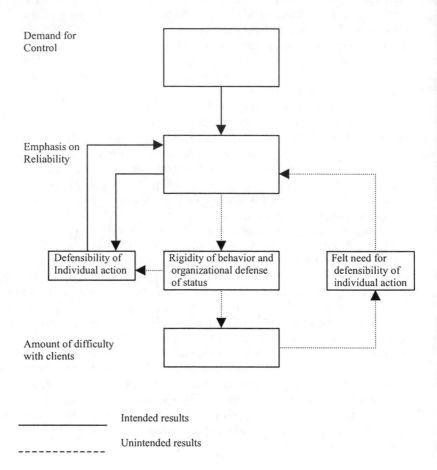

Demand for
Control

Emphasis on
Reliability

Defensibility of
Individual action

Rigidity of behavior and
organizational defense
of status

Felt need for
defensibility of
individual action

Amount of difficulty
with clients

_____ Intended results

- - - - - - - - - Unintended results

Source: D.S. Pugh, *Organization Theory: Selected Readings.* (London:
Penguin Books, 1984), p. 32.

"problem of maintaining intensive instrumental and expressive interpersonal relations."
In this model, the top hierarchy makes the demand for control. As a result of the demand, increased delegation of authority is instituted and on the one hand, ratified. Delegation of authority increases the chances for training in specialized competencies. Such competence improves an employee's ability or capacity to deal with more sophisticated problems. As a result, "delegation tends to decrease the difference between organizational goals and achievement, and thus to stimulate more delegation" (p. 33). On the other hand delegation stimulates the creation of "departmentalization and increased bifurcation of interests among the subunits in the organization" (p. 33). The maintenance needs of the subunits dictate a commitment to the subunit goals over and above their contribution to the total organizational program. Many individual needs depend on the continued success and expansion of the subunit.

Bifurcation of interests is stimulated by the specialized training which delegation produces. Training results in increased competence, increased costs of changing personnel, and in further differentiation of subunit goals. The "bifurcation within the organization leads to increased conflict among organizational subunits" (p. 33). Consequently, the content of organizational decisions depends increasingly on the nature of internal strategic options especially if the is "little internalization of organizational goals by participants" (p. 33). Consequently, there is an increase in the difference between organizational goals and achievement. This difference results in an increase in delegation. This influences daily decisions. First, the struggle for internal control not only affects directly the content of decisions, but, it also causes greater elaboration of ideologies that are used to legitimize subunits. Second, each struggles to succeed in fitting its policy in consonant with the official doctrine of the larger organization for the legitimization of its demands. This tactic increases the internalization of subgoals by participants of the subunits.

Internalization of subgoals is reinforced by a feedback from the daily decisions it influences. Making daily decisions is necessarily a process of precedent setting. Decisions that become precedential are organizationally operational in terms of the applicability of their subunit goals. Precedents are habitually relevant because they consistently reinforce the internalization of subunit goals. Since internalization of subgoals is relatively dependent on the operationality of organizational goals, it is more likely than otherwise, to observe and test how effectively goals are achieved. "Variations in the operationality of organizational goals affect the content of daily decisions" (p. 34) and the extent to which subunit goal decisions are internalized daily.

Evidently, it is clear, based on this analysis, that delegation of authority or responsibility has both functional and dysfunctional consequences in relation to the achievement of organizational goals. Delegation contributes to the "realization and deflection" (p. 34) of the goals in question. Theoretically, it is hypothesizable that both increases and decreases in goal achievement cause an increase in delegation. In other words, even when goals are not attainable, bureaucratic authority tends to delegate responsibility in spite of the expectations to the contrary. This happens because within the framework of the "machine model" (p. 34) delegation is the correct and the only alternative response. Figure 2.2 illustrates the highly simplified Selznickian model.

Gouldner's Model

Gouldner's model or paradigm (1954) is simpler than Mertonian and Selznickian models though they all have certain similarities. Like Merton, Gouldner is concerned with the consequences of bureaucratic rules for the maintenance of organizational structure. He, like Merton, tries to portray how a "control technique designed to maintain the equilibrium of a subsystem disturbs the equilibrium of a larger system, with subsequent feedback on the subsystem" (Pugh, 1987, p. 36).

Due to the demand for control created by the hierarchical structure, general and impersonal rules are used to regulate organizational norms, procedures and precedents. One consequence of such rules is to decrease the visibility of power relations with the group. The visibility of authority differences in the context of the work group interacts with the extent to which equality norms are held to affect the legitimacy of the supervisory role. Subsequently, it affects the degree of impersonal tension within the work group. Sociologically, because American culture is egalitarian, the power and visibility of the worker decreases with the legitimate increase in supervisory role. Such a relationship helps to decrease tension within the group. According to Gouldner, the above-mentioned anticipated consequences of rule-making take place in order to allow the survival of the work group unit. The unit uses rules that are reinforced. The work rules provide cues for organizational members beyond those intended by the authority figures in the organization. The rules enable the organizational members to know what acceptable and unacceptable behavior means. Oversupervision

Figure 2.2. The Simplified Selznick Model

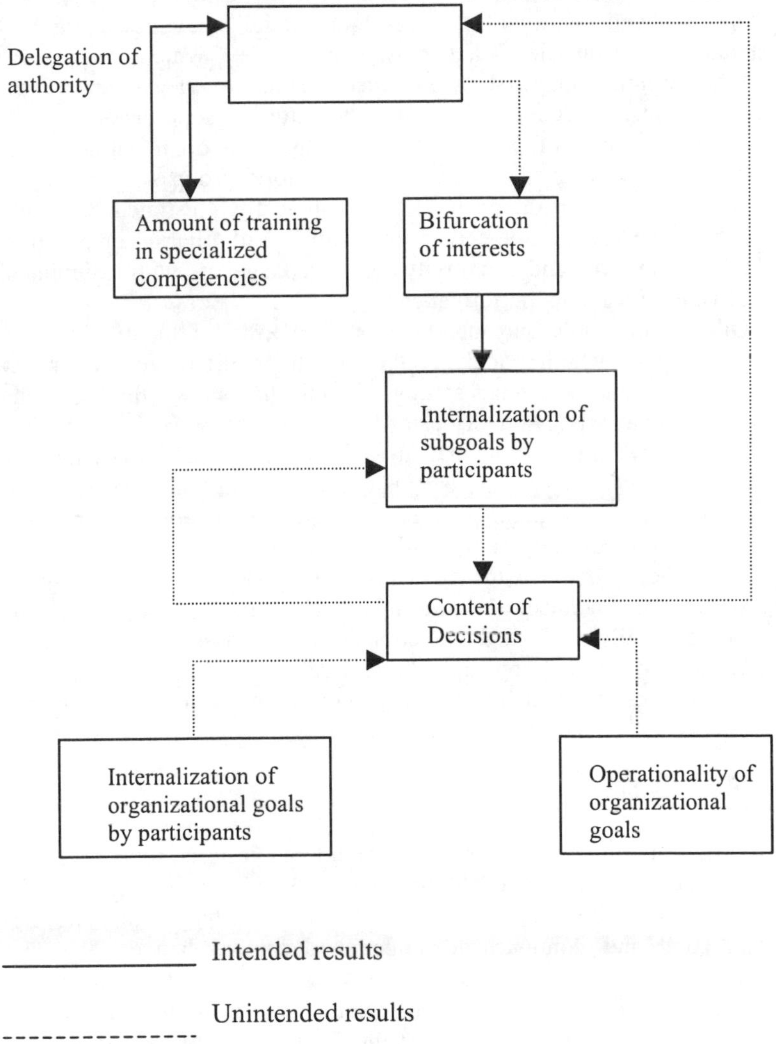

Delegation of
authority

Amount of training
in specialized
competencies

Bifurcation
of interests

Internalization of
subgoals by
participants

Content of
Decisions

Internalization of
organizational goals
by participants

Operationality of
organizational
goals

_____ Intended results

_ _ _ _ _ _ _ _ _ _ _ _ _ _ Unintended results

Source: D.S. Pugh, *Organization Theory: Selected Readings.* (London:
Penguin Books, 1984), p. 35.

and closeness of supervision may cause organizational disequilibrium. Organizational disequilibrium may take place due to the mechanistic nature of Gouldnerianism. If performance is low or poor, more detailed inspection and control of the "machine model" may be required. It should be made clear that close supervision, which may cause disequilibrium, may stimulate that element of organizational dysfunctionalism due to the fact that the nature of supervision tends to increase visibility of power relations within the organizations. This tends to raise tension level within the work group – resulting in disequilibrium. Gouldner's model is graphically illustrated on p. 48. Intense supervision is perceived to be either authoritarian or punitive. Authoritarianism and punitivity are inconsistent with stimulated motivation for higher performance.

Other comparable bureaucratic models worthy of mention include Bendix (1947) who has analyzed the limitations of technical rationality in organizational and other settings. Bendix has shown the intriguing problems that arise with the use of spy systems of control. Dubin's (1949) model is similar to that of Merton. Blau (1955) evaluated the changes in operating procedures that take place at the lower levels of the bureaucratic pyramid. Such an examined evaluation is carried out due to the pressure exerted by work group needs.

In all these three and the other previous models, the elaboration of evoking their connections, the inherent unintended cues, and the organizationally evolved dysfunctional learning associated with these models tend to be responsible for a large part of the unanticipated consequences with which these theories or models articulate. Figure 2.3 is an illustratively simplified Selznick's model.

T. Burns Model

Burns has shown that the history of modern Western industrialization is about two centuries old. Within this period, industrialization, just like other institutions (family, church, government, military force, etc.) has undergone and continues to undergo dynamic change. The two technologies of industrialization are material and social forms of engineering. The third successful technology was the creation of the first factory by Strutt and Arkwright. Factory means "the combined operation of many work people, adult and young, in tending with assiduous skill, a system of productive machines continuously impelled by a central power. It is the constant aim and tendency of every improvement in machinery to supersede human labour altogether" (Pugh, 1987, p. 41).

Figure 2.3. The Simplified Gouldner Model

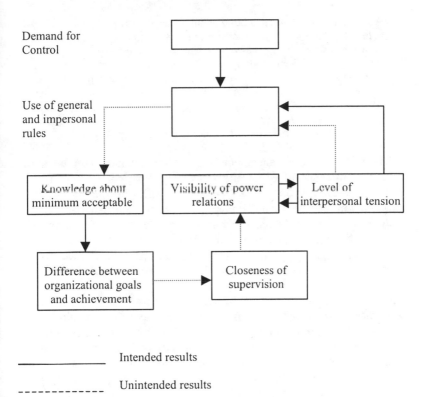

Source: D.S. Pugh, *Organization Theory: selected Readings* (London: Penguin Books, 1984), p. 37.

Karl Marx, in his *Das Kapital*, has described the factory in the following manner:

> a collection of machines in a building all driven by one prime mover, and preferably, of the same type and engaged on the same process. Attending the machines were men and women who themselves were attended by 'feeders', most of them children, who fetched and carried away materials. There was also a 'superior, but numerically unimportant' class of maintenance and repair workers. All of these worked under a master, with perhaps a chief workman or foreman. The primitive social technology of the factory system still confined it, even by the 1850s, largely to the mass production of textiles (Pugh, 1987, p. 41).

With the technical advancement in transportation and communication, with the influence of cultural, political and commercial centers like London and Paris, with the coming of the free trade and the introduction of the manufacture, distribution and consumption of military hardware, these new technical advances were used to produce and revolutionize industrial development. Machine tools of iron and steel boomed in the market. Advancement in chemical technology evolved first in Germany and later in other countries. These evolutionary and infantile industrial beginnings (1850-1860s) became the base or springboard from which more advanced and historically evolutionary methods and forms of industrialization developed. In essence, the gradual improvement of material technology and the attendant social techniques of industrial organization had been established. "With the extension of the factory system into engineering, chemical, iron and steel processing, food manufacture and clothing, an organizational development took place which provided for the conduct and control of many complex series of production processes within the same plant" (p. 41). One positive development which came as a result of the evolution of the factory system was the increase in the number of "salaried officials employed in industry" (p. 41). Comparatively speaking, the number of factory managers and supervisors (administrative employees) as compared to that of line workers (production employees) in England had risen from 8.6% in 1907 to 20% in 1948. In general, similar increases were repeated in Western Europe and the U.S.A.

The fact that industrial managers (administrative officials) were so many may be a reflection of the growth of the organizational structures or "bureaucracies." This patrimonial structure was characterized by a variety of "department managers, sales managers, accountants, cashiers, inspectors, training officers, publicity managers, and the rest emerged as specialized parts of the general management function as industrial concerns increased in size" (p. 42). This hierarchical system evolved out of the 18th century masters system. At every level, all rights and powers were derived from the leader or boss. "Fealty or responsibility is owed to him; all benefits are 'as if' dispensed by him. The bond is more easily and more often broken than in pre-feudal polities, but loyalty to the concern, to employers, is still regarded not only as proper, but as essential to the preservation of the system" (p. 42). Even Chester Barnard has emphasized that loyalty, which is the acceptance that the organization or corporation is dominant, is the universal qualification of the organizational man – employee.

The second phase o industrialization was stimulated by the growth of bureaucratic structure and bureaucratic rationality, and the development of material technology. Industrial development was marked by a major breakthrough in technological advancement. Initially, rapid technological advances accompanied by immense industrial production led to a significant death rate of the smaller and in some cases, larger enterprises. Industrial growth occurred when the rate of technical development slowed down because less capital and labor intensive techniques, industrialists and entrepreneurs had saved or invested in profit-making business climates and "consumer demands" tended to have become more "standardized through publicity and price reductions, and the technical progress" became consequently restrained (p. 42). These happenings enabled companies to remain stable while "large-scale production was built up by converting manufacturing processes into routine cycles of activity for machines or semi-skilled assembly hands" (pp. 42-43).

Under these conditions specific industrial companies grew in size and manufacturing processes became permanently routinized, mechanized and quickened. Consequently, various management functions became not only routinized, but they also became technologically specialized. These functions for which the attendant bureaucracy was supervisorily charged with included "specialized management tasks: those of ensuring employee cooperation, of coordinating different departments, of planning and monitoring" (p. 43). In recent years, the second phase of industrialism has continued to dominate the institutional and organizational life of Western and other societies. Its bureaucratic character, however, belongs to the first phase of the industrial organization.

The third industrial phase which J.K. Galbraith has called the *Affluent Society* is about 30 or 40 years old. This industrial phase is new and has "more insecure relationship with the consumer which appears as production catches up and overtakes spontaneous domestic demand. The 'propensity to consume' has had to be stimulated by advertising, by styling, and by marketing promotions guided by research into the habits, motives, and potential needs of consumers" (p. 43). Industrial expansion and governmental spending on the military industrial complex may have enhanced elements of sizeable influx in industrial and information technology which constitute, because of domestic malaise and competition from Europe and Asia, a "challenged technological leap" in the United States.

Japanese-Asian Industrial Revolution Model

The history of technological transformation of Japan, which is technological evolution of the country, has been written by Morris-Suzuki (1994). The author shows that in its evolutionary technological transformation, Japan went through three major technologically connected industrial revolutions between the 17th and the 20th centuries. What is remarkable about Japanese historic – technological advance is the fact that it started with the use of simple machines and tools that were processually used in its backward stage of evolution. This 17th and 18th century stage became the base or springboard from which Japan has technologically evolved in order to catch up with the West and yet use that technological and economic superiority to chart new directions in the well calculated technological frontier. The three stages of Japanese technological transformation are: the Togugawa Heritage of 1603-1867 which used labor-intensive methods for a limited market, the Technological Stage of Industrializing Japan, 1868-1945. According to Fujita (1994), the Japanese hired more than 3,000 experts from Western and other countries for advice on how to transform Japan. From the Western world, British, American, French, and German foreign advisers were hired and consulted. It is likely that the contributions of these experts (1868-1912) may have planted the seeds of technological advance in Japan. The third stage is the Making of a Technological Superpower, 1945 to the present. Throughout the 400 years, there has always been a fair amount of technology in Japan irrespective of the "biased and shallow" rhetoric about imitation and transfer of technology. Japan invested heavily in education which became the vehicle for capitalizing on resource constraints in terms of choices, modifications and indigenization of technology.

Why have the Japanese, who industrialized relatively late, caught up with the West and surpassed the West in many cases? According to Morris-Suzuki (1994), Japanese are good at organizing in the sense of using social networks for the distribution of productive information. The center of the network system is characterized by, on the one hand, large powerful and advanced organizations of which the state, major universities, laboratories, experimental stations, leading private corporations, national trade associations and research and consulting groups are members. On the other hand, the periphery comprises of a variety of subnational groups and organizations like prefectures, municipalities, specialized and training educational institutions, regional and local trade associations and a variety of smaller enterprises in both the public and private sector of the economy.

The network structure is also highly pronounced in Japanese bureaucratic system (Kim, Muramatsu, and Pempel, 1995). The three authors indicated that this bureaucracy exercises interpersonal competition in the context of the overall cooperative effort of the bureaucratic structure. Unlike the U.S. or other bureaucracies that are wasteful, mediocre, incompetent and red-tape like (McKenna, 1998) the Japanese bureaucracy is "small, efficient, creative," and adaptable (Kim et al, 1994, p. 939). According to Yamamura, the Japanese bureaucracy has played a major role in national economic development during the last 150 years. It intervenes in the market to reduce information acquisition costs and to stimulate efforts to catch up with the West. The bureaucracy reduces the cost of capital for firms and industrial sectors viewed to be potentially more export oriented and less import oriented. In other words, emphasis is on promotion of exports and reduction in imports.

Though senior bureaucratic officials retire early, most join the private sector (*amakudari* where they become useful and productive within this bureaucracy, competition is exercised at individual, intraministerial and interministerial. Further still, it is allowed to compete at the central and local political levels. In doing that, it contributes to helping institutions to become less lethargic and more efficient, nimble, innovative and accountable. Notwithstanding the Japanese bureaucratic reputation of protectionism and an antimarket perspective, it is characterized by a strong element of market competition which is beneficial to the national economy and its strategic economic development objectives.

Because of Japanese bureaucratic involvement in the market and the national economy, neoclassical economists feel that the government interferes in the market in order to allocate values regardless of its long term implications in terms of consequences. This involvement of the bureaucracy in the management of the national economy, which they regulate with some rigidity, may fearfully backfire particularly as this influence has provoked American trade negotiations to demand more influence for the promotion of bilateral relations including that of trade imbalances and the need for their correction. Prominent students of Japan's political economy emphasize the importance of the "revisionists" or "Japan-bashers" by their critics.

It has been argued that Japan's miraculous management of economic and technological empowerment was not necessarily the by-product of imitation and importation of Western technology. Rather, this great genius for creativity, motivation, and productive hard work is essentially cultural and Confucian in Japanese tradition (Amsden, 1993). The Japanese spirit of economic and technological empowerment has been reflected on by (Nishiguchi in his 1994) *Strategic Industrial Sourcing*. Nishiguchi affirms how Japanese firms work synergistically with their supplies to create world-class manufacturing systems. The author and his book explain how the Japanese supplier relations system creates competitive advantage in both the automobil: and electronic industries. The text paradoxically indicates that "strategic flexibility in the Japanese system of supplier relations enables firms to use extensive outsourcing to produce a great variety of goods with breathtaking speed and quality. Exit barriers are meaningless in this vertical value-adding system, despite very high asset specificity" (Shrivastava, 1996, p. 286). In other words, strategic industrial sourcing as a system relies on the flexibility of human capital. For instance, in relation to industrial sourcing, it is instructive to compare the behavior of British and Japanese subcontractors. Based on the merit of this study which involved the interviewing of 1,000 people, British subcontractors were viewed, in their trade relations with customers, to be "precarious" (p. 287) because evaluation was based on the price of their wares. Also, very short notice was given when their orders were canceled. Suppliers were treated with a sense of triviality rather than dignity and respect – as important assets whose organizational stature should be preserved continuously. Instead, they were used as "buffers against fluctuations to protect customers' workforces" (p. 287).

In comparison, Japanese customers encouraged their subcontractors to modernize facilities by assisting them with technical and financial assistance. The "team spirit characteristic of most firms and the mutual problem solving facilitates continuous improvements in product quality, cost control, and technological excellence for both supplier and buyer" (p. 287). Even though, it does not make some trade-offs explicit. This system of team work and network which Nishiguchi has described is called *Keiretsu*. This type of strategic industrial sourcing requires permanent improvements in physical capital (capital outlay) as well as flexibility of workers. Because of the prevailing subcontracting opportunities, Japanese workers, unlike those of other industrial countries, are likely to become entrepreneurs.

Political and economic conditions have been analyzed and attributed to Japanese pre-eminence in techno-nationalism (Farnsworth, 1995). Economists, political scientists and social scientists argue that Post War Japan was politically dominated for a long time, by the Liberal Democratic Party which laid a strong foundation for political stability and economic progress. On the other hand, Japan's relative isolationism from major areas of international conflict including the Cold War, Korean War, Vietnam War, the Gulf War, the Bosnian war, the Serbian war, and African and Central American regional conflicts contributed to her meagre defense expenditures. While the U.S. was deeply involved in these costly wars, Japan invested heavily in industry, education, research and economic development.

According to Samuels (1993), *fuan* (insecurity) which is a national concern that enabled pre-War Japan to mobilize the entire state in a military related industrialization is the same situation which has propelled post-War Japan to excel techno-economically. Samuels hypothesizes that insecurity has stimulated the development of Japanese techno-national ideology whose tripartite constants include the "struggle for independence and autonomy through indigenization of technology (*kokusanka*); the national commitment to diffuse this learning throughout the economy (*hakyuu*); and the national, regional, local, and sectoral effort to nurture and sustain Japanese enterprises to which technical knowledge can be diffused (*ikusei*)" (Farnsworth, 1995, p.1170). Techno-nationalism is an ideology that is basic to the security of the nation. The inseparable three constants are what make the rich and formidable in the world of 'pervasive anxiety' (p. 1170). Both the "War machine of the 1930s and the economic machine" of the 1990s are the product of imitation and indeginization of an industrial society whose generic basic technology underwent protectionism, subsidizes research and development and supports political and bureaucratic involvement.

Given the historical understanding (according to Adam Smith and J.M. Keynes) that there is a 'direct causal link between warfare and economic prosperity' this understanding may serve as an explanation for the apparent Japanese techno-national ascendance in the face of American decline particularly in defense technology and innovative products that are of vital strategic military importance. In the light of such understanding, the United States needs to revolutionize the way it conducts business. It needs to: (1) reinvent government to ensure that it works efficiently, effectively and rationally; (2) reinvent its national culture by rediscovering the vitality and spiritual power of its social, cultural, and religious traditions; (3) creatively establish a machinery that will facilitate the interdependent linkage between military and commercial applications by promoting their economies of scale and removing barriers that separate the two institutions; (4) construct a supranational technical unit comparable to MITI which will coordinate the strategic importance of national science, business and industrial technology by using education, research and development, and bureaucratic technocracy. Though MITI has, in recent times, been viewed to be notorious and ineffective in some ways, its historic contribution in terms of coordination of the strategic essence of Japanese techno-nationalism, particularly during Japan's formative techno-national period, cannot be underscored (Callon, 1995). Both MITI and the state need to play the dual role of entrepreneur and conflict manager (Chang and Rowthorn, 1995). Since an American MITI might introduce a national state-driven economic policy, a notion American individualistic and corporate capitalistic enterprise has never supported, might or could be instrumental for the resurrection of American techno-nationalism comparable to the recent congressional Republican political and cultural resurgence.

Since the 1920s, Japan has, according to the public testimony of Hitachi Corporation, been trying to nurture the capability to develop advanced technology independently. For instance, since 1877 all Japanese industrial policy was tied to the growth of a powerful military force. Military demand (military Keynesianism) stimulated the Meiji economic revolution. State military research and investment promoted industrial progress in "steel, machines, metal fabrication, automobiles, aircraft, and weapons of all kinds" (Farnsworth, 1993, p. 1171). Foreigners were hired to assist Japan in the process of indigenization which involved the creation of university departments of technologies that gave training on 'disassembly, reassembly' and training (p. 1171). They used this kind of technology for torpedo construction and perfectability. According to Samuels, this pattern of learning and indigenization by doing has been a major element of Japanese international cooperation and diffusion. The diffusion of innovation was the product of "privatization of government arsenals and other heavy industry investments and subsequent government orders, of transfer of skilled laborers from the government sector to the private sector, and government research transferred to the private sector" (p. 1171). Japan interdiffused military and commercial technologies, subordinated individual gains for the benefit of the nation. By the end of the Second World War, her advanced industry had made her the fourth most powerful nation on earth with specialization in "rocketry, turbojets, missiles and jet engines" (p. 1171).

In spite of Japanese pre-War achievements, the country was criticized for its radical techno-nationalistic ideology which nearly destroyed the state due to politics, bureaucratic sectionalism and parochialism and due to the fact that Japan was fighting against a more technologically advanced enemy. However its post-War technology, in spite of the moderate defense buildup, has largely been used for economic and peaceful purposes. These purposes have enabled Japan to become an economic superpower and have also enabled Japan to cultivate a propensity for military superiority. The nation also has potential to develop hypersonic and supersonic transport aeroplanes. LDP dominated the political climate between 1955 and 1993. During this time, three major defense buildups were carried out (1958 to 1976; 1950s to 1970s; and 1980s to the present). Since the LDP has dwindled due to defections to other movements, bureaucrats have again started to dominate Japanese public and private life. The end of Cold War politics has helped to alter the security needs and policies in the region. Japan has become an interdependent ally of the U.S. Though the socialist movement is influential (because coalition government had a socialist prime minister in 1955), other parties might defeat the socialist influence soon. With the exception of LDP and the Socialist Party of Japan, other political candidates are new and centrist but less influential.

Japan's "structural learning" and its current national and cultural interest rather than Confucianism per se, have influenced its post-War demand for lifetime employment and close cooperation between government and business. The role of government is carried out through MITI which as we saw earlier, has been criticized for inefficiency and corruption. In brief, the techno-nationalistic ideology, as Samuels and others have argued, happens to be the driving force for Japanese nationalism and industrial cooperation rather than competition. Japan uses a lot of common sense to emphasize the importance of cooperation of their market system while the U.S.'s competitive element is an aberration because it is anti-cooperative in bias and pro-competitive. The U.S. cannot avoid to ignore or emulate Japan. Mutual understanding and borrowing in terms of intercountry or intersectoral or interorganizational emulation or exchange of ideas, information, skills, and innovative models might revitalize the weaker systems of either nation.

Keys, Denton, and Miller (1994) have argued that since Japan has invested heavily in other countries, and since this investment is a reflection of economic superiority, she does not know the fate of her next destiny. In other words, Japan is in the jungle groping to conquer or to be conquered by her next frontier. This jungle theory argues that external and internal forces that have synergistically impelled Japan to economic and technological prominence will enable her to survive in the jungle as she pursues its next frontier. The external forces that have shaped Japanese management practices are the uniform or homogeneous culture that is different from pluralist societies, the industrial organization particularly the Keiretsu, and the government especially (MITI). Each of these triadic influences on techno-nationalism can be highlighted.

Japanese Culture

Culture is one of the triadic external and strategic forces that help to drive Japanese management practice toward change. Culture also serves as the foundation of the nation's management practice. Collectively, the cultural elements that tend to enhance management practice include the "presence of a collective mentality, a great persistence in the face of difficulty, a strong emphasis on social reciprocity as the governing principle of relationships, a physically concentrated and culturally homogeneous society, and an uncommon appreciation for education and learning" (p. 375).

Philosophically, Confucianism and Zen Buddhism are part and parcel of the rich Japanese cultural heritage which influences their work ethic. Confucianism views the ideal society as one in which relationships and associations are based on family and hierarchy. These social experiences are harmoniously and permanently maintained. Since a person's identity is derived and perceived to be a group's value, social and occupational or professional organizational activities are also group activities (Alston, 1989; Barnland, 1993; Condon and Kurata, 1987; and Durlabhji, 1993). Prevalent, individual, and private motives can be sacrificed for the public good (Befu, 1989). Japanese companies are like families. This familial element of the culture has become the resource that companies use for social and economic well being. For instance, since every worker is a member of the family (company), he/she is guaranteed lifetime employment, at least in the past.

Folk heroes in Japanese culture use their ability to demonstrate that Zen can be used to overcome human emotion that is a barrier to the pursuit of honorable goals. Currently, Zenism is used to "discipline the mind within the Japanese educational and social systems. According to Zen thinking, life is a process rather than a destination. The process (life) is to be improved by using strategic (long term) planning.

Japanese attach special value to personal relationships with business friends and associates and tend to maintain these relationships reciprocally. The relationships do not have to be rational as that of the Westerners. Foreign participants are, initially, accepted gradually while "inefficient distribution systems" are kept for a long time (Vzinkota, 1985a; 1985b; Lazer, Murata and Kosaka, 1985; and Tsurumi, 1982). Strong emphasis place is on resolving conflicts amicably and this culturally tends to eliminate litigation. Informal relationships between corporate managers and their subordinates are extensively used for expressive rather than instrumental purposes. The Western World uses formal and meritocratic influences for promotional and salary increases (Befu, 1989; Kumara, Hara and Yans, 1991, and Lincoln, 1989). These influences are also instrumental.

Japan's physical limitations of land availability has contributed to her cultural homogeneity and population concentration. As group membership determines one's status, material products define the role of one's group identity. The land and housing scarcity has influenced Japanese to invest conspicuously. These investments reflect not only the superior status of the products, but those products are evidences of individual and social status (Mueller, 1987).

Japan's scarcity of natural resources is a need that has motivated it to promote trade with foreign markets. This situation has spurred it to make and use technological innovations for logistics. Space and energy-efficient products were internationally attractive in markets during the 1970s largely due to the oil embargo, auto downsizing and environmental issues (Near and Olshavsky, 1985; and Porter, 1990).

Japanese education is second to none. Japanese students are academically superior to the students in other countries. The excellence of their schools, colleges, institutes and universities prepare students for lifetime corporate and public employment. Family involvement, high personal discipline and high expectations have contributed to their continual higher test scores (Porter, 1990; Tung, 1984a; Warner, 1991; White, 1989; Stevenson, Chen, and Lee, 1993; and Neelankavil, 1992). Though both Confucian and Zen philosophical systems reinforce family values and responsibility in respect to educational study habits and mental discipline, Japanese academic success is the result of diligence and persistence rather than innate ability which Darwinian evolutionists contradictorily promote (Ohmae, 1987 and Whie, 1989). In recent years, the promotion of ideas related to inferiority as an innate or genetic category rather than a socioeconomic and ecological phenomenon is shunned. Their association with eugenic movement has lost the claim and validity of universality.

Japanese zest for international education and training has sprung from cultural and strategic imperatives associated with the nation's involvement in World War II (Ibe and Sato, 1989). The persistence of Japanese expatriates in remaining in international assignments for lengthy periods influences Japanese companies and corporations to invest heavily in international training (Tung, 1984a).

Industrial Organization: Keiretsu

Leading organization analysts believe that the secret to Japan's global economic dominance or success can be attributed to the emergence of the post World War II Keiretsu (Ferguson, 1990; Gerlach, 1987; Kearns, 1992; and Rapoport, 1991). Prominent Keiretsus are the same as the Zaibatsu which existed before World War II. Keiretsus are centered around large banks which are a financial lineage (*Kinyu Keiretsu*) or enterprise or entrepreneurial group (*Kigyo shudan*) that include members several financial institutions, a highly diversified set of large manufacturing firms, a principal player, and a general trading company (Sarathy, 1985). With the influence of the post World War II McArthur administration, the family owned *Zaibatsu* was destroyed for forming the military machine of Japanese imperialism. In spite of the history of the past, six large Keiretsus have gained control over 30% of industry. They have concentrated power that parallels that of the pre-War situation (Kearns, 1992).

Because of their economic, political and industrial or organizational power, *Keiretsus* can assist their affiliates in several ways. They can provide a considerable economies of scale and highly integrated vertical relationships within the Keiretsus (organizations). They can provide a networking strategy which limits the competition of, with, or against other competitors. They can provide leverage which has favorable repayment schedules. They can provide a strategy and create a climate conducive to foreign direct investment. And finally, Keiretsus have plenty of government and political influence which they are capable of manipulating in their favor (Genay, 1991; Johnson, 1986). Small or medium sized Japanese firms are important supplier firms called *chu-shokigyo*. These firms have made Japan technically adaptable and proficient. As small subcontractors who negotiate with a Keiretsu, the small ones share design and development costs of large firms. These small firms (*dai kigyo*) "absorb losses and layoffs when business encounters a recession, agree to prices imposed from above, and often provide jobs for retiring executives when central companies are unwilling to retain them" (Cutts, 11992; and Keys, Denton and Miller, 1994, p. 377). Smaller firms hire corporate managers who are 50-55 years of age. Retiring senior officials from public service are hired by the same corporations. Through this kind of interdisciplinary, intersectoral, interprofessional and synergistic enterprise, "strong political and legal skills are passed on to top managers. Strong information networks are insured between them and interorganizationally regulated flow of information and human capital from the top to the lower institutional echelons, this is a form of emanation called *amakudari*. Emanation is a 19th century theological doctrine involving the descendance of the Deity from heaven for the purpose of reaching out to save, help, and promote the welfare of the relatively disadvantaged. This thinking, as we have seen in recent times, is not uncommon in Japanese elitist and imperialist circles.

The Japanese MITI

Japanese government exercises power through the strength and coordination effort of the twenty-one ministries. The most powerful one is the Ministry of International Trade and Industry (MITI) (Morgan and Morgan, 1991). Several prominent scholars have argued that MITI articulates the economy in the context of a five-year plan cycle. In this arena, MITI rewards strategic "industries that fit well into Japan's vertically integrated economy, promoting a planned emphasis and guiding new technology development and implementation" (Cutts, 1988; Green and Larson, 1992; McGraw, 1986 and Sullivan, 1992; and Keys et al., 1994, p. 377). According to Cutts (1992), this managed and competitive relationship tends to foster the "acceptance of informal cartel management" (Keys et al, 1994, p. 377).

The role and influence of bureaucrats in Japanese decision making arena have been the subject of debate for 35 years. The triadic bureaucratic power elite (bureaucracy, big business, and LDP) are the ones who share power in Japan. According to Chalmers Johnson (revisionist) (1982), MITI's dominant role in industrial policy making contributed to the emergence of Japan's economic miracle. The revisionist position was challenged with considerable evidence which empirically showed that institutions, organizations, processes, and participants of different industrial sectors provide(d) explanations of certain policy outputs or charges in policy outputs showing why attempts to change such outputs succeed or fail. This counter-revisionist critique of bureaucratic dominance is a more sensitive, interpretive and radical explanation concerning the implementation of industrial policy in Japan.

As unabashed counter-revisionist, Callon (1995) has thematically argued that MITI's industrial policy regime collapsed when the Japanese economy was transformed from a catch-up follower to a caught-up economic superpower during 1975-1985. The paradigm of coherence and cooperation that formerly marked the relationships among MITI, private companies and other bureaucratic actors was displaced by one of competition and conflict. Evidence indicates that MITI's industrial policy for microelectronics was neither cooperative nor successful. The powerful degree achieved by Japanese companies occurred despite of and not because of MITI.

Since the 1970s MITI's main industrial policy was to promote the knowledge-based industries. The major instrument that developed during the 1960s was the research consortium through which MITI brought together the leading companies to do joint research and development (R&D). MITI provided leadership and organization, dictated the research agenda of projects and issues, and provided half the funding. This competitive collaboration apparently worked. The country's quick rise in microelectronics during the 1960s and 1970s was widely attributed to the conspiracy in the public interest organized by MITI. Building on that success, MITI set up four more consortia for high-technology projects, and those provided the empirical evidence to support the analysis' central argument.

The relationships between MITI and the participating companies as well as among the latter were marked by continual conflict concerning the aims of research, funding and organization. Companies were unwilling to join the consortia, they minimally and grudgingly cooperated. As involvement in projects became less consistent with their interests, they tried to lessen their participation with MITI. These companies refused to provide matching funds to the second tier body of researchers. The same companies refused to participate in joint laboratory experimental ventures with MITI. MITI was forced to make major concessions. For instance, in the supercomputer consortium, the concept of a joint lab with MITI was abandoned. Though MITI was obligated to fund the whole project; the companies dictated the research agenda.

In this arena, only the VLSI consortium achieved the goals set by MITI. The goals were achieved largely due to the fact that the size and effectiveness of subsidies rather than the existing cooperation of the participating companies in joint R&D. What made them successful was not the joint lab. Rather, it was the work accomplished by companies in their private labs with the use of MITI funds. Both the supercomputer and Fifth Generation consortia rejected unproductive exotic technologies whose goals were impossibly and ambitiously unaccomplishable. The consortia produced specialized machines that were unusable because nobody wanted them. For instance, the failure of the TRON Consortium to install a standard educational PC in Japanese schools exposed the limits of MITI's powers. Consequently, a bitter and prolonged bureaucratic conflict over the jurisdiction of the Ministry of Education (MOE) resulted in MITI's defeat. Bureaucratic turf wars characterized the operation of the other three consortia, with MITI's claim to industrial policy jurisdiction disputed, as R&D issues crossed organizational boundaries and policy jurisdictions. MITI's policy change, away from the applied technology R&D conducted by its consortia in the 1960s into basic research, brought it into direct conflict with MOE which is responsible for all research in national universities. Its policy initiatives in the supercomputer, Fifth Generation and TRON Consortia were hamstrung by MOE's unwillingness to allow its academic researchers to work in MITI-financed labs or to contribute to MITI projects. There was conflict, too, between MITI and the companies as well as among the latter.

MITI's failure derived from the profound change in its policy environment. First, the transformation of the Japanese economy changed MITI's relationships with big companies. Once dependent upon the ministry to protect their domestic markets, the companies grew in size, competitiveness, and independence. Second, as microelectronics companies moved to the edge of the technology frontier, catching up and then overtaking U.S. firms, these companies could no longer rely on U.S. patents, licenses, and know-how despite the fact that their political and entrepreneurial operatives tried to influence top U.S. public officials, through lobbying activities for the purpose of restructuring operations for commercial concessions. These Japanese companies were pressured to be innovative, to increase their own R&D spending for the creation of new technologies. In essence, they had no need for MITI's seed money. Third, the deterioration in trade relations with the U.S. particularly during the 1970s, 1980s, and early 1990s was the result of Japan's increasing market share in high-tech industries, and the accumulating surplus on the trade account meant that MITI's former aggressive promotion of Japanese industry could no longer be tolerated. The ministry's loss of power and prestige forced it to attempt to expand its policy jurisdiction into new areas, such as telecomunications and venture capital, as it searched for a new role. Both here and as elsewhere, MITI has been frequently rebuffed by other more competitive bureaucracies.

In conclusion, the triadic marriage between and among the bureaucracy, industrial and technological organizations and the corporate sector have capitalized on the homogeneous Japanese culture to create internal and external organizational structures for the pursuit of their ambitious domestic, global and strategic objectives. The internal elements that enable the triadic triangle to be competitive include the "overlapping Japanese organizations, long term planning horizons, decision making and control, just-in-time manufacturing, TQC, QCs and continuous improvement, aggressive R&D, lifetime employment, generalists career paths, company unions, and women as temporaries and support groups" (Keys et al, 1994, p. 373). Alternatively, the external strategic forces that have influenced the performance of Japan's economic miracle are:

> the relative cultural homogeneity of the Japanese people makes culture a more powerful and uniform force in Japan than in more pluralist societies. Second, Japanese managerial and political elites have played a critical role in choosing, from available local and foreign cultural options, those practices which suited their own ends. They used traditional values to legitimize such practices, powerful socialization processes to inculcate associated behaviors, and material and moral incentives to reinforce these behaviors (Dunphy, 1987, p. 454; and Keys et al, 1994, p. 378).

In recent years, despite Japanese closure rather than full and free openness of its market, more American goods have started to enter Japan's market. The anti-Japan political and media rhetoric has dwindled in the U.S. because the two superpowers have started more meaningful bilateral negotiations on trade and geostrategic restructuring of the balance of forces for world stability and global coexistence. Such restructuring may be appropriate because it is in the best interest of China and its sphere of influence.

Japan's insidious propaganda release and use of funds to establish think tanks in U.S. universities and its attempt to influence the curriculum of U.S. elementary and high schools including the Japan-paid trips for social studies teaching that may rewrite World War II history and its atrocities (Choate, 1990) are questionable but less important issues of the geostrategic triadic dialectic (Americo-Japanese, Sino-American, and Sino-Japanese triangle).

The most unique characteristic of the traditional Japanese management system is its highly integrated and intrinsically consistent nature (England, 1983). The management system is like a finely tuned machine whose strategic forces are intertwined for the production of historically unparalleled economic gains. As a highly integrated and fine compensatory system, it is not, due to its unique cultural, politico-bureaucratic, and industrial aspects, very difficult to transplant. However, within itself, the system is domestically and internationally adaptable, relatively open but very efficient in entrepreneurship, trade, R&D and investment. Scholars and scientists who investigate the system should not overlook its culture, government and organizational (industrial) alliances that are influenced by its management structure— that is currently challenged for change in the context of Theory-jungle. Futuristically speaking, the United States should work hand in hand with Japan by strengthening each other in areas where either of the two superpowers is weak. Evidently, the cultural ways of Japanese society are shifting toward Western values though the shift has no cultural uniformity in all facets of national life. The Japanese industrial organization (Keiretsu) will tend to be competitive both at home and abroad. American corporations and companies have an opportunity to integrate an innovative and producer culture that parallels its largely consumerian mentality. The American market is open to Japanese goods while the Japanese market is relatively closed to Western goods. The West must seek a balance in trade in order to offset the deficits in their balance of payments and revitalize economic growth and competitiveness.

Organizational structure in Japan overlaps both product and project management team organizations; the benefits of this arrangement are associated with product development and effective implementation of operations. The presence of overlapping boundaries in project and product development enhances information sharing and creativity. Though Japanese planning models are similar to those of the Western formal corporate structure, their planning system is more visionary and sophisticated.

Decision making and control systems of the Japanese are not built on employee-manager participation and consensus decision-making, but instead they are based on consultative or persuasive decision styles. The strength of this model lies more with the structural systems that are essential for the promotion of information amplification and control and creativity. Some of these are being duplicated in the West. Manufacturing productivity per employee in the United States is rapidly approaching or is exceeding parity with Japan. Japanese companies have comparative advantage in research and development, and product design. These areas of Japanese comparative advantage are supported by MITI and other vertical alliances like Keiretsus. The

Japanese have some advantages in the management of quality processes because they evaluate product quality, critique quality management processes, assess product quality perceptions of buyers, evaluate R&D management and involvement outcomes. The U.S. corporations have started to learn to catch up in these areas.

Asian and European countries which purchase American and Japanese products have affirmed that the quality image of Japanese products is higher than that of U.S. products because of distribution, promotion and service advantages. The Japanese will continue to invest more heavily in R&D than U.S. firms because the latter spends more money in military related technologies. Japan also introduces new products faster and more economically than the U.S. The former uses "superior organizational, communicative and integrative arrangements, discriminatory patent protection, superior governmental funding and exceptional support by Keiretsus" (Keys et al, p. 392). Through their creative inventiveness, the Japanese have exemplified the integration of product R&D with manufacturing R&D both of which are strengthened by inhouse experienced workers (Hull and Azumi, 1991).

In relation to the utilization of human resources issues, HRM practices are superior for European rather than those of American and Japanese transplantation arena (Bamber, et al, 1992; Beechler and Yang, 1993; Maruyama, 1992; Tachiki, 1991). Notwithstanding the attempt to draw conclusions on the basis of a few scholarly studies, it is apparent that Japanese HRM adaptation strategies are likely to succeed in foreign countries when management conditions similar to those used in Japan are applied. Lifetime employment and seniority based employment have progressively and increasingly been declining in Japan largely due to a rapidly aging workforce (Akira, 1987; McCune, 1990; Wakabayashi and Kido, 1986; Tachiki, 1991; Hori, 1993; and Mroczkowski and Hanaoka, 1989). This decline in lifetime employment and security in hiring and promotions is largely attributed to the "movement of Japanese employees out of unionized manufacturing industries and into service industries and by implementation difficulties in foreign labor markets" (Keys et al, 1994, p. 394). Transplanted Japanese organizations have had limited success in implementing these practices and are likely to make few attempts in future. Qualitative evidence shows that the Japanese have a passion for self-improvement and a confirmed claim and persistence in rigorous educational pursuits (Ohmae, 1987; Warner, 1991 and 1992). Most Japanese major in science and engineering before obtaining graduate inhouse training in management. Very few go for postdoctorates. Internationally, they are not being criticized for their cultural homogeneity, but about the "rule and culture based learning style—often absent of a personal ethical foundation" (Keys, et al., 1994, p. 394). Japanese organizational learning theory is based on the theory of action (managers gather and process information they understand and share) and *Kaizen* (continuous improvement and perfectability). Overall, because of the rapidly converging parity of U.S. and Japanese productivity and quality, and diminishing HRM advantages, future competitive advantages of the Japanese, as they persist, will accrue largely from managerial and organizational excellence and other technologically and politically structured elements of the Japanese society.

Rationalism in the Islamic Organizational Tradition

Roxanne L. Euben (1997) has argued that rationalism is not necessarily the monopoly of the Western intellectual and analytical tradition. He refutes the affirmative of this assertion by arguing that an Islamist fundamentalist (original, biblical) critique of rationalism can be used to critique Western rationalism to demonstrate that rationality is not a monopoly of a specific racial or ethnic group. This antienlightement position is a form of antifoundationalist political discourse whose deconstructive tone may be viewed to be an element of postmodern and extreme radicalism whose norms denigrate Western and monocentric imperialism and colonialism (Euben, 1997).

Fundamentalist Theory of Political Islam

This critique is an analysis of the political theory of an "influential Islamic fundamentalist theorist" (p. 28). The critique shows that in spite of divine influence on Muslim socioeconomic and intellectual sphere of life, it is irrelevant and immaterial to assume that Islamic ideas are "irrational or purely epiphenomenal" (p. 28). Actually, these fundamentalist political ideas contain and need to be understood "as an apparently compelling ...ethicopolitical vision for the future, one that, furthermore, is part of a broader critique of rationalism and modernity that we in the West not only recognize, but in which we often participate" (p. 28). In other words, Islamic fundamentalism should not only be viewed as "reactive, defensive," and Fischer, 1982; Ibrahim, 1980; Richards and Waterbury; Tussler, 1993, and Euben, 1997, p. 30), but a genuine and rational system similar to Western rationalism. According to Sunni and Shiite Islamic fundamentalist thought, the challenge of modern political and economic sovereignty in the Middle

East is also the same challenge for the Western countries. Such challenge is a form of crisis that is attributed to the failure of Western Marxism, liberalism, and socialism. The failure of these Western socioeconomic systems also portrays the failure of Western "rationalist discourse" (p. 31) which is the incubator of reason from which "truth, knowledge and authority" emanate (p. 31). Hence, "the rationalist rejection of transcendent foundations is the source of modern malaise in general, and the impoverishment of community, authority and morality" (p. 31).

The failure of fundamentalist political practice will continue to challenge liberal and democratic ideas of all political communities. This form of thinking is a system of comparative political theory that shows how human and Western systems challenge each other on the ladder of social progress and how they are challenged due to their own ignorance. Ignorance is a condition that is characterized by "crisis, decay and malaise" (p. 33) in Western Society.

According to Qutb (1991), the problem of modern civilization is *jahiliyya*—ignorance. This type of ignorance has made society to descend by deviating from the Islamic path of progress. The *jahili* (ignorant) society has refused to submit to the will of Allah—God. As a result, "Allah's sovereignty in the realm of belief, worship, and law, through a denial of his existence, restriction of his authority or dilution of His sovereignty with false 'gods'" (Euben, 1997, p. 35) has been undermined. In addition, the Muslim community has decayed like some eras of early Islam. In other words, contemporary jahiliyya in terms of "people's ideas, their beliefs, habits, traditions, culture, art, literature, rules and laws .... Islamic sources, philosophy and thought are jahili constructs" (p. 35; and Qutb, 1991, p. 17). Universally, according to Islamic world view (*tasawwur*), the values of Islam have corrupted the souls of the entire Islamic society.

Qutb argues that the Islamic community has morally, spiritually, and socially degenerated because it is inspired by Western material, scientific, and technological achievements rather than by morality, real freedom, and authentic Islamic justice. To gain moral, spiritual, and social ascendance, the Islamic society must perceptively realize a new vision and redefinition of its true "progress, true civilization, true justice and genuine freedom" (p. 35). The same society should challenge Western cultural hegemony, valuelessness and inhumanity with values that will enable it to regenerate, become humane and built a strong civilization. In other words, Muslims should not "struggle to imitate alien models" which make them to "replicate the ills of Western society in the Islamic world" (p. 36). This usurpation of divine authority by man-made authority unites communists, liberal, socialist and nationalist systems" (p. 36). Legislative and political authority of these systems is secular rather than divine. Such authority supplants the divine sovereignty of humanity by alienating its moral discernment that makes him/her beastly. People in the West have become beastly because they are morally bankrupt. Moral bankruptcy is characterized by family alienation, disintegration, disorganization, disunity and social dislocation rather than family love, unity, nurturance, family values, social integration and tolerance. The family is the smallest social unit in civilized and backward society. It fortifies the young through social conventions and transmission of cultural heritage. The abuse, rejection and destruction of the family in liberal Christian systems is equivalent to the rejection of heaven, denial of the sovereignty of God on earth and the cultivation of an abysmal civilization.

Sovereignty belongs to God alone. It needs to be expressed in the context of Islamic law (*Shariah*) which includes the thoughts and practices of Mohammed the Prophet. Every believer knows and utters the *Shahadah* (confession of faith) by pronouncing that "There is no God but Allah, and Muhammed is His Prophet" (p. 38). The prophet is the teacher of God's will (Qutb, 1991). Contemporary authority has lost his Islamic path for progress because he has become more political and less spiritual instead of vice versa. In doing that, the authority has become an unbeliever.

Islamic path is a form of Islamic law. The "law provides guidelines for everything from ritual washing to dispensation of property to political treaties. Since it dictates the principles of administration, justice, morality and social and domestic norms, it governs as a totality" comparable to contemporary Western political theory (rationality) which separates 'public' from 'private' sovereignty (*hakimiyya*) (p. 38).

Islam as Freedom and Equality

According to Qutb, real Islamic civilization is based on freedom and equality for everyone in society. Freedom is positive and negative liberty (Berlin, 1986) for the *Umma* (all Muslims). Freedom for the Umma (in a supranational sense—without political or geographical boundaries) "is freedom from obedience to tyrannical rule, the essence of which is a absence of (Sovereign's) restraint, an evil ...." that is "intrinsic to human sovereignty" (Euben, 1997, p. 39). Secondly, it is also "freedom to submit to membership in God's community, to repudiate the dominance of passion and license that has passed as freedom" for full humanhood (p. 39; and Qutb, 1991, p. 125).

The Islamic traditions of equality under the divine sovereign are grounded on the idea that "each member is equal by virtue of common submission to God, as opposed to a society in which one man rules another or where certain races or nationalities claim supremacy" (Euben, 1997, p. 39). The Islamic doctrine of equality is different from "Locken idea of equality" in which "all persons are free and equal in that each has a natural right to life, liberty and property" (p. 39). In this case, Lockeanism is not only natural law derived from 13th century Christian thinkers such as Aquinas (McKenna, 1994), but that natural law and legal right is not indiscriminately applied in capitalistic, competitive and racist environments in which the weak, poor, and minority are, through no fault of their own, less competitive. In other words, in individualistic, competitive, and liberal environments, equality is de facto and relatively materialistically determined in terms of the collectivity within each class stratum of the socioeconomic structures. Natural rights are human or civil rights. These rights are also individual rights or the "rights of man" though they are not the only rights for individuals and their respective social collectivities. However, in the Islamic tradition, all Muslims are equal and subject to the Call of Allah. They have equal citizenship. This citizenship is citizenship of belief through which all "are equal under the banner of Allah" (p. 39;and Qutb, 1991, p. 25). Those who submit to the will of God are free and equal because of their membership in the Islamic and Godly community. This freedom and equality brought about by their membership in a theocratic community transforms the believers' status that becomes "both the precondition to and fulfillment of the" collective "actualization of the Umma" (Euben, 1991, p. 39). Though righteous servitude is far more preferable rather than unjust slavery, police coercion, and constitutional rationality (regulation of social behavior), faith and conscience (God's wrath and pleasure and reward of paradise), which are carried out in the context of the jihad (holy war) are the constraints that can appropriately control social behavior and the character or "condition of the Soul" (p.39). Jihad is pious martyrdom that liberates people by bringing God's kingdom on earth. It makes the world a better place by eradicating the jahili society replacing it with a Godly one. Analogically, as the communist state withers in a state of distributive "perfection," the Islamic state would also wither if Islamic law were to be applied strictly and blindly.

Science, Philosophy, and Freedom

Though the scientific and philosophical sciences have been used to make "human history and the universe devoid of divinity" (p. 40) these disciplines are expected to be used in such a way that humanity can be drawn to rather than dissuaded from Allah. It is true that what is Western science, that which has deflected people's attention from Allah, was originally and characteristically Islamic or Middle Eastern. The West may have antagonistically used it linguistically, metaphysically, and epistemologically in order to create or cause transgressive and corrosive contradictions in Islamic reason, interpretation, and definition of the world. Having been the cause of such chaotic contradictions means that man's viceregency (Khalifa or stewardship) of the world in which he or she is God's "deputy," has been mismanaged. Such mismanagement of God's world makes it difficult to distinguish humans from beasts. The bestiality of humanity has been demonstrated through the use of "modern technology, mass media, and weaponry" (p. 40) for the dissemination of fundamentalist ideology, the carrying out of assassinations, and mobilization for the control of the masses.

Semanticontexually, when the jahili society has been eradicated, people can exercise their sovereignty in the name of God by practicing the prescribed teachings of the Revelation. Though this looks like the use of force or compulsion, this phenomenon sounds like "Rousseau's claim "that humanity "must be forced to be free" (p. 43). In other words, "coercion is justified in the pursuit of liberation from slavery: Islam not only has the right, but the obligation to realize human freedom" (p. 43). In any case, the Qur'an shows that 'oppression is worse than killing' (p. 43) because oppressive jahiliyya has multiple power to oppress morally, educationally, technologically and coercively. In addition, modern jahili Islamists do not see the contradiction between those who advocate the "practices of veiling of women while encouraging believers to use modern methods of warfare. These corrupting influences of the jahili society make the *jamaal* (group of Muslims to carry out a jihad for change and stage a periodic *hijrah* (emigration or separation) from the corrupting tendencies of the society governed by jahiliyya. Therefore, "Islam means freedom from jahiliyya, freedom from the enslavement of one individual to another," and by another, "freedom to exercise the freedom to choose ... Islam, of course" (p. 44). Islam is not only din (way of life) about personal and public belief, this faith or way of life, "attacks institutions and traditions to liberate humanity, but does not force individuals to accept its beliefs" (p. 44). In authentic Islamic environments, belief, like individual conscience is a strong statement "about the locus of sovereignty" (p. 44).

Morality and Politics

In accordance with Islamic moral philosophy, part of the 'divine program' (p. 44) is to establish an Islamic system whose authority radiates from Allah though individuals have a right to interpretively and empirically exercise their freedom of conscience (freedom of sentiment – hurriyat al-wijdan) as they please. They exercise it in the context of the vaguely defined "Universal Law" (p.44). Universal law comprises of the laws that are essential for human "biological being," his or her involuntary functions; Shariah is part of the universal law; the physical laws of nature embody these laws" (p. 44). To say the least, universal law is divinely ordained and it is deeply intertwined with the physical and biological sciences. Like Western and Lockean presuppositions, these physical and biological sciences are reflections of natural law.

Morality and political power are inextricable aspects of Islamic life that becomes the path to cosmic integration for the Muslims.

> In this way the just community is morally and philosophically prior to the individual: the righteous jamaa .. is the 'vehicle of redemption for the society' and 'the Umma and its destiny ... supersedes all individual considerations' ... Hence, there is a simultaneous sublimation and elevation of the self through action aimed at establishing God's nation. The Umma, in turn, creates righteous relationship on earth, endows life with special significance. Individual commitment and faith are strengthened through participation in collective action whose righteousness, in turn, guarantees the triumph of the community over hostile forces. Transformed through membership in the righteous community, man's noblest intellectual, moral and spiritual characteristics find their fullest expression. Neither evil/inferior nor divine, humans occupy a place above other creatures, endowed with God's viceregency on earth, but whose knowledge is nevertheless circumscribed by the limits of his nature. There is an essence called 'humanity' which is immutable and divine creation. This essence constitutes a fixed standard by which actual human behavior may be judged deficient or worthy (p. 45).

The State in Islam

Symbolically, Qutb (1991) has likened the Islamic state to a far-reaching, deep-rooted and extremely valuable and productive tree. To illustrate his empirical symbolism, he asserts that "Islam is just like a strong, towering tree which casts a long shadow, its intertwined branches striking the sky. By nature, its roots penetrate deep into the earth, extending to its farthest recesses, in proportion to its splendor or greatness" (p. 31 and Euben, 1997, p. 46). Qutb has used metaphorical symbolism of the state. This tree is "organic and dynamic" (p. 46) because it is comprised of a variety of live organs whose growth is singly patterned and whose universal and immutable outlook is comprehensive enough to accommodate prevailing circumstances and needs. In other words, there are no theoretical specificities for its applicable empirical explanation due to the fact that Islam is more of a practice than a scientific or speculative theory. An actualized Islamic community has only one God, Allah and no other. Given the fact that such a belief has been canonized for hundreds of years, it is self-evident that all Islamic political, bureaucratic, economic and philosophical organizational structures, values, and norms derive their essence and vitality from this type of belief system that tends to be mythologically rationalizable. In other words, Islam is "a model or universally recognized religious or scientific accomplishments that provide problems and solutions to a community of scholars, believers, and practitioners…(Sagini, 1996, p. 93 and Kuhn, 1962).

Though Qutb does not, for obvious reasons, specify the political institutions of the Islamic state, for this would be viewed as a form of theorizing that is "a jahili tactic designed both to distract believers and to neutralize the essential practicality of the Islamic worldview" (Euben, 1997, p. 46) and was destructive and sophisticated gamesmanship and sophistry, he conceived it as a dynamic and continuous program whose active and transforming capacity is beyond theoretical intellectualization in its practice. Theorizing is against the authority of Islamic legal philosophy. In other words, the statehood of Islam is oriented to its "religious doctrine … oriented praxis" (p. 47). Government must practice social justice in Islam (Al-Adala al-Ijtima 'iyya fi-l-Islam) and the principle of consultation (*Shura*). The Qu'ran indicates that Allah expects believers to 'settle their affairs' "by" 'mutual consultation' (p. 47). Sura "42:38" admonishes believers to 'seek counsel' from their brethren in all affairs (Sura 3:159)" (p. 47). In other words, all human activity is regulated by divine law. Government does not legislate but administers the given religio-politically inspired Islamic law that keeps the theocracy afloat. It is clear that the system resembles "Plato's philosopher kings ... selfless instruments of timeless truths" (p. 47) that are deeper than "human legislators" (p. 47 and Wolin, 1960, pp. 53-55).

Though the Islamic theocracy is an extended and tyrannical function of the state, its extreme and monolithic element resembles its Marxian counterpart whose bankruptcy in democratic theory does not invalidate the superiority of democratic rationality. The "responsibility of the ruler is thus mediated by the Shar'iah: justice flows from adherence to Islamic law alone, not from adherence, for example, to the terms of a political contract. Because the ruler's authority is entirely derivative, he has no claims to hereditary succession, special privileges, or elevated status" (Euben, 1997, pp. 47-48). Even when a political leader uses his own discretion, he does so in consonant with Islamic Shariah. If Reform and innovation are justifiable in "reference to Islamic principles and can facilitate the realization of the ethico-political worldview implicit in Islamic Law" (p. 48) it will be carried forward through legally and officially recognized channels of authority.

Economically, Islamic law regulates property ownership. Ownership of common property is viewed as a form of stewardship. Islamic government redistributes the property as it sees fit. This theocratic and socialistic tendency does not only reject the ideal concept of free market competition, but, it also rejects the laws of self-interest through which individuals, groups, and corporations can accumulate wealth and exchange it for cash or for goods and services.

Qutb and other scholars believe that the Islamic state's fundamental political purpose is the provision of social justice. Its community has the moral responsibility to maintain and protect weaker members. This is a collective legal and moral obligation. In essence, "Islamic social justice is the natural expression of an organic worldview; it is but one practical corollary of the universalistic ethic of unity, mercy, love and mutual responsibility" (p. 48). The way in which wealth is redistributed expresses responsibility. In Qutbian analysis, Marxist economic equality is philosophically reductionist in the context of Islamic understanding of justice, for in Islam, "equality must be manifested simultaneously in the social, political, and spiritual realm. Therefore, when justice is abundantly available in all life's facets," attentiveness to social justice is the path to Allah's pleasure and avoidance of his vengeance for both the individual and ... the community" (p. 48). Though justice is viewed as an "expression of and catalyst for the solidarity" (p. 48) of human beings, it is mitigated through the distribution of property to the community. Much like John Locke's philosophy, ... the right of ownership of property, i.e. acquisition is gained through labor. However, acquisition is not only attained through "hunting, irrigation, mining, and wage-labor" (p. 48), but, it is also the "appropriation of the possessions of unbelievers killed by a Muslim" (p. 48 and Qutb, 1953, p. 110). In other words, both Islam and Christianity can kill or enslave in order to acquire property and redistribute it as they see fit. Since Marxism lacks moral justification for redistributive justice, it will cease to be.

The Marxist tradition of historical materialism or dialectical materialism has some moral affinity with the Qur'anic revelation of the economic principles of the Islamic community. The principles assert that each Muslim should be able to earn a living. "One of the five Pillars of Islam is an obligatory poor-tax (*Zakat*, literally meaning purification, but also charity), a property tax that provide a kind of safety net for the poor" (Euben, 1997, p. 49). According to (Sura 24:56) of the Qu'ran, when believers observe their devotional obligations by paying the Zakat and obeying the Apostle, they will be shown mercy. In other words, they generously practice piety because they minimally care for the poor. Such generosity, piety and caring spirit tends to militate against the love of selfish personal gain. In a Western sense, personal or selfish gain is self-interestedness that is characteristic of basic elements of human nature. In Islamic traditional religious and political culture, both the individual and the community, group, or collectivity need to resist the selfish instincts of human nature for the successful construction of a just society. Even ancient Greeks and Medieval Europeans agree with what Averroes has affirmed, that the autocratic *Wazir* (prime minister) managed their resources in terms of wealth and prosperity of the empire in order to support the military and the commercial population. The peasantry and merchant classes were not heavily taxed for this world adversely affect commerce and productivity. Municipal market managers (*muhtasib*), according to hisba literature, supervised business activity in line with the business principles of Roman Sensors (*aediles*) and Greek market regulators (*agoranomai* and *metronomai*). When the demand was low (*talaqqi*) merchandise was sold cheaply. Sometimes, this state of affairs encouraged hoarding activities that encouraged the sale of goods to intermediaries to take place. In spite of the extended family agriculture and stock-raising activities, particularly commercial credit, use of checks and bookkeeping are originally Arabic rather then European. Additionally, old terms like storehouse, warehouse, and magazine are Arabic rather than European. In other words, both economic theory and intellectual historical legacy seem to have evolved in Muslim or Arabic lands rather than Caucasian ones (Essid, 1995).

As an eminent critic, Qutb condemns monopolies and usury. His vilification of capitalism has been observed in the *book Marikat al-Islam wa al-ra 'smaliya (The Battle of Islam and Capitalism,* (1952)). This form of economic and political rationality is not only shared by Islamic and Western peoples, but, it was also immensely exercised by the magnetically bureaucratic Egyptian empire of antiquity whose spirit of intellectual and mythical rationalism has been inherited in the West (Redford, 1992, pp. 48-55; and Sagini, 1996, pp. 1-37).

Intolerance

Jews and Christians (Gentiles) are called the People of the Book – The Holy Bible. These people are supposedly, viewed on the historical plane, protected minorities in Muslim lands. They are the ahl al-dhimma whose rights are based on Public law. However, since the rights are not firmly enforced, the *ahl al-dhimma* are treated as "unequal, as evidenced by their differential treatment in the realms of taxation, military service, and job opportunities, as well as in popular suspicion of minorities" (Euben, 1997, p. 49). These Zionist and Christian (Egyptian coptics) minorities are religiously tolerated in spite of the claims of toleration by the majorities for diversity and inclusiveness. A just and tolerant Islamic society is one which is not only characterized by diversity and inclusiveness, but also one which "incorporates and builds upon a plurality of histories, cultures, and identities united by each individual's equal relationship with the creator" (p. 50). The language of pluralism should be diversity rather than unity or uniformity and plurality rather than solidarity or unanimity. Though Qutb, in the book *Social Justice in Islam*, argues that individual equality is a function of common individual humanity, in essence, that that form of common individual humanity is imperialistically incorporated into assimilationists rather than integrationist socio-cultural morphology. As a result, "Qutb's emphasis on unity out of diversity is more an expression of his monistic vision of a community that has transcended the 'base' divisions of class, clan, tribe, race, and country than a discussion of tolerance in the classic Lockean sense" (p. 50).

The five pillars of Islam are *zakat* (charity), *salat* (prayer), *shahada* (the profession of faith), the *hajj* (pilgrimage to Mecca), and *saum* (fasting). The pillars place emphasis on active practicality of the Islamic religious spirit. In the context of the spirit, the state responds in two established cultural traditions. "On the one hand, ... the state as the vehicle to transform natural harmony into communal solidarity is a direct challenge to political theories of 'conflict,' that is, theories of the state that build upon a conception of human nature as inherently contentious, and progress as the outcome of tension and discord between species, classes, or interests" (p. 50). On the other hand, Qutb's intellectual and monistic rhetoric asserts that Islamic practicalism was characterized by chaotic parochialism (*fitna*). Fitna is a state of rebellion or war carried out against the divine law or threat against the moral purity and belief of Islam (Euben, 1997). Such is the condition of rationalistic empiricism of the Islamic tradition. The tradition, which may be influenced by ascetic and mystic irrationalism is reaffirmed by the rationality of its transcendentalism.

Rationalism in Human History

According to Hegel (1997), rationality, which is to say, reason, or thinking is experienced in the form of "sensation, cognition, intellection, in our instincts and violations" (p. 955). In other words, rationality is

reason is the law of the world and that, therefore, in world history, things have come about rationality. This conviction and insight is a presupposition of history as such: in philosophy itself it is not presupposed. Through its speculative reflection philosophy has demonstrated that reason and this term may be accepted without closer examination of its relation to God – is both substance and infinite power, in itself the infinite material of all natural and spiritual life as well as the infinite form, the actualization of itself as content. It is substance, that is to say, that by which and in which al reality has its being and substance. It is infinite power, for reason is not so impotent as to bring about only the ideal, the aught, and to remain in an existence outside of reality – who knows where – as something peculiar in the heads of a few people. It is the infinite content of all essence and truth, for it does not require, as does finite activity, the condition of external materials, of given data from which to draw nourishment and objects of its activity; it supplies its own nourishment and is its own reference. And it is infinite form, for only in its image and by its fiat do phenomena arise and begin to live. It is its own exclusive presupposition and absolutely final purpose, and itself works out this purpose from potentiality into actuality, from inward source to outward appearance, not only in the natural but also in the spiritual universe, in world history. That is, the Eternal, the Absolute Power and that it and nothing but it, its glory and majesty, manifests itself in the world—this, as we said before, has been proved in philosophy and is being presupposed here as proved (pp. 955-956).

Comparative Critique of Rationalism

Europeans have incorporated their religious ways of life into their constitutional, institutional, cultural and organizational structures. This happened during the Byzantine and Scholastic periods of European emancipation from the cultural influences of Egyptian, Greek, and Roman antiquities. In America, the constitutional "Wall of separation" between church and state is both real and superficial. This condition of moderation has left the secular Republic to assert its robust influence in domestic and global affairs without a strong sense of moral consciousness whose soul is spiritually bankrupt, ethically hollow, and materialistically unsatisfied because it is ceaselessly wanting. In Islam, the patriarchal authority of the theocratic state has crafted the political, economic, religious and cultural climate whose total community beliefs in the inseparability of church and state. These influences of incorporation, separation and inseparability between the rational and the irrational aspects of human nature have not been rationally reductionistic in spite of the rhetoric to the contrary. For instance, though, the previous rationalist analysis of Islam was based on modern ideas of Enlightenment Philosophy, socialism, liberalism and colonialism, the ideas are not "pure" enough to the extent that they can water down "the understanding of social systems in terms of the dynamic social processes, the incorporation of the ideal progress, the pronounced concern for social justice, modified historicism, the dialectical vision of history and the very concept of modern jahiriyya" (Euben, 1997, p. 50). In other words, in spite of their modifications, these ideas are as original as Islam itself. In their contemporary manifestations, the jahiriyya of these ideas and their malaise can be understood in the context of "Nasserism, liberalism, socialism, Marxism and Arab nationalism" (p. 51). The *ajahiri* nature of these ideas has made the Islamic authority not only to recognize the hegemonic essence of their significance, but also, to realize that such rationalist and hegemonic constructions of the religious state have contributed to making it less and less divine, more and more alienating of the elite from the masses of society. By doing that God's sovereignty has been repudiated. That is why Western ideas concerning political, cultural, economic, liberal, nationalist and socialist theory have been used to dominate the *ajahiri* culture wherever it has been.

In the absence of God's sovereignty, Western scientific reason has been used to unite a plethora of the particularity with the universality of world spirits of rationalism. That rationalistic experience is energized by human interest and guided by human love, reason, wisdom, truth and knowledge which collectively have made the world to be a more safe, stable and habitable environment for humanity. Even though, regardless of what has been the apparent, peaceful and stable socioeconomic and cultural stability of the modern and contemporary society, there have been severe times that were marked by instability of the age whose spirit of secular intellectualism – "Old Intellectual, the Anti-Intellectual and the New Intellectual" (Johnson, 1988, p. 306) shifted society's rationality from utopianism to hedonism. Old intellectuals were committed to utopian and socialist ideas. The anti-intellectual age is the period of pop relativism. The New Intellectual Age is characterized by the society's dependence on science and technology, relativism, UFOs, psychics, valuelessness, anti-family and political correctness. The intellectuals who promote these ideas are highly individualistic and non-conformist categories of people. Their behavior has a regular pattern of operation. As a group, they are ultra-conformists who support and who are supported by significant others. Ultra-conformality tends to make them collectively dangerous because they can create popular and influential "climates of opinion and prevailing orthodoxies" (p. 342). These opinions and orthodoxies tend to generate irrational and destructive consequences regardless of the lot of society. Just as it has been demonstrated by the 20th century events on warfare, the tyranny of ideas and those who execute them can be heartless and despotic. When ideas lose their rationality by being forcefully imposed on the peoples cultural institutions and organizations, the results of rationality become irrationality, tyranny, despotism, and dangerously full of holocaust. Such a climate demonstrates humanity's *de facto* flight of reason (Johnson, 1988) which is devoid of freedom. Such a form of freedom includes the freedom to express ideas, think idealistically, theologize or philosophize or intellectualize freely and idealistically. Such form of Hegelian thinking has parallelism in Platonic love – the love of using ideas – that are the essence of things (Sagini, 1996).

This form or mental way of thinking is monistic and processually dialectical. The dialectical method is a system of understanding reality from which truth emanates epistemologically. The dialectic consists of triads each of which consists of the thesis, antithesis and synthesis. The initial proposition is the thesis. If the thesis is inadequate in resolving the problem, the opposite is generated. This opposite premise is the antithesis. If it also proves inadequate in resolving the problem of the essence of something or things, the thesis' and antithesis' dialectic produce the synthesis or the third triadic balance, equilibria or resolution. In abstract Hegelian sense, right is the thesis, morality is the antithesis, and ethics are the synthesis. In this case, the idea of right is one of rationality. Being right is being rational. However, because there is no reference to the individual's conscience, the idea of right is both abstract and legalistic. In Hegelian and Rousseauist terms, a thing or something is right as long as it does not violate the conscience of the individual or society. In addition, since this is a form of subjectivism because the right thing to do is also the rational. Most aspects of rationality are reflections or connotations of legal universality. The two contradictory views (right-moral or thesis-antithesis) neither of which is adequate are sublanted in the ethical life and subsequently in the concept of right with which society and its individuals are accustomed. This society's concept of right is not or may not be as abstract as abstract right might be. In addition, if philosophical doctrine, e.g. Marxism, is false due to the fact that it cannot be refuted by counter-arguments, its internal weakness will make it to collapse or become valueless. Dialectically, logical processes through which the construction of dialecticism is accomplished include the being, essence, and notion of something or a thing. Then theory of being deals with quality, quantity and measures. Marxist dialects was the result of the transformation of quantity into quality or ability into need. Why questions deal with the essence of thing(s). Finally and in other words, essence is inferior to notion. In other words, at the level of notion, the sustenance is the subject i.e. mind – "the self developing conscious whole" (Flew, 1979, p. 141). While Hegelian dialectics can be used to resolve contradictions, Lockean empirical, experiential, and reflective thought can compliment the former without necessarily addressing Islamist concerns which find lasting solutions in rational and patriatheoretic fundamentalism.

References

Adachi, K. 1989. Problems and prospects of management development of female employees in Japan. *The Journal of Management Development* 8, 4: 32-40.

Adams, R.J., R.B. Peterson, and H.F. Schwind. 1988. Personal value systems of the Japanese trainees and managers in a changing competitive system. *Asia Pacific Journal of Management* 5, 3:169-179.

Akira, E. 1987. Lost: Illusion about Japanese management. *Japan Quarterly* 34: 419-423.

Alston, J.P. 1989. Wa, guanxi, and inhwa: Managerial principles in Japan, China, and Korea. *Business Horizons* 32: 26-31.

Amsden, A.H. 1993. Asia's industrial revolution. *Dissent Summer:* 324-332.

Anderson, W.S. 1981. Meeting the Japanese economic challenge. *Business Horizons* 24, 2: 56-62.

Bamber, G.J., M.A. Shadur, and F. Howell. 1992. The international transferability of Japanese management strategies: An Australian perspective. *Employee Relations* 14, 3: 3-19.

Barnland, D.C. 1993. Public and private self in communicating with Japan. In *Japanese Business: Cultural Perspectives,* eds. Subhash Durlabhji and Norton E. Marks. Albany, N.Y.: State University of New York Press.

Basadur, M. 1992. Managing creativity: A Japanese model. *Academy of Management Executive* 6, 2: 29-42.

Beatty, J.R., J.T. McCune, and R.W. Beatty. 1988. A policy-capturing approach to the study of United States and Japanese managers' compensation decisions. *Journal of Management* 14, 3: 465-474.

Beechler, J.R. 1992. International management control in multinational corporations: The case of Japanese consumer electronics firms in Asia. *OECD Economic Journal* November: 20-31.

Beechler, J.R., and S. Taylor. 1993. The transfer of human resource management systems overseas: An exploratory study of Japanese and American maquiladoras. In *Japanese Multinationals: Strategies and Management in the Global Kaisha,* eds. Nigel Campbell and Nigel Holden. London: Routledge.

Beechler, J.R., and J.Z. Yang. 1993. The transfer of Japanese-style management overseas contingencies, constraints, and competencies in Japanese-owned firms in the United States. Paper submitted to the Journal of International Business Studies.

Befu, H. 1989. A theory of social exchange as applied to Japan. In *Constructs for Understanding Japan,* eds. Yoshio Sugimoto and Rass E. Mouer. New York: Kegan Paul International.

Bendix, R. 1947. Bureaucracy: The problem and the setting. *American Sociological Review* 12, 493-507.

Blau, P.M. 1955. *The Dynamics of Bureaucracy.* Chicago: Chicago University Press.

Borrus, M. (1988). Chips Wars: Can the U.S. Regain Its Advantage in Microelectronics? *California Management Review* 30, 40, 64-78.

Callon, S. 1995. *Divided Sun: MITI and the Breakdown of Japanese High-Tech Industrial Policy, 1975-1993.* Stanford: Stanford University Press.

Chang, H.J., and R. Rowthorn. 1995. *The Role of the State in Economic Change.* Oxford: Clarendon Press.

Choate, P. 1990. Political advantage: Japan's campaign for America. *Harvard Business Review* 68, 5: 87-103.

Cole, R.E., and D.R. Deskins. 1988. Racial factors in site location and employment patterns of Japanese auto firms in America. *California Management Review* 31, 1: 9-22.

Condon, J., and K. Kurata. 1987. *What's Japanese About Japan?* Tokyo: Shufunotomo Company, Ltd.

Crump, L. 1989. Japanese managers-western workers: Cross-cultural training and development issues. *The Journal of Management Review* 8, 4: 48-55.

Cusumano, M.A. 1988. Manufacturing innovation: Lessons from the Japanese auto industry. *Sloan Management Review* 30, 1: 29-39.

Cutts, R.L. 1992. Capitalism in Japan: Cartels and keiretsu. *Harvard Business Review* 70, 4: 48-55.

Cutts, R.L. 1988. The construction market: Japan slams the door. *California Management Review* 30, 4: 46-63.

Czinkota, M.R. 1985a. Distribution in Japan: Problems and changes. *Columbia Journal of World Business* 30, 3: 65-71.

Czinkota, M.R. 1985b. Distribution of consumer products in Japan. *International Marketing Review* 2: 39-51.

Deming, W.E. 1980. What can American manufacturers learn from the Japanese? *Iron Age* 6, 3: 51.

Diesing, P. 1962. *Five Types of Decisions and Their Social Conditions.* Urbana: University of Illinois Press.

Dillon, L.S. 1983. Adopting Japanese management: Some cultural stumbling blocks. *Personnel* 60: 73-77.

Drucker, P.F. 1981. Behind Japan's success. *Harvard Business Review* 49, 2: 83-90.

Dubin, R. 1949. Decision-making by management in industrial relations. *American Journal of Sociology* 54: 292-297.

Dunphy, D. 1987. Convergence/divergence: A temporal review of the Japanese enterprise and its management. *Academy of Management Review* 12, 3: 445-459.

Durlabhji, S. 1993. The influence of Confucianism and Zen on the Japanese organization. In *Japanese Business Cultural Perspectives,* eds. Subhash Durlabhji and Norton E. Marks. Albany, N.Y.: State University of New York Press.

England, G.W. 1983. Japanese and American management: Theory Y and beyond. *Journal of International Business Studies* 14: 131-142.

Essid, Y. 1995. *A Critique of the Origins of Islamic Economic Thought.* Leiden and New York: E.J. Brill.

Euben, R.L. 1997. Comparative political theory: An Islamic fundamentalist critique of rationalism. *The Journal of Politics* 59, 1: 28-55.

Farnsworth, L.W. 1995. Japan in political and economic change: Foundations for understanding. *Journal of Politics* 57, 4: 1169-1175.

Fegurson, C.H. 1990. Computers and the coming of U.S. keiretsu. *Harvard Business Review* 68, 4: 55-70.

Flew, A. 1979. *A Dictionary of Philosophy.* New York: St. Martin's Press.

Garvin, D.A. 1986. Quality problems, policies, and attitudes in the United States and Japan: An exploratory study. *Academy of Management Journal* 29, 4: 653-673.

Genay, H. 1991. Japan's corporate groups. *Economic Perspectives* 15, 1: 20-30.

Gerlach, M. 1987. Business alliances and the strategy of the Japanese Firm. *California Management Review* 30, 1: 126-142.

Gortner, H.F, et al. 1997. *Organization Theory: A Public Perspective.* Fort Worth, TX.: Harcourt Brace College Publishers.

Gouldner, A. 1954. *Patterns of Industrial Bureaucracy.* New York: Free Press.

Green, R.T., and T.L. Larson. 1987. Only retaliation will open up Japan. *Harvard Business Review* 65, 6: 22-28.

Gulick, L.H., and L. Urwick, eds. 1937. *Papers on the Science of Administration.* New York: Institute of Public Administration.

Hegel, G.W.F. 1997. Reason in history – classics. In *From Plato to Nietzsche: Philosophic Classics,* eds. Forrest E. Baird and Walter Kaufmann, 955-985. Upper Saddle River, N.J.: Prentice Hall.

Hori, S. 1993. Firing Japan's white-collar economy a personal view. *Harvard Business Review* 71, 6: 157-172.

Ibe, M., and N. Sato. 1989. Educating Japanese leaders for a global age: The role of the international education center. *The Journal of Management Development* 8, 4: 41-47.

Johnson, P. 1988. *The Flight of Reason. Intellectuals.* New York: Harper Perennial.

Johnson, C. 1986. *MITI and the Japanese Miracle: The Growth of Industrial Policy 1925-1975.* Tokyo: Charles E. Tuttle Co.

Kearns, R.L. 1992. *Zaibatsu America: How Japanese Firms Are Colonizing Vital U.S. Industries.* New York: The Free Press.

Keddell, J.P. 1993. *The Politics of Defense in Japan.* Armonk, N.Y.: M.E. Sharpe.

Keys, J.B., et al. 1994. The Japanese management: Theory jungle – revisited. *Journal of Management* 20, 2: 373-402.

Kim, H.K., M. Muramatsu, and T.J. Pempel, eds. 1995. *The Japanese Civil Service and Economic Development. Catalysts of Change.*

Kuhn, 1962. *The Structure of Scientific Revolutions.* Chicago: The University of Chicago Press.

Kumara, U.A. Y. Ha, and M. Yano. 1991. On understanding behavior characteristics of Japanese manufacturing workers: An analysis of job climate. *International Journal of Intercultural Relations* 15: 129-148.

Lazer, W. S. Murata, and H. Kosaka. 1985. Japanese marketing: Toward a better understanding. *Journal of Marketing* 49, 2: 69-81.

Lincoln, J.R. 1989. Employee work attitudes and management practice in the U.S. and Japan: Evidence from a large competitive survey. *California Management Review* 32, 1: 89-106.

March, J.G., and H.A. Simon. 1958. *Organizations.* New York: Wiley.

Maruyama, M. 1992. Lessons from Japanese Management Failures in Foreign Countries. *Human Systems Management* 11, 1: 41-48.

McCraw, T.K. 1986. *America Versus Japan.* Boston: Harvard Business School Press.

McCune, J.C. 1990. Japan says sayonara to womb-to-womb management. *Management Review* 3: 112-116.

McKenna, G. 1998. *The Drama of Democracy: American Government and Politics.* Guilford, CT: Dushkin Publishing Group, Inc.

Merton, R.K. 1940. Bureaucratic structure and personality. *Social Forces* 18: 560-568.

Merton, R.K. 1936. The unanticipated consequences of purposive social action. *American Sociological Review* 1: 894-904.

Morgan, J.C., and J.J. Morgan. 1991. *Cracking the Japanese Market: Strategies for Success in the New Global Economy.* New York: The Free Press.

Morris-Suzuki, T. 1994. *The Technological Transformation of Japan: From the Seventeenth to the Twenty First Century.* New York: Cambridge University Press.

Mroczkowski, T, and M. Hanaoka. 1989. Continuity and change in Japanese management. *California Management Review* 31, 2: 39-53.

Mueller, B. 1987. Reflections of culture: An analysis of Japanese and American advertising appeals. *Journal of Advertising Research* 27, 3: 51-59.

Near, J.P., and R.W. Olshavisky. 1985. Japan's success: Luck or skill? *Business Horizons* 28, 6: 15-22.

Neelankavil, J.P. 1992. Management Development and training programs in Japanese Firms. *Journal of Management Development* 11, 3: 12-17.

Nishiguchi, T. 1994. *Strategic Industrial Sourcing: The Japanese Advantage*. New York: Oxford University Pres.

Ohmae, K. 1987. *Beyond National Borders: Reflections on Japan and the World*. Homewood, IL: Dow Jones-Irwin.

Porter, M.E. 1990. *The Competitive Advantage of Nations*. New York: Free Press.

Pugh, D.S. ed. 1987. *Organizational Theory: Selected Readings*. London: Penguin Books.

Qubt, S. 1991. *Ma' alim fi- Tariq* [*Signposts Along the Road*]. Beirut: Dar al- Shuruq [Originally published in 1961].

Qutb, S. 1953. *Social Justice in Islam*. Translated by John B. Hardie. Washington, D.C.: American Council of Learned Societies.

Rago, W.V. 1994. Adapting total quality management (TQM) to government: Another point of view. *Public Administration Review* 54: 61-64.

Rapoport, C. 1991. How the Japanese are changing. *Fortune* 122, 8: 15-22.

Redford, D.B. 1992. *Egypt, Canaan, and Israel in Ancient Times*. Princeton, N.J.: Princeton University Press.

Reed, S.R. 1993. *Making Common Sense of Japan*. Pittsburgh: University of Pittsburgh Press.

Samuels, R.J. 1993. *Rich Nation, Strong Army*. Ithaca, N.Y.: Cornell University Press.

Sagini, M.M. 1996. *The African and the African-American University: A Historical and Sociological Analysis*. Lanham, MD: University Press of America.

Scott, W.R. 1981. *Organizations Rational, Natural, and Open Systems*. Englewood Cliffs, N.J.: Prentice-Hall.

Selznick, P. 1949. *TVA and the Grass Roots*. Berkeley: University of California Press.

82   *Organizational Behavior*

Shrivastava, P. ed. 1996. *Academy of Management Review* 2, 1: 286-301.

Stevenston, H.W., C. Chen, and S. Lee. 1993. Mathematics achievement of Chinese, Japanese, and American children: Ten years later. *Science* 259, 5091: 53-58.

Sullivan, J.J. 1992. *Invasion of the Salarymen: The Japanese Business Presence in America.* Westport, CT: Praeger.

Sullivan, J.J. 1983. A critique of Theory Z. *Academy of Management Review* 8: 132-142.

Sullivan, J.J., and I. Nonaka. 1986. The application of organizational learning theory to Japanese and American management. *Journal of International Business Studies* 17, 3: 127-147.

Suzuki, N. 1986. Mid-career crisis in Japanese Business Organizations. *The Journal of Management Development* 5, 5: 23-32.

Suzuki, N. 1984. Japanese MBAs: Frontrunners in the multinationalization of Japanese business. *The Journal of Management Development* 3, 4: 12-22.

Tachiki, D.S. 1991. Japanese management going transnational. *Journal for Quality and Participation* 14, 6: 96-107.

Taylor, F.W. 1947. *Principles of Scientific Management.* New York: W.W. Norton.

Taylor, F.W. 1911. *Principles of Management.* New York: Harper and Row.

Tsurumi, Y. 1982. Managing consumer and industrial marketing systems in Japan. *Sloan Management Review* 24, 1: 41-50.

Tung, R. 1984a. *Key to Japanese Economic Strength: Human Power.* Lexington, MA: Lexington Books.

Warner, M. 1991. Japanese management education and training: A critical review. *Human Systems Management* 32, 2: 41-47.

Weber, M. 1947. The theory of social and economic organization. In *Organizational Theory: Selected Readings,* ed. D.S. Pugh, 328-340. New York: Free Press.

Weber, M. 1946. *From Max Weber: Essays in Sociology.* Translated by H.H. Gerth and C.W. Mills. Oxford University Press.

White, M. 1989. Learning and working in Japan. *Business Horizons* 32, 2: 41-47.

Wolin, S. 1960. *Politics and Vision.* Boston: Little Brown and Company.

Chapter 3

The Organization as a Natural or Behavioral System: 1920s - 1960s

The natural systems model of the organization is a reactive critique of the rational systems model. It is also called the informal organization. Though the natural systems model is not a dialectical critique of the rational model, the former has its own merits. The natural organization is predominantly influenced by the behaviorist and other schools of thought. The natural system has four major schools rationalize it. These schools include behaviorism, organizational humanism, human relations and the open systems. A variety of minor but influential theories such as McGregor's theory X and Y, Ouchi's theory Z, Lowe's theory of participatory leadership compliment systems theory. The open systems theory has been excluded in this chapter because it is a whole chapter in itself.

Behaviorism

The behaviorist tradition is methodologically empirical and data concerning human or animal behavior is collected through observation of natural phenomena. Behaviorism is rooted in the positivist intellectual tradition (of observation). Since the 1940s, the behavior and theory has been a scientific methodology that places emphasis on objectivity, valid results, efficiency, and economy. The ideological roots of the behaviorist theory can be traced in philosophical realism, the positivist tradition and the materialistic view of society (Knight, 1980). In the light of the realistic ideological inclination, humankind and the laws of nature are expressions or impressions of the behaviorist theory. "The task of the behaviorist is to observe living organisms, including man, in an attempt to discover the laws of behavior" (p. 118). The discovery of behaviorist laws creates a need for the technology of behavior. Second, the next root of behaviorism is positivism which was initially advanced by a Frenchman who was a mathematician and philosopher, Auguste Comte (1798-1857). Comte generally categorized the history of humanity into three major eras. The first was the most primitive era of theology in which life is explained in the light of and dominated by spirits and gods. The middle era is the metaphysical in which situations are "explained by essences, causes, and inner principles" (p. 118). The third, highest and most complex period is the positive one characterized by observation and measurement of facts.

Comte was an authority in contemporary science which he studied at Ecole Polytechnique. He was a secretary to Saint-Simon. His six volumes were the *Cours de Philosophie Positive* (1830-42). Since Comte was interested in the development of a science of society, which the behaviorists have built on, he rejected its intuitive character in terms of theology and "essences, feelings and inner causes" (p. 119) because these are not scientifically measurable and verifiable. Behavioristically, empiricism is the central tenet of verification. In other words, the behavioristic philosophical and scientific doctrine assertively argues that "sense perceptions are the only admissible basis of human knowledge and precise thought" (*Webster's II New College,* 1995, p. 861). Behaviorism is also applied in logic, epistemology and ethics. In other words, this scientific and Comtean system of thought was designed to be superior to theological and metaphysical methodology and presuppositions. Its preeminence is based on a hierarchy of the sciences that begins with the science of mathematics and culminates in sociology. Comte's radical philosophical intellectualism made him unable to teach in universities. He only lectured to private audiences.

Third, the historical root of behaviorist theory is infused in materialism. Materialistically speaking, the reality of behaviorism is explainable and explicable in the context of laws of matter and motion. Its scientific eminence rejects "the beliefs of the mind, spirit and consciousness. It rejects them because these beliefs, with the exception of the Freudian school, belong to pre-scientific and pre-industrial age. These cannot be observed and analyzed scientifically.

Ivan Pavlov (1849-1936) was a Russian psychologist who used a reflex reaction to "condition dogs to salivate by ringing a bell if the dog had previously been trained to associate the sound of the bell with the arrival of food" (Knight, 1980, p. 119). In his advancement of Pavlov's work, John B. Watson (1878-1958), an American psychologist, asserted that human behavior is a construction of reflexes that are conditioned. He argued that psychology should not concentrate on thinking and feeling, both of which are largely cognitive in reality and unobservable, instead, psychology should concentrate on what people do. Watson believed that the environment influenced and shaped human behavior. He argued that when the child's environment is controlled, the child could be molded to meet the desire of the adult.

In the United States, the behaviorist theoretical perspective was first propounded by the psychologist J.B. Watson in *Behaviorism* (1925). In this book, Watson asserted that psychological functioning can be defined in terms of observed behavioral data. This position was initially introduced for the purpose of establishing a firm scientific basis for psychology. Since then, behaviorism has been extensively elaborated by many eminent social scientists including B.F. Skinner.

Behaviorism covers three major and separate doctrines. The first one is metaphysical behaviorism which argues that consciousness does not exist. Organisms and humans only behave. Second, methodological behaviorism holds that "whatever the truth about this metaphysical question, a truly scientific psychology can only study publicly observable behavior and may not deal with introspection" (Flew, 1979, p. 39). In recent memory, introspection is associated with cognitive psychology or cognitive awareness which on the contrary is a form of intellectual consciousness (Posner, 1989). Third, analytical behaviorism claims the "Psychological concepts can be analyzed in exclusively behavioral terms and that is what such words mean" (Flew, 1979, p. 39). Of the three types of behaviorism, analytical behaviorism appeals to most philosophers and psychologists. For instance, in his prominent work, *The Concept of Mind* (1949), Gilbert Ryle contends that the Cartesian myth of the ghost in the machine is a product of a category mistake about the exclusivity of the mental and the physical, and that in reality, mental concepts could be analyzed in terms of overt acts and utterances. Epistemologically, even Wittgenstein reasonably argues that the criteria for the occurrence of mental processes is not private or introspective acts, but is rather publicly accessible as a form of behavior. For instance, the criterion for identifying and measuring pain is pain related behavior.

The two philosophical intricacies of the behaviorist tradition include: what precisely the concept of behavior identifies, e.g. physiological movements or voluntarily performed acts. Second, speaking in first person terms, can pain as an inner experience, be an outward manifestation of behavior as it was inferred to earlier. In other words, if inner feelings cause a certain manifestation of behavior, isn't behaviorism a form of operationalism? In other words, under these circumstances, behaviorism may be viewed as neither monistic nor pluralistic but in a sense, a dualistic concept (Flew, 1979) that is introspectively and operationally instrumentalized.

According to the *New Webster's Dictionary and Thesaurus of the English Language* (1992) the term behavior means "action, attitude, bearing, breeding, carriage, conduct, deed, demeanor, deportment, disposition, manner, strategy, tactics" (p. T4). In other words, the term behavior refers to "manners, deportment, moral conduct, the way in which a machine, organ or organism works with respect to its efficiency," or "the way in which something reacts to environment" (p. 87).

The positivist behaviorist tradition is limited due to its rejection of truth whose sources are nonempirical or nonobservable and scientifically unverifiable. Its thought process influenced the emergence of pragmatism, behaviorism, scientific naturalism and the analytic movement in philosophy. The scholars (20th century Vienna circle) are scientists, mathematicians and symbolic logicians who coined the term logical positivism. The main goal of these scholars and scientists has been an attempt to discover an inclusive terminology and intellectual framework common to all sciences. All positivists feel that human or scientific observers can achieve neutrality in their findings. The behaviorist tradition studies behavior by using the individual as the unit of analysis. In his *Administrative State*, Herbert Simon indicates that decisions are the unit of analysis. He argues that decision making is multidisciplinary in approach which calls for rigor in scientific and systematic research which is comparative and empirical. Simon argues that the behavioral approach is normative. Normativity is the logical positivist tradition in academia. In this intellectual and scientific tradition, we use observation to prove propositions. The practice of proving is a value free dichotomy of values and facts. Simon argues that the principles of administration (proverbs or wise sayings) are maxims that enable the political and administrative elite to rationalize power as they run the affairs of government. What is observable must be separated from what ought to be observed. Originally, Weber supported the "ought" position. However, behaviorism, which is more descriptive than normative was asserted. The diversity of themes behaviorism incorporates involve the human relations theory, the contingency theory, the organizational humanism theory and Simon's decision making model.

In recent years, the most influential behaviorist was B.F. Skinner. Skinner's work in behavior modification, teaching machines and programmed learning has had far reaching impact in academic, counseling and in scientific circles. Of the 20 works he composed, the most influential ones were *Science and Human Behavior* (1953), *Beyond Freedom and Dignity* (1971), and *Walden Two* (1948). *Walden Two* is a utopian story book which publicizes the virtues of a behaviorally influenced society. His writings on behavior modification views behaviorism as a way of psychologically changing personal relations based on motivation, for instance, determining real needs, providing the sense of belonging, accomplishment, and teamwork.

Skinner's ideas of behaviorism made him to be the center of controversial debates for two decades because he "repudiates the freedom and dignity traditionally ascribed to human beings, and seems to indicate that some individuals should decide how others will be conditioned" (Knight, 1981, pp. 119-120). In other words, Skinner's contentions may appear to have been less critical of slavery and abusive irrespective of the moral, constitutional and humanitarian considerations. His position parallels George Orwell's *Animal Farm* (1984) in which humanity is reduced to objects or organisms that exist to be manipulated in and by the environment that is controlled by the laws of nature and behavioral technology.

According to Skinner, when humans are governed through the process of conditioning, by the laws of behavioral technology, the chances of human survival can be maximized as opposed to when humans are governed by other laws that apply at random.

The presuppositions of behaviorism are rooted in naturalistic science; behavioralists aspire to develop a science of humankind. Behaviorism is not a science of human behavior, but rather, it is a theory of human behavior which has affinity with scientific philosophy in terms of methodological and analytical constructs. Behaviorists argue that humans do not have special dignity or freedom. Although these human beings are complex natural organisms, they are part and parcel of the animal kingdom. The animal kingdom is analyzed or analyzable through evolutionary theory which behavioristic psychology and other social sciences theoretically affirms. Educationally, learning can be engineered behavioristically by using positive or negative reinforcers. Positive reinforcers reward learners to repeat the rewarded behaviors which are associated with success. Negative or aversive reinforcement punishes undesirable behaviors whose existence becomes extinguished in the long run. Some of the aversive forms of reinforcement are forms of control, e.g. "corporal punishment, scolding, extra homework, forced labor, the withdrawal of privileges, and examinations designed to show what the student does not know" (Knight, 1981, p. 121). Such aversive behaviors lead to aggressiveness, daydreaming and dropout behaviors. According to Ozmon and Craver (1976, p. 149) the procedures for classroom behavior modification are:

(1) specify the desires outcome, what needs to be changed, and how it will be evaluated; (2) establish a favorable environment by removing unfavorable stimuli which might complicate learning; (3) choose the proper reinforcers for desired behavioral manifestations; (4) begin shaping desired behavior by utilizing immediate reinforcers for desired behavior; (5) once a pattern of desired behaviors has begun, slacken the number of times reinforcers are given; (6) evaluate results and reassess for future development.

In recent years, both philosophic orientation to behaviorism and the materialistic mentality of the business community have put a manipulative emphasis on education to provide efficiency, economy, precision and objectivity as elements of accountability. Behavioral techniques are used in business practice. Some of these include systems management, advertising, sales and promotion and even online production performance.

Skinner

Skinner's creative and strange model is scientifically and technologically designed to be instrumentally responsible for mechanistic and orderly human Behavior. He argues that all human behavior is caused and controlled by external agencies rather than by the human being as an individual. He argues that humans do not have the freedom of choice because "there are no arbitrary, uncaused, ultimately mysterious, or inherently inexplicable human acts" (Nash, 1968, p. 407). Skinner's main point is the argument that "it is not a question of freedom or control, but who controls us" (p. 407). What he has in mind is that science in terms of manipulative and rational scientific experimentation, business, politics, organized religion and the mass-media have a strong interest in controlling and nurturing humanity. Humanity is planned and controlled by agencies that are external to him/her. Revelation and traditional authority have no place in human planning and control. Skinner's model society is one that is a product of scientific genetic experimentation described in Walden Two (1948). The values of such a society must be tested scientifically in order to judge the validity of their conventionality by effortlessly enhancing the goodness and happiness of society. Such a situation will eliminate the "struggle, competition and punishment, we shall have secure contentment, painless virtue and cheerful efficiency" (p. 408). All of these things can be achieved through the application of positive reinforcement. Positive reinforcement rewards people for promoting the nurturance of a virtuous society that is controlled from without rather than from within. Skinner further argued that:

> In such a society there will emerge a new model of the educated person. Although Skinner's plan allows for great diversity of types of educated people, they will possess certain common characteristics. Scientific knowledge of the control of human behavior will be used to create a planned man, one who will behave in the way best calculated to achieve society's goals. For Skinner, the ultimate value is the survival of mankind. Hence the educated man will be capable of cooperation with his fellows, since it is this, rather than aggressive competitiveness, that will lead to survival. He will not be a fanatical zealot but a rational, critical, and creative thinker. Behavioral engineering will have removed his antisocial tendencies and he will want only what is good for himself and his society (p. 408).

Skinnerian model of humanity was constructed during America's golden age (1945-1970) but popularized during the 1970s and early 1980s. It is a very abstract and romantic view of what society should be in the era of scientific pre-eminence in terms of its use to solve society's problems in the face of East-West competition during the Cold War. The model is kind of reductionist because it underscores human capabilities including freedom of choice and individual autonomy. This led many to attack Skinner out of ignorance, fear, misinterpretation and sheer malevolence. Even though, psychologically, some scholars tend to argue that his model of society is loftier because it epitomizes the dreams of the Great Society Programs of the 1960s with which Lyndon Johnson was concerned. The Programs were also designed to address and pacify the pathologically oriented internal and external crises of the nation's domestic and foreign policy of which the Civil Rights Movement, the Vietnam War, the student rebellion and the post-Nixonian aftermath were classic. Those who attacked Skinner revealed that he touched a sensitive nerve with his utopian idealism. Happiness does not necessarily come from mechanistic structural functionalism as much as it does come from experimental and informal unpredictability.

In Walden Two, ethics are inculcated during early childhood only. The possibility of adult moral development is nonexistent and undesirable since it was pre-programmed during childhood or at infancy. Since Skinner's model fails to recognize morality and maturity, which are questions of free choice and decision-making, the model is so mechanistic and inhuman to allow the development of adult morality and maturity. In addition, testing values is scientifically untenable.

1920s-1930s: The Human Relations Model: Elton Mayo

It has been argued that organizations are systems of interdependent and interrelated human beings. Organizational members are a resource that is actively involved in the functioning processes of the organization. Members play certain roles that affect organizational aims, methods and goals that are essential for accomplishing organizational missions. According to Blau (1956), it is unreasonable to assume that the criteria of technical rationality is the best solution to all human problems. Contrary to this assumption, Blau shows that "To administer a social organization according to purely technical criteria of rationality is irrational, because it ignores the nonrational aspects of social conduct" (Blau, 1956; and Scott, 1981, p. 79).

The father of the human relations school of thought is Elton Mayo. During the 1920s and early 1930s, a variety of detailed studies and scientific experiments were conducted at the Hawthorne plant belonging to the Western Electric Company near the City of Chicago. Though these scientific studies on the subject in question have been meticulously described by Roethlisberger and Dickson (1939), this descriptiveness was scholastically interpreted and popularized by Elton Mayo (1945). Both Roethlisberger and Mayo were colleagues of the Harvard Business School. Mayo was a specialist in industrial psychology and his early research interests evolved from Taylorist Industrial and mechanistic tradition of scientific management school. Like Taylor's School, "Mayo studied individual factors such as fatigue in an attempt to determine the optimum length and spacing of rest periods for maximizing productivity" (Scott, 1981, p. 86). The purpose of the Hawthorne research experimentation was to "determine the optimal level of illumination for the assembly of telephone relay equipment" (p. 86). The results of the research indicated that

> The conditions of scientific experiment had apparently been fulfilled—experimental room, control room; changes introduced one at a time; all other conditions held steady. And the results were perplexing...Lighting improved in the experimental room, production went up; but it rose also in the control room. The opposite of this: lighting diminished from 10 to 3 foot-candles in the experimental room and the production again went up; simultaneously in the control room, with illumination constant, production also rose (Mayo, 1945, p. 69; and Scott, 1981, p. 86).

It should be noted that this experiment's results, initially confused the researchers because they did not understand why production went up in the experimental and control rooms. At least, production should have remained low in the control room. This confusion influenced Mayo to comment like this:

> After inspecting the results of the bank wiring observation room study at the Hawthorne plant, Mayo concluded: It is unfortunate for economic theory that it applies chiefly to persons of less, rather than greater, normality of social relationships. Must we conclude that economics is a study of human behavior in non-normal situations, or alternatively, a study of non-normal human behavior in ordinary situations? (Scott, 1981, p. 86).

In other words, the results of Hawthorne research ironically proved that individual workers were not influenced by economic rationality. Their behavior was collectively, psychologically, and individually driven by feelings and sentiments rather than economic factors of the Taylorist and Wilsonian mechanistic and classical traditions of management theory in which "the only best way" of mechanistic structural functionalism was the order of the day. Individual interviews proved that workers' productivity did not increase in both cases because workers were well paid or were committed to the ethics of organizational industrial production; on the contrary, these unmotivated alienated and underpaid workers produced well because they felt good for being singled out for the interviews and wanted to show management and their interviewers that they had unmet needs that were being addressed through the interviewing process. The feeling and realization that their individual and collective needs were being articulated influenced productivity. In other words, the Hawthorne experiments and their observations, analysis, and interpretation enabled Mayo to discover the interlockage of the natural (behavioral) and the informal organization in the formal or rational one.

The circumstances under which these experiments were conducted involved three major factors. First, post-World War II economic conditions characteristic of inflation, stagflation and industrial sluggishness were paramount. Second, with the successful evolution of the 1917 Communist Revolution in the USSR, the subsequent development of a strong Socialist Movement in the U.S. during the 1920s and 1930s dictated such a form of intellectual inquiry into organizational and industrial settings. Third, in spite of the massive unionization of labor, workers felt that the owners of capital used the factors and forces of production to exploit them through the monopoly of the means of production, misappropriation of labor surplus and inequitable distribution of economic resources (Marx, 1954). As a result of the alienation, exploitation, the poor working conditions (low wages, poor housing, slave-like labor) of workers, most of whom were new immigrants in the central cities, further social problems were ignited in terms of exchange of citizenship for votes during subsequent and ideologically based general elections in the United States. To hit the nail on the head, the 1924 Immigration and Naturalization Act was not only passed in order to respond to the scarcity of labor, but that form of scarce labor was extrapolated in the context of the nature of workers output which was affected by the way in which they were treated. Naturally enough, how people feel about their work affects how they perform. The way they feel affects their co-workers and affects their productivity. How you feel about your boss outside the work environment or inside it affects your productivity. The affectation of the worker by the working climate of the work environment influences workers' "hearts, feelings and attitudes" that in turn affect their productivity (England, Lecture Series for 3-6-1997) on the informal school of thought at Oklahoma State University.

Workers' dilemma, before the Hawthorne inquiry was carried out, conditions of work were largely determined by the structure of organizational culture. Nearly all organizations have norms and implicit rules which influence governance and productivity. These norms and rules are part and parcel of the formal organization which is inextricably "married with" the informal organization. The informal organization is a set of shared attitudes, feelings, group solidarity, similarity of attitudes and above all, organizational culture. The discovery of informal group processes in organizational settings has been extensively studied by social psychologists and sociologists during the last fifty years. For instance, studies on the subject in question have been done by Maier (1952), Katz, Maccoby, and Morse (1950), Katz, et al. (1951), Homans (1950), Whyte (1951 and 1959), and Sayles (1958). They wrote on small group behavior in organizational settings. Their work centered on the organizational environment, group perceptions of leadership behavior, "impact of worker background and personality attributes on organizational behavior" (Scott, 1981, p. 87) and how "organizational factors affected the number, types and tactics of groups that emerged" (p. 87). Also, Roy (1952) and Seashore (1954) focused on the consequences rather than the determinants of group membership, "group cohesiveness on individual conformity to production norms" (p. 87). According to White and Lilpitt (1953), groups perform more effectively under democratic as opposed to laissez-faire or authoritarian leadership. Stogdill and Coons (1957) investigated how trust, friendship and respect are values that characterize supervisors who are well organized and who get things done. This type of value system was called "initiating structure" (Scott, 1981, p. 87). The two men were at Ohio State University when they completed the study. Effective leaders create a climate for high morale.

In 1961, Likert's findings showed that supervisors' ability to influence their subordinates made them linking pins (p. 88) within the bureaucratic hierarchy of organizational settings. According to Blau, managers have authority and leadership skills which give them power in formal organizational settings. The distinctive characteristic of authority which differentiates it from informal leadership, is that it is rooted in the formal powers and sanctions which the organization bestows on managers (Blau, 1964). It is in "keeping with the natural system perspective to ignore this distinctive component of leadership in formal organizations" (Scott, 1981, p. 88).

Studies have been conducted by Collins (1946) on race, Warner and Low on class, and Dalton (1950) on the influence of culture. These studies show that the human relations theory influences organizational behavior in respect to the roles individuals play in organizations.

Also, in her analysis of corporations in the United States, Kanter (1977a) established that "men are systematically allocated to career lines allowing extended upward mobility while women tend to be placed in low-ceiling or dead-end tracks" (Scott, 1981, p. 88). Although objective social conditions do not cause existing behavior, individuals vary in their "interests, values, intelligence, sensitivity, and many other properties" (p. 88).

In the light of these circumstances, the purpose of the evolution of the human relations school is to sympathetically understand the workers' dilemma (Roethlisberger and Dickson, 1939) and provide professional advice and insight that are conducive to organizational change and adaptability. In addition, and in human relations perspective, formalization is a function of extreme functional and rational specialization which has its own shortcomings because it alienates. To eliminate such side effects, "job enlargement or job rotation tends to reduce alienation (Argyris, 1957). In addition, participatory management and motivation (Lewin, 1948; Coch and French, 1948; Blumberg, 1968; and Tannenbaum, et al, 1974) theories are viewed as better solutions in terms of their reduction of organizational and industrial alienation. Recent observations on the subjects indicate that Japanese and Western Europeans are culturally better placed in using participatory and motivational techniques than Americans. Participatory management eliminates alienation.

In spite of its promises, the human relations theory as a movement has been severely criticized on ideological and empirical planes. Though it evolved to humanize the "cold and calculating rationality of the factory shop" (Scott, 1981, p. 89) it has been attacked for being "a more subtle and refined form of exploitation" (p. 89). It de-emphasized the legitimate interests of the worker. The actual conflicts of interests were not only denied, but they were 'therapeutically' managed. Management's new roles became more elitist than instrumental. During the 1940s and 1950s, the movement was nicknamed 'Cow sociology' which meant that as contented cows produced more milk, the manipulated and satisfied workers tended also to be more productive (Bell, 1960; Bendix, 1956; Landsberger, 1958; and Strauss, 1963).

Irrespective of these criticisms, research conducted by Brayfield and Crockett (1955) has shown that there is no clear relationship between worker satisfaction and productivity. Schwab and Cummings (1970) indicated that the relationship between supervisory behavior or leadership style and worker productivity is not clear either. Hollander and Julian (1969) have argued that there is no clear relationship between job enlargement and worker satisfaction or productivity. Hulin and Blood (1968) have demonstrated that there is "no clear relationship between participation in decision making and satisfaction or productivity" (Scott, 1981, p. 90). Based on the theoretical and empirically synergistic view for reform, the human relations model has done little, in spite of the rhetoric to the contrary, to be instrumental to organizational humanism in the areas of motivation, morale, and leadership (Scott, 1981).

Comparison between Behavioral and Classical Models

Nowadays, managers do not use POSDCORB—the behavioral paradigm that challenged the classical approach with respect to the place of the individual in the organization. The classical approach to organizational management was either structural rationality or mechanistic Taylorism which were articulated along rational and hierarchical levels of the organization. These classical models concentrate on executive decision making responsibilities that maintain organizational hierarchical structures. The behavioral approach seeks to enhance better and more effective participatory leadership. Supervision in classicalism was task and production oriented. The classical approach placed emphasis in specialization of labor (division of labor) by applying the scientific management principles. Antithetically, the behavioral approach emphasized job enlargement and responsibilities of the individual. Job-enlargement or broad-banding is beyond the field of specialization. It is assumed that job-enlargement gives the employee a sense of satisfaction in the organization particularly when he/she may use unionization policy or work rules to reject expanded responsibilities. The classical approach advocates the use of a narrow span of control, centralization and coordination of organizational functions. The organizational person or worker is rewarded extrinsically (Herzberg, Mausner, and Snyderman, 1959). This mechanistic view of humankind allowed segmental involvement of the worker who is (was) oversupervised, exploited and alienated. In this environment money is the primary motivation for work. Contrary to the perceptions of the individual in the mechanistic worldview, the behavioral arena provides the employee with a wide span of control. Power is decentralized in organizational settings to warrant flexible response on the part of supervisory management. Although decentralized and participatory management tends to be more productive than its centralized mechanistic counterpart, recent, intensive and extensive utilization of artificial intelligence (computer usage) tends to neutralize the traditional promises, in terms of effectiveness, of decentralized operations. In addition, despite its commercial, vocational and instrumental promises, the negative consequences of high-tech information use in terms of massive unemployment and Taylorist technocratic and mechanistic inclinations is enigmatic.

Behavioristically, people's, workers, or employees' behavior is variable and therefore less manipulatable within the organization. This type of behavioral variability is responsible for the practice of both the formal and informal organizational dynamics. Informal organizational settings have informal groups whose success depends on intrinsic incentives and rewards. The importance of informal groups is based on their motivation which originates with the satisfaction of employee needs and effective management of their attitudes, feelings and dreams. A wealthy variety of behavioral literature which talks about organizational humanism is subject to misuse for psychological manipulation of clients and organizational employees in the name of the human relations theoretical movement, improving organizational climates, and promoting fairness and equity.

Irrespective of the three comparative differences in respect to the application of the classical and behavioral models, neither school of thought distinguishes public from private administration. In other words, the concurrent and competitive application of the two schools of thought in both public and private arena was the genesis of the contingency approach in terms of application (theoretical) to multiorganizational modeling. The logic of the classical mechanistic model is deductive. Its orientation runs from the general to the specific. It promotes normative values and it is based on the "one best way" Taylorist approach to organizational management. Gulick's POSDCORB is also a classic example of organizational rationality whose dynamics were employed to perpetuate structural functionalism in organizations and society at large (Scott, 1981).

Parenthetically, the logic of inquiry of behaviorism is descriptive rather than deductive. The orientation of behaviorism, unlike that of the classical models, runs from the specific to the general. Herbert Simon's decision theory is a classic example to this model. Simon theorized that managers do not optimize decisions. Instead decisions are made in the form of "bounded-rationality" fashion (Simon 1960; and March, 1994). In this case, bounded-rationality is the same thing as limited rationality (March, 1994). The behavioral logic is value free but inundated with facts that logically become the assorted corpus for theoretical formulation. For instance, Abraham Maslow who was an organizational psychologist observed organizations, collected and empirically analyzed factual data and arrived at the conclusion that when basic human needs are met, such a situation becomes the natural base for the satisfaction of higher needs that motivationally propels the "animal" to experience self-actualization. As a humanistic scholar, he was able to use behaviorism to penetrate the bio-psychosocial dynamics of human personality and reconstruct a theory of human motivation conducive to superior and creative productivity. This is contrary to the classical thinking in which money was thought to be the only motive for superior performance.

Anthony Down's (1967) *Inside Bureaucracy* argues that the evolution of the classical and behavioral management models of the organization had nothing to do with the prevailing political environment. In other words, these theoretical models evolved in the private environment of the factory system where they were implemented or applied and scientifically evaluated for their effectiveness. As compared with the classical model, Mayo's conceptual and behavioral theory is relatively simplistic. Its simplicity is largely common sensical. It also may be psychologically used to manipulate employees who can be exploited further by the organizational system. For instance, based on Herzberg's (1966) motivation-hygiene theory, workers or employees who are motivated to work due to "achievement, recognition, work or task itself, sense of responsibility and an apparent climate for growth and advancement" may be frustrated by 'dissatisfiers' (Herzberg, 1966) of which "company policy and administration, supervision, interpersonal relations, working conditions and salary" contribute to job dissatisfaction (Pugh, 1984, p. 339). In most organizations, workers' or employees' lot is influenced by the two categories of variables respectively. This indicates that they pursue different goals that are based on individual needs. Informed high-level management should sensitize this element of organizational dichotomy and establish effective mechanisms to address specific individual and organization concerns and try to reconcile their antagonistic inclinations. These antagonistic inclinations are forces whose dialectical dynamics might "drown the organization into a dungeon." In brief, natural (behavioral) systems analysts point out that highly centralized and formalized systems are ineffective and irrational because they waste the organization's resources, intelligence and initiative. If this criticism is true, then the evolution formalization and institutionalization of behaviorism is questionably unquestionable.

Structural-Functional Analysis—1930s - 1960s

Classical British Colonial Anthropology

Other than Mayo's human relations theory, the structural functional model is a form of behavioral naturalism in terms of the effect of heredity and environment on human behavior and action. British sociological and anthropological theories of Merton (1957) and Malinowski (1939) and Radcliffe-Brown (1952) may be organizationally paraphrased to view the organization as a social unit or system. The organization has certain "needs or requirements that must be met if it is to" (Scott, 1981, p. 84) survive in its present form. This school places emphasis in the maintenance of functional structures, needs that must be met and functions that must be performed by the organization's units in order for the system to survive. Given structures perform functional needs to maintain the existing wholistic structure. Biologically, if the human body is to survive, oxygen must reach the blood stream. Oxygen cannot reach the blood stream if the lungs and heart do not perform their normal vital functions of purification and pulsification respectively. Or, historico-politically, if the superpower has to survive, it must use its structures to act imperialistically. By using its resources to colonize, extract raw materials from its client states and colonial subjects, it must produce the raw materials for the empire. Effective exploitation of these resources requires the maintenance of political, legal, economic, military, educational and technological structures that enforce the colonial or neocolonial model for the salvation of the superpower in terms of its protection of higher standards of living. In other words, if colonialism is an organization, then its effective maintenance requires the functional arrangement of well maintained structures that will ensure its survival (Mudimbe, 1988). The colonial regime is a functionalistic and mechanistic establishment that uses all forms of power including the power to control, oppress, enslave, suppress, frustrate and dehumanize in order to maintain the structures that ensure imperial, i.e., organizational (societal) survival. Such an exploitative organizational model farther alienates people particularly in class societies which are insensitive to the "needs of the significant others" in the colonial and empirical jungle.

Social Systems Theory—Parsons

Like any organism's, or the human body's role, the organization's structural elements are themselves mutually interdependent. Variation in one element or part results in the modified imbalance of the other parts or structural elements. Pareto, Henderson (1935) and Buckley (1967) argue that such systems tend to strive toward a state of balance - equilibrium. With the exception of biological systems, the functionalist paradigm fails to clarify the context in which needs and the concept of survival apply. In other words, its ethics are jungle-like and primordial. Though some social structures are more specialized in the degree of their social differentiation, others are less structurally differentiated to perform a certain range of functions.

This functionalist and classical paradigm of the British anthropological and sociological school of thought has been expanded by Talcott Parsons (1951). Parsons argues that societies are in a state of equilibrium. This originally organic and Spencerian theory views the *whole* as predominant over all of its parts. As dynamic social systems, the survival or maintenance of the systems, is dependent upon meeting important needs or *functional imperatives*. The functional imperatives are a necessary precondition of survival. A basic requirement for meeting these needs is the articulation of certain *structures or uniformities*. These structures are specified in the form of *social organization as social institutions*, e.g. the family, religion, education, economy, and government—called by the society. However, societal needs dictate the organization of these structures into a *system of interrelated activities* that are, in turn, *mutually supportive*.

The components of *systems* theory are a functional utility that maintains the whole system even the system's institutional patterns, deviance, conflict, and subcultural forms. Within each system formal and informal socialization, structures of social control, defense mechanisms and other devices provide continuity of the system because these *three* devices are relatively constant. As such, the social system, hence, is a configuration or a network of interrelated parts organized into a whole. The components relatively exist in a form of homeostasis which lacks a perfect equilibrium (Blackwell, 1991).

Parsons spent the whole of his life trying to perfect a general analytical model for small and primary groups and larger societies—and formal organizations (Parsons, 1960 and 1966). He asserted that social systems suffer from four basic problems that include "adaptation, goal-attainment, integration and latency or pattern-maintenance (Scott, 1981, p. 95). Parsons' model is based on his analysis of organizations' ecological, structural and socio-psychological levels. He argues that each organization (system) has subsystems that are farther divided into finer subdivisions. However, the top part of the organization that can mobilize resources and implement them for goal attainment deals with "policy decisions" (p. 96). Lower level decisions that are concerned with allocation of responsibilities and resources are allocative decisions (Scott, 1981). Making attempts that motivate and integrate personnel for effective roles are responsibilities that result in "coordinative decisions" (p. 97). The values that serve to authorize and legitimize the right to make decisions within the subsystem are "supporting values" (p. 97).

Parsons model of functional differentiation is applicable to organizations in general and to societies and subcultures in particular. In other words, at the organizational level, the bottom structural layer is the "technical" (p. 97), that is epitomized by the "workers on assembly lines, scientists in the laboratory, and teachers in the classroom" (p. 97). The managerial system is above the technical level. The functions of this system are to "mediate between the organization and the immediate external situation, including those who consume the organization's products and supply its raw materials, and administer the organization's internal affairs" (p. 97). Above the managerial level of the organization "is the institutional system whose function is to relate the organization to the larger social system" (p. 97).

Though Parsons' model is largely universalistic rather than particularistic, its universalism analogically helps to see its structural parallelism between societies and organizations that make them or by which they are made respectively. For instance, both particularistic and universalistic elements of the system are characterized by formal, rational and informal elements of systemic and organizational dynamics respectively. Though he has difficulty to translate his "global" concepts into operational variables, a factor that is largely explained by the fact that his work is substantive theory, the predictions of Parsons' analysis are difficult to test. This may explain why Parsons is not a contemporary theoretical and organizational icon. Irrespective of this criticism, his hypothesis that "unless the system's needs are met the organization will not survive" (p. 98) is true.

Institutional Theory—Selznick

Philip Selznick studied bureaucracy at Columbia where he was mentored by Merton. He was intellectually influenced by Michels to develop the natural systems model. Although Selznick is not as well known as Mayo was, the former's model is completely developed and coherent. Selznick's students who popularized his works include Burton Clark, Charles Perrow, and Mayer Zald. According to Selznick's understanding, the paramount element in organizations is that they are "tools" and each organization (tool) has a life of is own" (Scott, 1981, p. 91). Selznick accepts the rational system analysts that the distinctive nature of formal organizations is that

> they are rationally ordered instruments designed to attain goals ... these formal structures can 'never succeed in conquering the nonrational dimensions of organization behavior'... The sources of these nonrational dimensions are (1) individuals, who participate in the organization as 'wholes' and do not act merely in terms of their formal roles within the system; and (2) the fact that the formal structure is only one aspect of the concrete social structure that must adjust in various ways to the pressures of its institutional environment ... In short, organizational rationality is constrained by the 'recalcitrance of the tools of action': Persons bring certain characteristics to the organization and develop other commitments as members that restrict their capacity for rational action; organizational procedures become valued as ends in themselves; the organization strikes bargains with its environment that compromise present objectives and limit future possibilities (Scott, 1981, p. 91; and Selznick, 1949, pp. 253-259).

Pictorially, Selznick sees organization structure to be similar to an adaptive organism which plays its role relative to other participants and in the light of the pressures of the internal and external environments. He embraces structural functionalism. In other words, the organization is an empirical system which has basic needs that are essential for self-maintenance, repetitive self-defense, and daily functional operations (Selznick, 1948). Selznick emphasized that the most important need of all organizational systems was 'the maintenance of the integrity and continuity of the system itself' (Scott, 1981, p. 91). Specifically, Selznick argued that organizational 'imperatives' (p. 91) included the "security of the organization as a whole, ... the stability of lines of authority and communication, the stability of informal relations within the organization, and homogeneity" rather than heterogeneity of outlook with respect to the meaning and role of the organization (p. 91). In Selznick's conception, these needs and imperatives were more suggestive than definitive. The concept of need is paramount because it allows attention to be directed in meeting the "internal relevance of organization behavior, including behaviors that are ostensibly directed outward" (p. 92).

Selznick's model is akin to the general natural systems model discussed earlier. However, his model slightly differs from the natural systems one on the grounds that he "proposes we will learn more interesting things about organizations if we do not attempt to examine the satisfaction of all needs of the organism" but, like Freud, he focused on those needs 'which cannot be fulfilled within approved avenues of expression' (Scott, 1981, p. 92; and Selznick, 1948, p. 32). Selznick also focused his attention on the informal and irregular rather than the formal and regular organizational structures. These informal structures include but are not limited to informal social structures, ideologies and cooptation. Selznick did not use experimental psychological processes to analyze his system. Instead, he used clinical psychology to analyze the dynamic adaptation of the organisms and people in organizations. Critical decisions made in such a setting enabled organizations to change structures. "The pattern of these critical decisions, viewed over time, results in the development of a distinctive character structure for each organization, just as an individual's critical decisions and typical mode of coping with problems give rise to the development of a distinctive personality" (Scott, 1981, p. 92; and Selznick, 1957).

According to Selznick, the process through which an organization develops a unique character structure is institutionalization. This is the infusion of organizational values with the technical requirements for accomplishing available tasks. The classic institutional model of Selznick was the Tennessee Valley Authority (TVA) which FDR constructed in the light of his New Deal Philosophy of eradication of poverty and joblessness during the Great Depression of the 1930s. TVA was a highly decentralized and privately managed government corporation which was built in a chronically depressed and flood ravaged area of Tennessee. The hydro-electricity that was generated by the TVA was used for southern electrification, mechanization and industrialization. The project created 10 million jobs and partially became instrumental to the economic recovery of the 1940s. Democratic ideology was employed to recruit and motivate gifted participants in a democratically conservative region. To gain legitimacy and political support, the cooptation strategy was employed. Cooptation was a system by which external factors were incorporated into the decision-making structures of the organization in order to provide and promote the success rather than failure of the program.

Selznick's model influenced four other scholars to adopt, adapt and popularize it. First, Clark (1956) selectively used it to introduce adult education program in Los Angeles to enrich the intellectual and cultural needs of an economically marginalized community. Second, Messinger (1955) used Selznick's model to analyze the Townsend's economic interests whose movement during the 1930s was transformed from radicalism to noncontroversial recreational programs. Third, Zald and Denton (1963) used the model to transform YMCA from a religious organization which provided rehabilitative and welfare for the inner cities into a social and recreational center for suburban and middle class "youth."

This model enables organizations to change gradually. Its methodology is case study oriented that relies on documents, informants and history of the organization respectively. For the organization to sell its goals, to grow and survive (Perrow, 1979), it needs to focus on the forces that undermine its impersonal principles ("pathologies like deviance, abnormality, friction, dilemma, doubt and ruin" (Selznick, 1948; and Scott, 1981, p. 94). By subverting its formal ends to narrow interests rather than sustaining the values that bolster rationality (Gouldner, 1955), this clinical sociologist discovered destructive organizational forces and laid down mechanisms for alleviating them in order to enhance the "health and goals" of the organization.

The Principle of Supportive Relationships; The Linking Pin

In an organization, Likert (1961) has shown that managers can be high producing, mediocre or low producing. Since organizations are interested in high productivity, he has commented on the professional character of the high producing managers and the components of their organizational environment. These managers create a climate characterized by a preponderance of favorable attitudes on the part of participants, toward all members, superiors, workers, the organization and all things related to the job. The managers create a climate that is conducive for participants to be motivated, to be cooperative, for nurturing ego motives, security motives, economic motives and even for attempting to satisfy curiosity, creativity and desire for new and productive experience. The managers establish organizational goals and objectives that integrate the needs and desires of organizational participants and others who are directly or indirectly related to it or benefit from or through it. Such a climate promotes organizational morale which can be harnessed to unleash massive leadership and productive energy for coordination, motivation and cooperation that are essential for optimum productivity.

According to Likert's conclusions, managers and supervisors should treat people as "human beings" instead of treating them as "cogs in a machine" (Pugh, 1984, p. 297). In other words, the relationship between superiors and subordinates reflects this:

(a) He is supportive, friendly and helpful rather than hostile. He is kind but firm, never threatening, genuinely interested in the well-being of subordinates and endeavors to treat people in a sensitive, considerate way. He is just, if not generous. He endeavors to serve the best interests of his employees as well as of the company.

(b) He shows confidence in the integrity, ability and motivations of subordinates rather than suspicion and distrust.

(c) His confidence in subordinates leads him to have high expectations as to their level of performance. With confidence that will not be disappointed, he expects much, not little ... (supportive rather than critical or hostile condition).

(d) He sees that each subordinate is well trained for his job. He endeavors also to help subordinates be promoted by training them for jobs at the next level ...

(e) He coaches and assists employees whose performance is below standard. In the case of a subordinate who is clearly misplaced and unable to do his job satisfactorily, he endeavors to find a position well suited to that employee's abilities and arranges to have the employee transferred to it (Pugh, 1984, p. 297).

In other words, the high producing manager plans and schedules work activities, trains subordinates, provides them with resources for work and initiates work activity and tasks to be performed. Plans, schedules, activities and resources alone do not produce competent workers. Competent, loyal and motivated workers are the ones who implement plans, schedules, and resources to provide activities and accomplish tasks, invent solutions for solving organizational problems in order to enhance productivity. The team and group spirit is a tie that binds. According to Argyris (1957), March and Simon (1958), and Viteles (1953), subordinates react favorably when they are supported and when the support they receive from their superiors contributes to "their sense of importance and personal worth" (Pugh, 1984, p. 298). In their conclusions on personality development (Argyris, 1957; Rogers, 1942; and Cartwright and Zander, 1960) concluded that each human being (employee-employer) "wants appreciation, recognition, influence, a feeling of accomplishment, and a feeling that people who are important to us believe in us and respect us" (Pugh, 1984, p. 298). In a sense, organizational employees expect managers to behave in accordance with their personalities (managers) even when managerial background, cultural experience and expectations may be inconsistent with organizational perceptions of these managers and the objective reality of the environment. The principle of supportive relationships states that:

> The leadership and other processes of the organization must be such as to ensure a maximum probability that in all interactions and all relationships with the organization each member will, in the light of his background, values and expectations, view the experience as supportive and one which builds and maintains his sense of personal worth and importance (Pugh, 1984, p. 299).

This principle of supportive relationship is a group or team approach principle in which each organizational participant belongs to a work group characterized with group loyalty, effective skills for interaction and "high performance goals" (p. 301). Well knit and effective groups have several characteristics. Each individual accepts the goals of the group. Each employee/manager tries to influence goals and decisions by comparing them with their own experience and personal goals. Each employee communicates clearly and effectively. Each employee responds to others by communicating effectively. The behavior of each employee is critical to the successful implementation of goals, decisions and ideas of the group. Each employee's behavior influences not only the group, but also the "significant others" whose power and status help to determine the organizational destiny of each individual employee in the group. In other words, in every organization, even that which is led by an autocrat, there is evidence of functional competition, cooperation, decision-making, strategic, tactical and operational goals to be attained, in the face of conflict. The role of dynamic structures and processes is to constructively use conflict and harmony to bring change. Each group leader in the organization and the supportive relationship experienced within and without the organizational functional structures in order to enhance productivity, is like Likert's concept of the "linking pin." An organization which uses a single linking pin is likely to fail or collapse and disintegrate. One which uses several or many is likely to prosper in its evolutionary development.

D. McGregor's Theory X and Theory Y and Ouchi's Theory Z

McGregor (1960) and Ouchi (1981) have formulated interesting assumptions concerning human nature and human behavior. The assumptions have been popularized in organizational literature that is used as a guide for current managerial decision-making and practice. In particular, McGregor's theory X asserts that workers have to be directed and controlled in order to be productive. His theory Y which is the opposite of theory X and behaviorally based, states that self-motivated and productive workers are those whose goals are integrated with organizational goals. The third and most recent managerial theory is Ouchi's (1981) theory Z which is essentially a product of Japanese humanistic, cultural and team oriented management practice emphasizes a participatory rather than the mechanistic, functionalistic, and autocratic orientation employed by McGregor (Pugh, 1984; and Davis, 1977).

Theory X

There are three major assumptions around which theory X is centered. First, average human beings have an inherent tendency to dislike work and can try to avoid it if they can. Second, because humans inherently and characteristically dislike work, most people must be coerced, controlled, directed, and threatened with punitive measures in order to exact the efforts that are essential for the achievement of organizational objectives. This theoretical assumption criticizes the "permissiveness and democracy" (Pugh, 1984, p. 317) of the human relations school that is viewed to be indirectly reinforced by theory X and recentralization rather than post-War II decentralization measures. Third, the average human being likes to be directed, wishes to avoid responsibility, has relatively little ambition, and wants security.

Relative to theory Y, theory X is managerially autocratic. It portrays workers and employees negatively by showing that they avoid work because they are lazy and indolent. They are lazy and indolent because they lack ambition or motivation. Such unambitious people are self-centered, indifferent to organizational needs and expectations, and resistant to change. Regardless of how organizations may compensate them, they will not overcome their indolent, unambitious and irresponsible behavior. As a result, the only option left to management is to secure high employee performance by using autocratic and aversive methods.

Unfortunately, this crude way of viewing human behavior in industry and other organizations has both merits and demerits. Some of the scientific theories that support the existence of theory X are either fallacious or have half truths. For instance, even in science, it has taken a long time to discover that some of Newton's laws of motion are half truths. Einstein's theory of relativity has brought more understanding about these laws that Newton partially and inadvertently falsified about. Since humans have needs that need to be perpetually satisfied, or since needs are human deficiencies that require drives to animate them, organizational management practices, decision-making processes, operating practices and organizational designs should be structured in order to integrate employee concerns with managerial goals and objectives. Using the "carrot and the stick" (Pugh, 1984, p. 323) or autocratic and aversive measures alone are two simplistic solutions to the complexity of the corpus world of human nature. In addition, the fact that the human relations theory is "abusable" requires the discovery of more effective way of understanding and managing human complexity in organizational management.

There are few rewards that can be employed to satisfy needs in a competitive and multifaceted work environment. For instance, most fringe benefits such as "overtime pay, shift differentials, vacations, health and medical benefits, annuities and the proceeds from stock purchase plans or profit-sharing plans – yield needed satisfaction only when the individual leaves the job" (Pugh, 1984, p. 322). Given this reality, workers – employees view work as an unrewarding and aversive experience. These benefits are means of control and direction for the worker to whom the benefits might be rightly viewed in terms of the "stick and carrot" metaphor of substance. Though management has provided physiological and safety needs, this provision has "shifted the motivational emphasis to the social and egoistic needs. The work environment may provide opportunities that satisfy primary needs. If the satisfaction of primary needs does not create an impetus for the satisfaction of higher level needs, employee behavior will show a persistent deprivation. Deprived people are coerced and threatened to produce due to the fact that they are not productively motivated by physiological (basic) needs alone. Assumptively, such a situation validates theory X largely because effects have been misinterpreted for causes. To say it in another way, thwarted needs will not be nurtured in ineffective organizational climates. Satisfied needs will.

Theory Y

Unlike theory X whose assumptions are based on ecological and physiological pathologies of the organizational environment, this environment can be improved psychodynamically in order to produce new assumptions for which theory Y is known. McGregor's theory Y undergirds humanistic and supportive values of the workplace environment. The evolution of this management theory in the scientific as well as in the social and behavioral sciences has become an imperfect and major theoretical and philosophico-scientific tradition which informs management practice concerning the expenditure of human resources in organizations. The six major assumptions by which theory Y is rationalized include:

1. The use of physical and mental effort to work is as natural as either play or rest. Generally, this means that most human beings, if at all, like work. If the work is perceived to be a source of satisfaction, people can do it. On the contrary, if it is viewed aversively, it will be avoided.
2. External control and the threat of punishment are not the only means for bringing about effort toward organizational objectives. Man will exercise self-direction and self-control in the service of objectives to which he is committed (Pugh, 1984, p. 326).
3. "Commitment to objectives is a function of the rewards associated with their achievements" (p. 326). For instance, rewards such as those used to satisfy "ego and self-actualization needs" (p. 326) may directly be a product of functional organizational objectives.
4. In general, the average human beings have the capacity to learn to accept responsibility. If people avoid responsibility, they have no ambition but show a need for security, this happens because of nurture rather than their nature. Past experience has taught them negatively rather than positively.
5. Those who profoundly use imagination, ingenuity and creativity to solve organizational problems are widely rather than narrowly spread out in the population.
6. In modern industrial life, the intellectual potential of average people are partially rather than impartially utilized.

Theory Y assumptions about management and their perceptions of employee behavior are radically different from those of theory X. Theory Y assumptions are dynamic as opposed to static view of theory X. They view human potentiality to be promising in terms of growth and development. These assumptions necessarily place emphasis on selective adaptation and change rather than "a single absolute form of control" (p. 327). Unlike theory X assumptions of the factory model, theory Y assumptions are constructed to theoretically and managerially facilitate the resourcefulness of human personality.

Theory Y framework of assumptions does not give management an easy reasoning logic about ineffective organizational behavior (performance). Largely, this happens based on the available nature of human resources at management's disposal. In addition, theory Y heaps problems squarely on the face of management. The fact that employees are regarded to be lazy, indifferent, irresponsible, intransigent, uncreative, and uncooperative, these X related assumptions are an aversive product of management's methods of organizational communication and control. Though theory Y assumptions are not permanent or temporary elements of organizational behavior, they are, based on the synergistic analysis of their practical and theoretical reasoning, more consistently applicable than theory X assumptions. With further research and theory development on these assumptions (Y), they are likely to be refined, expanded and modified rather than contradicted, falsified, or fabricated. Superficially, these assumptions are acceptable as they are portrayed. In practice, their implications are phenomenal because they challenge managerial philosophy, attitudes, feelings and actions.

The Integration Principle

Integration is the organization of organic, psychological or social traits and tendencies of human personality into a harmonious whole. The main principle which underpins theory Y is integration. An integrative organization creates a climate for organizational members to achieve their own goals individually while seeing that they strive for organizational success as well. However, given the fact that the established industrial and high-tech environment is very pervasive and externally controlled and directed, at times, the notion of integration and self-control remains to be a remote objectification and perpetual fixation in the workplace. Such pervasiveness and external control and direction contribute to the existence of theory X mentality which management authority utilizes to justify "the scalar principle" (p. 328). In real practice, large theory X promotions and transfers are, most of the time, made unilaterally rather than multilaterally and otherwise. Since the organization is negatively affected when individual needs and goals are ignored, the principle of integration requires that the goals and needs of individual participants be recognized and matched with those of the organization. When the organization is integrated, management works together with labor, shares rewards and contributes to organizational success. However, management feels that working together with labor will force the former to make adjustments that are contrary to its managerial philosophy and that will "lead to anarchy, chaos, irresponsible conflicts of self-interest, lack of responsibility, inability to make decisions and failure to carry out those that were made" (p. 330). In other words, management favors unilateral action more than integration regardless of the fact that the unintended consequences of its costs or gains and vice versa might crop up.

Although it is difficult to find a perfect organizational system, theory Y type of management and the professional people they deal with tends to recognize employee worker needs, test assumptions, and refine techniques and processes in order to enhance organizational productivity. In doing that, the organizational system develops mechanisms for identifying its pathological elements of "indifference, irresponsibility, minimal compliance, hostility, sabotage" (Pugh, 1984, p. 32) and constructively learns to manage them synergistically in order to enhance productivity. In other words, for the enterprise to succeed, management must learn how to continuously use its managerial capacity, skill and ingenuity in order to eliminate problems and strive to survive, remain competitive and productive in a turbulent environment. Doing that enables management to make theory Y a prerequisite for continuous innovation.

Does integration lead to job satisfaction? Three scholars (Herzberg, Mausner and Snyderman, 1959) have argued that "job satisfaction and dissatisfaction among managerial and professional people suggests that these opportunities for self-actualization are the essential requirements of both job satisfaction and high performance" (Pugh, 1984, p. 332). The wants of employees fall into two groups. The first group has needs that are occupationally or professionally viewed as the source of personal growth. The second group which is the more important element to the first is concerned with fair treatment in terms of "compensation, supervision, working conditions and administrative practices. Even when the needs of the second group are fulfilled, the group cannot be motivated to high levels of job satisfaction. In addition, this second group cannot go an extra mile in order to excel on the job. To satisfy this group's needs, the organization must prevent their "dissatisfaction and poor job performance" (Herzberg, Mausner and Snyderman, 1957, pp. 114-115).

Theory Z—Organizational Learning: C. Argyris and D.A. Schon

When, why and how do organizations learn? This is one question in three which lays the framework for explaining the structure and values of organizational learning. Organizational participants, management and scholars collectively agree on the importance of organizational learning. Given the fact that the costs of health care, sanitation, police, housing, education, welfare and cities have risen astronomically, the agencies that provide them with services must learn to be accountable, efficient and productive in order to keep these organizations a float. Government, corporations and business need to work together, as Al Gore's national initiative has demonstrated, in order to solve problems effectively.

It is self-evident that in many organizations, more problems are triggered by the methodological and analytical tools used for the generation of solutions. For instance, when industrialized and urban communities try to eradicate slums for urban renewal, or when Nazi forces malevolently tried to eradicate the Jewish race, or when the Russian government tries to introduce statecentric openness (glassnost), restructuring (perestroika) and democratic liberalization of society and its institutions, more problems are created by those who are trying to bring desired change. In other words, strategies used to solve problems are not sociotechnically, psychologically and socioecobiologically effective at the local, regional, national or global environment. Environmental turbulence makes it difficult if not impossible to eradicate the actual and potential organizational problems. Consequently, organizations tend to perpetually exist and operate in economically, politically and technologically unstable environments. To solve these problems requires learning organizations to learn how to solve problems, make adjustments, create opportunities and synergistically reconcile conflicting organizational forces in order to manage them creatively and productively.

The theory of organizational learning is rooted in action rather than explanation, prediction or control theories and goals of the traditional research universe respectively. The theory of action, apart from its purposive and inherent elements of cognitive and normative construction, testing and reconstruction of knowledge, is essentially, like all other theories, broadly characterized by "generality, centrality and simplicity. For clarity purposes, the theory of organizational learning is theoretically and scientifically interdependent rather than autonomous and exclusive. As a theory of action, organizational learning is influenced by "espoused theories and theories-in-use" (Pugh, 1984, p. 355). The two types of theories may or may not be compatible.

Organizational learning is a metaphoric expression because we know that organizations as such, unlike individuals, do not, in a literal sense, behave, remember, think, memorize or learn. However, because the metaphoric expression conveys the underlying concept more powerfully and clearly, we use metaphors to talk about organizational trust, gossip, "sleeping or breathing." Organizational learning can be viewed as a concrete or abstract phenomenon.

What happens when change becomes a problem?

Individual members frequently serve as agents of change in organizational theory-in-use which run counter to organizational entropy. They act on their images and on their shared maps with expectations of patterned outcomes, which their subsequent experience confirms or disconfirms. When there is a mismatch of outcome to expectation (error), members may respond by modifying their images, maps, and activities so as to bring expectations and outcomes back into line. They detect an error in organizational theory-in-use, and they correct it. This fundamental learning loop is one in which individuals act from organizational theory-in-use, which leads to match or mismatch of expectations with outcome, and thence to confirmation or disconfirmation of organizational theory-in-use (p. 361).

For instance, if turnover or marketing strategies appear to threaten the performance of an organization, management may be forced to reexamine the factors that may create organizational instability and perhaps, entropy. Factors like "salary levels, fringe benefits and job design" (p. 361) may be evaluated to judge the relationship between productivity and potential instability.

Single-Loop Learning

The three types of organizational learning are single-loop learning, double-loop learning and deutero-learning. In examples of single-loop learning, "members of the organization respond to changes in the internal and external environments of the organization by detecting errors which they then correct so as to maintain the central features of organizational theory-in-use" (p. 361).

Double-Loop Learning

Double-loop learning is the organization's identification of emerging conflict, ability to analyze the conflict by changing organizational norms. The organization is given a new structural design. New strategies and assumptions are matched with the newly established norms. The norms must be "embedded in the images and maps which encode organizational theory-in-use" (Pugh, 1984, pp. 198, 364-365). There is a double feedback loop notion which "connects the detection of error not only to strategies and assumptions for effective performance but to the very norms which define effective performance" (p. 365).

Deutero-Learning

When organizations continuously become aware, through creativity, innovation, or the scientific management of change, they are not only consciously aware, but this form of ongoing self-evaluation and self-correction, if you like, cybernetic sense of mind is called deutero-learning (Bateson, 1972). Deutero-learning is second-order learning which is learning how to learn. The organization uses single-loop and double-loop as the basis for deutero-learning. Behaviorally, organizations may be described as "less open, experimental, confronting, demanding, or defensive" (p. 370).

Conclusion

Theoretically, organization behavior is influenced by the five major schools of thought, namely, positivistic behaviorism, organizational humanism, human relations, open systems theories and the three theoretical assumptions (X, Y, and Z). Through the concept of organization behavior, management is viewed as the organization of individual's behavior in relation to the physical means and resources for translating goals and objectives of the organization into meeting desired targets. To achieve desirable targets, managers are bound to control the behavior of members in order to produce and provide service efficiently and effectively. Viewed in this light, subjects organizational behavior to two functional and controversial debates. The first debate concerns the mechanistic view which asserts that organizers (managers) need to apply more and better control mechanisms in order to realize efficient performance. Such organizational managers place emphasis on "specialization, clear job definitions, standard routines and clear lines of authority" (Pugh, 1984, p. 10). The second ones are the behaviorists who continuously believe that too much control over behavior is rigid rather than flexible, self-defeating because it stifles creativity which consequently retards productivity because there is lack of freedom to experiment. Such behavior does not only demotivate employees, but demotivation makes them apathetic to perform. In other words, counter-control imposed through informal relationships eliminates the chances for increased efficiency. If efficiency is enhanced, it is likely to be costly conflictual and tactical rather than strategic. Both sides are inevitable aspects of the organizational dilemma with which it is continually challenged.

Managing organizational behavior during the new millennium will be challenging for several reasons: "(1) the increasing globalization of organization's operating territory, (2) the increasing diversity of organizational work forces, (3) continuing technological innovation with its companion need for skill enhancement, and (4) the continuing demand for higher levels of moral and ethical behavior" in the market place of the employees and workers (Nelson and Quick, 1994, pp. 18-19).

One of the major issues of organizational behavior is work place diversity. Diversity is an element of organizational change and globalization. Not all organizations will experience all forms of diversity. However, the main forms of the globalized and diverse workforce of the

New Millennium will comprise of "age, race, ethnicity, gender, physical abilities and qualities, and sexual and affectional orientation" (Hellriegel, Slocum, and Woodman, 1998, p. 30).

Diverse forms of workforce diversity of which customers, gender, race, ethnicity and age will affect many employees, managers, teams, departments, and organizations. These types of diversity are important because they are reminiscent of employee differences in perspectives, lifestyles, attitudes, values, and behaviors. The manner or degree with which managers and employees will embrace and respond to issues of diversity will help to chart new directions of organizational effectiveness, innovation, and change.

Further still, issues of diversity, quality, technology, organizational culture, ethics, management and globalism will require organizations and employees to change their traditional practices and behaviors. To be productive and effective organizations, professionals and managers must cultivate a lifetime attitude for learning. The five core competencies which learning should articulate include but are not limited to mobilizing innovation and change, managing people and tasks, communicating, achieving technical proficiency and management of self. The traditional approach of managing people and tasks will not be the exclusive province of managers and supervisors alone.

The theoretical plurality which influences organizational operations in terms of diverse peoples, resources, technology and culture will configure a dynamic interplay with strategic factors, individual processes, group and interpersonal processes all of which will synergistically propel the living organization into its image of the future and the unknown future's future.

References

Argyris, C. 1957. *Personality and Organization.* New York: Harper and Row.

Argyris, C., and D.A. Schon. 1978. *Organizational Learning: A Theory of Action Perspective.* Addison-Wesley: 8-29.

Argyris, C., and D.A. Schon. 1974. *Theory in Practice.* Fossey-Bass.

Bateson, G. 1972. *Steps to an Ecology of Mind.* Ballantine.

Bell, D. 1960. Work and its discontents: The cult of efficiency in America. In *The End of Ideology.* Glencoe, IL: Free Press: 222-262.

Bendix, R. 1956. *Work and Authority in Industry.* New York: John Wiley.

Bennis, W.G. 1959. Leadership theory and administrative behavior. *Administrative Science Quarterly* 22: 1-21.

Blackwell, J. 1991. *The Black Community: Unity in Diversity.* Boston: University of Massachusetts Press.

Blau, W. 1964. *Exchange and Power in Social Life.* New York: John Wiley.

Blau, P.M. 1956. *Bureaucracy in Modern Society.* New York: Random House.

Blumberg, P. 1968. *Industrial Democracy: The Sociology of Participation.* New York: Schocken Books.

Brayfield, A.H., and W.H. Crockett. 1955. Employee attitudes and employee performance. *Psychological Bulletin*, September, pp. 396-424.

Buckley, W. 1967. *Sociology and Modern Systems Theory.* Englewood Cliffs, N.J.: Prentice-Hall.

Burns, T., and G.M. Stalker. 1966. *The Management of Innovation.* London: Tavistock.

Cartwright, D., and A. Zander. eds. 1960. *Group Dynamics: Research and Theory.* Ron Peterson.

Coch, L., and J.R.P. French, Jr. 1948. Overcoming resistance to change. *Human Relations* 1, 4: 512-532.

Collins, O. 1946. Ethnic behavior in industry: Sponsorship and rejection in a New England factory. *American Journal of Sociology* 21: 293-298.

Dalton, M. 1950. Conflicts between staff and line managerial officers. *American Sociological Review* 15: 342-351.

Davis, K. 1977. *Human Behavior at Work: Organizational Behavior.* New York: McGraw-Hill.

Downs, A. 1967. *Inside Bureaucracy.* Boston: Little Brown.

England, R. 1977. Informal School of Thought. Lecture Given at Oklahoma State University, Department of Political Science, on March 6, 1997. Stillwater, OK.

Flew, A. 1984. *A Dictionary of Philosophy.* New York: St. Martin's Press.

Gouldner, A.W. 1955. Metaphysical pathos and the theory of bureaucracy. *American Political Science Review* 49: 496-507.

Hellriegel, D., J.W. Slocum, Jr., and R.W. Woodman. 1998. *Organizational Behavior.* Cincinnati, OH: South-Western College Publishing.

Henderson, L.J. 1935. *Pareto's General Sociology.* Cambridge, MA: Harvard University Press.

Herzberg, F. 1966. The motivation-hygiene theory. *Work and the Nature of Man.* New York: World Publishing Company.

Herzberg, F., B. Mausner, and B.B. Snyderman. (1959). *The Motivation to Work.* New York: Wiley.

Hollander, E.P., and J.W. Julian. 1969. Contemporary trends in the analysis of leadership processes. *Psychological Bulletin* 71: 387-397.

Homans, G.C. 1950. *The Human Group.* New York: Harcourt.

Hulin, C.L., and M.R. Blood. 1968. Job enlargement, individual differences, and worker responses. *Psychological Bulletin* 69: 41-55.

James, P., and A. Hristoulas. 1994. Domestic politics and foreign policy: Evaluating a model of crisis activity for the United States. *The Journal of Politics* 56, 2: 327-348.

Kanter, R.M. 1977. *Men and Women of the Corporation.* New York: Basic Books.

Katz, D., and R.L. Kahn. 1951. Human organization and worker motivation. In *Industrial Productivity,* ed. L. Reed, 146-171. Cambridge, MA: Industrial Relations Research Association.

Katz, D., N. Maccoby, and N. Morse. 1950. *Productivity, Supervision and Morale in an Office Situation.* Ann Arbor, MI: Institute for Social Research.

Katz, D., et al. 1951. *Productivity, Supervision and Morale among Railroad Workers.* Ann Arbor, MI: Institute for Social Research.

Knight, G.R. 1981. *Philosophy and Education: An Introduction in Christian Perspective.* Berrien Springs, MI: Andrew University Press.

Landsberger, H.A. 1958. *Hawthorne Revisited.* Ithaca, N.Y.: Cornell University Press.

Lewin, K. 1948. *Resolving Social Conflicts.* New York: Harper.

Likert, R. 1957. An integrating principle and an overview. *New Patterns of Management,* McGraw-Hill: 97-118.

Likert, R., and J.M. Willits. 1940. *Morale and Agency Management.* Life Insurance Agency Management Association.

Maier, N.R.F. 1952. *Principles of Human Relations.* New York: Wiley.

March, J.G. 1994. *A Primer on Decision Making: How Decisions Happen.* New York: The Free Press.

March, J.G., and H.A. Simon. 1958. *Organizations.* New York: Wiley.

Marx, K. (1954). *Capital.* Moscow: Foreign Language Publishing House. First Published in 1867.

Mayo, E. 1945. *The Social Problems of an Industrial Civilization.* Boston: Graduate School of Business Administration, Harvard University.

Mudimbe, V.Y. 1988. *The Invention of Africa: Gnosis, Philosophy, and the Order of Knowledge.* Bloomington: Indiana University Press.

Nash, P. 1968. *Models of Man: Explorations in the Western Educational Tradition.* New York: John Wiley and Sons, Inc.

Nelson, D.L., and J.C. Quick. 1994. *Organizational Behavior: Foundations, Realities, and Challenges.* Minneapolis/St. Paul: West Publishing Company.

New Webster's Dictionary and Thesaurus of the English Language. 1992. Danbury, CT: Lexicon Publications, Inc.

Ozmon, H., and S. Craver. 1976. *Philosophical Foundations of Education.* Columbus, OH: Charles E. Merrill Publishing Co.: 149.

Parsons, T. 1966. *Societies: Evolutionary and Comparative Perspectives.* Englewood Cliffs, N.J.: Prentice-Hall.

Parsons, T. 1960. *Structure and Process in Modern Societies.* Glencoe, IL: Free Press.

Parsons, T. 1951. *The Social System.* Glencoe, IL: Free Press.

Perrow, C. ed. 1979. *Complex Organizations: A Critical Essay.* Glenview, IL: Scott Foresman.

Petz, D.C. 1951. The Influence of the Supervisor within His Department as a Conditioner of the Way Supervisory Practices Affect Employee Attitudes.Ph.D. dissertation. University of Michigan.

Posner, M.I. 1989. *Foundations of Cognitive Science.* Cambridge, MA: The MIT Press.

Pugh, D.S. 1984. *Organization Theory: Selected Readings.* London: Penguin Business.

Roethlisberger, F.J. and W.J. Dickson. 1939. *Management and the Worker.* Cambridge, MA: Harvard University Press.

Rogers, C.R. 1942. *Counseling and Psychotherapy.* New York: Houghton Mifflin.

Roy, D. 1952. Quata restriction and goldbricking in a machine shop. *American Journal of Sociology* 57: 427-442.

Sayles, L.R. 1958. *Behavior of Industrial Work Groups.* New York: John Wiley.

Schwab, D.P., and L.L. Cummings. 1970. Theories of performance and satisfaction: a review. *Industrial Relations* 9: 408-430.

Scott, W.R. 1981. *Organizations: Rational, Natural, and Open Systems.* Englewood Cliffs, N.J.: Prentice-Hall, Inc.

Seashore, S.E. 1954. *Group Cohesiveness in the Industrial Work Group.* Ann Arbor, MI: Institute for Social Research.

Selznick, P. 1957. *Leadership in Administration.* New York: Harper and Row Publishers.

Selznick, P. 1949. *TVA and the Grass-Roots.* Berkeley: University of California Press.

Selznick, P. 1948. Foundations of the theory of organizations. *American Sociological Review*, 13, pp. 25-35.

Simon, H.A., ed. 1960. *The New Science of Management Decision.* New York: Harper.

Simon, H.A., ed. 1957. *Administrative Behavior.* New York: Macmillan.

Skinner, B.F. 1976. *About Behaviorism.* New York: Vintage Books: 3.

Stogdill, R.M., and A.E. Coons eds. 1957. *Leader Behavior: Its Description and Measurement.* Research Monograph 88, Columbus,

OH: Bureau of Business Research, Ohio State University.

Strauss, G. 1963. Some Notes on Power Equalization. In *The Social Science of Organizations,* ed. H.J. Leavitt., 39-84. Englewood Cliffs, N.J.: Prentice-Hall, Inc.

Tannenbaum, A.S. 1974. *Hierarchy in Organizations.* San Francisco, CA: Jossey-Bass.

Viteles, M.S. 1953. *Motivation and Morale in Industry.* New York: Horton.

Warner, W.L., and J.O. Low. 1973. *The Social System of the Modern Factory.* New Haven, CT: Yale University Press.

White, R., and R. Lippitt. 1953. Leader behavior and member reaction in three social climates. In *Group Dynamics,* eds. D. Cartwright and A. Zander, 586-611. Evanston, IL: Row, Peterson.

Whyte, W.F. 1959. *Man and Organization.* Homewood, IL: Richard D. Irwin.

Whyte, W.F. 1951. Small groups and large organizations. In *Social Psychology at the Crossroads,* eds. J.H. Rohrer and M. Sherif, 297-312. New York: Harper.

Zald, M.N., and P. Denton. 1963. From evangelism to general service: The transformation of the YMCA. *Administrative Science Quarterly* 8: 214-234.

Chapter 4

Organizations as Open Systems

> That a system is open means, not simply that it engages in
> interchanges with the environment, but that this interchange is an
> essential factor underlying the system's viability (Walter Buckley,
> 1967 and Scott, 1981 p.102).

The open systems theory evolved from the post World War II
intellectual currents though it may have started earlier. The new area of
study this intellectual movement created is cybernetics and information
theory. The movement stimulated new applications of which **systems
engineering and operations research** were classic. This movement
changed the then existing disciplines; the study of organizations as a
discipline evolved. The theory (systems) proposed closer linkages
among, within and between existing scientific disciplines.

The "father" of open systems theory was a biologist namely, Ludwig
von Bertalanffy who was concerned with the increasing fragmentation
or compartmentalization or increasing division of the scientific
disciplines. Each discipline in other words, was "encapsulated in a
private universe, and it" was 'difficult to get word from one cocoon to
another' (Scott, 1981, p. 102). Bertalanffy and his coevals argued that
certain general ideas were applicable to all scientific disciplines, it was
scientifically and professionally sound to create linkages or open the

disciplinary systems and subsystems whose encapsulation in "personal" cocoons made them less interdependent, less dynamic, less cybernetic, less morphogenetic and less characterized with equifinality. The argument for the open systems theory and its linkages or interconnectedness started to hold much water when scientists proved that "nuclear particles, atoms, molecules, cells, organs, organisms, ecological communities, groups, organizations, societies" and "solar systems—are all subsumable under the general rubric of system" (pp. 102-103). Systems are interdependent assemblages. The same systems have fundamental similarities. The parts of each system are chemically or physically or genetically or socially structured in either simple or complex or variable perspectives. For instance, "as we move from mechanical through organic to social systems, the parts of which systems are comprised become more complex and variable. Similarly, the nature of the 'relations' among the parts varies from one type of system to another" (p. 103).

The "father" of cybernetic theory is Norbert Wiener. He argued that systems or organizations, particularly the open systems, should exhibit functional, spatial, and temporal interdependence. However, in

> **Mechanistic** systems, the interdependence among the parts is such that their behavior is highly constrained and limited. The structure is relatively rigid and the system of relations determinant. In **organic** systems, the connections among the interdependent parts are somewhat less constrained, allowing for more flexibility of response. In **social** systems, such as groups and organizations, the connections among the interacting parts become relatively loose: less constraint is placed on the behavior of one element by the condition of others. Social organizations, in contrast to physical or mechanical structures, are loosely coupled systems" (Ashby, 1968 and Buckley, 1967, pp. 82-83).

Progress or development of systems from simplicity to complexity enables the systems to exchange 'flows' (resources) with their environment. The major types of "system flows are materials, energy, and information" (p. 103). According to Buckley (1967), the relations in terms of components of mechanical systems are functionally and primarily spatial and temporal. Energy is transmitted from one component to another. The interactive relationships of higher levels of the system increasingly depend on effective transmission of information. In his book the *Living Systems*, Miller (1978) has identified the seven levels of a system. These include the "cell, the organ, the organism, the group, the organization, the society, and the supranational system" (Scott, 1981, p. 103).

Boulding (1956) has constructed a nine-point typological classification of systems based on their level of complexity. These include:

1. Frameworks – Systems have static structures such as the arrangements of atoms in a crystal or the anatomy of an
2. Clockworks – Simple dynamic systems with predetermined motions such as the clock and the solar system.
3. Cybernetic system. A system capable of self-regulation in terms of some externally prescribed target or criterion, such as a thermostat.
4. Open systems. A system capable of self-maintenance based on a throughput of resources from its environment, such as a living cell.
5. Blueprinted-growth systems. Systems which reproduce not by duplication but by producing seeds or eggs containing preprogrammed instructions for development, such as the acorn-oak system or the egg-chicken system.
6. Internal image systems. Systems capable of a detailed awareness of the environment in which information is received and organized into an image or knowledge structure of the environment as a whole, a level at which animals function.
7. Symbol processing systems. Systems which possess self-consciousness and so are capable of using language. Humans function at this level.
8. Social systems. Multi-cephalous systems comprised of actors functioning at level seven who share a common social order and culture. Social organizations operate at this level.
9. Transcendental systems. Systems comprised of the 'absolutes and the inescapable unknowables' (Boulding, 1956, pp. 200-207 and Scott, 1981, pp. 103-104).

Illuminatingly, Boulding's typology of systems is universally variant and persuasive. Levels four to six are about biological systems. Seven and eight concern human and other social systems. Finally level nine indicates that Boulding's classification system will remain open rather than closed to ununderstandability of the unknown.

Nine mutually inclusive levels have been clearly identified by Boulding and have been associated with existing systems. In this multisystem constellation, "each higher level system incorporates the unique features of the lower level systems. For instance, "it is possible to analyze a social organization as a framework, a clockwork, a cybernetic system" (p. 104), an open system, a blueprinted-growth system, an internal image system, a symbol processing system or a social system. Level eight is "the most complex or higher level processes occurring in organizations" (Scott, 1981, p. 104). Theoretically, most social science schemes are at level two and three despite the fact that the subject matter is at level eight.

Organizations as Cybernetic Systems

Two examples are used for illustration. First, cybernetic systems function, according to Boulding, at level three. Cybernetic systems are capable of self-regulation. Self-regulation is a feat reached through the evolutionary development of specialized parts or subsystems that are connected with certain processes and resource flows from the environment. In the case of a thermostat (Scott, 1981, p. 106), the cybernetic system has three parts. First, it has a mechanism for converting inputs into outputs. Second, it has a mechanism for comparing the level of outputs with some desired target level (e.g. thermostat regulate temperature at a given target-criterion by switching the heater on or off). Third, it has a mechanism for setting the desired target level that governs the activity of temperature regulation in the room.

In abstract terms, the cybernetic system's view of the organization emphasizes three elements. These are "the operations, the control, and the policy centers" (p. 105) that are influenced by the flows.

The policy center sets goals for the system. Goals are administratively set in response to demands and preferences that arise from the environment. Organizational goals are set on the basis of "information about preferences in the environment so that exchanges between the environment and the organization can occur" (p. 106). The control center monitors the performance of the operations level, keeping its outputs in line with the goals established by the policy center.

The cybernetic system is goal-directed rather than goal-oriented system.

Viewed from the natural systems perspective, "the normative structure of an organization is only loosely coupled with its behavioral structure" (p. 108). The goals and actions of the individual are weakly linked. Above all, March and Olsen (1976a), Cyert and March (1963), and Pfeffer and Salancik (1978) have theoretically proposed that the key participants in organizations are not the "unitary hierarchy or organic entity but a loosely linked coalition of shifting interest groups"

(Scott, 1981, p. 108). In recent times, given the fact that hierarchies have been criticized, ridiculed, and blamed for their obstructionism of productivity and innovation, management specialists have advised for their elimination, reduction or streamlining.

Pfeffer and Salancik (1978) assert that the organization is not only a coalition of groups and interests each of which tries to get something from the whole through interaction with others, but each of the "interested" groups has its own objectives, goals, and preferences. The interests, in other words, do not pursue "consistent or common objectives" (p. 108). These coalitions continuously change their purpose and domains to accommodate new interests while sloughing off parts of themselves to avoid some interests and of necessity, they tend to be involved in activities that have no relationship with their stated mission or purposes. In brief, contrary to the assumptions of the rationalists, open systems theorists assert that "loose coupling in structural arrangements can be highly adaptive for the system as a whole" (p. 108).

Open systems are capable of self-maintenance because of a "throughput of resources from the environment. The system is open or closed depending on how one defines openness and closure.

Thermodynamically, closed systems move toward the condition called entropy; the second law of thermodynamics states that entropy is "energy loss or energy that can not be turned into work" (p. 109). The elements of a closed system are randomly arranged. Its stratified structures are dissolved (e.g. former USSR). It exists in a state of maximum disorderliness. Contrary to closed systems, open systems have no boundaries. They receive energy from the environment, experience "negative entropy or negantropy" (p. 110). Open systems acquire "inputs of greater complexity than their outputs." They "restore their own energy and repair breakdowns in their own organization" (p. 110).

Burkley (1967) has indicated that open systems are morphostatic and morphogenetic. Morphostasis are processes which preserve or maintain the system's established "form, structure, or state" (p.110). Morphostatic processes in biological systems may include "circulation, respiration; in social systems, socialization and control of activities" (p. 110). Morphogenesis "refers to those processes that elaborate or change the systems," for instance, "growth, learning, and differentiation" (p. 110).

The source of system diversity and variety is the environment. There is a close connection between the condition of the environment and the characteristics of the systems within it. A complex system can not maintain its complexity in a simple environment. Open systems are subject to what is called the **law of limited variety.** This means that "a system will exhibit no more variety than the variety to which it has been exposed in its environment" (Pondy and Mitroff, 1979, p. 7 and Scott, 1981, p. 111).

Schools of Open Systems Theory

There are four schools that rationalize the open systems theory. These schools are the systems design, the contingency theory, environmental approaches, and Weick's model of organizing.

Systems Design

Theorists have shown that general systems theory is the source of ideas that are used to improve the design of organizations – "determining proper workflows, control systems and planning mechanisms, and their interrelations" (Scott, 1981, p. 111). This pragmatic and applied school seeks to "change and improve organizations as viewed from a managerial perspective, not simply to describe and understand them" (p. 111). The school deals with the simple and deterministic behaviors and the complex and probablistic ones. The behaviors of open systems are dealt with by simulation processes that utilize statistical manipulations for operations research in the fields, of cybernetics and systems design. Information processing (gathering, transmission, storage, and retrieval) and flow is critical to the organizations and design. As information processors, individuals exhibit "low channel capacity, lack of reliability and poor computational ability' (Haberstroh, 1965, p. 1176 and Scott, 1981, p. 113). In addition, Arrow (1974) and Williamson (1975) indicate that the "very existence of organizations is explained by the information processing limitations of individuals confronted by complex situations" (Scott, 1981, p. 113).

Contingency Theory

There are three assumptions that succinctly underpin contingency theory. Galbraith (1973) states that:

1   There is no best way to organize as mechanistic Taylorism, and Wilsonianism assert.
2.   Any way of organizing is not equally effective.

3. The best way to organize depends on the nature of the environment to which the organization must relate.

These three assumptions are analogous to the three theories of X, Y, and Z (see behaviorism or natural systems theory).

Environmental Approaches

In the light of open systems perspective, environmental influences help to shape or determine the "structure, functioning and fate of the organization" (Scott, 1981, p. 115). Specifically, the environment is a force on its own right. The same environment is "a source of resources and constraints controlled by actors capable of behaving independently of the organization and in ways that profoundly shape the activities and outcomes of the organization" (p. 115). Several scholars such as Hofstadler (1945), Hawley (1950), Campbell (1969), Hannan and Freeman (1977), Aldrich (1976), and Scott (1981) view the organization from the biologically traditional and Darwinian natural selection model. Though Darwin's natural selection model which deals with organizations as populations rather than individual systems has a biased and checkered history. This kind of extrapolation of a universal law to explain an organization may be an exercise in scientism rather than the application of a scientific law. If it explains why certain forms, types or species of organizations survive and prosper while others decline and vanish, it is questionable whether the cause of their unsurvivability is entropy, or genetic resilience rather than natural selection whose law of the "fittest" is a form of speculative scientism rather than scientific and empirical reality (see Scott, 1981, p. 115-116 and Campbell).

The resource dependence model of organizations and their environments put emphasis on adaptation processes that in strategic planning perspectives (organizations are active, malleable, and responsive to their environment). The resource-dependence model of the organization and its relationship to the environment is viewed as political economy (Zald, 1970; Wamsley and Zald, 1973). Thompson (1967) and Jacobs (1974) called environmental approaches, i.e., political economy a "power-dependency model" (Scott, 1981, p. 116).

Environmentalists (both natural section and the resource dependency groups) theoretically indicate that the open systems model is powerfully and innovatively responsible for shaping the form and function of organizations.

Weick's Model of Organizing

Environmentalists developed their version of the open systems on the basis of ecological analysis. Karl Weick's socio-psychological perspective of the organization views the organization not in terms of using nouns, but rather, in terms of using verbs. In other words, Weick uses the verb organizing rather than the noun organization. If nouns are "stamped out," the right concept is realized. He asserts that:

> The word organization is a noun and it is also a myth. If one looks for an organization one will not find it. What will be found is that there are events, linked together, that transpire within concrete walls and these sequences, their pathways, their timing, are the forms we erroneously make into substances when we talk about an organization (Scott, 1981, p. 117 and Weick, 1974, p. 358).

Both Scott and Weick may have read Bateman. Bateman's shift from using organization to using organizing (nouns to verbs) is an attempt to deemphasize structure while putting more emphasis on process. While structures and hierarchies tend to convey Taylorist, mechanistic and rigid forms of classicalism of the organization, processes tend to signify open, organic, loose, flexible, adaptible and changing organizations of the post-structural, post-communist, and post-industrial world. According to Weick, organizing is the "the resolving of equivocality" in an empirical environment whose "interlocked behaviors" are intertwined with "conditionally related processes" (Weick, 1969, p. 91). Weick adds that the organization uses basic raw materials "to operate. The basic raw materials include informational inputs, which are "ambiguous, uncertain, and equivocal" and misleading. The information may be infused with "tangible raw materials, recalcitrant customers, assigned tasks," or "union demands" that are used to enhance organizational goals and mission.

The interlockage of organizational behaviors is repetitive, reciprocal and contingent on a variety of factors whose evolutionary activities of enactment, selection, and retention radiate from naturalistic presuppositions (Campbell, 1969 and Scott, 1981). The organization will continue to exist if it maintains a balance of adjustment and stability (Weick, 1976). The organization receives information and retains it or discredits or questions it. The information about the organization and its open systems viewpoint is based on the assumption that the cognitive processes of perception and attentional selectivity and meaning are used by the meaning of the term organization. Interpersonal processes of coordination and control are influenced by "interlocked behaviors" (Scott, 1981, p. 118) that are perceived to be individual systems of flexibility and strategic implementation (Weick, 1976).

Weick uses the concept of equifinality which argues that any organizational outcomes could be the synthetic product of radically different processes other than those commonly known or used by organizational people. In other words, contrary to closed systems, open systems, which display the principle of equifinality, have a tendency for achieving a final state independent of the original state. Specifically, "open systems tend to resist perturbations that take them away from" they experience or "exhibit homeostasis" (Rapaport, 1972, p. 53). In essence, contingency or open systems theorists argue that the significance of equifinality in organization design could be functional and structural. Given the degree of conflict in "functional demands of the organization, also given the latitude of structural options available," there are three different types of equifinality; these include but are not limited to "suboptimal, tradeoff, and configurational" (Gresov and Drazin, 1997, p. 403). Functionally, this shows that a different agenda for research, structure, and design could have normative implications regarding how managers should design for superior performance. Since suboptimal, tradeoff, and configurational forms of equifinality could be epic, technofuturist and purist elements of strategic rationality; this form of rationality is part and parcel of open systems theory which could be narratively and fictionally or imaginatively improvable or advanced. Also, given the possibility that the future organization might be more "virtual" than concrete, then strategic planning and management is likely to be narratively and fictionally or fictitiously advanced to create a "certain reality" whose virtuality is fictionally or narratively rationalizable to reconstruct further reality (Barry and Elmes, 1997).

Recent studies in work unit design (Gresov, 1989) small businesses (Eisenhardt, 1988) and tests of sophisticated strategic typologies (Doty et al, 1993) assert that functional equivalence promotes equifinality. Functional equivalance takes place when functional demands conflict or when structural latitude is high. Such observable behavior influences the three kinds of equifinality mentioned above and which are part of the traditional contingency theory. While equifinality is the product of different processes, "causal arc" which is the product of the "likelihood of reciprocal rather than unilateral causation" (Weick, 1974; Buckley, 1967; and Scott, 1981) is different from equifinality.

Compared to the rational and natural systems, the open systems model of organizational management and creativity started late. Ever since it started, it has attracted a large following whose perceptions of reality has altered our meaning of organizations and their essential, fundamental, and postmodern processes. The open systems perspective of organizational structure puts emphasis on complex and viable components and individual participants and small groups rather than structures. The connections among and within all these are loose rather than rigid or inflexible. The components of the system are inherently semiautonomous in action. This makes the components of the system to be "loosely coupled to" each other (Scott, 1981, p. 119). Within the context of human organizations, the open systems approach has many heads that receive information, digest it, make decisions and direct organizational operations. In these organizations, people form coalitions and leave them more often than not, coordination and control are difficult but not impossible to manage. The internal and external boundaries of the system are collectively amorphous. The activities of "actors or actions to either the organization or the environment often seems arbitrary and varies depending on what aspect of system functioning is" being considered (p. 119).

Open systems theory may romantically be viewed as a form of living imagery or process whose conventional views of organizational structure are newly perceived in verbal terms like organizing, saticificing, optimizing and strategizing as opposed to nounal terms. The functioning of these processes are carried out. The "former emphasize self-maintenance and stability, the latter, development and elaboration of structure" (p. 119).

The organization is an arrangement of roles and relationships that fluctuate daily. For it to survive, it must adapt. Once it has adapted, it has to change. If this process of survival does not take place, the organization will experience entropy. Figuratively, the complex organization is more like a modern weapons system than a classical and fortified citadel, or "more like a mobile than a static sculpture, or more like a computer than an adding machine" (p. 119 and Leavitt, Dill, and Erying, 1973, p. 4). Above all, the open systems-based organization is symbiotically interdependent with its supraecological environment as well as organic, cybernetic, equifinal, morphogenetic and morphostatic. Finally, open systems are the informal management of the external socioeconomic environment of the organization that places emphasis on processes as opposed to structures.

Gulick (1937) asserts that the informal organizational management of the external environment is a form of administration. Administration is politics. The science of politics is political science whose traditional roots radiate from history and political philosophy. In its intellectual analysis, objectification, abstraction, and methodological and theoretical standardization, political science is paradigmatically deductive (specific and empirical) and inductive (general and normative). In addition, the second paradigm or model for the standardization of political science is theoretically normative and empirical. The specificity and empiricism of deductive reasoning has a dialectical analytical relationship with the generality and normativity of inductive reasoning. Both ways of reasoning are behaviorist and socialization mechanisms for scholarly and scientific inquiry.

Trist's Model

For instance, Gulick was an inductive theorist. Pasmore and Khalsa's (1993) work on the contributions of Eric Trist in the logic of social science is worthy of mention. Trist's major works comprise twelve books and articles. As a major contributor in the enrichment and advancement of open systems, Trist has used social science disciplines to creatively talk and write about "Sociotechnical systems theory, self-managing teams, assessment centers, the causal texture of organizational environments, social and organizational ecology, and intervention in interorganizational domains" (Pasmore and Khalsa, 1993, p. 546). Trist's research and experience with global communities and environments in terms of learning from and contributing to groups, organizations, communities, and society in general, enabled him to scholastically formulate sociotechnical systems theory and conceptualize the notion of self-directed work teams. Such form of learning enabled him to see organizations as open systems of the environment that are uniquely, socioecologically, and textually produced. The complex interaction of the social, technical, ecological and environmental variables and processes cause the individual, group, organizations and society to change (Getis, Getis, and Fellman, 1998 and Pasmore and Khalsa, 1993).

By profession, Trist was a clinical psychologist who graduated from Cambridge in the United Kingdom, collected data with Wilfred Bion and Jock Sutherland in order to deal with war time mental casualties and try to offer psychotherapy to World War II fatigued victims (POWs). Evidence indicates that he was a boundary spanner who linked "science with humanism, theory with practice and vision with pragmatism" (Pasmore and Khalsa, 1993, p. 547). He also studied coal miners and mining processes in Britain where he found that each mining group used different mining methods but arrived at the same results. In his observations, behavior is a function of the individual and his or her environment. The leaderless group is self-regulating while the group which has a leader tends to follow the norms established by the leader. By comparing the two groups, Trist's scholarly contributions assertively argued that the

(a) behavior of individuals was affected by the groups of which were members; individual performance and group performance were therefore directly related to the ability of the group to be self-regulating in accomplishing tasks; (b) noting that "basic assumptions" (regressive) behavior is omnipresent in environments where strong leadership control is the operating paradigm, and that these effects permeate not just leader-subordinate relations, as McGregor (1960) would later explicate, but entire systems, be they organizations or society (p. 549).

When a strong leader has powerful control, the group tends to regress because it becomes less innovative and unproductive because the autocrat destroys motivation—the engine of creativity.

Trist strongly believed that "individuals, groups, organizations, communities, and society, are "capable of undertaking remarkable change when made aware of the choices before them" (p.549). Because of conscious and unconscious forces, humans construct group and organizational structures that are unsatisfactory and ineffective. In spite of these unattractive states, "deep psychological resistance causes them to deny these negative effects" (p. 550). If the effects are pointed out, "paradigms can be shifted ... processes can be used to involve people in constructing their social arrangements to make them more effective, healthier, more responsive, and more satisfying" (p. 550).

Trist conducted research in India at Calico Mills, Norway at Norsk-Hydro, Britain at Cornwall, and United States at Procter and Gamble, General Foods, and Rushton Mining. He co-authored *Organizational Choice* with G. Higgin, Hugh Murray, and A.B. Pollock in 1993. By largely observing the coal mining industry, he postulated the following generalizations:

Social systems and technical systems are highly interdependent; therefore, the design of the production system as a whole must consider the impact of technology on the social system in order to achieve maximum effectiveness. When social systems are designed into highly fragmented roles without common pay or goals, external control is required to assure compliance with intended behaviors, but external control is typically less effective than internal control and produces regressive rather than productive behavior. Change is best accomplished through the direct involvement of those affected. Social and psychological stress is associated with absenteeism, sickness and accidents. The design of work determines the level of stress experienced. Despite the importance of successful social innovations, managers are more likely to pay attention to technical than social innovation. Organizations are typically poor at both learning from experiments and at communicating the results of experiments internally. Organizational culture, including the history of working relationships and expectations regarding working arrangements, influences the ease with which new ways of working can be introduced, irrespective of the need for change in working arrangements. Teams that lack social unity and technical ability will experience difficulty in self-regulation. Teams as large as 40 members, which possess unity and skills, are capable of effective self-regulation (Pasmore and Khalsa, 1993, p. 557).

Socioecological and sociotechnical systems are interdependent and part and parcel of the theoretical and practical organizational domains (Trist, 1963). Domains are complex processes of change that influence a variety of aspects in organizational operations. The contextual environments of organizational operations change at increasingly complex and sophisticated rates (Emery and Trist, 1965). This requires continuous personal, organizational and social understanding of the "systemic implications of these changes" (Pasmore and Khalsa, 1993, p. 558).

Emery and Trist (1965) have intelligently argued that organizational environments have causal texture. Their argument is based on the sound belief that the character of internal and external dialogues of the organization and its environment has causal texture. Since environments tend to be more independent and self-sufficient by "taking on lives of their own" (Pasmore and Khalsa, 1993, p. 558), organizations can neither control nor predict their destiny and influence of environments. Because of their unpredictability and uncontrollability, organizational environments tend to be viewed as a "turbulent field" that is distinguishable from three other causal textures "placid random, placid clustered, and disturbed reactive" (p. 559). In this case, the contextual interdependence between the organization and its rapidly changing environment is causally and contextually challenging to organizational stability, growth and adaptability. In other words, organizations, in order to survive and prosper, need to be innovative by capitalizing on efficiency and the dynamics and interdependence between them and their environments on one hand and between them and other alliances within the environment. These organizations need to learn and adapt in order to stay afloat when the "ground is in motion" (p. 559). They can stay afloat if they internalize and integrate "greater requisite variety" (p. 559, Re and Ashby, 1960). Managers should manage rather than being managed by the social system. Both the social system and organizational managers may buy into each other's system and become the enemies of organizational adaptability, creativity and innovative change.

Trist has made great strides by contributing to the notion that causal texture of organizational environments may be responsible for turbulent fields. This thinking has not only influenced postindustrialism, but its turbulent temper was, in one way or the other, responsible for the collapse and disintegration of the Soviet State and empire. In the wake of such organizationally disruptive, destabilizing, and paralyzing environmental fields of turbulence, a classic case of which took place in the whole of East Asia (stock market) (Thailand, Singapore, Malaysia, Hong Kong, South Korea, and even Japan), shows that alternative forms of organizing are imperative. New alternative forms of organizing will, it is hoped, enhance organizational effectiveness, promote industrial survival, enhance cooperation and competitiveness, and strengthen field and organizational welfare (Trist, 1977). The purpose for organizational reorganization is to redesign, reinvent and empower bureaucratic structures, values, and organizational forms which cannot "adapt to conditions of persistent and pervasive environmental turbulence, however large they become or massive the power they wield" (Trist, 1977, p. 167 and Pasmore and Khalsa, 1993, p. 559). In the light of Trist's looking glass:

> The basic reason why bureaucratic organizations show diminishing adaptive capabilities in the face of rising environmental turbulence is that, though they can cope with risk they cannot cope with uncertainty, which throws them off the carefully programmed courses they have prepared. Furthermore, "the greater the resources – human, material and financial – sunk in these programs, the more difficult it becomes for them to change direction" (Trist, 1977, p. 167).

In Trist's understanding, the concept of organizational ecology is the mutual interdependent relationship of organizational entities and units. When organizational entities and units acceptably learn to share the limited resources of a common environment, they tend to survive in spite of the potentially existing turbulent environments (Trist, 1987). In respect to organizational ecology, it will be illogical to think, though his research was conducted in India, U.K., U.S. and Norway, that Trist is ignorant of the Keiretsu model of the Japanese industrial, economic, and technocultural corporation (Ouchi, 1981) which forms network alliances with government (MITI), industry, and other corporations and banks for its own survival and strategic competitiveness.

The sociotechnical systems of Trist was a group approach to the adaptation of capabilities and conditions necessary for the optimization of group effectiveness. This is a team approach which enhances participatory management. However organizational ecology, contrary to sociotechnical systems, is the extension of group values to the field of organizations. Such collaboration between sociotechnical systems and organizational ecology violates the principle of competition. However, in a turbulent organizational environment, where no organization will survive without collaboration and sharing of resources with other organizations, to forgo competition, which is an external ingredient, is a wise strategic action that will have far reaching positive influence on the organization(s) and its or their environment(s), respectively ... "in understanding systems of organizational ecology, social networks are as fundamental as the primary work group is to understanding single organizations" (Trist, 1977 and Pasmore and Khalsa, 1993, p. 560). In this arena, 'interface relations, which require negotiation rather than compliance, are as basic to systems of organizational ecology as superior-subordinate relations are to bureaucratic organizations" (p. 560).

Between 1950s and 1970s Trist's action research that was concerned with client systems, used data from large and complex social systems (e.g. National Union of Farmers of England and Wales). In other words, beyond organizational ecology, more complex interdependencies (social ecology) emerged. This new socioecological paradigm has structural components but "lacked cultural values, organizational philosophies and ecological strategies" (Emery and Trist, 1973, p. 158) of the postindustrial world. In other words, the new values of postindustrialism must:

> be ones which enhance our capability to cope with the increased levels of complexity, interdependence and uncertainty that characterize the turbulent contemporary environment. Evidence is mounting that the individual by himself, or indeed the organization and even the polity by itself, cannot meet the demands of these more complex environments. A greater pooling of resources is required; be communal rather than individualistic regarding access to amenities, cooperative rather than competitive regarding the use of scarce resources; yet personal rather than conforming regarding life styles and goals (Emery and Trist, 1973, pp. 172-173 and Pasmore and Khalsa, 1993, p. 561).

Trist is a polemicist who argues, and rightly so, perhaps, that the structural, cultural values of society during the industrial era were achievement, self-control, independence and perseverance (Emery and Trist, 1973). Other societal strengths like the Protestant Ethic have been eroded by the causal texture of the postindustrial era. The classical organization theories like Taylorism and Weberian rationalism, structuralism and functionalism have become so mechanistic and rigid to allow competition to healthfully flourish and enable the West to exercise industrial and economic dominance. These classical theoretical models tend to cause organizations and society in general, to become inhibitive and unable to organize organically and collaboratively. Since interdependence has become a principle for sharing our scarce global and environmental resources of our planet, ecologically based strategies can potentially become salient features of our organizational, institutional and societal operations. These strategies are solvent in "anticipating crisis, planning over longer time horizons, enacting more comprehensive (holistic) measures" rather than "specific ones that address only symptoms" (Pasmore and Khalsa, 1993, p. 562). The promise of these socioecological and sociotechnical strategies is grounded on the assumption that the organization and society are actively involved in participatory rather than in consenting and conformist behaviors alone. Trist argues that planning models are rooted in historical and empirical industrialism. These models view planning to be "comprehensive, technocratically devised and centrally imposed from the top" (p. 563). The resources used for control are hierarchical. The thinking systems of the models are closed rather than open. The goal of this machine theory of organizing is maximization of power in terms of authority, profit, and tenure respectively. Unfortunately, such complex hierarchical and closed organizational and societal systems have proved to be "unworkable" and full of "messes" (pp. 562-563). Such systems can work if they are made participatory by using adaptive planning approaches (Ackoff, 1974). Adaptive planning models are innovative and purposeful systems that tend to create new climates of organizational culture and politics conducive to group, organizational and social innovation (Trist, 1979).

According to Ackoff (1974), the main and current organizational pathologies and problems are so intertwined and interlocked with each other, so much so that the notion of "meta-problem or mess" (Pasmore and Khalsa, 1993, p. 563) is used to describe them. The issues inherent in meta-problem are extensive, many sided, and complex for any organization to cope with. Since these issues and problems are inter- and multi-organizational, they can be analyzed at the interorganizational domain perspective (Trist, 1983). The members of the fields of these organizations have common experiences.

Because societies are weak at the interorganizational level, institution building at the domain level is required to deal more effectively with meta-problems. In some cases, a new *referent organization* is created by the members of the domain, controlled by all but dominated by none, which allows it to contribute optimally to meta-problem appreciation and responsive domain development (e.g., the Labor-Management Committee of the City of Jamestown) (Trist, 1977). Referent organizations serve three broad functions: (a) regulation of relationships, (b) appreciation of issues and development of shared vision, and (c) infrastructural support (Trist, 1983).

In other cases, no single referent organization exists and the coherence is provided less structurally by shared values within a *social network* (e.g., Marilyn Ferguson's notion of the *Aquarian Conspiracy*, 1980). In this case, there is a recentering of organizational life—away from bounded single organizations and toward unbounded networks in which members of a domain are linked (Trist, 1977).

To make this shift, individuals are needed who are willing and able to break out of fixed organizational molds and to cultivate the skills of the boundary spanner, thereby becoming "network men" [and women] rather than "organization men" (Trist, 1977). It also demonstrates the key interdependence between personal development and social development, be that at the level of the organization, the community, or an industry (Trist, 1979).

In the context of interorganizational domains, adaptive planning becomes focused on the creation of adaptive social organizations capable of continuous learning via acts of *appreciation* (Vickers, 1965), multiple interest group engagement, and relevant domain formation. In this mode of planning, judgments of value and fact are normatively wedded (Trist, 1976). The driving normative decisions involve selecting a set of intended and desirable *consequences* (distant outcomes, including ecological effects in the wider social system) as *distinct from results* (immediate outcomes of specific courses of action) (Ozbekman, 1971).

Table 4.1 emphasizes the necessary changes in social life patterns as societies experience the transitional move to postindustrialism (Trist, 1976). Such transitional change requires the fulfillment of four conditions: (a) starting to bring change on the periphery is simpler

Table 4.1. Changes in Emphasis of Social Patterns in the Transition to Postindustrialism[a]

Industrial Era	Postindustrial Era
Cultural Values	
Achievement	Self-actualization
Self-control	Self-expression
Independence	Interdependence
Endurance of distress	Capacity of joy
Organizational Philosophies	
Mechanistic forms	Organic forms
Competitive relations	Collaborative relations
Separate objectives	Linked objectives
Own resources regarded as owned absolutely	Own resources regarded as society's
Ecological Strategies	
Responsiveness to crisis	Anticipating crisis
Specific measurements	Comprehensive measures
Requiring consent	Requiring participation
Damping conflict	Controlling conflict
Short planning horizon	Long planning horizon
Detailed central control	Generalized planning control
Small local government units	Enlarged local government units
Standardized administration	Innovative administration
Separate services	Co-ordinated services

[a] Note: From *Towards a Social Ecology: Contextual Appreciation of the Future in the Present*: 174, 182, 186, by F.E. Emery and E.L. Trist, 1973, London: Plenum Press. Copyright 1973 by Plenum Press. Reprinted by permission.

because there is less complexity, less overload and has more room and freedom for experimentation and error; (b) work from the bottom upwards rather than from the top downwards; (c) concentrate on "middle level of society between the single organization and the nation state" (p. 565); and work across networks rather than through formal hierarchies in order to reach social fields" (p. 565).

Table 4.2 is a categorized reflection of the emerging societal patterns that shows how different levels are interconnected or interlinked. These social patterns are socioecologically, philosophically and strategically reflective of the social patterns in Table 4.1. This paradigmatic feature corresponds with the current and paramount causal texture of

Table 4.2
Features of an Emerging Societal Pattern[a]

Present	Emerging
Policies	
Centrally formed	An innovative periphery
Statutory bodies allocate resources	Power is shared with nonstatutory bodies
Party politics	Community politics
Passive electorate	Active participation
Organizations	
Technocratic bureaucracies	Democratized organizational forms
External controls	International controls
Low QWL	High QWL for the many
Domains	
Discrete problem solving	Meta-problem appreciation
Independent objectives	Interdependent objectives
Competing interests	Collaborative interests
Individuals	
Privatized	Shared values
Dissociated	Network connectedness
Powerless though autonomous	Empowered, socially responsible

[a] From "New Directions of Hope: Recent Innovations Interconnecting Organizational, Industrial, Community, and Personal Development" by E.L. Trist, 1979, *Regional Studies*, 13: 449. Copyright 1979 by *Regional Studies*. Reprinted by permission.

environmental turbulence. It is critically important, according to postmodern and postindustrial thinking, to apply these approaches to change in order to avert chaos, and institute order for sustaining livelihood, society, and planet of the only habitable environment we know of. As a scientific humanist, Trist places emphasis in action research whose knowledge and results have been used to restore hope and the "ability of the average worker to be responsibly self-regulating." Trist's conclusions have offered principles and values that guide society for the better. The core values of self-regulation and freedom from oppression, democracy, and self-determination of working arrangements, and fair treatment in terms of dignity for all in the workplace, participation in change and collaboration" (p. 567) are imperative.

Above all, self-regulating groups, sociotechnical systems theory, causal textures of the global environment, national and regional environment, organizational ecology and social ecology have become the new testament for "biblical" ideas in the field of revolutionary and innovative management thought. Their implications for open systems practice and praxis could be far-reaching.

Conclusion

Open systems theory is based on the premise that the parts of one system or the existence of many systems have their being in the principle of interdependence in terms of resource expenditure, input and output respectively. The father of open systems theoretical model is Ludwig von Bertalanffy. He argues that open systems theory is a scientific model of self-regulation and self-maintenance of scientific organizations," natural systems and social systems. The five major schools of thought on which the social systems model is grounded differ in their intensity and variability and in terms of their explanatory power concerning the open systems model and its utility. Respectively, these five major schools of the open systems model of organizational management include but are not limited to systems design, contingency theory, environmental approaches, Weick's concept of organizing as opposed to organization, and Eric Trist's sociotechnical and socioecological interdependence.

Though the open systems model evolved relatively late as compared to the rational and natural (behaviorist) traditions in organizational management, the former has rapidly attracted followers and has radically changed the human notion of organizations and their characteristic components and processes. The open systems theory places emphasis on complexity, variability of individual components, participants and subgroups by which the organization is comprised of. The model stresses looseness of the connecting linkages among and between the components. Organizational parts and structures have the capability to be semiautonomous. Each part is loosely, indirectly or directly, connected to other parts. In this respect, the organization is like the human body whose nervous system is uniquely structured to sensitize the pressures of the environment which may stimulate its many organs by stimulating it to respond consciously or unconsciously. Organizations are multicephalously constructed. This means that human organizations have many people who use their heads to receive information, data and ideas for decision-making and viable performance. In these organizations, people behave formally and informally in terms of groups, coalitions and networks. They plan, coordinate, control and integrate organizational activities. Depending on the character and personalities of people in charge, the organization can be viewed as open rather than closed, processual rather than structural oriented, cybernetic (self-regulating) rather than static, morphostatic (self-maintaining and stable) rather than mechanistic, classical, and morphogenetic (changeable evolutionary development of structure) and equifinal.

The open systems perspective of the organizational realm assumes an abstract and empirical interdependence of the organization with its environment. Unlike the rational system which overlooks the environment, and the natural system which is "alien and hostile" (Scott, 1981, p. 120) to the open systems, the latter stresses reciprocity "that binds and interrelates the organization with those elements that surround and penetrate it" (p. 120). The environment is the "source of materials, energy and information, all of which are vital" to the survival and development of the system (p. 120). This same environment could also be the source of order as well.

It is self-evident that open systems theory is an offshoot of the general systems paradigm which evolved fifty years ago. The general systems theory is too general to be specific and esoterically explanatory. It heavily relies on analogies which are symbolic and parallel generalizations that lack scientific specificity. In other words, the universality of general systems theory grossly suffers from the dynamic particularity and sophisticated complexity of the open systems perspective.

Although the open systems perspective employs complex terms such as "cybernetics, morphogenesis, morphostasis, equifinality, sociotechnical and socioecological systems, the complexity and abstractness of these terms shows that research scholars are progressively trying to come up with new concepts to explain how the system works. The invention retention and application of such new vocabulary indicates that the organization is no longer "closed, self-contained, and self-sufficient" (p. 120). This very organization uses processes and structures. The processes are dynamic rather than static forces that continually change existing operational structures.

References

Ackoff, R.L., and F.E. Emery. 1972. *On Purposeful Systems*. Chicago: Aldine Press.

Aldrich, H.E., and Jeffrey Pfeffer. 1976. Environments of organizations. *Annual Review of Sociology* 2: 79-105.

Arrow, K.J. 1974. *The Limits of Organization*. New York: W.W. Norton and Co.

Ashby, W. 1960. *Design for a Brain*. New York: Wiley.

Ashby, W.R., and W. Buckley, eds. 1968. Principles of self-organizing system. In *Modern Systems Research for the Behavioral Scientist*. Chicago: Aldine: 108-118.

Barry, D., and M. Elmes. 1997. Strategy retold: Toward a narrative view of strategic discourse. *Academy of Management Review* 22, 2: 429-452.

Bertalanffy, L.V. 1956. General system theory. *General Systems: Year-Book of the Systems Theory*. Edited by Ludwig von Bertalanffy and Anatol Rapoport 1: 1-10.

Boulding, K.E. 1956. Systems Theory—The skeleton of science. *Management Science* 2: 197-208.

Buckley, W. 1967. *Sociology and Modern Systems Theory*. Englewood Cliffs, N.J.: Prentice-Hall.

Campbell, D. 1969. Variation and selective retention in socio-cultural evolution. *General Systems: Yearbook of the Society for General Systems* 16: 69-85.

Cyert, R.M. and James G. March. 1963. *A Behavioral Theory of the Firm*. Englewood Cliffs, N.J.: Prentice-Hall.

Doty, H.D., W.H. Glick, and G.P. Huber. 1993. Fit, equifinality, and organizational effectiveness: A test of two configurational theories. *Academy of Management Journal* 3: 1196-1250.

Eisenhardt, K.M. 1988. Agency and institutional theory explanations: The case of retail sales compensation. *Academy of Management Journal* 31: 488-511.

Emery, F.E., and E.L. Trist. 1973. *Towards a Social Ecology: Contextual Appreciation of the Future in the Present*. London: Plenum Press.

Emery, F.E., and E.L. Trist. 1965. The Causal Texture of Organizational Environments. *Human Relations* 18: 21-32.

Galbraith, J. 1973. *Designing Complex Organizations*. Reading, MA: Addison Wesley.

Getis, A., et al. 1998. *Introduction to Geography*. Boston, MA: McGraw-Hill.

Gortner, H.F., et al. 1997. *Organization Theory: A Public Perspective.* Fort Worth, TX: Harcourt Brace College Publishers.

Gresov, C., and Robert Drazin. 1997. Equifinality: Functional Equivalance in Organization Design. *Academy of Management Review* 22, 2: 403-428.

Haberstroh, C.J. 1965. ed. Organization design and systems analysis. In *Handbook of Organizations.* James G. March. Chicago: Rand McNally.

Hannan, M.T., and John Freeman. 1977. The population ecology of organizations. *American Journal of Sociology* 82: 929-964.

Hawley, A. 1950. *Human Ecology.* New York: Ronald.

Hofstadler, R. 1945. *Social Darwinism in American Thought, 1860-1915.* Philadelphia: University of Pennsylvania Press.

Jacobs, D. 1974. Dependency and vulnerability: An exchange approach to the control of organizations. *Administrative Science Quarterly* 19: 45-59.

March, J.G., and Johan P. Olsen. 1976a. Ambiguity and choice in organizations. Bergen, Norway: Universitetsforlaget.

March, J. and H. Simon. 1958. *Organizations.* New York: Wiley.

McGregor, D. 1960. *The Human Side of Enterprise.* New York: McGraw-Hill.

Miller, J.G. 1978. *Living Systems.* New York: McGraw-Hill.

Ozbekhan, H. 1971. Planning and human action. In *Hierarchically Organized Systems in Theory and Practice,* ed. P.A. Weiss, 123-230. New York: Hafner.

Pasmore, W.A., and Khalsa, G.S. 1993. The contributions of Eric Trist to the social engagement of social science. *Academy of Management Review* 18, 3: 546-569.

Pfeffer, J., and G.R. Salancik. 1974. Organization decision making as a political process: The case of a university budget. *Administrative Science Quarterly* 19: 135-151.

Pondy, L.R., and Ian I. Mitroff. 1979. Beyond open systems models of organization. In *Research in Organizational Behavior,* ed. Barry M. Staw. Greenwich, CT: JAI Press.

Rapaport, A. 1972. The uses of mathematical isomorphism in general system theory. In G.J. Klir (Ed.) *Trends in General System Theory.* New York: Wiley, 52-65.

Scott, R.W. (1981). *Organizations: Rational, Natural and Open Systems.* Englewood Cliffs, N.J.: Prentice-Hall.

Thompson, J.D. (1967). *Organizations in Action.* New York: McGraw-Hill.

Toffler, A. 1970. *Future Shock.* New York: Random.

Trist, E.L. 1987. Intervention strategies for interorganizational domains. In *Human Systems Development,* eds. R. Tannenbaum, N. Margulies, F. Massarik, and Associates. San Francisco: Jossey-Bass.

Trist, E.L. 1983. Referent organizations and the development of interorganizational domains. *Human Behavior* 36: 269-284.

Trist, E.L. 1981. The sociotechnical perspective: The evolution of sociotechnical systems as a conceptual framework and as an action research program. In *Perspectives on Organizational Design and Behavior,* eds. A.H. Van de Ven and W.F. Joice, 19-75. New York: Wiley.

Trist, E.L. 1980. The environment and system-response capability. *Futures*: 113-127.

Trist, E.L. 1977. A concept of organizational ecology. *Australian Journal of Management* : 162-175.

Trist, E.L. 1976. Action research and adaptive planning. In *Experimenting with Organizational Life,* ed. A.W. Clark, 223-236. New York: Plenum Press.

Trist, E.L. (1970). Social science policy and development of research in the social sciences: The organizing and financing of social research. In *UNESCO Committee on Research Trends in the Human and Social Sciences, Main Trends of Research in the Social and Human Sciences,* 695-811. Paris: Mouton/UNESCO.

Trist, E.L., and H. Murray. eds. 1967. *The Social Engagement of Social Science: A Tavistock Anthology: The Socio-Psychological Perspective.* Vol. 1. Philadelphia: University of Pennsylvania Press.

Trist, E.L., et al. 1963. *Organizational Choice: Capabilities of Groups at the Coal Face Under Changing Technologies: The Loss, Rediscovery and Transformation of a Work Tradition.* London: Tavistock.

Wamsley, G.L., and Mayer N. Zald. 1973. *The Political Economy of Public Organizations.* Lexington, MA: Heath.

Weick, K.E. 1976. Educational organizations as loosely coupled systems. *Administrative Science Quarterly* 2: 1-19.

Weick, K.E. 1974. Middle range theories of social systems. *Behavioral Science* 19: 357-67.

Weick, K.E. 1969. *The Social Psychology of Organizing.* Reading, MA: Addison-Wesley.

Williamson, O.E. 1975. *Markets and Hierarchies: Analysis and Antitrust Implication.* New York: Free Press.

Zald, M.N. 1970. Political economy: A framework for comparative analysis. In *Power in Organizations,* ed. Mayer N. Zald. Nashville: Vanderbilt University Press.

Section Two: Organizational Structure

Section Two deals with organizational structure, goals, culture and diversity of the organization. Goals are targets, standards, objectives and rationally established yardsticks for making judgments concerning the progress, success or failure of the organization. Organizations and institutions are anchored in society's cultural assumptions and presuppositions from which the goals, which are society's thoughts, feelings, perceptions, and aspirations, are filtered. The filtration of these goals can be conducted legislatively, corporately, ceremonially, symbolically or ritualistically for the purpose of enhancing organizational values. Organizational values which members hold are entrenched in societal culture. It is through a variety of formal and informal socialization mechanisms used for enhancing civilization, productivity, adaptability, innovation and turnover that this culture is reproduced to enhance change, mobility, and restructuring.

The mission of the organization whose culture is rooted in society's complex life is to articulate the goals in question. The wholistic articulation of specific organizational goals requires certain resources in terms of people, time, funds and technology for realizing the organization's programmatic structure. Organizational structure comprises roles, authority and communication which are instrumentally essential for effective interactive coordination of fragmented functional specialties, utilization of technology of production, and centralized and decentralized integration and socialization of a variety of participants in organizational departments, divisions, and their units.

Organizational models of which the pyramid, matrix and team are paramount, are characterized by specialization of functions, standardization of procedures, roles and processes of centralization of authority, restructuring of roles and values, and unity of command and control. Often times, these management functions do not run smoothly because of political, economic, administrative, and ideological contradictions within specific organizations and their cultural niches and climates.

Organizational goals, structures and culture are a microcosm of society's norms, values and ethics that are reminiscent of its diversity. Diversity management is a conscious process of introducing variety by increasing the worth of people, both qualitatively and quantitatively, into the organizational environment, for the purpose of enhancing organizational equilibrium, synergy, and productivity. Though organizations at large are anthropologically and socially constructed "objects" of the larger socioeconomic, cultural and political systems, their cultures, social climates, and power groups create opportunity and disincentives or social traps that inherently produce the irreconcilable contradictions of their anticipated consequences. Only when the mechanisms of socialization, restructuring and training through organizational learning are put in place do effective organizational management functions managerially become solvent.

Chapter 5

Organizational Goals: The Mission of Langston University

Organizations are systems built on partial involvement of their members, functional specialization and structural differentiation. They use goals. A goal or objective, is a broader, specific, and a "specialized function" (Scott, 1981, 18) or element. Organizational elements are components of the social structure of the organization that is reflective of the features of its environment, e.g., structural forms and technology. Specifically, these organizational elements are social structure, participants, goals, technology, and environment.

The organization is a social system which must meet many needs one of which is to pursue its goals (Selznick, 1948; Etzioni, 1961; and Parsons, 1960). These are output goals or product goals or self-maintenance goals (Gross, 1968; and Perrow, 1970). Those who design and implement goals have authority and power in terms of knowledge for bringing them to fruition.

It is rational to ask questions like these: What are goals? If organizations have goals, who sets them? Are there organizations that exist without goals? Are goals a basis for control? How are organizational goals set? These questions can be answered in the course of this chapter's analysis.

Types and Uses of Goals: The Problem Setting

Analysts, entrepreneurs, and employees have difficulty, due to confusion, to understand, conceive or correctly interpret the complex nature of organizational goals. As a result, goals are at times identified based on the theoretical underpinnings they are based on. For instance, rational system analysts argue that goals provide the criteria for generating and selecting from many alternative courses of action (Simon, 1957). The rationalist intellectuals emphasize that the "cognitive functions of goals" are based on providing "directions and constraints on decision making and action" (Scott, 1981, 261). Second, natural (behavioral) system analysts championed by Barnard (1938) and Clark and Wilson (1961) stress that goals are used for identifying and motivating organizational participants. Third, Selznick (1949) points out that goals are an ideological system for overcoming opposition. Opposition is overcome when resources are garnered from the environment and utilized to process organizational inputs to produce outputs. Clark, Barnard, Wilson, and Selznick emphasize the cathartic (emotional) nature of goals because they serve as a basis of attachment for internal and external publics. Cathartic goals are different from other goals. At times, vague and general goals may be enough for motivational purposes but unsuitable for cognitive endeavors. Weick (1969) and Festinger (1957) have argued that:

> Rationality seems better understood as a postdecision rather than a predecision occurrence. Rationality makes sense of what has been, not what will be. It is a process of justification in which past deeds are made to appear sensible to the actor himself and to those other persons to whom he feels accountable (Weick, 1969, 38; and Scott, 1981, 262).

In a sense, behavior can precede goals and goal statements may be used to justify specific actions. Human choice is a process for discovering goals for action (March, 1976). Goals are statements that are used for evaluating the behavior of participants. Individual or personal goals are called motives. These are different from organizational goals. Both individual motives and organizational goals are "purposive" goals. There are no collective goals. Organizational goals can be set in an entrepreneurial, consensual or coalitional settings. In other words, goals have many uses that meet the needs, designs and controls of organizational participants. The goals can be used for cognitive functions, for "guiding the selection of alternative courses of action; they have cathartic properties ... they provide present justifications for actions taken in the past; they provide criteria for the evaluation of performances, participants and programs of action; and under some conditions, they provide ideological guidance for the contributions of participants" (Scott, 1981, 289). Though individual participants come with their motives (goals) into the organization, these are hardly similar to those of the organization. However, if the organization has to be productive, individual motives should be reconciled with organizational goals. This is difficult to realize unless individuals are willing to sacrifice their views, positions and influence for the success of the whole (organization's) goals.

Goals are a product of the views of dominant coalitions which determine organizational trajectory. Through these coalitions, mysteries of goal setting are laid down. Doing that helps to avoid reification of the organization as a purposeful actor whose goals and preference structures differ from those of its participants and clients. The concept of coalition creates a climate for individuals, groups, and participants to articulate a variety of interests and agenda. This coalitional organizational variety shows how through negotiation and the making of side-payments, bargains can be struck for the purpose of evolving a common strategic action. The concept of dominant coalitions is an evidence to the promise that individual participants do not have equal power in decision-making. Also, the preferences and interests of some will receive more attention than those of the rest. Although individuals and groups bring preferences and interests with them into the organization, organizations are more than a seat of common interests. They are institutions which create new interests as opposed to old ones.

The size and shape of the dominant coalition tends to change over time. The change is a response to the pressures exerted by external conditions which influence organizational adaptability. As new sources of uncertainty and challenge evolve in its surroundings, the organization creates mechanisms for dealing with them. Officials are capable of coping with problems. They may be expected to acquire power within the organization because other people depend on them for crucial and critical contributions. With the evolution of environmental turbulence, dominant coalitions tend to grow in size and shape and gradually incorporate a variety of specialists who are capable of managing a variety of problems. When the demographic composition of the dominant coalition changes, the goals of the organization change too because such change is a form of shift in power as well.

What happens or what is likely to happen if organizations do not have goals? This is an interesting situation. Several things are likely to happen. Since they lack goals and efficacious technologies, such conditions are not conducive to organizational formation and maintenance. First, organizations are likely to suffer for a long time while awaiting a charismatic leader who can clarify goals and provide means and vision for achieving them. Second, the situation may become more ambiguous due to the fact that participants do not have the capacity to identify problems and provide relevant solutions. Third, some organizations might seek to create institutionalized organizational subsystems in which "meaning and matter are" fed by "rationalized myths" (Scott, 1981, 290). Other organizations may falter and disintegrate. Finally, others may consensually agree on "proximal or procedural goals that provide a stable framework which coexistentially tolerate substantive differences.

Any organization is a collectivity which controls its members. Goals in themselves may be viewed as organizational controls which participants are responsive to and accountable for. Those who design goals for implementation have power and ability for sanctioning them. The sanctioning requirement could be legally, politically or socially constructed. The power to sanction or enforce is a form of authority. This authority is normatively regulated as a form of power as well. The authority of informal groups is a form of endorsed power. This power is normatively constrained and enforced by subordinates—the organizational employees. However, in informal organizations, authority exists in terms of being authorized power. This power is interpreted and "supported by norms enforced by officers superior to the power wielder. Most organizations attempt to regulate the contributions of participants by developing evaluation systems that link performances to organizational sanctions" (p. 290). Though such control systems are ubiquitous, they are cumbersome, complex and flawed, particularly when organizational goals are unclear. The control systems of some of the organizations may be more consensually defined, and interpreted than they are individually defined or positioned. As cathartic, ideological, cognitive and control mechanisms, the goals of higher education enterprise need some elucidation.

Goals of Higher Education Organization

Higher education is academic, technological, and professional education beyond high school level. In this arena, goals are designed for giving direction and for being ends. A goal is an aim or purpose which guides or directs an orderly and progressive process. Goals emanate from the mission of the university. The process is activated within a short, medium, or long-range time span. Within any given time, an institution's goal must be given the opportunity to experience successive and "cumulative growth and maturation" (Dewey, 1966). If the institution is to experience effective and efficient performance, then the goals, which emanate from it, for it, and with it, should be formulated, implemented, and evaluated by experts of vision and professional principles. Goals are perceived to be "ends or outcomes" (Grambasch and Gross, 1968). Such goals direct activity in a step by step manner until a successful end is reached. Success is reached because goal planning and goal administration are carried out with foresight. Foresight involves careful observation of the given conditions to see what the means for reaching the end are; to discover obstacles in the process, and to use means sequentially and properly in such a way that economy can be maintained. Finally the planners of higher education goals use their foresight to predict the outcome of implementing specific goals, compare the value of two courses of action in respect to each goal, and evaluate their relative desirability. Employment of relevant, predictable, and measurable goals is intelligent organizational and management behavior.

Good "goals must have criteria" (Dewey, 1968). First, the goals must outgrow from existing internal conditions. When goals emanate from external conditions, they limit the intelligence of those who apply them because they are foreign to them and, imposed on them.

Secondly, goals must be flexible. Flexibility makes them capable of alteration or modification to meet prevailing situations. Externally oriented goals are rigid and difficult to implement or adapt. They result in failure. On the contrary, the value of good goals lies in the fact that we can use them to change circumstances. It is a formula for dealing with circumstances so as to effect desirable alterations in them. The goals are experimental and therefore constantly growing as they pass the test of time, pomp and circumstance.

Thirdly, good goals must be used in such a way that specific objectives or (targets) can be hit. The target is the end in view. Deviation from good goals result in no end at all.

How should education goals be applied in higher education? In the first place, education per se has no goals. Only persons, i.e., parents, teachers, professors, and education directors and administrators have goals upon which they erect the foundation of the educational system. Good educational goals are founded upon the intrinsic activities, needs and abilities of students. Secondly, the goals must appeal to the expectations of adults who advocate them and contribute to them. They should be designed to suit the ordinary student at large. Thirdly, goals must correspond with curricula and instructional methodologies of the institution. In this case, externally imposed goals are a vice with deep roots. Fourthly, educators must discard goals that are too general, ineffectual, and ultimate. General goals tend to be detached from the reality of situational specificity and from reality itself.

Fixing educational goals is one of the first steps in planning. Absence, vagueness or incoherence of goals could result in serious national education or institutional consequences. Any country with a good system of higher education, has goals which are a reflection of national development not only in moral, political, social, technological, industrial, intellectual and professional competence, but also in "international cooperation and understanding" (*Educational Planning*: UNESCO, 1970). The university produces competent minds because it is a "power house and clearing house of new ideas" (Brubacher, 1977, 18). It is a source of inspiration. Next to government, it is the chief instrument of social change. Good goals must bring constructive change because change is inextricable from development. It is intertwined with it.

Goals of higher education are connected with a specific brand of philosophy or with brands of philosophies. To what extent should a university concern itself with a particular philosophical thought? What stand should the university have concerning a particular philosophy and why? In what way and to what extent should the philosophy be exemplified through inculcation of students, tests for teachers etc.? Is the university responsible for the philosophies its members cherish? In the opinion of Moberly (1949), a higher institution of learning should exercise neutrality in ultimate issues. Its neutrality should be positive rather than negative. This positive stand should have a unity of thought from men and women alike. Such a form of neutral solidarity is a fascade for its survival during critical situations.

The process of attaining university education is a complex phenomenon. It is complex because the knowledge is sophisticated. In view of this, the following questions which Brubacher (1977) raises have relevance: Who is responsible for offering sophisticated knowledge? How do we know whether the claim to sophistication is legitimately genuine? Since only experts in higher education are the only competent evaluators of their sophistication, should the community of scholars be an autonomous body? For the constant improvement of sophisticated learning, should the faculty of these institutions enjoy academic freedom? Is there a useful sense in which the pursuit of higher learning could have religious implications? To answer these questions successively, it will be proper to formulate some of the philosophical principles which govern the administration of higher education in the democratic world. Subsequent analysis will answer these questions in a more elaborate manner.

The Functions of Higher Education

Higher education is a republic of scholars. All its disciplines, as Newman (1925, Chapter 9) asserts, are not isolated and independent of each other; instead, they form a whole system. The parts of the system are complementary and interdependent irrespective of their secular or religious persuasions. Taking into its charge all the sciences (disciplines), methods, data, principles and doctrines which are the reflections of the universe upon the human intellect, he admits them all, disregards none, and, allows none to exceed or encroach. In essence the functions of the university are threefold: research, teaching, and community service.

As far as research is concerned, it is a science of systematic and logical inquiry or "exclusive investigation" (Ortega, 1963). The researcher poses problems, works them out empirically or philosophically and reaches the right conclusion. From the moment a conclusion is reached, all that may subsequently follow is unscientific. That is why it is not scientific to learn, teach or apply science. For instance, a competent science professor knows science. As far as his competence is concerned, to know is to investigate and to investigate is to discover truth and, or, demonstrate error. The truth which has been discovered is to be assimilated into his consciousness. In doing this scholarly work, the university has become a home of creative, scientific, and philosophical thought.

"The university is the intellect, it is science erected into an institution" (Ortega, 1963, 74). The sciences are the soil out of which higher learning grows and from which it draws its sustenance. Scholarly and scientific findings should create ferment and stimulation in the university. Its science is the dignity of the university; for development is impossible without dignity. Therefore sensitivity to scientific learning is the soul of the institution. University scientific findings need perpetual contact with existing science, public life, and historical reality in terms of the past, present and future. This reality is its totality which it must illuminate. To illuminate it well, the university which uses science must be open rather than closed to that reality.

Because the university is a guiding light, it must intervene in current affairs and treat important current issues objectively. The issues could include cultural, professional and scientific phenomena. The study earlier cited (Ortega, 1963) points out that the university must assert itself as a major spiritual power, higher than the press, standing for serenity in the midst of frenzy, for seriousness and intellectual honesty in the face of frivolity and unashamed stupidity. In brief, it must be an uplifting principle in the history of humankind.

The university or the republic of scholars is a constant intellectual critic of dogmatism, irrationality, and incorrect ideas. When intellectual pursuits are intensively cultivated, they result in intellectual passion. The pursuit of intellectual passion generates reasonable efficiency which inspires the uninspired dogmatic intellectuals. This inspiration leads them to intellectual thoroughness and meticulous accuracy in dealing with empirical evidence. When evidence has been found, no matter how unwelcome it is, the way of seeking the truth is made more widely open and finally real truth or knowledge is established. Nash (1944) indicates that within that empirical procedure, the established or creatively discovered truth hardly bears its contextual meaning. Meaningless truth should be reexamined, made or altered to become meaningful, internalized by the community of scholars and scientists.

Finally, the creative discovery of the republic of scholars is not for most ordinary minds. It is for the gifted and "dominant minority" whose chief responsibility is to focus the community's intellectual conscience. This ability to focus the community's intellectual conscience is not a monopolistic feature of the university, but the university cannot be equaled or rivaled in its possession of it. The creativity of scholars is the work of research and excellent researchers are excellently creative teachers as well.

We have seen that the university is research and research is the university. Subsequently, the following paragraph indicates that the university is not only research and vice versa, it is also teaching and vice versa. Ortega (1963) indicates that the primary and basic function of the university is to teach the ordinary person to become, in the first place, cultured. When the person is cultured, he or she can see the paths of life in a clear way. Secondly, the function of the university is to teach a person to become professional. A professional person has a skill which reinforces his or her competence. Doctors, judges, historians, geographers, and political scientists, and what have you, are competent professionals. Finally, its esoteric role is to produce researchers and scholars of the finest type.

Grambasch and Gross (1968) show that professors and teachers should cultivate the intellect of students. The educated students should become well rounded, that is, because of their cultivation, students should be physically, socially, morally, intellectually and aesthetically adjustable. The students should be familiarized with the great minds and ideas of history. They should develop objectivity about themselves, and their beliefs and they should examine those beliefs critically. Their exposure to the world of learning and scholarship should enable them to make sound and correct moral choices.

Professors and teachers should prepare students for specific useful careers by providing them with skills, attitudes, contacts, and experiences which maximize their potential for societal leadership. They should train students to become scholars, creative and scientific researchers. Such trainees should later on become good and selective consumers, who are culturally elevated, who have good taste. Above all, the educated student should be able to perform his citizenship responsibilities effectively.

The selection of the professors and teachers should depend not only on their rank as investigators but on their talent for synthesis and teaching. In emphasizing this thought, a study by Kneller (1955) indicates that the university must assist in integrating and interpreting knowledge; it is unreasonable to expect students to synthesize a culture which has been fragmented by the multifarious types of analysis that emanate from powerful minds. The programs of the university must be based upon the student, and not upon the professor or upon knowledge. The student need to be encouraged to learn what is necessary with thoroughness and understanding.

Autonomy Academic Freedom and Tenure

A productive university must exercise the principles of autonomy, academic freedom and tenure. This section will be devoted for the definition and function of these terms as understood by modern institutions of higher learning. Less competitive and patronage or dogmatic clad institutions are foreign to these ideas. Their foreignness could be attributed to their lack of exposure or standards.

Autonomy

Autonomy is the degree of independence or freedom for self-direction, self-determination or political control possessed by a minority—"in its relations to the state or political community of which it forms a part" (*Webster's Dictionary*, 1961). Numerically, the university is a minority in every state or country. It is mainly composed of students, faculty, and the actual and supportive administration, and the Board of Trustees. The constituency may be considered part of the university as well. When each of these five organs of the university plays its role effectively, the university may be said to be exercising its autonomy. This autonomy is realized because the university is a hierarchical rather than an egalitarian community, dedicated to the principles of discovery, publication, teaching, and service. Its citadel is reason rather than violence, or force. Without the respect for reason, the university cannot be itself. As users of reason, and consumers of higher education, students are influential in deciding on the curriculum, on the appointment, promotion, and dismissal of the faculty. In a sense, they constructively exercise autonomy extended to them by the university which also exercises autonomy irrespective of administrative and governmental encroachments.

It is impossible for the university to exercise absolute autonomy because those who finance its programs and employ the administration and faculty have a stake in it. Brubacher (1968) indicates that absolute autonomy might encourage lethargy, prejudiced conservatism, and intolerance of innovation. In spite of the fact that the state is the logical legitimator, benefactor, and protector of the university, the former must recognize a self-interest in the university's independence to criticize the status quo. Its autonomy to criticize constructively, and the societal acceptance of this constructive criticism, does not only strengthen its autonomous character, it also provides security which fosters the maturity of the university.

Perceived as a super-culture or, as an intellectual arm or the store house of the ruling class, which criticizes the establishment in its unending devotion for the search of truth, the university may indirectly be criticizing itself although this criticism is directed at the society which owns the university. By implication, the above analysis reveals that both the university and the state need each other if society has to develop and advance. If the development and advancement are the criteria for the existence of a university, then relative autonomy must be an accepted principle which governs good, mature and productive universities.

Brubacher suggests that there can be no autonomy where the higher learning is an instrument of the church. Autonomy lacks here because sectarian views infiltrate the ranks of the university and violate the autonomous principle. Likewise, higher learning should not be an instrument of unproductive secularism either. The ultimate legitimation of autonomy must be loyalty to the truth. Since truth is defined differently by private, independent, and public universities, Brubacher's definition of higher learning seems to be narrow and particularistic rather than synergistically broad and universal.

Academic Freedom

Academic freedom is the autonomy the scholar must enjoy in teaching higher learning and expanding its frontiers through creative and explorative "research, publication, painting and performance" (Freeman, 1963). For his/her evaluation, the list of publications determines whether a person will be kept on the faculty, be promoted, be given salary increments, be allowed to teach certain courses, or otherwise be rewarded in terms of the various possibilities which obtain at that time. Publication is a sign that the scholar is ready to submit himself to the judgment of his/her colleagues.

The chief problem of publishing is the fact that it requires the professor to neglect his teaching which is basically his professional responsibility. Those teachers and professors who do not publish should not be regarded as lazy, incompetent or indifferent, many cannot organize themselves for provocative and analytical research. Institutions which compel professors to publish or perish (Freeman, 1963) encourage the proliferation of trivial scholarship. Their students graduate without vital intellectual and moral animation. Some do not finish college learning successfully. Essentially, teaching and publishing are integrally interrelated because teaching grows out of research and research grows out of teaching. Both are complementary to each other.

Academic freedom can be justified epistemologically, politically, and morally. First, looking at academic freedom epistemologically, its major function is to insure the accuracy and validity of knowledge. To do this thoroughly, the scholar must be able to pursue his or her activities under the guidance of truth. The purpose of seeking the truth will protect him in his search for it, against the pressures of the church, state, and economic or administrative interests. To deserve academic freedom in higher learning, scholars must reflect a high degree of meticulous expertise in the techniques of processing knowledge. The sophisticated knowledge of experts makes academia an aristocracy of trained intellect rather than an egalitarian democracy. Obviously due to their mission, community colleges and some four-year institutions tend to be more egalitarian and open-door policy oriented institutions which differ from the more elitist institutions. With such training, however, the autonomy of applying the canons of truth should be employed in the context of law. Effective lawful employment of academic freedom should be interpreted to mean constitutional provisions, their amendment, and the successive interpretations of the law by the courts and the judiciary. For instance, in 1959, chief justice Warren spoke that: to impose any straightjacket upon the intellectual leaders in our colleges and universities would imperil the future of the nation. No field of education is so thoroughly comprehended by man that new discoveries can not yet be made. Particularly is that true in the social sciences where few, if any, principles are accepted as absolutes (Brubacher, 1977, 41).

Secondly, this epistemological aspect has clear and profound political implications. Thirdly, academic freedom can be justified morally. For the public interest, society relies on its institutions of higher learning as the principal agency for gaining new knowledge as a means both of understanding the world and as using its resources to improve the human condition. One of the main sources of moral perplexity is lack of knowledge about the facts connected with any moral dilemma. By giving scholars the freedom and security to research these facts as a vocation, institutions of higher learning put themselves in a more insightful position to perceive the right thing to do on behalf of society.

Let us paraphrase this example to illustrate the limits of academic freedom in the politicization of higher education (Brubacher, 1977). A campus professor may:

1. objectively compare a variety of social ideas in different systems.
2. describe their differences, similarities and show commonalities among one or some of them.
3. degrade one system while praising an alternate one.
4. suggest the desirability or even the necessity of violent overthrow of a bad system.
5. incite students to form a revolutionary conspiracy against it.
6. actually participate in organizing and directing revolutionary activity.

The first three options are within the context of academic freedom. In the last two or three cases, academic freedom is abused because the professor has gone over the realm of action. In this case, because it has been abused, academic freedom will be limited by the law. In brief, academic freedom is not a right but a privilege of the minority. If it is abused by employing revolutionary activity instead of employing persuasive and convincing logical reason, then the spirit of higher education will be jeopardized. Academic freedom protects professors in all their identities as teachers, scholars, scientists, citizens and consultants. Society gives them this privileged exclusivism because it has a stake in the integrity of their expertise of it.

Tenure

The last but not least of the three academic principles is tenure. Tenure, as *Webster's Dictionary* (1961) indicates, is the status granted to a person after a probationary period, to one holding a position, especially a teacher or professor and protecting him from dismissal except for serious misconduct or incompetence determined by formal procedures. The major purpose of tenure is to allow a scholar freedom to pursue his academic aims without interference from administrators, board of trustees, and the local community. In a way, tenure guarantees academic freedom. This means that when a professor is genuinely original with his findings, he may differ drastically with the established opinions in his entire field. The difference in opinion will not cause him the fear of losing his job in spite of his dissent, innovation, nonconformism or eccentricity. On the other hand, tenure reminds administrators not to whimsically and arbitrarily fire or control professors whose views they perceive to be unwelcome, unpopular or unacceptable.

Tenure protects the entire university community and not merely the individual professor. Unless he feels secure while pursuing his teaching and research, the entire university suffers. It suffers because knowledge on which there is any restriction is not knowledge. A professor who cannot do all relevant research and read freely cannot be a professor in the real sense of the word. The application of tenure is one of the major factors responsible for the growth of higher education in modern times.

Administrators become extremely hesitant about granting tenure because they think that some professors might turn out to be bad as soon as their appointments become permanent. In respect to this inherent fear, the Board of Regents chairman becomes overcautious about granting tenure to new people. In some cases, to give tenure is to make the university less creative, lethargic, and exceedingly uninnovative because professors come under the influence of complacence, excessive gossip, and ultimately, intellectual inertia. In other cases, giving tenure gives the university a name and a place in the starry constellation of the republic of scholars and scientists. In the U.S., where most senior executives are white, male and Protestant, long tenured executives tend to make less risky decisions because tenure is proxy for risky aversion; it may result in action constraining commitments; or it can enable more conservative administrators survive organizational attrition by getting promoted (Finkelstein and Hambrick, 1996).

The Moral Goals of Higher Education

Higher education in a liberal sense, liberates a person to be a free thinker who separates truth from ignorance and error. It enables the individual to think logically, to be a prudent judge or evaluator, to discriminate between good and bad, and to appreciate his culture, religion, race, sex and those of other peoples. Hesburg (1977) claims education should enable a "person to humanize every thing that he or she touches in life" (p. 117). He should constantly improve his/her relations to God, fellowman, his wife, her husband, their children, associates, neighbourhood, country and the world. In the positive humanization of things, great virtues and values which are the synthetic product of epistemology and metaphysics should be cherished in thought and practice. Of these, the most outstanding include love, power, sanctity, truth, wisdom and above all "mutual help, decency, social justice, trust, freedom and respect for persons" (Moberly, 1949, 119). The virtues and values should be transmitted to the youth through their academic disciplines and exemplified when they are taught. When this is done, education is geared to uplift rather than debase the dignity and conscience of the individual and prepare him for his destiny or high calling.

To teach the values effectively, the university should "teach what is most real and most universal" (Kneller, 1955, 225). The study earlier cited (Moberly, 1949) points out that the university should not inculcate a philosophy of life; instead, its duty is to assist students to form their own philosophies of life, so that they may not go out into the world maimed and useless. I think that this philosophical viewpoint might appear repugnant to some sectarian and conservative religious institutions which inculcate their philosophies to students. The inculcating schools do so because they have goals and objectives they want to achieve. Some of the questions related to those goals and objectives may include: How should a man live? What are the things which really matter and what is their relative importance? To what sort of world have we to adjust ourselves? These questions focus on the responsibility of the university which, like the Greeks of antiquity, replies that the unexamined life is no life for a person. Emphatically, Socrates said that an "unexamined life is not worth living."

To teach and transmit morals through cherished values, the university should not, foster defective discussions which omit vital issues by treating them superficially. The superficiality and omission of the reality destroy the virtues of intellectual and moral innocence by encouraging vice and propaganda. To encourage intellectual innocence and growth, as Meland (1953, 47) indicates, "the culture of the human spirit should reinforce the culture of the mind to open man's mind and imagination to strive for power to turn energy into purposeful and beneficial ends."

In the Western world, especially in America, higher education has reached a "crisis of legitimacy" (Brubacher, 1977, 1). The crisis of legitimacy is one in which education has been made ineffective; that is, it does not respond to the moral needs and desires of the majority. It lacks moral fiber because it concentrates only on the "mental aspect of man's development" (White, 1952, 13).

In the study earlier cited, Kneller (1955) points out that the crisis in British universities is termed moral, a cultural and regional matter, a social crisis, a crisis in study values, essence of university integrity threatened, and a relaxation of cultural foundations. Others see it happen due to lay invasions, others call it crisis cosmic, and others see no crisis at all. Whatever it is called, the university which is second to none in expertise should foster good values for the development of the individual, preservation and advancement of his culture, and maintenance and development of technology. This development, offered in a physical structure, should assume not just the intellectual, but also the "social, physical and spiritual aspects of the development of students" (White, 1952, 13).

Allegorically, the university is "a church" (Brubacher, 1977, 116) which practices scholarship as a way of life. The higher learning which the university harbors is a religion. Higher criticism, scientific empiricism and the theory of evolution have undermined the patriarchal ecclesiastical order and emancipated the higher learning from the authority of the church. The emancipation of higher learning caused it to be highly secularized. The humanistic, scientific and existentialistic secularization of the university has not been without positive and negative consequences.

Sociologically, the university acts like a church in the feudal system. It has lost its innocence, lost control of its destiny and it lacks the quality of integration. In spite of these weaknesses, the university must go on and transmit the higher learning into wisdom. Wisdom emerges from knowledge when what is true about the nature of things is reshaped to human need and oriented to human hope and dreams.

In a Deweyan, scientific and secular sense, faith is the continued disclosure of truth through scholarly investigation. This form of faith is ipso facto thought to be more religious in quality than any faith in a completed revelation. The scholar in a university is like a high priest of truth. The university is the temple of the human intellectual spirit. The 'university is the transcendental institution in society because it seems to promise the nation of community' (Bell, 1970, 254). The spiritual attachment to intellectual things is all the closer for those who think that there is a basic unity to knowledge in the university. The branches of knowledge are united together as the work of the Creator. The university is like an organism because its parts and the whole are relatively diametrically opposed and yet inextricable and compelling.

While the church has ecumenical problems, the university, in its unfettered search for truth, has no fear of criticism as indicated through the principles of autonomy, academic freedom and tenure. Its intellectual prophecy only leads to progress in higher learning and this progress itself is institutionalized. Institutionalization of intellectual prophecy creates a rich reservoir of institutional wisdom reflective of society's cultural and scientific heritage. In the West, even when the personal touch misses or becomes neglected, the students less and less consult the parish priest or church pastor and more and more the university counselor or psychiatrist, who hears some of the confessions and in his psychotherapy advises different but comparable forms of absolution (Brubacher, 1977).

With standards of morality in government, business, medical work, and science and the church at an unprecedented low, the university must provide new leadership. If it is a super culture, then it is the church of super cultural values. The super culture may even conflict with folk-culture because the former is more universal while the latter is more local. This secular church is the conscience of society. Its four interdependent functions are teaching, consultancy, research, and community leadership and service. The university and the church are the least corrupt institutions in the world. Because of that, they serve the needs and interests of society in its quest for truth, empowerment and salvation.

In general, administrators tend to value more highly than do the faculty members the goals relating to the student's moral development and his/her roles of consumer and citizen. This difference probably results from the more purely scholarly orientation of the faculty, which tends to scorn all student output goals except those connected with intellectual development and scholarly skills. Where there is disagreement over the value of a particular goal, there also tends to be a disagreement over the emphasis it receives.

In brief, it should be emphasized that the few differences that exist over the values and attitudes of administrators and faculty, as revealed in their ratings of preferred goals, are too slight to warrant any inference of deep-seated conflict. All three comparisons of background and personal characteristics, of perceived goals and of preferred goals suggest that administrators and faculty are not such different breeds as they appear to be treated. They value and work toward essentially the same goals. The power of administrators does not appear to jeopardize the interests of the faculty either. Above all, Dresel (1967) who was John Hannah's provost at Michigan State University for three decades, has summarized the outcome goals of the university in terms of (1) acquiring advanced knowledge, skills and standards; (2) attaining an intellectual orientation that intellectually promotes learning; (3) placing emphasis on personal development in goal setting, self-worth and self-confidence; (4) transmission and appreciation of cultural forms; (5) using curriculum to plan for vocational, career planning and advanced training in research to extend the frontiers of learning; (6) providing education which meets the needs of the local population by liberating its mind; (7) using science, democracy and academic freedom in the context of the law; and (8) with a sense of accountability, use innovation, ferment, and experimental discovery to responsively serve the community. The articulation of process and outcome goals do not only enable the university to rationalize its mission, but the rationalization of it makes the university competitive, alive, and afloat.

Goals and Their Origins: A Case Study

Langston University is one of the 117 historically black colleges and universities (HBCUs) that are predominantly located in the South of the United States. Of the twenty-seven colleges and universities in the State of Oklahoma, Langston stands alone as the only predominantly black university. Though more than ten HBCUs were founded between 1854 and 1888, Langston was founded in 1897. Most HBCUs were created in this century. Langston's founding was essentially based on the 1890 Morrill Act through which a variety of land grant colleges were established (Sagini, 1996; and *Langston University Self-Study*, 1997). Land grant colleges were originally designed to offer mechanical, agricultural, and vocational education to citizens and communities of rural America. This original mission has significantly been expanded at Langston. The expanded change of the mission will be addressed later. However, in consonant with its original purpose, Langston University was established as the Colored Agricultural and Normal University by the Oklahoma Territorial House Bill No. 151 which still constitutionally retains its land grant legacy.

For the last 300-400 years, American societal institutions are and have been known to be exclusionary, segregationist and highly biased against people of color and all minorities in particular. Such an institutional and racial climate could not allow the development of harmonious relations in interracial interaction to prosper and warrant exchange of ideas and learning in academic scholarship. As a result, uneducated black people who had no leaders continued to remain intellectually undeveloped and leaderless. In other words, the original purpose of the HBCUS was not only to develop the intellectual capabilities of blacks and other minorities, but that form of development of their minds was a form of uplift (Woodson, 1990) and intelligent, trained, and responsible leadership (Sagini, 1996).

Goals and Objectives of the University

The goals and objectives of Langston University are an analytical byproduct of socio-cultural values and historico-political evolution of the African-American community in America. These goals and objectives are enshrined in the institution's mission statement (*Langston University Catalog,* 1996-1998). The mission is the institution's historic purpose, and reason for its existence. In its descriptive and prescriptive terms of mission, the statement qualifies "the institution's major area of interest, its scope of intended actions, the basic market needs it intends to satisfy, its primary values, current performance, vision of leadership, and its distinctive competencies" (Sagini, 1987, 10). Langston University's land grant mission articulates rural, urban and international components of its instructional, research, and public service elements. The institution offers associate, baccalaureate and masters degrees that are recognized by all institutions in the country and the world and that are at the same time accredited to state, regional, and national accreditation agencies. The multicampus institution has three campuses at Langston, Tulsa, and Oklahoma City. Its academic heart is at Langston. The institution's mission has eight major goals whose plethora of objectives are programmatically, disciplinarily, and departmentally defined in the light of the five major schools of the University. The schools are Arts and Sciences, Business, Nursing and Health Professions, Agriculture and Applied Sciences, and Education. The goals through which the mission is ratified and rationalized articulate educational issues in urban, rural, and global environments.

The goals were constructed to guide the University in charting new directions during the industrial era. Because that historical period has relatively declined with the evolution of the technological age, the ninth goal of the University should be: To prepare the University system to accept being challenged by its willingness to acquire and use new technology whose skills are in great demand. Finally, the tenth goal should be: To prepare the University in such a way that it can become competitive, adaptable, and global in its futuristic outlook. Being futuristically oriented will not only need continuous instructional and self-criticism, but in doing so, the University will have established a dynamic machinery for self-regulation, adaptability and change. A change oriented University will remain to be an effective school. Also, the University should have clear goals for massive fund raising that will enable it, in the era of retrenchment, to remain viable, competitive, and alive. It will be fruitless if the university will raise millions of dollars and yet remain unaccountable, extravagant and irresponsible.

Substantially, goals may be viewed as management frames that are organizationally structural, human resource, political, and symbolic expressions of the human heart and aspiration (Bolman and Deal, 1984). The purpose of setting goals is to provide a good example for organizational planning, goal setting, decision making, evaluation, and motivation. Structurally, goal-setting keeps the organization focused in charting a new and specific direction. From human resource perspective, goal-setting keeps people involved and communication channels open. Politically, goal-setting provides the opportunity structure for individuals and groups to publicly express their interests. And, last but not least, symbolically, the purpose of goal-setting is to develop shared or common organizational values.

Employees

Langston University has 137 faculty and 275 staff members. Sixty to sixty-five percent of the faculty have terminal degrees in terms of Doctor of Education, Doctor of Philosophy, or another doctoral degree. The rest have masters degrees. Nearly 33 percent of the faculty are foreign-born. These professionals have no American origins. In spite of their naturalization credentials, they originated in more than 30 countries of the five continents of our globe. Though some are administrators, their primary functions are either research or instruction. They received their academic credentials from a variety of Third World, European, and American elitist and nonelitist academic institutions respectively. Their contributions in terms of teaching, research, and public or community service reflect a rich academic and intellectual background in disciplinary and interdisciplinary specialization. One of the most interesting scientific observations I have made is that more internationals are more active in fund raising, teaching, and research while national faculty are predominantly teaching and service oriented. This difference in terms of faculty involvement in institutional endeavors could be largely attributed to motivational, cultural, and organizational mission and structure rather than its design and patterns of communication, decision making, and control (Gortner, 1997).

Though a small portion of the service staff belongs to the professional class, the majority are a support group whose administrative, clerical, advisory, and counseling roles are supplementary to and complementary of the instructional, research, and service roles of the University. Unlike 33 percentage ratio of the faculty that has international connections, the number of staff with such connections is less than five percent. This indicates that the globalization of professionals and professions is carried out at a higher level of organizational sophistication and specialization. Sophisticated specialization requires the mastery of scientific, linguistic, and disciplinary competencies which the competitive U.S. professional and academic market demands.

Organizational Structure

The structure of the organization is used for reorganization, design, effective coordination, centralization/decentralization, differentiation and integration. The University is pyramidally structured along the Weberian model of bureaucratic hierarchy. The authority of creation and legal operationalization rests with the state of Oklahoma.

The State Board of Regents for the Oklahoma Higher Education System establishes policy guidelines in consultation with the superintendent for education in the State. The Board of regents, which is statutorily created by the Governor, is a coordinating or regulatory agency responsible for making sure that resources are available for translating the mission of higher education consistent with the politically, fiscally and academically established values of the public. In addition, the president of the University, in consultation with the OSU and A&M Colleges Board of Regents, design specific policy guidelines for the colleges one of which is Langston. As a mediator, the president communicates to and interprets for the Boards, the internal and external issues and policies that affect the University. For it to be productive, he delegates the implementation of Board policy in a chain command to the vice-presidents, deans, department chairpersons, and faculty. All workers within the hierarchy are supposed to be efficient, effective, responsible and above all, accountable. Less responsible and less accountable people are warned, demoted, or dismissed. Depending on how close one is to the center of patronage, and given the fact that one is accountable, such a person can be promoted or tenured as long as the person has worked for some years.

Clientele

The University serves students from all races, classes, continents, age groups, gender groups, and other groups. During the Fall of 1995, the African-American student body was 46.8 percent while the Caucasian student population was 45.68 percent. The rest, who were either American Indians, Hispanics, Asians, or Internationals accounted for 7.5 percent (*Langston University Self-Study,* 1997). The 1954 Brown vs the Board of Education Topeka Kansas Act has enabled the University to desegregate and to accommodate a higher degree of multiculturalism in all its facets. The University is an academic institution of higher learning that offers programs in schools of environmental sciences, business administration, physical and health professions, education, and arts and sciences. The above named statistics vary from year to year based on a variety of internal and external variables.

Budget

In higher education and the public sector, budgeting techniques are formula, incremental, decremental, zero-based budgeting, planning programming budgeting systems, and several other techniques. Langston University uses incremental and line item approach that shows the decision making relationship between institutional and regulatory bodies, or the academic and political, or the university and state agencies respectively. Since the major goal of the University is teaching rather than research and public service, most of the budget allocated annually is used for instruction. Graphically speaking, the tabular statistics of the institution's budget are self-explanatory. However, because the research and extension unit of the university, which was independent of the institution, has become integrated (1998) with it, such integration has forced the administration to alter some priorities and create new opportunities for integration to materialize.

External Support

Langston University is externally supported by a variety of political, funding and accreditation agencies. Politically, both the State of Oklahoma, the Oklahoma Board of Regents for Higher Education, and interest groups of members of African-American community at large support the institution's existing power structure whose charismatic leadership has been instrumental in negotiating the morphology for the opportunity structure of the institution's viability in a pluralistic society. In terms of funding, and based on the President's recommendations, Langston receives funds from state appropriations that are specifically allocated for the University. These funds are part and parcel of the Board's allocation budget for higher education in the State. The budget is legislatively, governatoraly and bureaucratically approved before the Board or regulating agency authorizes the State treasurer or auditor general to allocate funds for each public institution including Langston. In other words, institutions request, the Governor recommends, and the legislature appropriates funds before the auditor general makes allocations based on board decisions. Through the alumni, corporations, faculty, federal government subsidies and students fiscally contribute to support Langston.

Langston University is accredited to and has membership in many national and local organizations. Nationally or regionally, the University is accredited to the North Central Association of Colleges and Secondary Schools and National Association for Equal Opportunity in Higher Education. Other organizational levels with which Langston is affiliated to or has membership in at departmental, programmatic, or school rather than institutional levels are many. Though accreditation and membership status of Langston are not directly related to bringing money into the University, these two conditions testify that the University is responsibly accountable for excellence of the academic program it offers. It is also, given the fact that it is continually funded by the state, federal, and other agencies, indicative of the efficiency and effectiveness with which it has managed to run its operations in spite of the fact that it is one of the most poorly funded institutions in the state. State funding formulas are political and bureaucratic techniques that are used to make decisions and financial allocations to state institutions of which colleges and universities are classic examples. Given the fact that Langston is predominantly a black institution, and given that blacks are a minority segment of the American population that has been historically and racially discriminated and segregated against by the white majority, the design of funding and allocation formulas are normally used to quench the thirst for competition with main stream institutions by preferentially using inequitable and partial designs to make allocation decisions. Whether those decisions are made incrementally or rationally or aggregatively, does not matter much, what matters is how such approaches are designed to benefit, reward, or punish or prevent particular groups from receiving a fair share of funds for their institutions. In spite of the small amounts given by corporations, the state, alumni, federal quotas, faculty, and students, Langston's academic program has tended to improve by leaps and bounds. The institution uses cost-effective strategies which have enabled it to experience effective, i.e., goal oriented accomplishments. It is debatable to what extent such accomplishments may be said to have been carried out with efficiency. Efficiency is high or effective production that is done with minimum waste and less effort (*Webster's II New College Dictionary*, 1995).

Line versus Staff and Centralization versus Decentralization

Langston University is a designed, complex, coordinated, integrated, and structured institution. Line supervisors are departmental chairpersons who oversee faculty performance. Each department is organized on the basis of policy or program areas, management function, and type of specialization. In other words, the chairs and their faculty are grouped into offices based on their specialties, political, technical, and professional designs. Though the role of chairpersons is supervisory and managerial in character, most of the time, they are not different from faculty with whom they experience similar challenges on a daily basis. Langston University is more centralized than it is decentralized. Centralization provides senior administrators with greater control in monitoring organizational operations and clarifying policy-making and communication channels. However, since it is lowly decentralized, units and departments are less autonomous in decision making. Fewer people make decisions. Due to the nature of charismatic leadership, ecological environment, and HBCUs traditions, it is viewed that the decentralization of the authority might generate unaccountability and conflict which might be detrimental to the effective functioning of the institution's system. As a result, centralization is there to stay and nobody has the guts to openly question it by challenging its status quo.

Process and Issues

The process and issues deal with the organization's intelligence system; communication patterns, leadership styles and decision making. First, the intelligence system is highly centralized because the institution's leader, more likely than not, receives qualitative and quantitative information from trusted student, faculty, administrative, and staff agents who are members of a variety of campus and community groups. It is more likely that most intelligence agents are self-appointed for attention getting and for meeting their personal sociopsychological needs. Others are the leader's advisers though most of the time, he does not use their advice especially when it is too parochial and prejudicial. Second, communication is in essence, a process through which the University informs and clarifies goals, provides a system for organizational coordination and control, and it is a primary medium for the exercise of power. At this University, most upper-level, middle-level, and line staff people are members of fraternities or sororities to which institutional leaders pledge allegiance. These informal networks are good for instrumental and expressive purposes. Leadership styles are influenced by the intelligence gathering system and communication patterns of the administrative regime and vice versa. Leadership is either a group thing or process through which the leader influences his/her followers. Followers provide "the consent of the governed" or the leadership role to "the wearer of the mantle" (Gortner 1997, 318). Through his informal and formal influence, the leader uses his influence, power, and authority to persuade rationally, inspire, consult, ingratiate, exchange favors for targets that need accomplishment, and uses coalition tactics, legitimating tactics, and pressure to get things done. The commonly used leadership styles in government and academia are "Bureaucratic, organized anarchy, compromise, debate, rational, consensus, and conflict resolution" (Sagini, 1991, 78). Though none of these are autocratic as the leader's style, his autocracy, charisma, and entrepreneurship, are not totally unique at Langston. He uses these styles interchangeably and when it is necessary.

Decision Making

The dominant decision making models in academia and public sector are the rational, incremental, aggregative and garbage can techniques. Langston University uses incremental approach for budgeting. Downward and upward formal communication network is more commonly practiced than horizontal because this is a system that favors patronage more than academic authority and specialization. For instance, professors who are selected as teachers of the year are those who retire, those who have worked for many years, or those who raise more money. Excellence in teaching, as student evaluations show, and faculty research do not count much. In most institutions of higher learning, excellence in teaching is determined by student evaluations rather than by the cumulative years of service. Age or duration of service is no index for excellence and competitiveness. Such a strong system of patronage tends to serve the leader and his cronies more than the student and faculty who are the core of learning in the academy. Is Langston unique in its operational performance? Let us look at history.

Although we do not have enough evidence concerning the relationship between the administration and the faculty in the Egyptian temple universities, Plato's Academy, Aristotle's Lyceum, or the Chinese, Arab, and Indian universities, the available scanty evidence suggests that the goal of successful higher learning in the ancient civilizations was to create an organizational climate for faculty and students to learn, create, discover, invent and disseminate the products of their intellectual digestion. With the inspiration of these ancient academic models, the modern university evolved from the mists of antiquity during the 13th century. The political, constitutional and academic values of the modern university are more than seven hundred years old. These modern universities are relics of medieval rather than ancient antiquity. Chronologically, they are modeled on the French, British and German universities respectively. In America, mainstream institutions, particularly the elite and comprehensive universities are representative transplantations of the University of Paris and Oxbridge models. In other words, white American colleges and universities are constitutionally, structurally and substantively rooted in continental and transcontinental traditions. These academic transplantations have provisions which enable them to guarantee the faculty power to exercise academic freedom and academic governance. Departmentally, they also determine who is qualified to teach, who is qualified to earn a degree from the university and who is qualified to be tenured. Their administrations have flexible power, if at all, concerning democratic faculty participation and decision making which affects their professional responsibilities.

Unlike the former institutions, Historically Black Colleges and Universities (HBCUs) have neither parallel nor model of inspiration as their mainstream counterparts. These African-American institutions are uniquely modeled on are autocratic plantation model of slavery of antebellum South. During slavery the slave masters allowed the mulattos, who were culturally and genetically "closer to them," to exercise "delegated" power over the slaves. This houseboy and field boy dichotomy enabled the mulattos to use their delegated leadership power to suppress opposition, oversee production and prevent slave revolts that were stimulated by inhumane, oppressive, racist, and draconian society. In antebellum society, institutional leaders of the platocracy used authoritarian power to make decisions for administration, supervision, and control. Since this system of draconian laws was private, undemocratic, antiparticipatory and exclusionary in decision making, slavery was continued for a long time. Slavery, unlike freedom, does not animate people to think. It forces people to work hard for free or for very little material and nonmaterial gains. Slavery alienated the intelligent and creative "trouble makers." It also tortured and executed extremist or radical slaves. The slaves were not expected to be literate, to excel in poetic, literary and scientific scholarship, or have positions of power and influence in society. They were not expected to be intellectually intelligent since in those days "they had no conscience or humanity." They were viewed as objects of chattel slavery kept for private or domestic use and for provision of menial services. Slave masters feared intelligent and revolutionary slaves. Instead of giving them freedom and opportunity to lead the system for greater productivity, they suppressed this inherent genius and preferred the status quo – only to be taught lessons by the events of the Civil War (*Editorial*, 1997).

After the Civil War, the Federal government, private organizations and philanthropic organizations joined hands with ex-slave populations and constructed the HBCUs. These institutions were started without any model for emulation. The purpose of creating them was to "train leadership for the purpose of uplifting African-American community. In other words, unlike mainstream academic institutions which are modeled on continental and transcontinental intellectual and academic traditions in terms of leadership styles, decision making, communication and control processes, and theoretical and structural postulates, the HBCUs are modeled on the autocratic plantation model of inferiority, oppression, fear, privacy, exclusion and alienation.

Why do these institutions of promise and hope use feudal structures and values to manage what are supposed to be modern universities? This question is complex. It requires a complex answer. The answer is that these institutions of "privilege and opportunity" are part and parcel of the societal values that have shaped the evolutionary history, politics, and socioeconomic and constitutional structures that collectively form the superstructure from which ideological and substantive values of running the universities and other institutions of society emanate. In other words, the past influences the present and the present will influence the future. This is a scientific law of history.

Does this law change? Yes. Only when revolution or reformation is intelligently carried out. And either of the two approaches is not without consequences.

Conclusion

In some cases, organizational goals of different systems are not clearly and logically structured. Such goals do not distinctly portray the mission of the organization or university. In some higher institutions of learning, the goals become a private property of a few ruling elite which may be disinterested with the machinery for their application. In other cases, goals are neither understood nor critically and periodically evaluated to validate their worth and reliability.

For both private and public institutions, the principles of tenure, autonomy, and academic freedom, as they have been treated in this chapter, appear to make the university an independent institution. In reality, this apparent independence of the university is not absolute because the various publics of public and private institutions contribute in material and nonmaterial forms to the universities, and this contribution makes universities dependent on them for support. This dependence reduces their complete autonomy. Universities and their publics or communities are interdependent.

The application of moral and ethical virtues in societal institutions enhances their functional efficiency and effectiveness. Unfortunately, the leaders of society at all levels including the church have become less moral because their world, particularly the West, is living in a post-Christian era. In this era, scientific materialism, totalitarian humanism, and individualistic existentialism and claims for democracy occupy the vacuum of humankind's moral conscience. The innocent and young generations of students and scholars are guided by leaders of moral blindness and intellectual anomie. These shortcomings might lead the world to disaster. To solve these problems needs a moral reformation in every leader, parent, teacher and student. Only a totally moral and reformatory situation will save the world from a bottomless abyss into which it is drifting fast. The moral revolution must not be handled carelessly or propagandistically. It must be dealt with synergistically, systematically and analytically. The world needs men and women of integrity and singleness of purpose to bring about the regeneration of human values by establishing new and better standards for the young and humanity in general.

As necessary guidelines, goals direct the entire philosophical and actual operation of higher institutions of learning and other organizations. Good goals must be definitive, evaluative and flexible. They should show the mission of the organization in terms of short, medium, and long range time span. Above all, they should have a criteria or machinery for accomplishing the mission. University goals can enable it to accomplish its mission well if it exercises the principles of autonomy, academic freedom and tenure. In themselves, these three principles are not an index of efficiency and effectiveness. The application of these principles should be consistent with the established goals and organizational philosophy. This consistence should be based on moral intellectual and scientific virtues which consolidate and empower rather than venomously pollute, disfigure and weaken the conscience of society.

Internally, one of the major and distinctive characteristics of the University is the conflict generated by the pressures arising from the competing claims for bureaucratic and professional roles and priorities (Birnbaum, 1983). With the use of Etzionian philosophy, such as conflict can be constructively managed by appointing administrators who have both professional training and management experience. The administrators may use a variety of techniques of which garbage-can is one of the best that enables decision makers to solve organizational problems.

The governance system needs more attention in developing governance patterns to preserve traditions of informal consensus and try to prevent regular campus conflict. Such conflict can be minimized if faculty is actively allowed to participate in governance, budgetary decision making, academic bargaining, and the Boards. Such a form of self-regulation will enable the university to protect itself against external forces that might erode its autonomy and compromise its integrity. Doing that will protect some of the most cherished values of the faculty.

Overall, the total organization works together for the attainment of the clearly established goals and objectives. Organizational communication is generally carried out more in a downward and upward way than the horizontal way. Due to its cultural diversity, interpersonal relationships may not be fully open and frank. The organization is structured around functional schools, departments and units. The administrative and operational system is dictated by functional needs rather than by where action is needed. Decision making is more centralized than decentralized. The absence of well-established conflict resolution procedures could encourage backbiting, empire building and power politics. Though the organization is results oriented, there is no strong desire or need to reward those who produce. At times, since the organization becomes a prisoner of its own form and process, some changes are stimulated by spasmodic crises. There is no strong effort to facilitate human growth of capacities of individual units. New employees need to be effectively recruited, hired, developed and promoted on the basis of their abilities and accomplishments rather than on the basis of patronage. Above all, the public has the right to demand that higher education goals should be politically, economically, professionally, and morally justifiable.

References

Barnard, C.I. 1938. *The Functions of the Executive.* Cambridge, MA: Harvard University Press.

Bolman, L.G. et al. 1984. *Modern Approaches to Understanding and Managing Organizations.* San Francisco: Jossey-Bass.

Brubacher, J.S. 1977. *On the Philosophy of Higher Education.* San Francisco: Jossey-Bass Publishers.

Clark, P.M., and J.Q. Wilson. 1961. Incentive systems: A theory of organizations. *Administrative Science Quarterly* 6, 129-166.

Dewey, J. 1966. *Democracy and Education.* New York: Macmillan Publishing Co.

Editorial. 1997. The Faculty is Not the Enemy. *University Faculty Voice,* 1, 10, 5.

Educational Planning. 1970. UNESCO.

Etzioni, A. 1961. *A Comparative Analysis of Complex Organizations.* New York: Free Press of Glencoe, 1975.

Festinger, L. 1957. *A Theory of Cognitive Dissonance.* Evanston, IL: Row, Peterson.

Finkelstein, S., and D.C. Hambrick. 1996. *Strategic Leadership: Top Executives and Their Effects on Organizations.* Minneapolis/St. Paul: West Publishing Company.

Gortner, H.F., et al. 1977. *Organizational Theory: A Public Perspective.* Fort Worth, TX: Harcourt Brace College Publishers.

Gross, E. 1968. Universities as organizations: A research approach. *American Sociological Review,* 33, 518-544.

Gross, E., et al. 1968. *University Goals and Academic Power.* Washington, D.C.: American Council on Education.

Harvey, L.J. 1976. *Managing Colleges and Universities by Objectives.* Wheaton, IL: Ireland Educational Corporation.

Hesburgh, T.M. 1979. *Higher Values in Higher Education.* Kansas City: Andrews and McMeel, Inc.

Hutchins, R.M. 1936. *The Higher Learning in America.* Yale: Yale University Press.

Kneller, G.F. 1955. *Higher Learning in Britain.* Los Angeles:

California Press.

Langston University Catalog: A Century of Excellence From Langston to the World. Langston: 1996-1998.

Langston University Self-Study: Prepared for the Commission on Institutions of Higher Education, North Central Association of Colleges and Schools. (1997). Langston.

March, J.G., and J.P. Olsen. 1976a. The technology of foolishness. In *Ambiguity and Choice in Organizations.* Bergen, Norway: Universitetsforlaget.

Meland, B.E. 1953. *Higher Education and the Human Spirit.* Chicago: The University of Chicago Press.

Moberly, W.S. 1949. *The Crisis in the University.* London: S.C.M. Press Limited.

Nash, A.S. 1944. *The University and the Modern World.* New York: Macmillan Company.

Newman, J.H.C. 1958. *The Scope and Nature of University Education.* New York: E.P. Dutton and Co.

Newman, J.H.C. 1925. *The Idea of a University-Defined and Illustrated.* London: Longmans Green Co.

Niblett, W.R. 1950. *Higher Education—Demand and Response.* San Francisco: Jossey-Bass Inc.

Ortega, G.J. 1963. *Mission of the University.* Translated by H.L. Nostrand. New York: Routledge and Kegan Paul Limited.

Parsons, T. 1960. *Structure and Process in Modern Societies.* Glencoe, IL: Free Press.

Perrow, C. 1970. *Organizational Analysis: A Sociological View.* Belmont, CA: Wadsworth.

Sagini, M.M. 1996. *The African and the African American University: A Historical and Sociological Analysis.* Lanham, Washington, D.C.: University Press of America, Inc.

Sagini, M.M. 1987. *Comparative Perceptions of Planners of Four Michigan Community Colleges.* An Unpublished Doctoral Dissertation for Michigan State University, East Lansing, MI.

Scott, W.R. 1981. *Organizations: Rational, Natural and Open Systems.* Englewood Cliffs, N.J.: Prentice-Hall, Inc.

Selznick, P. 1949. *TVA and the Grass Roots.* Bekerley: University of California Press.

Selznick, P. 1948. Foundations of the Theory of Organization. *American Sociological Review* 13, 25-35.

Simon, H.A. 1957. *Administrative Behavior.* New York: Macmillan.

Weber, M. 1904-1905. *The Protestant Ethic and the Spirit of Capitalism.* Translated by T. Parsons. New York: Scribner.

Webster's II New Collegiate Dictionary. 1995. Boston: Houghton Mifflin Company.

Weick, K.E. 1969. *The Social Psychology of Organizing.* 2nd ed. Reading, MA: Addison-Wesley.

White, E.G. 1952. *Education.* Mountain View: Pacific Press Publishing Association.

Woodson, C.G. 1990. *The Miseducation of the Negro.* Trenton, N.J.: Africa World Press.

Chapter 6

Organizational Structure and Design — NATO

Introduction

The structure and design of any organization is determined by economic and ideological forces that are classifiable, or professional and occupational interests or ideological and ethnic values, or resources in terms of physical units and outputs within the whole system. In this light, this chapter deals with theories of organization structure. The chapter overviews traditional theories and presents a detailed review of the more contemporary research and theoretical analysis on organizational design. Of specific interest is the agency's (bureau's) needs for programmatic support, its program technologies and its environment. The purpose of this chapter is to examine both the traditional and contemporary models of organizational structure from the literature in the organization theory. Emphasis is placed on the technical as opposed to the political uses of rationale behind a reorganization of structure. To some extent, the rationale behind a reorganization (structure and design) is political and what scholars have called "rational" (Gortner, et al., 1997, p. 92) organization designs. A wealthy variety of a body of research and theory on the advantages of designs that use most technical, programmatic and political objectives is abundantly available.

Organization structures are organized in order to "improve their efficiency by removing duplicative offices and improve the level of coordination" (p. 91). These structures serve more than political ends. Administrators analyze and choose structures on the basis of technical efficiency and other matters. These structures may differ in their "capacity to adequately coordinate task activities, in their degree and form of specialization" (p. 92), and in their capacity to allow agencies "to respond adequately to changing environments and program technologies" (p. 92). Above all, three major contemporary schools of thought concerning how best to "design innovative and responsive organizational structures" will be highlighted. These schools of thought which evolve from the mission of the organization include the traditional Weberian structuralism, centralization versus decentralization and differentiation versus integration.

Sources of Structure in a Bureau

The formal structure of any organization, e.g., the bureau is the officially prescribed distribution of authority and task responsibility among its offices and officials. The authority of officials to decide, to act, or to delegate responsibility is prescribed in the structure, and there is often some further specification of the conditions or bases for action, command, and intelligence gathering structures which specify how new policies and procedures are to be communicated to the appropriate level for official action. Formal structures prescribe how the bureau's work is to be divided into individual tasks and grouped into departments, offices, and other subdivisions. The relationships between and among all the subdivisions, their unique responsibilities, and their coordination are prescribed in the structure. The prescriptions that define structure are a product of legal, managerial, and professional decisions that evolve with political responsibility.

Internally as well as incrementally, executive and mid level managers develop structures of which rules of procedure for the creation of new projects, routing activity reports, and monitoring compliance are examples. In addition, professional program specialists develop the codes, regulations and procedures for programs that determine specific reporting and generate command structures for program implementation. All written rules are usually inscribed in manuals which form the yardstick for bureau's operation. Job description, civil service laws of specific jurisdiction, specify the division of task responsibilities. These procedures and rules determine the specific activities of each bureau and how its structure will operate. The next few paragraphs will answer the following questions: (1) What models are used in the creation of these structures? (2) What principles of good and useful structure form and guide the original design and subsequent reorganization of bureaus?

(1) Traditional Structural Principles

Organizational people belief that an ideal structure should conform to the theory of administrative science school. This school of thought believes that a set of universal principles of structure are the key to successful management which is well structured and self-regulating. Max Weber's model has always been used as an analytical tool of bureaucratic management. The main structural elements of the model are hierarchy, delimited authority, and specialization or division of labor (Weber, 1947).

Specialization of functions promotes the efficiency of bureau operation. It enables officials to become highly proficient and esoteric. It allows workers to become more productive because complex work is organized into simple and repetitive tasks that increase the speed of production. The ideal type bureaucracy is professionally, technically, and rationally designed. This rational order produces stability, consistency, and efficiency. It also enhances predictability. Because of their inherent simplicity, these principles replicate organizational design. Simon (1965) and Simon and March (1993) have called these principles "vacuous and inconsistent" (Gortner, et al., 1997, p. 93) because they show lack of understanding, intelligence and serious purpose.

(2) Centralization and Decentralization

Centralization and decentralization refer to the degree to which decision-making authority is confined to the top echelon offices and officials of the organization. Centralization is the process of achieving greater control for the purpose of monitoring operations and for clarifying policy making and communication channels. In other words, centralization facilitates control and uniformity in service delivery. Such uses can be critical to the survival and effectiveness of the organization. Organizations decentralize in order to enhance participatory management as articulated in the *National Performance Review* of 1993. Decentralized structures allow greater autonomy in the bureaus' divisions and units. More people participate in decision making. Decentralization generates mechanisms for unaccountability and conflict because many decision-makers do not make consistent policies in bureaus. However, it allows managerial flexibility and responsiveness to clientele. Over the years, Alfred Sloan of General Motors has tended to concentrate on using a model called "centralized control of decentralized functions" (p. 97). He used the best of the two "worlds." Based on the observations of contingency research, the effectiveness of any model including centralization versus decentralization depends on the ecological, technical and environmental conditions. In relation to bureaus and other organizations, some of the major "principles of Administrative science" (p. 96) are unity of command, line staff, span of control, and functional and scalar principles.

Principles of Administrative Science

Delegation of Authority – is the transfer of authority and responsibility from a higher to a lower administrative official for purposes of decision-making. Due to accountability constraints, people do not like to delegate authority. They resist by refusing to relinquish power in order to delegate it. Those who delegate do so because they know or, assume that someone will manage the affairs of the organization with a sense of efficiency, accountability and effectiveness.

Unity of Command – Each official is expected to receive commands from and be responsible to only one supervisor in order to avoid confusion, unfair expectations, divided loyalties, and potential for uncoordinated action. Even though the span of control, i.e., the optimal number of subordinates, should be successfully commanded by one supervisor only. In this regard, the American bureaucracy which serves the President and Congress may have difficulty to coordinate its activities due to the fact that its loyalty may be divided between the two masters it serves. This generates conflict, ambiguity and frustration on the part of bureaucrats because they may be confused as to whom they are accountable.

Line Versus Staff – Line services are direct in their contributions to the organization. Staff services are advisory and supportive in nature. Most of the time, contemporary organizations are limited in their ability to distinguish line versus staff issues.

Functional/Scalar Principles (Tall Versus Flat Hierarchies) – This connotes the search for the optimal basis determining the appropriate type and degree of specialization in subordinate officers, and the optimal point at which to add another layer in the hierarchy.

Functional Consolidation – is merging of two or more administrative units that perform similar tasks into a single agency, e.g., fire and defense departments.

(3) Differentiation and Integration

Closely related to centralization and decentralization are two basic theoretical concepts of organizational structure that underpin contemporary organization theory and design. The concepts are "differentiation and integration" (Gortner, et al., 1997, p. 97). The two terms express finer or smoother and hierarchical task distinctions. Differentiation is the vertical and horizontal degree of specialization found in organizations. A more differentiated organization has a more complex structure because the volume of work distinguish a variety of clientele groups. The degrees of ways of specialization have policy implications and technical consequences. In other words, all organizations that are socially differentiated, due to technical specialization, are, according to Trist (1963 and 1977), not only sociotechnical systems, but they also are social ecologies.

The greater the level of differentiation, the more formidable the task of integrating or coordinating all these distinct and specialized tasks within and among the subdivisions of the organization. The integration process includes all the mechanisms and procedures by which the differentiated tasks are coordinated and ordered to achieve the organization's purpose. Integration is achieved through the hierarchical chain of command, communication system and also through the processes for task coordination specified in rules, program regulations, plans, and schedules. Staff meetings, program task forces, procedures for circulating memos about policy changes, informal consultations, and even departmental grapevines, all contribute to organizational integration" (Gortner, et al., 1997, p. 97). The greater the level of differentiation, the greater the need for integration and coordination of activities.

When differentiation and integration are balanced, the organization structure can be viewed to be effectively designed. The "greater the level of differentiation, the greater the need for integration" (p. 97). Although organizational members may complain about cuts, programs and procedures, more often than not, what is required is to understand the levels and patterns of differentiation and learn how to make tradeoffs. Alternative structural forms exhibit different solutions to the balancing of differentiation and integration.

(4) Bases of Departmentalization

Division of labor at the individual level results in specialized tasks that must be grouped together to form departments, offices, and other subdivisions. Departmentalization is a basis for grouping tasks and effective utilization and implementation of resources in consonant with specific elements of its jurisdiction. In a traditional sense, bureaus were departmentalized on the basis of policy area or program area, management function, client type, and geography or regional considerations. In the U.S. and in several other countries, departmentalization is based on similarity of program policy (Gortner, 1997). Second, in order to make departments or their units more functional, ""officials are grouped into offices based on their management specialty" (p. 98). Such specialty may include "program management, policy education, personnel, budgeting or planning" (p. 98). Generally departments, among other things especially the political, technical and professional factors are largely based on either programs geography or program functions (e.g., personnel) (Filley, House and Kerr, 1976); Management (process), client type (e.g., for corrections – juvenile offenders or criminals); and geography (e.g., soil conservation districts).

Organizational forms may include; the "Matrix like NASA" (p. 101). Which has several departments each of which deals with projects handled by organizational teams. Second, TQM which according to Hackman and Wageman (1995) deals with cross-functional problems. The pyramid is the third type of organizational form that is common but radically different from the rest.

(5) General Concerns of Traditional Approaches

The traditional approach to organizational structure places high value on stability, symmetry, clarity of lines of command, and on fully rationalizing the structure of the bureau. Generally, the universal principle of structure and management sought by the Administrative science still guides many management practices. Its Weberian origins are classic but somehow irrelevant and confusing. As a result, current approaches attempt to flexibly create an organizational form that is responsive to circumstances rather than to find a form that will be universally applicable everywhere. Structure can be crafted to accommodate specific environments and work flow reflected in the new trend toward organization design. The new trend will put emphasis on processes of management and production rather than hierarchical structure which disempower, demotivate and alienate employees.

Organization Design: Perspectives on Structure

Organizational design is complex coordination and integration of organizational structure. Theoretically, program goals, processes and procedures rest on the universalistic principles of Administrative Science School. Solutions to problems are handled in strategic and technologically based designs: Administrators, according to Thompson's (1967, p. 114) view and Gortner et al. (1997), "need a rationale that creates linkages between the environment, technology and structure." Unlike the industrial setting of hierarchy, which is currently under fire for causing a lot of problems, the post industrial organizational forms are increasingly becoming more "Organismic" (Burns and Slalkers, 1994) and learning "Organizations" (Senge, 1990; and Gortner, et al., 1997, p. 115). Complex organizations encourage "interdependency among agencies ... and a more stable, effective, interorganization system" (p. 114). The new structures should emphasize "a network rather than a hierarchy of authority and control relations, with open, lateral, and upward communications based on consultation, not just downward commands ... tasks and workflow are flexible and subject to continual redefinition on the basis of new information" (Perrow, 1960, pp. 33-34).

In the new economy (high tech) self-correcting organizations (Landau, 1973), organizational learning through single-loop, double-loop (conflict stage) and deutero learning stages, (Argyris and Schon, 1978) and self-designing organizations (Hedberg, Nystrom and Starbuck, 1976) must have "a different culture than the traditional, hierarchical, authoritarian ones of the past" (Gortner, et al., 1997, p. 118). These approaches include the traditional and the universalistic prescriptions of the administrative science school and antidesign theories which are increasingly becoming irrelevant. Structures can be designed with the use of technology and application of interdependency models. Given this reality, it is important to know that structure can support or impede the efficient coordination of work process although the former does not define the process. Careful planning should match structures to technology, environments, and program design and development. In such structure, there is need to reinforce rather than hinder program administration, implementation and evaluation.

All organizations create mechanisms for carrying on activities that are instrumental to their goal achievement. The regularity of the activities are centered around the processes of allocation, coordination and supervision of the organization's structure. Organizational structure may be viewed as a form of bureaucratic technical efficiency (Weber, 1947) or bureaucratic dysfunctionalism (March and Simon, 1958). March and Simon have tried to assertively show that imperfections of the bureaucracy could be, paradoxically and ironically speaking, "just as great a cause for its perpetuation as its efficiencies" (Pugh, 1987, p. 13). In his studies of firms in stable and adaptive environments, Burns (1963) comparatively contrasted bureaucratic with organismic structures. Bureaucratic structures are mechanistic in orientation. For instance, in relation to organismic authority, task allocation and communication are very adjustable while the bureaucracy's rules and procedures are extremely rigid – due to their constitutional and political mandates. Woodward (1958) strongly suggests that the structure of the manufacturing arena is strongly related to the technology of production. This proposition provokes debate concerning whether all organizations are similar in their possession of the basic principles of structure. Pugh (1987) has described the research he carried out with his colleagues by measuring "the range of degrees of specialization, standardization and centralization of authority structures" (pp. 13-14). They also investigated the "effects of contextual factors such as size, technology, ownership, interdependence, etc., on the characteristic differences found" (p. 14). Lawrence and Lorsch (1967) analyzed the degree of structural differentiation that is necessary for "a firm to function in a particular environment and the corresponding integration mechanisms required for it to be a high performer" (Pugh, 1987, p. 14). Crozier (1976) used organizational structure to analyze "recurring strategic and tactical games played by individuals or groups in organizations" as they use power for bargaining purposes. Finally, in relation to the structure of organizations, Jaques (1976), in his *A General Theory of Bureaucracy* shows that the basic depth-structure of an organization is established by and based on "the manager-subordinate relationships which have different time-spans of work discretion" (Pugh, 1987, p. 14). All these scholars have shown that structure has nothing to do with processes, but something(s) to do with hierarchy.

Hage and Aiken (1970) conducted case study research on organizational change and dynamics. Having studied a variety of firms, these authors identified seven points for strategic organizational climates. The Hage and Aiken's seven structural characteristics of adaptive or dynamic organizations include:

1. Organizational complexity, defined as the number and professionalism of occupational specialties in the organization, is positively associated with the ability of the organization to respond to external change, because professionals are often extremely oriented to the developments in their fields as they bring them to the agency.

2. Centralization of authority in the upper echelons of the bureau slows the rate of change because decision criteria are static and lower ranking personnel, who often see the need for change, are most directly excluded from decisions.

3. Formalization, the degree to which tasks are highly codied into rules and standard operating procedures, slows the rate of program change. When large portions of program and management activities are rule governed, change is delayed and perceptions of the possibility of substantial change are limited. Extreme formalization also slows the process of implementing change, as a whole set of rules must be developed and coordinated with existing ones.

4. Stratification, the differentiated distribution of rewards among employees to emphasize rank, decreases the rate of change. Stratification creates insecurities and fears of loss of status. It also discourages negative reports on organizational performance and open discussion of problems with superiors.

5. Emphasis on a high volume of production lowers the rate of change since change, almost of necessity, disrupts production.

6. Greater emphasis on efficiency delays change because new program ideas are usually oriented first to improvements in quality, not efficiency. Thus, program changes will only be adopted when they have developed to the point of high operating efficiency.

7. Higher levels of job satisfaction are also associated with greater rates of change since satisfaction increases commitment to organizational success and enables the organization to overcome the strains involved in change (Gortner, et al., 1997, p. 113).

Self-Designing Bureaus and Organizations

Complex public and private organizations (firms) could be part and parcel of the boundary—spawning, cooperative, coordinating or competitive institutions for resources and program jurisdictions. Informed organizational administrators would tend to create a climate of or a climate for stable and effective interdependency of organizational systems (Litwak and Hylton, 1962; Benson, 1975; and

Lindblom, 1965). Thompson (1967), who argued that organizations are professionally and technologically managed in order to accomplish certain organizational and structural processes of the environment, tend to "boundary-span" between the bureau and the environment. The boundary spanners are roles that are played by certain individuals for the purpose of "buffering" the core technology from external interference. In relation to external interference and possible disruption of organizational operations, "under norms of rationality, organizations facing heterogeneous task environments seek to identify homogeneous segments and establish structural units to deal with each" (Thompson, 1976, p. 70).

Korten's (1980) organizational model of self-designed structures that "learn" (Gortner, et al., 1997, p. 116) advocates "emerging knowledge of program development needs rather than ... to traditions or excessive needs for internal security and control" (p. 116) of structures and technologies. These structures need to be tailored to meet program needs.

Korten studied effective Third World programs in terms of their diversity of goals, sponsorship, size and funding sources. He argued that with the exception of those which did not succeed, the successful programs that were developed depended "on the learning capacity of the implementing organization" (p. 116). Korten (1980, p. 498) discovered that "The learning organization embraces error." This organization does not deny if the program identifies problems, corrects them, and uses available means, regardless of source, to solve the problems. Second, the learning organization capitalizes on existing local knowledge, expertise and technology in order to remedy the program problems. The program targets and means for reaching them enable program developers to be informed about the priorities and hardships of the target group. Third, for learning organizations, linkage of knowledge to action enables the organization's implementation leaders and users to socialize with "the teams that created the original program" (Korten, 1980, p. 429). In other words, this approach tends to ensure that the dedication and enthusiasm of the project initiators (champions) is not lost but is "used and rewarded" (Peters and Waterman, 1982). Also, policymaking teams should never be separated from the implementation teams because these "clients, researchers and administrators" (Gortner, et al. 1997, p. 116) form the necessary reservoir for viable and creative adaptation of the program. In the Third World, program planning, development, implementation and evaluation can be a participatory endeavor. In the U.S., program development clients lack a set of unified demands. As a result, several problems related to program procedures, staffing, and funding may create constraints in the process of program development and implementation. Some of these problems are associated with American judicial, legislative, executive and bureaucratic mandates that take a long time to satisfy ambitious, parochial and diverse political constituencies.

Hedberg, Nystrom, and Starbuck (1976) and just as Landau (1973) have shown that self-designing bureaus and organizations use program development processes which put pressure on them to enhance flexibility and create mechanisms for sensitizing opportunity and knowledge that are necessary for organizational self-redesign. In some ways "Perrow's nonroutine structure or Burns' and Stalker's 'organismic' system (Gortner, et al., 1997, p. 117) are the scholars less interested in structural forms common in decision-making channels which will unrigidify organizations by forcing them to reappraise themselves continuously. The "minimalist" processes that prevent complacency and promote the continuous drive for organizational self-design or "self-renewal" include but are not limited to:

1. Acting on minimal consensus rather than waiting for unanimity.
2. Striving for only minimal contentment among personnel, which sharpens their desire for change and their search for alternatives.
3. Working toward only minimal affluence since even though a 'small buffer of flexible resources is an asset, ... too much affluence breeds complacency and contempt for new opportunities.
4. Placing only minimal faith in plans or goals. Even though they are needed to direct immediate action, they should be discarded easily.
5. Attempting to be only minimally consistent since total consistency impeded the pluralistic bargaining process that produces incremental changes, thereby forcing a delayed and destructive revolution to achieve any change.
6. Aiming only for minimal rationality in procedures. Even though basic managerial processes must be established, highly coherent and fully rationalized structures convey a false sense of control and prematurely define new problems and opportunities rather than encouraging their exploration. Some structural and procedural ambiguities will keep the organization in a state of readiness for change (Gortner, et al., 1997, p. 118).

Having studied learning organizations, Senge (1990) argued that they "must have a different culture than the traditional, hierarchical and authoritarian one of the past." His concept of culture means "the perspectives, values, beliefs, myths, behavior patterns, and so on commonly held within an organization" (Gortner, et al., 1997, p. 18). Senge asserts that learning organizations have five technologies that are critical to organizational success. They consist of:

1. Systems thinking. The ability to contemplate the whole of a phenomenon instead of any individual part of the pattern.
2. Personal mastery. The discipline of continually clarifying and deepening one's personal vision, of focusing one's energies, of developing patience, and of seeing reality objectively.
3. Mental models. The process by which individuals learn how to surface and challenge the other individuals' mental models (deeply ingrained assumptions, generalizations, pictures or images) that influence how one understands the work and, therefore, takes action.
4. Building shared vision. The skill of unearthing a shared 'picture of the future' that binds people together around a common identity and sense of destiny, therefore fostering genuine commitment and enrollment rather than compliance.
5. Team learning. The skill of sharing 'dialogue,' the capacity of members of a team to suspend assumptions and enter into a genuine 'thinking together,' and learning how to recognize the patterns of interaction in teams that undermine learning (Senge, 1990, pp. 6-10; and Gortner, et al., 1997, pp. 18-19).

The underpinning concept behind the self-designing organization is for it to remain with tension and radical dynamism like the organismic model. However, the self-designing organization is different from the organismic one because the former uses different strategies for the creation and maintenance of its dynamism. Such dynamism has power that makes the status quo difficult through rule setting that makes change easier and achievable. Such kind of dynamism is inherent in TQM processes whose synergistic vision is shared with self-designing organizations.

Organismic and Mechanistic Systems

To effectively define the organismic system requires the need for its comparison with the mechanistic systems. First, organismic organizational system is characterized by:

1. The contributive nature of special knowledge and experience to the common task of the concern.

2. The realistic nature of the individual task, which is seen as set by the total situation of the concern.
3. The adjustment and continual redefinition of individual tasks through interaction with others.
4. The shedding of responsibility as a limited field of rights, obligations and methods. (Problems may not be posted upwards, downwards or sideways.)
5. The spread of commitment to the concern beyond any technical definition.
6. A network structure of control, authority, and communication.
7. Omniscience no longer imputed to the head of the concern; knowledge may be located anywhere in the network; this location becoming the center of authority.
8. A lateral rather than a vertical direction of communication through the organization.
9. A content of communication which consists of information and advice rather than instructions and decisions.
10. Commitment to the concern's tasks and to the "technological ethos" of material progress and expansion is more highly valued than loyalty.
11. Importance and prestige attach to affiliations and expertise valid in the industrial and technical and commercial millieu external to the firm (Burns, 1963; and Pugh, 1984, pp. 46-47).

Organismic organizational systems are suitably adapted to unstable organizational climates which are prone to a variety of prevailing problems. Specialist roles that exist in hierarchically mechanistic settings are unheard of in organismic organizational environments. Responsibilities, functions, methods, and powers of organizational participants require continuous definition and redefinition. The definition and redefinition of these tasks is a group or collective rather than an individual exercise. Collective or group activity enables the organization to learn, share responsibility and tasks and try to solve common problems. Individuals work for a specific and overall purpose of the organization. "Interaction runs laterally as much as vertically, and communication between people of different ranks tends to resemble lateral consultation rather than vertical command. Omniscience can no longer be imputed to the boss at the top" (Pugh, 1984, p. 45). Unlike the individual in mechanistic systems, the person in the organismic organizational realm is committed to the organization. The mechanistic system tells the individual what to do, how to do it, what does not concern him/her, what is not expected of him/her, and what others are responsible for. Contrary to the mechanistic system, the organismic organization allows the individual to be "independent," exploratory, boundaryless, responsible, competent and curiously innovative and productive. In other words, organismic systems create a climate for open and free exchange of information flow that can be used for dynamic change.

Second, the mechanistic Taylorism is adapted to stable organizational environments. In mechanistic systems, specialists handle problems, tasks and concerns. Each specialist "does his or her own thing" regardless of the overall purpose or mission of the organization. Only the top person approves or appraises the job and work of the individual by seeing its relevance to the whole organization. "The technical methods, duties and powers attached to each post are precisely defined and a high value is placed on precision and demarcation" (p. 44).

Vocational and professional interaction in the organization is vertical (superior-subordinate) rather than horizontal and collegial. An individual operates in the context of the dictates and prescriptions that govern the role he/she plays in the organization. Such a hierarchy of values portrays the top person to be omniscient. This charted and complex hierarchical management system works like a control system that allows decisions and instructions to "filter" as they descend "through a succession of amplifiers" (p. 44). In other words, mechanistic systems are rationally bureaucratic and characterized by malaise. For instance, the mechanistic system is characterized by:

1. The specialized differentiation of functional tasks into which the problems and tasks facing the concern as a whole are broken down.
2. The abstract nature of each individual task, which is pursued with techniques and purposes more or less distinct from those of the concern as a whole.
3. The reconciliation, for each level in the hierarchy, of these distinct performances by the immediate superiors.
4. The precise definition of rights and obligations and technical methods attached to each functional role.
5. The translation of rights and obligations and methods into the responsibilities of a functional position.
6. Hierarchic structure of control, authority and communication.
7. A reinforcement of the hierarchic structure by the location of knowledge of actualities exclusively at the top of the hierarchy.
8. A tendency for vertical interaction between members of the concern, i.e., between superior and subordinate.

9. A tendency for operations and working behavior to be governed by superiors.
10. Insistence on loyalty to the concern and obedience to superiors as a condition of membership.
11. A greater importance and prestige attaching to internal (local) than to general (cosmopolitan) knowledge, experience and skill (p. 46).

As a rational and mechanistic "jungle," to be effective in communications, and in spite of its insistence on using mechanistic principles, the ideology of bureaucratic formality which is also the ideology of industrial management—the bureaucracy, tends to employ liaison specialists in order to penetrate bureaucratic tough and enhance effective communications. Sometimes special committees are selected to expedite the communications structural operations without which the system may develop pathologies that may "strangle" the organization. In general, "out of date mechanistic organizations are perpetuated and pathological systems develop, usually because of one or the other of two things: internal politics and career structure" (p. 50).

Structure, Culture and Function of NATO: A Case Study

This section of the chapter illustratively analyzes the origin, structure, culture and functions of NATO during the last fifty years. This illustration will show the design, purposes and rationale behind its formation. World War II was coming to a close when 50 nations signed the United Nations (League of Nations) Charter in San Francisco on June 26, 1945. It was seven weeks after the surrender of Nazi Germany, six weeks before the Hiroshima and Nagasaki bombs, and the world hoped that there would finally be peace. Within four years, ten European nations were faced with the threat of war. Since the United Nations was and is a League of Friendship without military and state-centric authority, it could not guarantee their security. They turned to the United States and Canada to sanction their pledge of mutual security. As a result, on April 4, 1949, the North Atlantic Treaty Organization (NATO) was signed. NATO was created, structured, and made to ensure peace and security of its signatory countries through continuous cooperation and for an indefinite duration.

One might ask what happened in those three years and about nine months that convinced twelve countries of the need for a regional defense alliance. Collectively, the defeat of Germany and Japan left a window of opportunity for the Soviet Union. The British prime Minister, Sir Winston Churchill, in his telegram of May 12, addressed to President Truman, expressed his anxiety in the following terms: "What will be the position in a year or two when the British and American armies have melted, and the French have not yet been formed on any major scale, and when Russia may choose to keep 200 or 300 divisions on active service?" He added, "An iron curtain is drawn down upon their front," 'Russia.' "We do not know what is going on behind" (NATO Information Service, 1969, p. 14).

As predicted, in 1945, when Germany and the Western democracies began to demobilize and withdraw their armed forces from Europe, the Soviet Union kept its armed forces prepared for potential war. With the combined strength of the red army and world communism, the Soviet Union began to act upon an expansionist policy. The United Nations tried to reach peaceful agreements with the Soviet Government without success.

However, in November 1945, after making concessions, the Western Powers were able to reach an agreement with the Soviet Union on a procedure for framing peace treaties with Italy, Finland and Germany's former satellites in the Balkans. The Peace Conference opened in Paris on July 29, 1946, and the peace treaties with Italy, Finland, Bulgaria, Hungary and Rumania were not signed until February 10, 1947 (NATO Information Service, 1997, p. 15).

Foreign Ministers met at the 1947 Moscow Conference to discuss the drafting of peace treaties with Germany and Austria, but were unable to agree on what Germany's role and fate should be. A new Foreign Ministers' Conference was held in London in November 1947, and accomplished no more than the first. Shortly after came the end to the cooperation which had developed between the USSR and the Western democratic countries during the War. The signing of the United Nations Charter on June 26, 1945,had raised hopes of the peoples of the Western countries, but the Soviet Union abused the right of veto at the Security Council (NATO Information Service, 1997, p. 15). The Soviet Union vetoed decisions taken by the Security Council, and drafted resolutions recommending United Nations action on more than one hundred different occasions.

Soviet expansion under Stalin had already begun during the War. With the incorporation of the territory of Estonia, Latvia and Lithuania, together with certain parts of Finland, Poland, Rumania, North-Eastern Germany and Eastern Czechoslovakia, the Soviet Union had gained more than 180,000 square miles of land occupied by more than 23 million inhabitants. The Soviet domination effectively compelled Albania, Bulgaria, Rumania, Eastern Germany, Poland, Hungary and Czechoslovakia to relinquish their sovereignty and identity into the circle of Soviet supremacy. Such expansionist Soviet behavior raised the eyebrows of some Western leaders such as Truman's.

On March 12, 1947, President Truman told Congress: "It must be the policy of the United States of America to support free peoples who are resisting attempted subjugation by armed minorities, or by outside pressure" (NATO Information Service, 1997, p. 19). This statement became known as the "Truman Doctrine." The Truman Doctrine was designed to strategically and economically deal with the specific threat to Greece and Turkey by authorizing the allotment of $400 million for aid up to June 1948.

In spite of the aid received by some of the free countries of Europe from United States, the European economy was close to economic and recessionary collapse. On June 5, 1947, in a speech at Harvard University, the then Secretary of State for the United States, General George C. Marshall, initiated the idea of a Programme for European Recovery (NATO Information Service, 1997). Truman also said that this policy was "directed not against any country or doctrine but against hunger, poverty, desperation and chaos" (NATO Information Service, 1997, p. 19). His tone was intended to de-escalate tension and suspicions. This offer of economic assistance was also open to the Soviet Union and the countries behind the Iron Curtain but Stalin refused all American aid. Finally, in response to the Marshall Plan which was referred to as "an instrument of American imperialism," Stalin set up the Cominform. The Cominform was a communist information bureau that was set up to coordinate the communist parties of Bulgaria, Czechoslovakia, France, Hungary, Italy, Poland, Rumania, USSR and Yugoslavia. It was dissolved in 1956 due to the fact that coordination and integration of their ideological and political character was contradictorily irreconcilable.

The idea of a defensive alliance within the framework of the United Nations had already been contemplated in 1946. So when the world found itself split in two, the free countries of Europe came together. On March 4, 1948, representatives of Belgium, France, Luxembourg, the Netherlands and the United Kingdom met in Brussels to consider the terms of a treaty of mutual assistance. Belgium, France, Luxembourg, the Netherlands and the United Kingdom signed the Brussels Treaty on March 17, 1948. Russians started the 323-day blockade of West Berlin in June 1948, and was only counteracted by the strategic order of an air-lift by Western powers which reinforced their defense needs.

On April 28, 1948, the idea of a single premium defense system, including and superseding the Brussels Treaty, was publicly put forward by Mr. St. Laurent in the Canadian House of Commons

(NATO Information Service, 1947, 1997, p. 21). In order to join the Atlantic Alliance, the United States needed to have constitutional permission. To this end, in consultation with the State Department, Senator Vandenberg drew up a resolution which recommended, in particular, "the other collective arrangements as are based on continuous effective self-help and mutual aid" and "its contribution to the maintenance of peace by making clear its determination to exercise the right of individual or collective self-defense, under Article 51 of the United Nations Charter should any armed attack occur affecting its national security" (NATO Information Service, 1997, p. 21). After preliminary talks, which started on July 6, 1948, and ended on September 9, 1948, the Consultative Council of the Brussels Treaty announced complete unity of views on the principle for defensive alliance for the North Atlantic area.

In spite of that memorandum to the signatory countries of the Treaty, the signing seemed to have immediate results when just one month later the USSR raised the Berlin blockade. For over 40 years there would continue to be great tension between NATO and the Soviet Union without a breakout of war, and the ideological, economic, and military rivalry between the two camps was called "The Cold War." The character of Soviet political leadership has been discussed in Chapter 9. In 1985, a new Soviet leader, Mikhail Gorbachev, began to seek better relations with the U.S. and other NATO countries. The Communist Party lost control of the Soviet Government in 1991 and democratic forces under the banner of Yeltsin and his protegee—Putin have controlled elected governments ever since.

The Treaty was ratified five months after it was signed and came into force on August 24, 1949. Now the signatory countries were faced with two immediate tasks. One was to create a structure capable of putting the Treaty into action. The other task was to work out a common defense strategy for Western allied security.

The North Atlantic Council was formed and consisted of Foreign Ministers of member countries. It met for the first time in Washington, D.C. on September 17, 1949. It began to design a civilian and military framework. I accordance with article 9 of the Treaty, the Council created a Defense Committee composed of the Defense Ministers of member countries, responsible for drawing up coordinated defense plans for the North Atlantic area. In addition, a number of military bodies were set up: a Military Committee, a Standing Group, and five Regional Planning Groups. Figure 6.1 shows the graphic structure of NATO and its international staff.

Figure 6.1. NATO International Staff

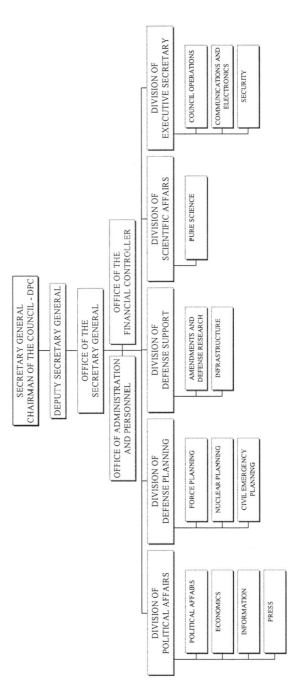

Source: NATO Handbook. 1985. Brussels: Information Service, p. 160.

The Military Committee was in charge of advising the Council in military matters. The Standing Group was the Military Committee's executive body which was responsible for strategic guidance in areas where NATO forces operated. The five Regional Planning Groups were responsible for developing defense plans for their respective areas. These areas included Northern Europe, Western Europe, Southern/Western Mediterranean, Canada/USA and North Atlantic Ocean. The structure of NATO's military force was organized into three main commands: Atlantic Command, Channel Command, and Allied Command of Europe.

The Supreme Allied Commander Atlantic headed Atlantic Command. His most important task was to provide for the security of the Atlantic area by protecting the sea lanes and denying their use to an enemy in order to safeguard them for the reinforcement and resupply of NATO Europe with men and material. This area of attention covers about 12 million square miles extending from the North Pole to the Tropic of Cancer and from the coastal waters of North America to the coast s of Europe and Africa. The Supreme Allied Commander of Atlantic is also in command of the Standing Naval Force Atlantic. It is a permanent international naval squadron reinforced and regulated on a continuous basis.

The Supreme Allied Commander Channel's mission is to control and protect merchant shipping in the area, while cooperating with the air defense of the channel. He also has under his command the Standing Naval Force Channel. The Channel Command covers the English Channel and southern areas of the North Sea.

Allied Command Europe covers the area extending from the North Cape to the Mediterranean and from the Atlantic to the eastern border of Turkey. The Supreme Allied Commander Europe's "main functions are to prepare and finalize defense plans for the area under his command, and ensure the combat efficiency of forces assigned to him in the event of war" (*NATO Handbook*, 1985, p. 37). General Dwight D. Eisenhower, who later became the President of the United States (1952-60), was the first Supreme Allied Commander Europe elected by the Council. The Supreme Allied Commander Europe is always a U.S. general and most of NATO's forces are in Allied Commander Europe.

The Civil and Military Structure of the Alliance consists of the North Atlantic Council, the Defense Planning Committee, and the Nuclear Planning Group. The North Atlantic Council is composed of representatives of the 19 member countries, and is the highest decision-making body whose forum is used for consultations within the Alliance. The Defense Planning Committee is also composed of representatives of the member countries and deals with matters specifically related to defense. Fourteen countries participate in the Nuclear Planning Group which discusses crucial nuclear matters.

The International Staff is composed of the Office of the Secretary General, the Office of Management, and the Financial Comptroller. The Office of the Secretary General has five divisions: Political Affairs, Defense Planning and Policy, Defense Support, Infrastructure Logistics and Council Operation, and Scientific Affairs. There is an Assistant Secretary General for each division to carry out several responsibilities. The Director of Management is responsible for all matters regarding the organization and structure of the International Staff. Finally, the Office of Financial Comptroller is an independent office headed by the Financial Comptroller who is responsible for the control of budgeted expenditures.

The International Staff is composed of the Office of the Secretary General, the Office of Management, and the Financial Comptroller. The Office of the Secretary General has five divisions: Political Affairs, Defense Planning and Policy, Defense Support, Infrastructure Logistics and Council Operation, and Scientific Affairs. There is an Assistant Secretary General for each division to carry out several responsibilities. The Director of Management is responsible for all matters regarding the organization and structure of the International Staff. Finally, the Office of Financial Comptroller is an independent office headed by the Financial Comptroller who is responsible for the control of budgeted expenditures.

The Alliance is an association of free states joined together to preserve their security through mutual agreements and collective self-defense as recognized by the United Nations Charter (*NATO Handbook*, 1985, p. 21). The organization provides the forum in which they discuss and reach decisions on political and military issues. On the political side security policies are coordinated in accordance with the goals of the North Atlantic Treaty. The military side formulates joint defense plans, forms the infrastructure needed to enable their forces to act, and arranges for joint training programs and exercises.

The Alliance does not base its security on military strength alone but focuses on two principles; deterrence and defense. The primary role of the Alliance is to safeguard the security of members by deterring aggression. However in the event of aggression NATO will have sufficient forces to respond to any level of aggression with an appropriate response.

In 1998, Poland, Hungary and the Czech Republic joined this body of sixteen original members. Here is a list of current signatory countries.

Belgium	Iceland	Portugal	Canada
Italy	Spain	Denmark	Luxembourg
Turkey	France	The Netherlands	United Kingdom
Germany	Norway	United States	Greece
Poland	Czech Republic	Hungary	

The Alliance celebrated its 50th anniversary in 1999 and has effectively managed to keep peace in the Euro-Atlantic area and has provided security to its members all throughout the high-tension years of the Cold War. The Cold War has ended with the coming down of the Wall and unification of Germany in 1990, the disintegration of the Soviet Union in December 1991, the expansion of NATO territory and membership changes in Central and Eastern Europe. So, therefore, the NATO Heads of States and Governments have since adapted its overall strategy to fit the changing political strategic environment. In Rome, in 1991, they adopted a Strategic Concept which outlines a broad approach to security based on dialogue, cooperation, and the maintenance of a collective defense capability. The Concept provides for reduced dependence on nuclear weapons and major changes in NATO's integrated military forces, including substantial reductions in their size and readiness, improvements in their mobility, flexibility and adaptability to different contingencies and greater use of multinational formations (*NATO Today*, 1996, Online Version, p. 1)

The Alliance's basic goal of enhancing security and extending stability throughout the Euro-Atlantic area has been strongly apparent through initiatives such as the creation of the North Atlantic Cooperation Council (NACC), Partnership for Peace (PFP), and the establishment of new Euro-Atlantic Partnership Council (EAPC), which replaced the NACC. On May 27, 1997. NATO and Russia signed the "Founding Act on Mutual Relations, Cooperation and Security between NATO and the Russian Federation." The Founding Act reflects the changing security needs between NATO and Europe and constitutes an enduring commitment between NATO and Russia to build together a lasting and inclusive peace in the Euro-Atlantic area.

The Study of the Alliance's Enlargement was initiated by NATO's Foreign Ministers in December 1994. The Alliance's decisions on NATO's enlargement were taken by NATO Heads of State and Government in Madrid in July 1997, when Czech Republic, Hungary and Poland were invited to begin accession negotiations in accordance with Article 10 of the North Atlantic Treaty Organization.

There has been a lot of debate over the joining of former enemies and Warsaw Pact members, Czech republic, Hungary, and Poland. Not only do people believe that NATO should not expand, they also see no reason for the Alliance to continue. With the collapse of the Soviet Union and an estimated beginning cost of NATO expansion to be $125,000 billion, many see the disadvantages of keeping and expanding NATO strongly outweighing the advantages of ending it.

On the other hand, others take into account the dangerous legacy of nations and international problems, and see this as a lack of stability. There are still a variety of dangers such as ultranationalism, ethnic differences, terrorism, and the proliferation of weapons of mass destruction. Although an aggression against NATO seems extremely unlikely, Russia will retain land, air, and sea forces with the capability to conduct a wide range of operations. In addition, Russia will still remain the dominant military power in Europe and only NATO has the defensive capabilities to counterbalance these residual forces.

Although the cost of keeping and expanding NATO is significant, it may be the price that Americans and fellow signatory countries have to pay in order to guarantee their safety and security as free countries. The Alliance was created in a time of high tension with Russia and has succeeded to prevent war for almost 50 years. Ever since 1991, when the Communist Party lost control of the Government, there have been questions about the future role of NATO. NATO seems to be the reason for the gradual improvement of relations between Russia and the Alliance countries, so it is apparent that continuing the Alliance will only keep the peace. In a way, until there is another way of ensuring peace for those that want it, NATO will most likely continue to exercise the validity of its existence.

In spite of the collapse, disintegration, and apparent disappearance of the Soviet threat, NATO plans to expand its military alliance towards the East and thereby strengthen the integration and political enlargement of Western Europe. This expansion has not eliminated the potential for escalation of regional conflicts which tend to erupt into violence. Such violence results in massive casualties, millions of psychologically, economically and socially helpless refugees and poverty and hatred epitomized by former Yugoslavia as reflected by international relations experts (e.g., Kolodziej and Kanet, 1996). These experts predict that the potential for war and peace is a concomitant coexistence. For instance, most neorealist international political scientists argue that NATO's survival and potential expansion is not only an anomaly and product of neorealist power whose existence will dispel the "threat-based models of alliances," but such neorealism is associated with or influenced by neoliberal institutionalism (Barnett, 1997) and cybernetic theory as viewed and interpreted in the light of

NATO's cooperation from Suez in 1956 to Sarajevo in 1994, and lately to Pristina in 1999. Since the threat to NATO is largely external rather than internal, the cooperation of the alliance does not depend on the existence of a perceived threat from within; but rather, one that is from without. Given this reality, continual cooperation of NATO leadership of the United States and effective communication command structure, NATO members count on the peaceful relations among all the great powers.

Duffield (1995) constructed *Power Rules* which provocatively tests neorealist thought against the backdrop of NATO's historical legacy. Like Risse-Kappen (1995) who authored *Cooperation among Democracies,* both authors deal with intra-alliance decision-making dynamics from a neorealist intellectual platform which challenges other theoretical models. Duffield exhaustively deals with a historical analysis of NATO's conventional force posture and structure by exploring the evolution of its contributions for European, and more importantly, Western security interests particularly during the Cold War era. Duffield gives three complimentary explanations which assert that the (1) balance of power politics, that is, neorealism, which predicts that its force posture is a function of changes in Soviet power and behavior, (2) intra-alliance politics, that is, public choice theory, which explores the differential contributions of alliance members to the public good and NATO strategy over time, and (3) institutional theories, i.e., regime theory, which suggests that NATO's norms, rules, and decision-making processes will produce stability in the overall posture and differential contribution despite the fact that environmental changes would lead the first two theories to predict an altered force posture and contribution profile (Barnett, 1997).

Though NATO is also an instrument of American foreign policy for global security and empirical coexistence, its moral and logical power rested in understanding the principles of détente, ostpolitique, and neorealism. NATO's conventional force posture relied on the doctrines of Mutual Assured Destruction (MAD) which meant massive retaliation during the 1950s and the enforcement of flexible response of the 1960s which, with strategic containment of the USSR, had served the cause of humanity with distinction, by the end of the Cold War. In this arena, while intra- and inter-alliance politics did not greatly and negatively affect member countries, differential contributions were more or less influenced by the strategic rationality and institutionalist (customary or cultural) practices. Such instrumental practices have helped to explain the "impressive stability of NATO's force posture when both intra-alliance and balance of power theories have been used to predict NATO's dynamics for change. In other words, theoretical pluralism in terms of neorealism, institutionalism and NATOISM help fully to explain why they constrain the behavior of states and thereby "institutional content is conditioned by international structure and national interest" (p. 275). Duffield searched for when intra-alliance state behavior accounted for and helped to define state or national interests instead of concentrating on how norms might shape the meaning and substance of state security and how frequent interaction among NATO members conceptually shaped state identities, relationships and interests. He made a strong case for institutionalism's contributions for NATO's existence largely not due to neorealist promises and opportunities it offers for analysis, but due also to the subject, its research design and inherent limitations of rationalist perspective.

On the contrary, Risse-Kappen (1995) argues, in *Cooperation among Democracies* of this trans-Atlantic Alliance, that state identities and interests of NATO consist of an international structure characterized by values of normative integration and material forces. The normatively integrative and material forces are used as a guide for NATO's interactive and inter-alliance socioeconomic, scientific, and strategic dynamics.

Radical debates of neorealist, sophisticated realist and liberal theories of inter-alliance interaction clash over big versus small states' contributions to European and alliance security interests. The extent to which how effective these theories explain European influence on American foreign policy could be a matter of contradictory conjecture. In spite of such contradictory and conjectural presuppositions, neorealist presuppositions assert that the state which has more power than the rest could be the final arbiter. Alternatively, the sophisticated realist school of thought, contrary to neorealist untheoretical intransigence, shows that small states which are allies, tend also, to wield a lot of influence in inter- and intra-alliance affairs.

In the light of liberal international relations theory, "republicanism, institutionalism, and transnationalism" work jointly to construct "an architecture" which is seen as a community rather than an alliance (Risse-Kappen, 1995). If NATO is a democratic alliance of liberal states, it has distinctive norms which help to provide a credible explanation of the processes and outcomes of the disputes, conflicts and disagreements among the member states. On the other hand, if NATO is not an alliance of states, then it is a community of liberal democracies that are characterized by "distinctive norms that revolve around consultation and codetermination" (Risse-Kappen, 1995). The externalization of the states' domestic concerns and the above mentioned norms tend to clarify the dynamics of NATO's decision-making processes and how, why and when conflicts between and among member states are ironed out in order to continually maintain their vitality and the strategic supranationalism of the community's alliance. In other words, at times, the theoretical models of liberalism's and sophisticated realism's predictions converge to cause the same outcome while neorealist theoretical underpinnings tend to hold no water in both cases.

As a profound intellectual analyst, Risse-Kappen needed to use his theoretical alliance in a constructivist way for his own benefit. For instance, his theoretical overview places a lot of emphasis on the "consensual nature and codetermination of alliances among liberal states" and offers a stylized world that exclusively makes the language of power to be realism and that of norms to be liberalism respectively. This dichotomous relationship appears and tends to be unfair to sophisticated realist overtures that tend to create problems for democratic liberalism. For instance, a "sophisticated realist hypothesis might argue that self-interest and power-seeking behavior might generate such norms of consensuality" (Risse-Kappen, 1995). Further still, liberalism, which places emphasis on coalition-building, communicative processes, and codetermination, omits power asymmetries and coercion" (Risse-Kappen, 1995). By doing this, realism is effectively tested against the backdrop of liberalism. Consequently, "realists are granted a monopoly on power" and liberalism is "stripped naked" (Risse-Kappen, 1995). Given this scenario, and in defense of the worth of liberalism, liberal theorists need to "incorporate the role of power into their conceptual analytical framework and firmly argue how power asymmetries can be "tamed, modified, and defined" to reflect the logic of community rather than the one of anarchy. For instance, James and Hristoules (1994) have shown that as a leading member of NATO and the international system, the United States plays and has played a major role particularly during the Cold War era. They assert that:

> External influences on foreign policy, consistent with the tradition of political realism...These elements are combined in model crisis of activity. Using data pertaining both to the United States as a polity and an actor in the international system, propositions derived from the model are tested in the crisis domain. The results are encouraging: crisis activity is explained by a combination of internal and external factors. Significant internal influences, with potential cross-national relevance, include explicit forms of behavior by the public, perceptions of international

tension and public approval of the president. At the external, the gravity and importance of crises underway in the system affect its receptiveness to activity by the United States. The study concludes with some recommendations for the research on the linkage of domestic and foreign conflicts with particular reference to the explanation of crises in world politics (p. 327).

Based on a constructivist perspective, Risse-Kappen (1995) constructed a form of theoretical alliance in the light of constructivism while emphasizing communicative processes. In this arena, he has also emphasized the significance of "identity for understanding the definition and content of interests and norms, and the transactional coalitions that are structurally enabled" (Barnett, 1997). Though he does not identify the origins of these norms, for the known liberal democracies, their essentialist and constructivist origins are not only contradictory at best, but the manner in which he historicizes and objectifies them indicates their contingent underpinnings whose construction and institutionalization tend to animate various domestic actors in the United States. Overall, through communicative processes, the actors are enabled to construct, debate and repair concepts of the group and their own place in it.

As the leading member of NATO, and contrary to the well-known assumptions and expectations based on bureaucratic power, central decision-makers developed a consistent strategy which guided U.S. nuclear weapons between 1960 and 1993. Though most people thought that MAD was the strategy, the real strategy was Nuclear Utilization Theory (NUTS) which "involved the targeting of Soviet Military assets" instead of population centers (Mlyn, 1995). MAD was both a description and prescription policy that was popular but could have never been used instead of NUTS which the statist theory approved of for its benefits in terms of limited rather than indefinite nuclear war.

The popularity of MAD as a war fighting policy was always opposed by Congress and the public while the central state decision-makers also found it difficult to use NUTS which lawmakers who approved the use of force were not aware of and could have made the fighting capability of the U.S. more difficult if they were to approve its use. During the 1960s and 1970s, the Soviet Union "achieved nuclear parity with the U.S." Its technology improved the warhead delivery, accuracy and efficiency of the nuclear missiles. It is questionable how effective any nuclear exchange with the Soviets would have been if war had occurred. To avert a catastrophe, sophisticated technology allowed the United States to structure forces in accordance with strategy (NUTS) short of a declaratory policy (MAD). In doing that the state which wanted to be autonomous in the use of NUTS for action and procurement purposes found itself constrained by the dialectics from both Congress and the popular polity.

The historic, dramatic, and recent collapse of the Soviet Empire and its political, economic, ideological rather than military disintegration has created a new world of multipolarity perceived in terms of untraditional East-West tensions. In the New World, they are perceived in terms of major players (led by the U.S.) versus small multipolar world tensions. Given this scenario, there exists a theoretical vacuum in terms of international organizations. This theoretical vacuum is filled with a theory of international regimes most of which are interdependent rather than dominant, powerless rather than powerful, and controlled by the realist, neorealist and liberal democratic ideologies, norms and values of the dominant members of the United Nations. In the light of this assessment, there is little opportunity for international organizations like the UN or NATO or any other regional organizations to "intervene effectively and independently of great power interests, even for humanitarian purposes" (Esman and Shibley, 1995). In addition, with the dramatic collapse and disappearance of the empire's communist East-Europe, and the subsequent reunification of Germany, the evolution of EEC into the European Union (EU) has not helped E.U., in this climate of rapid political transition, to establish the capacity for solving the most serious ethnic tensions in former Yugoslavia and its belligerent provinces. The European Union has to "shop" elsewhere particularly in the U.S. which is a powerful and remote actor that has the capacity to work with NATO allies in order to resolve the crisis in Central Europe. The NATO-Serbian confrontation over Kosovo is a case in point.

In this political arena, dialectical partisan interests have demonstrated that the United States becomes extremely sensitive to the costs of global leadership in which other powers define the limits of their regional interests. In other words, the effectiveness with which the United Nations and interregional organizations act in order to provide security, peace and prosperity is highly limited by the willingness of the major players to "cooperate, open up their wallets, and sacrifice lives" (Chernoff, 1996; and Kolodziej and Kanet, 1996). The reason why the powers that be (U.S., Russia, Japan, China, and the European Union) have problems to deal with these crises is due to the fact that they "lie in deeply rooted domestic and regional dynamics" which are extensively independent of international (global) control.

Conclusion

Organization structure consists of the pattern of roles, authority and communication structure, which are instrumental to the effective coordination and utilization of technology and organizational participants. Its functional form is organized around the functional specialties that are essential for mission accomplishment. Organizational structure allows intensive and extensive use of functional expertise, which may inadvertently create coordination problems. "The product or service form is organized around the products or services" the organization provides. Functional specialists may reduce coordination problems though it may be difficult to eliminate the endemic and systematic duplication of organizational resources. For instance, the widespread elements of downsizing, though beneficial in some cases, have not enabled corporations and public organizations to create sizeable savings (profits) that can be used to strengthen U.S. industrial competitiveness. In addition, because of the interaction barriers generated by the hierarchical organization structures and unproductive sociotechnical organizational climates, there is decreased opportunity for collegial interaction among functional specialists who perform the same or relevant activities. The matrix organizational "form is organized around both functions and products." The structure of the matrix organization form is given a matrixial form so that the organization can "profit from the advantages of both functional and product structures." Such a classical mechanistic organizational theory may not be suitably beneficial to the needs and issues advanced by multiculturalists and globalists of our contemporary environment. The rigid boundaries the organization creates for itself make it firmly exclusionary and "permanently" impenetrable with glaring "outsider" alternatives for flexibility, challenge and change. Worse still, since both the product boss and functional boss is the same person, such a structure has in recent postindustrial memory, become the source of confusion and conflict. It cannot be gainsaid that these structures have been largely attributed to mass failures and closures of business organizations, the flight of the currency during the decades of the 1970s and 1980s, and a sluggish, inflationary and recessionary economic environment particularly in the West. It may also be argued that the failure of Western organizations to coordinate and integrate their resources for productive domestic investment may not have been the sole cause of the closures, failures and currency flight. Big power politics and the forces of geo-strategic rationality influenced corporations and banks (including IMF and the World Bank) to shift resources and invest them in areas that were viewed as a buffer of Western economic and geostrategic interests during the scary and uncertain Cold War days. This shift of resources from the center to the periphery enabled economically competitive Japan-modeled South East Asia to developmentally benefit at the detriment of the former European colonies whose mass poverty, fragile technology, unstable political climates and postindependence cultural nationalism dissuaded Westerners to invest elsewhere. The effects of these high-tech and Space Age planning strategies on inner city and African economies and other Third World nations were far-reaching (Boansi, 1997).

Organization structure is a formal design characterized by "formal rules, formal hierarchy" and "formal targets and goals." Formalized planning structure is the degree to which a system or an organization is prespecified in terms of its membership, responsibilities, authority and discretion in decision-making. Strategically speaking, formalized planning correlates with cost, comprehensiveness, accuracy and success (Johnson, 1975; and Sagini, 1987).

The three basic organizational structures of formality that display different types of authority are the classical pyramid, the matrix, and the team (Johnson, 1975). Although it is found in most organizations, the pyramidal form is a product of preclassical and classical organization theory in which both the team and the matrix were inextricably interlinked. The team theory on which Theory Z (Ouchi, 1981) which the cultural Japanese management corporation (*saibatsukeiretsu*) uses, places emphasis on participatory management in which leaders and followers have authority to effectively and creatively contribute to decision-making. This collective and humanistic decision-making model motivates personnel, through active involvement and sharing of tasks and responsibilities and through collective awareness of expectations, opportunities and rewards for commitment and quality production. Collective decision-making is not only humanistic in its approach, but, it is also neo-Marxian, anti-Western, and anti-mechanistic Taylorism. Contrary to these archaic models, the team approach evokes feelings of belonging, responsibility and ownership. Belonging, responsibility and ownership are manifestations of group unity, solidarity and professional and psychological satisfaction rather than exclusion and alienation.

In every formally integrated organizational structure, there is an existence of informal structure in terms of norms, hierarchy, individual needs and goals. The informal structure analyzes the primary and secondary needs of the organization and uses informal norms to eliminate pathologies and to motivate personnel (Maslow and

McGregor) and create a tolerable industrious, manageable, and conducive climate for productivity. Maslow's motivation theory is a form of organizational humanism, which shows that if basic needs of humanity are taken care of first, mechanisms for motivation are established for realizing basic and higher goals. In other words, due to lower need satisfaction, motivation is attained for realizing higher need satisfaction. In some ways, human relations theory of Mayo, which addresses individual attitudes, pathologies, feelings and conflicts tends to integrate the formal and informal organizational structures for more effective exploitation by top organizational bureaucrats and technocrats, in static organizational cultures and climates. During most of the new millenium, these structures, models and cultures will be obsolete because they are risky to implement, ineffective to be solvent, and unsuitable to the postindustrial organizational paradigm whose values are ecologically sound and sustainable.

In spite of the criticisms of the classical organization models, the six primary and dimensional variables of organizational structure are the specialization of activities and roles, standardization in terms of employment practices, formalization—writing down of instruction, procedures, etc., centralization in terms of top management being the authority to make certain decisions for the hierarchy, and configuration in terms of the organization'' size, shape and role structure relative to unity of command and span of control (Pugh, 1984).

References

Ambrose, S.E. 1985. *Encyclopedia of the American Presidency.* New York: Simon and Schuster.

Argyris, C., and D. Schon. 1978. *Organization Learning: A Theory of Action Perspective.* Reading, MA: Addison-Wesley.

Barnett, M.N. 1997. Bringing in the new world order: Liberalism, legitimacy, and the United Nations. *World Politics* 49: 526-551.

Benson, K. 1975. The interorganizational network as a political economy. *Administrative Science Quarterly* 20: 229-249.

Betts, R.K. 1997. Should strategic studies survive? *World Politics* 50: 7-33.

Boansi, K.O. 1997. Africa in the Changing International Political Economy. Paper presented at the New York State Political Science Association Conference, New York, April.

Burns, T., and G. Stalker. 1994. *The Management of Innovation.* Oxford: Oxford University Press.

Chernoff, F. 1996. *After Bipolarity: The Vanishing Threat, Theories of Cooperation, and the Future of the Atlantic Alliance.* Ann Arbor: University of Michigan Press.

Duffield, J.S. 1995. *Power Rules: The Evolution of NATO's Conventional Force Posture.* Stanford: Stanford University Press.

Esman, M.J., and S. Telhami. 1995. *International Organizations and Ethnic Conflict.* Ithaca: Cornell University Press.

Fayal, H. 1949. *General and Industrial Management.* Translated by Constance Storrs. London: Pitman.

Filley, A., R. House, and S. Kerr. 1996. *Managerial Process and Organizational Behavior.* 2nd ed. Glenview, IL: Scott Foresman.

Galvin, J.R. 1991. *NATO Review: From Immediate Defense Towards Long-Term Stability.* Web Edition, No. 6.

Gortner, H.F., et al. 1997. *Organizational Theory: A Public Perspective.* Fort Worth: Harcourt Brace College Publishers.

Hackman, J.R., and R. Wageman. 1995. Total quality management: Empirical, conceptual and practical issues. *Administrative Science Quarterly* 40: 309-342.

Hage, J., and A. Aiken. 1970. *Social Change in Complex Organizations.* New York: Random House.

Hage, J., and A. Aiken. 1969. Routine technology, social structure and organizational goals. *Administrative Science Quarterly,* 14: 366-376.

Heads of State and Government. 1989. *Declaration. Treaty North Atlantic Council.* Brussels, May 29-30. Internet Address: www.nato.int/docu/comm/c890530a.htm.

Hedberg, B., P. Nystrom, and W. Starbuck. 1976. Camping on seesaws: Prescriptions for a self-designing organization. *Administrative Science Quarterly* 21: 41-65.

Johnson, J.W. 1975. An Examination of the Management and Planning in Higher Education. Ph.D. dissertation. University of Arkansas.

Kolodziej, E.A., and R.R. Kanet. 1996. *Coping with Conflict after the Cold War.* Baltimore, MD: Johns Hopkins University Press.

Korten, D. 1980. Community organization and rural development. *Public Administration Review* 40: 480-511.

Landau, M. 1973. On the concept of a self-correcting organization. *Public Administration Review* 33: 533-542.

Laurence, P.R., and W.L. Jay. 1986. *Organization and Environment: Managing Differentiation and Integration.* Boston: Harvard University Press.

Legge, M. 1991. *NATO Review: The Making of NATO's New Strategy.* *Web Edition, No. 6.* Internet Address: www.nato.int/docu/review/article/9106-2.htm.

Leonardi, R. 1995. *Convergence, Cohesion and Integration in the European Union.* New York: St. Martin's Press.

Levine, C., R. Backoff, A. Calhoon, and W. Siffin. 1975. Organizational design: A post-minnowbrook perspective for the new public administration. *Public Administration Review* 35: 425-435.

Lindblom, C. 1965. *The Intelligence of Democracy.* New York: Free Press.

Litwak, E., and L. Hylton. 1962. Interorganizational analysis: A hypothesis on coordinating agencies. *Administrative Science Quarterly* 6: 397-420.

Lubbe, H. 1992. European unification is irreversible: Adelbert Reif in conversation with Hermann Lubbe. *Universitas* 36: 298-305.

March, J.G., and H.A. Simon. 1993. *Organization.* 2nd ed. New York: John Wiley and Sons.

Mlyn, E. 1995. *The State, Society, and Limited Nuclear War.* Albany: State University of New York Press.

Mosher, F.C. 1982. *Democracy and the Public Service.* 2nd ed. New York: Oxford University Press.

National Performance Review (U.S.) 1993. *Creating a Government that Works Better and Costs Less: The Report of the National Performance Review.* New York: Plume/Penguin.

North Atlantic Treaty Organization (NATO). 1998. *The North Atlantic Treaty.* Web-Archive. Internet Address: www.nato.int/docu/basictxt/treaty.htm.

NATO 1998. *NATO Handbook.* Online Version. Internet Address: www.nato.int/docu/handbook/htm.

NATO. 1996. *Handbook Preface. NATO A to Z, The Fundamental Tasks of the Alliance.* Online Version.

NATO 1996. *NATO Today,* Online Version.

NATO Information Service. 1985. *NATO Handbook.* Brussels.

NATO Information Service. 1969. *NATO Facts and Figures.* Brussels.

Osborne, D. and T. Gaebler. 1992. *Reinventing Government: How the Entrepreneurial Spirit Is Transforming the Public Sector.* Reading, MA: Addison-Wesley.

Perrow, C. 1970. *Organizational Analysis: A Sociological View.* Belmont, CA: Wasdworth.

Perrow, C. 1967. A framework for the comparative analysis of organization. *American Sociological Review,* 32: 194-208.

Peters, T., and R. Waterman. 1982. *In Search of Excellence.* New York: Warner.

Pressman, J., and A. Wildavsky. 1984. *Implementation: How Great Expectations in Washington Are Dashed in Oakland.* 3rd Ed. Berkeley: University of California Press.

Pugh, D.S. ed. 1984. *Organization Theory: Selected Readings.* London: Penguin Books.

Ross, R.S. 1995. *Negotiating Cooperation: The United States and China 1969-1989.* Stanford: Stanford University Press.

Risse-Kappen, T.R. 1995. *Cooperation among Democracies: The European Influence on U.S. Foreign Policy.* Princeton: Princeton University Press.

Ritter, J. ed. 1971. *Historiches Worterbuch der Philosophie [Historical Dictionary of Philosophy].* Schwabe: Basel.

Rutter, S.D., Jr. 1998. NATO Expansion fueled by U.S. capital. Internet Address: www.gl.umbc.edu/~sruttel/NATO.txt.

Sagini, M.M. 1987. Comparative perceptions of planners of four Michigan community colleges. Ph.D. dissertation. Michigan State University.

Schwarz, B. 1997. Why Russians are worrying. *Boston Globe,* October 21. Internet Address: www.robust-east.net/NET/usa/russians.html.

Senge, P.M. 1990. *The Fifth Discipline: The Art and Practice of Learning Organization.* New York: Currency/Doubleday.

Skibbins, G.J. 1983 *Organizational Evolution.* New York: AMACOM, Endpaper.

Sloan, A.P., Jr. 1990. *My Years with General Motors.* Garden City, N.Y.: Reprinted by Currency/Doubleday.

Swiss, J.E. 1992. Adapting total quality management (TQM) to government. *Public Administrative Review* 52: 356-362.

The New World Order: Opposing Viewpoints. 1991. San Diego: Greenhaven Press.

Thompson, J.D. 1967. *Organizations in Action: Social Science Bases of Administrative Theory.* New York: McGraw-Hill.

Urwick, L. 1943. *Elements of Administration.* New York: Harper.

Vollmer, G.B. 1992. Order into chaos? How scientific knowledge shapes our world view. *Universitas* 34: 256-267.

Walton, M. 1990. *Deming Management at Work.* New York: G.P. Putman's and Sons.

Weber, M. 1947. *Theory of Social and Economic Organization.* Glencoe, IL: The Free Press.

What Is NATO? NATO Basic Sheet No. 12. 1997. Internet Address: www.nato.int/docu/facts/what.htm.

Wilson, J.Q. 1989. *Bureaucracy. What Government Agencies Do and Why They Do It.* New York: Basic Books.

World Book. 1996. *The World Book Encyclopedia.* Vol 14. Chicago: Scott Fetzer Company: 387.

Woodward, J. 1980. *Industrial Organization: Theory and Practice,* 2nd ed. Oxford: Oxford University Press.

Chapter 7

Organizational Diversity: The New Theory

Diversity is a process of introducing variety by increasing the worth of organizational members. Some organizations have inclusive rather than exclusive value systems. Others are exclusive value systems only. Some have both value systems. Regardless of its essence, diversity can be divisive though its dynamics can enhance creativity, productivity and synergy. Based on the available, tangible, and interdisciplinary scholarly evidence, the Northeast of the United States holds more tolerant views of other peoples than the West, South, and Midwest. In other words, these are areas where ethnicity and cultural differences, even in a global context, tend to evoke unique mindscapes or cultural differences that influence different logic systems of operation. Given effective management models, diversity can become an opportunity or a usable and organic resource.

Diversity is a multicultural representation of the organizational make up reflective of our cultural and ethnic composition as a nation. Organizationally, the thesis of this chapter argues that though minorities and women who are managers may hold important positions in society, both groups are discriminated against. However, such discrimination may not necessarily prevent them from using cultural and other strategic avenues for successfully dealing with such discrimination. In a culturally diverse society, such forms of discrimination are and can be anecdotally generalizable.

Global Theory of Diversity

Diversity at the work place is needed to make people come to grips with today's reality. In a highly competitive, demographically changing, and changing labor force market, an agency or organization that successfully manages its diverse labor force will not only do well, it will also attract and retain highly skilled and trained work force. It has been realized that whereas individuals in the past were willing to assimilate to the work place culture, such as corporate culture, in what has traditionally been considered to be the U.S.'s melting pot, employees nowadays refuse to assimilate. Increasingly prospective employees are being taught to be proud of who they are, and are therefore, unwilling to compromise their uniqueness. Thomas (1991, p. 8) suggests that although there will always exist some aspects of assimilation, enforced assimilation is largely unattainable and bad for business. The assimilee becomes uncomfortable trying to live in two worlds, and doing very badly in both of them.

Thomas (1991) further warns against trying to force today's reality, that is, increasing diversity at the work place, into yesterday's management patterns of assimilation. Diversity is a resource that can be managed properly using a comprehensive managerial process that can develop an environment that works for all employees. Diverse workers need to be attracted, retained, promoted, and empowered to make some decisions. Likewise, for managers to be effective, they need to be sensitive to the strategic realities of organizational culture (Schein, 1991) and organizational restructuring (Traxler and Unger, 1994; Zajac and Kraatz, 1993). Diversity is a catch phrase used in understanding the issues of race, ethnicity, and gender (cultural diversity). But in this study, its meaning includes age, sexuality, religion, natural identity, cultural modality, physical disability, and class.

Diversity at the work place, when managed properly, is the greatest asset for any organization and/or corporation (Thomas, 1991). The market place, in terms of competition and demographics, is changing very fast in the United States and elsewhere. By the turn of the century, 85 percent of the new entrants into the job market will constitute women, minorities, and immigrants (Blockstein, 1990; Johnston, 1988; U.S. Department of Commerce, 1989). Yet, the minorities and women are or may not be well represented in the upper end of the economic spectrum, a situation that is visibly reflected in nearly all work places (Blackwell, 1991; Brief, 1993).

In decision making, there is a risk. According to Thomas (1991, p. 3)

Those at the helm of their organizations have a choice: they can treat all members as if they were the same (or try to force them to *become* the same), or they can view the diversity as an opportunity, a strategic lever. If they can take the first course, they risk seriously jeopardizing the strength of the organization, possibly its very survival. If they take the second course—and if they do so before the competition does—they will have an enormous strategic advantage.

Therefore, rather than "kill" diversity, managers should try to work with it because it is the way of the future. Diversity here, goes beyond the issues of gender and race (Andersen and Collins, 1995; Thomas, 1991). A diverse work place in the United States has the presence of women, African Americans, Asian Americans, American Indians, Alaskan Eskimos, Pacific Islanders, and White men. But diversity goes beyond race and gender to include age groups, life styles, and those individuals who are physically, mentally, emotionally, and visually challenged, who avail themselves to the serious endeavors rendered by a given organization.

Diversity management is the process of introducing variety by increasing worth, both qualitatively and quantitatively, into organizations, for the purpose of effecting organizational balance, productivity, and synergy (Sagini, 1991; Thomas, 1991). Organizations whose culture is reflective of diversity are inclusive rather than exclusive value systems (Schein, 1991). Such inclusive organizations value individual differences in their management of diversity.

People differ in different ways. The same is true for workers. Sometimes managers negatively or positively use stereotyping instead of training and use of objective analysis to determine how employees perform. When rational or bureaucratic organizations do not objectively analyze their internal and external weaknesses and strengths in order to capitalize on the strengths they already have, they risk their changes of survival in the competitive and hostile but strategic environment.

In the strategic environment, recent trends in the collapse of the Soviet system of communism and the subsequent reorganization of the world into major global competitors in terms of NAFTA, WTO, EU, APEC, and the Third World, have influenced all organizations in business, industry, government, education, and labor to restructure and reform in order to sustainably compete and effectively position themselves for their own survival. This is the era of serious organizational retrenchment, readaptation and renewal.

Successful organizations will be those that will foster cooperation, multicultural teamwork, mentoring, and inclusion, rather than assimilation, alienation, and cooperative competition. Workers in such a restructured and reformed environment are more productive. They cultivate a sense of belonging to the organization. Because they feel, think and know that they belong, they are naturally motivated to work harder to enhance the productivity of the organization.

Managers who use group dynamics, teamwork techniques, and participatory decision making styles are more likely to foster a productive work force than those who do not (Ouchi, 1981). They work in organizations that are flexible, open, and result-oriented. The organizational benefits that accrue from the use of diversity as a form of effective interpersonal and interactive communication include, but are not limited to, workers who are prepared to compete in the twenty-first century; managers and employees who gain practical knowledge about using cultural differences as resources rather than barriers; and an organization that develops strategies to attract and retain the best work force (Bienvenu, 1974).

The United States has, in the past, both socioeconomically and psycho-politically viewed itself as predominantly biracial society. This kind of national and cultural self realization was and has been an interesting and complex dialectical dichotomy. Though integrationist and egalitarian attempts have been made to metamorphically unify and rationalize the positive elements of its biracial dichotomy in order to subsequently absorb and assimilate negative ones, the evolutionary and progressive development of its multicultural structure has made the situation more complex. Consequently, and in spite of conservative claims to the contrary, racial attitudes have continued to become more diverse and more complex. Scholars may have started to address these changes not only in black and white paradigms, but also, in addition to these, in Asian and Hispanic configurations. The totality of perceptual racial configurations of the American cultural and ethnic landscape is increasingly becoming less and less biracial and more and more diverse and multicultural. Differences in terms of cognitive images whites may hold of minority groups in respect to themselves could have a significant influence in the construction of issues which in turn influence the construction of social policy for the whites as opposed to other minority groups in society.

Within the social science policy oriented disciplines, the normative and evaluative images (e.g., poor, elderly, black, lazy, hardworking, intelligent, etc.) accorded certain groups viz-a-viz others is called "Social construction differential" (Link and Oldendick, 1996, p. 150). Social construction differential is the "difference between how whites view their own race as a group and how they view different minority groups in society" (p. 150). Such perceptions of the dominant or powerful group of other groups enable the former to make social policy decisions on the later groups. Such decisions, which are largely prescriptively distributive, may be viewed to be reflections of symbolic racism or covert racism, or elements of tokenism by minority groups. The letter groups are given that kind of treatment because the dominant group believes that minorities violate American traditional values such as "individualism and self-reliance, the work ethic, obedience, and discipline" (McConahay and Hough, 1976; McConahay, 1986).

The above argument which blames the victim does not seem to hold much water. Group conflict theorists argue that minorities are socially and distributively victimized not because of their violation of traditional American values, but because they have become a threat to white dominance in the struggle for power and opportunity in American society (Bobo, 1988; Glaser, 1994). The traditional way of stereotyping them could be a weak indicator of psychologically denying feelings of hostility that are repressed subconsciously (Toews, 1991).

Socioeconomic status and demographic characteristics determine the concept of social construction differential. Social construction differential is high or low depending on the negative or positive contributions and ratings of minority groups by the majority respectively. The multiculturalism of all the racial and ethnic groups influences group related policies such as those in education which are designed to promote understanding and equality in the instruction of various cultural traditions and values. Multiculturalism also means the "effects and consequences of increasing racial and ethnic diversity in American social institutions and organizations" (Merelman, 1994). While the structure of equal opportunity is rooted in individualistic experience of the U.S.A., such concept of equal opportunity tends to place emphasis on the similarity or lack of inherent difference among members of different groups. Conversely multiculturalism reflects the support for "racial group equality" (Link and Oldendick, 1996, p. 154) and the "preservation of differences among groups" (p. 154). Multicultural views are received more negatively in the South, Midwest, and West than in the Northeast. This indicates that attitudes held on racial diversity are more tolerable in the Northeast than in other regions of the country. This could have significant local and regional implications for social policy including educational opportunity.

Diversity, when viewed from a traditional paradigm evokes issues of ethnicity and cultural difference reflective of various racial/natural groups in society. Contrary to this traditional idea of ethnicity, Maruyama

(1994), has constructed an equally competitive idea of ethnicity by using global perspectives or logics called "mindscapes" to describe what individuals bring to markets and organizational settings and situations. Maruyama argues very convincingly that individuals bring four types of mindscapes (H, I, S, and G). Each mindscape looks at or interprets the environment through different types of lenses or looking glasses. For instance, H types see the world in a very well "ordered, hierarchical, zero sum fashion," whereas G types understand the world to be more "holistic, integrated and positive." I types are more "individualistic, negative-sum, everyman/woman"-for-himself or herself respectively. Finally, the fourth mindscapes are the S types that view the world — marketplace to be "interactive, simultaneous, and cooperative." Maruyama also adds by saying that while these mindscapes may possibly overlap, other more mindscapes could be in existence about which research has not been done.

The author asserts that though the mindscapes are culturally rather than genetically determined, they are not culturally dependent. Maruyama specifies that Europeans and Americans are predominantly H type while Japanese are predominantly S/G type. He further argues that despite the dominant influence of culture in the formation of an individual's mindscape, variation in individual mindscape within given countries and cultures anecdotally infers that mindscapes could be innate.

The mindscape paradigm is a form of heterogeneity. In this case, heterogeneity refers to both differences in mindscapes across cultural individuals and the existence of different mindscapes within a single individual. This mindscape typology is a complex system reminiscent of human, social, psychological, and organizational diversity. Maruyama believes that some people are biscapal because they can see or interpret a situation by using two or more mindscapes. "Biscapalism" or mindscape heterogeneity needs to be reinforced because through its integrated form (using different perspectives), humans create and invent. Through creativity and invention, new structures or patterns of knowledge are developed. They are developed because of the inherent integration of mindscapes. In the light of mindscape idea, the specialization, isolation and in fact alienation that are practiced in England and North America are based on H type mindscapes. These inhibit innovation and creativity by increasing "discord between individuals and divisions" (Barr, 1996, p. 558).

Looking at diversity from an internal and perceptual way of understanding situational reality, it might be argued that Maruyama has conceptually constructed a globally internalized theoretical structure of culturally constructed cognitive differences that influence and determine human knowledgeability, habituation, and performance.

The diversity of the American and global landscape may not only be viewed in ethnic and biscapal paradigms alone. Other paradigms which help to analytically define the forces of diversity and its vitality in the American or global scene are warrantable. One of these could be the element of multiculturalism (Bowser, Jones, and Young, 1995). These three authors, inspired by two conferences that were held at California State University at Hayward in 1989 and 1991, wrote a book entitled, *Toward the Multicultural University.* The conferences were sponsored by the Center for the Study of Intercultural Relations and the Extension Division. The authors assert that the university, as the producer of the elite and the intelligentsia, cannot only continue to be a reflection of Eurocentric values in a society that is progressively and dynamically becoming more and more multicultural viz a viz monocultural. The major argument or premise reads that the Eurocentric institution needs to be changed in order to accommodate, for its vitality and raison d'être, the legitimate values of our multicultural society. The university should, in that change, be guided to become more and more American rather than statically remaining to be Eurocentric, perpetually and parochially narrow in its structure, content, and operational morphology.

As a result, what is required is the creation of a multicultural university which will enable the synergistic evolution of competitive multicultural values whose fusion will stifle division, exclusion and alienation (Moore and Johnson, 1989). One of the challenges of such a university, if it comes to fruition at all, will be the collective reaction of the traditional Eurocentrists who may be tempted not to give up "a hard-earned, well-learned belief system for widespread acceptance of others' beliefs and cultures" (Bowser, Jones, and Young, 1995).

Between 1979 and 1989, Japan transformed itself into a superior global economic superpower. Within the same period, Japanese direct foreign investment (FDI) was $67.5 billion (Organization for Economic Cooperation and Development (OECD), 1991). Fifty percent of all Japanese foreign investment was in the U.S. In 1993, and based on the figures reported in *Business Week's Global* (1993), 281 of the 1000 largest firms were Japanese. In spite of dominance of Japan's performance in the global market place, Western scholars' ethnocentrism has not allowed them to aggressively investigate or massively reflect on the magnitude of this kind of performance which has dethroned Western supremacy in international commerce, business, and trade. Judging by the number of Western scholarly contributions in *Administrative Science Quarterly, Strategic Management Journal,* and *Academy of Management Review,* only less than 3 percent of the publications dealt with Japanese domestic and international firms and their employees. The journals were investigated between 1980 and 1994. Books rather than journals written by established Japanese management scholars discuss these issues. In other words, Westerners' silence about Japanese economic superiority and contributions may be an admission of the inevitable but bitter reality.

Abo (1994), Aoki and Dore (1994), and Mason and Encarnation (1994) have tried to analyze the centrality of the Japanese management and economic system. They found out, through introspection, that during the 1990s, management scholars, companies, industry associations, and government agencies tried to better understand what made Japanese companies successful. Having analyzed the cultural trappings in foreign and domestic circles, they found the answer to their question in a report delivered by the Japan Federation of Employees (Doyukai, 1992). The answer broke down managerial practices into two categories:

> Practices with positive benefit and practices with uncertain or no benefit. These in turn, were broken into two classes each: (a) practices with certain benefit that ought to be strongly promoted in overseas operations and practices that ought to be maintained domestically and applied overseas where possible and (b) practices with uncertain benefit that should only be applied in Japan and practices that ought to be done away with even in Japan (*Academy of Management Review,* 1996: 565).

These five analysts arrived at these conclusive observations after respectively analyzing the firm as a system that uses employee training, incentive systems, research and development, corporate groupings, career employment, seniority promotion, and enterprise unions. In addition, these conclusive observations were the work of integrated interdisciplinary scholarship by Japanese, Europeans, and North Americans in fields of political science, sociology, and economics. Anthropologists and psychologists were not used. Their contributions could have enhanced a more balanced analysis. Evidently, this study proved that a majority of international Japanese corporations are reluctant multinationals whose economic transplantation could, if poorly managed, threaten their own productivity and survival. However, because Japan has managerially been able to deal with diverse elements of its organizational management, it continues to remain economically competitive and relatively dominant.

By authoring *Management in China During the Age of Reform,* Child (1994) has convincingly argued that although Chinese management theory and practice have been a rudimentary rather than an established discipline in recent years, the last 18 years of their economic and administrative reform have witnessed the evolution of organizational management theory and practice that have enhanced the scale of organizational change and development. The reformed transformation of economic and administrative practice of the Chinese system have contributed to making China to become the third largest global economic power, after the United States and Japan.

Since 1984, 'developments in the management of state-owned enterprises'...operated 'on a national scale." To view management through national rather than through complex Chinese culture, regional variation, history, politics, social heritage and size and diversity of China's heterogeneity is a monumental management feat. This complex form of heterogeneity has contributed to certain unique types of organizational forms of which leadership, decision making structures, input-output transactions, the role of management, human resource management, joint-ventures, and compensation are but only a few classic elements of Chinese organizational innovation.

In spite of all these influences, the most powerful ideas and values of Chinese management style have been those advanced by Confucius and Chairman Mao Zedung (Child, 1994). Confucian ideas are traditional and Mao's are modern. The integration of these ideas into Chinese management philosophy and organizational rationality has contributed to the flexibility of organizations and the vitality of China's economic system.

From the traditionalist perspective, Chinese ethical and moral philosophy of organizational and administrative management is rooted in Confucian Analetics (Lun-yü) and thought. Confucius (551-479 BC) was a venerable master teacher whose dialogues and sayings were collectively reconstructed by his disciples for cultural empowerment and organizational theory. These teachings (Analetics) became the basis of social and political order. In principle, the Analetics defended the way (tao) of antiquity and the ancients. They became the ethical and moral foundation of Chinese society when the piety and vitality of old religions and ritual practices which governed social and political intercourse had been eroded.

Given that kind of erosion of Chinese moral fiber, the stability, and orderly development of society was threatened. To fill the vacuum and avoid social instability, disorder, and anomie, Confucianism provided moral and ethical justification for humane consciousness (Flew, 1979).

Confucianism presupposed that the pyramidal structure of the old society was consonant with the natural moral order. The onus of that order assumed that each individual was responsible for the moral obligations inherent in his position (son, father, subject, ruler, etc.) (Flew, 1979). The cardinal virtue (jen) is "benevolence or humanity." Benevolence (humanity) is the homophone of Chinese for "man." Man, that is, jen or benevolence embraces all the moral qualities of the real man. The qualities of real or true manhood include "loyalty, reciprocity, dutefulness, filial and fraternal affection, courtesy, good faith, and friendship" (p. 72). This is a philosophy of familism. Although Confucius knew that he had failed to popularize and institutionalize his (these) teachings, his students (disciples) reconstructed them, for cultural diffusion and institutional fusion. Mencius (371-289 BC) successfully used neo-Confucianism (Confucian morality) to argue that human nature is innately good and rulers should capitalize on that form of goodness to reproduce a Confucian society.

Though Confucian morality and capitalism are inconsistent, the utilization of capitalistic forms of production, organizational functionalism, and scientific management have been synergistically influenced with the politically Maoist, collectivistic, and scientifically socialistic values of a reformed command economy. That economy uses free enterprise practices, in an ideologically hostile, totalitarian, and communistic climate to foster modern forms of economic capitalism and organizational rationality, bureaucratic hierarchy and productivity. China's reformist strategy can be explained in the light of politicians, rather than business entrepreneurs or corporate leaders, who have made decisions in the context of complex institutional norms and rules. In spite of the dominance of the political elite in economic decision making and in growth oriented Chinese economic enterprise, the economic logic of the transition to market oriented economy has demonstrated that these policy makers have limited abilities related to the management of economic expansion. Regardless of this conflicting element in "Sino-socioeconomic egoism," both the dynamics and dilemmas of the Chinese political economy are better explained in the context of market competition and free enterprise rationalism (Yang, 1996). Since collectivist centralization has been replaced with fiscal decentralization, the Chinese market has not only become highly segmented, but that form of capitalist economic segmentation has led to the evolution of political involvement in the management of economic productivity and industrial reforms. The game-theory role the U.S. played to make China an ally and dispel the fears of Soviet expansionism and enhance Americo-Japanese global economic compatibility has not only contributed to the economic and political stability in South East Asia, but that form of geostrategic thinking has contributed to the friendly and capitalistic China which has peacefully gradually, and permanently helped in the containment and dissolution of the USSR (Langlois and Langlois, 1996). While the degree of friendship with China is measurably enigmatic, the dissolution of the U.S.S.R. is an irreversible dialectic.

A question may be raised concerning the collapse of the centrally-administered Soviet system and the clear sustainability of the Chinese one though both systems had employed far reaching reformist measures for their own viability. Why did China's central political and administrative hierarchy remain intact in the wake of Soviet collapse? Viewed from a neo-institutional model of the breakdown of authority within hierarchies (Solnick, 1996), or from an agency model of hierarchy, the Soviet system created a political context in which property rights remained ambiguous, authority relations were unclear, and risk sharing climate prevailing under communism persisted after its demise. Given these conditions of the model, decentralizing and modernizing reforms were so powerful and far reaching that they triggered the system's "bank run" or "big bang" or "shock therapy" (Solnick, 1996; Langlois and Langlois, 1996). Consequently, Soviet local agents held organizational assets under their control. The reputation-preserving strategies of central authority became too eroded to warrant, rather than avert, system disintegration. Soviet political, bureaucratic, industrial, state, fiscal and military hierarchies collapsed. It should be made clear that these reforms shifted substantial autonomy from central to local field agents. In spite of the collapse in the USSR, by contrast, and as it was mentioned earlier, the Chinese center "preserved both its capacity for monitoring and its reputation for disciplinary transgressions, and for the rise of hybrid ownership forms that made expropriation of state and party assets far less attractive" (Solnick, 1996, Abstracts). In other words, under a reformist climate, the integrative management of communist Chinese political, economic, military, bureaucratic and fiscal affairs at the national, regional, and local levels legitimized the powers of the centrally entrenched political elite who have been responsible for system management, transitional change, political stability, and economic growth. The successful management of the diverse elements of Chinese society in its critical moment of transition to market reforms was superior strategic planning. This is dialectical and paradoxical (Handy, 1994).

Paradox is a central feature of modern life. While the Chinese case survived as a paradox, the Russian case collapsed and vanished due to gradual and internal decay of the system (Sagini, 1994). In other words, Russian political, military, and bureaucratic elite failed disastrously to innovatively manage internal economic and ideological forces upon which the structure and culture of society rested on. In the absence of a strong economic and unifying ideological force, the cleavages of ethnicity, racism, class, nationalism, and economic hopelessness "widened perilously only to invite the collapse and fall of the empire." Russians were poor power managers of diversity and irresponsible imperialists than the Chinese. Confucianism, collectivistic Maoism, and capitalist ideas and ideals have synergistically been used by the Chinese to enhance economic reforms. Chinese political leadership is culturally, philosophically, and ecologically proficient in the sense of being able to digest the diverse elements of Chinese society and integrate them for organizational synergy and culturally designed economic productivity.

Women and Racial Minorities in Organizations

Jacobson (1995) has reviewed two books which deal with a multidisciplinary, feminist, global, and scholarly approach that is very revealing about the challenging role of women in management. In this endeavor, she has articulated individual and organizational issues which women of color who are managers face. She penetratingly portrays a situation as characterized by "stress, romantic relationships in the workplace, and work-family role conflict; and systemic issues ... discrimination and legal and political realities faced by women managers" (Jacobson, 1995, p. 742).

The literature on the subject has mixed and inconclusive findings concerning the role of women in management. First, some scholars argue that although there are very few women executives, many will climb the ladder of promotions as they acquire seniority. Lack of enough women in executive positions is a form of inequality between men and women. In spite of such concerns for equality of social mobility, scholarly research has not found any significant differences between women's and men's management styles. Global competition has influenced American corporate sector to adopt a 'human resources approach...emphasizes interpersonal communication, collaboration, and the development of subordinate potential' (Jacobson, 1995: 743). In addition, the fact that American men and other men have started to participate more liberally in "family matters, flextime, telecommuting, organizationally offered day care" (p. 743) and, given the implications and potential of demographic shifts, organizations are being influenced to promote women for the sole purpose of meeting their needs as managers.

Even if this were not the case, there is evidence to suggest that "overt and subtle discrimination against women" (p. 743) in the workplace will continue for quite some time. Their uniqueness in family responsibilities could be a factor that exacerbates discrimination against them. Also, workplace forces such as "occupational segregation, relocation as a job requirement, the seemingly lower expectations of women vis-a-vis men, and pay differentials" (p. 744) are forces that are used to discriminate against women.

Management is also segregated. "Women managers have been recruited and hired primarily to manage other women" (p. 744). As a feminist scholar, Jacobson feels that organizations are hegemonically male oriented because both males and masculinely constructed organizational norms and values tend to be not only dominant but also "monolithic" vestiges of organizational socialization. To encourage an atmosphere of community and cooperation, Martin (whom Jacobson cited) de-emphasized "winning and losing, status differences, and invidious comparisons" (p. 744). Martin also asserted that democracy and participation should be made to animate organizational life, subordinate groups, and "organizational nurturance and caring" (p. 744). Baum and Singh (1994) argue that organizations that overly display inequality practice satisficing rather than optimizing evolutionary tendencies. Satisficers are normal planners while optimizers are efficient planners. Through their organic evolution (adaptation and problem solving) or learning, and adaptation, the organizations can change their course. In other words, corporate restructuring (Donaldson, 1994) should be made a continual process of adaptation. These organizations employ wisdom which "is the capacity to endure despair, and ... endure despair means to face and to bear the hopelessness" (p. 265).

In this case, nonevolutionary organizations, or organizations which do not deconstructively change are more likely to create and perpetuate weak personal networks of women and minorities in management than those which do. In other words, it is evidently arguable that the organizational context in which interaction networks are embedded produces unique constraints on women and racial minorities. These organizational constraints cause the networks of these minorities to differ from those of their white male counterparts (Ibarra, 1993). They differ in composition and characteristics of their relationships with network members. These constraints make organizational contexts to directly or indirectly affect the personal networks and strategies of these women and minorities. In the light of such circumstances, women and minorities make strategic decisions in a structurally and functionalistically limiting but scarcely "navigable" work place environment. The networks in question tend to "allocate a variety of instrumental resources that are critical for job effectiveness and career advancement as well as expressive benefits such as friendship and social support" (Ibarra, 1993, p. 56).

The Role of Woman in American State Government

During the nationalist phase of United States of America, the political scene was fully dominated by the male. The women had no chance to participate in politics. It is hard to believe that they only got the right to vote in 1920. Before that, women were even devoid of their right to participate in such fields like welfare, education, and in many other social activities and organizations. But once they were progressively allowed to participate, they tended to excel and compete like men. At present women are trying to be at par with them in the political race. They are interested in almost every aspect of American politics but their progress in American State Government is particularly remarkable.

Nowadays, if we focus our attention on state houses and senates we can observe a significant number of female legislators in comparison to their negligible number seen a few years back. For example, in Washington State Senate, of the 49 legislators, 22 are female. They now also hold 4 of every 10 seats in Washington State legislature. In other states, they are not very far behind. Among them are Arizona, Colorado, Connecticut, Minnesota. Here, they occupy 3 of every 10 seats. This indicates that people are accepting the leadership of women at legislative levels.

But things were not easy as they are now. Woman had to struggle hard to achieve their present position. Before their arrival at this level, women received little or no attention from their counterparts, even on such issues like maternity leave, domestic violence and divorce law. The women in state houses also used their votes to tip the balance in favor of a bill raising the minimum wage and also enact laws that require life imprisonment without the possibility of parole for someone convicted of two violent crimes. The women also passed a bill that requires the police to make an arrest when some violence occurs.

The influence of female lawmakers is gradually increasing as seen when they have been credited with more and more governmental responsibilities to state government. Overall, women hold 1593 of the nation's 7,424 state legislative seats (21.5%) and they hold 24 top legislative posts nationally. But the scene was different 20 years back when they only possessed 10% of the national total and a handful of top legislative posts. In 1975, only 604 (8%) served in state government.

Since the early 1970s, each election has raised the percentage of female legislators by a point or two. At present 60% of female legislators are Democratic and 40%, Republican. This difference may be due to economically and socially constructed political ideology. Unquestionably, women are the critical mass of today's political power. No longer can they be ignored. Now, their political power may tip the balance of forces on either side, on any issue. In other words, in spite of their relatively less influence in private organizations, their dynamic influence in the public arena is not a thing of the past.

The participation of women in American politics is in pubertal stage in comparison to man's political experience, but their progress in this field surely draws attention from every politically-conscious citizen. They are gradually bringing down the gender gap closer. In the next decade or so, they might be fighting neck to neck with men in state and Federal legislatures. And it would not be surprising to see a woman as President of the United States of America in future. Women's freedom of access to political opportunity and freedom to attain status for governance is an expression of organizational and cultural diversity.

Instrumental Resources

With the use of an expressive "network analytic literature" (Fombrum, 1992; Monge and Eisenberg, 1987; Tichy, Tushman, and Fombrun, 1974), views concerning minorities and gender in formal and informal (emergent) settings of network organizations have been observed for analysis and reflection. The network organizations with which the analysis will place emphasis are the informal or emergent organizations. The two different levels of analysis of the emergent networks are systemwide (organizational) network and personal network.

Instrumental network relationships or ties develop "in the course of work role performance and involve the exchange of job-related resources, including information, expertise, professional advice, political access, and material resources" (Ibarra, 1993: 59). Instrumental ties also include developmental relationships or ties that enable the worker to function in his/her "career direction and guidance, exposure to upper management, help in getting challenging and visible assignments, and advocacy for promotion" (p. 59). Instead of exclusively depending on one mentor or sponsor for access to the benefits which obtain, individual workers usually devise multiple mentoring relationships (Hill, 1991; Thomas, 1990). In spite of the overlapping instrumentalism of network contacts and formally prescribed relationships, the former are not limited to the latter. For instance, peer ties often are a major source of instrumental support and developmental advice (Hill, 1992; Kotter, 1982).

The difference between instrumental and expressive network relationships is very important. First, the nature of the relationship gives a definition of the primary resource that is being exchanged. This happens in the context of structural and limiting constraints mentioned earlier. Second, on the basis of network literature, "conflicting types of relationships and personal networks provide access to instrumental versus expressive benefits" resources (Ibarra, 1993: 60). Any investigative inquiry which does not take into consideration the two types of this dialectical and concomitant network of relationships will be impartial and inconclusive. In addition and spuriously speaking, a variety of ties could be multidimensional rather than instrumental and expressive per se.

Expressive Resources

In essence, expressive network relationships involve the exchange of friendship and social support and care characteristic of higher levels of closeness and trust than those relationships that are exclusively instrumental (Ibarra, 1993). Since people "have more leeway in choosing their friends, expressive relationships tend to be less closely bound to formal structure and work roles" (p. 59). Under normal conditions, a large variety of network relationships are both instrumental and expressive. For instance, most Japanese management executives may establish mentor protégé relations that enhance opportunities "for career advancement and psychological support" (Ibarra, 1993: 59; Kram, 1988; Thomas, 1990). As noted by Lincoln and Miller (1979: 106) friendship networks are not merely sets of linked friends but also "systems for making decisions, mobilizing resources, concealing or transmitting information, and performing other functions closely allied with work behavior and interaction." The "degree to which a personal network provides access to instrumental and expressive resources is contingent upon characteristics of the individual contacts and of the relationship among parties to the network" (Ibarra, 1993: 60).

Characteristics of Personal Networks

The extent to which a personal network provides access to instrumental and expressive resources is based on the characteristics of individual contacts and on the ties of the network members. Network theory delineates characteristics of personal networks that are "associated with a variety of costs and benefits" (p. 60). The characteristics have implications for access to network benefits at two levels of inquiry. First, benefits may come directly from particular dyadic relationships. Second, benefits stem from the indirect access provided by the contact as well as from structural features of the entire network. In the work of limited time and energy for network evolution and maintenance (Wellman, 1988), network individuals should be expected to manage basic tensions arising from the network relationships that provide access to a variety of benefits and resources.

The Composition of the Network

The characteristics and scope of opportunities for personal network depend on network composition (organizational or identity) group connections. Organizational groups include "hierarchical levels and functional or departmental subunits; identity groups include gender, racial, and ethnic groups" (Ibarra, 1993: 60). These groups are appropriately relevant because differences and commonalities rooted in ascribed (formal) attributes and available resources determine the nature of intra organizational intercourse (Blau, 1982). Likewise, identity characteristics produce common interests and world views and best explains the spontaneous ties for interpersonal attraction (Marsden, 1988; McPherson and Smith-Lovin, 1987). In these relationships, the structural and functional interdependencies that arise from vertical and horizontal mobility, by contrast, enable individuals to establish "links and ties" for having access to labor opportunities whose market has scarce resources (Laumann, Galaskiewicz, and Marsden, 1978; Lincoln, 1982).

When organizational and identity group members interact in pairs that are interpersonally similar in communication, behavioral predictability, and that exercise mutual trust and reciprocity (Kanter, 1977; Lincoln and Miller, 1979), the pairs become homophiliacs. Homophiliacs view the world in the same way. They derive instrumental and expressive benefits in the same way because they share demographic characteristics within the "chain-command" of the network connections (Kaplan, 1984; South, Bonjean, Markham, and Corder, 1982; Tsui and O'Reilly, 1989). During periods of uncertainty and turbulence individuals direct their networking strategies to those who have comparable personal attributes (Galaskiewicz and Shatin, 1981; Kanter, 1977). When the network of interaction is restricted to some network members, such an action makes it difficult for information to be received from the various parts of the system.

The degree of diversity contained in the personal network is called range (Burt, 1982). While homophily is a restrictive and narrow network relationship, range is a broad network of relationships. The range provides greater access to instrumental resources than the homophily. Evidence suggests that people whose network contacts extend beyond their required places of work (work flow interactions), immediate work groups, or immediate work units tend to be perceived as more powerful (Blau and Alba, 1982; Brass, 1984). Similarly, "a network that includes peers, superiors, superiors of superiors, subordinates, and subordinates of subordinates provides greater support for the implementation of a manager's agenda and the development of power" (Ibarra, 1993: 61). According to Lin (1982) and Brass (1984), network contacts with an organization's "dominant coalition" is an important correlate of perceived power and future promotion. Broad-ranging networks rather than narrow-ranging networks, take more time and effort to develop and maintain than those drawn from a more restricted group. For instance,

> Semantically, though the term homophily is commonly used to mean individual preferences or characteristic of a dyadic nature, it can also be used to describe the whole plethora of personal network. Range also is used to describe relationships on standard deviations or variation. In respect to the former:
> Homophily and range may not always be strongly correlated: When the variable of interest is multivariate, rather than bivariate (e.g., peer, superior, or subordinate versus male/female), the negative correlation between homophily and range can be diminished substantially. For example, two managers who have the same proportion of network relationships within their departments have equally homophilous networks (from an organizational group standpoint) but may differ dramatically in range, depending on the extent to which the remaining network contacts are different organizational groups" (Ibarra, 1993: 61).

Tie

Tie power or strength is a function of "the amount of time, the emotional intensity, the intimacy (mutually confiding), and reciprocal services that characterize the tie" (Granovetter, 1973: 1361). In reality, tie strength is the balance of personal network relationships that are characterized by closeness, stability and restrictiveness as opposed to weaker, superficial and emotionless investment. Ties can be multiplex— i.e., involve the exchange of multiple resources like job-related advice and friendship for career support and mobility.

In organizational settings, strong ties are instrumentally beneficial. They bond similar people who are connected. The disadvantage of strong ties is that information obtained through them is redundant because it instrumentally contributes to gross forms of inefficiency. In spite of their expressive nature, strong ties between co-members of an organization also serve a range of significant instrumentally oriented functions. For instance, tie links to powerful organizational people could be centrally critical to organizationwide networks (Brass, 1984; Ibarra, 1992). Through intense influence and persuasion, strong ties can be used to provide assistance during crisis or uncertain situations (Granovetter, 1982; Kaplan, 1984; Krackhardt, *in press*). Frequent transactions of strong ties reinforce trust, predictability, and persistence as opposed to transactions conducted through weaker ties (Ibarra, 1993). Above all, "the strength of a tie is indexed as some combination of frequency of contact, level of closeness, and degree of reciprocity" (p. 63).

Weak ties, in spite of their infrequency, relative casualness, and emotionlessness are channels through which socially distant ideas, influences, or information reach the organizational individual and the system at large. The value of these ideas, influences and information lies in the weakness of the relationship rather than the conflict in the relationship.

Density

Density is the extensiveness of interaction or contact between and among the members of an individual's personal network (Marsden, 1990). Density is high if an individual's network connections or contacts are closely linked with each other. Density may have weak ties and sparse networks for interaction with other individuals or groups that provide various or specific resources (Aldrich, 1989). Low density is indicative of "efficiency or maximal coverage in return for the time and energy invested in maintaining a finite set of relationships" (Ibarra, 1993: 64). By contrast, densely fixed "networks provide greater social support and solidarity" (p. 64). Personal networks may be completely connected or completely disconnected (Burt, 1983). Density is specifically useful for enabling individuals to distinguish the relationship between and among different segments of the personal network. Generally speaking, strong tie sets "constitutes a high-density subnetwork, whereas a set of weak ties will constitute a low density subnetwork" (p. 64). Large groupings are called friendship clusters or resource-dense clusters (e.g., primary work dense or executive committee). These resource dense clusters are inherently redundant but powerful cliques in organizational settings. In spite of their power and influence, they cannot effectively exercise social control over the structurally untrusted but/and influential brokers who try to penetrate the "organizational mind" and assert their influence for gaining expressive and instrumental resources.

In the context of density, a person's contacts are mutually interconnected. These contacts cannot be played off at each other in negotiations, and the person cannot broker relations between the contacts in question (Burt, 1982, 1992). Vocal and radical individuals loose power but keen managers broker and make deals to enhance effective organizational management in decision-making (Kanter, 1989).

In brief, homophily, range, tie strength, and density are inter and intra connected in conceptual and empirical subnetworks. Conceptually, all these network units share the notion of access to different or diverse viz-a-viz redundant resources. Empirically, homophilous ties are stronger than heterophilous ones particularly when it involves individuals who have a diversity rather than homophilous experience. In other words, similarity in homophily, tie, density and range builds intimacy and networks that are characterized by strong ties. Also, broad-ranging networks have weak ties because their members are loosely interconnected (Granovetter, 1982; Marsden, 1990). It should be made clear that instrumental and expressive benefits can be "gained from mutually exclusive features of personal networks, and all managers, regardless of race and gender (Ibarra, 1993), need to negotiate by making deals and trade-offs in order to balance dialectical issues or competing tensions for the development of an optimally constructive network. Evidently, the relationships that evolve through these types of networks in terms of their implications to individual accessibility to "expressivism" and "instrumentalism" varies for men and women and, for whites and minorities.

Situation centered structural or organizational contexts influence the structure of women's and minorities' personal networks. Indirectly, the same contexts help to shape interaction dynamics between race and gender groups. Consequently, these groups influence network characteristics, roles, and interaction dynamics whose interplay contributes to limiting the "victim's" alternatives that are used for shaping network strategies.

By contrast to situation centered contexts, person centered contexts are dispositional situations which place emphasis on individual differences in preferences or skills. These individual differences in preferential skills include personality characteristics and socialization patterns. Structurally, it can be argued that "characteristics of the organizational and societal situations in which individuals operate, rather than their traits, account for most observed differences (Ibarra, 1993: 65). Essentially, what is regarded as individual preferences in network decision-making could be a product of human interaction through which men, women, whites, and minorities, in the U.S.A.'s case, express themselves.

Organizationally, women and minorities share three main commonalities. First, both groups are numerical minorities within societal and organizational power elites (Morrison and Von Glinow, 1991). Second, minorities and women experience negative stereotypes and "Attributions concerning work-related competencies or aptitudes and fitness for managerial responsibilities" (Ibarra, 1993: 66). Third, both groups are prejudicially relegated to lower social status in society. As a comparatively and relatively poorer and collectively more numerous political collectivity, minorities and women can translate their class status into political power and use it to restructure organizational and economic opportunity for themselves. The Clinton-Gore administration is a classic reflection of the political marriage between minorities and women whose union was not only harmful to Dole-Kemp camp, but, whose union could be used to restructure and reform economic opportunity for the "new majority."

Contextual Effects on Personal Network Structure

Structurally, two principles determine the gender and race differences in interaction in organizational settings. First, social relations occur within an opportunity context that determine the type of social contacts. Though people tend to interact with others who are like them, this type of contact is highly constrained by the availability of similar others within the various subnetworks that accept the individual. Second, demographically, the higher the correlation of one of the group members in the network nexus, the "greater the social distance among members of any given group, producing a constricted opportunity context for interaction" (p. 66).

There are four ways of understanding opportunity in terms of formal structure and organizational demography. In relation to minority's and women's work-setting network issues...

> the extent to which women and racial minorities are present in any particular organizational context...the extent to which women and racial minorities are represented in the upper echelons of the firm...the extent to which functional or departmental groups are segregated by sex or race, such that group members are systematically overrepresented in certain subunits and underrepresented in others; and...the mobility and turnover rates of minority relative to majority group members. Because within most American corporations, women and minorities are still relatively underrepresented in positions of power and authority (p. 66).

Above all, the organizational factors that influence or determine operational behavior could be reflectively viewed "as moderators of the relationship between race and gender and network structure" (p. 66). In terms of the effects of the composition of the network, the exclusion of minorities and women from interaction networks is due to a universal preference for homophily or interaction with other people whose race and sex is the same. In other words, and demographically speaking, the social system puts constraints on the practice of individual preference by selectively limiting access. As a result of the dominant homophilous practices, women and minorities have a smaller set of "similar others" (p. 67) from whom and with whom they can professionally interact (networkwise) and advance.

Based on minority and women interaction networks, any potential preference for interacting with "same-sex or same-race" (p. 67) persons is greatly constrained by their availability. Given this reality, it can be theorized that women and minorities have a meager percentage of same-sex or same-race network ties than their white male counterparts. In addition, identity group homophily and range of organizational subunits that are represented in the network will be positively associated for women and people of color than for white men. Third, identity group homophily and positional power of network contacts will be negatively associated for women and other minorities as opposed to white men. Since women and minorities have fewer strong and multiplex ties than their white male counterparts, the former's networks are less stable than the latter's. Also, given the fact that women's and minorities' networks are sparser than those of white men, the former have a higher proportion of same-sex/same-race network contacts than the latter. Paradoxically, and based on the expectations of their structural availability, this is an anomaly. Since important cross-sex and cross-race relationships are weaker and less permanent than homophilous ones, women and minorities are less likely than their white male counterparts to share network ties with their most critical network contacts. Finally, it is quite evident that weak ties have less instrumental value for women and people of color than they do for white male counterparts. Figure 7.1 and Figure 7.2 help to illustrate the categories of structural constraints that challenge women's and minority interaction networks.

Network Strategies for Advancement

In spite of the existing constraints that restrict a person's rage of options, structure is not totally deterministic of the individual's potential for mobility. Individuals have a role to play in structuring social networks to achieve their goals and maximize rewards and benefits. Different people use a variety of ways to pursue their goals and calculations by gaining access to certain benefits regardless of cost. In other words, they use strategies that are alternatives shaped by the social context in spite of its apparent, deterministic, and structural functionalism or internal colonialism (Kennedy, 1996). As they pursue their goals, minorities and women use strategies and make choices and trade-offs in order to circumvent certain network dilemmas. One of the common strategies they use is functional differentiation of the networks. This works like this:

> In order to be effective in their jobs without forfeiting access to social benefits "and negative costs" associated with close work relationships and

Figure 7.1. Summary Model of Factors that Shape the Personal Networks of Women and Minorities

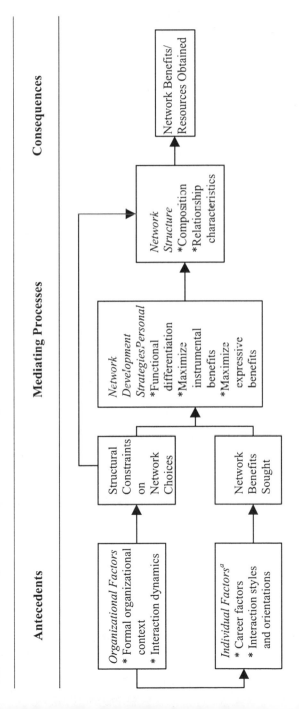

Antecedents   Mediating Processes   Consequences

[a]Indicates that an extensive review of individual factors is not provided in this chapter.

Source: Ibarra, H. (1993). Personal Networks of Women and Minorities in Management: A Conceptual Framework. *Academy of Management Review,* 18, 1, Figure 2.

Figure 7.2. A Social Trap Model of Trap Model of Diversity Management

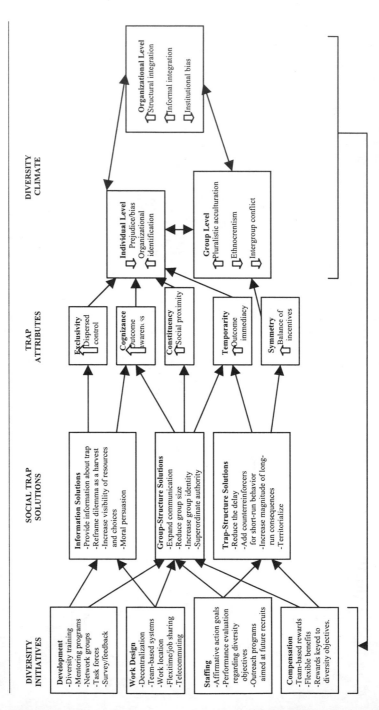

Source: Barry, B. (1996). A Social Trap Analysis of the Management of Diversity. *Academy of Management Review*, 21, 3, page 771.

critical advice from others who share similar experiences, many women and minorities logically choose to navigate a course between two different social circles. A functionally differentiated network, therefore, includes a homophilous circle or relationships that provide expressive benefits as well as alternate channels for information and advice...ties to the majority group constitute a second circle, cultivated to provide access to important organizational resources and information (Ibarra, 1993: 75).

Also, the extent to which two circles may overlap or have common members of the same network assumes a homophilous relationship. In respect to this phenomenon, Ibarra (1992) observed that homophilous women largely selected other women to be their friends and sources of support. The same women heavily depended on "men for professional advice and as sources of influence, but got organizational information from roughly equal members of their male and female contacts" (Ibarra, 1993: 75). As opposed to the two previous statements, Ibarra (1993), Bell (1990) found that career oriented black women who had very few homophilous relationships had nonoverlapping instrumental and expressive circles.

The strategy of functional differentiation has high costs and benefits. Managing a differentiated social structure is not only time consuming but also stressful. It is stressful due to the fact that "moving too close to either circle can lead to guilt, feelings of alienation, and loss of resources or support from the other group" (p. 75). Stress usually originates from conflicting information and advice regarding career decision and job performance. In brief, when a person uses a functionally differentiated strategy it indicates that a preponderance of uniplex relationships will be concentrated on due to the reduction in the benefits associated with strong and multiplex ties (Ibarra, 1992). When a person seeks to maximize on either instrumental or expressive benefits rather than both, the person becomes more effective because he/she manages the uniplex network with ease as opposed to the more complex and functionally differentiated multiplexity.

Some of the unintended consequences of managing the functionally differentiated network could be like this: "liking and support are the direct resources exchanged via friendship ties, friends' instrumental contacts may be viewed as indirect resources for the focal individual" (Ibarra, 1993: 75). The dilemma for both women and minorities is that gender and race have greater influence on expressive ties. In addition, organizationally, instrumental and expressive networks tend to be interconnected. Hence, at the organalytic (organizational analysis) level, closeness in one network increases the chances of closeness in the network. Evidently, Lincoln and Miller (1979) and Ibarra (1992) observed that functionally differentiated strategies have unintended consequences that contribute to the reduction of women's centrality and viable visibility in organizationally inclined expressive networks.

It should be noted that differentiation does not necessarily imply that expressive support may be obtained only in homophilous relationships or that homophilous relationships cannot provide access to instrumental resources. However, for female and minority managers, most instrumental access is obtained through heterophilous relationships that, under normal circumstances, are weaker in expressive resources.

Frequently, intergroup interaction dynamics may make it difficult to maintain two different work related social circles. Organizational tokens are pressured to avoid interaction with or turn "against members of their own group as demonstrations of loyalty to the dominant group and their 'fit' with the corporate culture" (Ibarra, 1993: 76). These tokens also experience intergroup sanctions against those who align themselves with "the men" or "the white boys" (p. 76). In other words, elitist organizational women and people of color could be "prisoners" of their own consciousness. In other words, although they are free to talk about or write about, or handle situations in a manner consistent with their beliefs, the sanctions placed on accepted tokenism could be so socially and psychologically binding that minorities and women might find themselves to be professionally risky but tolerable.

Kanter (1977) has argued that functional differentiation theory or strategy requires the availability of "similar others" for the "skewed" versus "tilted" organizational contexts to be perceived as either extreme or less extreme respectively. For instance, skewed organizational contexts are viewed as creating severe dilemmas as more women and minorities gain positions of power and influence. In this case, and proportionally speaking, a minority group is negatively related to its frequency of contact with and amount of social support received from the majority (South et al., 1982). In turn, this behavioral relationship effectively serves to diffuse biased accusations (Ridgeway, 1991).

As observed by Cox, Lobel, and McLead (1991), Asians, African Americans and Hispanics tend to be more "collectivist-cooperative" (Ibarra, 1993: 77) as opposed to "individualistic" (p. 77) Anglo-persons. Though these behavioral differences are culturally attributable, structural analysts interpret them to be "a manifestation of deference to higher status others" (Ibarra, 1993: 77). The implications of this kind of behavior on Western and American bureaucratic, industrial management, and corporate culture could be contradictory at least and futuristically ineffective at most. However, one way of responding to such behavior is to do further research on comparative cross-cultural studies and use the findings from the behavior of culturally diverse groups for policy construction by top management in organizations (Riordan and Vandenberg, 1994). Second, research scholars should try to find out why problems, dilemmas, and obstacles which face minorities and women are rooted in the structure of organizations rather than in the personal characteristics or attributes of individuals. Third, the research should empirically and methodologically concentrate on emergent (informal) interaction patterns and the impact of such interaction on organizationally and normatively sanctioned exclusionary practices. Minorities and women should influence organizations to learn that "all roads lead to Rome."

Fourth, in recent times, more women than racial minorities have taken management positions though they are equally discriminated against in wages, promotions, tenure, and in entry into scientifically oriented professional disciplines (Barber, 1995; Ibarra, 1993). Though "white women interact frequently with white men in their daily lives, racial minorities tend to be segregated from whites outside the workplace" (Ibarra, 1993: 82). This happens because normatively established socialization patterns of mainstream culture reinforce cross-sex interaction rather than interracial interaction. Hill (1991) has argued that because there are difficulties that are unique to cross-gender interaction, these difficulties make organizational men to be sensitive to "workplace interactions, potential sexual tension and public perceptions of a sexual relationship" (Ibarra, 1993: 82). Though the social networks of single men and single women are similar, parental and family responsibilities tend to drastically alter their similarity. Fifth, since the literature or organizational research relevant to minority women and minority groups other than African Americans is scanty (Cox and Nkomo, 1990; Ely, 1991), further research on the subject could produce valuable findings that could be essential in post-industrialism. Even if that were the case, Bell (1990), Thomas (1989), and Fernandez (1981) have suggested that organizational experiences differ in intra-group and intergroup settings of minorities. Though Hispanic and Asian managers are also subjected to negative evaluations and stereotyping (Ferdman and Cortes, 1992), "they are less likely than Blacks to report exclusion from informal networks" (Ibarra, 1993: 83). Taboos associated with cross-racial sexual relationships might create a sensitive environment whose intellectual realization discourages minority women from engaging in mentoring relationships with white men (Thomas, 1989).

Cultural Masculinism

Schaum (1995) has edited Mencken's 18th and 19th century works on women and has drawn a comparative element on them with men. He has used an antifeminist stance—called heroic vitalism to portray, all along to the present century, man's prejudices against women, and how these prejudices are "naturally and culturally prescribed. The description satirizes women's intelligence, humanity, and social and cultural accomplishments. In some cases, the same author sees women as cunning slaves who use mediocre wit to cause intrigue. For instance, the following prejudicial quote is self-explanatory:

> Mencken posits the male/female relationship as fundamentally inimical, delimiting the sexes' antithetical directions in life, literature, abilities, goals, ethics and standards. The antithesis goes deeper than the clash between individuals or groups, to the very concept of "the feminine" as an element potentially within men, symbolizing the seductive forces of mediocrity, triviality of thought, domesticity (the "vegetable security" of the feminine/bourgeois home) along with materialism and libidinousness, the last an element...weaker less civilized feminine. At stake in this contest are male creativity, freedom, genius, progress toward the superman—in short, culture itself—potentially undermined by both the female without and the "female" within (Schaum, 1995: 190).

He further argues that if women become dominant in society, their practical participation in human affairs will contaminate masculine ideals of justice, honor, and truth. To contaminate human affairs effectively, women will use feminine ideals of dissimulation, equivocation, and intrigue to deceive men in order to perpetuate mediocrity and feminine myopism. Evidently, Mencken's equation of feminine with the decline of cultural and intellectual standards and psychic threat is a reflection of the well known historical and cultural tradition of misogyny. Contextually, the 20th century critical backlash to feminine growth in emancipation and influence further illuminates the psychic threat men have started to sense with the increasing and challenging influence of the modern woman.

These writings about women express an inner anger, fear, and disbelief of what had happened — "the domestication of refinement" (Clark, 1993: 738) had been shattered asunder. The values of capitalism, republicanism, and Christianity which flourished in a climate of "virtue and talents...bodily strength,...beauty, good humor, politeness and other accomplishments...auxiliary ground[s] of distinction" (p. 740) are being challenged by women and the forces of poverty and disillusionment. Among these, viewed from a domestic standpoint "commentators feed ideological debates and moral panics about the problems of crime, drugs, family values, ethno-racial balkanisation and multiculturalism" (Kennedy, 1996: 87). Externally, the end of the Cold War and the evolution of economic superpowers in Asia rather than in Europe or the Americas, has "encouraged requiems for the American Empire" (p. 87). Imperialism thrives on the interdependence of political and economic processes. These processes are "inseparable from the social relations" of production, distribution, and consumption and the "discourses of race, gender, ethnicity and class at home" (p. 88). In other words, the American domination of "international others has depended on mastering the other at home — and in oneself: an internal colonization whose achievement is fragile at best and which is often exceeded or threatened by the gender and racial arrangements on which it depends" (p. 89).

Internal colonization and the strategic racial arrangement for its maintenance has created avenues for potential instability and lack of opportunity that has made white males paranoid and fearful of their future place in society. That psychic fear is viewed to be the reactive imperial subconsciousness for the reassertion of white manhood.

In recent years, white manhood has been challenged by affirmative action that is viewed as reverse or positive and opposite discrimination. The "decline in real wages and growing job insecurity in an age of post-industrial restructuring which has deprived many of this class of the benefits long associated with capital growth" (p. 89) are factors that psychically threaten white middle-class males. They fear losing control of themselves, society and the standards they have created for themselves. They are confronting "their diminishing ability to assume normative roles of power and authority and transcend the politics of identity formation" (p. 89).

White males have become the "victim culture" (p. 100) that decries the growing polycentricism of the United States. For instance, in academia, where "canon wars" (p. 89) are being waged, the wars are viewed as attacks on "white, male, heterosexual humanities by politically correct fundamentalists who press issues ethno-racial and gender identities and difference" (p. 89). On the other hand, the assertiveness with which these academic and intellectual wars are being waged may be viewed as the challenge of masculinity by aggressive and "spiritually paralyzing" intellectual aspects of femininity. For instance, a scientific academy (culture) values manly attributes like "independence, emotional toughness, objectivity, and...rational thought" (Barber, 1995: 231). These attributes , in spite of their historic attribution to men, are increasingly being cultivated by the woman of the academy despite the fact that she is discriminated against in wages, promotions, and numerical composition in this great American organizational and scientific enterprise. Despite that form of discrimination, and based on 1990 statistical calculations by the National Science Board and the U.S. Department of Education Statistics, women have increasingly cultivated the masculine intellectual attributes that have enabled them to sizeably penetrate the "masculine intellectual empire." Though they are "tortured" before entering it, their contribution in the destruction of exclusionary systems is a feat for humankind. They need to mentor more women and minorities rather than "they themselves." After all, despite the struggle to enter and succeed in science, women have been mentored by men who were interested in their development. In return, they should or need to mentor minorities, other women, and men of good will.

This kind of masculine view of the feminine world does not influence men to see women as belonging to a different "race and subspecies," but such perceptions have become the epistemological and psychological forces that influence men to formulate domestic policies that affect the welfare of women both at home and in the market place of ideas, production, distribution, consumption and professionalism. In doing so, men contribute to the eternal colonization and control that helps to avert the threat of their decreasing authority and power in the market and society in general. In other words, men and women tend to view the world in gendered terms because they are socialized in gendered ways (Kathlene, 1995). For instance, recently, a "study of prisons and recidivism rates was presented to 47 Colorado legislators during a taped interview...Men and women in this study conceptualized the origins of and solutions to crime differently" (p. 698). These differences were interpretively understood to originate from developmentally oriented gendered socialization in Western society.

In another study (Reingold, 1996):

> Compared female and male legislators' self-reported strategies for getting bills passed, their descriptions of the bases of their own power and influence, and their orientations toward hard-ball politics. I find that these men and women were equally likely to endorse feminine or feminist leadership styles and concepts of power that stress the value of compromise, consensus-building, equality, and honesty. In addition, they were equally critical of and reluctant to participate in stereotypically masculine behavior involving hierarchically based manipulation and coercion of others. The power of institutional norms, as opposed to gender norms, of behavior is offered as the primary explanation for the lack of sex differences among the legislators (p.464).

In other words, organizations whose culture, that is, norms, procedures, practices, values, standards, expectations, and precedents, are codified or institutionalized into law may be viewed as a "constitution" from which organizational behavior, leadership norms, decision making styles and normative structure produce patterned channels through which performance is expressed and formalized. In democratic, open, and competitive societies in which the law, human rights, and the constitution have provisions that guarantee the rights of the individual, nothing less, other than the inhibition of gendered differences, could influence the "professionalism" of such high echelon political barons in their conduct as decision makers of their respective state legislatures. The constitutionality of their authority legitimized the manner in which they exercised their power including that of making decisions. The legitimization and exercise of power is a lawful and culturally inscribed process. The process is carried out by elected representatives whose role, behavior, and actions are sanctioned by law, political tradition, and institutional norms. Without the constitutional provisions for the protection of "diversity" in legislative chambers, academic halls of learning, corporate, bureaucratic, and military citadels, the environment could create a less democratic, less competitive, and more exclusionary society in terms of participatory and other endeavors. If there were no laws that could guarantee such provisional protections, racial, gender based and other laws of the jungle might prevail over participatory diversity.

Kahn (1996) of Arizona State has authored *The Political Consequences of Being a Woman: How Stereotypes Influence the Conduct and Consequences of Political Campaigns.* In her conclusions, she has argued that at present, 20 percent of seats in state legislatures are held by women. However, only 6 percent of U.S. Senate and governorships are held by women. Women's negligible inelectability to senatorial and gubernatorial offices seems to be caused by the stereotyping of women candidates in statewide and national campaigns. Having focused on candidates, the media, and voter behavior, Kahn found that state electorates perceived women not only to be politically incapable (incompetent) but they also were viewed to be a liability. "Politicizabilism" (public and political manipulation of the feminine influence which also means "poliantifeminism") were pre-electorally designed by editors and reporters before voters were "fed" with stereotypical and prejudicial perceptions. Though women candidates do not seriously, at least initially, consider such negative attitudes about their electability these stereotypes significantly contributed to limiting women's mobility in public office. Such limitation of opportunity is a denial of diversity.

Diversity in Formulation of U.S. Foreign Policy

Participatory diversity is a form of political hyperpluralism of the American Society (Ahrari, 1987). In relation to the contributions to American foreign policy by various ethnic groups in the United States, Ahrari's book *Ethnic Groups and U.S. Foreign Policy* deals with characteristics, organizations, issues, policy, and political influences which help to facilitate or stifle the influence of ethnicity in American foreign policy arena. Respectively, and in a descending order, the eight chapters of the book deal with the most and least effective ethnic influence in the global construction, through active participation of American foreign policy. One chapter deals with how pro-Israel groups restrict the influence of pro-Arab groups in constructing the various aspects of the foreign policy process. Public image stereotypes and media hype are comparatively used to show stronger and weaker competitors. In spite of the organizational, political, and media advantages, the success of pro-Israel groups is crucially determined by the congruence as opposed to the antithesis of U.S. and Israel strategic objectives and interests. The success of the pro-Israel lobby relies in asserting more effort and influence in terms of clear objectives, prudent strategies, provision of ample resources and organizational dynamics.

Contrary to the pro-Israel/Arab foreign policy controversy, the behavior of African American diplomatic and political elite, in respect to American foreign policy toward Africa, is characterized by the low priority of African issues in the foreign policy making arena. African American elite, like Americans in general, may be practicing the "policy of indifference" or the "policy of benign neglect" (Hale, 1995: 4).

Between World War II and Helsinki Accords, this period was marked by an effective organizational development of American foreign policy toward Poland. Though the nature of the policy was defined by East-West configurations, twenty senators and twenty-four members from congressional districts were equally involved in influencing American foreign policy toward Poland. In addition, elite political and intellectual operatives like former President Carter's National Security Advisor, Zbigniew Brzezinski, helped to chart Poland's new directions within the leftist and Soviet dominated geopolitical and strategic umbrella. Such calculations enabled the Polish state to opt for democratic, economic and political institutions whose ratification by the West became the genesis for the dissolution of the Soviet Empire.

Like the African American community, the Mexican or Latino Hispanic American community is very sizeably large and electorally influential. In spite of that, its influence is stronger in domestic rather than in foreign policy. They are more limited by their "low saliency" in articulating Latin American policy issues within the Mexican Americans, i.e., within their ethnic community rather than within the policy-making arena. Neither substantive, cultural, nor political issues appear to have a compelling case for effective articulation of the Mexican American role in the foreign policy concerns of the American government. Even in the formulation, articulation, and implementation of NAFTA, Hispanics may have played a minimal role, if at all.

Contrary to the behavior of Mexican American ethnic group, the Cuban Americans are more constantly aggressive in and committed to exerting their influence on American foreign policy making process. The ideological conditions of the world influenced the Carter and Reagan administrations to allow Cuban American influence in the foreign policy decision making forum. In other words, Cuban Americans' influence in American foreign policy depended on the concurrence of Cold War world views of the Cuban Americans and the specific administrations. Given this reality, the "convergence of interest...is the key variable."..."ethnic group influence is dependent and variable instead of independent and constant" (pp. 116, 132). In other words, Cuban Americans who fled Cuba because of political reasons have ideological views that concur with those of the American government in terms of what should be done to alienate Castro, destroy Cuban communism, and annex Cuba into the Western free enterprise socioeconomic system.

In the case of Irish Americans as contributors to American policy making process, they are less effective in spite of, or due to the unclarity of the issues in their foreign policy agenda, organizational ineffectiveness, and the complexity of changes in the American political structure. The historic colonization of the Irish by the British makes American approach to Irish affairs more contradictory and less clear. Both US and UK are allies whose alliance neutralizes their antagonistic perception of the Irish situation.

Finally, the growing hyperpluralism of the American polity may have enabled various ethnics to be involved in the evolution, structure, and scope of the foreign policy debate without significantly promoting it effectively. For instance, in spite of the active involvement in foreign policy construction by the ethnic elites, executive and legislative proceedings largely help to formulate the structure and scope of American foreign policy. In addition, ideological and philosophical beliefs of the U.S. and its allies must concur in terms of their "congruence of strategic interests" in order for the U.S. to successfully facilitate its foreign policy. The synergistic integration of diverse views contributes to the relative and continuous success of American diplomacy in the foreign policy debate.

If anything, ethnic contributions to this debate is not only small but also highly marginalized.

Major Theories

Organizations which are exclusive need to know about the factors that affect the "treatment of disabled individuals" in organizational settings. The model of factors that affect the treatment of organizational people includes the following:

> Person characteristics (e.g. attributes of the disabled person, attributes of the observer environmental factors e.g. legislation and organizational characteristics (e.g. norms, values, policies, the nature of jobs, reward systems) combine to affect the way disabled individuals are treated in organizations. Furthermore, the model indicates that the relationships just noted are mediated by observer's cognitions (i.e. categorization, stereotyping, expectancies, and affective state).

Finally, it is expected that the people who suffer from disability or challenge could make certain personal adjustments to "modify the observer's expectancies and organizational characteristics" (Stone and Colella, 1996, p. 352).

The organizational integration of disabled persons requires specific tasks of socialization and animation if individuals are expected to be productive. Recent management research on the subject has shown that "diversity in the composition of organizational groups affects outcomes such as turnover, and performance through its impact on affective, cognitive, communication, and symbolic processes" (Milliken and Martins, 1996: 402). Definitively, organizational diversity is rooted in observable and non-observable attributes ((Milliken and Martins, 1996). The diversity of observable characteristics include race, ethnic background, age, gender, and body size. Diversity based on the detectably less observable attributes is influenced by "education, technical abilities, functional background, tenure in the organization, socioeconomic background, personality characteristics, or values (p. 404).
The most relevant form of organizational diversity is the skills or know-how type of top management officials. See Figure 7.3 concerning diversity in the public sector.
Any type of diversity is very difficult to understand because of its inherent complexity, implicit, philosophical orientations, assumptions,

Figure 7.3. Major Sources of Advantage and Disadvantage in Managing Diversity in the Public Sector

1. *Legal:* failure to manage diversity will result in high costs of litigation as well as of diverse judgments by the courts.
2. *Costs:* the costs of doing business will be higher with failure to manage diversity—communication will be more difficult, employee involvement will be reduced, relationships will be strained if not adversarial, and so on, as organizations become more diverse.
3. *Intergroup Conflict:* a special case of costs, with broad implications for the quality of working life, labor-management relationships, the quality of unionization—conflict will be greater where managing diversity is less successful.
4. *Attractiveness to Potential and Actual Employees:* failure in managing diversity will be a major disincentive for existing as well as potential employees, which is of special significance in the public sector which has well-known disadvantages in recruitment and retention. The attractiveness holds not only for minorities, who will form large portions of the pool of employees, but also for others interested in a public work force that "looks like America."
5. *Attractiveness to Budgeting Authorities:* government agencies derive their life's blood from complex executive-legislative views of requests for appropriations, and poor performance in managing diversity may well become a growing factor in adverse reviews.
6. *Attractiveness to Clientele or Customer:* unsuccessful diversity efforts may well have direct implications for how an agency serves its clients or customers. The latter will become increasingly diverse over time, their needs presumably will be more accessible to diverse work forces and management, and the comfort level for both service provider and client/customer should increase.
7. *Attractiveness to Managers and Executives:* more managements are not only tasking subordinates with diversity goals, but performance on those goals is taken into increasing account re promotions and salary judgments.
8. *Creativity and Problem-Solving:* many observers argue that organizations successful in managing diversity will bring broader perspectives, different experiences, and lessened attachment to past norms and practices, all of which can be expected to have a positive effect on creativity and problem-solving.
9. *System Flexibility:* agencies with successful diversity efforts will be more accustomed to dealing comprehensively with a changing environment, and hence more fluid and perhaps less standardized, as well as arguably more efficient and effective in responding to environmental turbulence.
10. *System Legitimacy:* success in managing diversity is associated with core values in our political and social philosophy, and hence that success also should have regime-enhancing tendencies.
11. *System Image:* successfully managing diversity provides another opportunity for government to exercise leadership as model employer.

Sources: Golembiewski, R.T. (1995). *Managing Diversity in Organizations.* Tuscaloosa: University of Alabama Press: 47, and Gortner, H.F., J. Mahler, and J.B. Nicholson. (1997). *Organization Theory: A Public Perspective.* Harcourt Brace College Publishers: 389.

and causal beliefs "with which the more superficial or observable differences are correlated" (p. 404). Such types of diversity involve the existence of schematic (cognitively speaking) differences in consciousness, unconsciousness, thought, and conscience all of which cause coordination difficulties in organizational settings. These difficulties can, as it was mentioned earlier, be a source of organizational homogeneity and stability or, organizational heterogeneity, instability, innovativeness, and change which may come through organizational adaptation.

Scholarly opinion has suggested that more functionally diverse teams may be better linked with external networks that enable them to have access to information. Information is generated through specialized occupational diversity. As inferred earlier, occupational diversity may or may not "create interaction difficulties and a low level of behavioral integration" (p. 411).

In terms of organizational cohorts, which is a form of diversity, individuals identify with others who enter an organization or department at the same time. This cohort identification influences behavior. Also, individuals who differ from others in job classification or tenure are more likely to turn over. Employees with the shortest tenure resort to "good behavior" to compensate for their "high difference scores."

Zenger and Lawrence (1989) have found that diversity in organizational tenure is negatively related to the number of times an employee communicates with external agencies. "Variation in organizational tenure is positively related to group processes" (Milliken and Martins, 1996, p. 413) like ability to clarify goals, develop implementable plans, and prioritize objectives. It also has "an indirect positive impact...on team rated performance and a direct negative impact on adherence to budgets and schedules" (p. 413).

Diversity in group tenure is negatively, as opposed to positively, associated with group-level social integration as well as with individual integration. Though team tenure heterogeneity is supposed to reduce groupthink and increase organizational creativity and positive restructuring, scholarly evidence has shown that "diversity in group tenure may reduce social integration among group members and increase turnover" (p.414). In spite of its deterrence of homophily bias, diversity helps to structure the in-group out-group aspects of organizational dynamics that could be managed wisely to convert homosocial reproduction (groupthink) into organizational productivity.

In the United States, as in elsewhere perhaps, it is a challenge to function in a culturally diverse environment while using issues of diversity for reflective and integrative multiculturalism (Nemetz and

Christensen, 1996). For instance, recent memory has witnessed the growth of formally established diversity-training programs in the country. These programs have negatively attracted unpopular attention for their 'political correctness' and 'white-male bashing.' Viewing the individual from a multicultural niche upon which multicultural theories of the 19th and 20th centuries are rooted, radical structuralism, functionalism, functional pluralism, and other eclectical theories inform this analysis.

Burrell and Morgan (1979) have defined these isms (theories) by viewing how individuals perceive reality through polarized epistemologies. First, "polarity is labeled the sociology of regulation and the other the sociology of radical change. The term sociology of regulation refers to explanations of society that emphasize its underlying unity and cohesiveness. Sociology of radical change refers to explanations of deep seated structural conflict and modes of domination characterizing modern society" (p. 437). Organization theoreticians and analysts who try to give rationale for social relations and events by articulating the sociology of regulation are named functionalists. Those who articulatively assert the sociology of radical change are called radical structuralists (Burrell and Morgan, 1979). These diametrically opposed views make radical structuralists to articulate sudden change while functionalists defend the status quo of cohesion and stability.

Radical structuralism is a Marxist theory. The theory views capitalism and its organizations to be repressive, oppressive, and enslaving. It condemns gross economic inequality in society and views conflict resolution to be "an opiate and a tool of domination whose purpose is to prevent revolution and shift of power to the oppressed" (Nemetz and Christensen, 1996: 437). In opposition to the former theory, functionalism places paramount emphasis on the maintenance of social order and stimulation of gradual and evolutionary change in the context of problem-solving (Burrell and Morgan, 1979).

The third theory is functional pluralism. Its articulation is aimed at creating the balance through conflict and power structures of the social order. The theory places emphasis in using pluralism to control conflict and thereby build viable and consensual democratic institutions. They view conflict resolution to be a useful exercise in creative problem solving. Change comes as a result of debate and consensus. This orientation brings reform rather than revolution in the eyes of the oppressed and the oppressor alike. The existence and application of these theories in a multicultural society, as inferred earlier, creates a climate for new immigrants and all types of diverse or ethnic groups to experience assimilatory and acculturative influences that enhance "intergroup diversity on the left and absence of multicultural diversity on the right"

(Nemetz and Christensen, 1996, p. 438). Therefore, both theoretically and practically, the dialectical relationship between functionalism and radical structuralism or pluralism appear to change nothing in the light of multiculturalism. Other minor theories that influence social order and organizational behavior include but are not limited to:

1. Population variation which is the degree of interactive relationships among subgroups and their members. Emphasis is placed on separation and integration. An integrated population shows that relationships are "randomly distributed" regardless of "race, ethnicity, gender, religion, or sexual orientation" (p. 439).
2. Population separation occurs on these same categories (race, ethnicity, etc.).
3. Cultural variation is the existence of many values, behaviors, and attitudes of society.
4. Cultural particularism (similarities within a group or differences "between groups" in society); it is parochial, isolationist and prejudicial. "Solidarity is obtained against outsiders, fanaticism, obedience to a hierarchy and obliteration of individual self" (p. 439).
5. Cultural separation - e.g., Apartheid—is a condition of cultural preservation.
6. Cultural pluralism—co-existence of many cultures, minority and majority culture adopt each other's norms, or minority culture can adopt norms from both majority or, any other culture for its own identity.
7. Cultural homogenization—an integrated and modernist conception of common language, currency, and cosmopolitan behavior that is blendable into a harmonious mixture of diverse components. A culturally homogenized society minimizes group or ethnic differences by using structural institutions of society. In such a society, "religion, culture, and nationality" are marginalized in people's identities at work (Barber, 1992). Cultural homogenization is animated by "industrialization and commercialization" (Barber, 1992). In America, the culturally homogenized society is dominated by "Eurocentric and technologically driven culture" that takes advantage of minorities (Worseley, 1985). This culture, according to Bloom (1987) and Lasch (1979) wallows in the "basest instincts" ever known to humans. This elevates the individual above the group and thereby creates avenues for pathological alienation of some people and marginalizes their cultural and religious identity. Minority groups may be inevitable victims of cultural homogeneity.
8. In terms of moral philosophy, relativism and comprehensive

universalism are extensions or offshoots of multiculturalism. Relativism is moral neutrality and group and class belief of the whole community that advocates tolerance of differences that creates avenues for openness in society. The moral relativist looks for the common ground. Such relativism may create gender, racial, ethnic, and religious conflicts in total society during interaction. Due to lack of objective truth and abundant liberty, moral relativists define their cause in economic and political (power) terms that polarize the liberal democracy into "oppressors and victims" dichotomy (Nemetz and Christensen, 1996, p. 441).

9. Comprehensive universalism—is a fundamentalist school of thought that has evolutionist views that assert that certain societies are more advanced than others. Advancement is viewed as a form of Enlightenment in such issues as "freedom, equality, human rights, meritocracy and the rule of law" (p. 441).

In brief, radical structuralists use reasoning, morality, and cultural practices to choose leaders who hold power. In contradistinction, functionalists sense that the greatest societal threat is based on conflict and inability to put society together. Hence, they prefer hierarchically regulated unity and social or institutional cohesion. They advocate cultural homogenization, comprehensive universalism, population variation, and in some cases integration. For instance, in relation to integration, "American South came with the recognition that Christianity applied universally, even to slaves, but it was perfectly acceptable to separate black churches from white churches" (p. 443). Evidently, the "correlation between functionalism and separatism is unpredictable. Strong functionalist-multiculturalists tend to support culturally homogenized and comprehensively universal perspectives. In a culturally diverse organizational setting where established cultural and theoretical underpinnings influence workers' beliefs, values, attitudes and patterns of behavior, workgroup interactions can be enhanced through the construction and utilization of monolithic, plural, and multicultural organizational models that are structured, enforced and supervised for their workability, effectiveness (Larkey, 1996; Cox, 1991) and cognitive processing. Organizational models that specify work enable workers to understand and be evaluated positively while those organizations which categorize work increase misunderstanding and negative evaluations.

In some organizations, whenever duties, responsibilities and expectations are categorized rather than specified, categorization becomes an element of the social trap particularly in situations that involve management of diversity. As a resource, diversity issues originate from organizational social traps. Social traps "are situations where decision problems involve conflicts between-individuals or near term outcomes and collective or long-term consequences. The management of diversity is conceptualized in terms of the social traps created by workplace diversity issues" (Barry and Bateman, 1996, p. 757). The social trap model (Figure 7.4) identifies the defining attributes of social traps in diverse organizational environments. "Social traps are situations within which individuals or groups face the prospect of adopting seemingly beneficial behaviors that have negative consequences over time or for a larger collective" (p. 758). In other words, social traps exist when 'some of the costs or damages of what people do occur beyond their purview, and they either don't know or don't care about them' (Schelling, 1978: 112). For instance, if a common grazing pasture is overgrazed by the community's cows, "short-term individual gain-seeking behavior leads to long-term collective disaster" (Barry and Bateman, 1996, p 758). Further still:

> Like social traps, diversity issues...often require organization members to make behavioral choices that place self-interest and the interests of others in conflict,...often challenge decision makers to manage inconsistencies between the short-term and long-term consequences of the choices they make, ...may compel choice making without the benefit of explicit knowledge of the conflicts of interests and of the consequences of the choices to be made, and...typically involve social issues having substantial societal implications" (pp. 758-759).

Diversity is a human resource management issue or initiative. Issues and initiatives are expressively articulated to solve problems in the management of diversity in organizations. To solve the problems effectively, management should address such topics as "organizational demography, the dynamics of cross-gender (Raggins and McFarlin, 1990), and cross-race (Thomas, 1993), development relationships, and the impact of diversity training programs (Rosen and Rynes, 1995), the impact of diversity on work-team composition (Jackson 1992), and the development of race- and gender-based employee network groups" (Friedman, 1996).

Diversity issues, initiatives and traps are social dilemmas that are conceptualized or behavioristically perceived in terms of individual, group, or organizational frames of reference and have been articulated by Cox (1991, 1993). Cox specifies social traps in the following manner:

> Factors at the individual level include attitudes and behaviors manifesting prejudice and/or bias toward outgroups and their members, as well as

Figure 7.4. Structural Constraints on Properties of Women's and Racial Minorities' Interaction Networks

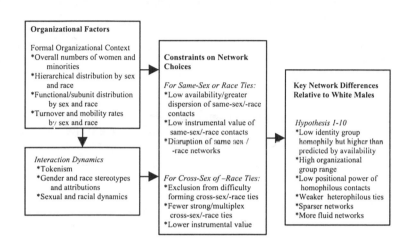

Source: Ibarra, H. (1993). Personal Networks of Women and Minorities in Management: A Conceptual Framework. *Academy of Management Review,* 18, 1, Figure 1.

attitudinal commitment to (i.e., identification with) the organization as a whole. At the group level, climate reflects the degree to which majority and minority cultures retain their identities yet achieve interdependence and mutual identity (pluralistic acculturation), group tendencies to view organizational behavior through an in-group/out-group lens (ethnocentrism), and the extent of friction between cultural groups (intergroup conflict). At the organizational level, climate encompasses diversity in the organization's hierarchy and formal structure (structural integration), the inclusion of minority-culture members in informal social networks (informal integration), and the extent to which management systems generate obstacles to minority-culture participation institutional bias) (Barry and Bateman, 1996, p. 761).

In general, Cox, Barry and Bateman have evidently argued that although there is no clear standard or criterion for assessing the effectiveness of diversity initiatives, it is empirically and behavioristically observable that workplace climates that address diversity issues and initiatives tend to enhance "career achievement and satisfaction" (p. 761) for individual organizational members. Improved climates promote organizational effectiveness and efficiency in terms of realizing "productivity, quality, less turnover, problem-solving, and profitability" (p. 761). In other words, when organizations try to eliminate social traps, they tend to motivate and empower people to maximize or optimize their performance. Organizationally, the term minority culture refers to workforce attributes like "race, gender, age, and ethnicity" (p. 765).

According to Barry and Bateman (1996), there are five main attributes which influence the trap-model of the climate of organizational diversity. These attributes are:

1. Constituency (social or psychological distance).
2. Temporality (time lapse that separates the initial effects of a person's actions from the manifestation of ultimate consequences; given the complexity of sociological and socio-cognitive issues involved in successful diversity management, solutions are gradual.
3. Symmetry (experimentally, traps are symmetric—i.e., "Each participant has a common base of personal resources to contribute and equivalent incentives; each one also stands to suffer the same consequences." Asymmetric traps are external traps (Cross and Guyer, 1980). Unlike countertraps (defence), external traps constitute heterogeneous outcomes among participants because of their varying resources, preferences, and self-interests. Asymmetric outcomes inhibit cooperative behavior because individuals know that workers will receive unequal outcomes despite the fact that their risks and

contributions seem to be the same. Asymmetric social trap model reflects the "real-world conflict" that has greater complexity than symmetric traps (Wit, Wilke and Oppewal, 1982; Murnighan and King, 1992). These things happen because barriers like attitudes and organizational bias help to create a "glass ceiling" that hampers the development of women and minorities. Asymmetric "preferences, incentives, and outcomes reinforce dysfunctional organizational" norms that are exclusionary.

4 Cognizance—Cultural ignorance, and cross-cultural inexperience, or low levels of enculturation may make managers and supervisors incapable of sensitivity issues in their management of organizational diversity (Gordon, 1964). Extensive and intensive educational and training programs may help organizations "seeking to modify individual attitudes and behaviors that create barriers reinforced by intolerant values, stereotypes and policies" (Barry and Bateman, 1996, p. 768).

5. Exclusivity—If "diversity issues are suppressed or minimally managed in organizations, power imbalances between majority and minority groups persist (Cox, 1993). Naturally, such a case results in the "concentration of control over relevant resources" like "information, opportunity advancement, satisfaction, and commitment" "within the decision makers who hold power. The trap is perpetuated, rather than solved, to the extent that relatively few members of the organization possess both motivation and the control over resources to defuse it" (Barry and Bateman, 1996: 768). Scholarly research suggests that "dispersion of control is more likely to result in decision making that enhances the organization's diversity climate (p. 769).

Conclusion

An organization is an assemblage of buildings or artifacts, people and organizational culture or climate in which and through which certain organizational functions and purposes are structurally, and substantively accomplished. On a microscale or macroscale, almost every organization reflects a diverse workforce whose values and climate affect its operations. Diversity climate comprises of individual, group, and organizational attributes that influence the impact of employees whose culturally heterogeneous attitudes, norms, behaviors, and structures bring to bear on organizational dynamics and performance.

The major elements of organizational diversity consists of the complex issues that arise as a result of individual interaction, intergroup conflict and the character of both the internal and exogenous factors that influence organizational operations, strategy, productivity, accountability, dynamics, and adaptability. Of the most important organizational elements, issues of class, race/ethnicity, gender, age, mindscape, and social trap or social dilemmas are commonly classic. Organizations establish systematic machinery for providing solutions to these problematic issues. Most organizations, particularly those in the West, tend to use the social trap to solve their problems but end up in either contributing to their unsolvability, maintaining the status quo, making minimal change, or doing nothing at all. For instance, social pressures exerted at the individual level could combine "with performance pressures at the unit level to lock in behavior and create obstacles to change. Even if the individual overcomes the social pressures that feed the trap, cross-level disincentives remain" (p. 769). Workplace change is resisted and the trap is reinforced by powerful and entrenched interests struggling to maintain power at various levels of the organizational pyramid. Resistance to change may also come from "legalistic mechanisms and systems that exacerbate power disparities, bias decision making or impede innovation" (p. 769). If diversity is to be addressed but not resolved, "these mechanisms can take the form of normal procedures, rigid affirmative action guidelines, or fears of discrimination litigation that lead decision makers to prefer narrow or short-term remedies over broader or more precedent-setting strategies that would break the trap" (pp. 769-770).

There are group, trap, diversity and climate oriented solutions that will and that do enhance the synergistic evolution for organizational diversity. First, group strategies will change the design, hierarchy, norms, and interaction features of the organization and its departments or subunits. These solutions will also tend to lessen the social distance between policy makers, employees, and constituents, i.e., organizational clients. These new organizational features should be used to create trap-results awareness climate. Such a strategy enables communication to be openly conducted, and creatively used for moral power that creates a sense of group identity and cohesion. The second structural aspect of restructuring of the organization is to recognize that individuals are more cooperative than groups and individual participants in small groups are more cooperative than those in larger units and organizations. Individual, group, and organizational units should be managed to increase personal accountability, group identity and cohesion in order to enhance the value of group membership. Group membership is a collectivity which may not be very cohesive if the group understands that it is distinctive, prestigious and competitive. Such elements of organizational restructuring (design, hierarchy, norms, structure, identity, cohesiveness, cooperation) can be integrated and internalized by a superordinate authority in order to control the allocation of organizational resources.

Any trap that involves short-term gains and long-term loss should be treated in such a way that decisions regarding noncooperation will be made and effected immediately. In addition, managers should "territorialize" resources equitably, eliminate the trap and undermine or eliminate "mutual dependence."

Diversity issues and traps can be addressed effectively when organizational workers developmentally trained in positive interpersonal interaction, use of employee network groups, the selection of diversity task force(s) to monitor the quality and degree of organizational change, and use of organizational consultants and techniques to manage change. These workers need to be trained to understand the value and essence of decentralization which enhances participation, elimination of unnecessary and cumbersome management structures, creation of team-centered systems and workgroups, and restructuring of work assignments in terms of place, space, and time. Decentralized organizations should adhere to the legal and institutional requirements that enhance the fair recruitment, selection, promotion, tenure, and evaluation of organizational employees. These employees should be compensated in terms of wages, salaries, rewards, benefits that accrue with their qualifications, contributions and commitment. Compensation in monetary and nonmonetary ways and the use of incentives help to eliminate or alter the "structure of the trap culture."

Social traps influence the organizational climate. Informal and formal integration helps to eliminate individual bias and prejudice because the side effects of interpersonal and intergroup differences and attitudes tend to be learnt and de-emphasized for integration, motivation, and productivity. Theoretically, the socio-psychological theory of intergroup bias used for its analysis is contact theory or hypothesis (Allport, 1954). Such an analysis which articulates intragroup, intergroup or cross-cultural dynamics helps to attenuate intergroup conflict. More better results in inter-group cooperation as opposed to conflict will mature. The maturity of diversity initiatives and issues promote "equal status between groups," enhance cooperation, interpersonal and professional interaction and creation of intergroup norms that constructively enhance interaction.

Points To Remember

1. Organizations should specify rather than categorize work in order to eliminate the possibility of negative evaluations.
2. Minorities and women should hire experts to analyze organizations

they work for in order to identify and expose social traps.

3. This analysis should re-evaluate the short and long-term implications of the trap situation particularly when it is permanently confusing or conflicting.

4. It should be made clear that diversity issues are initiatives, biases, social traps or social dilemmas that evolve with individual, group or organizational interaction.

5. The degree of applied diversity depends on the underlying organizational or societal ideological theory from which attitudes, values, decisions and actions that warrant it emanate.

6. Workplace situations that enhance diversity issues promote productivity, quality, higher retention rates, problem-solving, and profit.

7. Elimination of social traps motivates employees and empowers them to maximize or optimize performance.

8. Traps can be asymmetric (external), counter-asymmetric (defense).

9. Organizations should be cognizant of their cultural ignorance due to cross-cultural inexperience.

10. Organizations should use group, trap, diversity and climate oriented solutions that address complex organizationally entrenched diversity problems.

11. Effective enforcement of diversity proposals should use group strategies to change the design, hierarchy, norms and interaction styles of the organization and its units.

12. When managers territorialize resources equitably, they eliminate the trap.

13. Organizations should use consultants and superior techniques to train managers and employees about the worth of diversity.

14. Organizations should use formal and informal integration to socialize employees and eliminate bias and prejudice.

15. Employees should curiously understand the society's culture in which organizational culture is based.

16. Employees should analyze organizational culture, purposes, and goals and match these goals with their own individual goals.

References

Abo, T. ed. 1994. *Hybrid Factory: The Japanese Production System in the United States.* New York: Oxford University Press.

Academy of Management Review. 1996. 2, 2: 565.

Adler, N.J., and D. Izraeli. ed. 1994. *Competitive Frontiers: Women Managers in a Global Economy.* Cambridge, MA: Blackwell.

Ahrari, M.E. eds. 1987. *Ethnic Groups and U.S. Foreign Policy*. New York: Greenwood Press.

Aldrich, H. 1989. Networking Among Women Entrepreneurs. In *Women-Owned Business*, eds. O. Hagan, C. Rivchun, and D. Sexton, 103-132, New York: Praeger.

Andersen, M.L., and Collins, P.H. 1995. *Race, Class, and Gender*, 2nd ed. Belmont, CA: Wadsworth Publishing Company.

Abo, T. ed. 1994. *Hybrid Factory: The Japanese Production System in the United States*. New York: Oxford University Press.

Aoki, M., and Dore, R., eds. 1994. *The Japanese Firm: Sources of Competitive Strength*. New York: Oxford University Press.

Ayres, B.D. 1997. At the Washington Statehouse women lead a tide. *The New York Times* April 14, 1.

Barber, B.J. 1992. Jihad vs. McWorld *Atlantic Monthly*, 269, 3: 53-63.

Barber, L.A. 1995. U.S. women in science and engineering, 1960-1990. *Journal of Higher Education* 66, 2: 213-234.

Barr, P.S. 1996. Mindscapes in management: Use of individual differences in multicultural management. *Academy of Management Review* 21, 2: 558-579.

Barry, B. 1996. A social trap analysis of the management of diversity. *Academy of Management Review* 21, 3: 757-790.

Baum, A.C., and Singh, J.V. eds. 1994. *The Evolutionary Dynamics of Organizations*. New York: Oxford University Press.

Bienvenu, M.J. 1974. Interpersonal communication inventory. In *The 1974 Annual Handbook for Group Facilitators*. University Associates Publishers, Inc.

Blackwell, J. 1991. *The Black Community: Unity in Diversity*. Boston: University of Massachusetts Press.

Blau, P.M. 1982. Structural sociology and network analysis: An overview. In *Social Structure and Network Analysis*, eds. P.V. Marsden and N. Lin, 273-279, Beverly Hills, CA: Sage.

Blau, P.M. 1977. *Inequality and Heterogeneity: A Primitive Theory of Social Structure*. New York: Free Press.

Blau, J.R. and R.D. Alba. 1982. Empowering nets of participation. *Administrative Science Quarterly* 27: 363-379.

Blockstein, D.E. 1990. Women and minorities — how are the AIDS societies doing? *BioScience* 40, 8: 607-609.

Bloom, A. 1987. *The Closing of the American Mind*. New York: Simon and Schuster.

Bobo, L. 1988. Group conflict, prejudice, and paradox of contemporary racial attitudes. In *Eliminating Racism: Profiles in Controversy*, eds. P.A. Katz and D.A. Taylor. New York: Plenum.

Bowser, B.P., Jones, Jones, T., and Young, G.A. 1995. *Toward the Multicultural University*. Westport, CT: Praeger.

Brass, D.J. 1984. Being in the right place: A structural analysis of individual influence in an organization. *Administrative Science Quarterly*, 29: 518-539.

Burrell, G., and G. Morgan. 1979. *Sociological Paradigms and Organizational Analysis*. London: Heinemann.

Burt, R.S. 1992. *Structural Holes: The Social Structure of Competition*. Cambridge, MA: Harvard University Press.

Burt, R.S. 1983. Range. In *Applied Network Analysis. A methodological Introduction*, eds. R.S. Burt, M.J. Minor, and Associates, 35-74, Beverly Hills, CA: Sage.

Burt, R.S. 1982. *Toward a Structural Theory of Action*. New York: Academic Press.

Child, J. 1994. *Management in China During the Age of Reform*. Cambridge, England: Cambridge University Press.

Clark, C. 1993. Culture, ideology and social change in America, 1700-1800. *The Historical Journal* 36, 3: 737-744.

Colella, A. and D.L. Stone. 1996. A model of factors affecting the treatment of disabled individuals in organizations. *Academy of Management Review* 21, 2: 352-401.

Cox, T.H., Jr. 1991. The multicultural organization. *Academy of Management Executive* 5: 34-47.

Cox, T.H., Jr. and Nkomo, S.M. 1990. Invisible men and women: A status report on race as a variable in organization and behavior research. *Journal of Organization Behavior* 2: 419-431.

Cox, T.H., Jr.,Lobel, S.A., and McLeod, P.L. 1991. Effects of ethnic group cultural differences on cooperative and competitive behavior on a group task. *Academy of Management Journal* 34: 827-847.

Dean, J.W., and M.P. Sharfman. 1993. Procedural rationality in the strategic decision-making process. *Journal of Management Studies* 30, 4: 587-610.

Donaldson, G. 1994. *Corporate Restructuring: Managing the Change Process From Within*. Boston: Harvard Business School Press.

Edsall, T.B., and D.E. Mary. 1991. *Chain Reaction: The Impact of Race, Rights, and Taxes on American Politics*. New York: Norton.

Essay Review: Critical postmodern studies of gay and lesbian lives in academia. *Harvard Educational Review* 66, 2: 368-382.

Fagenson, E.A. ed. 1993. *Women in Management: Trends, Issues, and Challenges in Managerial Diversity*. Newbury Park, CA: Sage.

Flew, A. 1979. *A Dictionary of Philosophy*. New York: St. Martin's Press.

Friedman, R.A. 1996. Defining the scope and logic of minority and female network groups: Does separation enhance integration? In *Research in Personnel and Human Resources Management,* ed. G.R. Ferris. Greenwich, CT: JAI Press.

Galaskiewicz, J., and Shatin, D. 1981. Leadership and networking among neighborhood human service organizations. *Administrative Science Quarterly,* 26: 343-448.

Glaser, J.M. 1994. Back to the black belt: Racial environment and white racial attitudes in the south. *Journal of Politics* 56: 21-41.

Golembiewski, R.T. 1995. *Managing Diversity in Organizations.* Tuscaloosa: University of Alabama Press: 47

Granovetter, M. 1973. The strength of weak ties. *American Journal of Sociology,* 6: 1360-1380.

Hale, W.M. 1995. Africa and the United States: An Historical Perspective. Paper Presented at Langston University as part of the Distinguished Lecture Series.

Handy, C. 1994. *The Age of Paradox.* Boston: Harvard Business School Press.

Hill, L. 1992. *Becoming a Manager: Mastery of a New Identity.* Cambridge, MA: Harvard Business School Press.

Hill, L. 1991. *Beyond the Myth of the Perfect Mentor: Building a Network of Developmental Relationships.* Boston: Harvard Business School Case Services, Case No. 9-491-096.

Ibarra, H. 1993. Personal networks of women and minorities in management: A conceptual framework. *Academy of Management Review* 18, 1: 56-87.

Jackson, S.E. 1992. Team composition in organizational settings: Issues in managing an increasingly diverse work force. In *Group Process and Productivity,* eds. S. Worchel, W. Wood, and J.A. Simpson, 138-173. Newbury Park, CA: Sage.

Jackson, S.E., and E.B. Alvarez. (1992). Working through diversity as a strategic imperative. In *Diversity in the Workplace: Human Resources Initiatives,* ed. S.E. Jackson, 13-29. New York: Guilford Press:.

Jacobson, S.W. 1995. *Academy of Management Review* 20, 3: 741-748.

Johnston, W.E. 1988. *Civil Service 2000.* Indianapolis, IN: The Hudson Institute.

Kahn, K.F. 1996. *The Political Consequences of Being a Woman: How Stereotypes Influence the Conduct and Consequences of Political Campaigns.* New York: Columbia University Press.

Kanter, R.M. 1989. The New Managerial Work. *Harvard Business Review* 67, 6: 85-92.

Kanter, R.M. 1977. *Men and Women of the Corporation.* New York: Basic Books.

Kaplan, R.E. 1984. Trade routes: The manager's network of relationships. *Organizational Dynamics,* Spring: 37-52.

Kathlene, L. 1995. Alternative views of crime: Legislative policymaking in gendered terms. *The Journal of Politics* 57, 2: 464-485.

Keizai, D. 1992. *O-Pun Shisutemu e No Kigyo [Enterprise Reform Toward an Open System].* Tokyo: Author.

Kennedy, L. 1996. Alien nation: White male paranoia and imperial culture in the United States. *Journal of American Studies,* 30, 1: 87-100.

Kotter, J.P. 1982. *The General Managers.* New York: Free Press.

Krackhardt, D. *In press.* The strength of strong ties: The importance of philos in organizations. In *Networks and Organizations: Structure, Form and Action,* eds. N. Nohria and R.G. Eccles, Cambridge, MA: Harvard Business School Press.

Kram, K.E. 1988. *Mentoring at Work: Developmental Relationships in Organizational Life.* New York: University Press of America.

Langlois, C.C., and Langlois, J.P. 1996. Rationality in international relations: a game-theoretic and empirical study of the U.S.-China case. *World Politics* 48, 3: 358-390.

Larkey, L.K. 1996. Toward a theory of communicative interactions in culturally diverse workgroups. *The Academy of Management Review* 21, 2: 463-491.

Lasch, C. 1979. *The Culture of Narcissism.* New York: Warner Books.

Laumann, E.O., Galaskiewicz, J, and Marsden, P.V. 1978. Community structure as interorganizational linkages. *Annual Review of Sociology* 4: 455-484.

Lin, N. 1982. Social resources and instrumental action. In *Social Structure and Network Analysis,* eds. P.V. Marsden and N. Lin, 131-145. Beverly Hills, CA: Sage.

Lincoln, J.R. 1982. Intra- and inter-organizational networks. In *Research in the Sociology of Organizations,* ed. S.B. Bacharach, 1-88. Greenwich, CT: JAI Press.

Lincoln, J.R., and Miller, J. 1979. Work and friendship ties in organizations: A comparative analysis of relational networks. *Administrative Science Quarterly* 24: 181-199.

Link, M.W., and Oldendick, R.W. 1996. Social construction and white attitudes toward equal opportunity and multiculturalism. *The Journal of Politics* 58, 1: 149-168.

Marsden, P.V. 1990. Network data and measurement. *Annual Review of Sociology* 16: 435-463.

Marsden, P.V. 1988. Homogeneity in confiding relations. *Social Networks* 10: 57-76.

Maruyama, M. 1994. *Mindscapes in Management: Use of Individual Differences in Multicultural Management*. Aldershot, England: Dartmouth Publishing Company.

Mason, M. and Encarnation, D., eds. 1994. *Does Ownership Matter: Japanese Multinationals in Europe*. New York: Oxford University Press.

McConahay, J.B. 1986. Modern racism, ambivalence, and modern racism scale. In *Prejudice, Discrimination, and Racism*, ed. J. Dovidio and S.L. Gaerter. New York: Academic Press.

McConahay, J.B., and Hough, J.C., Jr. 1976. Symbolic racism. *Journal of Social Issues* 32: 23-45.

McPherson, J.M., and Smith Lovin, L. 1987. Homophily in voluntary organizations: Status distance and composition of face-to-face groups. *American Journal of Sociology* 52: 370-379.

Milliken, F.J., and Martins, L.L. 1996. Searching for common threads: Understanding the multiple effects of diversity in organizational groups. *The Academy of Management Review* 21, 2: 402-433.

Moore, K.M., and Johnson, M.P. 1989. The status of women and minorities in the professoriate: The role of affirmative action and equity. *New Directions for Institutional Research*, 63: 45-63.

Nemetz, P.L., and S.L. Christensen. 1996. Challenge of cultural diversity: harnessing a diversity of views to understand multiculturalism. *The Academy of Management Review* 21, 2: 434-462.

Ouchi, W.G. 1981. *Theory Z: How American Business Can Meet the Japanese Challenge*. New York: Avon Books.

Raggins, B.R., and D.B. McFarlin. 1990. Perceptions of mentor roles in cross-gender mentoring relationships. *Journal of Vocational Behavior* 37: 321-339.

Rehab Brief. 1993. Cultural sensitivity rehabilitation. XV, 8: 1-4.

Reingold, B. 1996. Conflict and cooperation: legislative strategies and concepts of power among female and male state legislators. *The Journal of Politics* 58, 2:464-485.

Rosen, B., and S. Rynes. 1995. A field survey of factors affecting the adoption and perceived success of diversity training. *Personnel Psychology* 48: 247-270.

Sagini, M.M. 1994. The process of the causes of the fall of the soviet empire. Paper presented at the Oklahoma Political Science Association Meeting, Tulsa, Oklahoma.

Sagini, M.M. 1991. Planning models: The challenges of strategic imperatives in higher education. *Community/Junior College*

Quarterly of Research and Practice 15, 1: 71-85.

Schaum, M. 1995. H.L. Mencken and American cultural masculinism. *Journal of American Studies* 29, 3, 379-398.

Schein, E.H. 1991. *Organizational Culture and Leadership*. San Francisco: Jossey-Bass Publishers.

Schelling, T.C. 1978. *Micromotives and Macrobehavior*. New York: Norton.

Sievers, B. 1993. *Work, Death, and Life Itself: Essays on Management and Organization*. Berlin-New York: de Gruyter.

South, S.J., C.M. Bonjean, W.T. Markham, and J. Corder. 1982. Social structure and intergroup interaction: Men and women of the federal bureaucracy. *American Sociological Review* 47: 587-599.

Thomas, D.A. 1993. Racial dynamics in cross-race developmental relationships. *Administrative Science Quarterly* 38: 169-194.

Thomas, D.A. 1990. The impact of race on managers' experience of developmental relationships (mentoring and sponsorship): An intra-organizational study. *Journal of Organizational Behavior*, 2: 479-492.

Thomas, R.R. 1991. *Beyond Race and Gender: Unleashing the Power of Your Total Work Force by Managing Diversity*. New York: AMACOM.

Toews, J.E. 1991. Historicizing psychoanalysis: Freud in his time and for our time. *The Journal of Modern History* 63, 3: 504-545.

Traxler, F., and Unger, B. 1994. Governance, economic restructuring, and international competitiveness, *Journal of Economic Issues* XXVIII, 1: 1-23.

Tsui, A.S., and O'Reilly, C.A., III. 1987. Beyond simple demographic effects: The importance of relational demography in superior-subordinate dyads. *Academy of Management Journal*, 32: 402-423.

U.S. Department of Commerce. 1989. *Population Profile of the U.S. 1989. Series P-23, No. 159*. Washington, D.C.: Bureau of the Census.

Welch. L.B. ed. *Perspectives on Minority Women in Higher Education*. New York: Praeger.

Wellman, B. 1988. Structure analysis: From method and metaphor to theory and substance. In B. Wellman and S.D. Berkowitz (Eds.) *Social Structures: A Network Approach*. Cambridge, England: Cambridge University Press: 19-61.

Worseley, P. 1985. *Introducing Sociology*. New York: Penguin Books.

Yang, D.L. 1996. Governing China's transition to the market: Institutional incentives, politician's choices, and unintended outcomes. *World Politics: A Quarterly Journal of International Relations* 48, 3: 424-

452.

Zajac, E.J,. and Kraatz, M.S. 1993. A diametric forces model of strategic change: Assessing the antecedents and consequences of restructuring in the higher education industry. *Strategic Management Journal*, 14: 83-102.

Chapter 8

Organizational Culture: The New Theory

Every organization has a culture that reflects its own image or identity. Organizational culture is the training, cultivation, and development of the organizational mind, the people who serve the organization and by whom the organization is served (organization field). The organizational mind is refined in taste, beliefs, manners, and practices. The beliefs, practices, and actions are embedded in the religious, social, economic, and cultural structures of society in which the organization exists.

The practices and actions are, in one way or another, the intellectual, artistic, and aesthetic manifestations of the organization which the culture claims (New Webster Dictionary and Thesaurus, 1992). The culture of an organization, in essence, is a pattern of basic assumptions invented, discovered, or developed by a given group as "it learns to cope with its problems of external adaptation, and internal adaptation, internal integration that has worked well enough to be considered valid and, therefore, to be taught to new members as the correct way to perceive, think, feel" (Schein, 1991 P. 9) and Conceptualize. In this light, the minds of new members are refined through the process of systematic socialization. Such a form of Socialization enables the new organizational members to be assimilated into or enculturated with organizational values, assumptions and artifacts (Schein, 1991).

The socialization process is a powerful form of cultural embedding and reinforcement through which culture is transmitted. Cultural transmission depends on what organizational leadership pays attention to, measures, and controls. The culture influences leader reactions to critical organizational events and crises; intentional role of modeling, instruction, and mentoring or coaching by organizational leaders. It also determines the criteria for the allocation of rewards, privileges and status, the criteria for recruitment, selection, hiring, training, retention, promotion, and retirement or dismissal (Schein, 1991).

Organizational socialization is the 'process in which people learn the rules, norms, culture of the organization, roles that were provided by the organization they join, and technical skills that were inevitable to well perform their job(s)' (Takahashi and Watanabe, 1997, p. 1). The people who are socialized are socializees who are organizational outsiders. Those who socialize them are organizational leaders or insider socializers who establish viable structures for the socialization of organizational "foreigners."

An organization exists to be perpetually challenged by problems of external adaptation and survival and by problems of internal integration. The first set of problems are strategic in character because they arise with the formulation and application of the mission, strategy, goals, means, measurement, and correction of the organization whose goals clarify it for simplification. The goals are targets to be reached. The means are elements of organizational structure, design, division of labor, reward system and authority structure through which the organization measures its performance and accomplishments on the one hard, and through which it develops consensus for correctional remediation, renewal and adjustment.

The second set of problems by which and through which the organization is perpetually challenged are problems of internal integration for its being. Of these, common language and conceptual schema, group boundaries and criteria for inclusion and exclusion, power and status, intimacy, friendship, and love, reward and punishments, and ideology and religion are paramount (Schein, 1991). Linguistically, if communication between and among organizational members lacks clarity, purpose and effectiveness, then it is difficult to define the organization's rationality and raison d'etre. Second, the insider-outsider organizational psychosis is based on definite criteria of inclusion and exclusion which dialectically contributes to organizational animation. Third, every organization has its own criteria and rules, regulations, or procedures for the conferment, acquisition, maintenance and loss of power, privilege and, status. A consensual understanding of the purpose of the criteria helps members to appropriately manage feelings of aggression and insecurity. Fourth, a each organization must create a structure through which intimacy, friendship, and love are appropriately expressed. For instance, there should be a system or framework through which existing rules of the game allow peer relationships, relationships between the sexes, and openness and intimacy to be expressed in order to reduce tension and enhance organizational goals. Such activities create a climate which motivates workers to promote organizational creativity, loyalty, and productivity as opposed to organizational inertia, disorder, burnout, and entropy. Fifth, organizational members or groups need to know that heroic deeds are rewarded with property, status, privileges and power. Also, the members should know the consequences of sinful or negative behavior that are punishable with withdrawal of love or intimacy, rewards or final excommunication.

Finally, like any society, the organization needs to use religious or/and ideological elements to explain the unexplainable and inexplicable events, "which must be given meaning so that members can respond to them and avoid the anxiety of dealing with the unexplainable and uncontrollable" (p.66). Religion gives a justificatory context for what appears to be meaningless.

Religious ideas provide guidelines that specify and reinforce the heroic and what is regarded to be sinful or undesirable. Such situation and contextual dichotomy of events creates an "ideology" (p. 79) that explains a variety of assumptions about "human nature, the nature of relationships, the nature of society"(p. 79 and the nature of reality. Such an ideology helps to explain the essence of superstitious behavior. The ideology may reflect the current ideals and futuristic aspirations. It may also show current reality. By so doing, an ideology functions as a guide and an incentive system to members. Most ideologies are couched in linguistic terminology that connotes the organizations central mission and the respective goals which emanate from it . The ideology shows preference in terms of how means will be accomplished and how organizational members should relate to one another. Because ideologies have powerful influences which generate cohesion and momentum, they are important values from which organizations can hardly be disentangled. Ideologies are found in official institutional documents in which organizational culture, at least from a literary perspective, is preserved.

According to Posner.(1989), humans are good at learning complex conceptual structures. Some of the complex structures that are learned include a variety of cultural models and the ways in which these structures of cultural models are explained and utilized. Organizational models are cultural models which people depend on. Even personal models are cultural model that are more than some kind of packaged information about the world. Cognatively and logically speaking, this implies that both personal and organizational models are cultural models that are preculturally espoused and culturally designed. Empirically, the linguistic terms which tend to explain these complex models reflect a high degree of abstraction in terms of logical, spatial, or temporal priority by culturally based associations (Lakoff, 1987). Cultural models are, in the actual cognitive sense, little machines organized in software programs that are not necessarily data per se. The brain which has mental machines runs the little cultural machines. The little programs are also important because when they are activated, a variety of procedures such as searching, chuncking, storage, and recalling would not work without them. In other words, the science of cultural intellectual culture, is the science of cultural information and cultural programs which interact with the more general programs of intelligent systems (D'Andrade, 1989).

Within the framework of organizational culture, colleges of education, particularly in the U.S. have engaged in activities that constitute cultural disempowerment of the youth in their institutional settings. One would be tempted to think that such institutions which are comprised of educators who would not professionally, through implementation of curricular or other means, disempower those who badly lack empowerment notions of educational processes. In particular, (Giroux, 1994) has assertively argued and theorized that scholars working within the area of education are not pedagogically serious in playing a role that could shape institutional culture and politics. Secondly these scholars in colleges of education have not utilized a wealthy interdisciplinary and interpostdisciplinary resources to positively analyze teaching and learning. Because these institutions have not used these opportunities which are rampant in cultural studies (literature, film, media, Communications and philosophy), within the humanities and social science fields, popular multimedia experts who have exploited the educating processes reinforce dominant racist and cultural stereotypes in the wake of escalating changing economic conditions, hopelessness, normlessness and anomie (Giroux, 1994).

Educators have not only abstained from utilizing interdisciplinary scholarship in the field of cultural studies for the purpose of empowering their students, but, they have also helped to cultivate an anti-intellectual spirit in the name of professional and scientistic objectivity. They have failed to challenge or reform "narrow technocratic models that dominate mainstream reform efforts and structure education programs" (p. 279). Since cultural studies challenge the dogmatic, ideological and political nature through which the educators claim scientific objectivity, they either fail to realize, or reaffirm that professors work and speak "within historically and socially determined relations of power (p. 279). Theoretically, professional cultural studies of professionals reject the traditional practice of teaching as a specific fixation or technique or set of unique skills in a specific discipline. They affirm that as a social practice, teaching is better understood through thoughtful notions of history, politics, cultural studies, whose constitutive essence is deconstructive and empowering because it articulates interdisciplinary issues. Their texture and representation are refracted through "the dynamics of gender, sexuality, subordinated youth, national identity, colonialism, race, ethnicity, and popular culture" (p.280). Both unwillingness to reform and the social and intellectual practices that reinforce the statues quo are not only aspects of cultural disempowerment of these institutions, but also they are the culture that determines the terrain of inclusion, exclusion, and alienation (Giroux, 1994).

As Schein stated earlier, organizational culture may be viewed as assumptions, values, and artifacts of the organization. This definition of organizational culture is essentially symbolic and processual. According to (Hatch, 1993), Schein's organizational theory could be functionally advanced by using the cultural dynamics model of organizational culture to deconstructively enrich organization theory. The cultural dynamics model originates from anthropological and sociological dimensions of symbolic interaction and cognitive interpretation school. Though Schein views organizational culture to be unitary systems that are normatively fashioned, to maintain social structure (Feldman, 1991; Martin, 1992; Meyerson, 1991a and 1991b, Berger and Luckmann, 1966) who are symbolic interpretivists, think that organizational culture can be understood by focusing on "symbols and symbolic behavior in organizations and interpreting these phenomena in a variety of ways"(p. 658).

Cognitive Anthropology

The major elements within the cultural dynamics model or theory include manifestation, realization, symbolization, and interpretation. Each of the elements of the cultural dynamics model are processes extrapolated from cognitive cultural anthropology. The expression cultural dynamics means that the issues which deal with organizational culture may include "origins and evolution of cultures, enculturation processes, and the problem of change versus stability (e.g. through diffusion, innovation, cultural conservatism and resistance to change (p.660). Hence, by using the term culture, this concept has been advanced or extended in the context of "origins, evolution, and enculturation and in the dialectic of change and stability" (p.660). This line of thought was originally advanced by such great cultural anthropologists as Redfield (1941),

Kroeber (1944), Malinowski (1945), and Herskovits (1948) (p. 660).

The manifestation processes of organizational dynamics are actively constituting and reconstituting the role of assumptions in organizational culture. This concept of manifestation means any process through which the "essence reveals itself, usually via the sense, but also through cognition and emotion"(Hatch, 1993, p. 662). In other words, in terms of the cultural dynamics framework of the organization.

Manifestation permits cultural assumptions (the essence of culture in Schein's theory) to reveal themselves in the perception, cognition, and emotions of organizational members. That is, manifestation contributes to the constitution of organizational culture by translating intangible assumptions into recognizable values. This constitution occurs through the advantage that manifestation gives to certain ways of seeing, feeling, and knowing within the organization. The cultural dynamics model suggests that manifestation occurs in two ways: "through those processes that proactively influence values and through those processes that influence assumptions via the retroactive effects of value recognition" (p. 662).

To clarify how the ways organizational dynamics theory works, Figure 1 vividly illustrates this phenomenon. Manifestations are either proactive or retroactive. Proactive manifestations constitutes of what organizational members assume to be true features and shapes of what they value. The shaping occurs through the processes of proactive manifestation through which assumptions provide "expectations that influence perceptions, thoughts and feelings about the world and the organization" (p. 662). Assumptions engage in manifestations simultaneously, and interactively in order to reveal values. The assumptions are taught to organizational members as "the correct way to perceive, think, and feel' (Schein, 1985, p.9).

In this case, Schein (1985) shows that values are a sense of what ought to be as opposed to "what is"(Hatch, 1993, p. 663). The values may be influenced by aspirations. The same values are not experienced on a one by one basis. Instead, they are experienced as a collectivity or as a gestalt. For instance, organizational environments which success depended on frequently employed systematic effort that would consider laziness negatively. Consequently, because laziness is perceived negatively, organizational thoughts and feelings about laziness may create or evolve a value system for controlling laziness. In brief, proactive manifestations generate values and expectations that culturally organize action and experience in the context of perceptual, cognitive and emotional field.

Figure 8.1. The Cultural Dynamics Model

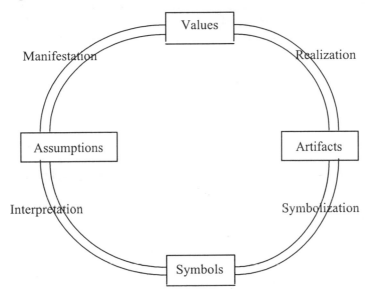

Source: Hatch, M.J. (1993). The Dynamics of Organizational Culture.
Academy of Management Review, 18, 4, p. 660.

Retroactively, the manifestation process is the contribution of values to
assumptions. In one sense, values retroactively maintain or alter
prevailing assumptions. In reciprocal terms, values and assumptions are
harmonious. Organizational members are happy with the world which
harmoniously confirms their culture. However, assumptions may be
altered if new values are initiated by organizational managers and
executives. If new values result in desirable accomplishments, the
maintenance of such values, in the long run, will result in their being
taken for granted. At this juncture, the values become part and parcel of
the culture's core assumptions. In other words, within the context of
cultural dynamics perspective of organizations, values that emerge from
basic assumptions have a retroactive effect for reaffirming and buttressing
the assumptions from which they emerged. If new values are not
retroactively taken to be part of the culture, the manifestation process will
ignore them.

Evidently, it is clear that values are manifestations of the assumptions of culture. Other cultures which are nonsocialized in and independent of the organizational culture may show up within certain individuals. These may produce random variation or innovation (Herskovits, 1948; Kroeber, 1944; and Malinowski, 1945). Such random variation or innovation does not necessarily constitute values; it is a production of artifacts of which objects, ideas, or actions that rationalize retroactive realization are associated with.

To realize is to bring something to life or to vivify. In the context of cultural dynamics model of the organization, proactive realization is the process through which expectations and values are transformed into artifacts. The example of artifacts may include but are not limited to rites, rituals, organizational stories, humor, and a variety of physical objects.

Hence, cultural realization is the process of making values real by transforming expectations into social or material reality and by maintaining or altering existing values through the process of artifacts. Materialization of reality is cognitively constructed. Cultural dynamics process is perceptually and emotionally realized. Within an organization, the realization of expectations may include the production of things or objects like company products, official reports, internal news letters and buildings. Also, involvement in organizational events like meetings, organizational picnics, award banquets and office parties are forms of realized expectations.

Finally, involvement in formal speeches, informal conversation, and joking are forms of realized expectations. If objects are imported, or when events are carried out and language artifacts imitated or transported from other cultures, these are evidences of realization of expectations.

The realization process can be proactive or retroactive. Proactive realization is the process through which culturally influenced activity generates artifacts that are representative of some tangible values and expectations. In this process, the activity and artifacts of the organization that are left behind are infused with cultural values but do not unequivocally indicate them.

Retroactive realization concerns the *post-hoc* or *exo-posto facto* "contribution of artifacts to values and to expectations of how things should be. Similar to manifestation, two distinct possibilities should be examined. In one case, artifacts realized from values and expectations maintain or reaffirm these values and expectations, whereas artifacts produced by another culture or by forces not aligned with cultural values could introduce artifacts that retroactively challenge values and expectations". (Hatch, 1993, p.667).

The third major process in the cultural dynamics model of

organizational culture is symbolization. All symbols are artifacts. According to symbolic interpretivists like Tompkins (1987), every artifact has symbolic importance. Based on symbolic and scholarly interpretation, a symbol is a thing which represents a "conscious or and unconscious association with some wider, usually more abstract, concept, or meaning" (Hatch p. 669). According to Gioia (1986), organizational symbols include but are not restricted to corporate logo, slogans, stories, actions and nonactions, visual images and metaphors"(p.669). Eisenberg and Riley (1988) commented that "organization charts, corporate architecture, rites and rituals"(p.669) also are part and parcel of the symbolization processes. According to Ott(1989), symbols and artifacts are not only indistinguishable, but they also are in their physical form, static manifestations of symbolization. Within the Clinton administration's regime, while president Clinton's symbolic view to strategically cut the size of white house bureaucracy by about ten percent to address retrenchment concerns would have been politically questionable, and while these cuts would have been officially viewed in a literal sense, the congress and media continued to view them in pejorative terms. The administration's symbolic gesture was criticized with hostility and cynicism. Such treatment did not result in significant cuts though such cuts would have set a productive precedent for the efficient and effective management of public institutions (Hart, 1995).

Further still, the giving of roses as for a gift is not only an expression of appreciation but the objective form of the symbol of the rose flowers could have a literal meaning associated with smell, color, texture and pattern or arrangement. Subjectively, such a symbolic gesture may be viewed either positively or with neutrality depending on the receivers experience, personality, and history of roses(Barthes, 1972).

In brief, symbolic forms are not imitations. They are objects of reality. Through the agency of symbolic forms, things are made real in intellectual and visible terms. Symbolization is useful for the adaptation of aesthetic techniques used to study the organization (Bjorkegren, 1991; Strati, 1990, 1992; Van Maanen, 1988; Witkin, 1990). Symbolization processes can be methodologically studied with the use of aesthetic techniques such as acting, writing, drawing and photography.

Finally, the fourth process of the dynamics of organizational culture is interpretation. Hermeneutically, interpretation relies on assumptions that are dominant in symbols. With the cultural dynamics Paradigm, interpretation reconstructs symbols and revises basic assumptions in terms of both current experience and the prevailing assumptions. Interpretation processes are investigated by using a variety of well known techniques. The most important of these techniques include "ethnographic interviews

(Spradley, 1979), scripts (Barley, 1986; Martin et al; 1983), semiotics (Barley, 1983; Fiol, 1991), deconstruction (Carla's and Smircich, 1991; Martin, 1990) and discursive analysis (Coulthard, 1977)" (Hatch, 1991, p. 676).

In terms of its theoretical domain, cultural dynamics as an intellectual construction, tries to bring together, as a paradigm, ideas that have historically been kept separate in organization theory. The processes of cultural dynamics are simultaneously cognitive and social. These processes also are perceptual, emotional and aesthetic. Cultural dynamics is both an objectivist (aspects of culture are not objectable but they are theorizable in subjective terms) (Gioia and Pitre, 1990). The dynamism of objective and subjective dialectic is theoretically useful and distinctive.

In this field, symbols and values invoke objectivist theorizing because their relationship to artifacts is experienced as external. They also invoke subjectivist theorizing by referring to basic assumptions that have no direct external referent. For instance, theories of environmental determinacy such as resource dependency theory which largely affects Third World nations are evidences of "objectivist appreciations of organizational reality" Hatch, 1993, p. 684). However, social constructivist theories like enactment are evidences of subjectivist rationalization.

Theoretical interpretation and symbolization are built around the discourse of reflexivity. In contradistinction, theoretical manifestation and realization are framed or constructed in the discourse of activity. Values and symbols are similarly distinguishable. While values are connected with the action frames, symbols invoke reflexive discourse. Both discourses enrich our understanding of the "Wheel" (See Figure VIII.2) by which organizational culture is represented and rationalized. Its theoretical orientations are subdivided by the discourses of activity and reflexivity.

Talking about recent theories of justice in organizations, Young (1992), argues that the paramount issues of justice, which are elements of organizational culture, involve class, race, gender, sexual groups, and the systematic social relations that reproduce relations of power, privilege, and oppression. Within such a setting, many "laws, policies, actions, prejudice, symbols, images,... come together to provide a set of very real constraints on the actions of men and women, even when no one in particular intends to constrain them" (p. 78). In the light of this argument, these theories and what they entail constitutes organizational culture.

Figure 8.2. The Objectivist and Subjectivist Domain of the Cultural Dynamics Model

SUBJECTIVIST
Subjectifying activity

OBJECTIVIST
Objective activity

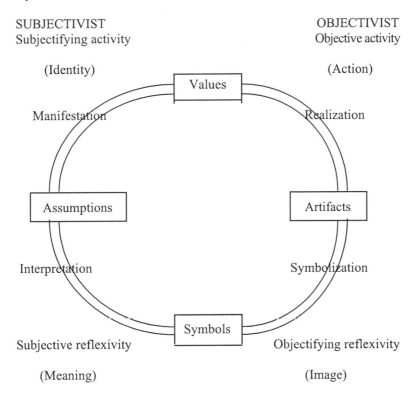

(Identity)

(Action)

Values

Manifestation

Realization

Assumptions

Artifacts

Interpretation

Symbolization

Symbols

Subjective reflexivity

Objectifying reflexivity

(Meaning)

(Image)

Source: Hatch, M.J. (1993). The Dynamics of Organizational Culture. *Academy of Management Review,* 18, 4, p. 685.

Rafaeli and Pratt (1993) have suggested that dress is an ubiquitous element in organizations. Dress reflects or creates a variant of organizational dynamics. The variety of dynamics dress creates in organizations may depend on its attributes, homogeneity and conspicuousness. Dress indicates the degree to which an organization could be influenced by, or could seek association with a particular culture or institution. Its attributes may distinctively and enduringly convey the lasting values of the organization. Homogeneity of dress indicates the value of organizational consistency. When dress is homogeneously stratified, workers and management know that organizational labor is permanently specialized.

When an organization is homogeneously stratified in dress, it is more mechanistic than humanistic or behavioristic etc. If organizational dress is conspicuous, it tends to influence greater compliance with given role requirements. Homogeneity in dress tends to enhance the extent to which individual behavior is driven by organizational rather than individual goals, values, and priorities. Organizations that are homogeneous and conspicuous have dress which tends to increase the extent to which employees are identified as valid representatives. The attributes of dress, especially colors, materials, and styles influence the external image of the organization: Conspicuous organizational dress that identifies an institution will attach the image of the institution to organizations displaying this dress. Within the organization, the attributes and stratification of dress can identify distinctions of status within the organization and help direct demands of organizational personnel.

Finally, in certain settings, the conspicuousness of organizational dress can promote service delivery because dress helps to identify both members and nonmembers. Further still, stratification of dress may reinforce organizational members to be more loyal, accountable, and respectful.

Using a management perspective of organizational culture, Gannon (1994), has used an interdisciplinary literature review to examine and try to understand global culture from seventeen countries. Through the disciplines of sociology, anthropology, psychology and political science, the cultures were examined to identify the "cultural mind set of a nation" and how that culture influences its social institutions. Gannon concluded that the best way to understand others' culture and their institutions is to us the comparative strategy to elucidate the "cultural metaphor." Anthropologists are particularly proficient in using cultural metaphors to thematically and abstractively covey meaning pregnantly.

Religious Philosophy

In the light of cultural dynamics theory, the influence of Gandhi on social institutions in India and elsewhere has been anything but classic. Though Gandhi was a brilliant and practical man, he was not a systematic philosopher or an academic scholar. Those who, in recent times, have written extensively about Gandhi have said that he was a contradictory person. Leftist critics and Hindu conservatives distrusted his inclusivism, multiculturalism, and the toleration of non-Hindus. These critics of the left and right sides of the dialectical intellectual spectrum resented his criticism of traditional and orthodox Hindu way of life. With sensitivity and resentment, these critics attacked his attitude toward "Untouchability, various practices of the caste system, and the oppressive treatment of women" (Allen, 1993, p. 291).

Gandhi rejected utilitarianism for its unethical irrelevance to Indian life, Marxism for its collectivistic and anti Indian way of life and capitalism for its oppressive, exploitative, and enslaving influences on the soul. He preferred the universalistic form of Gandhian socialism which his critics and admirers alike have called Utopia. Through his abstract and utopian approach, he saw universal formulations about Truth (Satya) God, the Self (Atman), Religion, Tolerance, non-violence (ahimsa), method of non-violent resistance (satyagraha) "welfare of all" (sarvodaya), "self-rule" (swaraj),"self-reliance" (swadeshi)...as detached from any cultural context (Allen, 1993, p. 93). They were specifically and holistically Indian.

According to Richard (1985) Gandhian philosophical and religious ideals, though apparently utopian, were, in reality, abstract concepts or assumptions, which his political estate and government identified with as they had a risen from "specific contradictions and dynamic confrontations situated within contingent cultural contexts of global and indigenous structures of inequality and domination" (p. 93). In other words, this context was the genesis of his 19th and 20th century ideas on colonization and decolonization of India, South Africa and the Asian continent.

According to Gandhi, means and ends are convertible. Gandhi used non-violence (passive resistance), "non-injury, non-destruction of life" (p.94) to talk, teach, and rationalize about truth. Truth was internalized fulfillment of non-violence. He reasoned that the essence of the individual person is the lofty universality of the self. This form of a higher self is in unison with truth or God or reality. Given this state of affairs, then it is morally, spiritually and philosophically irresponsible or unnecessary to inflict violence, pain and suffering on the individual. Causing these problems on individuals would not only be viewed as hostility toward humanity, but as a form of negativism that violates the laws of "Truth, God, Reality and One's Self" (p. 94). This concept of truth and its inseparability from non-violence is the paramount approach to understanding "Gandhi's creativity of ideas of satyagraha (Truth force, Soul force; the techniques of non-violence and applications of non-violence) and sarvodaya (Universal Uplift, Welfare of all" (p. 94) It is interesting also to understand where and how Dr. King got his ideas of nonviolence with which he championed the cause of civil rights in the United States.

Gandhi also believed that non-violence was or is inextricably intertwined with truth. Truth is an absolute ideal. Such an ideal may or

Organizational Behavior

may not be perfect. The imperfection of such idealistic truths could be historically or culturally conditioned. Such was Gandhi's concept of truth which was applicable to India's social, economic, political, educational and other issues.

Gandhi discussed theories and practices which did least harm on castes and untouchables. Some of the theories were colonialism, untouchability, educational goals, socialism, Marxism, and a decentralized economy. He analyzed these theories in the light of truth, oneness to existence, self and non-violence to see whether there was contradiction. He asserted that venomous snakes can be killed to save life. Violence may be used to protect life or resist the perpetrator. Ahimsa (non-violence) should not, as a principle of philosophy of life be taken for granted. In this case, Gandhi was both flexible and absolute or rigid. Truth is indivisible. Truth is interrelated. Unity is the essence of existence.

Though Gandhi's original source of his ideas are believed to be Tolstoy, Ruskin and other Westerners, his Indian and Orientalist beliefs of Hinduism enabled him to be a complex but creative, contradictory, syncretistic, and above all, synergistic. He was also influenced by the traditional advaitin philosophy which is non-dualistic. Traditional Advaita Vedanta tended to be more contemplative than practical. This is a world in which action is viewed as maya or illusion. To him, practical action could be illusionary or deceptive and therefore irrelevant and unwarranted.

As a prominent and devout nationalist, Gandhi opposed, during the struggle for independence, the partition of India into the current states of (Pakistan, India, and Bangladesh). He also rejected exclusivism, chauvinism, intolerance, and others form of radical nationalisms. He sought self-rule (swaraj) and national self-reliance which were (Swadeshi) a form of Gandhian socialism. Gandhi believed that nationalism was a unifying force in life. With the Indian community bound together via common understanding of the social or cultural institutions, the glimpses of Truth i.e. God were realized. Largely, due to Gandhi's philosophy and leadership during the 1940s, 50s, and 60s, Indian life was highly unified. Currently, it is difficult to conceptualize what keeps India together since Hindu nationalism has become contradictorily divisive, intolerant, violent, antimulticulturalism and anti-welfare.

The ability of Gandhi to internalize cultural history, orientalism, and elements of postmodernism, in order to analyze western hegemony and the world system for the social reconstruction and restructuration of India, was heroic feat. Though Westerners thought that Indians were "fatalistic, other worldly spiritualists who lacked the superior concept of the modern, autonomous, rational individual" (p. 302), Gandhi saw his people to be more spiritually superior than the depraved Western materialists. These "organic, harmonious, and oceanic Indians were responsible and consensual humans. With the influence of Gandhian utopian thinking, the orientalized world system of cultural domination was penetrated. The penetration of the "dominant orientalized Western system by the Gandhian Eastern but universal and utopian culture produced a value structure of conflicted intimacy" (p. 304) that enabled the synergistic evolution of a new "hegemonic discourse" (p. 304) that resulted in important "cultural innovations (p. 304). These innovations were carried out and rationalized by organizational structures conversant with the eastern mind and its ecological reality.

Though Gandhian thinking was more radically leftist and was viewed by many as a form of Utopianism, its radical leftist extremism helped to change India. In recent times, Fox has argued that Indian consciousness also contains certain elements of Gandhian philosophic thought that utilizes "a militant and ideologically structuring Hindu nationalism." This brand of nationalistic consciousness greatly appeals to Hindus, Urban and lower middle class. These groups are viewed as "progressive or forward castes." In addition, the educated classes like the urbanized upper class castes, merchants, money lenders and small scale entrepreneurs have all "joined hands" with the forward castes to strategically restructure Indian socio-economic, political and spiritual life in order to build abase for ruling and remaining dominant in Indian affairs. These two categories of groups have united against evolving classes or caste such as the Muslims, untouchables, "Kulaks" and other rural and backward groups of Indian society. Sometimes, such dichotomous and ideologically uninspired social structure creates a synergistic dialectic from where Indian communal violence emanates. Hindu communal nationalism greatly appeals to universities because it represents the interests of the sophisticated, urban, educated, and privileged elite. When such dialect dichotomy of the Indian social structure erupts into violence, it does so when the system tries to de-emphasize or demystify Gandhian tolerance, compassion, non-violence, inclusivism, multiculturalism and the unity of diversity.

Recent Indian social and institutional beliefs and practices have been shaped by a political culture dominated by Hindu nationalists. These nationalists have tried to ignore or de-emphasize the Gandhi of tolerance, compassion, non-violence, inclusivism, multiculturalism and unity with respect for differences. Their policy emphasizes conservative Gandhian elements like the deification-or-veneration of the cow and preservation of certain traditional Hindu values. On the other hand, there is a lot of "modern and western" Gandhi whose values are dominant:

This Gandhi has a revolutionary commitment to personal and social transformation; a non-elitist capacity to empathize with and communicate with India's Village masses and to reclaim what is positive in the indigenous culture; a focus on non-western alternative model for development and appropriate technology, decentralization, and a healthier relation to nature; and resistance to domination, hatred, violence, economic exploitation, gender and caste and religious oppression (pp. 310-311).

In a way, people like the Gandhian way because it confronts oppressive ways of life of which inequality and injustice are classic. In spite of its multifaceted socio-economic and political limitations, the Gandhian approach presents a powerful critique to a lot of unwanted features of modernism. Of these, models of development, domination, and the bureaucratic state are cases in point that were profoundly penetrated by Gandhian thinking.

Organizational culture is rooted in basic societal assumptions that are regarded to be valid and that are taught to new organizational members so that they can be helped to perceive, think, feel, and conceptualize organizational reality. The elements of this reality are visible and cultural artifacts of the organization which include personal enactments, ceremonies, rites, stories, rituals and symbols used to enable the participants to have a sense of identity, increase their commitment, reinforce organizational values and become a control mechanism that influences behavior.

Theoretically, leaders apply specific models to influence, change and reinforce organizations whenever they allocate rewards and hire, promote or fire individuals. Those who receive the rewards are effectively socialized and proactively and retroactively mentored. The management of organizational culture is the main challenge for contemporary organizations. With the trend that emphasizes downsizing and restructuring, maintaining organizational culture in the wake of change and uncertainty in the turbulent and global environment is not easy. The challenges of globalism, work force diversity, technology and the management of ethical behavior require the imperative for organizational adaptability. Adaptive organizational cultures create organizational climates which enhance creativity and performance.

Managers can use many techniques to manage organizational culture. They can manipulate the artifacts of culture, communicate values that foster the organization or use socialization to shape behavior. Managers are models who interactively and interpersonally communicate organizational culture to employees. They establish and reinforce organizational norms and standards. As leadership models, they develop a culture which values diversity, emphasizes empowerment, nurtures innovation in industry, service and professions, and promotes ethical behavior.

Between 1981 and 1996, bell hooks whose real name is Gloria Watkins composed fourteen books that are severe critiques on organizational culture and diversity. The books have been esoterically edited by Irene Duhaime of the *Academy of Management Review*. Duhaime views bell hooks as a thoughtful race, cultural, and gender critic who heretically, deconstructively and incisively portrays both masculine, feminist, and gender elements of organizational social construction to be characterized by "racism, patriarchy, class, heterosexism, sexuality, sexual identity, religion, postcolonial issues, and physical ability" (Duhaime, 1997, p. 553).

Though hooks' aim is to use her writings to decolonize mainstream's 'white supremacist capitalist and patriarchal values' that are oppressive (p.553). This is an objective she theoretically, critically and anatomically achieves. By dissecting American culture, her revolutionary conscientization (Freire, 1964) tactics are etically (professional elitist) and emically (universally) dialectical. The dialectical polemics her writings evoke are central to the issues that articulate white and black dichotomy, women and men dichotomy, white women and black women dichotomy, mainstream and minority dichotomy and the poor versus the rich dichotomy, and race and class related gay, lesbian, and religious dichotomies. In other words,

Her heresy early in her career had gotten hooks' books banned by "bourgeois feminists" (Euro-American, middle-upper class, college educated, heterosexual) in charge of upper class white women's studies programs; she had deconstructed their race, class, and heterosexual privilege. Within the civil rights movement, she discusses the undiscussibles by pointing out how the former activists have colluded with the white supremacist heterosexual capitalist patriarchy by adopting its values and seeking to replace Euro-American male dominance with Euro-American female dominance with African-American male dominance, thus maintaining the oppression of African-American women and other diverse peoples (p. 555).

In other words, since the social elite, regardless of their race, ethnicity, and sexual orientation are capable of oppressing the disadvantaged classes, by ironically camouflaging in an oppressive state in order to win mainstream masculine sympathies for better treatment, jobs, promotion, money, and power, the feminist cause, viewed in male/female dialectic, seems to articulate a changeless status quo agenda since women, just like men in the past, have gained power to oppress their oppressors.

Methodologically, since hooks who is a public intellectual attacks "her class" by revealing the irreconcilable contradictions within it and thereby effectively deconstructing feminist theology (Betty Freidan's [1963] *The Feminine Mystique*), her critique is more reductionistic rather than constructivist. Given this reductionist element of her work, it is understandable why hooks' works were initially banned in certain intellectual and feminist circles. The banning was an emotionally charged atmosphere aimed at silencing her revolutionary literature which painted bourgeois women as "reactionary and opportunistic enemies" who have patrayed the cause of the Civil Rights Movement for their own advantage. Unlike those who have been conquered militarily, politically, economically, and culturally, the unity of the bourgeois men and women, most of whom are mainstream folk, gives them significant leverage over the masses of the disadvantaged and economically marginalized groups. By attacking the reactionary forces and playing the conscientization role of the public intellectual, philosopher, and enlightener, she messianically tries to empower the dispossessed with hope, knowledge and power for self-and collective humanistic and neo-Marxian liberation of the lumpen proletariats.

Since the masculine dominated capitalist and patriarchal system is culturally hegemonic, the only language that can be used to liberate this system of oppression and enhance justice is heuristic deconstruction which hooks has attempted to rationalize. Its relative closure, superior ego, bias and fear of postmodern imperialism may produce barriers whose analysis may either promote or hamper hooks' radical but timely and reasonable cultural critique for cultural and organizational diversity. For instance, though the majority of Americans support diversity especially in higher education, campus diversity education measures tend to "emphasize our differences" rather than our commonalities. In doing so, it "breeds conflict" that is connected with either liberal or conservative agenda (*The Chronicle of Higher Education*, May 2, 1997, p. A32). In addition, in order to enhance the survival and productivity of minorities in homogenous organizations, these institutions should provide external mentors who can provide support, friendship, acceptance, counseling, and role modeling to the neophytes.

Conclusion

In its semantic and anthropological usage, culture is a humanly constructed reality of its environment. The term culture is used in a wide a ray of interdisciplinary fields, both general and esoteric. Scholars such as Kroeber, Clyde and Kluckhohn suggest that culture is a comprehensive totality which enumerates elements of the content of "culture. Boas argues that culture embraces all manifestations of social habits of a community, the reactions of the individual as affected by the habits of the group in which he lives, and the products of human activities as determined by these habits." Linton concluded that culture is the total social heredity of mankind which is also a rule, or way of life or design for living. Biologically Paul Sears, said that culture is a way through which people do or a group does things, make and utilize tools, get along with each other and with other groups, the language and words they speak, and how they express or do not express the thoughts which they think. Psychologically, culture is a process of adjustment, learning and habituation. This definition cognitively connotes problem solving capacity of culture and how culturally attuned problems can be solved.

Piddington asserts that culture is the "sum total of material and intellectual equipment whereby People satisfy their biological and social needs and adapt themselves to their environment." Gillin has argued that culture is "patterned and functionally interrelated customs common to specifiable human beings composing specifiable social groups or categories." Kimball Young calls culture" a precipitate of man's social life". Leslie White defined culture as "the name of things and events" which depend on extrasomatic symbolization. Based on the research arena, Claude Levi Strauss pointed out that culture is practically observable and characterized by sharp discontinuities.

In its contextual sense, culture is culturally relative. This also gives way to the possibility of ethical relativity of specific cultures even that of organizations. Anthropologists tend to recognize not only the existence of cultural diversities, but also the existence of cultural universals which are caused by similarities in the human station through time and space. A constant physical environment and common biological endowments can influence species to replicate universal cultural commonalities of the ecosystem and vice versa. This does not mean that culture is static. The possibility of cultural discontinuity is assumed.

Culture also means ethos, customs or civilization. Philosophers and sociologists say that culture is the sun total of ideas, symbols, and values of a particular people. Psychoanalytically Sigmund Freud, writing to Albert Einstein, said that culture is a system of defenses that consist of " a progressive displacement of instinctual aims and a restriction of instructual impulses." Arnold (1869) wrote *In Culture and Anarchy* and concluded that culture is "the study and pursuit of perfection."

Behaviorally, Elliot asserted that culture is " that which makes life worth living." As a physicist and novelist, Snow (1959) argued that scientific culture is both intellectual and at the same time anthropological. In more recent times and especially in the USA, the term culture has taken a more scientific than humanistic or evaluative meaning. Culture is more increasingly and frequently defined and displayed in novels, film, TV, comic strips, popular media and more recently, in cyberspace. These images of American or global culture are reflections of the artifacts of humanly constructed technological handiwork.

Sociologically, Comte, Spencer, Weber, and Durkheim argue that the term society is synonymous with culture. Edward Taylor, the English anthropologist, published the *Primitive Culture* in 1871. His definition of culture says that culture is "that complex whole which includes knowledge, belief, art, law, morals, custom, and any other capabilities and habits acquired by man as a member of society." In the light of this definition, different social classes are carriers of different cultural traditions and orientations. For instance, every social structure particularly the organizational intellectuals tend to speak for itself and for the rest of society (nonexperts) in order to provide individual and collective cultural meanings. Individual and collective meanings evolve from cultural systems that are either conventionally or ontologically designed.

Therefore, and in essence, culture is who you are, where you come from, where you are going, and what you wear. As an individual, you are an offspring of a particular cultural tradition, group, or organization. Several or many individuals who belong to the tradition, group, or organization are natural rather than artificial reflections of its inevitable and uncontradictory representation. Such natural and inevitable representation is a social, interpersonal, and interactive law of nature and social custom. In its finest representation, the organization or group perfects itself by creating a climate conducive to the diverse satisfaction of or self-actualization of the biologically or culturally learned material, instinctual, psychological, social, and vocational needs of its members. If the needs of these members are not met, the group or organization will progressively and gradually decline, disintegrate and vanish.

References

Adler, N.J., and Izraeli, D., eds. 1994. *Competitive Frontiers: Women Managers in a Global Economy*, Cambridge, MA: Blackwell.
Alderfer, C.P., and K.K. Smith. 1982. Studying intergroup relations embedded in organizations. *Administrative Science Quarterly* 27: 35-

65.
Allen, D. (1993). Gandhi's Philosophy: The struggle over many contradictory philosophies. *Social Theory and Practice* 19, 3: 289-313.

Barley, S.R. 1986. Technology as an association for structuring: Evidence from observations of CT scanners and the social order of radiology departments. *Administrative Science Quarterly*, 31: 78-108.

Barthes, R. 1972. *Mythologies* (Translated by A. Lavers). New York: Hill and Wang.

Barry, B. 1996. A social trap analysis of the management of diversity. *The Academy of Management Review* 21, 3: 757-790.

Bjorkegren, D. 1991. *Postmodernism, Its Enemies and Defenders*. Paper presented at the 8th International SCOS Conference, The Valhalla Conference. Copenhagen, Denmark.

Blau, P.M. 1977. *Inequality and Heterogeneity: A Primitive Theory of Social Structure*. New York: Free Press.

Bork, R.H. 1996. *Slouching Towards Gomorrah: Modern Liberalism and American Decline*. New York: Harper Collins.

Calás, M.B., and Smircich, L. 1991. Voicing seduction to silence leadership. *Organization Studies* 12: 567-602.

Chao, G.T., P.M. Walz, and P.D. Gardner. 1992. Formal and informal mentorships: A comparison on mentoring functions and contrast with nonmentored counterparts. *Personnel Psychology* 45, 619-636.

The Chronicle of Higher Education May 2, 1997: A32.

Colella, A. and Stone, D.L. 1996. A model of factors affecting the treatment of disabled individuals in organizations. *The Academy of Management Review* 21, 2: 352-401.

Dean, J.W., and Sharfman, M.P. 1993. Procedural rationality in the strategic decision-making process. *Journal of Management Studies*, 30, 4: 587-610.

DeMuse, K.P., and W.W. Tornow. 1990. The tie that binds – has become very frayed! *Human Resource Planning* 13, 3, 203-213.

Donaldson, G. 1994. *Corporate Restructuring: Managing the Change Process From Within*. Boston: Harvard Business School Press.

Duhaime, I. ed. 1997. A review essay on the books of bell hooks: organizational diversity lessons from a thoughtful race and gender heretic. *Academy of Management Review* 22, 2: 553-574.

Edsall, T.B., and Mary, D.E. 1991. *Chain reaction: The Impact of Race, Rights, and Taxes on American Politics*. New York: Norton.

Fagenson, E.A. Ed. 1993. *Women in Management: Trends, Issues, and Challenges in Managerial Diversity*. Newbury Park, CA.: Sage.

Federal Bureaucracy. *American Sociological Review* 47: 587-599.

Flew, A. 1979. *A Dictionary of Philosophy*. New York: St. Martin's Press.

Freldman, M. 1991. The meaning of ambiguity: Learning from stories and metaphors. In *Reframing Organizational Culture,* ed. P. Frost, L. Moore, M. Louis, C. Lundberg, and J. Martin, 1145-156. Newburg Park, CA: Sage,.

Gannon M.J. 1994. *Understanding Global Cultures: Metaphorical Journeys Through 17 Countries.* Thousand Oaks, CA: Sage

Gioia, D. A. 1986. Symbols, scripts, and sensemaking. In *The Thinking Organization,* ed. H.P. Sims, 49-74, San Francisco: Jossey-Bass.

Giroux, H. A. 1994. Doing cultural studies: Youth and the challenge of pedagogy. *Harvard Educational Review*, 64, 3: 278-308.

Halsey, W.D., and B. Johnson. Eds. 1989. *Colliers Encyclopedia.* 17. New York: Macmillan Educational Company, 558-562.

Harnessing a diversity of views to understand multiculturalism. *The Academy of Management Review* 21, 2: 434-462.

Hart, J. 1995. President Clinton and the politics of symbolism: Cutting the White House staff. *Political Science Quarterly* 110, 3: 385-403.

Herskovits, M. J. 1948. *Man and His Works: The Science of Cultural Anthropology*. New York: Knopf.

Hunt, D.M., and C. Michael. 1983. Mentorship: A career training and development tool. *Academy of Management Review* 8: 475-485.

Jackson, S.E. and Alvarez, E.B. 1992. Working through diversity as a strategic imperative. In *Diversity in the Workplace: Human Resources Initiatives,* ed. S.E. Jackson, 13-29, New York: Guilford Press.

Kanter, R.M. 1989. *When Giants Learn to Dance: Mastering the Challenge of Strategy, Management and Careers in the 1990s.* New York: Simon and Schuster.

Kanter, R.M. 1989. The New Managerial Work. *Harvard Business Review* 67, 6: 85-92.

Keizai, D. 1992. *O-Pun Shisutemu e No Kigyo [Enterprise Reform Toward an Open System].* Tokyo: Author.

Kram, K.E. 1985. *Mentoring at Work.* Glenview, IL: Scott, Foresman and Co.

Kroeber, A. L. 1944. *Configurations of Culture Growth.* Berkeley: University of California Press.

Lakoff, G. 1987. *Woman, Fire, and Dangerous Things. What Categories Reveal about the Mind.* Chicago: University of Chicago Press.

Malinowski, B. 1945. *The Dynamics of Cultural Change.* New Haven, CT: Yale University Press.

Martin, J. 1992. *Cultures in Organizations: Three Perspectives.* New York: Oxford University Press.

Martin, J. 1990. Deconstructing organizational taboos: The suppression of gender conflict in organizations. *Organization Science,* 1: 339-359.

McDonough, P.M., and McLaren, P. 1996. Essay review: Critical postmodern studies of gay and lesbian lives in academia. *Harvard Educational Review,* 66, 2: 368-382.

Meyerson, D. 1991a. Normal ambiguity? In *Reframing Organizational Culture,* eds. P. Frost, L. Moore, M. Louis, C. Lundberg, and J. Martin, 31-144. Newbury Park, CA: Sage.

Meyerson, D. 1991b. Acknowledging and uncovering ambiguities in culture. In *Reframing Organizational Culture,* eds. P. Frost, L. Moore, M. Louis, C. Lundberg, and J. Martin, 254-270. Newbury Park, CA: Sage.

Mintzberg, H. 1983. *Power In and Around Organizations.* Englewood Cliffs, N.J.: Prentice-Hall.

Munch, R. and Smelser, N.J. Eds. *Theory of Culture.* University of California Press.

Ott, J.S. 1989. *The Organizational Culture Perspective.* Pacific Grove, CA: Pacific Brooks/Cole.

Posner, M.I., ed. 1989. *Foundations of Cognitive Science.* Cambridge, MA: The MIT Press.

Rafaeli, A., and M.G. Pratt. 1993. Tailored meanings: On the meaning and impact of organizational dress. *Academy of Management Review* 18, 1: 32-55.

Raggins, B.R. 1997. Diversified mentoring relationships in organizations: A power perspective. *Academy of Management Review* 22, 2: 482-521.

Raggins, B.R., and D.B. McFarlin. 1990. Perceptions of mentor roles in cross-gender mentoring relationships. *Journal of Vocational Behavior* 37: 321-339.

Richard, T. 1985. *Discourse/Counter-Discourse.* Ithaca: Cornell University Press.

Schein, E.H. 1991. *Organizational Culture and Leadership.* San Francisco: Jossey-Bass Publishers.

Sievers, B. 1993. *Work, Death, and Life Itself: Essays on Management and Organization.* Berlin-New York: de Gruyter.

Spradley, J.P. 1979. *The Ethnographic Interview.* New York: Holt, Rinehart and Winston.

Strati, A. 1992. Aesthetic understanding of organizational life. *Academy of Management Review* 17: 568-581.

Strati, A. 1990. Aesthetics and organizational life. *Academy of Management Review* 17: 568-581.

Takahashi, K., and N. Watanabe. 1997. The emergence and development of a psycho-dynamic approach to Japanese managerial operations: The unconscious process of organizational socialization. Japan: Jimbun-Gakubu Mie University and Keio University. *The Academy of Management Review* 2, 2: 565.

The Chronicle of Higher Education May 2, 1997, A32.

Van Maanen, J. 1988. *Tales of the Field: On Writing Ethnography.* Chicago: University of Chicago Press.

Welch, L.B. ed. 1992. *Perspectives on Minority Women in Higher Education.* New York: Praeger.

Wellman, B. 1988. Structure analysis: From method and metaphor to theory and substance. In *Social Structures: A Network Approach,* eds. B. Wellman and S.D. Berkowitz, 19-61. Cambridge, England: Cambridge University Press.

Witkin, R. W. 1990. The aesthetic imperative of a rational technical machinery: A study in organizational control through the design of artifacts. In *Symbols and Artifacts; Views of the Corporate Landscape,* ed. P. Gaglaiardi, 325-338 . Berlin: Walter de Gruyter.

Young, I.M. (1992). Recent theories of justice. *Social Theory,* 18, 1: 64-79.

Section Three: Organizational Processes

Section Three is about organizational processes. This section addresses seven major organizational processes, namely organizational leadership, organizational communication, organizational decision making, organizational technology, organizational work motivation, organizational control, and organizational change. Organizational processes are forward looking, sequentially organized and step by step procedures, ways, techniques, and hierarchically constructed belief systems and activities that are collectively activated to serve as the "engine" of productivity and performance. This engine of organizational production and development is willed to accomplish the mission of the organization. In the post-modern world, organizational processes are the means to an end. Historically, these processes have evolved with the advancement in technology, culture and theoretical development. This development is a form of instrumental rationality because it is concerned with how to use organizational means (processes) in order to achieve organizational goals.

Chapter 9

Organizational Leadership

A leader is a person who wears many hats. Naturally, he/she has a following of loyal supporters, moderate supporters and enemies to whom he/she is wisely advised to reach out. In doing that, both friends and enemies call the leader—our leader. A leadership model is a strong rather than weak personality. That is why he/she models. To model is to be an "archetype, copy, criterion, design, duplicate, an example, form, image, gauge, mold, original, paragon, pattern, prototype, replica, representation, specimen, standard or tracing." Leadership models lead the family, the group or team, the organization, the nation or the world at large *(New Webster's Dictionary and Thesaurus,* 1995, p. T-38). This chapter has three sections. The first section concerns theories of leadership. The other two sections are a comparative analysis of Western and Eastern public (political) leaders.

Theory

Martin Buber, a British existentialist philosopher once told a story about Rabbi Baer of Radoshitz. The Rabbi (Baer) said to his teacher, "Show me one general way to the service of God." The teacher replied, "It is impossible to tell men what way they should take. For one way to serve God is through learning, another through prayer, another through fasting, and still another through eating" (Martin Buber). As an intellectual philosopher and leader, Buber used this illustration to show that the individual should be himself/herself without being irrationally suffocated by the unnecessary dogmas, doctrines or ideologies of the moment. In other words, the individual needs to create self-identity for personal awareness. Past models are valuable examples that need to be selectively emulated to articulate our contemporary tastes, needs and aspirations. For instance, past models or standards may have been only good for the past rather than the present. This aspect makes leadership theory or model to be a situational affair rather than the traditional fixation with the trait theory of personality (in which leaders were viewed to be wise and eclectic) (Nash, 1968). In other words, leaders, for instance Roosevelt, Truman, and Kennedy and others, were not only integrated, self-respecting, expressive, self-confident, charismatic, bold, courageous, tenacious and visionary etc., but, contemporary leaders should rise above this trait theory and possess the capability to solve problems that are unique, situational or of special circumstances.

Leadership is effective management of culture. The diversity of cultural differences in individual, group, organizational, or societal realms are immense. Each individual, group, organization or society identifies itself in terms of the underlying cultural assumptions, beliefs and values that determine how people "perceive, feel, and think" (Schein, 1991). These perceptions, feelings, and thoughts are commonly shared by group, team and organizational members who predominantly are cultural "insiders" rather than "outsiders." Cultural outsiders can become insiders through socialization, enculturation and in some cases, through assimilation. Effective management of culture is accomplished when leaders establish the mission, goals and objectives of the organization and strive to attain them. The mission, goals and objectives are organizational, institutional or societal standards which have been superstitiously, intellectually, scientifically or philosophically analyzed to filter the unwanted from the wanted cultural aspirations members want to reach (Allen, 1993). Leadership models manage culture to make life worth living and enhance "knowledge, belief, art, law, morals, custom" (Taylor, 1871) and civilization which they have inherited from their ancestors.

In the corporate world, model leaders use many techniques to manage organizational culture and performance. They can manipulate artifacts and symbols. They can communicate values that foster the organization. They can use socialization to shape behavior. In other words, they interactively and interpersonally communicate organizational culture to employees. By doing so, they reinforce organizational norms (expectations) and standards. Effective and visionary leadership models develop a culture or organizational climate which values diversity, emphasizes empowerment, nurtures innovation in industry, service, and professions and promotes ethical behavior (Nelson and Quick, 1994).

It is wise to differentiate management from leadership. Mintzberg (1973) asserts that management functions involve planning, organizing, coordinating and controlling. In a general way, he views managerial roles to be interpersonal, informational and decisional roles and subroles. Leaders who manage play the following roles: interpersonal figurehead, leader, liaison, informational monitor, disseminator, spokesperson, decision entrepreneur, disturbance handler, resource allocator and negotiator (Mintzberg, 1973).

Managers should portray effective interpersonal, technical and conceptual skills (Mann, 1965). Contrary to the roles of management, the essence of leadership is "responsibility for motivating and activating subordinates and staffing, training, and associated duties" (Siegel and Lane, 1987, 484). Without followers, the leader leads nobody or nothing. Every organization requires a leader whose training, experience and temperament are relevant to its unique culture needs, and aspirations. French and Raven (1959) have shown that leaders (supervisors) need (reward, coercive, legitimate, expert and referent power) for supervising subordinates. Yukl (1981) has shown that effective leaders tend to rely more on expert (specialization) and referent (identification) power. On the contrary, Podsakoff and Scriesheim (1985) who have critiqued leadership models, argued that effective leaders are those who place emphasis on such variables as productivity and satisfaction of members and clients.

Theories of Leadership

During the 1950s, the two radically different theories of leadership were the trait theory which identifies *characteristics* of effective leaders and the behavioral and human relations theory which identifies *actions* taken by effective leaders. The trait theory was advanced by Landy (1983) who used such characteristics as "age, ambition, dominance, empathy, height, intelligence, motivation, self-confidence, verbal facility" and charisma (Siegel and Lane, 1987, 486). Kenny and Zaccaro have argued that these traits reflect members' needs and goals which the organization learns to identify and promote or change.

Behavior theory was analyzed at Ohio State University during the 1950s. The scholars studied educational, military, business, and industrial organizations. They concluded that effective leaders display dimensions of consideration (respect for subordinate ideas, mutual trust, and warmth) and initiating structure (roles) which different individuals are expected to play (Fleishman, 1953). Effective leadership is a joint function of characteristics of the leader and features of the situation in which leadership is exercised. The leader is an organizational engineer (Fiedler, 1967).

Situational Theories: Fiedler's Contingency Theory

Situational theories are based on contingency theory. Contingency theory is characterized by its likelihood of uncertainty, probability, unforeseeableness, or incidental quality. The three common situational theories—include the path-goal theory, the contingency theory and the normative theory. Effective leadership (style) is contingent (dependent) on the situational context in which it must be utilized.

Path-goal theory is grounded on the belief that leaders motivate subordinates. Different styles are appropriately used to motivate different subordinates under different circumstances. Theoretically, "effective leaders clarify the path to subordinate goal attainment" (Siegel and Lane, 1987, 497). Path-goal theory is cognitively influenced by the expectancy theory of motivation in which the leader is responsible for motivating subordinates. To do so effectively, the leader becomes directive, supportive, participative and achievement oriented rather than cold, aloof, calculating, exclusionary and nongoal oriented.

Implications for the Organizations

Path-goal theory emphasizes effective leadership as a major element for subordinate motivation, job satisfaction, and performance. As a contingency theory, it stresses that the leader is a diagnostician who should identify the needs of subordinates and structure outcomes in order to satisfy those needs. Second, the diagnostic leader should eliminate obstacles which hinder subordinates from attaining their goals. Third, the leader coaches and counsels subordinates individually. Fourth, the leader must reward subordinates for achieving their goals.

Path-goal theory is ambitiously theorized and constructed because it tries to integrate expectancy theory of motivation, ideas on consideration and initiating structure which were used at Ohio State University during the 1950s, and Fiedler's contingency theory of leadership. Path-goal theory is relatively weak as a subfield of inquiry because the terms which describe it are rather technical to operationalize. These terms are definitively ambiguous (Yukl, 1981). With its intuitive and integrative appeal, and for it to be used effectively, path-goal theory requires critical intellectual refinement in the fields of industrial organization psychology and social science.

Normative Theory

The normative theoretical model concerns decision-making. A leader's quality decisions can influence other people to react in relation to commitment, turn over and productivity. Such a leader's job can be viewed to be decision-making. The model is situational because decision-making processes are seen as appropriate for solving a variety of organizational issues and problems. Normative theory is normative because it is decisionally prescriptive (Vroom and Yetton, 1973).

Taxonomically, Vroom and Yetton have classificationally indicated that autocratic, consultative and group strategies are commonly used to operationalize the model. While consideration and initiation of structure are needed for the effective implementation of normative theory, consultative strategy capitalizes heavily on consideration. This situational theory was designed to assist the leader to rationally make decisions after weighing a variety of alternatives, situations and people for whom and to the decisions that are to be made. The optimal choice will influence the formation of a decision that is qualitatively superior, rapidly constructed and approved or ratified. Such a decision will be effectively implemented by the subordinates.

Vroom and Yetton have constructed seven rules for strategically constructing the model. Three rules protect the quality of decisions that are being made. Four rules promote the chances of their being accepted by the subordinates. Decision processes for groups can be taxonomically illustrated with Fig ABCD (Siegel and Lane, 1987, 501-503).

Since the real world is more characterized by participative and autocratic situations rather than managers, decision-making behavior is contingent upon a variety rather than a uniformity of situational variables. The normative model is coherent, useful for training, and empirically significant in statistical reliability (Field, 1979, 1982). Role-playing is not the only function leaders do. Effective leadership also means appropriate scheduling, planning, encouraging, evaluating performance, developing subordinates' skills, ironing out interpersonal conflict and saying "Hi" to those around you.

Leadership as Reciprocity of the Vertical Dyad Model

The vertical dyad linkage (VDL) model (Dansereau, Graen, and Haga, 1975) and the social exchange leadership theory of Hollander (1978) place emphasis on mutual influence which exists between leaders and followers. The mutual influence idea is currently popular in basketball team mentality. Both the coach and the players, whatever they do, influence each other. Though these theories superficially assume that the subordinates in this supervisor-subordinate dyad or relationship behave or respond homogeneously (Dansereau et al, 1973), that form of homogeneity is misconstrued since each dyad crosses many layers of organizational hierarchy.

Supervisors use leadership when they exert influence without using their authority (Dansereau et al, 1975; Jacobs, 1971). For instance, supervisors can persuade, advise, etc. On the contrary, supervisors use supervision when the substance of their influence "is formal organization, policies, procedures, and rewards" (Siegel and Lane, 1987, 506). Sociologically speaking, a supervisor leads or supervises depending on the status of his/her social network status. In other words, the "supervisor will either lead or supervise depending upon whether the subordinate is perceived to be a member of the in-group or the out-group" (p. 506). As reality indicates:

> the relationship in a particular supervisor-subordinate dyad is regarded as reciprocal. In-group members are viewed by the leader/supervisor as having greater competence and skill, having earned the privilege of being trusted, and as deserving of greater responsibility. Consequently, in-group members are permitted more latitude to negotiate job-related matters and receive more attention and support. In essence, in-group members are led, whereas out-group members are supervised (pp. 506 and 507) (comparatively).

As evidence has shown, extreme in-group interdependence leads to group think which is detrimental to organizational vitality and innovation. Managerial leaders should not totally ignore the role outsiders play when issues of change, innovation and quality are at stake.

Based on scholarly evidence, in-group subordinates tend to agree more closely with their supervisors about the nature and tasks of their job (Graen and Schiemann, 1978). In a sense, subordinates and supervisors influence each other regardless of their status in the organizational hierarchy (Liden and Graen, 1980). When the same supervisor interacts more frequently with their supervisees, evidence indicates that more job satisfaction and less turnover is experienced. This happens because there is high quality rather than low quality leader-subordinate interaction (Vecchio and Gobdel, 1984). Such regular and interactive exchanges significantly contribute to improvement in "subordinates' job satisfaction, supervisor satisfaction, and productivity" (Siegel and Lane, 1987, 507).

To be effective, the VDL leadership model must be tailored to meet the needs of the unique situation of each supervisor-subordinate dyad. Though the VDL approach is time consuming and costly to implement, it is suitable for higher-level dyads rather than those of the supervisor-blue-collar dyadic type.

When a leader's behavior is substituted for leadership, variables such as subordinate characteristics, task characteristics and organizational characteristics are used as neutralizers which collectively, are a form of "supportive leadership" (p. 509). Supportive or substitutive leadership is not necessary if subordinates are competent in terms of experience, capability and training. Supportive leadership is stronger than instrumental leadership because the former is value driven while the latter is agency driven. In organizations, values are more preeminent than agencies and agents. Intrinsically satisfying tasks and cohesive work-groups are effective substitutes. Leaders are those who are in charge because they have a command over their followers. Their effectiveness or ineffectiveness of leadership is a function of follower-perceptions and leader actions.

Leadership as Ultrapreneurship

In the private sector, leadership is not only enterpreneurship but also a form of ultrapreneurship. Ultrapreneurship is extreme entrepreneurship. Ultrapreneurs are more productive than other executive entrepreneurs are. Though they "get twice the work done in one work-hour as other executives their work is better and more productive" (Marino, 1997, 11). The factors which influence their success could include but are not limited to the "health of the economy, the unique product advantages a company has over its competitors, the efficiencies of its manufacturing processes, the lack of strong competitors, better customer knowledge and service, or just plain luck" (p. 11).

As leaders in business and industry, ultrapreneurs have been described by psychologists as follows:

They love what they do—and would rather be doing it than doing anything else. They have a psychological urge to lead. They are self-confident. They know themselves well—both their strengths and their weaknesses. They play to their strengths, and they bolster their weaknesses with people who possess the skills they lack. They are great communicators. They share information with all employees. They have little time or inclination for socializing. In fact, they avoid intracompany friendships and relationships. They are geared to systems, new technologies, and team approaches to problem solving. They measure performance results. They enjoy sound mental and physical health which allows them to carry their workloads comfortably and happily. They are generalists rather than specialists; they have broad knowledge of a wealth of subjects. This enables them to comprehend complex situations quickly and to conceptualize problems easily. It also keeps them from concentrating on just one facet of the business. It encourages them to delegate. They are adept at political maneuvering and at building loyalty among their employees. They are realists who size up people and situations quickly and accurately. They rarely take "no" for an answer. They have confidence in their ability to achieve their goals. When they run into unforeseen problems, they improvise. They thrive on challenges presented by calculated risks. But they take risks only when their mental, physical, and organization's resources can be applied effectively against those risks. They are able to channel their frustrations into constructive effort. They have little need for status. Luxurious cars, expensive homes, and impeccably tailored clothes are at the bottom of their lists of priorities, unless those items work constructively to benefit their businesses (p. 11).

Ultrapreneurs have rapport with people because people accept their agenda. They praise honestly and appreciatively, they accept mistakes directly before mentioning the mistakes of others. They ask questions rather than ordering people. They make people feel better about themselves and interested in organizational pursuits. As policy entrepreneurs, ultrapreneurs use a variety of activities to promote their ideas in public and private arena. These activities include but are not limited to "identifying problems, networking in policy circles, shaping the terms of policy debates and building coalitions" (Mintron, 1997, 739). Though they may be perceived as superficial specialists, their superficiality is broad and comprehensive enough to enable them to effectively muster authority and power to lead.

Based on industrial organizational and psychological perspectives, leadership is social and intellectual cognition that is perceptively associated with individual or organizational performance. Executive leadership shapes organizational culture to absorb information processing (Lord and Maher, 1991) which helps to define the extent to which top executives are characterized by leadership competence. Competent leaders achieve their goals due to "ability, effort, task difficulty or luck" (Siegel and Lane, 1987, 512). People, tasks and contexts influence performance. Perceptually, subordinates are treated differently depending on whether their success or failure is internally or externally caused. For instance, if a person is known to be high in ability, he/she is likely to be punished if he/she performs poorly. Supervisors see poor performance to be internally caused while subordinates see the opposite view.

Gary Yukl (1994) has listed nine terms which tactical leaders (managers) use to influence performance, action, or behavior in public organizational settings. These influence tactics include:

1. Rational persuasion:- the leader uses logic and facts to persuade the target that the proposal is strategically achievable.
2. Inspirational appeals:- the leader proposes a target and creates an enthusiastic climate through which target values, ideals, and aspirations can be confidently articulated.
3. Consultation:- the leader involves target participation by strategizing activity or change for which target support and assistance are desired, or is willing to modify a proposal that deals with target issues.
4. Ingratiation:- the leader uses praise, flattery, friendly behavior, or helpful behavior to get the target in a good mood or to think favorably of him/her before asking for something.
5. Personal appeals:- the leader targets feelings of loyalty and friendship toward him/her when seeking help.
6. Exchange:- the leader exchanges favors and shows that he/she is willing to reciprocate later or promise a share of the benefits if the target is instrumental.
7. Coalition tactics:- the leader seeks the help of others to influence the target to do something or uses the support of others as a reason for the target to be in agreement.
8. Legitimating tactics:- the leader seeks to establish the legitimacy of a request by claiming authoritative power to make it or by ascertaining that it is consistent with organizational policies, rules, practices or traditions.
9. Pressure:- the leader tends to use demands, threats, frequent checking, or persistent reminders to influence the target to do what he/she wants.

The above nine mentioned tactics of influence are comparable to (Robert Nakamura's and Frank Smallwood's, 1980) five kinds of policy implementers in public organizations. The five include:

1. Classical technocrats are directed by policy makers to implement goals in the context of the former's specialization and effective hierarchical and organizational command structures. These technocrats have technical capabilities for achieving goals.
2. Instructed delegates are implementers who operationalize the specific goals of policymakers. The former are authorized to implement the goals because they have technical, administrative and negotiating capabilities to implement and rationalize the goals and achieve them.
3. Bargainers are implementers whose negotiating power, relative to the power of policymakers, is considerable and full of clout because they are capable of issuing threats of noncompliance and nonimplementation. Although formal policymakers determine policy goals, the desirability of the goals does not necessarily enable bargainers and policymakers to agree. To resolve their differences over the goals in question, both implementers and policymakers have to bargain with each other and over goals and means.
4. Discretionary experimenters are implementers who dramatically receive abundant delegated power from uninformed policymakers to refine goals and develop the means for accomplishing them.
5. Bureaucratic entrepreneurs are powerful implementers who generate and control information. Because they have continuity, they can outlast and wear down policymakers. They possess entrepreneurial and political skills which they use to construct and dominate policy formulation.

Managerial traits, motivations and skills which characterize managers were studied by Bass (1981). Bass's Stogdill's *Handbook of Leadership* (1981, 1990) is a product of Stogdill's 45-year study of leadership. Stogdill researched 124 articles dealing with personal factors concerning leadership. These articles were 1904 through 1947 publications. Between 1948 and 1970, Stogdill also surveyed 163 articles for traits on leadership. Though the *Handbook of Leadership* was the result of the study, the specific leadership traits for which Bass is canonically known include:

1. Capacity: intelligence, alertness, verbal facility, originality, judgment.
2. Achievement: scholarship, knowledge, athletic accomplishments.
3. Responsibility: dependability, initiative, persistence, aggressiveness, self-confidence, desire to excel.
4. Participation: activity, sociability, cooperation, adaptability, humor.
5. Status: socioeconomic position, popularity.
6. Situation: mental level, status, skills, needs and interests of followers, objectives to be achieved, and so on (Gortner, Mahler, and Nicholson, 1997, 335).

Bass summarized the results of his own work and concluded that the organizational leader is characterized by a strong drive for responsibility task completion, vigor and persistence in pursuit of goals. The same leader tends to be venturesome, original in problem solving and possesses a drive which enables him to exercise initiative in socially constructed organizational settings. The leader has self-confidence and a strong sense of personal identity. His drive for leadership propels him to be willing to accept consequences of decision and action. He is prepared and destined to absorb interpersonal stress, willingness to tolerate frustration and delay and ability to influence other people's behavior. Above all, the leader has the "capacity to structure social interaction systems to the purpose at hand" (Bass, 1981, 87).

Closely related to the trait theory of leadership is the theory of motivation and values which managers and executives hold. David McClelland (1975) and Winter (1973) have argued that the three major factors which contribute to managerial effectiveness are needs for achievement, power, and affiliation. For instance,

In established bureaucracies, the dominant motive of most successful organizational managers is the need for power. Along with a drive for power appears to go the self-confidence and assertiveness that are necessary to lead and control a large and complex group. The power drive, however, needs to be moderated by a sense of concern for the group, or a social sense, that generates a use of power to benefit others, and not simply for one's own advantage. A leader with a power drive that is moderated by social concern is usually more open to advice, to active participation in decisions by subordinates, to the development of clear and understandable organization structures, and therefore, to a general pride in belonging to the organization (Gortner, Mahler, and Nicholson, 1997, 336).

Any successful leader has a need for affiliation that will enable him to fulfill the social and public relations activities that are essential for managerial executive positions. Affiliation is paramount for the "leader's effective interpersonal relationships with subordinates, peers, and superiors" (p. 336).

Motivation is closely interwoven with the values managers hold on to tightly. The values create motivation. According to L. Gordon (1975, 76), there are six major organizational values. These include but are not entirely limited to:

Support: Being treated with understanding, kindness, and consideration; receiving encouragement from other people.

Conformity: Following regulations; doing what is accepted, proper, or socially correct.

Recognition: Attracting favorable attention; being admired, looked up to, or considered important.

Independence: Being free to make one's own decisions or doing things in one's own way: experiencing freedom of action.

Benevolence: Being generous and other directed; sharing with and helping those who are less fortunate.

Leadership: Having authority over people; being in a position of influence and power (Gordon, 1975, 22-25; and Gortner, Mahler, and Nicholson, 1997, 336-337).

Conclusive evidence has frequently shown that effective managers and executives have higher leadership ranking but lower support, conformity and benevolence scores. Though human relations components such as "rationality and individuality, and ethical factors are important, these are not comparable to the six values mentioned above.

In relation to situational theories of group leadership, the "managerial grid" (Blake and Mouton, 1994) is well-known model of supervisory management. The grid is based on two dimensions of organizational behavior. First managers must have a genuine concern for people. Second, they also must demonstrate a genuine concern for productivity. These concerns are parallel consideration and initiating structure principles of management for which Ohio State University was known for during the 1950s and 1960s.

Three important questions the supervisor needs to ask should read as follows: "What are the important factors that must be taken into consideration if a particular individual is going to be successful in leading this group? How many of these factors can be combined and still be manipulated by the individual who is attempting to lead? How does the leader keep track of newly developing factors that may prove important to leadership success? (Gortner, Mahler, and Nicholson, 1997, 344).

Blake and Mouton (1985) have argued that teamwork is essential in organizational productivity. Based on management theory, the team gets involved in the theory of managing which "presumes an essential connection between organizational needs for production and the needs of people for full and rewarding work experiences. The leaders desire is to contribute to corporate success by involving others so that they too may contribute. Such a 'can do' spirit is contagious, inspires a 'win' attitude in others, and promotes enthusiasm, voluntarism, spontaneity, and openness. Contributions with caring in the sense of a genuine desire to help others reach their highest potential is basic to creativity, commitment, and cohesion" (Blake and Mouton, 1985, 82).

Gary Yukl (1994) has identified a comprehensive "multiple linkage model" for supervisory management (p. 295). He has constructed situational variables that contribute to effective individual and group performance. Of the most important variables (factors) are the following:

1. Subordinate effort. The extent to which subordinates strive to attain a high level of performance and show a high degree of personal responsibility and commitment to task objectives.
2. Subordinate ability and role clarity. The extent to which subordinates understand their job responsibilities, know what to do, and have the skills to do it.
3. Organization of work. The extent to which effective performance strategies are used by the group to attain its task objectives and the work is organized to ensure efficient utilization of personnel, equipment and facilities.
4. Cooperation and teamwork. The extent to which group members work together smoothly as a team, share information and ideas, help each other, and feel a strong identification with the group.
5. Resources and support. The extent to which the group has the budgetary funds, tools, equipment, supplies, personnel, and facilities needed to do the work, and necessary information or assistance from other units.
6. External coordination. The extent to which the activities of the work unit are synchronized with the interdependent activities of other subunits in the same organization and those of outside organizations (e.g., suppliers, clients, joint venture partners,

thereby avoiding unnecessary delays, disruptions, and wasted effort (Yukl, 1994, 295-296 and Gortner, Mahler, and Nicholson, 1997, 346).

Individual subordinates' performance largely depends on the first four above mentioned Yuklian factors. The last two factors relate to the group as a whole. The interactive behavior of the six factors help to ascertain the nature of individual and group commitment, morale and productivity. Leadership, as Gulick (1937) has demonstrated, works better when organizational leadership promotes the 'dominance' of an idea (Gortner, Mahler, and Nicholson, 1997, 347).

Strategic leaders are, in a sense, also, transformational. They like to challenge the status quo and inspire a shared vision. They enable others to act by modeling the way and drawing people forward. Such leaders search for opportunities, tend to experiment and take risks. Behavioristically, they are visionaries because they visualize the future. They foster collaboration, empower others and become the example. Their plans produce small but cumulative gains that are like "quantum leaps." These strategic leaders recognize the contributions of others and encourage organizations to celebrate major accomplishments (Nutt and Backoff, 1993).

Introspectively, strategic leaders have certain values. They superstitiously believe in the importance of the strategy, the need for it, its enemies and its efficiency. Rhetorically, they craft metaphors that enable others to visualize or become sensitive to change. They use stories and linguistic parlance that fit the audience (Conger, 1991).

Interpretively, strategic leaders are zealously attentive to vision realization which is their trajectory. They are sensitive to meaning which they vehemently and constantly communicate. They can be trusted through positioning and commitment (Bennis and Nanus, 1985). When they take action, these leaders search for vision, chart new directions, challenge others to be committed, recognize the institutional and organizational architecture and the possibilities for growth and innovation. They discover their niche and use it to move the organization toward the desired trajectory while constructively reducing the fear of failure.

Leadership is a form of exemplary followership. Exemplary followers are co-creators of strategic vision. The leaders support followers to share information, co-create vision, share risk and reward and to experience a supportive environment. Such followers are makers of leaders. According to Kelley (1991), both leaders and followers mold each other contractually.

Kelley's research findings from a variety of public and private organizations showed profound "dissatisfaction with leaders in a wide variety of organizations ... The findings suggest that 50 percent of all leaders have questionable abilities. Few provide positive role models and even fewer instill trust. Feeling threatened by talented subordinates, these leaders respond to their insecurities by refusing to share the limelight (Nutt and Backoff, 1993, p. 331). Talented and exemplary followers are largely instrumental to organizational success. Speaking to this effect,

These individuals must do the work that carries out plans which will transform an organization. Before someone can ride the winds of change, exemplary followers are needed to fill the sails. An exemplary follower is an active, independent and critical thinker who responds to challenges with energy and commitment. They find ways to increase their worth to the organization and to work within an organization's network of relationships while retaining strong values which Kelley calls a 'courageous conscience.' These traits make exemplary followers stand out from other followers who are passive, conformist, alienated, and even the pragmatic follower who does what is required without passion and commitment. Leaders do not create exemplary followers, but must sustain and nurture them if they are to make transformation" (p. 331).

The following two sections are a comparative analysis of the most popular twentieth century political leaders in the Western and communist or post-communist Soviet societies. Their personalities, societal environments and experiences may have helped them to exercise leadership in the way they did.

Organizational Leadership: The Western Experience

The purpose of this section is to make an attempt to analyze the sources, characteristics, functions, styles, and challenges of the presidency in academic, political and corporate world. Although the analysis will be based on an "outsider" rather than an "insider" perspective, a condition dictated by economic and logistic rather than intellectual illumination, the analysis will be kept informative and enlightening.

Every presidential regime is characterized by complex structures, complex organizational cultures, and complex needs which the leadership of that regime, through its various upper, middle, and lower echelons, tries to nurture and change. Every type of nurturance of the structures, culture, and needs depends on who is in power, what philosophical theory of leadership dominates his thinking, who his closest advisors and what their backgrounds are, what his social, psychological, and genetic sources of his leadership dreams are, what his ability to integrate information wisely is, and what state of simplicity or sophistication the cultural, scientific and technological evolution his society (followers) finds itself in.

If a national president is a transforming leader, he possesses seeds of intellectual, reformative, revolutionary, heroic, or ideological orientation. If he is a transactional leader, his orientation to opinion, group, party, legislative (parliamentary) and executive leadership will radically differ from the former (Burns, 1978). The terms (transforming and transactional) express the relationships which exist between leaders and their followers. Transactional leaders create a situation in which and through which their followers exchange one thing for another with them, e.g., jobs for votes. On the contrary, transforming leaders identify the needs and demands of their followers by examining their potential motivations. Having identified their needs and demands, the transforming leaders establish a viable machinery for satisfying the higher needs of their followers. This process of follower need satisfaction results in the conversion of followers to leaders and leaders to moral agents. Ecologically, the respective transformational and transactional relationships between leaders and followers is a symbiotic and reciprocal phenomenon. This phenomenon and social relationship is not only dynamically interdependent, but the interdependence is symbolic of a fair social contract, deal, or order (Burns, 1978).

When presidential leaders lose their creativity and become mere leaders, their followers take over the leadership from them and the former remain to be mere power holders. They resemble "barking dogs which have no teeth."

Scholarly evidence indicates that all presidential leaders are elitist in nature and most of them are transactional rather than transformational characters. Philosophies, styles, adversaries, backgrounds, environments, followers, and orientations per se, do not determine the effectiveness of a particular presidency. Instead, effective presidents are identified by the type of power they display and how the kind of power displayed contributes to effectively addressing important social needs, social change, and unsatisfied psychological wants and expectations (Burns, 1978, Hargrove, 1974).

Secondly, effective presidents became effective because of the nature of their personality. For instance, Franklin Roosevelt, Truman, and Kennedy "were happy, integrated, self-respecting, and expressive people who were capable of growth and learning" (Hargrove, 1974,

50). Johnson and Nixon were active but ineffective because both men suffered from a low opinion of themselves and gained little personal satisfactions from their work. The circumstances under which Nixon got involved in the Watergate scandal after Johnson's defeat due to the events of the Vietnam War and the implications of the Kennedy Association compel us to understand the sources of their low self-esteem.

Roosevelt, Truman, and Kennedy were energetic and powerfully ambitious. Their energies were externally geared toward success, not bound up in defensive manifestations.

As for Franklin Roosevelt, he was a political and democratic man who developed a healthy childhood personality. He received love and discipline from parents. From them, he learned trust and affection—skills he later developed in his successful political career. He loved himself and he was self-confident. He was a happy warrior, a warm person, and both a lion and a fox.

Franklin Roosevelt was eclectic, empirical, and operationally flexible. "His political virtues were his policy deficiencies" (Hargrove, 1974, 57). His other greatest virtues were his ability to communicate courage to others and ability to be spiritually very healthy. He had high self-esteem and a great capacity to identify with others. Roosevelt was an effective administrative leader because he possessed the above-named qualities.

In contrast to Roosevelt's personality, Richard Nixon's personality was quite different. Contemporary American presidency is viewed as one faced with crisis. For instance, 1972's Nixon's Watergate scandal was in essence "a crisis of the President's style of authority, isolation, contempt for opponents, encouragement of toughness and vindictiveness, and a sense of himself and the White House as besieged by enemies" (Hargrove, 1974, 41). The Nixonian style was typical of his personality. As a congressman, senator, vice president, and presidential candidate, Nixon's "real" true self was never known. Over the years, he was a chameleon who capitalized on specific political contexts although he appeared to have no inner moral convictions which he rhetorically used to fight his political wars. Because he had no inner convictions, he treated his opponents ruthlessly. He also developed a view that he was surrounded by enemies rather than friends. As he remained to be inwardly uncertain, he compensated his uncertainty by use of rhetoric, attack, and will. He was a fastidious "loner and an outsider" (Hargrove, 1974, 42).

Nixon's personality may be rooted in his family background. Nixon's parents were poor. His father was an authoritarian person. Nixon's two brothers died in childhood; at that time, "there was little in the way of established community or subcultural tradition to rely on as a source of personal identity beyond anomic lower-middle class society" (p. 43). In college he struggled with his classes. Both in high school and college he always ran for office by using his weakest strategies and turning them into strengths. Although Nixon was a courageous man, his strongest drive was not for power, it was for fame and respect. It is an irony that he won the highest office in the land, influenced national and international power, and yet felt weak and defensive.

The reason for the comparative contrast between Franklin Roosevelt and Richard Nixon is not only to show the differences between a strong and weak president but to clarify that specific family, childhood, and school backgrounds which helped to determine their personalities also prominently featured during their adult lives of political careerism.

Nixon and Roosevelt were politicians who evolved within a particular geo-political and cultural framework. Their rise to prominence in leadership was nurtured within the western geo-political and cultural framework. Since their rise within that framework was motivated, largely, by their political and historic ambitions of the time, and since their ambitious manifestations of leadership and power inspired their regimes and followers to support them, it might be said that their typical administrative leadership styles and power differentials were expressions of political authority. The authority (will) was given to them by the people. The manner in which their governments displayed authority by defending freedom, protecting the weak and the strong, dispensing justice for the good of all, raising taxes and distributing them for economic development and welfare programs, etc., does not only show the essence of power differentials between the two presidents, but the positive rather than the negative essence of these differentials determined the impact of their leadership as a form of political expression. The impact lies hidden in the annals of history as courage, boldness, tenacity, and vision. This is the meaning of the impact when it is translated in terms of effectiveness. Without the leadership of towering presidents, who are men and women of unusual ability, the problems of the future which such men may help to create will catastrophically haunt society and its institutions. President Clinton's behavior of lying under oath to cover up sexual immorality is a classic example which has created a crisis that has destabilized congressional politics and national ethos.

Technically, leadership may be viewed as cultural expression. In some societies, leadership is a reflection of wider conceptions and practices of societal management. Certain values, e.g., "efficiency, specificity, rationality, measurability, objectivity" (Sergiovanni, 1984), and "effectiveness" (Sagini, 1987) are combined with the understanding that good management is responsible cultural accountability. In such an arena, leadership theory places emphasis on the leader's behavior and on results of management. During the management of leadership processes, it is theoretically expected that uncertainty and ambiguity are both natural and desirable outcomes of strategic phenomena in management. Within this realm, what the leader stands for is more important than what he/she does. The meanings a leader communicates to his juniors and colleagues are more important than his leadership style. Leaders take actions based on preconceptions, assumptions, and motives, all of which are embedded with meanings. The leadership acts are in themselves and of themselves, expressions of culture. As cultural expression, leadership seeks to build unity and order within an organization by giving attention to purposes, historical and philosophical tradition, and ideals and norms which define the way of life the organization emulates for socializing its members and obtaining their compliance. To develop and nurture organizational value patterns and norms represent a response to felt needs of individuals and groups for orderliness and stability of purpose and meaning. As he demonstrated, Shils (1961) described organizational need by showing that every organization has a "center." Organizational centers represent the focus of values, sentiments and beliefs which provide the cultural cement needed to hold people together in groups and groups into an organizational federation. If an official center does not exist, "wild" centers develop within the organization and act as a natural response to felt needs. Since wild centers are accidentally compatible with official centers, the "domestication" of the former centers is crucial to leadership as cultural expression. Shils boldly argues that

> Organizations often resemble multicultural societies and that subgroups must of necessity maintain individual and cherished identities, the domestication process seeks minimally to build a cultural federation of compatibility which provides enough common identity, enough common meanings and enough of a basis for committed action for the organization to function in spirited concert (Shils, 1961, 107).

To function effectively, the president, then, should be the one who establishes a domestication machinery which, according to Shils (1961), can operationalize its strategy by employing ten tactical and strategic principles (prerequisites, perspective, principles, platform, politics, purposing, planning, persisting, peopling, and patriotism). All aspects of leadership do not only have an indestructible essence, but they also evoke a cultural and historical consciousness symbolic of what people believe in, why they function as they do, what they value, and what their identity is.

Characteristics of the Leader

The characteristics of a presidential leader can be as many as there are traits of leadership theory. Several authorities have offered some of the characteristics. The former president of the University of Oklahoma, asserts that a leader must possess "insight, initiative, cooperation, originality, ambition, persistence, emotional stability, judgment, popularity, and clear communication skills" (Kamm, 1982, 13). According to Kamm (1982, 13), the greatest attributes of an American political president include but are not limited to "honesty, integrity, decency, common sense, courage, and ability." Other qualities, says Kamm, are "vision, humility, understanding, patience, strength, dependability, confidence, statesmanship, pragmatism, objectivity, patriotism, and charisma" (p. 14).

A leader who has the above-named qualities is more likely to help the group to define its tasks, goals, and purposes; help the same group to realize its tasks, goals, and purposes; and help the group to be cohesive in order to gather momentum for realizing individual needs. By so doing, the leader shares power with the group. When the group has met its needs and realized its goals, their leader has also succeeded in realizing and meeting them.

Viewed from Burn's (1988) perspective, a leader should enable followers to develop faith in his/her leadership. The qualities characteristic of such a leader include vitality and endurance, decisiveness, persuasiveness (ability to change objective incentives into subjective values), responsibility and satisfactory intellectual capacity, character (moral excellence, integrity, courage, sincerity, and intelligence), motivation, and experience. In case the president is a university leader, he has to be a manager, an energizer, envoy and an intellectual. His example is equal to a guiding and authoritative directive.

Leadership may be viewed as power and conflict. Leaders of all persuasions do not and should not overlook conflict. They confront it exploitatively, embody it, and use it as a catalyst for organizational change. Leaders who shape, express, and mediate conflict capitalize on its potential benefits. Such leaders initiate the creation of mechanisms for people's identity, self-esteem, human rights, justice, and human dignity. In a sense, they help followers by leading them to see their own contradictions and to resolve these contradictions. When conflicts are resolved, change is the result. Change as an end becomes the evident resultant because the leader analytically integrates theory and moral values to produce an intellectually clear and articulatable cause. Such analytically integrated, theoretical, and practical causes are reflections of successful transformational and strategic leadership.

According to Lall and Lall (1979), a leader needs to have a sense of humor, a profound knowledge of human nature, self-control, fairness, impartiality, energy, enthusiasm, tact, sincerity, frankness, positiveness, decisiveness, dignity, likableness, pleasantness, friendliness, desire to excel, strength of will, belief in one's own powers, originality, forcefulness, memory, and keen observation.

Both Thorndike (1940) and Stogdill (1948) argue that leaders should not only be alert, dependable, persistent, sociable, popular, adaptable, knowledgeable, economically strong, initiating and aggressively assertive, but they also should be inspired by a sense of human brotherhood, expertise in leadership, and insensitivity to slander and ingratitude.

Describing the qualities of a university president, Clark Kerr (1963) said the following when he was the President of Harvard University:

> The university president in the United States is expected to be a friend of the students, a colleague of the faculty, a good fellow with the alumni, a sound administrator with the trustees, a good speaker with the public, an astute bargainer with the foundations and the federal agencies, a politician with the state legislature, a friend of industry, labor and agriculture, a persuasive diplomat with donors, a champion of education generally, a supporter of the professions (particularly law and medicine), a spokesman to the press, a scholar in his own right, a public servant at the state and national levels, a devotee of opera and football equally, a decent human being, a good husband and father, an active member of a church. Above all, he must enjoy traveling in airplanes, eating his meals in public and attending public ceremonies. No one can be all of these things. Some succeed at being none.
>
> He should be firm, yet gentle; sensitive to others, insensitive to himself; look to the past and the future, yet be firmly planted in the present; both visionary and sound; affable, yet reflective; know the value of a dollar and realize that ideas cannot be bought; inspiring in his visions, yet cautious in what he does; a man of principle, yet able to make a deal; a man with broad perspective who will follow the details conscientiously; ... but ready to criticize the status quo fearlessly; a seeker of truth where the truth may not hurt too much; a source of public policy

pronouncements when they do not reflect on his own institution. He should sound like a mouse at home and look like a lion abroad (Hesburgh, 1979, 4).

In brief, the university president is a man of distinction, an educator, a respected countryman and an intellectual scholar and leader. It is in his capacity that he is challenged with willingness to act boldly, share credit for successes, absorb the stress of failure, and tolerate frustration and delay. When his institution experiences conflict, it should be viewed as an attempt by competing interests which try to establish boundaries, channel hostility, counteract social ossification, invigorate class and group interests, encourage innovation, and define and empower leadership. Conflict shapes stability and harmony because, when structural levels of wants, needs, and motivations are integrated with hierarchical values that are sharpened by conflict, dynamic leadership emerges as a byproduct of conflicting interests. Any leader who integrates charismatic, expert, legitimate, reward, and coercive power with his/her administrative style, especially in a university setting, achieves maximum effectiveness.

Contemporary Images of the Western Presidency, Especially in the U.S.A.

The last 60 years have witnessed a more powerful, expanded, and problematic presidential office in American politics. Success or failure of a presidential era is influenced by the constraints of and the character filling the office or by both. For instance, scholarly evidence affirms that Franklin D. Roosevelt's tenure was a watershed. After the Second World War, scholars assert, the problems which faced America were multivarious and difficult; the tasks were more complicated. As chief executive, Roosevelt managed domestic policy responsibly, became involved in world affairs, dealt with an intractable budget, made contributions in the elusive international peace market, and increased the bureaucracy of the presidential office.

The president initiates policy. However, today, his office is not only weak, but it is also one that distrusts institutional reform, hence, futuristically a likely source of strength or weakness. The president has become too visible to be an impartial public servant. The presidency has become so much personalized that it looks like a tribal plebiscite. He uses the media to misinform, disinform, and distort reality. As a result, the presidency misleads the nation because such propaganda lacks not only the critical analysis but also the taste for higher moral and ethical standards.

Because the personalized presidency lacks peer review, it raises unrealistic expectations that will never be realized, weakens political parties by going around them, plays down coalition building in support of using the media to appeal to the electorate and exalts presidential skill at campaigning over governmental administration. A president who relies more on the mass-media and less on the political parties or voters makes the electorate less informed because he relies on media consultants rather than experienced political and opinion leaders.

The expansion of the bureaucracy, executive office, and White House staff do not only offer great various institutional and specialized policy framers, but the policymakers nexus has become so fragmented that it has made the policymaking process a nebulous affair characterized by contending (antagonistic) policymaking interests. Policy formation has, hence, become more complicated and difficult. The Carter, Reagan, and Nixon administrations are classic examples.

A fragmented and policymaking group of specialists is a highly politicized and ideologically inclined bureaucracy which brilliantly, for its own survival, isolates the president from conflicting interests; the Iran-Contra and Monica Welensky scandals are cases in point.

Although the judicial, legislative, and the executive branches of government attempt to constitutionally provide checks and balances, the presidency has become weaker because an opposing party in either of the houses of Congress can form a majority which can neutralize presidential powers and vetoes.

The fact that the United States system of government is maligned by cycles of economic boom followed by recession, of liberalism followed by conservative ideological underpinnings, of governmental public confidence, followed by capitalistic private enterprise—all are phenomena that are beyond the control of a president.

One of the reasons why the presidency is elusive is that the framers of the Constitution deliberately did not define it; the definition of the office was or is done or given by its incumbent. Historians define the presidency in terms of presidential personality rather than the philosophical, cultural and historical perspective.

Reagan's is an example of a personalized presidency. He used the media to build a base for personal power. How well this strategy served him could be explained, largely, by an analysis of his Hollywood experience. It is arguable that his use of the media enabled him to translate his personal popularity into political power. To extend this power further, he appointed a large bureaucracy on the basis of ideological grounds in order to impose this power on the political system. Although he earned credit for conservative economic reforms and peacetime strategic militarization of land, air, and sea, in order to neutralize communism, a goal he masterfully achieved largely through propaganda, his failures in managing the budget, the Iran-Contra Scandal, inability to help conservatives become the majority in both houses, and his lack of foreign policy initiatives appear to have been overshadowed by his popularity.

With the evolution of polycentricism, multipolarity and interdependence, the post-modern presidency needs to be sensitive to the articulation of domestic and foreign policy agenda in a coalition manner in order to accommodate a variety of interests that are essential forces for securing support to avert national and international constraints on critical national policy (Smith, 1997). The use of a coalition of interests will enable the U.S. to globally reassert its influence in the wake of its relative decline in political and economic hegemony. This presidency is viewed to be "imperial, imperiled, impossible, plebiscitary, symbolic, rhetorical, coalitional, and administrative" (p. 220).

In the European setting, both Walesa (Poland) and Yeltsin (Russia) try to use extra constitutional powers but fail to use it. Walesa in particular, threatened to dissolve parliament in April 1994 and in February 1995 but lacked authority to do so as his re-election popularity contest had gone as low as 9%. As a president, he was neither the impartial arbiter nor a guardian of political equanimity. Many saw him as a "divisive and disruptive" rather than one who moderates, harmonizes and heals (Baylis, 1996, 318). His counterpart, Havel of the Czech Republic appears to be unpredictable rather than "dignified, diplomatic and paternalistic chief of state" (p. 319). In spite of the popularity of the rest of the presidents of Eastern European new democracies, they have not institutionalized their charisma. Since the presidents have come to office from dissident roots, their prestige and respect has yet to be observed, questioned and tested. Though their prime ministerial counterparts are more popular, stable and respected because they come from ethnically homogeneous regions, the recency of their countries politico-economic and social stability has not been fully tested by historical conflicts and economic and constitutional emoluments.

Each president has a particular leadership style and strategic leadership versatility. According to Blakeley (1995), presidents exhibit telling versus directing, selling versus coaching, participating versus supporting, analyzing versus delegating, organizing versus delegating, and endorsing versus abdicating behavior. In terms of their administrative styles (driver, expressive, amiable, analytical, institutionalist and stoic) Presidents Nixon, Reagan and Carter were low in these styles while Clinton and Eisenhower were high. These behaviors were observed rather than procured from psychological constructions.

Strategic leadership is a form of magnetic and pragmatic statesmanship. The statesman/woman makes wise and prudent decisions based on a sound theory and informed or visionary opinion. For instance, after World War II, to reconstruct Europe, President Truman made a series of practically wise, visionary, and historic decisions. He reconstructed Europe by means of the Marshall Plan, contributed to the creation of NATO, and conceived how Russian expansionism would be controlled, at least for several decades, by the strategic policy of containment (Magstadt and Schotten, 1988) which was theoretically and rationally envisioned by using a hypothetical triadic museum of strategic thought (Okle, 1989) and translated into practical terms.

As indicated from the analysis, leaders are differentiated in accordance with character, ability, methods, and purposes. Strategic leaders are able to distinguish error from truth, superficiality from reality, and substance from foolish, unrealistic, and utopian ideas. For instance, throughout his political career, Winston Churchill, the man who had "a colorful personality, ... brilliant, charming, witty, controversial, cantankerous, courageous" (Magstadt and Schotten, 1988, 302) outlook, was preoccupied with German's continental and global ambitions. Churchill's foresight, experience, and analytical skills enabled him to vehemently articulate that perceived threat for which he became isolated by the Conservative Party for a long time. The conservative government which isolated him between 1930 and 1939 for consistently pointing out the grave dangers inherent in Nazi Germany gave in in the final analysis and appointed him Prime Minister in 1940. As Prime Minister and statesman, Churchill helped save Britain and the rest of the world from German NAZI dominion during World War II. In addition, Churchill, Roosevelt, Truman and Dugal laid a framework for rebuilding Western Europe in order to contain Communistic Russian Expansion.

The Process of the Causes of the Fall of the Soviet Empire: The Challenges of the Dynamics of Leadership (Case Study)

The internal and historic decay of the rigid Soviet socioeconomic structure was caused by its elitist nomenchlatura (elite Bureaucracy) which divided society into the "haves and have-nots" of the classless society. The struggle between the two unique social classes was identified when the system's economic base declined and failed to use the base to appease or revitalize mass creativity. Absence of system creativity created avenues for mass frustration, disillusionment, and hopelessness. Pockets of imperial dissention did not only capitalize on the fragile economic base, but these dissenting vassal states also capitalized on nationalistic, ethnic, racist, and political cleavages which the system's declining essence and efflorescence had let loose. In the absence of a vibrant and unifying ideological fabric, the faltering superstructure and the "strangling" global containment strategy forced member states out of the black box. In doing so, the forces of disunion killed the "global elephant." The implications of this disunion and the permanent dismemberment of the USSR produced far-reaching and classic implications on Eastern Europe and Yugoslavia in particular.

Much of the USSR was comprised of the 15 republics excluding its satellite states of Eastern Europe. The former socialist countries of Eastern Europe are East Germany, Czechoslovakia, Poland, Hungary, Rumania, Bulgaria, and Yugoslavia. After World War II, these nations were forcefully annexed by the Soviet totalitarian and monolithic communist empire. This socialist empire lasted only for 73 years. The father of communistic socialism was Marx whose theory of historical (dialectical) materialism affirmed that history is a process of conflicting opposites particularly in social and economic spheres. To translate dialectics into practical life, the history of the world was viewed as a class struggle between the haves, and have-nots. To eliminate class structure and enforce egalitarian equality, the proletariat and the peasantry united and destroyed the bourgeois capitalist and feudal state, nationalized property, and collectivized productivity and its distribution. By doing so, the state was run by the dictatorship of the proletariat. Such dictatorship was supposedly rationalized to eliminate the capitalist exploiters by replacing the system with a classless society that would provide mechanisms for the withering away of the state. Though Marx was influenced by Engels, the former was a more devout writer and intellectual popularize of these irrational ideas (Sica, 1990). The irrational ideas could include but may not be limited to "anxiety, jealousy, ambition, pride, vengeance, love, enthusiasm, devotion and appetites of all sorts" that are glamorized to supplant objectivity, empiricism and reason. In other words, there are numerous non-rational factors in human experience and creativity particularly in aesthetic perception and imagination, in moral judgment, in political and religious belief and commitment, and even in scientific and philosophical thinking. If and when the state withered, for lacking rationality, and based on the logical but irrational theory of Marx and Engels, the communist society would evolve into a state in which it would be ruled by things rather than by the exploitative human and state driven hierarchical structures of the capitalist society. The institutions of the capitalist society suffer from moral decay, corruption, and "laws of motion," e.g., inflation and recession, which continue to enhance its relative instability. Though the state never withered for this unrealized prediction about which Marx and Engels were at fault, and though the state never became a democratic confederation as Lenin had intended, the state's elite cadres particularly the Nomenchlatura, created a "fence" or barrier around itself. This social but exclusive and bureaucratic barrier was a form of social distance intentionally devised to eliminate the proletariats and the masses from the inner and logical dynamics of communist economic, political, and technological empowerment. Such a division between the autocratic and totalitarian rulers on the one hand and the rusty masses and lumpen proletariats on the other, separated them from each other. The division between the two classes of society alienated the majority, from the supposedly productive and politically active and dominant center within the USSR and the periphery (Soviet Union and its vassal states) respectively. This division made it difficult if not impossible for the two groups of nationals to effectively communicate or exchange ideas and information from and to either side. The lack of effective communication between the two forces of society and the lack of the free flow of information between them and their institutions paralyzed the communication channel and in turn paralyzed the national spirit of creativity, morale and optimism. In turn this "confusion" bred a climate of resignation, frustration and stagnation within the empire. The nurturance of an exploitative and exacting class system within the "classless" society exacerbated continuous stagnation. Gradual stagnation and decline bred gradual disintegration which started during the 1960s when Yugoslavia and Hungary paved a different path of development. During the 1980s, solidarity and Walesa steered Poland into the Western camp. Poland had increasingly reached catastrophic and alarming proportions in terms of system decay during the 1980s. The USSR's communist system, among other things, concentrated in military related production industries and failed to diversify industry, appease nationalities or reform Russification laws, reduce the cost of military expansion during the Cold War and encourage efficient food production and distribution methods in the empire in order to lessen dissent and maximize, through ideological indoctrination and party discipline, the unification of the Soviet Union. Coupled with the fragile ethnological relationships and nationalistic dissent arising from past forced Russification, assimilation, and discrimination of ethnic minorities, system decay influenced the withering away of the empire. The state that Marx said would wither did not wither away. Instead, it "camouflaged" and ossified to cause the empire to wither away. The speed of withering away of the empire was spectacular and dramatic. Its latent tensions caused the disintegration (disunion and dissolution) of the Russian empire. The Soviets who owned it were shocked to witness "the passing of a thick cloud." The world whose interpretive and creative genius became staggeringly petrified for lack of quick and logical analysis of these dramatic events was shocked. On hindsight, it is a historic illusion. Was it real? Were they dreams? Who dreamed about them? Were they true dreams? What happened to those glorious days of Lenin and Stalin? A hard look at the personalities and the role they played could be instructive. The three most important include Stalin, Gorbachev, and Yeltsin.

Stalin

Based on the scholarly writings of Tucker (1973) and Medvedev (1989), Stalin's personality was crucial in the formation of the Soviet system after the death of Lenin. These two scholars assert that Stalin's personality was a "triffle" which made him to deflect from the path of principles of the Leninist revolution. It is argued that Stalin was

> An obsessive and damaged individual whose defence against cruelty and rejection in childhood was to create an idealized image of himself through projections on to 'hero' figures from Russia's past. To add to his troubles, Stalin was diminutive in stature (like Alexander the Great, Napoleon, Hitler, and numerous other male go-getters of history, pockmarked and had a crooked arm) (Merridale, 1993, 234).

It is also commented that Stalin had great lust for power and boundless ambition. He possessed extreme self-hate. His "denial and repression of failures, faults, errors, wrongdoing and ... villainies" (p. 234) were an expression of self-hate. Stalin was not only "rude, ill-tempered, self-centered, and cruel, he was a morbidly suspicious man" (p. 234). Stalin's personality world was private. Both Tucker and Medvedev do concur in their psychoanalytic description of Stalin's personality, but they also assert that the childhood and youth experiences were always so projected that they became part of his second nature. In this assertion, Medvedev argues that:

> Stalin had a charming, even domestic side, that he could be a solicitor host, serving, guests with his own hands from dishes he had chosen himself, cutting roses for them from the garden which he occasionally cultivated (and from which he drew many tiresome political metaphors). He could also play childish tricks, humiliating his political allies by placing ripe tomatoes on their seats or forcing them to dance for the entertainment of himself and their peers" (p. 235).

Stalin behaved as if he had no dignity. He attended and concentrated in drunken parties. At his desk, he told stories about pathetic and empty lives of his children. Though his daughter tried to defend his "piety" and moral integrity, Stalin was a devoted and great purger. He used tyrannical methods to create pseudo socialism whose basic tenets were fundamentally irrelevant and different from the ones Lenin had in mind for a true socialist society. This analysis will do injustice if Lenin's views are not mentioned. As a founder of the first communist system in the world, he may have not succeeded in bringing it about had he not shown that it was necessary to apply "intolerance and irascibility" (p. 236). He used and advocated repression in 1917. Though he advocated a just system in which people make sacrifices and "worship" selflessly, the single-party state he established inherited anti-democratic elements upon which Stalin capitalized to fashion Soviet society. In this case, the origins of Stalinism are deeply rooted in Leninist-Marxist philosophy. Hence: "the revolutionaries, once propelled by insurrection into the role of the ruling party, proceed forthwith to form a regime that would use force and violence to quell the displaced but still active enemies of the R evolution from the former ruling class" (p. 236).

Lenin's Revolutionary leadership was elitist in character. It was led by intellectuals and party ideologies who shared his vision of communism. Stalin built socialism of a communist society using the KGB, the party, the proletariat, the ideology, and scientific socialism. Stalin's use of brutality and other purging methods may be viewed as an attempt to search for himself through personal discovery. Since he used past Tsarist models to modernize society from above, he discovered that his exemplars were Peter the Great and Ivan the Terrible (Grozny). Ivan, whom he read extensively turned out to be "an inspiration for his cruelty and the whole-scale and scope of the purges" (p. 238) which took place between 1936 and 1938. Ivan was his role model. His reign of terror was emulated by Stalin. Stalin carried out the extirpation of his enemies and their families in order to have his way. It may be argued that Stalin's use of the five-year plan economic strategy and his reign of terror may have helped him to transform a rural and feudal state into a modern industrial and scientific superpower. While he has been given credit for creating such a society which transformed the Tsarist empire into a Russian or Soviet Empire, such a feat has been viewed as a vindictive and capricious accomplishment whose motives were rooted in Stalin's guilt rather than prudence or innocence. During his reign, anti-Semitism, anti-intellectualism, anti-disability, anti-Kulukism and anti-revolutionarism were society's economic attitudes or ethos of Stalinization that were used to suppress the unwanted. In a nutshell, he used his father and Ivan the terrible as models for the administration and expansion of the Russian empire.

Gorbachev

Gorbachev inherited power from a socioeconomic socialist system whose post-revolutionary and Leninist-Stalinist leadership he had helped to create. The foundation of this socialist system, though different in ideological, scientific, economic and political character, was deeply rooted in ancient Tsarist traditions of which political and cultural models that were emulated by 20th century leaders are classic. For instance, from a Russian perspective, the term "union and Russia" (Dunlop, 1993-1994, 604) mean the same thing. However, the terms "Russian and Soviet" (p. 604), though semantically similar in meaning to Russians, had different meanings in the 14 Russian republics or vassal states. The communist regime, with the influence of Russia, did not only use force or purges to annex and Russify the republics within the empire, but the Russians who viewed their leadership role to be superior for the civilization of the republic and other ethnic minorities within the empire, encouraged 25 million ethnic Russians to migrate to the republics, "create a supra-ethnic Soviet People" (p. 604) who would speak Russian but "be ethnically and culturally mongrelized" (p. 604). This policy of Russification which started during the reigns of Alexander III and Nicholas II was aggressively continued by Stalin particularly during the 1930s. This meant that the nonethnic Russians were inferior and subject to both the Tsarist and Russian empire respectively. On a gradual scale, post-Stalinist Russian rulers' attitudes towards the role of nationality laws, the economy, the military, the party, and the KGB were not only liberalized, but this more liberal attitude, was clearly noticed in leaders like Khruschev, Gorbachev, and lately in Yeltsin. The liberal stance also scared the Nomenchlatura—

elite for pending or potential trouble in terms of receiving less of their privileges to the extent that they looked inward and created the "fence" in order to protect their tuff and thereby polarizing society into the haves and the have nots of the "classless" society.

Gorbachev is a product of the Soviet society and culture that gave him elite status. When he assumed the reigns of power in 1985, unlike the other post-Stalinist gerontocrats, he was the one who would try to revitalize the decayed system's dynamics in order to save the "Soviet Soul." Despite the important strain in Marxist-Leninist development theory as well as declared and implemented Soviet policy of denigrating nationalism, post-Stalin Soviet program including Gorbachev's promoted it for years. Widespread opportunities for education engendered groupings of individuals able to elaborate and communicate national appeals and platforms. The foundation of republics, autonomous provinces, and the like provided national groups with a structural base for organization that advantaged some people over others (Lapious and Zaslarsky, 1992). Public policy created grievances that served as rallying points. Some of these ranged from dissatisfaction with the stress on cotton growing in central Asia to the anguish over the effects of the Chernobyl nuclear disaster and the material and human drain of the war in Afghanistan. Others included the beliefs that non-Russians were insensitive to what they owed Russians and the Russian minorities in these republics. Other public policies, in combination with the history of ethnic groups before they were included in the USSR, fostered different aims and methods for gaining them among national movements and their leadership (Barry, 1992).

Further still, before Gorbachev came to power, and in spite of the Balts' courage and successful efforts in fighting for their independence during and soon after the First World War, the Baltic states did not get full international recognition until 1921. Though Britain was sympathetic to their course which the Red Army wanted to destroy in 1918/1919, sooner or later, the three small states of Lithuania, Latvia and Estonia were Russified by force. In this case, Lithuania about which Lieven (1993) has focused attention on was distinguished, both then and in the more recent past, from Estonia and Latvia as the leading Baltic state in their "rebellion" from the Russian empire. The Russian images of the rebellion, in Western perceptions, became more real because of Lithuania's earlier and more powerful union with Poland in 1569 (Lieven, 1993).

Given this kind of modern and contemporary socioeconomic reality, and like several communist reformers before him, Gorbachev's strategies of perestroika, glasnost (openness and restructuring) and democratization created both resources and opportunities for proponents of nationalism to get greater autonomy and statehood.

On the other hand, an analytical observer is struck by the impact of unforeseen results of programs grounded in well-articulated philosophies, as well as in strategies based upon crass calculations of political advantages. Stalin's purges of republican communist leaders, apart from being the exploitation of one class by another within the "classless" society, provided martyrs for nationalist movements in the Baltic, Slavic and Muslim pockets of the Russian empire. These nationalist movements increased the chances to proselytize and seek adherents in Gorbachev's world of openness and restructuring. Moreover, the greater empowerment of individuals and groups that he fostered in hopes of strengthening the Soviet system helped to destroy it. Like other communist reformers before him, Gorbachev found that he had unknowingly used his elite class status to create conditions for emergence and support of undesirable alternatives.

No matter how hard he tried, he could not retain control of subsequent developments. His philosophy of perestroika and openness had underpinnings that espoused Western materialism while maintaining the communist system. He wanted Russia to remain an empire which "practices double standards." Such a philosophy of wanting to serve "two masters" violated, according to Basancon (1986) an imperial principle: "To have an empire, ... one must have a privileged people, an essentially military means of conquest, and limited goals" (Dunlop, 1993-1994, 605).

The Russian leaders who contributed to the system's decay were myopic rulers. For instance:

> With the exception of the Central Asian Muslims, Russians in the Soviet Union did not live noticeably better than did the titular peoples of the minority republics. Debilitating poverty, wretched roads, and environmental degradation were the norm in the Russian Republic as they were throughout the USSR. The Russian national religion, Orthodox Christianity, was as zealously repressed as say, Judaism and Islam. Russian patriotic thought was watchful censorship. Some Russian nationalist spokesmen, such as Vladimir Osipov, editor of the well-known *Samizdat* journal *Veche,* found themselves undergoing long prison sentences for preaching the Russian idea (Dunlop, 1993-1994, 606).

Given this reality, Russians were willing to accept Yeltsin's maverick but apparently creative initiatives for devolution, disunion and dismemberment of USSR in exchange for the democratic autonomy of separate Soviet republics. Six years after the defeat of Gorbachev by Yeltsin, Gorbachev spoke at Oklahoma State University's Executive Management Briefings Lecture Series. He talked about the deindustrialization, the brain drain of Russian scientists and corruption and mismanagement. He blamed Yeltsin and the West for these failures but advised Americans this way: "Business is an ocean, and you cannot expect calm waters. You cannot expect to set sail only when the weather is calm. Go into Russia because the time is good for it. I believe our people now know what business is. Our people are ready to act" (Perry, 1997, 1). He had no options except to invite the super capitalists to transform Russia from poverty and confusion to capitalism. Viewed in Marxist, Leninist and Maoist frame of ideological philosophy and doctrines, this apparent reverse to the past is enigmatically ironic and antithetically contradictory as well as inevitable.

Yeltsin

With the decline of the mobilizing power of the communist official ideology during the Brezhnev era and after it, and given the tempo of events which Gorbachev's liberalization strategy had produced, the Soviet society had set itself an irreversible and uncontrollably indeterminable destiny. People in the republics and the Russian minorities (Beilarus, Moldava, etc.) whose religious freedom was repressed for the benefit of the communist imperial ideology were determined to reverse this trend. Those Russians whose patriotism had been silenced repressively rallied Yelstin's idea for an independent Russian and anti-union republic. Though these Russians are proud of their ethnicity, the system's loss of economic credibility, and imperial supremacy enhanced their spirit of the search for better economic opportunity. That search was thought to be found in the permanent disintegration and dismemberment of the Soviet Empire. In other words, successor states would establish their autonomy and deal with issues of social and economic development. Using Western capitalist economic menus as models for recovery has become a major strategic and democratization philosophy for which successor republican state's strategy of revitalization might capitalize on.

The last days of imperial collapse and disintegration of the Soviet Empire were momentous. The positions Yeltsin, Gorbachev, conservatives and hardliners took in the struggle for imperial survival help to explain their role in it and what could have been done to save the empire, if at all.

As a conservative and patriotic change agent of the Soviet Union, and like Brezhnev before him, Gorbachev, though insensitive and uninformed about ethnic issues in the empire, wanted both during the pre- and post-perestroika, to preserve the Russian and Soviet Unitary State. However, a coalition group of conservative alliance of neo-Stalinists, National Bolsheviks, and Conservative Russian Nationalists who wanted to resurrect the policies of Tsars Alexander III and Nicholas II, opposed his ideas. This group advocated the development of institutions in Russia which did not have any of them and which would parallel those found in minority republics. Some of the institutions that were later created included the Russian KGB, Russian MVD, Russian Academy of Sciences and Russian TV and Radio. Though Yeltsin did not identify himself with this conservative coalition, the issues they raised were instrumental for the administration of Russia when he became the president of this autonomous republic.

In addition, a coalition of democrats led by Yeltsin assertively advocated to, contrary to the expectations of Gorbachev and the hardliners, turn Russian Soviet Federated Socialist Republic (RSFSR) into an economically and politically independent republic. The USSR, as indicated earlier, was to become independent. The conservative coalition, by contrast, wanted Russia to suppress separatist elements in the periphery. Throughout this period, and as evidence shows, Gorbachev was fighting against two powerful and diametrically opposed coalitions. In 1990, Yeltsin was elected the chairman of the RSFSR and later, 1991, as president of the Russian Republic. Though Gorbachev wanted such Russian government to be politically and economically fragmented and thereby fail to break away from the union with "his Russian," Yeltsin's popular election as president of a united Russia underscored Gorbachev's'' tactical strategy. In essence, party hardliners sided with Yeltsin to strengthen Russian autocracy (autarchy). On the other hand, the reason why Yeltsin succeeded to destroy the empire and create his own state was based on this; the intellectual leader of the confederate idea that Yeltsin bought (Kozyran) thought that this move would lead the "unitary Soviet state" into an evolving and intergroup system like the current Western European one. However, the momentous spirit and the uncontrollability of the anti imperial events and incidents helped to wipe out the empire from existence.

Together with the Gorbachev's "center" and the Yeltsin's "democrats," the so-called hardliners represented a third major political force impacting the future of the Russian Republic. With a strong representation in such elite institutions such as the KGB, the party bureaucracy, the military command, and the Soviet military-industrial complex, this group was in a position to attempt to impose its will on the Russian Republics and on the union as a whole. In January 1991, the hardliners seemed to have played the key role in attempting a putsch in the Baltic and they were, of course, supporters of the August 1991 abortive coup. There was, however, as it has been mentioned, a basic contradiction in their position. On the other hand, they were vehement champions of the unity of the Soviet state; on the other hand, and paradoxically so, they were ardent defenders of Russian autarchy, a stance which de facto served to weaken the very cohesion of the USSR which they sought to preserve. In other words, the term Soviet state and how it was to be preserved was contradictory to Russian autarchy in terms of how and who could effectively implement it on diverse and complex millieux. Such contradiction contributed to the withering away and decay of the empire.

The factors which caused the decay and disintegration of the Communist empire have been discussed. Some were direct. Others may have been indirect. A few have been a combination of both. A number of them may be unknown in the field of scholarship. Those which are known could include fatalism (belief that their situation was naturally or supernaturally predetermined), lack of effective communication between the elite (leaders) and the masses, Western strategic disinformation and containment of the Soviet Union and its satellite states, and economic and ideological bankruptcy. The first two factors refer to the role played by Stalin, and others, including Gorbachev and Yeltsin.

According to Brzezinski (1987), the causes that resulted in the gradual decline and death of the empire are seven. First, socialism lost its salt in the eyes and tastes of the masses. Second, their future looked pessimistic as standards of living progressively continued to decline. Third, the Communist Party of each of the socialist countries lost its vitality in terms of spirit and ideological commitment while vitality was being replaced by polarizing elements of nationalistic and religious awakening. Fourth, because people found that religious values filled the facets of their atheistic lives, their apostasy, which they capitalized on, undermined the nationalistic and ideological fiber which used to cement and strengthen the elements of imperial nationhood and the promises and tenets of revolutionary and internationalist socialist universalism. Fifth, some aspects of economic privatization and the platonic love (Neale, 1991) for free market conditions mushroomed across the empire. Sixth, such developments produced a new climate of active political opposition within the ranks and file of society. Seventh, the demand for political pluralization from below became real. Such factors or forces made the authoritarian regimes defensively reactive and more abusive of human rights. Explosively and collectively, these factors were and are major crises which evolved with the decline and collapse of the system that undermined the imperial and social mission of communism.

Summarizing Lucian Pye, Adkins (1991), has extensively analyzed the literature on Third World political development. In his conclusions, he has identified six crises characteristic of the current crises in Africa, Eastern Europe and the former USSR. These crises include the identity crisis, the legitimacy crisis, the penetration crisis, the integration crisis, the participation crisis, and the distribution crisis. Though Poland, Hungary, Czech, and Slovak republics seem to have relatively weathered the crisis (Dyba and Svejnar, 1991), it has been, up until recently, increasingly intense in the former Soviet Union, and Yugoslavia. In the first crisis, the political regime has difficulty to identify itself with its homeland national territory. For the second crisis, there is widespread perceptual consensus that the authority and responsibility of government are not legitimate functions. Thirdly, in relation to the penetration of the system, it lacks a formal machinery for establishing governmental institutions that enjoy the confidence and rapport of both the rulers and the ruled. Fourthly, the integration crisis concerns difficulties of relating popular politics to governmental performance and how answerable intergovernmental agencies are to each other and to groups seeking governmental support. Fifthly, the participation crisis is a situation in which existing institutions are unable to accommodate more participants due to the multiplicity of interest groups and political parties. Finally, the distribution crisis arises as a result of the inability of the system to effectively and efficiently exercise its power for the massive and orderly creation of an equitable distribution of goods and services. Over all, all these problems did not only make it difficult for the empire to function ineffectively, but they collectively became so unmanageable that they contributed to the erosion of Marxist theory and practice.

In Eastern Europe and the entire fallen Soviet Empire, such a complex crisis ridden situation failed to be contained during the last ten years (1981-1991) of communist hegemony. Though the Brezhnev, and the short-lived Chernenko, Andropov, and the Gorbachev administrations attempted to reform the system as indicated earlier, the cumulatively catastrophic effects of its political and economic mismanagement outweighed the abortive reforms. The system's failure to function effectively and competitively produced a spirit of disillusionment, skepticism, and hopelessness in the viability of communist empire. The "mortal blow that struck a wound on its economic base," the moral decay of its political and ideological institutions, the ineffective bankruptcy of its centrally planned economic affairs and its invalid communist ideology, may have caused the system's essence, efflorescence, and superstructure to mightily falter, "prostrate asunder," rapidly disintegrate, and perpetually dismember the Soviet Empire.

The structure and dismemberment of Russian imperial disintegration has become a reality. The transition to democracy is not likely to be easy because East Europeans and the other "relics" of the former empire have neither practiced nor theoretically managed credible democratic institutions in recent memory. This system, which East Europeans have rejected was without historical precedent at home. The system evolved in Russia from whence it flourished and whence henceforth it declined. Its foreignness was imposed on Eastern Europe. Lacking the roots of originality and authentic historicity, the consequences of its imposition on Pan-Slavic, Baltic and Muslim civilizations have had far reaching effects. That is why previous political leadership was challenged by revolts in Czechoslovakia, Poland, Chechnya and other states. The causes of the revolts were superficially interpreted to mean that the revolting states were concerned with the empire's economic slowdown and disloyalty to the USSR.

Based on the intellectual interpretation of the current state of affairs, the replacement of socialist by capitalist Eastern Europe, Eastern European scholars argue that the current pro-Western situation was partly created or exacerbated by the pressure exerted by dominant Western nations for their own political, economic, and technological interests (Barrows, 1991). In a sense, if this interpretation is correct, it is a reincarnation of the containment strategy which strengthened Western Europe, (NATO) Japan, and the Third World in order to undermine the official mind and the vitality of the critical tenets of communist expansion—the ideology, the communist party, scientific socialism, the base, and the superstructure (Hunt and Sherman, 1986). Though Western political, economic, and technological experts and governments have prescribed liberal models for revitalization of Eastern European economic and political systems, these culturally biased blueprints which, in themselves may be as foreign as those which caused the demise of communism, if applied without relevant and domestic evolutionary experimentation might be instrumental to post-communist economic recolonization called neo-colonialism. Both economically and sociopolitically, the essence of neo-colonialism is post-structuralism and post-modernism. Its survival is dictated by the geostrategic rationality and the calculated relationship between unipolarity and multipolarity of our global existence (Miller, 1992). The progressive intellectualization of bipolarity as a theory of international relations and peaceful coexistence does not hold water any more. The extent to which a unipolar system, dominated by the United States can become a viable mechanism for the effective promotion of equilibria within the global multipolar structure and yet survive, will be tested by time, courage, caution, and prudence. Neocolonial but pluralistic and democratic institutions are more likely to promote economic vitality and political stability reflective of contemporary and strong Western societies whose social, political, economic and cultural values have remained sustainable for centuries.

Conclusion

There are a variety of theoretical models upon which leadership is based and constructed in the social and behavioral sciences. Of these theories, the trait theory of personality, the situational theories of Fiedler, the path-goal theory, the contingency theory and the normative theory are paramount. The last three theories are situational because their universes are characterized by uncertainty, probability and incidentalism. These theories are dominantly used in industrial organizational psychology. Other theories such as transforming leadership, transactional leadership and autarchy or autocracy are the basic hypothetical underpinnings that inform the realm of practical and theoretical political science and public administration.

The interdisciplinary nature of this chapter is an intellectual analysis of leadership in the academic, corporate and political (public) environments. Though some scholars see leadership as a form of cultural expression, others see it as complex, interactive and expressive reflections of the exercise of power and conflict. Theoretically speaking, leadership theory has been used to critically observe the empirically based comparative aspects of Western and Eastern public administration leaders and the political and cultural history which produced them. These leaders were the chief stage actors and twentieth century world leaders who were the makers of history.

Western leaders are democratic, pragmatic, prudent and geostrategically manipulative. They can sacrifice lives, resources and other things to protect Eurocentric values of which democracy, human rights, individual liberty, rule of law and free enterprise are paramount. Eastern leaders are largely, as are opposed to Western ecological environments which produce Western leaders, products of their unique ecological, cultural, political, economic and ideological systems. These leaders are autarchic, overly irrational products of economically and culturally deterministic systems that are, with the exception of India and modern Japan, very undemocratic. These authoritarian systems from which the leaders receive inspiration, other leadership values and their legitimacy are totally and diametrically opposed to other systems in their parliamentary, constitutional, bureaucratic and cultural ethos. Organizations which evolve from such systems are true replicas of the systems themselves rather than external transplantations. Though the newly established democratic and free enterprise economies have flourished on the ruins of ex-communism, their lack of experience in democratic and entrepreneurial economies will require time, effort, strategy and political stability that are necessary for their evolutionary transition.

James MacGregor Burns (1978) has assertively argued that contemporary leadership is mediocre rather than meticulous and meritorious, irresponsible rather than responsible, reckless and lacking in intellectual discernment which is essential for change. Social institutions and organizations need to evolve strong philosophical, historical, intellectual and practical traditions on which modern and contemporary leadership theory will be based. Although humanistic psychology has attempted to define leadership much better than any other disciplines, it is time for other disciplines such medical anthropology to do likewise.

The leadership power base is equated with cultural and political innovation, inspiration, mobilization of followers, setting goals for the organization, achieving goals, defining values, satisfying needs and leading followers through an open as opposed to a blind alley. Such leadership is a form of collective purpose. Leaders do not shun conflict, they confront it, exploit it and finally embody it (Burns, 1978). These leaders lead by consensus as opposed to dissensus. The leaders help followers to be conscious of their sexual, communal, ethnic, class, national and ideological identity. By doing so, they help their followers to discover their contradictions and resolve them by themselves. Intellectual leaders attempt to do so.

The ideas of an intellectual leader have moral, scientific and social power. As a devotee of ideas, knowledge, values and intellect the leaders are characterized by a critical, creative and contemplative mind. Their intelligence grasps, manipulates, reorders, and adjusts. The leader's intellect "examines, ponders, wonders, theorizes, criticizes and imagines" (Burns, 1978). Effective leadership identifies levels of wants, needs and other motivations. The same leader integrates these with the Masloic hierarchies of values. These values may be clarified by crisis and conflict in order to undergird the dynamics of leadership itself.

As described by an unknown author, scientific scholarship has shown a quickened interest which conflict plays in the leadership arena, as it "establishes boundaries, channels hostility, counteracts social ossification, invigorates class and group interests, encourages innovation and ultimately defines and empowers leadership." Stability and harmony are not stimulants for growth. The first task of the leader is to arouse, both in theory and practice, the consciousness of true psychological reality of the sense of people's needs, values and purposes irrespective of conflict which is a byproduct of leadership and management. Given this understanding, it is essential to conclusively distinguish the existing differences between managers and leaders. The distinctions are as follows:

> The manager administers; the leader innovates. The manager is a copy; the leader is an original. The manager maintains; the leader develops. The manager focuses on systems and structures; the leader focuses on people.
> The manager relies on control; the leader inspires trust. The manager has a short-range view; the leader has a long-range perspective. The manager asks how and when; the leader asks what and why. The manager has his eye always on the bottom line, the leader has his eye on the horizon. The manager imitates; the leader originates. The manager accepts the status quo; the leader challenges it. The manager is the classic good soldier; the leader is his own person. The manager does things right; the leader does the right thing (Bennis, 1989, 45, and Gortner, Mahler, and Nicholson, 1997, 353).

Organizations and institutions which operate in an ideologically dominated system (communism) tend to use ideological purity rather than rationality training, competence and ability as the yardstick for recruiting, hiring, promoting and tenuring the bureaucracy and other state-run corporations and enterprises. As indicated in this chapter the personalities who ruled the Russian empire and its aftermath used either the communist ideology or the crude democratic ideology (in the case of Yeltsin and Putin) to lead and manage public and private organizations.

In the former Soviet Union, while the nationalism of the majority and their dominant values was treated with empathy, the nationalisms of the minorities were considered divisive and therefore unwarranted and suppressed. The Republics, contrary to Lenin's advice on autonomy and dissent, were subjected to brutal colonial Russification, and linguistic and cultural assimilation during the Stalinist era. The destalinization of these measures witnessed the development of national administration units based on ethnic territorial boundaries and the racism of indigenous leaders in the central government. Such less cohesive and disuniting creations were the cultural infrastructure of nationalist sentiments that helped in the dissolution of the Soviet Empire. Contrary to the leftist and non-leftist expectations, the process of modernization and change has inevitably increased a strong element of ethnic consciousness in both Eastern Europe and the world as a whole. The thought of popular sovereignty has made the demands for national self-determination more legitimate. Democratization has catalytically served as an activator for unique and reinforced ethnonationally inspired demands (Jalali and Lipset, 1992-1993) for complete autonomy.

During the Cold War, many ethnic movements particularly in the Third World, were, others argue, supported by East-West competition. The movements led many countries to become independent. The global realignment following the disintegration of the Soviet Union has heightened as opposed to reduced, ethnic tensions to a smaller number especially in Central Africa, Iraq, Eastern Europe, and the former USSR. This realignment appears to be precipitating a new era of state making that is likely to set into motion a nationalist-subnationalist dialectic in which ethnic minorities, enclosed in newly formed states, challenge new regimes for autonomy or self-determination and thereby creating further division, fragmentation, and disunion. If these ethnic movements are caused by nationalistic and subnationalistic sentiments, socio-cultural offshoots of irrationality rather than prudent creations of reason, design, and order, their influence will be rampant, disruptive, but short-lived. However, if the democratization process with which these global movements are characterized by reflect vision, courage, and positive aspects of political tolerance, fairness, human rights and economic and technological improvements, they are more likely to stand the test of time and accomplishment. Such accomplishments, viewed in the light of Soviet development experience of historico-politcal and cultural nationalism, will be challenged in the long or short run by the internal and external forces of decay whose natural and artificial character destroy great empires and their organizations. Some of the these forces of decay could be identified with the presence of war in human reason. This warlike element is a form of irrationality of the social movement struggles that are forms of progressive disenchantment of bureaucratically oversized and over-rationalized institutional iron cages. Such iron caged regimes are the essence of cyclical movements of which the Soviet experience is classic. The experience made the management and leadership of public and private organizations difficult if not impossible to manage. Using the iron hand, or the ideology rather than reason, sound judgment, democracy or human relations were anathema to the well functioning of the system that was subject to autocratic management of public and currently sustained private organizations and institutions. Regretably, though autarchy or autocracy is not comparable to democracy, mechanistic consensus, human relations or contingency and transformational theories, its impact has been negatively far reaching than otherwise.

Above all, acording to McFarland, Senn and Childress (1993), public and private organizations should prepare their communities to compete in the 21st century. 'Old leadership tools' should be discarded because they are ineffective. Many leaders are mobilizing their people around empowerment, vision, shared values, a healthy culture, total quality, superior service, diversity, social responsibility and strategies for global competitiveness. When creating a vision, values, culture, empowerment, total quality, or any critical organizational building block, the top leadership team needs to be the first to take part in training and education, setting the example for the entire enterprise. Great leaders, particularly in academia and public life, promote values which inspire others to demonstrate a sense of responsibility, dependability, friendship, human brotherhood, high expectations, courage, hope, self-esteem and self-actualization.

References

Adkins, R.L. 1991. East European economic reform: Are new institutions emerging? *Journal of Economic Issues* 25, 2 (June), 589-595.

Barrows, L.C. ed. 1991. Higher education in Eastern Europe. Bucharest: CEPES-UNESCO.

Barrows, L.C. ed. 1990. *Higher Education in the USSR.* Bucharest: UNESCO-CEPES.

Barry, D.D. ed. 1992. *Toward the "Rule of Law" in Russia?: Political and Legal Reform in the Transition Period.* Armonk, N.Y.: M.E. Sharpe.

Bass, B.M. ed. 1981. *Stogdills Handbook of Leadership.* New York: Free Press.

Baylis, T.A. 1996. Presidents versus prime ministers: Shaping executive authority in Eastern Europe. *World Politics* 48: 297-323.

Bennis, W. 1989. *On Becoming a Leader.* Reading, MA: Addison-Wesley.

Bennis, W., and B. Nanus. 1985. *Leaders: The Strategies for Making Change.* New York: Harper and Row.

Besancon, A. (1986). Nationalism and bolshevism in the USSR. In *The Last Empire,* ed. Robert Conquest, 10-11. Stanford, CA: Hoover Institution Press.

Blake, R.R., and J.S. Mouton. 1994. *The Managerial Grid.* Houston, Texas: Gulf Publishing.

Blake, R.R., and J.S. Mouton. 1985. *The Managerial Grid III.* Houston, Texas: Gulf Publishing.

Blakesley, L. 1995. *Presidential Leadership from Eisenhower to Clinton.* Chicago: Nelson/Hall.

Blaney, J. and M. Gfoeller. 1993. Lessons from the failure or perestroika. *Political Science Quarterly* 108, 3: 481-496.

Bradley, J. 1988. *The Russian Revolution.* New York: Bison Books Corp.

Brzezinski, Z. 1989. *Communities of Discourse: Ideology and Social Structure in the Reformation, the Enlightenment, and European Socialism.* Cambridge, MA: Harvard University Press.

Burns, M.J. 1978. *Leadership.* New York: Harper and Row Publishers.

Conger, J. 1991. Inspiring others: The language of leadership. *Academy of Management Executive* 5, 1: 31-45.

Conquest, R. 1990. *The Great Terror: A Reassessment.* London: Oxford University Press.

The Daily Oklahoman. 1996. Bosnian Muslims, Croats sign peace plan, p. 3.

Dansereau, F., J. Cashman, and G. Graen. 1973. Instrumentality theory and equity theory as complementary approaches in predicting the relationship of leadership and turnover among managers. *Organizational Behavior and Human Performance* 10: 184-200.

Dansereau, F., G. Graen, and W.J. Haga. 1975. A vertical dyad linkage approach to leadership within formal organizations. *Organizational Behavior and Human Performance* 13: 46-78.

Dunlop, J.B. 1993-94. Russia: Confronting a loss of empire, 1987-1991. *Political Science Quarterly* 108, 4: 603-634.

Dyba, K., and J. Svejnar. 1991. Economic developments and prospects in Czechoslovakia, Yugoslavia and East Germany. *American Economic Review* 185-190.

Fiedler, F.E. 1967. *A Theory of Leadership Effectiveness.* New York: McGraw-Hill.

Field, R.H.G. 1982. A test of the Vroom-Yetton normative model of leadership. *Journal of Applied Psychology* 67: 523-532.

Field, R.H.G. 1979. A critique of the Vroom-Yetton contingency model of leadership behavior. *Academy of Management Review* 4: 249-257.

Fleishman, E.A. 1953. The description of supervisory behavior. *Journal of Applied Psychology* 38: 1-6.

French, J.R.P. and B. Raven. 1959. The bases of social power. In *Studies in Social Power,* ed. D. Cartwright. Ann Arbor: Institute for Social Research, University of Michigan.

Furtado, C., Jr. 1994. Nationalism and foreign policy in Ukraine. *Political Science Quarterly* 109, 1: 81-104.

Gibbon, E. 1983. *The Decline and Fall of the Roman Empire.* New York: Penguin Books.

Gibson, J.L. 1993. Perceived Political Freedom in the Soviet Union. *The Journal of Politics* 55, 4: 936-974.

Gordon, L.V. 1976. *Survey of Interpersonal Values: Revised Manual.* Chicago Science Research Associates.

Gordon, L.V. 1975. *The Measurement of Interpersonal Values.* Chicago: Chicago Science Research Associates.

Gortner, H.F., J. Mahler, and J.B. Nicholson. 1997. *Organization Theory: A Public Perspective.* Fort Worth: Harcourt Brace College Publishers.

Graen, G., and W. Schiemann. 1978. Leader Member Agreement: A Vertical Dyad Linkage Approach. *Journal of Applied Psychology* 63: 206-212.

Gulick, L. 1937. Notes on the theory of organization. In *Papers on the Science of Administration,* ed. Luther Gulick and Lyndall Urwick. New York: Institute of Public Administration.

Hargrove, E.C. 1974. *The Power of the Modern Presidency.* New York: Alfred A. Knopf, Inc.

Heller, M., and A. Nekrich. 1986. *Utopia in Power: The History of the Soviet Union from 1917 to the Present.* New York: Summit Books.

Heller, M., A. Nekrich, R.G. Hoxie. 1994. Forming a government: The prospects for democracy in Russia. *Presidential Studies Quarterly* XXIV, 4: 869-874.

Hesburgh, T.M. 1985. *The Hesburgh Papers: Higher Values in Higher Education.* Kansas City: Andrews and McMell Inc.

Hollander, E.P. 1978. *Leadership Dynamics. A Practical Guide to Effective Relationships.* New York: Free Press.

Hughes, J. 1991. *Stalin, Siberia and the Crisis of the New Economic Policy.* Cambridge: Cambridge University Press.

Hunt, E.K. and H.J. Sherman. 1986. *Economics: An introduction to Traditional and Radical Views.* New York: Harper and Row, Publishers.

Italian Journal. 1992. New York: Italian Academy Foundation Inc. 6, 5: 3-32.

Jalali, S.M., and R. Lipset. 1992-1993. Racial and ethnic conflicts: A global perspective. *Political Science Quarterly* 107, 4: 585-606.

James, H., and M. James. 1994. Communication—the origins of the cold war: Some new documents. *The Historical Journal* 37, 3: 615-622.

Joyner, C.C. 1993. When human suffering warrants military action. *The Chronicle of Higher Education* (January 27).

Kamm, R.B. 1982. *Leadership for Leadership.* Washington, D.C.: University Press of America Inc.

Katz, J. 1993. Contemporary Problems in Eastern Europe. Paper presented at a Spring Seminar. Langston University.

Kelley, R. 1991. *The Power of Fellowship.* New York: Doubleday.

Lall, G.R., and B.M. Lall. 1979. *Dynamic Leadership.* Mountain View, CA: Pacific Press Publishing Association.

Landy, F.J. 1983. *Psychology of Work Behavior.* Chicago: Dorsey Press.

Lapidus, G., and V. Zaslavsky, eds. 1992. *From Union to Common: Nationalism and Separatism in the Soviet Republics.* Cambridge: Cambridge University Press.

Laqueter, W. 1991. *Stalin: The Glasnost Relations.* London: Unwin Hyman.

Liden, R.C., and G. Graen. 1980. Generalizability of the vertical dyad linkage model of leadership. *Academy of Management Journal* 23: 451-465.

Lieven, A. 1993. *The Baltic Revolution: Estonia, Latvia, Lithuania and the Path to Independence.* New Haven and London: Yale University Press.

Lord, R.G., and K.G. Maher. 1991. *Leadership and Information Processing: Linking Perceptions and Performance.* Boston, MA: Unwin Hyman.

Magstadt, T.M., and P.M. Schotten. 1988. *Understanding Politics: Ideas, Institutions and Issues.* New York: St. Martin's Press.

Mann, F.C. 1965. Toward an understanding of the leadership role in formal organization. In *Leadership and Productivity,* eds. R. Dubin, G.C. Humans, and D.C. Miller. San Francisco: Chandler.

Marino, S.F. 1997. Straight talk: ultrapreneurs...work smarter—not longer—than other executives. http.//www.Industryweek.com.

McClelland, D.C. 1975. *Power: The Inner Experience.* New York: Irvington.

McFarland, L.J., L.E. Senn, and J.R. Childress. 1993. *21ˢᵗ Century Leadership: Dialogues with 100 Top Leaders.* Linc-Irvine, CA: Apple Computer Inc.

McNeal, R.H. 1988. *Stalin: Man and Ruler.* New York: New York University Press.

Medvedev, R. 1989. *Let History Judge: The Origins and Consequences of Stalinism.* George Shrives (Editor and Translator). New York: Columbia University Press.

Merridale, G. 1993. Glasnost and Stalin: New material, old questions. *The Historical Journal* 36, 1: 233-243.

Miller, B. 1992. Explaining great power cooperation in conflict management. *World Politics: A Quarterly Journal of International Relations* 45, 1: 1-46.

Mintrom, M. 1997. Policy Entrepreneurs and the Diffusion of Innovation. *American Journal of Political Science* 41, 3.

Mintzberg, H. 1973. *The Nature of Managerial Work.* New York: Harper and Row.

Moorehead, A. 1959. *The Russian Revolution.* New York: Bantam Books.

Nagel, J. 1993. Ethnic nationalism: Politics, ideology, and the world order. *International Journal of Comparative Sociology* 1-2: 103-111.

Nakamura, R., and F. Smallwood. 1980. *The Politics of Policy Implementation.* New York: St. Martin's Press.

Nash, P. 1968. *Models of Man: Explorations in the Western Educational Tradition.* New York: John Wiley and Sons, Inc.

Neale, W.C. 1991. The intellectual legacy of Karl Polanyi: Society, state, and market: A Polanyian view of current change and turmoil in Eastern Europe. *Journal of Economic Issues* 25, 2: 467-475.

New Webster's Dictionary and Thesaurus of the English Language 1995. Danbury, CT: Lexicon Publications, Inc.

Nutt, P.C. 1993. Transforming public organizations with strategic management and strategic leadership. *Journal of Management* 19, 2: 299-347.

Perry, J. 1997. Gorbachev urges U.S. policy shifts. *The Daily Oklahoman* 1. (October 16).

Podsakoff, P.M., and C.A. Schriesheim. 1985. Field studies of French and Raven's bases of power: Critique, reanalysis, and suggestions for future research. *Psychological Bulletin* 97: 387-411.

Rapoport, Y. 1991. *The Doctor's Plot. Stalin's Last Crime.* London: Fourth Estate.

Rancour-Lafferiere, D. 1988. *The Mind of Stalin: A Psychoanalytic Study.* Ardis Publishers.

Sagini, M.M. 1996. *The African and the African-American University: A Historical and Sociological Analysis.* Lanham, MD.: The University Press of America, Inc.

Schein, E.H. 1991. *Organizational Culture and Leadership.* San Francisco: Jossey-Bass Publishers.

Shils, E. 1983. *The Academic Ethic: The Report of a Study Group of the International Council on the Future of the University.* Chicago: University of Chicago Press.

Sica, A. 1990. *Weber, Irrationality and Social Order.* Berkeley: University of California Press.

Siegel, L., and I.M. Lane. 1987. *Personnel and Organizational Psychology.* Homewood, IL: Irwin.

Thompson, J.M. 1989. *Revolutionary Russia, 1917.* New York: Macmillan Publishing Company.

Trosky, L. 1941. *Stalin: An Appraisal of the Man and His Influence.* New York: Harper and Brothers Publishers.

Trucker, R. 1991. *Stalin in Power: The Revolution from Above, 1928-1941.* London: Norton.

Truckcr, R. 1973. *Stalin: As Revolutionary 1879-1929.* New York: W.W. Norton and Company.

Vecchio, R.P., and B.C. Gobdel. 1984. The VDL model of leadership: Problems and prospects. *Organizational Behavior and Human Performance* 34: 5-20.

Verdery, K. 1991. *National Ideology under Socialism: Identity and Cultural Politics in Ceausescu's Romania.* Berkeley, Los Angeles and Oxford: University of California Press.

Vroom, V.H., and P.W. Yetton. 1973. *Leadership and Decision Making.* Pittsburgh, PA: University of Pittsburgh Press.

Wallace, W. ed. 1991. *The Dynamics of European Integration.* London: Printer Publishers.

Winter, D.G. 1973. *The Power Motive.* New York: Free Press.

Yukl, G.A. 1994. *Leadership in Organizations.* Englewood Cliffs, N.J.: Prentice Hall.

Yukl, G.A. 1981. *Leadership in Organizations.* Englewood Cliffs, N.J.: Prentice Hall.

Zubek, V., and J. Gentleman. 1994. Economic crisis and the movement toward pluralism in Poland and Mexico. *Political Science Quarterly* 109, 2: 335-359.

Chapter 10

Organizational Communication

Introduction: Origin of the Discipline

Communications is a social and scientific study of human communication which evolved in the late 1930s in the U.S. According to Schramm (1983) the four founders of the communication movement were Harold Lasswell, a political scientist, Paul Lazarsfeld, a sociologist, and Kurt Lewin and Carl Hovland, both of whom were social psychologists. These "exotic" and interdisciplinary scholars were not responsible for much of the early research in the field, but they were the intellectual mentors of the second generation of scholars in the communication field.

Professors Lasswell, Lazarsfeld, and Hovland of Yale concentrated their research and teaching activities on the powerful and manipulative influence of the media. This model was called the "hypodermic needle." Metarphorically, this meant that as a doctor injected serum into the patient, the media's influence on the citizen made the person to have new reality and behave differently just as the human body responds differently to the injected serum. With the research conducted by the three men during the 1940s, a different and less communicatively hegemonous view of the mass media evolved. Since this view saw the media as one which transmitted information to opinion leaders who used it to influence others on a face-to-face position, this process was called "the two-step flow hypothesis" (Hovland, 1949; and Lazarsfeld et al, 1948). In essence, these scholars proved that both the hypodermic-needle model and the two-step flow hypothesis were highly oversimplified theories of the mass media on human behavior. In spite of the simplicity of these theoretical explanations, the two notions strongly influenced the thinking of mass communication scholars for over three decades.

At almost the same time, Lewin (1958) conducted famous empirical studies on the effects of group decision making at Iowa. Contemporaneously, Lewin (1939), studied group leadership, Lippitt and White (1943) conducted research on group morale in order to provide the political, military and scholarly enterprise with information essential for dealing with World War II crisis generated by the Axis Alliance. The science of communication emerged as an academic discipline during the 1950s. One of the first signs of its genesis came with the establishment of the Communication Research Institute at the University of Illinois which was being directed by Wilbur Schramm. The second major development in the evolution and expansion of social scientific studies in the communications enterprise was the establishment of the College of Communication Arts and Sciences at Michigan State University in 1955. A formal department for the discipline was chaired by David Berlo whose book *The Process of Communication* (1961) became one of the profoundest theoretical foundations of the discipline. This communication department had an interdisciplinary faculty whose specializations were journalism, speech, sociology, psychology, and political science.

Between 1960s and 1970s, communication as a scientific and higher education discipline developed rapidly. Two Annenberg Schools of Communication were founded at the University of Pennsylvania and at the University of Southern California respectively. Other centers which established schools of communication were at Ohio University, the University of Texas and the University of Kentucky. And last but not least, including their retention, other traditional, scholarly and professional components have evolved with departments of journalism, and speech communication.

Like in the other traditional and modern disciplines, consensus concerning theoretical underpinnings of the discipline has gradually and equivocally been delineated. Researchers of the discipline are interested in mass communication, organizational communication, small-group communication, interpersonal communication, intrapersonal communication, and most recently, in electronic (high-tech) communication systems.

During the late 1970s and early 1980s, two major theoretical paradigms were advanced in the communications field. The first one was the systems perspective (Monge, 1977; and Watzlawick, Beavin, and Jackson, 1967). This paradigm, as explained earlier, places emphasis on the structure and organization of all components of the systems rather than reductionistically focusing on it partially. The second paradigm is the rules perspective (Cronen, Pearce and Harris,

1982; Cushman, Valentine and Dietrich, 1982; and Pearce and Cronen, 1980). The rules perspective paradigm views the communicator as an actor. The actor is theoretically center-stage, that is assertively and theoretically based on such notions as intention, volition, motive and choice. In the light of this continuum, communicators negotiate new rules of the game and discard old ones. With the focus on our entry into the new millennium and the role of technology will play in it, more intensive research will be done to identify the interfaces between technologically mediated and face-to-face communication systems. Obviously, projective studies on these systems of communication will be more radically different than the hypodermic-needle and the two-step flow interpretation of media effects (Miller 1982). Since the focus of this chapter is on organizational communication rather than communication in general, delineation of the discussion under study is warranted.

In general, this chapter deals with the organization's intelligence system--communication, control, and decision making. The three terms deal with many types of formal and informal communication networks, their pathologies, and partial remainder -- the control system is dependent upon the communication structure which gathers and processes information. This indicates that problems identified in one part of the system do affect other parts of it. Control can be exercised through the use of quantitative, behavioral, and socio-psychological dimensions. Above all, theoretical descriptions and prescriptions for decision making and contingency theory are discussed. Their interpersonal, intercultural and electronic influences reveal the complex nature of the science of communicating messages in public and private organizations.

General Theory of Communication

Communication and organization are inseparable. Communication has a central place in the organization because "structure, extensiveness and scope of organizations are almost entirely determined by communication technique" (Barnard, 1938, 8). Communication is the essence of a social system or an organization (Katz and Kahn, 1978). As it is ubiquitously placed in organizations, it is a force for "defining the structure, process and culture of bureaus" (Gortner, et al., 1997, 135) that help shape the communication network.

Communication specialists are sophisticated and powerful individuals who use technology and research to reflect on and to rationally ratify the validity of the classical Tayloristic model of organizations. These are specialization, standardization, and formalization – "the classic concepts of the assembly line" (p. 135). These strategies which the specialists recommended or implemented were, most of the time, "suboptimal in solving the organization's problems; the very people most committed to new technology were also most responsible for its lack of impact" (p. 135). Likewise, the contemporary "high-tech" scene should be watched for lacking elements of effectiveness.

Communication and organization structure powerfully influence each other. Behavior and communication are patterned by the structure of the organization. In other words, organization structure introduces considerable predictability and stability into interaction. Major structural characteristics of bureaucracies include (1) a hierarchy of formal positions of authority, (2) the specialized division of tasks, and (3) rules and procedures. Members of this type of formal organization must accept direction from some individuals but not others, perform certain tasks (often in specialized ways) but refrain from others, and work and interact with some individuals rather than others. Their behavior, including communication, is different than it would be without the organization's structure" (p. 135).

Organization structure is differentiated in a variety of ways – hierarchical level, departments, task specialization, and organizational integration for goal realization. Information about goals, rules, the functioning of the organization's human and other resources, and its environment must be exchanged. Different activities and tasks must be exchanged. These activities and tasks must be coordinated. As indicated in the Chapter on structure, "the greater the organizational differentiation and complexity, the greater the need for integration" (p. 136). The organization's communication system is a key "mechanism for achieving integration and coordination" (p. 136). In complex public organizations, the communication, coordination, and integration processes are political in character. As policy and distribution of power are affected, expertise and control of information become the major elements of bureaucratic political influence (Rourke, 1984).

The communication act is interpersonal. Interpersonal communication is an "interactive process of exchanging information between sources and receivers for the purpose of conveying meaning" (Gortner, et al., 1997, 136). This form of communication may be instrumental, consummatory, or incidental (Zajonc, 1966). Instrumental communication is "purposeful or goal directed; the sender intends to have an effect (related to knowledge, attitude, and behavior) on the receiver" (Gortner, et al., 1997, 136). Consummatory communication is a product of emotional emission on the part of the sender (e.g., enthusiasm, fear, and uncertainty). Finally, incidental communication imparts information without the "sender being aware of having done so" (p. 136).

The purpose of effective communication is the "accurate transmission and reception of information between senders and receivers" (p. 136). Distorted information, though it may be unintentional, is dysfunctional, inaccurate and tends to make communication incomplete. Distorted information may also be a form of misinformation, error, or miscommunication. In this case, the message may have both truth and untruth both of which make its credibility ambiguous, unreliable and unwanted.

Interpersonal Communication

Even in antiquity, Aristotle "identified the speaker, the speech, and the audience as the principal features of communication" (p. 136). However, Greek or ancient modes of communication were, viewed from contemporary theoretical abstractions, quite simplistic. It is clear to demonstrate that communication is a "dynamic, on-going, ever changing and continuous" (Berlo, 1960, 24) process. Heraclitus observed rightly that a man can never "step into the same river twice; the man is different and so is the river" (Berlo, 1960, 23). Rogers and Agarwala (1976) view communication as continuous, sequential, and an endless process of change. The classical model of interpersonal communication process includes the elements of "Source-encoder, message, channel, receiver-decoder plus feedback" (Gortner, et al., 1997, 138). The strength of this model is based on the understanding that interpersonal communication is an interactive process in which the sender and the receiver are interdependent entities.

Linguistically, communication is a metaphoric and symbolic conduit (Reddy, 1979) that represents one thing in terms of another. In other words, if communication is not clear, language is the "enemy" of the communication process. Gortner et al (1997) show that in communication (1) language transfers thoughts and feelings from person to person, (2) speakers or writers insert thoughts and feelings in words, (3) words contain thoughts and feelings, and (4) people extract thoughts and feelings from words" (p. 138). Human thoughts and behavior are influenced by metaphors. Humans "do not transfer meanings to one another" (p. 138). The "receiver creates meanings in his/her own mind" (p. 138). Words have no meanings except those which evolve in people's minds. The evolution of meanings is an irrational, rational, interpretive and imitative experience.

Diagrammatically, this model (Figure 10.1) illustrates that complex phenomenon of communication.

Figure 10.1. Classic Interactive Communication Model

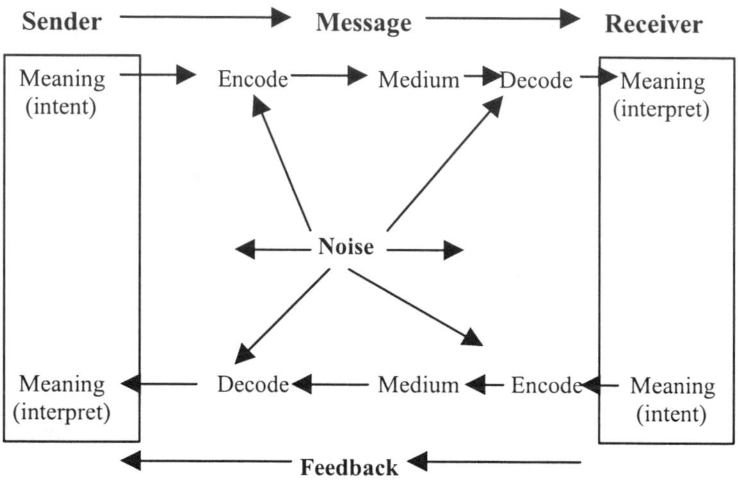

Sender ──────▶	Message ──────▶	Receiver

```
Meaning ──▶ Encode ──▶ Medium ─▶ Decode ─▶ Meaning
(intent)                                     (interpret)

                      ◀── Noise ──▶

Meaning ◀── Decode ◀── Medium ◀── Encode ◀── Meaning
(interpret)                                   (intent)

              ◀──── Feedback ◀────
```

Source: Gortner, H.F., J. Mahler, and J.B. Nicholson. (1997). *Organization Theory: A Public Perspective.* Fort Worth: Harcourt Brace College Publishers, Figure 5.1.

Formal and Informal Communication Networks

Formal and informal communication do coexist and are generally inseparable. Formal communication networks parallel the organization's formal authority structure that encourages its members and subdivisions to interact. Formal communications, like "organization charts, standard procedures, formal policy directives, orders, correspondence, report" are official (Downs, 1967, 113). No designed channel of communication can satisfy all communication needs of members. Informal channels emerge when there is "a need for organization members or officials to communicate and no formal channel exists" (Downs, 1967, 113). On the other hand, informal channels of communication "poses risks to personal or policy interests" (Gortner, et al., 1997, 141). Informal communication is "ubiquitous, sometimes overlapping with and sometimes existing outside the formal structure" (p. 141). Informal communication patterns are more wide ranging, flexible, dynamic and unpredictable than formal ones. This does not mean that informal organization is "random or without form" (p. 141). Nor does it imply that organizational individuals are linked to the rest in a similar fashion. It means that informal communication is either task oriented, formally unofficial, personal, and social. Its face to face character facilitates rather than impedes "trust, social support, informal learning and feedback" (p. 141). The results of informal communication enhance motivation. However, if loyalties and norms run at odds with formal goals and rules, the informal system will be dysfunctional. Recent research has shown that "informal communication channels are more effective for implementing change when risk and complexity are characteristics of that change" (p. 141). Informal channels "provide those adopting innovations with social support" (p. 141). The system of (informal communication) is better in meeting specific needs and questions "of the adoption unit because of the immediacy of feedback and the situation specificity of the communication" (p. 141) event.

In terms of bureau members and officials, informal (unofficial) communication is advantageous because it "can be withdrawn, altered, adjusted, magnified, or canceled without any official record being made" (Downs, 1967, 113). In the light of this behavior, new ideas can be encouraged. Policy "alternatives can be generated, program implementation problems anticipated, and support cultivated and marshaled without anyone being "locked into position" (Gortner, et al., 1997, 141). Due to new information or opposition, it is possible to change positions without giving an explanation for inconsistencies and formal statements. Internal control can be affected since subordinates avoid or delay exposing their ideas and problems before their superiors.

Though informal communication can be a boon, it can also cause a variety of problems when dealing with external publics. Organization leaders often attempt to restrict informal communications about sensitive topics which may involve journalists or officials of the bureau. In this case, specific officials may be appointed to become bureau spokes people.

Network Research

Network research analysis provides a fruitful approach to the study of human communication as an organizational process. Network analysis is the study of the structure of the organization's communication system rather than the structure of the organization. Unlike the formal communication channels, informal systems of communication are "more elusive and ephemeral" (Gortner, et al., 1997, 142). Small group communication networks may be viewed to be "chains, circles, and wheels" (p. 142).

The relationship between communication structure and task performance could be interesting. For instance, simple and routine tasks which have a centralized network (wheel) are more effective. In addition, decentralized networks are more accurate than the faster and centralized ones which also have a higher error rate. Also, the person who communicates more than others becomes central. Centralized persons and networks are not only independent, but they also are more satisfied. Saturation or information overload lowers performance in group tasks. This is the negative effect of centrality in communication matters.

A personal network may be "radial or interlocking" (p. 144). In a radial network, the "person interacts directly with others, but these people do not interact with one another" (p. 144). However, in the "interlocking network, the people with whom a person interacts interact with one another as well" (p. 144).

Communication occurs quickly and easily within interlocking personal networks, but the closed nature of such a network reduces its informational strength and power. Weak sociometric ties like those of the radial type promote the exchange of more information. Even researchers who use this approach collect more data for information processing.

Directions of Organization Communication

Organizational structure influences both the direction and substance of communications. Vertical communication occurs between superiors and subordinates. Communication may flow downward (from superior to subordinate) or upward (from subordinate to superior). Vertical communications are often formal because their substance is official. Generally speaking, the greater the degree of formalization or status and power differences, the higher the proportion of vertical communication, and the more likely the direction will be downward.

Horizontal (lateral) communication links relate tasks, work units, and divisions of the organization. Though most of the communication flow is vertically designed, some of it is horizontally oriented. Some horizontal communication is formal but to a lesser extent than the one used within vertical channels. Two structural factors, task specialization and the diversity of the organization's structure, stimulate internal horizontal communication. organizational diversity is interpreted as complexity and the number of occupations and professions and not as the micro-division of labor implied by task specialization (Thompson, 1961). Task specialization increases the need for coordination and integration. Likewise, the proportion of horizontal task communication is greater as the occupations in an organization increase in number and become more professional (Hage, Alken, and Marrett, 1971). The value of horizontal communications is that they are a check on the power of the organization's top leaders. Bureaus communicate externally, and informally when they permeably network with interest groups, politicians, clients and bureaucrats for the purpose of determining programs and formulating policy. This is called the "iron triangle" (Heclo, 1977) of administrators, politicians, interest groups and the military-industrial complex. President Eisenhower coined the military –industrial complex terminology. The term exclusively represents a coalition of interests of relevant politicians, bureaucrats, businesspersons and the defense industry. Inter-bureau rivalry for the scarce resources, budgetary cutbacks, programs and target clientele dictate the use of formal and informal channels of communication that are facilitated through multidirectional approach.

In brief, regardless of the structure of organizational communication and its directional morphology, the communication flow channels are dominated by gatekeepers, liaisons and bridges (linking pins), opinion leaders, and boundary spanners (cosmopolites or cosmopolitans).

Accurate exchange of information is the goal of communication. However, communication can be problematic and ineffective due to distortion and interference, perpetual distortion, erroneous translation, errors arising from abstraction and conventional or normative differentiation, lack of congruence, distrusted sources, intellectual and cultural jargon, inflated style, euphemism evasion, bias and propagandistic manipulation (Gortner, et al., 1997).

Electronic Communication

How does electronics help us from day to day? In today's society we use satellites for many different things. We use satellites to transfer information, radio waves, TV signals and various computer systems. We can reach all over the world with satellites. Satellites allow us to communicate anywhere at any time. The technology of satellites is becoming endlessly useful.

First before learning about this technology, we must learn the bases of satellite technology. The foundation of satellites is basic electronics. Electronics is the science related to the behavior of electrons in devices. The foundation of electronics rests on four basic roots or phenomena. These phenomena are known as current, voltage, resistance, and power. These all are related to one another and are used to make up electronics. These four roots of electronics are supplied with components. Components are devices or parts in a circuit or piece of equipment. Components make up circuits, a circuit is an interconnection of many components that provide an electrical path between two or more points. Circuits make up equipment. Equipment is electronic units used to perform a job. In understanding this concept, you must look at electronics as a tree. The roots of this tree is the current, voltage, resistance and power. The trunk of the tree is component, circuit and equipment. This tree also has branches. These branches of electronics are communications, data processing, consumer, industrial, military, government, biomedical, and tests and measurement. Out of all these different fields the one that satellites deal with is communications. Communication is the process of sending and receiving a message. Communication plays a big part in everyone's life. We communicate everyday and in different kinds of ways. Without a way of communicating we could not function right in life. Communications is a necessity in today's world. This is why technology is so important. Technology is the study of technique, of the way things work. Communication technology, then is the study of how communication works. That is, it is the study of communication tools and how messages are sent. The purposes of communication are different in many ways. Basically, there are five purposes for communication: to inform, educate, persuade, entertain and to control machines or tools. The value of electronics is very important. Through electronics we are able to take communications to another level. Our life is made better through technology. Electronic technology helps to make our everyday jobs easier. Just think how life would be without some of the everyday electronics we use. For instance, let us say you wake up one morning, there was no telephone and you had to make an important call. You would have to write that person or go to them in person. This could take days to do. That is why we need electronics so much. Electronic technology is convenient because it enables us to communicate quicker and more efficiently.

About a million years ago the earth was covered with ice. This period of time became known as the Ice Age. Then came the Stone Age and

Iron Age respectively. The Stone Age was an era when people used stone tools. The current time period is becoming known as the Information Age. This is because communication technology gives us access to vast amounts of information. Computers, radio, telephone, fax and satellites make it possible for us to find information quickly. On television, we can watch events as they happen thousands of miles away. Our society depends on the efficient and effective communication of information more than ever before. Technology is changing communication at a very fast pace. This affects all of us. Whether you realize it or not, in one way or several, you depend on communication technology. For example, you may watch television to stay informed of current events. Or you may turn on the radio to hear the weather report or find out which team won the big game. Let us suppose an emergency situation arose at your home. You would probably reach for a telephone to call for help. Communication technology is also important in other ways. It makes communication simpler and clearer. You probably take for granted that you can clearly understand people you speak with on the telephone. Do you sometimes get angry when the television picture is fuzzy? That is because you are used to having it clear. The information age is affecting all of us. If we look at it more closely perhaps, we can better understand what this new era is all about. The Information Age has introduced many new tools. It is also the result of them. One of these recent developments that have helped create the Information Age is the microchip. The microchip has caused many changes in communication devices. It is responsible for most of the latest developments in telephones, radios, televisions and satellites. These now depend on microchips. A microchip is a very tiny electronic control device. It is only about four millimeters square. You could hold it on the tip of your finger. Microchips make it possible for complex machines to be made quickly and cheaply. They also make machines smaller and they work more efficiently. Microchips are the life sources for satellites. The invention of microchip made it possible for satellites to function the way they do today. Satellites were invented in 1960. During this time microchips had not been thought of. So they had to use other means to develop and control satellite communication.

Satellites are tools of telecommunication. Telecommunication is communicating over a long distance. Satellites have greatly influenced our modern communication systems. These devices are used in many aspects of today's message transfer systems. The telegraph, telephone, radio, and television are examples of our desire to transfer information more efficiently. Each of these systems has, in some way depended on changing the messages into electronic signals which make satellite communication possible. A communication satellite is a device placed into orbit above the earth. It moves at the same speed that the earth rotates. It also stays in the same relative position above the earth. This is called a geostationary or geosynchronous orbit. The satellite is positioned approximately 22,300 miles above the earth and acts as a relay station. This means it simply reflects signals back to earth. For that reason a satellite is often called a "mirror in the sky." Just as a mirror reflects your image, satellites reflect signals or microwaves back to earth. In order to do this, it must operate at an angle. Through this way, signals can be sent to many locations.

Signals are sent to orbiting satellites through earth stations. An earth station is a large pie-shaped antenna. They are sometimes called ground station or satellite dishes. It receives signals and transmits them to the satellite. This is called the up-link. The satellite receives the signals and transmits them back to earth. This is called the down-link. Receiving earth stations capture the signals and encode them. Imagine how many signals are passing through the air constantly! You may wonder how the right message gets to the right earth station. When a signal is transmitted the sender puts a certain code at the beginning of the message. The code directs the signal to the intended receiver. In addition, messages can be "scrambled." Satellites help transmit numerous types of messages including telephone and television signals. Satellites are used to transmit printed information as well. For example, the copy for the *Wall Street Journal* and *USA Today* newspaper is transmitted by satellite to many printing locations throughout the country. Satellites make it possible to communicate instantly. Live broadcasts depend on satellites to transmit messages as they are happening. Since their development in the 1960s, satellites have changed a great deal in design and efficiency. This is due to the technological developments taking place in electronics and communication. Satellite systems are being developed today with greater capacity. This means they can carry more messages. They also provide better quality transmission. Satellites can send and receive signals from other satellites. This makes it possible to send messages from one point on earth, to practically any other point without using ground relays. Satellite technology has provided unlimited power for communication which is particularly useful for learning, decision making, intelligence gathering, and control especially in civilian and geostrategic organizations. The communication structure and electronic communication can be elements of cross-cultural communication.

Cross-Cultural Communication

Effective cross-cultural communication is not only an interdisciplinarian intellectual proposition, but it is also metaphysically and a epistemologically a multi-cultural, multi-ethnic, or interracial awareness. Our domestic and global concerns for interrelated exchange in cultural, scientific, educational, diplomatic, technological, business, and professional pursuits do make it imperative for persons of diverse cultures to understandably learn from one another in order to create a conducive climate for realizing our domestic, organizational, and global objectives. In the light of this argument, learning from one another openly promotes a situation in which intercultural and professional conflicts and difficulties are identified and ironed out before they become personality, intergroup, or intragroup crises. By managing the conflicts and difficulties in advance, people are "harmonized," resources are effectively utilized, and organizational morale and productivity are enhanced because their strategic purposes and intentions are made clearer and energized for effective performance in a multicultural or global setting.

Effective Cross-Cultural Communication

Cross-cultural awareness is the communication process of persons whose cultural backgrounds are quite different in almost every aspect of life. To communicate cross-culturally, one has to have a knowledge of one's culture to be able to communicate effectively. There are four classic definitions of culture which cross-cultural communicators need to know and internalize. First, culture or civilization is, according to Taylor (1871), the holistic complex of knowledge, belief, morals, laws, customs, and other naturally or socially learned potentialities of any human being. Second, a society's culture consists of knowledge and beliefs whose practice reflects the values of its members (Goodenough, 1964; and Mehan, 1980). Third, culture is linguistic, scientific, or professional competence which enables a person to effectively articulate the duties and roles related to the office of his calling (Chomsky, 1965). Fourth, culture may be viewed as an adaptive, ideational, symbolic, structural, and sociocultural system (Keesing, 1974).

When people from two or more cultural backgrounds communicate interactively, vertically, or horizontally, communication becomes or is said to be cross-cultural. Cross-cultural awareness is, in a sense, cross-cultural communication. For example, where an individual transmits stimuli, it modifies the behavior and attitude of other individuals (Samovar, Porter, and Jain, 1981). If A represents a speaker who communicates a message, S, through a channel, T, which reaches listener U and elicits a response V, then the communication process is completed. This process oriented definition of communication states or assumes intentionality. The purpose of communication is to intentionally transmit knowledge, shape attitudes, impart conscience, influence character, gain acceptance, and produce human action.

There are situations in which messages are conveyed unintentionally or unconsciously. Awareness of this possibility is especially important in cross-cultural communication (intercultural communication) when we may be transmitting unknown, unwanted, and undesirable messages without realizing it.

Second, cross-cultural communication includes "all the processes by which people influence one another" (p. 11). Viewed psychologically, communication, or cross-cultural awareness, "is a process which is concerned with all cross-cultural situations involving meaning" (p. 11). In essence, communication, culture, and the linkage between them are inseparable, intercultural, and interlinked in perspective.

In the light of such understanding, managers or supervisors and other leaders who professionally deal with people from diverse cultural and professional backgrounds need to cultivate a particular perspective conducive to their communicative effectiveness. In essence, the leaders need to be cosmopolitans, universal communicators, ethically sound negotiators, synergistic and creative multicultural collaborators, cultural change agents, managers of organizational culture, and inspiring leaders of work and team culture (Harris and Moran, 1981). Cross-cultural awareness may be seen as the management of intercultural communication in the context of the "Global Village" (Samovar and Porter, 1988) concept. In other words, cross-cultural awareness is the effective management of multiculturalism or the intentional "domestication" and individualization of multiculturalism. This process of multicultural domestication is to be inclusively universalistic, as opposed to being exclusively particularistic.

Before successful intercultural communication occurs, existing multicultural communication problems must be understood. The problem areas arise from six sources: (1) language, including forms of polite usage; (2) non-verbal communication; (3) rules of social behavior, which include bribing and gift giving; (4) social relationships that govern family and work relationships; (5) motivation, which includes cultural concerns with achievement and face-saving; and (6) concepts and ideology involving ideas derived from religion, economics, politics, culture, and law (p. 4). These sources are both intra- and inter-institutional and interdisciplinary.

In any field of contextual and sociocultural dynamics, the synergistic fabric between culture and homo sapiens interactive styles results in social behavior tendencies that selectively screen what "insiders," as opposed to "outsiders," need to hear, know, and react to. In doing so, the communication style becomes "a cultural filter" (p. 4) which effectively designates what people are interested in and what they are not interested in. People from different cultural backgrounds learn to concentrate on the unique aspects of their environments. The ability of people to understand the communicative behaviors of others who come from different cultural backgrounds requires a knowledge of that culture's value system. Value differences in intercultural communication are immense. Their immensity tries to complicate cross-cultural awareness approaches. Since "values are powerful unseen forces that provide a set of basic assumptions used by a culture to deal with its problems" (p. 4), the mere admission of the existence of multiculturalism makes the value structure to change from compound to complex. A complex cross-cultural or multicultural environment makes interpersonal interaction more and more problematic. Even though understanding differences will help us determine sources of potential problems in such an environment, understanding similarities may help us become closer to one another (Samovar and Porter, 1988).

Because of the manner in which people are socialized, every human being is inevitably characterized by ethnic selfhood (Green, 1982). Ethnic selfhood is self-identity reminiscent of a person's ethnic cultural background, history, origin, and social, intellectual, scientific, and artistic persuasions. In multicultural societies where minority ethnic groups are viewed as subcultures, mainstream ethnocentricity (Samovar and Porter, 1988) is used to create a situation in which competition to win rather than to cooperate and share rewards and resources equitably becomes the motto. The way in which mainstream populations interact with other ethnic minorities does not only show how minorities are discriminated against in every sphere of life, but it also shows that discriminatory attitude is philosophically reflective of mainstream thinking about life and about mainstream concerns themselves. Since such a situation complicates communication, dialogue, and exchange, and even stifles progress, it is necessary for cultural awareness and cultural learning experiences to be flexibly, intentionally, and openly provided in planning, administration, and the social policy arena where institutional dynamics for effective communication are highly needed, and perhaps, could be highly articulated.

In the field of social work where managers and supervisors provide services and activities concerned with the investigation, treatment, and material aid of the economically underprivileged and socially, physically, and emotionally challenged groups, cross-cultural awareness exercises should emphasize the preeminence of specific cultures and the holistic nature of all cultures which are complex and comprehensive designs for living. Emphasis needs also to be placed on the power of the comparative method which can be used to generate insight into the complexity and variability of human needs and concerns. The entire rationale, however, should be viewed, tentatively, as the formulation about the relationship between people's "culture, the personal and collective problems, and the institutions and programs of organized benevolence" (Green, 1982, xiii) created by the larger society. In this light, there is a need for agencies to develop and provide culturally relevant services and for colleges and university programs to develop and implement culturally relevant curricula.

Within the context of the social work arena, cultural awareness as a way of carrying out professional responsibilities involves three aspects: (1) continuous discussion among workers of ways to design services so that they better match the backgrounds and expectations of clients; (2) opportunities to learn about ethnic and minority clients and particularly the minority-directed agencies that serve those clients; and (3) a long-term commitment to working with clients from particular cultural groups and communities, with worker energy focused on the ethnographic setting of clients and specific problem and service topics (Green, 1982).

In his study of human communication and cross-cultural effectiveness, Ruben (1985) has observed the work relationships between industrialized and Third World workers in the context of cross-cultural communication. The work setting concerned a situation in which Western advisors, technical personnel, and governmental and private agencies were involved in development projects in the Third World. The projects were located in the educational, governmental, agricultural, economic, and industrial policy sectors. If these Western technical advisors were to be effective in carrying out their projects, then, they needed to possess first-class skills in communication competence--ability to effectively relate to other people. This type of ability, as scholarly evidence suggests, includes, but is not limited to: (1) capacity to communicate respect; (2) capacity to be nonjudgmental; (3) capacity to personalize one's knowledge and perceptions; (4) capacity to display empathy; (5) capacity to be flexible; (6) capacity for turn taking; and (7) tolerance for ambiguity.

To be ineffective in cross-cultural communication, technical advisors who interact with professionals from other cultural backgrounds may indulge in displaying self-oriented behaviors that hamper the effectiveness of cross-cultural communication. Behaviors such as being highly resistant to ideas of others, returning to what the group has previously acted upon and rejected, calling attention to oneself, projecting a highly polished personal image of achievements and professional qualifications, and manipulating the group to assert authority. When such behavior patterns are displayed in one's own culture, they are a good predictor of potential problems when interacting with people from other cultures. There is need to learn from one's failures, weaknesses, successes, and strengths. Such a need calls for the availability of cross-cultural technical communicators who are alert and sensitive to the needs, orientations, values, aspirations, and communication styles of other cross-cultural interactants.

One of the factors which makes cross-cultural awareness more difficult is the prevalence of value differences in intercultural communication. Behavior patterns which last for a long time from a kind of mental programming are called values. Values can be regarded as good or bad, pretty or ugly, clean or dirty, valuable or worthless, right or wrong, kind or cruel, just or unjust, appropriate or inappropriate. Ethnographically speaking, mental programs that are cross-culturally shared by all human beings are universal or *etic* (Pike, 1967). Those that are unique and universally held by members of a particular group or culture are called *emic* (Pike, 1967). These collective programs are perceptual group orientations understood only within the context of a specific culture. They include cultural differences reminiscent of social equality, the importance of group harmony, the degree to which emotional displays are permitted, and the value of assertiveness. As viewed in this light, the intermarriage of value and culture are inextricably intertwined. They are intertwined because values form the basis of cultural differences, standards, and assumptions that guide thought, practice, and action. Decisions and actions are based on the prevailing values. The values are formed within a particular cultural setting where environmental adaptations, and historical factors, and socialization forces influence and are influenced by their formation. For instance, Hofstede (1980) argues that the four dialectical dimensions through which cultural value systems can be ordered include power distance, uncertainty avoidance, individualism-collectivism, and masculinity-femininity.

It is essential to conceptualize the role of communication theory in all forms of communication of cross-cultural type as an essential component. The communicator, the source of the communication act, can be a single person, a group, a collectivity, a newspaper, a legislative body, a formal organization, etc. A communicator is also a receiver. When communication is informal, the distribution roles of sender and receiver of messages tends to be socially regulated and related to the general distribution of values and power in a particular social context (McQuail, 1975).

The message which the communicator transmits is information. To transmit information effectively, uncertainty must be reduced, the message must be encoded (put ideas into appropriate form), and coded (use linguistic symbols). Thus, the message should clearly eliminate the possibility of misrepresentation. The encoding process may be a highly specialized process governed by rules and conventions. For instance, prayers, scientific theorems, poems, legal documents, and strip cartoons are produced to suit the taste and values of particular institutional settings. Such messages are transmitted by speaking, writing, using electronic devices, films, sculpture, and painting. These are the media that are viewed as means of transmission.

The receiver, more often than not, is also the one who initiates a message. Because the message is shared in a particular social, physical, and temporal environment in space over time, sharing it increases its commonality. The message that is communicated comes from a communicator whose intention it is to bring change. The anticipated change is futuristic. The communicated message or message acts are essentially inter-subjective, spontaneous, and creative. The conveyed message or act is also an event whose complex social, psychological, and sociological underpinnings are patterned to reflect cultural or subcultural reality (McQuail, 1975).

Communication and cross-cultural communication is not only a conditional reaction to external stimuli, but it is also an attempt by the communicator to adjust or release tension. The tension-release management is a process through which a social system's patterns of communication are governed by norms and conventions. Resolving tension is also influenced by logic and past experience. Effective tension-management communication contributes to environmental change and restructuring. The environment is acted on rather than being acted in.

At the international level, industrialized nations have a monopoly over communication and information flow to and from the Third World. They monopolize these means of cross-cultural awareness because they have power in terms of money, technology, and political influence which enable them to control Third World minds through misinformation, disinformation, distortion of reality, and manipulative propaganda. They are able to control them because they use their technical personnel and financial resources to subsidize the media needs in these countries so that it can report or publish communicable information which suits and serves Western rather than Third World interests, or both. The fact that the developed nations can view themselves as the center whose interests must be served by exploiting the periphery does not only negatively perpetuate the dependency theory, but this perpetuity is a form of political, economic, cultural, and imperialistic manifestations that are a violation of the fundamental principles of human rights, decency, dignity, and freedom. Western nations which claim to be democratic behave in ways that are very undemocratic and uncivilized in their dealings with Third World nations which are in search of models for evaluation and emulation. Such a type of communication is negatively and cross-culturally oriented. Negative cross-cultural orientation is not only negative cross-cultural awareness, but it is also, valuewise, the most ineffective type of communication. When communication is most ineffective, things remain at a standstill because proper decisions that effect change cannot be made, implemented, and evaluated for accountability and change.

There are many barriers to the communication process. The most important ingredients of the communication process, according to Plunkett (1976), are the message, the message sender (transmitter), the message carrier (medium), and the receiver. Whenever any of these four components of the communication process is interrupted, the communication process becomes defective, loses clarity of meaning, and becomes less intelligible for understandability. Disruption then is not only barrier to communication, but prejudice, vanity, illusions, superstition, and social age, linguistic, vocabulary, political, economic, psychological, educational, and financial barriers (Cutlip, 1955).

Another barrier to communication arises with compressed information. Compressed information is ready made from the press, radio, television, and hearsay. Such information is, as evidence has shown, normally produced from manipulated, distorted, misreported, and misinterpreted data. Communication which is provided from such a compressed setting will not be effective because it is less truthful and less realistic although truth and reality may be forged to create it.

Another study (Lall and Lall, 1979) shows that communication is made more difficult because it conflicts with other information which the receiver possesses. Instead of hearing the message, the receiver hears what his mind tells him the sender has said.

Communication in a School Setting

The communicating phase seeks to bring out the communion set forth as the original objective. It proceeds through common experience in knowledge, attitude, and emotion. Before communication is carried out, it needs enough publicity through reasonable balance in data, planning, and evaluation. Dynamic and effective communication is both human and public relations which should be exercised persuasively and diplomatically to foster a cooperative and motivating social climate-- conducive to productivity. Administrators in private and in public enterprise communicate with their audience in a given situation, time, and place. The type of media and techniques of communication, as Cutlip (1952, 1955) indicates, must be selected carefully because they become the basis of effective communication. It is therefore imperative to bear in mind that an effective communication program is that which impels originality, growth, and maturation in achieving its goals and objectives.

Communication is not only the giving and receiving of information, signals, messages, gestures, etc., but it is also carrying across of interpretable and understandable symbolic information. The communicating act is a two-way process whose chief purpose is to transmit knowledge, shape attitudes, impart conscience, influence character, and gain acceptance to produce action in man. In this process, the sender transmits information to the receiver. The latter will internalize it to gain his perception of reality. This reality is governed by his experiential knowledge based on his learning and interpreting ability. What he learns through internalization and perceptual experience becomes increasingly informative as it is kept out of emotions, values, expectations, and perceptions. However, it should be noted that not all communication is effective.

Public relations as a communication process, works from inside out, since any organization has many publics; the place to start in identifying them is at the center of the organization. It is there that the essential character of an organization's public relationships are determined. It is there that meaningful support and key policy makers are located. Working out from this inner circle, the communication specialist encounters junior staff, supervisors and teachers, home communities, consumers, investors, and all other publics directly affected by the organization. Communicating from inside out has a horizontal relationship in direction.

Purpose of Effective Communication

To serve a community effectively, the school administration, in many ways, either directly or indirectly, interacts with its immediate social environment in a form of students, staff members, board and library officials. In turn, these collective school units talk to their surrounding public about the happening multiplicity of school affairs. The nature of reaction of the community, staff, and students towards administrative policies and decisions reflects the nature of the existing feedback link, or the two-way process of communication which they use. To use effective communication effectively, there must be a defined purpose the school wants to see achieved. This purpose will be fully explored as it deals with each of these collective units in detail. However, an effective communication philosophy will enable the administrator to identify problems while they are still in their embryonic stages and try to solve them before they grow to grow to crises.

It might be necessary to make a community survey for obtaining feedback opinions by using questionnaires. Alternatively, some teachers, students, and lay citizens will be well informed about school problems, and will suggest constructive ideas for running the school when they are allowed by the administration to attend advisory committees in which they exchange opinions. Sharing ideas will not only enable them to understand the purpose and objectives of the institution, but also its problems, challenges, and achievements. Eventually, ways to solve emerging problems will be learned and the school's needs will be met. Such kind of involvement in participating in school affairs by the chief representatives of its publics builds believability when requiring money and enables the people to see the school as their own institution which demands their support.

Alternatively, the administration can communicate effectively if he allows the formation and function of respective student, staff, and lay advisory committees which will serve to let him know about possible problems before they become explosive. Since each advisory committee is representative of a larger section of the population, they will advise the administration accordingly. When instant problems are aired, they result in instant feedback. Collectively, these groups may form a study group to examine specific problems facing the community. A clever administrator will see to it that an advisory committee does not waste time discussing trivialities at the expense of major needs of the school and the community. The most pressing and common topics for discussion include building needs and school budgets.

In committees, people who both agree and disagree with school officials should be represented. In doing so, it will be easy to find out what the community is thinking on major educational topics. The size of an advisory committee should be between twenty-five and fifty people. From these, subcommittees studying different topics could be formed. Each subcommittee may have as many as three people. If many volunteers want to serve, they may be involved. From all of these subcommittees, a steering committee might emerge. By involving more people, the chances of public understanding of the needs of the school are increased.

There should be written by laws governing the structure and functional procedure of the committees. Majority and minority opinion has to be taken into consideration. Carefully written by laws will prevent all kinds of problems. Meetings which have no recommendations are not productive. In giving and making them realistic deadlines are necessary. School officials should not dominate in these committees. If they do, they lose credibility which is their asset. Recommendations and reports should include positive comments and constructive suggestions. When making recommendations, the advisory group should consider the cost of implementation. Ideas that have no support on financial grounds will lead to frustration. Recommendations should be given to the school board before they are released to any other person or group. Finally, the administrator should thank all those who serve on committees and publicize their contribution for the improvement of education.

How to Communicate with the Staff

When the administrator encourages staff morale through an open two-way communication procedure, the communication process is effective. When planning an internal communication program, the administrator should identify his various publics: other administrators, teachers, secretaries, custodians, bus drivers, cafeteria workers, paraprofessionals and anyone else on the staff. In doing this, the school will attract top teachers into its setting because these people convey the image of the school to the public.

Effective leadership is characterized by the efficiency with which correspondence with the public is handled. The office should reply all applications addressed to it and must specify formal application procedures needed. The principal should enlighten the staff on informative literature about his district's accomplishments, needs, offerings, and challenges. He should make proper arrangements for interviewing and recruitment of new teachers by expert senior faculty members. In freedom and dignity, he should notify staff members about the newly hired teacher who should be warmly welcomed, housed, and incorporated into the school family. The administration should not only greet each new teacher and communicate an open door policy that sets a cooperative tone, but he should also meet new faculty members and ask them suggestions for improvement.

Misinformation and rumors can breed morale problems and encourage the faculty to distrust school administrators. That is why an on-going communication program must be established. Several ways exist to keep communication flowing. Most require time and effort, but they can result in a smooth running school with a happy staff. They will eliminate the "What's the rumor this week?" To encourage a two-way communication system the following thirteen steps should be taken into consideration

1. The administration should eat some meals with various staff members as often as possible. In such informal moments, they can discuss some problems. The staff will learn that he is interested in the school, its problems, and their solutions. He should accept suggestions of teachers and implement them.

2. A staff's advisory committee should be established by an elective procedure and should meet regularly. The participants should be encouraged to speak openly in the meetings. This method solves many problems before they reach the peak.

3. All staff members should be encouraged to let the administration know current and potential problems. The administration should be available to staff members. Secretaries should not surround administrators with a protective shield that makes them inaccessible.

4. All staff members should get access to suggestion box in which they can place their comments and suggestions. An administrator who reacts to all questions and suggestions will avoid frustration and enhance morale among the staff.

5. He/she should encourage the faculty to be more innovative in teaching and in trying to meet the objectives of using the curriculum. This will indicate that he/she values classroom actions.

6. The school should summarize the key topics of the faculty handbook and distribute copies to faculty members.

7. To avoid misunderstandings that could cause severe problems, he should communicate the district's policy on reappointment and tenure.

8. He/she should prepare an easy-to-follow explanation of the employee's paycheck and explain each deduction in terms that he can understand.
9. He/she should not interrupt teachers in the middle of a point they are making.
10. He/she should pleasantly smile at workers every morning. It may be the only one they get.
11. He/she should thank staff members orally and in writing for a job well done. Each individual at any level likes to know that his boss recognizes and appreciates what he/she has done.
12. He/she should conduct an exit interview with people who resign. He/she might learn about some shortcoming that triggered the employee's leaving.
13. He/she should not forget to let the secretary know that although he/she is extremely valuable, he/she is not the assistant administrator.

How to Communicate with Students

An effective two-way communication system should be going on regularly between students and school officials. The communication should be both verbal and written. It should be honest and helpful. Students need correct information, expectations, and answers from school officials. Likewise, school officials need correct information, constructive opinions, and serious questions from students. To encourage dynamic and effective communication, the following observations should be registered:

1. School officials and board members should give students time and place so that hey can ask questions, register complaints, and state opinions. Officials should provide answers and information. In most cases, they should listen. If they must answer, the answers should be given quickly and honestly.
2. Student leaders should meet with school officials to iron out differences existing between them. In turn, the leaders will speak to their student counterparts.
3. To use the dead time more effectively, administrators, board members, and department chairpersons might periodically schedule rap sessions with interested students in study halls.
4. Teachers and administrators should spend time eating with students. The occasion should be used by the administrators to obtain or dispense information. In no case should a teacher or

administrator be used to spy on students. This will not create a favorable social climate for free expression on the part of students.

5. School officials should invite students and eat with them at regular intervals. A variety of students, not necessarily the clever and friendly ones, should be included in this group. Administrators will learn much by listening.

6. A committee of about six persons, composed of four students, an administrator, and a teacher can be established to produce a weekly paper for students. The newsletters should contain reports of events and policies that are of interest to students. Reporters for the school newspaper should be encouraged to ask probing questions and develop interpretive data rather than to accept generalities from the central office or departments.

7. Parent Teachers Association meetings should add students to their groups so that they can become active voting members of their organization. In doing so, parents and teachers not only introduce new life among them, but they also make the students feel that they are an integral part of the home and school within the community.

8. The administration may engage and empower an ombudsman. Since he is a staff member, he can answer students' questions and help in cutting through the red tape.

9. Finally, students like to be judged on the basis of their ideas rather than on the manner of their appearance. However, in our system temperance in dress should be part of the school's philosophy an administrator should constantly encourage.

How to Communicate with the Board

To run the schools effectively, school officials must have community resources and support. This means that public and private schools belong to the people who are also taxpayers, or shareholders in these institutions. Therefore, the role the board can play will be vital. To communicate well, the administration should send agenda to all board members and of necessity to reporters. Local radio stations can announce the agenda the day of the meeting.

Bagin (1972) recommends the following procedure for conducting a board meeting:

1. Distribute a copy of the agenda and welcome all members of the board. The agenda pamphlet should include information about each board member and the procedure to be used to address the board. It should encourage questions to improve the schools. For

instance, "these are our or your schools."

2. Do not be biased against anybody's opinions. Guidelines should be available and in writing, they will largely be acceptable to most members.
3. Use a large name card for board members so those attending can identify them.
4. Make sure that some educational topic is discussed. Invite school curriculum people to present new ideas to the board.
5. Tape the proceedings, in addition to having a secretary who keeps minutes. This eliminates questions about what was discussed. All people at the meeting should know that it is being taped. Their awareness will motivate most to make fair and constructive comments in public.
6. Observe common courtesies toward every one attending. Check the room temperature, and have proper ventilation and light.
7. If there is disagreement on an issue, communicate both sides of the issue. Too many times boards vote unanimously on every issue, never showing that the problem was discussed. People who disagree with a discussion will feel more comfortable if their side is publicly presented.
8. When a person addresses the board, ask him or her for their name and address, and if he/she represents any group. A person who identifies himself/herself may keep his remarks more rational than one who remains anonymous.
9. Keep the format of the agenda consistent from meeting to meeting to avoid confusion and the accusation of re-ordering the agenda for someone's special interests.
10. Involve various staff members at each meeting. By so doing, they can learn that they play an integral part in the operation.
11. Involve students in each meeting too even if only to start the meeting with a flag salute. Although they may be less influential in contributing satisfactorily, they should be made to feel that they are welcome.
12. The administration should not recess the executive board meeting when facing controversy. Recess provokes suspicion and mistrust and officials spending people's money should not contribute to such suspicions.

After the meeting is over a board spokesperson should meet with the press. The administration should prepare a follow-up list of things to do as a result of comments, questions, and suggestions offered at the meeting. The spokesperson should answer questions he/she promised to answer. All employees should get a one page publication showing highlights of the board meeting. It should be objective and through it, employees will realize that the management team cares about morale. Harrington (1967) cautions administrators in regard to raising funds for a school project. The board or audience may be composed of taxpayers, church members, voters, parents, professionals, and even unionists. In view of this, a carefully planned method of raising funds should be used. The administration should not use force or apply pressure to influence his audience to accept his ideas, instead, he/she should encourage a collective participating spirit which will guide them to reach a consensus. The administrator should not allow confidential information about fund raising to be advertised before a meeting has been held because this might distort information that will negatively necessitate the failure of the project. Sometimes failure testifies gross administrative inefficiency.

The Library

Public relations is communication which should be given enough publicity. If the essence of the library is communicated to the audience as a resource of inculcable value, a stable educational force, and a core of the school force for societal excellence and change, the audience or the publics of the library should modify their attitude towards it. They should make positive adjustments concerning how they use the library and become positive contributors for its continuous existence. The librarian or administrator, or the public relations specialist or information specialist, should either collectively or singularly be able to identify the many publics of the library and constructively communicate with them through radio, television, and newspapers and through student, staff, and community organizations.

The chief publics of the library include the book sellers, schools which train librarians for recruitment, the reading public, the universities which use the libraries, the policy and decision makers, and the general public whose opinions affect those of all the publics. The school library, as a source for creative teaching and innovative discovery, should be given administrative and financial support to strengthen its resources in meeting not only its goals and objectives, but also the goals and objectives of its wider public. Finally, those who use the library should know through the two-way communication process, about the school's philosophy of education, aims, and means of achieving them.

In colleges and universities, the library is a center of learning, conferences, workshops, scholarly and scientific research, and more recently, it has become a center for computer instruction and information processing, storage, retrieval and distribution. This valuable resource should be used, funded and protected with care.

Lines of Communication

Educators treat pupils or students as the prime agents in the transmission of information about the school to their parents, home, and community. The character, conduct, and achievement of these learners daily reflect the influence of the school, and would do so in spite of one's efforts to the contrary. Laying the foundation for both worthy attainments by its students and their good reputation is not only the privilege of the school, but is also its obvious duty. In the light of this argument, the school child has a lot to do with public relations and wise educators should capitalize upon student opportunities. Looking at communications in all its facets, a school which encourages motivating and interesting classroom and extra-curricular activities and practices fairness, has good human relations and does not only reflect a dynamic spirit of cooperation, but it also reflects the spirit's effectiveness which is the essence of communication.

Through parent teachers association meetings, parents learn or discover what teachers "feed" their children with. Useful parental programs on education are displayed. The association helps school districts to survey and secure public opinion on basic issues. It provides opportunity for teachers to learn about the parents, homes, and additional data about the children they teach. However, one observation should be made clear. Restricting the membership of a community organization as this one, to parents, establishes some limits; an over-dependence on the PTA may result in inadequate contacts with many citizens whose interest and support are essential.

In every society, there are community organizations which render service to the development of a school-community relations program. In smaller communities most of these groups possess, in diversity and competition, greater influence than others. The organizations or groups include civic, cultural, economic, political, professional, social, women's and welfare groups. Most of these organizations are national in scope and the local pattern of their organization and function is well standardized. In view of this the school's leadership must strive to project its image optimistically.

Every creative and dynamic school administrator should make a reliable and meaningful annual report and publication for public relations purposes. The reports tell the public what the school intends to do and how it spends public finance. A similar report should be prepared in a church school for church members to know how their money is spent.

The student's progress report is used to inform the parent and the student about his or her progress in school. Parents are often dissatisfied with reports that tell little about their child, and it is the responsibility of the school to prepare and distribute reports to parents. The reports must be legible, meaningful, and useful. Teachers put remarks on cards showing individual differences and academic achievements of the learner. Reports contribute to parental understanding about their children's performance and advise them accordingly.

The school authority should emphasize the importance of personal contacts between school personnel and the public. In some cases, home visitation by staff members can be an excellent device for promoting public or human relations. If regular teachers are used to make home visits, those with sympathy and understanding, interest and enthusiasm should go. Their teaching loads should be minimized.

Parents should also visit the school during school sessions. They should come in small invited groups to get where records and other materials concerning their children are available. The other purposes for parental visits will be:

1. To familiarize them with the personnel, plant, curriculum, and other activities available.
2. To provide teachers with opportunities for discussing student problems with them.
3. To give students a chance to acquaint parents with the school environment.
4. To help parents get information about school problems.
5. To encourage parents to regard school visits as part of their normal activity.
6. To educate learners to the fact that parents should take an active part in planning school activities.

Before they depart, parents should be requested to visit with the school administrators and discuss any part of the school programs they observed. The administrator may ask them for their evaluation.

Newspapers give publicity to school news and often contribute free advertising of forthcoming events. As a channel of communication, the newspaper must be given a high rating because so many people read the newspaper and probably receive as much. The information given and opinions expressed in it influence the thoughts and actions of the public. Administrators should use it frequently but cautiously.

The school radio is used to inform the public about what is going on around the world. The broadcasts are intended to be nonpartisan and inform the public about public issues and problems. The radio contributes much in helping the public to understand the problems and needs of the schools.

Most of the working relationships discussed with regard to newspaper editors and radio station managers apply to television. However, the potential for radio for classroom instruction are not as satisfactory as those of the television. In any case the use and significance of television on public relations are much greater than those of radio. The addition of sight to sound makes the program more personal and direct. As a medium of communication television has great potential. Lately, the computer and other multimedia techniques are excellent teaching tools which should be acquired.

On the whole, it is in the classroom, on school campus, and in the community that the most lasting and most vital public relations attitudes are based. In view of this, schools should be staffed with the best teachers obtainable. Teachers who are proud of their profession, convinced of their importance to society, well trained to do their job, and who understand the importance of developing attitudes and habits along with skills in subject matter are not only a potent force for public relations, but they are also the core for successful teaching and effective communication.

Barriers to Communication

Plunkett (1975, 1976, 50) pointed out that the "most important ingredients in the communication recipe are the message, the message sender (transmitter), the message carrier (medium), and the receiver. "If any of these components of the communication procedure is defective in any way, clarity of meaning and understanding will be lacking. Arising barriers will sport the ingredients and disrupt communication. If it is disrupted, it becomes less effective. Cutlip (1952, 1955, 123) has pointed out that "the existing barriers in communication include prejudices, vanities, illusions, and superstitions." Accompanied with these are social barriers, age barriers, language or vocabulary barriers, political and economic barriers, and the constant roar of competition for people's attention.

Lack of social contact may be due to imbalanced inclination, lack of finance, and lack of education. Sometimes the meager time people have daily to pay attention to the information coming from outside hinders communication. Alternatively, both sender and receiver must be in their right frame of mind and tuned in the proper way of transmitting and receiving the message respectively. In other words, improper timing will hinder rather than promote effective communication. In addition to this information, a lack of similar backgrounds in the sender and receiver, in regard to their education, previous experiences, or present environment may hinder receptiveness to a message and prevent the proper reaction to it. Atmospheric disturbances hinder communication when the atmospheric environment is characterized by noise, interruptions, and physical discomfort for both sender and receiver. On the one hand, when information is compressed it is easily distorted and misinterpreted. Compressed information is ready made, from press, radio, television, and hearsay. On the other hand, the fear of facing facts that threaten the established pattern may cause communication problems. Some of the things people hear are not only disturbing, but they also threaten the status quo, and the current trends of life's routine. The threat becomes a personal one to the receiver and who reacts negatively or positively and otherwise to such provoking situations.

As mentioned earlier Lall and Lall (1979) indicate that communication is hampered sometimes because it conflicts with other information that the receiver possesses. Instead of hearing the message, the receiver hears what his mind tells him the sender has said. It may be the same or different message. Each individual tends to have preconceived ideas of what others mean. Individuals tend to identify something new with something similar that they have experienced. The receiver tends to question the reliability of the source of information. The receiver may ascribe nonexistent motives or apply a status image to the sender. If the receiver distrusts the sender, he or she may reject the message irrespective of its value. As it has been mentioned earlier, the type of language used may be the barrier of communication. Language usage is associated with symbols which represent attitude, facts and feelings. An individual conveys words rather than their meaning. The same words may mean different things to different people. This is because meanings are in individuals rather than in words which they represent.

Physical objects such as walls and doors are barriers of communication because they act as conventional situational closure objects. Even though, some communication leaks out across these objects. Much misunderstanding can be traced out not only to misinformation but also due to lack of full and accurate information.

This lack can be the root cause of friction and aggression that block good relations. To avoid these barriers which render communication ineffective, there should be a shift of emphasis to people's interests and intellectual capacities.

Types of Communication

In the history of communication, there are three main tools of communication namely verbal, written, and non-verbal. Each has its merits and demerits. I think that the most effective speaker is one who uses all the three tools while communicating with his audience. In the preceding paragraphs, I shall try to analyze and describe each of them.

Verbal. The verbal tool of communication is one in which a speaker speaks through his/her mouth. In meetings, the spoken word is a vehicle that brings people together face to face. This medium not only provides an opportunity to communicate to a selected audience, but it also provides the opportunity to listen. To communicate effectively in a meeting requires purpose, careful planning and staging, and skillful direction. The speaker must be well prepared and well equipped with materials for giving important and interesting speeches. The materials may be for illustrative purposes. Interesting speeches are extemporaneously delivered.

Since the staging of meetings is often the task of public relations staff, which is also an administrative function, the following checkpoints are essential if effectiveness is to be achieved. There should be comfortable facilities, long sessions should have breaks between them in which displays, films, and charts can be exhibited. Members should be served with refreshments and should be encouraged to participate. Lastly, organizers of the occasion should be credited before a press release.

Written. The second tool of communication is the printed or written word. administrators and public relations experts must know that the printed word is produced either internally or externally for organizational function. Its composer must spend enough time to produce qualitative rather than quantitative information. He must thoroughly know their audience in composition, age, professional background, sex, racial and socioeconomic status, etc. He must avoid jargon, use common words and concrete terms. In writing he should use correct grammatical constitutions. He should personalize his message and keep the reader in mind. Although he may employ strong verbs, he should not use useless words. If communication is to be intelligible, he should write about what he understands. He should not write faster than he thinks because this will influence him to write ineffectively. Correct and clear thinking leads to correct and clear writing. When ideas have been thoroughly and exhaustively digested, they can be put on paper. But they should not appear or be written on paper if he does not have adequate and accurate data on which the basis of his logistically written word will depend. In the final analysis, writing should not only convey a dictionary meaning, but it should portray a contextual one too. The content of the written word should be interesting, timely, and enjoyable. It should include information about workers and their organization. Issues of a controversial nature should be left out. The context of a publication determines its character and impact. In view of this, sound journalistic principles should be used in editing such a paper. For internal interdepartmental communication, letter writing is an important tool of communication. Plunkett, (1975) writing on factory management and maintenance, indicated six advantages of the company letter; these are: inexpensive, direct, important looking, intimate, quick, and informal.

The letter used for public relations purposes is written by the chief official of an organization or the chief of a division for circulation among the members. The purpose is to establish a direct contact that bridges the gap between the chief administrator and those who do not see as much of him as they would like to. Letters support the line of communication. They insure the accuracy of the line transmission. Their content points up what is newsworthy and important within the organization. They give added importance to the line of communication by providing that the line is well informed.

The grapevine. The grapevine is another tool of written communication which may be either formal or informal. Since the method is characterized by rumors and gossip, it should be challenged with facts. Workers who willfully spread improper information should be discredited. The administrator should be available to and honest with his people. He should know when silence is golden.

Nonverbal. The fourth nonverbal tool of communication is the image. For about a century, motion picture film has been used in efforts to inform by transmitting ideas, persuade by stimulating imagination, and motivate by producing action. The television is a classical example and an effective and economical agent of film showing which communicates effectively.

Motion picture as a form of communication, has several advantages. It combines the impact of sight, sound, drama, and movement, color and music with group enthusiasm. It represents meanings involving motions. It clarifies the time factor in any operation or series of events.

It provides a reproduced record of events and presents processes that cannot ordinarily be seen by the human eye. The camera can bring the past and the distant to the observer. Finally it can magnify and reduce objects and can as well use cartoon to dramatize abstractions. Also, the computer, fax and telephone can be used to communicate electronically.

Because of the expense and effort involved in the production of a good film, the practitioner should weigh the purpose of the film, channels of distribution available, and the potential audience. If it is worth the while, he should mull over the questions which follow here under:

1. What is the film expected to do?
2. What necessary points are inclusive?
3. What research and information resources are available?
4. How long will the film take before it does its job?
5. Is it colored or black and white?
6. What type of treatment? Comic? Documentary? Entertainment? Serious? Series?
7. Music—the need? Kind? Recorded? Special? Costs?
8. Can we do it? Or, shall we hire a professional firm?

The Ten Commandments of Good Communication

The four tools of communication (verbal, written, grapevine and nonverbal) cannot harmoniously and effectively be utilized unless they are governed by rules. Plunkett (1975, 1976, 56) has enumerated ten rules or commandments for good communication. These commandments which he paraphrased and tabulated from the American Management Association say that the administrator should clarify his ideas before conveying them. He must state them truthfully and with a considerate spirit. In planning the communications act, he should consult his peers for advice. He should be aware of not only the content of the message, but also its implications in perspective. He should convey the message at a timely moment. He should follow up the communication to assess the results of the feedback. If the results are negative, he must alter the technique or tool of communication. If they are positive, he has to maintain the standard of communication to produce positive results always. The communication process should be a continuous one in order to make life worth living. Interrupted communication is disastrous. The techniques of implementing communication must support the process. Finally, as a communicator, you have not only to understand through listening and thinking logically, but you must be understood too.

In the history of human affairs, communication is expected to be effective to meet the goals and objectives of the organization. Unfortunately, the fact that most organizations fail to communicate effectively and run into serious problems testifies the fallacy of this theoretical expectation. In practice most communication is a fad. Some administrators communicate better at the periphery rather than starting from the center of things to the periphery.

Most of the ideas expressed in this chapter are relevant to a democratic country like the United States where freedom of speech, other freedoms, and academic freedom are legal provisions guaranteed by the constitution and violable by none in the context of the law. In the light of this practice, not all of these ideas are applicable to various parts of the world where political, cultural, economic, and legal barriers may prevent their desired practice. However, there is no reason why they may not be used anywhere if there is need. It is better for leaders to create this need sometimes. Since most of these ideas, at least on the theoretical plane, sound workable and are good for initiating change, they should be excellent; but of what use will they be if they cannot be put into practice. This is a challenge to all of us.

Finally, to translate these ideas from theory to reality necessitates the interdependent union or interrelated marriage between theory and practice. History has proved that the two do not always function harmoniously. This failure may be the result of humankind's defective nature or the misapplication of principles he does not understand. Whatever the case may be, it does not prevent him from striving for mastery and excellence in performance.

Conclusion

As a scientific discipline, communication evolved during the 1930s and has undergone immense transformation in terms of theory development and practice. Communication is essential in all organizations. It is the process through which organizations inform and clarify goals for members. Internally, communication provides a medium for organizational coordination and control and more informally for social support among members. External communication is especially vital to bureaus to (1) maintain political responsiveness and accountability, (2) foster coordination with other agencies and levels of government, and (3) promote external support. This chapter has discussed accountability and power as well as cross-cultural organizational communication. These ideas are closely related for public bureaus because communication is a primary medium for exercising power. Bureaus, schools, churches, and corporations and their members can raise smoke screens to evade accountability. Information can be withheld or its timing and content manipulated to protect organization's operating routines and policies from external scrutiny. By shaping the flow of information, bureaus and their members attempt to maintain or increase their power and resources, to avoid the control of others, and to reduce undesirable environmental turbulence. As a result, policy outcomes and power relationships inside and outside the organization are affected.

Communicative skill must be used to enhance professional, intellectual and organizational or institutional dynamics within and without cross-cultural settings. Cross-cultural communication is a two-way process and cannot be separated from effective cross-cultural thinking, learning, and acting. Within the human services profession, effective multicultural communication involves understanding cultural habits, understanding the communication process, trusting people, asking questions, expressing oneself with simplicity and clearness, being linguistically selective, listening attentively, respecting differences, and adapting to situations with a sense of flexibility. In the global arena, cross-cultural communication is mutual and responsive intercultural exchange and understanding. Regardless of the field in which one finds oneself, effective cross-cultural awareness is essential for one's meaningful interaction and survival in our global village.

This chapter has also provided information that the school administrator should use for the dynamic and effective functioning of the school through a two-way communication system. Through research, the administrator must know what the community is thinking about. The reflected thoughts of the community, staff, students, and the wider public should be used for adjusting not only the goals and objectives of the institution, but also the curriculum which influences their needs and by which their needs are influenced.

Experiential evidence has shown that most school administrators feel inadequate when it comes to communicating with the public. This happens due to the fact that few administrators have had the opportunity to learn how to communicate in ways that make their schools smoothly running and truly private or public. The lack of opportunity is attributed to two correlative factors; the paucity of materials and the scarcity of experts in the field. As a result, few administrators have confidence in their ability to communicate and their schools cannot have a planned and regulated communication program. Some do nothing to communicate.

Administrators who do not think of communications when they consider accountability, bond issues, student riots, teacher demands, complaints at board meetings, and community group pressures are not prepared for current challenges. Their leadership leaves much to be desired. It is therefore emphatic that any program of public relations, even when cooperatively arrived at and implemented, responsibility for communication and ways of involving the people in community planning and implementation should be administrative functions.

In the modern world, organizational communication particularly that of the mainstream media in reality represents the interests and what the propaganda model that stipulates a set of institutional and organizational variables, reflecting the elite power, which very powerfully influence the media. In this arena, to understand how and why the system works, one needs to look into its institutional/organizational structure. Also, attention should be focused on how it is organized, how it makes decisions, how it is controlled, and how it is funded. Both Edward Harman of the University of Pennsylvania (Business) and Noam Chomsky of MIT (Linguistics) in their video presentations on *The Myth of the Liberal Media* have deconstructively argued that the liberal media, as a tenet of American political culture, communicates in such a way that the news media are subordinated to the corporate and conservative interests reflective of elite propaganda. That elite is more conservative than liberal -- hence the subordination. In other words, effective communication should be methodologically, empirically or ethnographically grounded on research that is rooted in assumptions, epistemology and ideologies that can be analyzed, interpreted, and conveyed meaningfully.

References

Ager, M.H. 1980. *The Professional Stranger: An Informal Introduction to Ethnography.* Orlando: Academic Press Inc.

Angoff, A. 1973. *Public Relations for Libraries: Essay in Communication Techniques.* Conn.: Greenwood Press.

Bagin, D., et al. 1972. *School Communication Ideas that Work: A Public Relations Handbook for School Officials.* Chicago: Nations Schools Press.

Barnard, C. 1938. *The Functions of the Executive.* Cambridge, MA: Harvard University Press.

Bass, D. 1994. *Concepts of Electronics.* New York: Johnson.

Berger, C.R., et al. 1976. Interpersonal epistemology and interpersonal communication. In *Explorations in Interpersonal Communication,* ed. G.R. Miller. Beverly Hills, CA.

Berlo, D.K. 1961. *The Process of Communication.* New York.

Berlo, D.K. 1960. *The Process of Communication: An Introduction to Theory and Practice.* New York: Holt, Rinehart and Winston.

Brislin, R.W. 1979. Prejudice in intercultural communication. *Intercultural Theory and Practice: Perspectives on Education, Training, and Research.* December, 28-36.

Burns, C. 1995. *Satellite Concepts.* Dallas, TX: Excel.

Coffey, C. 1970. *PR: The Role of Public Relations in Leadership.* Mountain View, CA: Pacific Press Publishing Association.

Cook, N. 1993. *Introductory DC/AC Electronics.* New Jersey.

Cronen, V.E., W.B. Pearce, and L.M. Harris. (1982). The coordinated management of meaning: A theory of communication. In *Human Communication Theory,* ed. F.E.X. Dance. New York.

Cushman, D.P., B. Valenlinsen, and D. Dietrich. (1982). A rules theory of interpersonal relationships. In *Human Communication Theory,* ed. F.E.X. Dance. New York.

Cutlip, S.M. 1964. *Effective Public Relations.* 3rd ed. Englewood Cliffs, N.J.: Prentice-Hall.

Cutlip, S.M. 1952. *Effective Public Relations.* Englewood Cliffs, N.J.: Prentice-Hall, 1955.

Downs, A. 1967. *Inside Bureaucracy.* Boston: Little, Brown, 1994.

Ericson, P.M., and L.E. Rogers. 1973. *New Procedures for Analyzing Relational Communication.* Family Process, 12.

Fales, J. 1988. *Technology.* Peoria, IL: Macmillan.

Goffman, E. 1963. *Behaviour in Public Places.* New York: Free Press of Glencoe.

Gortner, H.F., J. Mahler, and J.B. Nicholson. 1997. *Organization Theory: A Public Perspective.* Fort Worth: Harcourt Brace College Publishers.

Green, W.J. 1982. *Cultural Awareness in the Human Services.* Englewood Cliffs, N.J.: Prentice-Hall.

Grey, J. 1996. *Wireless Communication.* Los Angeles, CA: Smith.

Hage, J., M. Aiken, and B.C. Marrett. 1971. Organization Structure and Communications. *American Sociological Review* 36: 860-871.

Harrington, J.H. 1967. *How to Administer a School Bond Tax Election Informational Program.* Englewood Cliffs, N.J.: Prentice-Hall.

Harris, P.R., and R.T. Moran. 1988. *Managing Cultural Differences.* Houston: Gulf Publishing Company.

Hovland, C.L., A.A. Lumsdaine, and F.D. Sheffield. 1949. *Experiments in Mass Communication.* Princeton: Princeton University Press.

Jones, J.J. 1966. *School Public Relations.* New York: Center for Applied Research in Education.

Katz, D., and R.L. Kahn. 1978. *The Social Psychology of Organizations.* 2nd ed. New York: John Wiley and Sons.

Keesing, R.M. 1974. Theories of Culture, *Annual Review of Anthropology* 3. B, edited by Siegel, et al., 73-97. Palo Alto, CA: Annual Reviews, Inc.

Lall, B.M., and G.R. Lall. 1979. *Dynamic Leadership.* Mountain View, CA: Pacific Press Publishing Association.

Lane, H.A. 1955. *Human Relations in Teaching.* Englewood Cliffs, N.J.: Prentice-Hall.

Lazarsfeld, P., B. Berelson, and H. Gaudet. 1948. *The People's Choice.* New York.

LeCompte, M.D. 1984. *Ethnography and Qualitative Design in Educational Research.* Orlando, FL: Academic Press Inc.

Lee, J. 1968. *The Diplomatic Persuaders: New Role of the Mass Media in International Relations.* New York.

Lewin, K. 1958. Group Decision and Social Change. In *Readings in Social Psychology,* eds. E.E. Maccoby, T.M. Newcomb, and E.E. Hartley. New York: New York University Press.

Lewin, K., R. Lippitt, and R.K. White. 1939. *Patterns of Aggressive Behavior.* New York.

Ley, W. 1980. *Satellites.* New York: Viking Press.

Lindlof, T.R. 1995. *Qualitative Communication Research Methods.* Thousand Oaks, CA: Sage.

McDermott, R.P. 1978. The possibility of equal educational Opportunity in American culture. In *Futures of Education for Exceptional Students: Emerging Structures,* ed. M.C. Reynolds. Reston, VA: The Council for Exceptional Children.

McQuail, D. 1975. *Communication.* London: Longman Group Limited.

Mehan, H. 1980. The competent student. *Anthropology and Education Quarterly* 11, 3:131-152.

Meloy, J.M. 1994. *Writing the Qualitative Dissertation: Understanding by Doing.* Hillsdale, N.J.: Lawrence Erlbaum.

Montague, A. 1958. *Educational and Human Relations.* New York: Grove Press.

Philips, S.U. 1983. *The Invisible Culture: Communication in Classroom and Community on the Warm Springs Indian Reservation.* New York: Longman.

Plunkett, R.W. 1975. *Supervision. The Direction of People at Work.*

Dubuque, IA: W.M.C. Brown Company Publishers, 1976.

Reddy, M. 1979. The conduit metaphor - a case of frame conflict in our language about language. In *Metaphor and Thought,* ed. A. Ortony. Cambridge, England: Cambridge University Press.

Rogers, E.M. 1973. *Communication Strategies for Family Planning.* New York: Free Press.

Rourke, F.E. 1984. *Bureaucracy, Politics, and Public Policy.* 3rd Edition. Boston: Little, Brown.

Ruben, B.D. 1977. Human communication and cross-cultural effectiveness. *International and Intercultural Communication Annual* IV: 98-105.

Samovar, L.A., and R.E. Porter. 1988. *Intercultural Communication: A Reader.* 4th ed. Belmont, CA: Wadsworth Publishing Company.

Samovar, L.A., R.E. Porter, and N.C. Jain. 1981. *Understanding Intercultural Communication.* Belmont, CA: Wadsworth Publishing Company.

Sonnaike, S.A. 1987. Communication flow in a democratic world. A Guideline Paper for a Brown Bag Seminar of Michigan State University, African Studies Center, April 23.

Thompson, V.A. 1961. *Modern Organization.* New York: Alfred A. Knopf.

Zajonc, R.B. 1966. *Social Psychology: An Experimental Approach.* Belmont, CA: Wadsworth.

Zimmerman, D.E., and M.L. Muraski. 1995. *The Elements of Information Gathering.* Phoenix, AZ: Oryx Press.

Chapter 11

Organizational Decision Making

Introduction

The purpose of this chapter is to offer a comparative, descriptive, and prescriptive variety of the paramount decision making (policymaking) theories in bureaus and other organizations. The comparison contrasts these theories (methods) in terms of search, analysis and choice perspectives. Regardless of the weaknesses, strengths, and criticisms of each technique and its underpinning assumptions, the prospects for contingency theory or synergistic theoretical evolution are examined in the implicit light of control and communication of the decisions made.

Decision Making

Decision making is one of the most complex and overtly political activities in organizations. Though most basic policy decisions are formally made by elected officials and courts, administrative decisions about program implementation, staffing, and budgeting have significant and lasting effects on public policy. The methods, or procedures, or theories or techniques that bureaus employ for decision making also have important political consequences. The decision method affects who participates, how agenda are established, which alternatives are considered, how they are compared and analyzed, and which values will dominate in the final selection. The selected procedures for administrative decision making affect the substance of choice. Whatever method is used depends on the problems it tends to solve and the purpose of the program articulated.

The bureaus, in order to be innovative, tend to rely on standard operating procedures, scenarios that March and Simon (1993) call *performance programs.* Performance programs are the ways in which officials come up with alternatives that are specified or programmed in advance. Programmed decisions are fully codified with respect to both the identification of options or preferences and the method and criterion for choice. The "high degree of programming does not only serve to make the bureau stable, consistent, and predictable, as required of an agent of law, but, it also makes the bureau rigid and reduces the possibility for innovation."

Table 11.1
Elements of Decision Making Process

Method	Search	Analysis	Choice
Rational	Preselected	Quantitative	Optimize Gains
Incremental	Linked to status quo	Resource distribution	Group Agreement
Aggregative	Brainstorming	Participation of Experts	Group Ranking
Garbage Can	Personal Agendas	Sequential Comparison	Choice is an Artifact

Source: Gortner, H.F., et al. (1997). *Organization Theory: A Public Perspective.* Fort Worth: Harcourt Brace College Publishers., 224)

The Methods

The Table above is an illustration of the paramount elements of decision making in public agencies. The differences which result in the success or failure of each of these methods could be understood in the light of the culture of "participation, accountability, and organizational setting" (p. 364).

The Rational Model – For Policy Analysis

The rational method of decision making is used in the public and private sectors. It is mainly used for analyzing efficiency and return on investment; in this respect the rational approach is the ideal model for decision making. The emphasis is on efficiency, which makes it possible for policy goals set by policymakers to be viewed in relation to the role of the bureaucracy. Research on administrative behavior has been used to criticize rationality for its unrealistic and idealized assumptions. Continually, it is challenged for objectivity, suitability, and description. The model has been modified for use in the context of policy analysis and systems analysis. These approaches are costly and elaborate.

Rational choice is rational because it tries to select the most efficient means or instrument to realize a given purpose or goal. The model is also called "instrumental rationality when it is used for identifying the alternative that produces the most of the desired effect or greatest level of return" (p.226). It promotes the value of efficiency. In contrast to instrumental rationality, substantive rationality is concerned with the values of 'goodness' (p. 226)of the goal or purpose itself. What is substantively rational is the subject of political philosophy and legislative, judicial and administrative inquiry. Generally, bureaus tend to be more concerned with instrumental rather than substantive rationality and deal more with "means rather than ends" (p. 226).

The four stages of instrumental rationality are as follows:

1. The goal (end) of the policy is considered a given for the situation under consideration. The assumption is that external policymakers set goals. Also feasible alternatives which are means for accomplishing goals are given. In principle. Search, which is the process for determining several preference-based alternatives is not controlled by administrators, who determine alternatives, but is controlled, through selection, by political and technical experts.

2. Second, alternative programs or procedures are "subjected to a thorough analysis to identify all the consequences, desirable and

undesirable, intended and unintended, that are associated with each alternative" (p. 226). The consequences may be uncertain and risky. The analysis of alternatives is experimentally and scientifically forecasted.

3. Third, the alternatives are ranked in accordance with consistent and consecutive preferences and their respective consequences. Each alternative has different consequences which are ranked to correspond with the right alternatives.

4. Finally, the choice criterion is to optimize rather than maximize benefits or to select the alternative with the highest value. In essence, the rational decision method is used as an advisory tool by policymakers when goals and policies are at stake. It is administratively, directly, and immediately used in order to identify efficient programs and operating procedures.

James March and Herbert Simon (1993) have criticized the rational method of policy analysis. They argue that three unrealistic assumptions characterize the model. First, "it is not clear how or by whom the alternatives" (Gortner et al., 1997, p. 227) that are to be analyzed and ranked are identified. Not all possible alternatives are examined. 'Imagination is limited, and selective perception is common. What sample of options is identified and studied? On what basis are the options selected? The model does not specify this; it assumes that the alternatives are selected by policymakers. The "objectivity of the search process and its fidelity to the principle of efficiency are called into question if political considerations determine which possible programs will be analyzed" (p. 227).

The second criticism, according to March and Simon is the false assumption based on the belief that "risk and uncertainty" (p. 227) will be known. In other words, consequences are either over or under estimated. On the other hand, "whole categories of consequences known as 'unanticipated consequences' (p. 227) are missed.

Finally, March and Simon have criticized the classical rational method for its assumption, that the decision maker (individual or group) "has a consistent preference ordering for the consequences of the alternative" (p. 228). Generally, "many consequences, desirable or undesirable, a company a program" (p. 228). To ensure the effective use of the rational method, comparisons among a set of alternatives and their consequences and vice versa, must be made.

The problem of finding a consistent preference ordering for the various consequences of different alternatives is an important theoretical stumbling block for policy analysis. Even though, "analysts transform all types of consequences into one, money" (p. 228). Cost-benefit analysis is a key form of policy analysis. This technique is based on "comparing the monetary value to society of all costs and all benefits of each alternative" (p. 228). The only one kind of consequence is monetary and the optimal solution alternative that maximizes net benefit to society is the 'best' one that can be selected. According to Pareto (Italian economist and sociologist), "Change should be made if at least one person benefits by it and none are worse off" (p. 288). This is kind of utopian. However, the Kaldor-Hicks (British economists) criterion which is applied very often states "that if a policy change makes the 'gainers' so much better off than they can compensate for the 'losers' and still come out ahead, the policy should be undertaken" (p. 288). In actual practice, this criterion suggests that "we maximize net benefits, that is benefits minus costs" (p. 288). This though is undemocratic since it does not deal with equity issues. As a rational policy analysis method, the drawbacks of this method raises issues as to whether its "intangible benefits and costs can be assigned monetary worth" (p. 288). As a result, the "debate raises questions about race, gender and other 'human' political issues about which there is intense disagreement" (pp. 228-229). Even when estimates are done or designed with statistical accuracy and plausibility, evidence indicates that the beneficiaries of the system are not minorities and women; but rather, white males.

Another drawback of cost-benefit analysis as the cornerstone of a decision-making method is that it substitutes judgment based on economic factors or technical efficiency for professional judgment (Cohen, 1980). Such a decision might undermine the psychological and political (strategic) importance of such a decision in the case of military related decisions that concern whether a ship is more effective even when it is more costly than a cheaper one which can do the same functions but less effectively because of its strategic vulnerability.

Finally, in spite of its politically inclined cost-benefit method, those who use rationality argue that it is an "objective and apolitical in a partisan sense" (p. 230). However, as a policy making tool, "its role is advisory rather than determinative" (p. 230). This shows not only who makes decisions and how the decisions are made, but it also shows that changes in the political system are inevitable. For instance, such changes may be associated with Democrats who tend to "favor low discount rates" (p. 230) while Republications tend to favor higher discount rates" (p. 230). Democrats argue that lower discount rates are components of cost-benefit analysis allows projects to be efficiently funded when viewed by budget agencies and taxpayers. Republicans argue to the contrary.

Essentially, the rational way of making decisions is based on individual reason. Individuals or groups of individuals may set goals and objectives for their organization. They can generate and examine all alternatives for achieving organizational goals. They can be able to predict the consequent consequences of each adopted alternative. They can compare the consequences in relation to the agreed goals and objectives. It is true that because of individual values which people choose for themselves, and devise a machinery for implementing and evaluating programs which promote the values, goals are "fluid and conflicting" (Van Vught, 1985, p. 596). They are fluid and conflicting because, as McNeill (1973) says, the rational model through which the values are articulated, lacks comprehensiveness of intellectual diversity. However, since an eclectic rationalist perspective of the rational model possesses collective views from other models, it can be used to criticize values in the process of decision-making; collective and rationally organized participatory discussions enable values to be collectively formulated, integrated, and shared by the group or by organizational members. In light of the collective rationalist view, values can be criticized, liberalized, "deauthoritarianized," and democratized. The liberalization, deauthoritarianization, and democratization of the rational model is a logical imperative, especially in   higher education and other public organizations and private corporations.

Lawrence, Pennings (1985, p. 375) argues that the rational planning approach rigidifies behavior because the future is unpredictable. This phenomenon of an unpredictability pushes behavior from its goals. As a result, organizational people spend much more time in executive behavior programs than they do in strategic planning. In this case, people's use of time to program behavior blocks rationality, hence its rigidity.

These strategies, according to Pennings, may be used to reduce the rigid aspects of rational planning. First, organizational behavior can be programmed to contain healthy rationality. Policy decisions can be made retrospectively to guide future behavior. Second, institutional planners should employ participatory decision-making strategies. The collegial decision-making strategies, like the collegial and the informed consensus, rather than the authoritarian-control and logic-driven models of judgmental and analytical reasoning processes should be used. Third, time strategic interdependence or eclectic rationality should be applied. Eclectic rationality is balanced and flexible management. Unlike the rational model and MBO, "eclectic rationality" will not stifle creativity.

Grandy and Warner (1986), writing on *Philosophical Grounds for Rationality*, indicate that rationality, notwithstanding its narrow and stifling intellectual base, could be understood better by examining its meaning, reasoning style, psychological explanation, and ethical reality. Rationality is communication which is "reason-governed activity" (Grandy and Warner, 1986, p. 1). It is also "a purposive reason-governed endeavor" (p. 1). As Grandy and Warner point out, Kant and Locke assert that rational reasoning consists of the entertainment and acceptance in thought and speech of a set of sequential ideas each of "which is derivable by an acceptance principle of inference from its predecessors in the set" (p. 9).

Rational reasoning has a narrow intellectual base which stifles creativity because many people who plan rationally, or for whom rational planning is done, are qualitatively selected. They are selected because of inherent conventional-situational or natural limitations of rationality which is ability to argue argumentatively. Arguing is a skill, more than the ability to see logical connections. A planner's ability to make argumentative utterances will be effective when the meaning of the words and intentions are known. The meaning is systematized and systemized if it is shared rationally and conventionally. Systematic and conventional rationality is elocutionary, persuasive, and effective communication (Grandy and Warner, 1986, p. 598).

One way in which rational planning is used is in the policy area of institutional management. In respect to policy-oriented issues, Van Vught (1985) suggests that actors who participate in the formulation, analysis, and integration of values can agree on the policies they make because they "purge the private, selfish, or idiosyncratic preferences in open and public debate" (p. 598).

Organizational theory has three main dimensions which characterize policy-networks within the rationalist tradition (perspective). These dimensions include: (1) centrality – the number and length of linkages between one organization and all other related organizations; (2) complexity—the extent of functional dissimilarity (differentiation) of goals, services, products, or target populations among related organizations; and (3) density—the extent to which members of a population or network are directly related (connected) cohesively. Rationality, a "policy-network can be seen as an operational elaboration and an institutional approximation of the rationalist idea of collective decision-making and policy development by means of the 'community of discourse'" (p. 602).

Ellen Chaffee authored *Rational Decision Making in Higher Education* in 1983. Summarizing the essential features of the rational decision, Chaffee concluded that there should be:

1. A clear set of specific values or objectives which serve as criteria for particular decisions
2. An organizational atmosphere of stability, confidence, and predictability
3. Consistency, on the part of the decision-maker, with prior practice and with understood principles of decision making within the institution
4. Provision for analyzing a particular situation as strategic, tactical, or operational and for determining whether the classification is permanent or temporary
5. Provision for determining who should make the decision, who will be affected by it, and to what degree each party should participate in the decision-making process
6. A mechanism for generating as many alternative solutions to the problem and for presenting those alternatives for simultaneous considerations
7. A means of assessing the likelihood that a particular alternative will produce results that correspond with the value structure
8. A process for evaluating the degree to which such correspondence has been achieved and for feeding the evaluation back into the decision process (pp. 60-61).

It is evidently clear that among other things, the rational model of planning is associated with institutional or societal goals. The goals rationally evolve from institutional operations and needs. Experienced goal farmers formulate goals in a social climate conducive to goal articulation, clarification, implementation, and evaluation. The purpose, intent, and implication of goals (ends) are focused on the needs and means of the organization which uses the goals. When these goals are constructed in a psychologically and socio-politically stable climate, they can hardly get into conflict with declared institutional and cultural values. The tendency to eliminate conflict between and among goals and values, enables management, irrespective of the rigidity and creativity-stifling characteristics of (rationality), to reduce or minimize its negative attributes (Chaffee, 1983).

The rational model, according to Havelock (1973), emphasizes a problem-solving process which has six stages: 'building relationships; diagnosing the problem; acquiring resources; choosing the solution;

gaining acceptance; stabilizing the innovation." By comparison, Halstead (1974) argues that the rational strategy has six components, namely "determining goals, identifying problems, diagnosing problems, establishing premises, searching for possible solutions, selecting the solution" (p. 17).

Kitchen, whom Halstead has cited, indicates that an alternative strategy of rational planning involves six of the following: "Sequential steps: (1) identification of problems; (2) diagnosis of the problem situation, (3) clarification of the diagnostic findings; (4) search for solutions, (5) mobilizing for change, and (6) making the actual change decisions" (p. 17).

James March (1994) is a renowned professor at Stanford and an authority in decision-making. He asserts that decision-making is fundamentally central to individual, group, organizational and scientific life and enterprise. Drawing from a broad interdisciplinary perspective of the social and behavioral sciences, March tries to vividly and paradoxically show how decisions are made as opposed to how they ought to be made. In this endeavor, he addresses four controversial and paramount issues that persistently affect the province of organization decision-making.

First, decision-making is based on alternative assumptions and actions whose expected consequences ... are not known with certainty" (March, 1994, p. 5). Rational choice decision-making processes are preference-based because the consequences are examined or evaluated relative to personal preferences. "Alternatives are compared in terms of the extent to which their expected consequences are thought to serve the preferences of the decision maker" (p. 2). Such rational choice processes are humanistically and theoretically rooted in "microeconomic models of resource allocation, political theories of coalition formation, statistical decision theories" and strategic, situational, demographic, and global survival theories (p. 3). For instance:

> Decision makers do not consider all consequences of their alternatives. They focus on some and ignore others. Relevant information about consequences is not sought, and available information is often not used. Instead of having a complete, consistent set of preferences, decision makers seem to have incomplete and inconsistent goals, not all of which are considered at the same time. The decision rules used by real decision makers seem to differ from the ones imagined by decision theory. Instead of considering 'expected values' or 'risk' as those terms are used in decision theory, they invent other criteria. Instead of calculating the 'best possible' action, they search for an action that is 'good enough' (p. 9).

Human inability to know about the possible consequences, to use incomplete and inconsistent goals, and to use a different set of rules for decision-making rather than decision theory shows that rationality is limited (bounded) at the individual, organizational, societal and scientific levels. Rationality is bounded (limited) because of "attention, memory, comprehension and communication" (p. 9) problems. As a result, decision makers tend to satisfice or use problem-solving heuristics rather than maximize or optimize (Sagini, 1987). This may result in slack or innovative organizational experiences.

Second, the bounded element of rationality tends to make the decision-making process to be characterized by inconsistency and ambiguity rather than clarity and consistency. Decision makers take risks inadvertently in order to avoid them. They make errors by estimating potential risks. Whether they are successful or less so, knowledgeable or ignorant, they have to make decisions in a competitive, global and sometimes turbulent environment. They do so in order to demonstrate that they are rational (intelligent, calculating, successful, spiritually and coldly materialistic or sane) in a procedural or substantive sense. Logically, the consequences are defined by alternatives, expectations, preferences and decision rules.

Third, though decision-making is thought to be an important and paramount organizational activity, leaders create climates for certain decisions to be implemented and for others, especially those which do not promote their interests, not to be implemented. The climate is political and conflictual. Trust and distrust are elements of "decision struggle."

Since inconsistencies lead to complications, decision makers need to "convert inconsistent partnerships into teams by aligning preferences and identities" (p. 139). This strategy may lead to concerns about "contracts, incentives, selection, socialization and attention" (p. 139) that tend to reduce or eliminate inconsistencies.

Ultimately, the significance of certain operational, tactical or strategic decisions is not necessarily based on the outcomes alone, but, it also is based on the individual, organizational or social meanings these decisions create and sustain. Metaphorically, decision-making is a power struggle concerning who gets what, when, where and how or coalition building or partnership making that is essential for group, team or organizational agreements.

Finally, the outcomes of decision processes may not be solely attributed to the actions of individuals alone. They are attributable to the iterative, synergistic, and interactive influences of a variety of factors, forces, and climates that are reflective of individual, organizational, societal, environmental or global conditions.

In other words, while decisions happen based on the logics of consequence and appropriateness, the same decisions are bedeviled with the calculus of interpersonal and intrapersonal ambiguity in the realm of preferences, identities, experiences and meaning. Using intelligence to articulate "anticipatory rationality and history-based rule following is a wise way of engineering decision making. To be effectively engineered, decision engineering is characterized by improved 'adaptiveness, the use of knowledge and the creation of meaning'" (p. 222).

The Challenger Disaster: A Case Study

The decision to launch the Challenger was an example of irrationality and irresponsibility. The blame of irresponsibility and irrationality has been critically examined by Vaughan (1996). If the political, bureaucratic and corporate elite had made launching decisions rationally rather than secretly, and irrationally, the catastrophe would have been averted. Making such a risky decision to launch when they knew that the O-rings were faulty is a clear demonstration of how the culture of deviance dominates organizational settings.

The Challenger tragedy represents an important case for understanding the social basis of technical failure. The technical reasons for the explosions are now well known: the failure under cold-weather conditions of a pair of O-rings used as seals in the solid rocket booster (SRB). The tragedy had a sociological, political as well as a technical cause. However, NASA and the SRB contractor, Morton Thiokol, had advance warning of the possibility of O-ring malfunction in cold weather. Yet, the decision was made to launch; understanding the tragedy thus requires understanding this decision. Diane Vaughan (1996) has written an exhaustive, theoretically sophisticated, and most persuasive account of the Challenger launch, which questions the conclusion reached by earlier investigators. The view that the tragedy reflected "amoral calculation" by mid-level managers who suppressed safety concerns makes little sense, she argues, in views of NASA's normal concern for safety and the disastrous consequences of ignoring risk. Understanding individual actors to explore the organizational and environmental context in which it was made. Invoking anthropological ideas about "thick description," she plunges the reader into the culture of NASA and engineering and the history of the ill-fated-O-rings. According to Vaughan, the Challenger launch decision was made by moral individuals who responded to production pressures but consistently abided by the set of rules governing the definition of safety and risk. Engineers and managers were aware of problems with the O-ring damage using consensual procedures consistent with engineering and industry principles. Incrementally, they came to the conclusion that the O-rings were "safe" because they were redundant (a second O-ring would back up the first). The work groups belief in the acceptability of this risk was supported by larger organizational and environmental contingencies. Engineering culture accommodated technical compromise, and the original "technical" culture of NASA had been modified to include bureaucratic and political concerns, requiring the balancing of all three. Vaughan also shows how "structural secrecy" made it difficult for NASA administrators to "know" that there was a safety problem. Organizational inertia made it difficult to overturn previous conclusions about safety; specialization limited understanding, as did technical jargon and the over-abundance of information; regulatory mechanisms were ineffective. On the eve of the launch, decision makers at NASA were concerned enough about the effects of cold temperature to ask a teleconference with Thiokol. Thiokol engineers recommended against the launch, arguing that risk increased unacceptably in cold temperatures. However, they did not have unambiguous hard data with which they were to back up their recommendations. This prevented an effective formal challenge to the brief in the O-ring safety. Various obstacles to communication limited the effectiveness of the warnings the engineers were able to send out. On the other hand, Vaughan mounts an effective critique of the amoral calculation hypotheses, she provides abundant evidence indicating that procedures were followed and that there was a pervasive belief in the safety of the O-rings; similarly, she shows that the view that rules were violated is based on an understanding of NASA's procedures. Nevertheless, Vaughan may read more into this than is warranted. She admitted in her conclusion that the normalization of deviance may, in other contexts, facilitate misconduct, so why not in the Challenger case? There is no clear evidence that individuals used the rules to cover up their conscious transgressions. But Vaughan's argument that there was no malfeasance too often boils to a simple insistence that actors followed the rules of decision-making which tends to assume what needs to be proven.

This is particularly important as Vaughan appears to have relatively limited access to events at Morton Thiokol. Since engineers there eventually cautioned against cold-weather launch, and since Thiokol managers excluded the engineers from the launch decision, it is conceivable that concern about the O-rings prior to the Challenger incident was greater than it appeared. Circumstantial evidence to this effect exists, since when NASA asked for a teleconference on the question, the Thiokol engineers responded with an extremely unusual no-launch recommendation, even in the absence of "hard" evidence. If nothing else, Vaughan's account does not allow us to dismiss completely this alternative hypothesis. These conclusions Vaughan draws from her analysis are also persuasive and reasonable, but could be expanded. She makes a strong case that the focus on the middle management malfeasance distracts from the real responsibility of organizational and political elite's (Reagan's) in shaping the decision-making environment. It also makes technical decisions seem deceptively routine. Most importantly, it draws attention away from the ways in which routine organizational practices can "normalize" deviance.

Vaughan could add that Thiokol's apparent willingness to express its concerns about the O-rings only after NASA asked and NASA's aggressive reaction to the unusual suggestion by a contractor that launch be delayed may suggest that interorganizational hierarchy played a role in structuring this (and perhaps other) technical decisions. Finally, her analysis reveals the limits of engineering culture. Engineer's willingness to balance technical, economic, political, and bureaucratic pressures reduced the chances that concerns about O-ring safety would be voiced in unambiguous ways. And engineering "craft," as Vaughan calls it, which construct lasting conclusions on the basis of necessarily imperfect knowledge and best estimates, may encourage certainty about matters which should be routinely questioned. In the realm of rationality, the decision to launch the Challenger was a political rather than a technical one. The business and political elite's interests rather than the interests of organizational managers and scientists dominated the launch decision-making machinery. The judgment of experts, the evaluation of consequences of a faulty decision was ignored. The decision was carried on hastily and secretly rather than professionally, and responsibly. These secretly and politically based influences which dominated technical and professional judgment of scientific experts were followed by ineffective, disastrous and irresponsible consequences whose responsibility was erroneously blamed on the technical experts as the real culprits were hiding behind the former's aprons.

Types of Strategically Designed and Rational Decision-Making

Ackoff (1970, pp. 6-22) described three organizational postures for strategic planning: satisficing, optimizing, and adaptivizing. By assessing an organization's historic posture toward rational strategic decision-making, planners are better able to understand the opportunities and pitfalls of undertaking rational planning within the institution. The characteristics of each of Ackoff's postures are discussed below.

1. Satisficing. Ackoff's first philosophy of rational planning is that of satisficing—attempting to do well enough, but not necessarily as well as possible. Ackoff (1970, p. 7) noted:

> The satisficer normally sets objectives and goals first. Since he does not seek to set those as "high" as possible, only "high enough," he has to revise them only if they do not turn out to be feasible. Once the objectives and goals are set, he seeks only one feasible and acceptable way of obtaining them; again not necessarily the best possible way.

Satisficers seldom formulate and evaluate sets of potential strategic alternatives since any feasible set will satisfy them. They are more apt to identify past deficiencies produced by current policies than define future opportunities. Satisficers tend to focus on the financial aspects of their operation, neglecting such elements as manpower planning, physical plant, and services. Financial forecasting and budgeting dominate their planning efforts. Satisficers shy away from organizational changes because of their potential for controversy and conflict. They typically deal with one forecast of the future as if it were a certainty. This type of planning seldom produces a radical departure from the past, usually leads to the comfortable continuation of current policies, and appeals to organizations more concerned with survival than with development and/or growth. Satisficing seems to be the traditional approach to strategic planning in higher education. It is not difficult to deduce, however, that this approach is not of much value in a dynamic environment. Change, "in itself," demands that an organization look not to the past but to the future in order to define opportunities and threats and the means to deal with them. Therefore, academic organizations which continue to operate from a satisficing posture will surely find themselves left behind by the rapid changes and economic pressures of today's environment. Preoccupation with budgets, bottom lines, and risk avoidances—all characteristics of the satisficing posture, breeds mediocrity and ultimately organizational decline. Satisficers are conventional rather than rational strategic planners.

2. Optimizing. An alternative to satisficing planning is optimizing planning. Optimizers make an effort not just to do well, but to do as well as possible. They are constantly searching for a better way, a better product, a better environment. Optimizing is based on the use of mathematical models of the systems being planned for, which attempt to translate organizational goals into quantifiable terms and combine them into a single performance measure.

Optimizers tend to take many elements of the organization and its environment into consideration when developing optimization models and therefore often have a deeper understanding of their organization as a system. However, they assume all parts of the system are programmable, and therefore, fail to control for unanticipated environmental responses. For this reason, optimization is more useful in shorter-range tactical planning than in longer-range strategic planning.

The planning models and systems of optimizers can be of immense value in providing data for the strategic planning process. However, it must be repeated that strategic planning is an intellectual exercise, not an exact science. Models provide useful data, but the well informed opinions and even hunches of experienced managers and professionals must be taken into account as well.

Planners who attempt to rely only on the results of quantitative analyses of organizations and environmental scenarios are well advised to note the cautions of Peters and Waterman (1982, p. 23), who reported that the nation's most successful organizations have a "bias for action." An organization preoccupied by quantitative analysis and data-based decision-making stifles the creativity and entrepreneurial spirit described above. In a dynamic and highly competitive environment, higher education institutions cannot afford to be overly rational. Successful organizations realize that environmental opportunities must be created, not simply reacted to. An over-reliance on optimal decision-making techniques and data analysis can paralyze the development of openness and flexibility in an institution. These characteristics are essential to organizational development and prosperity in a dynamic, competitive environment.

3. Adaptivizing. Ackoff's third planning philosophy, adaptivizing, has three tenets. The first holds that the principal value of planning is not in the plans produced, but in the process of producing them. This leads to the idea that planning cannot be done to or for an organization, but must be done by the responsible managers. The second tenet holds that the principal objective of planning is the design of an organizational management system which *minimizes* the need for *retrospective* planning—planning directed toward removing deficiencies produced by past decisions. The final tenet holds that our knowledge of the future can be classified into three types: certainty, uncertainty, and ignorance, each requiring a different type of planning.

For those aspects of the future about which there can be virtual certainty, an organization can develop plans committed to particular actions or strategies with specific policies and procedures. For those aspects of the future for which there is a high degree of uncertainty, contingency plans must be developed. That is, flexibility must be built into organizational policies to allow for response to the opportunities presented when "the future makes up its mind." Finally, for those aspects of the future which cannot be anticipated (for example, technological breakthroughs or radical economic shifts), responsivity, which allows the organization to quickly detect and adapt to environmental deviations, must be built into the organizational planning system.

Adaptive responses to the two latter situations can be of two types: (1) passive adaptation, in which the organizational system changes its behavior so as to perform more efficiently in a changing environment, as may be seen in current efforts to bring the computer into curricular throughout higher education, and (2) active adaptation, in which the organization changes its environment, perhaps by addressing new markets or designing new products, so that its own present or future behavior is more efficient.

An adaptive organization, therefore, possesses the characteristics of America's best managed organizations (Peters and Waterman, 1982, pp. 13-16): (1) a bias for action, (2) an orientation to the customer, (3) an encouragement of entrepreneurship, (4) a respect for the worker, (5) a value-driven philosophy, (6) a narrow product line, (7) a simple structure and a lean staff, and (8) simultaneous loose-tight properties. That is, the adaptive organization is always looking for opportunities within its defined scope of activities or mission. It encourages product and program experimentation within the bounds of its mission, and allows for occasional failures, for only through such errors can new developments be generated. The focus of the organizations realize that no matter how good a product may be, if it is not what the customer wants, it won't be consumed. Quality is the key value of the adaptive organization, and individuals are encouraged and appropriately rewarded to champion new ideas, products, and services that meet the organization's quality standards. Planning is done by the work units, not by the top managers, since the adaptive organization recognizes the value of hands-on experience in quality decision-making. The structure of the organization reflects a high degree of respect for and confidence in the workers and their ability to contribute to the development of the organization. Finally, commitment is encouraged by a focus on organizational excellence and the creation of a culture that reinforces experimentation, dedication, and involvement.

The Incremental Model

During the 1950s, behaviorism evolved as a study (theory) of decision-making with a concern for descriptive accuracy "not met by the prescriptively oriented rational model in its original form" (p. 2310). At the same time, decision theorists advanced other empirically accurate and classic models such as incrementalism and satisficing.

The incremental model is used to make decisions through the bargaining process. Participants use it to allocate resources in terms of "budgets, personnel, program authority or autonomy" (p. 231). Participants agree on one alternative because it is selected as the best one. Benefits of each alternative are incremental but small and status quo oriented (Lindblom, 1959). Such incremental decisions are reached through compromise. The decisions change programs and policies in small and sequential steps or stages in order to maintain the status quo. The bargaining participants employ "persuasion, debate, and negotiation" rather than rationality (Gortner et al, 1997, p. 231). Proposals, counterproposals, and negotiation may generate minimum conflict before new ideals are made.

Incremental solutions focus on "tangible programs and projects rather than on more abstract goals and policy statements" (p. 231). It is easier to "bargain over resources than over ideology, principles and goals" (p. 231). Consequently, decisions made through incremental approach "tend to be crisis oriented, internally fragmented, ... contradictory, and are characterized as a series of changes in program activities rather than a specific statement of policy or organizational outcome" (p. 231).

Though the incremental method is well suited to describing the activities of political decision-making groups such as legislatures, it also allows for a good description of budget and policy decision-making in bureaus, where multiple levels and divisions are involved in program development. In terms of administrative decision-making, persuasion and bargaining are part of the official linkages to professional, organizational, and constituency interest.

According to Lindblom (1959), the incremental model can be summarized as follows: First, "clear value preferences are rare despite what the rationalist model claims" (Gortner, 1997, p. 231). In general, decision makers can attach preferences only to specific proposals that may reflect abstract goals and values only indirectly. This is why incremental decision makers bargain over programs. Second, policies and programs are not distinguishable from ends (goals and values). Third, the test of 'good policy' is that the actors agree on it even though they may not be able to agree on its underlying values. Fourth, the analysis of alternatives is limited both in number and depth by considering only a few alternatives which are normally considered. Although the incremental model looks to be a fragmented process, in reality, it symbolizes a "decentralized pluralistic system that automatically coordinates itself as actors compete for support" (Gortner et al., 1998, p. 232). The pluralistic assumptions of the incremental model justify the essence of its existence. It reflects the working of the political system. Decisions portray a series of successive approximations to multiple desired ends or values. In brief, its multiple goals serve a pluralistic society better.

Innovation and Incrementalism

Lindblom (1959) shows that the method's bargaining process articulates limited change. Other theorists see the bureaucratic organization to be responsible for limited search that favors options close to the status quo. Incremental changes are easier to correct if found to be wrong. The tendency of administrators to spend time on immediately pressing projects and to react to crises rather than to plan is observable. Competition between the old and the new elite who use the model, is common in bureaus (Downs, 1967). The bureaus use rules that are imposed on them by external actors – legislators. The rules, which claim to be "fair" rather than "effective", are not bureaucratic but political in character (Wilson, 1989). Wilson argues that the bureau or agency, in addition to its major goals, must serve a large number of contextual goals – that is descriptions of desired states of affairs other than the one the agency was bought into being to create. For example, a policy department not only must try to prevent crime and catch criminals, it must protect the rights of the accused, safeguard the confidentiality of its records, and provide necessary health services to arrestees. These other goals define the context within which the primary goals can be sought (see p. 236 – criticism).

Satisficing-Incrementalism

Satisficing resembles the incremental method. The method is used for organizational decision-making offered by March and Simon (1993). It is simpler than rationality though it is closer to rationality than to incrementalism. Satisficing "takes the perspective of a single decision maker or a unified group and attempts to optimize, rather than maximize the returns or results from the choice among possible alternatives sequentially. Search is also sequential and is status quo oriented. Simon and March compare it with the rationalist model by saying that "the difference between searching a haystack to find the sharpest needle in it and searching a haystack to find a needle sharp enough to sew with" (p. 162). Satisficing tends to describe how individual decision makers act. The incremental model is a group and an interactive decision-making model as compared to larger groups particularly the political environments.

Mixed Scanning

Mixed scanning is a variant of the incremental model. It tries to rectify the limitations of the model. According to Etzioni (1967), mixed scanning is dualistic because it is a method of search and decision-making "which does not fully accept either the rationalist model, which is expensive and slow, or the incrementalist model, which is biased toward status quo groups and issues" (Gortner et al., 1977, p. 235). Mixed scanning is both fundamentally descriptive and prescriptive because it criticizes incrementalism at the "Value-ordering level of decision making."

Aggregate Methods of Decision-Making

Aggregate methods is a third strategy for decision-making in public and private settings. These approaches are descriptive and problem-solving oriented. Examples include the use of consultants, e.g., the Delphi technique and the normal group technique (NTG). Generally, these techniques are coached on how to generate a wide range of alternatives (p. 236). One alternative is finally selected through some voting or consensus process. The final choice is said to be an accurate aggregation of individual preferences rather than a negotiated synthesis of preferences characteristic of incrementalism. These aggregate methods allow groups to:

(1) generate a broader, more diverse, and more innovative set of alternatives than either the rationalist or incrementalist methods; (2) to avoid the stifling influence of status and claim of expertise by some participants; and (3) to avoid the constraints of overoutinized standard operating procedures (p. 237).

Brainstorming is encouraged, and premature criticism of new ideas is avoided. The "hallmark of these techniques is that they attempt to maintain a healthy, well balanced level of group interaction without impressing excessive conformity or allowing excessive conformity or allowing excessive conflict" (p. 237). The groups which use the techniques in question are "agency staff, external expert advisory councils, and elected boards and councils" (p. 237). These techniques are frequently used for "planning, for identifying and setting priorities among and resources, and for goal setting" (p. 237). For details, see pp. 237-239.

The Garbage Can or Nondecision-Making Model (Organizational Culture)

Garbage can decision theory tries to accurately describe decision-making in organizations. Doing that goes beyond the incremental model in identifying the limits of rationality. March and Olsen (1979a) have argued that "incremental and satisficing models posit a level of clarity of intentions, understanding of problems and predictability in the relationship between individual and organizational actions that is unrealistic for most organizations" (Gortner et al., 1997, p. 239). These scholars argue that decision-making is a rather unreliable and ambiguous process for selecting courses of action. In reality, it serves as a "forum for individual and group expression of conflict, values, myths, friendships and power" (p. 239). Hence, organizational decision-making is "more expressive of social and personal needs than it is strictly instrumental" (p. 239).

The garbage can model views rationality as a single-goal oriented model of decision-making. As such, the garbage can model views "A choice opportunity as a garbage can into which various problems and solutions are dumped ... by participants. The mix of garbage in a single can depends partly on the label attached to the alternative cans; but it also depends on what garbage is being produced at the moment, on the mix of cans available, and on the speed with which garbage is collected and removed from the scene" (Cohen, March, and Olsen, 1979, p. 26).

Nonmetaphorically, decision-making is an expressive human activity whose opportunity helps to fulfill roles and planned commitments. This "activity defines virtue and truth by interpreting events and goals, distributing glory and blame, reaffirming or rejecting friendships and status relations, expressing or discovering self-interest or group interest, socializing new members, and enjoying the pleasures of a group choice (March and Olsen, 1979b, pp. 11-12).

Based on the garbage can perspective, the rational and incremental models err in assuming too much certainty and knowledge in decision-making. Realistically speaking, "most decision-making situations are plagued with ambiguities of many sorts: objectives are ambiguous; there is no clear set of preferences that represent the organization's intentions; causality is obscure; technology is difficult to define, past events are not easily understood, past events are interpreted differently by participants; and attention and participation of key actors is uncertain since other activities and other decisions compete for their time" (March and Olsen, 1979b, p. 12). When using this model, "decisions reflect shifts in the goals, beliefs, and attention of participants. Goals are defined—to the extent that they are very clearly specified – only in the process of considering particular proposals and debating whether to accept or reject them" (p. 240).

Anderson (1983) asserts that decisions are made through a series of binary (Yes-No) choices of specific plans. Both Anderson and March and Simon (1993) indicate that the decision makers did not necessarily select choices they thought would solve the problems. Instead, they thought they would solve the problems. They predictably reasoned the consequences that are not expected to have either very dangerous or very successful results "a bland alternative" (p. 240).

Interpretively, and as Olsen (1979) has also observed, the garbage can model is an artifactual or non-decision model which focuses on the unconscious and unintentional aspects of decision-making. Phenomenologically, decisions are socially acceptable reconstructions of past reality that has occurred. It may be a fictitious reconstructing of social reality.

Contingency Theory

When each of these methods (rational, incremental, aggregate, and garbage can) is synergistically or syncretically used to make organizational decisions, they become contingent or an assemblage or theory. Theoretically and empirically, this is possible; however, the reality of it "involves political choices about who will control what kinds of decisions" (Gortner et al., 1997, p. 247). The more scientific name for garbage can is organizational culture. The chapter on organizational culture clarifies the values garbage can as a technique integrates to make decisions.

Decision-Making: The Role of Management

Every organization needs to be managed in order to effectively coordinate and control its tasks, processes and operations. Of the most classical and contemporary theoretical and management gurus who have controversially discussed the principles of management and yet, have remained current in their influence include but are not limited to Fayol (1949), Taylor (1947), Sloan (1964), Vickers (1961), Simon (1960), March (1976), Lindblom (1959), and Vroom (1974).

First, Fayol (1949) argues that there are 14 principles of management which influence managers to make decisions. These principles are "division of work, authority, discipline, unity of command, unity of direction, subordination of individual interests to the general interest, renumeration, centralization, scalar chain (chain of command), order, equity, stability of tenure of personnel, initiative and espirit de corps," i.e., unity of command because unity is strength. According to Fayol, the principle of authority, responsibility, unity of command, good order, espirit de corps, are paramount in management parlance. As elements of law, rules, procedures and regulations, these principles are proverbs of administration. If these proverbs are abused, misused or misapplied, they are sanctioned or sanctionable with "remonstrances, warnings, fines, suspensions, demotion or dismissal" (p. 139).

Second, Frederick Taylor asserts that when principles of scientific management are effectively applied, or when time is well managed in relation to their application, productivity is larger and better for both the employers and employees alike. The same productivity gets magnified when management provides a suitable climate that is conducive to "initiative and incentive" (Pugh, 1984, p. 157). Such incentive driven initiative becomes progressively instrumental to the implementation of four principles of scientific management. These principles include:

1. Immense and systemized knowledge based on realistic experience.
2. Labor must be selectively and progressively recruited, developed, trained and taught in order to retain those who are excellent in terms of natural ability, skills and accomplishments.

3. Principles of scientific management are rooted in an integrated theoretical and practical science.

4. Finally, scientific management is characterized by division of labor whose power and authority rests with its specialization and social differentiation.

Third, according to Sloan (1964), the management of General Motors, the largest American corporation in the world, was largely characterized by "decentralization with coordinated control" (Pugh, 1984, p. 177). Motivation and opportunity were critical to the success of the corporation. The former was provided by incentive compensation, the latter by decentralization. However, based on the success of recent Japanese management practice, decentralized centralization seems to hold much more water than coordinated decentralization of Sloan. Through decentralization, the organization prospered in terms of "initiative, responsibility, development of personnel, decisions close to the facts, flexibility—in short all the qualities necessary for an organization to adapt to new conditions" (p. 177). Coordinationwise, General Motors experienced magnificent efficiencies and economies of scale though its recent history speaks to the contrary.

The concept of decentralized coordination portrayed a strong relationship, in terms of decision-making, between the central administration on the one hand and the "autonomously" coordinated divisions and highly specialized staff. Major policy committees consisted of specialists from the central administration, coordinated separate divisions and the specialized line staff. Divisional goals were structured as miniature reflections of the strategic and centrally managed organizational policy whose operational objectives were implemented by the line staff. The staff's contributions touched the field of "styling, finance, technical research, advanced engineering, personnel and labor relations, legal affairs, manufacturing and distribution..." (p. 179). In a sense, decentralized coordination of the organizational structure was the "linking pin" and engine of productivity and adaptability. In recent memory, the pin and engine of productivity has undermined its adaptability due to the fact that it concentrates on traditional hierarchical structures rather than labor and the processes of productivity. In other words, the organization tends to use bad judgment (Vickers, 1961), and antiquated organizational designs (Simon, 1960) and rationally selected alternatives of choice whose reasoning and intellectual formulations may be based on ideological, cultural, traditional, economic, social and demographic biases rather than on scientific objectivity (March, 1976). Biased decisions are a product of "technology of foolishness" (Pugh, 1984, p. 224) rather than one of scientific rationality. In other words, made decisions, regardless of their inherent objectivity or subjectivity, may be a product of the science of "muddling through" (Lindblom, 1959, and Pugh, 1984, p. 238). One of the best decision-making models that will enhance managerial productivity is the normative model (Vroom, 1974). Its predictive utility rests on the deep and integrative foundation that is rooted in conceptual, empirical, and rational description and analysis. For instance, Vroom's decision tree tends to be so normatively dynamic that its influence remains to be continually solvent.

Scientific Visualization of Organizations

For centuries and even for several a millennia, organizations have been traditionally perceived as normative hierarchical structures whose processes intrinsically and stably maintain and perpetuate the status quo. A generation ago, recent scientific developments and inventions in the information sciences have immensely contributed to the perceptual logic and modeling of organizations. In the 21st century scientific visualization of organizations will dominate the field of organizational forms by superseding "antiquated" and dysfunctional bureaucracies (Benveniste, 1994; Bergquist, 1993; and Pinchot and Pinchot, 1993). In other words:

> The ability to simultaneously visualize both key variables of interest and relevant organizational entities should allow for easier and more widespread analysis and diagnosis of organizational issues…Many areas of science and technology, ability to mathematically visualize obscure or shrouded processes, which is the essence of scientific visualization, has led to innovations and insights (Markham, 1998, p. 1).

The development of graphical data which is amenable to simultaneous display of complex organizational structures as opposed to the traditional and simple hierarchical organizational charts is a major scientific and literary accomplishment (Keidel, 1995). These scientific innovations have enabled organizations to be analyzed through the use of multilevel procedures, develop their graphical display nomenclature, and to reconstruct a scientifically embedded explanatory philosophy for organizational modeling which is vital for research and practice. Human ability to scientifically visualize natural phenomena has dramatically increased with all types of research agenda. Some of the visualized organizational designs, processes, and forms may be biomolecular, spherical, microscopic (biomolecular modeling) or macroscopic (interstellar cartography) in their physicality. Such structural designs may influence their behavior. Further research on entities in terms of individuals, dyads, groups and departments requires interdisciplinary analysis.

In the medical field, the use of computer visualization has been dependent on "computer imaging in conjunction with new scanning technologies and ...the requisite software for visualizing intelligent volumes" (Hhone, Pommert, Riemer, Schiemann, Schubert, and Tiede, 1994). Moving beyond simple x-ray procedures, computerized tomography, through the application of Fourier analysis, help visualize the density of the 3-D layers of a human body by 'stacking' the 2-D x-ray slices. The same principles of computed tomography, when applied to position emission tomography (PET) can visualize metabolic activity (Friedhoff and Benzon, 1989).

Theoretically, visualization information processing can be visually and psychologically displayed to (1) increase information density of the display, (2) reduce elapsed study time of information, and (3) improve the corresponding level of understanding regardless of a person's inborn visualization ability (Markham, 1998).

In brief, in the next millennium, the traditional way of perceiving organizations in terms of the hierarchical chart may be challenged by new ways of viewing them. This single-level analysis approach (individual employees, supervisor work teams, project teams, profit centers, divisions, corporations, etc.) will be replaced with platonic geometric solids i.e., (individuals are represented by a circle, dyads, work groups or teams = polygon, departments = rectangle, the organization = triangle etc.). Their morphology, organizational cartography and virtuality may be elements of their "transorganizationalism".

The PC as a Decision Making Tool

Computers are intelligent systems which help modern organizations to make complex decisions. These systems are capable of organizing, processing and modeling difficult decisions. The role of PCs in the organization is that of decision-support and computation. This role is called decision support systems (DSS) (Gortner, et al., 1997) and has been in use since the 1960s. With the initiation of VisiCalc, managers were encouraged to use the spreadsheets such as Microsoft Excel,

Novell Quattro Pro and Lotus 1-2-3, all of which are programs that use high quality graphics to organize and impressively manipulate build in functions that are complex "statistical, mathematical and financial operations" (p. 403). These sophisticated operations of the DSS are expert systems regulated by programmed and "sophisticated logic, decision rules, and 'interference engines'" (p. 403). New managers need to be fully equipped with skills for operating these systems. They must be familiarized with "processing tasks that crosscut traditional job categories" (p. 403). Public employees must be well trained to assume roles formerly played by statistical analysts and accountants. Such training will enable them to detect abuse and be able to bring it under control.

The DSS are based on the use of artificial intelligence and decisions made are rooted in the rational model. Both DSS and expert systems are used by corporate offices and public agencies. In the public arena, the programs are built to deal with "harzardous materials management, land-use planning, utility grid planning, and contracts negotiation" (p. 404). As a decision making tool, the PC Tayloristically enhances their efficiency and effectiveness.

Conclusion

The prescribed decision-making process in bureaus and other organizations has undergone a good deal of change during the last three decades. It changed from classical rational model to incrementalism and satisficing to the reincarnation of rationalism as policy analysis, and now to the group method of expressive model. These changes are probably not due to more than shifts in theory and new research findings. But rather, they reflect new popular and political views on what constitutes a legitimate role for the bureaucracy in policymaking arena and what constitutes a legitimate process of choice.

The reasons for the recent shift to analytic and purportedly apolitical methods of decision-making in bureaus are not easily identified. One possibility may be that suspicion of the pluralist-bargaining method generally grows from disillusionment with interest group liberalism and pork barrel politics in an era of budgetary restraints. The move from acknowledging a political method to interest in the more technically deliberate methods may also be part of the larger recent interest in high technology and futurist thinking. Attempts in the past two decades to adopt more quantitative and analytic criteria of policy effectiveness may also be related to changes in decision processes.

The shifts in decision-making methods, in theory and practice, illustrate that the bureau's most fundamental processes are not static; they respond to a variety of internal and external political and technological changes. The search for a single best decision-making process in bureaus may, therefore, be based on an unrealistic assumption about the stability of bureaus and the environment in which they operate. These bureaus are agencies or independent establishments and government corporations that are hierarchically structured policy or goal oriented and publicly accountable in their operations. Like public schools and colleges, which are accountable to their communities (states) and the boards of regents, these bureaus are accountable to Congress and the federal government. The incorporation of intelligent technological systems into organizational operations will enable these organizations to become more efficient and productive in respect to the visualization of their virtual reality and information processing systems.

Herbart Simon is a scientific pioneer in the study of organizational decision-making. He was one of the first social scientists to advance the science of administrative decision-making. His purpose was to make an attempt to reconcile the rational choice model of economic theory with the emergent findings on human behavior in organizations. This approach was theoretically and implicitly classical rather than modern or contemporary. Simon invented the term satisficing. He emphasized that decision-making can maximize efficiency. When managerial leadership suboptimizes, the leaders do so because rationality is bounded in the context of time, monetary, ethnic or political environment. Bounded rationality is limited human capability which tends to satisfice rather than maximize or optimize. Hence, public bureaucracies refrain from carrying out effective performance evaluations, providing workload measures or evaluations. As a result, they tend to concentrate on routine work which stifles creativity and makes it difficult to innovate bureaucratic decision-making which is a form of documented public decisions.

These bureaucratic decision rules are standard operational procedures that are sanctioned by professional norms, procedures and processes for service delivery. Externally, Waldo and Appleby view administration as organizational politics characterized by open systems, organic, natural systems and cybernetic elements of behavior. In other words, both Waldo and Appleby normatively deviate from the classical and mechanistic approach to organizational decision-making in the public arena and place emphasis in natural or behavioral and cybernetic systems.

Katz and Kahn (1978) who reinterpret systems theory argue that it is impossible to separate politics from public administration. Politics is not only "who gets what, when and how," but it is also the authoritative allocation of values. Public administration in which decision-making models are used, is different from corporate or private administration because the former operates in the political millieux. This difference between the two systems raises the possibility of separating facts and values. The fact-value dichotomy is a demonstration that there is a true science of administration. Most of what goes on in politics is more artistic than scientific although both art and science are elements of the political. There is no one best way. The concern is not structure or individuals but how to use processes, principles and procedures of public administration and reconcile it with democracy. By so doing, the politics tends to allocate values.

References

Anderson, P. 1983. Decision making by objection and the Cuban missile crisis. *Administrative Science Quarterly* 28: 201-222.

Benveniste, G. 1994. *The Twenty-First Century Organization: Analyzing Current Trends—Imagining the Future.* San Francisco: Jossey-Bass.

Bergquist, W. 1993. *The Post-Modern: Mastering the Art of Irreversible Change.* San Francisco: Jossey-Bass.

Birnbaum, R. 1989. The cybernetic institution: Toward an integration of governance theories. *Higher Education: The International Journal of Higher Education and Educational Planning* 18 (2).

Chaffee, E.E. 1983. *Rational Decision Making in Higher Education.* Boulder: National Center for Higher Education Management Systems.

Clark, K. (1979). Administration of higher education in our era of change and conflict. In *Conflict Retrenchment and Appraisal: The Administration of Higher Education,* ed. J. Monroe. Champaign, IL: University of Illinois Press.

Cohen, E. 1980. Systems paralysis. *The American Spectator,* November.

Cohen, M.A., and B.F. Brawer 1986. Controversies and decision making in difficult economic times. *New Directions for Community Colleges* 53, Chapters 2 and 3.

Cohen, M., and J. Olsen 1979. Organizational choice under ambiguity. In James March and Johan Olsen (Eds.) *Ambiguity and Choice in Organizations, 2nd Ed.* Bergen, Norway: Universitetsforlaget.

Cohen, M., March, J., and J. Olsen 1979. People, problems, solutions and the ambiguity of relevance. In *Ambiguity and Choice in Organizations*, 2nd ed., eds. James March and Johan Olsen. Bergen, Norway: Universitetsforlaget.

Cope, R.G. 1981. *Strategic Planning, Management, and Decision Making: Higher Education Research Report No. 9.* Washington, D.C.: American Association for Higher Education.

Demaree, E.W. 1986. Keeping the open door open. *New Directions for Community Colleges.*

Doucette, S. et al. (1985). Defining institutional mission. *The Journal of Higher Education.*

Downs, A. 1994. *Inside Bureaucracy.* Waveland Press.

Dziech, W.B. 1986. Part-time faculty. *New Directions for Community Colleges* 53, March, 1-6.

Etzioni, A. 1967. Mixed scanning as a 'third' approach to decision making. *Public Administration Review* 27: 285-392.

Fayol, H. 1949. *General Industrial Management.* London: Pitman.

Friedhoff, R.M., and W. Benzon 1989. *Visualization: The Second Computer Revolution.* New York: Abrams.

Gormley, T.W, Jr. 1987. Institutional policy analysis: A critical review. *Journal of Policy Analysis and Management* 6: 151-169.

Gortner, H.F., et al. 1997. *Organization Theory: A Public Perspective.* Fort Worth: Harcourt Brace College Publishers.

Grandy, E.R., and R. Warner 1986. *Philosophical Grounds for Rationality.* Oxford: Clarendon Press.

Halstead, D.K. 1974. *Statewide Planning in Higher Education.* Washington, D.C.: U.S. Government Printing Office.

Harper, A.W., ed. 1981. *Community and Junior College Journal.* Washington, D.C.: 8, May, 51.

Higgins, M.J., and W.J. Vincze. 1983. *Strategic Management and Organizational Policy: Text and Cases*, 3rd ed. Chicago: The Dryden Press: 2.

Hohne, K.H. et al. (1994). Medical volume visualization based on "intelligent volumes." In *Scientific Visualization: Advances and Challenges,* eds. L. Rosenblum, R.A. Earnslow, J. Encarnacao, H. Hagen, A. Kaufman, S. Klimenko, G. Nielson, F. Post, and D. Thalmann, 21-35. San Diego, CA: IEEE Computer Society Press/Academic Press,.

Johnson, B.L. 1969. *Islands of Innovation Expanding: Changes in the Community College.* Los Angeles: Glencoe Press.

Johnson, J.W. 1975. An examination of the management and planning in higher education. Ph.D. dissertation, University of Arkansas: 50.

Karabel, J. 1986. Community colleges and social stratification in the 1980s. *New Directions for Community Colleges* 54: 13-30.

Katz, D., and R.L. Kahn 1978. *The Social Psychology of Organizations.* New York: Wiley and Sons.

Keidel, R.W. (1995). *Seeing Organizational Patterns: A New Theory and Language of Organizational Design.* San Francisco: Berrett-Koehler.

Keller, G. (1983). *Academic Strategy: The Management Revolution in American Higher Education.* Baltimore: The John Hopkins University Press.

Lall, G.R., and B.M. Lall. 1979. *Dynamics of Leadership.* Mountain View, CA: Pacific Press Publishing Association.

Lindblom, C.E. 1959. The science of muddling through. *Public Administrative Review* 19: 79-88.

March, J.G. 1994. *A Primer on Decision Making: How Decision Happen.* New York: The Free Press.

March, J.G. and J.P. Olsen. 1976. *Ambiguity and Choice in Organizations.* Oslo: Universitetsforlaget.

March, J., and J. Olsen Eds. 1979a. *Ambiguity and Choice in Organizations.* Bergen, Norway: Universitetsforlaget.

March, J., and H. Simon. 1993. *Organizations.* Cambridge, MA: Blackwell.

Markham, S.E. 1998. The scientific visualization of organizations: A Rationale for a new approach to organizational modeling. *Decision Sciences* 29, 1.

McNeill, B.L. 1973. A critique of the uses of the rational model in educational planning. Ph.D. dissertation, Columbia University.

Miller, E. and M.J. McQuire. 1986. Maintaining commitment to quality. *New Directions for Community Colleges* 53: 57-64.

Moore, M.K., and A.G. Baker, III. 1983. The critical link: from plans to programs. *New Directions for Community Colleges* 11, 75-86.

Mulder, A. 1987. President of Lake Michigan College. Tape-recorded personal interview conducted on March 16, 1987.

Olsen, J. 1979. Choice in an organizational anarchy. In *Ambiguity and Choice in Organizations,* 2nd Ed, eds. James March and Johan Olsen. Bergen, Norway: Universitetsforlaget.

Pennings, M.J. Eds. 1985. *Organizational Strategy and Change.* San Francisco: Jossey-Bass Publishers, Inc.

Peters, T.J. and R.H. Waterman, Jr. 1982. *In Search of Excellence: Lessons from America's Best Run Companies.* New York: Harper and Row Publishers.

Pinchot, G., and E. Pinchot. 1993. *The End of Bureaucracy and the Rise of the Intelligent Organization.* San Francisco: Berrett-Koehler.

Pugh, D.S. ed. 1984. *Organization Theory: Selected Readings.* London: Penguin Business.

Ramsy, L.W. 1981. Using research for planning. *New Directions for Community Colleges* 9: 25-34.

Rutherford, D., and W. Fleming. 1985. Strategies for change in higher education: Three political models. *Higher Education.* Amsterdam: Elsevier Science Publishers 14: 433.

Savage, D.D., ed. 1987. *Community, Technical, and Junior College Journal.* February/March.

Simon, H.A. 1960. The executive as decision maker and organizational design: Man-machine systems for decision making. *The New Science of Management Decision.* New York: Harper and Row.

Sloan, A.P., Jr. 1964. The management of general motors. *My Years with General Motors.* New York: Doubleday: Chapt. 23.

Spaulding, S. 1997. What is educational planning? *Journal of Comparative Education* 13, March, 55.

Taylor, F. 1947. *Scientific Management.* New York: Harper and Row, 39-73.

Uhl, N.P., ed. 1983. Using research for strategic planning. *New Directions for Instructional Research* 37, San Francisco: Jossey-Bass, Inc. Publishers.

Van Vught, V.F. 1985. Negative incentive steering in a policy network. *Higher Education: The International Journal of Higher Education and Educational Planning.* Amsterdam: Elsevier Science Publishers.

Vaughan, D. 1996. *The Challenger Launch Decision: Risky Technology, Culture and Deviance at NASA.* Chicago: University of Chicago Press.

Vickers, G. 1961. "Judgement" the 6th Elbourne Memorial Lecture. *The Manager*: 31-39.

Vroom, V.H. 1974. A normative model of managerial decision making: A new look at managerial decision making. *Organizational Dynamics* 5: 66-80.

Webster's New Collegiate Dictionary. 1979. New York: Merriam-Webster, Incorporated.

Wilson, J.Q. 1989. *Bureaucracy: What Government Agencies Do and Why They Do It.* New York: Basic Books.

Chapter 12

Organizational Technology

This chapter discusses the evolution of computer and internet technology. It describes how humankind began with counting on his fingers and moved on to the abacus which was used in ancient Egypt, Greece, Rome, and China. The abacus was a calculator which consisted of a frame with beads on wire rods. Modern engineers invented machines such as the Pascal calculator, the difference machine, the ENIAC, and the UNIVAC; and finally gave us the computer. The computer and internet have elevated education, government, industry, media, and the business world. It has also caused some controversies in government, the general public and the business environment. The government has felt the need for regulatory laws to protect people while buying and using computers and the internet. This new technology has taken us all the way to the wireless internet, or cyberspace or websites.

Broadly speaking, technology is a way of life in which scientific and social techniques are used to provide certain objects that are necessary for human sustenance and comfort. In this case, technology may be viewed as a technical method for achieving positive practical results. On the other hand, other scholars suggest that technology is an independent and out of control force that is risky because it drives civilization to social or literal doom. This neo-Marxist school asserts that technology is a pernicious instrument that possesses the capability for oppressing lower classes or destroying life enmass. Still other scholars particularly those from the realist school of thought think that technology is a powerful force for the revolutionary transformation of socioeconomic relations. Whatever technology is or is not, its effects are either neutral and status-quo reinforcing, or socially and economically negative for reinforcing class oppression, or socioculturally revolutionary for transforming the culture and structure of the consumer society. If this is what technology is, then its traditional and emergent models are not only contradictory at least, but their limited or unlimited utility could be radically dialectical. Such dialectics could be the essence of the computer industry and cyberspace "psychology" in a predominantly democratic world of the Third Millennium.

The Evolution of Computer Technology

Computers have made life easier for the human race by calculating, processing, and finding information needed quickly. New computer and telecommunications technology has made the development of the internet to improve the way education, government, industry, business and communication works. The internet has also become controversial in these institutional organizations due to regulatory threats which control freedom of speech although their good intentions are aimed at controlling computer crime.

According to Hussain and Hussain (1986), John Napier of Scotland invented Napier Bones in 1617. This was a mechanical arrangement of bones in which numbers were stamped out and used for direct multiplication. In 1964, Gottfried Leibniz, a German mathematical philosopher, created a general-purpose calculator that could multiply, divide, add, and subtract. Due to his invention, multiplication was performed by rapidly repeated addition while division was performed by rapidly repeated subtraction of numbers (Hussain and Hussain, 1986). On the other hand, Szymanski, et al. (1995) stated John Napier figured out how to manipulate numbers to perform multiplication and division by reducing them to addition and subtraction—logarithms. In the 1640s, Blaise Pascal, a mathematician and philosopher, developed the Pascaline. This first digital calculator added and subtracted whole numbers. His invention of the Pascal computer made him a financial failure because he was the only person able to fix the machine when it broke down and human labor was cheap. The calculator was made of wheels and gears with dials numbered zero to nine on each wheel and decorated with ten teeth on each gear (Hussain and Hussain, 1986; Szymanski, et al., 1995). The calculator performed the mathematical functions by moving the wheel ahead one-tenth of a revolution and by gears after a revolution was completed for addition and reverse revolutions performed subtraction (Hussain and Hussain, 1986). Between 1801 and 1804, Joseph Marie Jacquard of France invented the automated punch-card machine which was attached to the weaving looms and made of a belt of punch cards with data coded on them which blocked some rods and allowed others to pass through to complete the weaves (Hussain and Hussain, 1986, 1986; Szymanski, et al., 1995). The cards controlled the patterns of the weaves by changing cards each time the shuttle was pulled (Hussain and Hussain, 1986). The automation of the weaving loom caused many of the mill workers to lose jobs (Szymanski, et al., 1995). Around 1830, Charles Babbage, an English mathematician, constructed the difference machine (difference engine), the first mechanical calculator, out of steam-driven rods, ratchets, and gears for solving equations more accurately than human labor. This machine was more efficient on the hand-done mathematical tables and storing the results in mechanical memory (Capron, 1998; Hussain and Hussain, 1986; Szymanski, 1995). Babbage hoped the machine would be exactly accurate in making calculations that range up to twenty digits and would print out mathematical tables including logarithms (Hussain and Hussain, 1986). The difference engine was well received by the British government, and Babbage was awarded a grant to build a full-scale working version of the machine which was eventually withdrawn after spending the money to no avail when the smallest imperfections threw it out of whack (Capron, 1998). Babbage also envisioned but never built the analytical machine (analytical engine) that would solve general problems that required six tem engines which would take up a space the size of a football field in order to run. However, he foreshadowed current general-purpose digital computers (Capron, 1998; Hussain and Hussain, 1986; Szymanski, et al., 1995. The analytical machine had several features possessed by modern computers. These include an input device, a storage place to hold the numbers waiting to be processed, a processor, a control unit to direct the tasks to be performed and the sequence of calculations, and an output device. Babbage's son made a model of the analytical machine, and in 1991, a working version of the engine was built and put on public display in London (Capron, 1998; Hussain and Hussain, 1986; Szymanski, et al., et al., 1995). She understood Babbage's ideas and was able to help develop the instructions for programming and computations (Capron, 1998; and Hussain and Hussain, 1986). She got others interested in Babbage's work, refined the design of the analytical engine to create the loop, the automatic repetition of a series of calculations; published a series of notes and scientific papers enabling others to accomplish what Babbage could not; and suggested the use of the binary system for storage instead of the decimal system (Capron, 1998; Hussain and Hussain, 1986; Szymanski, et al., 1995). In the 1850s, George Brooke, an English mathematician, developed and published Boolean logic which was fundamental in designing future computer circuitry (Hussain and Hussain, 1986; Szymanski, et al., 1995). He figured out that complex mathematical problems could be solved by breaking them down into a series of questions answered affirmatively or negatively. This strategy led to the binary system of 1s for positive answers and 0s for negative answers (Szymanski, et al., 1995). In the 1880s, Dr. Herman Hollerith developed the tabulating machine, the first electromathematical punch-card data-processing machine, and won a contest held by the U.S. Census Bureau to speed up the calculation of census information. The officials were able to speed the results of the 1890 census within six weeks; whereas, it took them 7.5 years to calculate the 1880 census' results by hand (Capron, 1998; Hussain and Hussain, 1986; Szymanski, et al., 1995). The answers to the census questions were represented by holes punched in cards which he put into a circuit-closing press to read the answers which were assigned specific locations on the cards. The card press had rows of telescoping electrical pins that fell to the surface of the card, and depending on the card's information, an electromagnet advanced a counting dialed one or more spaces when the pins passed through the holes in the card to complete electrical circuits. The tabulating machine had forty dials in all that could tabulate the results of forty questions simultaneously, and at the end of each day, operators recorded the totals on the dials and reset them at zero (Hussain and Hussain, 1986). In 1896, Dr. Hollerith founded the Tabulating Machine Company that became the International Business Machines Corporation (IBM) in 1924 when it merged with several other companies (Capron, 1998; Hussain and Hussain, 1986; and Szymanski, et al., 1995).

The Simple Computer

In 1939, John Atanasoff, a physics professor at Iowa State University, and Clifford Berry built the Atanasoff-Berry Computer (ABC), the first digital computer that worked electronically. The purpose of inventing the ABC was to help Atansoff's students solve mathematical problems easier (Capron, 1998; Hussain and Hussain, 1986; Szymanski, et al., 1995). The computer could solve linear algebraic equations with the goal of being able to solve twenty-nine of the equations with twenty-nine unknowns simultaneously (Hussain and Hussain, 1986; Szymanski, et al., 1995). Alan Turning of England discovered how Enigma, a German message-scrambling device smuggled out of Germany by the Hungarian underground system, worked and used the vacuum-tube technology that Konrad Zuse, a German inventor, had purposed (but Hitler thankfully decided not to use this new technology which could have put him at an advantage during the war) in order to make a British machine that could process 25,000 characters per second (Szymanski, 1995). Turning built the Automatic Computer Engine (ACE) which represents the first (arguably) programmable digital computer according to Szymanski (1995), yet Cowan (1997) stated that he built the first computer that contained a stored program while at the University of Manchester in Great Britain. In 1937, Professor Howard Aiken of Harvard University designed and built the Harvard Mark I (Mark I) computer with $1 million in support from IBM, and he finished it in 1943 or 1944 depending on the source, and was made public in 1944 (Capron, 1998; Cowan, 1997; Hussain and Hussain, 1986; Szymanski, et al., 1995). According to Cowan (1997), the Mark I pioneered automatic operational sequences even though it was not electronic; whereas Szymanski, et al. (1995) claimed it calculated with electromechanical relays and used electricity which replaced Hollerith's gear mechanism. The computer was built to calculate cannon shell trajectories. According to Szymanski, et al. (1995), Hussain and Hussain (1986) claim that the Mark I could perform addition and subtraction of two numbers in three-tenths of a second, and Szymanski, et al. (1995) claim it could do calculations of 23-digit numbers in only three seconds while using paper-tape input and punch-card output making it possible to complete in one day what had taken six months to do calculating manually previously. Capron (1998) asserts that the Mark I was 55 feet long and made of streamlined steel and glass. On the other hand, Szymanski et al. (1995) say the Mark I was 51 feet long, eight feet high, contained 750,000 parts, and required over 500 miles of wire. In the 1940s, John von Neumann, a mathematician from Hungary, worked on the EDVAC project and proposed computer memories that store programs and the introduction of conditional transfer (Hussain and Hussain, 1986; Szymanski, et al., 1995). He wrote the definitive paper called the "First Draft of a Report on the EDVAC" which outlined the stored-program concept and served as a blueprint for future store-program computers (Szymanski, et al., 1995). John von Neumann contributed to the adaptation of binary arithmetic to represent decimal numbers so that computations could be reduced to a simple on-off switch (Hussain and Hussain, 1986). He also led a team at the Institute for Advanced Study in Princeton , New Jersey, that built the first digital computer, with funding from the U.S. government and the RCA Corporation, that was capable of performing parallel processing which is the ability to perform calculations simultaneously instead of serially. The Ballistics Research Laboratory of the Ordinance Department hired hundreds of women with mathematics degrees to calculate trajectory tables for the guns used during World War II for such variables as the correct aiming directions, the right angles, the locations of the targets, the air temperatures, and wind directions (Cowan, 1997). In 1942, Dr. John Mauchly, a physicist at the University of Pennsylvania, and John Presper Eckert proposed to build a machine that could compute artillery firing tables quickly and accurately for the government. They won a contract to build the Electronic Numerical Integration and Computer (ENIAC) (Capron, 1998; Cowan, 1997; Hussain and Hussain, 1986; and Szymanksi, et al., 1995).

The ENIAC was operated on the decimal system, making it easy for humans to read the punch-card output, and took operators as long as two days to manually unplug and replug hundreds of wires involved in changing from one operation to another which made it inefficient for general-purpose computer use (Szymanski, et al., 1995). The ENIAC was twice as a thousand times faster and twice as large as the Mark I at 80 feet long, 18 feet or two stories high, 30 tons in weight, and occupying fifteen thousand square feet of floor space with more than 17,000 vacuum, 1,500 relays, 70,000 resistors, 10,000 capacitors, and 174 KW consumption (Cowan, 1997; Hussain and Hussain, 1986; Szymanski, et al., 1995). The ENIAC cost between $450,000 and $486,840.22 (in 1946). It could multiply 333 ten-digit numbers a second, had a computing power equivalent to the 1990's average, digital watch; and performed additional and subtraction twenty times slower than a two thousand dollar modern kneetop portable computer. The ENIAC was finished and became operational three years later; several months after the war had ended (Cowan, 1997; Hussain and Hussain, 1986). In the winter of 1945-46, the Los Alamos National Laboratory requested that the ENIAC be programmed to calculate whether or not a hydrogen bomb could be built, and the ENIAC performed the calculations in a matter of weeks what would normally have taken physicists years which whetted the military's apppetite for more complex, high-speed calculators which needed to be developed fast. This led to the ENIAC team to visit Moore School in 1946 to explain how the computer would work for several organizations that were interested in advancing computer technology further (Cowan, 1997).

In 1946, Mauchly and Eckert had a dispute with the University of Pennsylvania about having to sign all their rights to their patents over to their employers (Cowan, 1997). The ENIAC was kept a secret until 1955 (Hussain and Hussain, 1986). Mauchly and Eckert based their design of the ENIAC on the ABC after Mauchly visited Atanosoff in Iowa in 1941 while the ABC was being constructed (Capron, 1998; Szymanski, et al., 1995). On October 19, 1973, they lost their legal claim of the patent priority of the commercial version of the computer to Eugene Atanasoff when the courts ruled that he deserved the honor of being considered the latter to be the originator of the general-purpose electronic digital computer (EDVAC), one of the first stored-program computers consisting of the following five units: arithmetical, central control, memory, input, and output. It could store its instructions electronically while using the binary system for instruction coding and input, and it contained less vacuum tubes than the ENIAC. The former had increased memory, was easier to use, and included a simpler and quicker way to set up new problems (Szymanski, et al., 1995). In 1951, Mauchly and Eckert organized a new company and created the universal automatic computer (UNIVAC) which was the first successful commercial computer designed specifically for business data-processing applications rather than for military, scientific, or engineering use (Capron, 1998; Cowan, 1997; Hussain and Hussain, 1986; Szymanski, et al., 1995). The computer was created with the idea that engineers would make a computing system which was a series of related machines that could be combined and adapted to the particular needs of customers. High-speed printers, magnetic-tape drives, card punchers, and converters could be added to the UNIVAC system (Cowan, 1997). According to Hussain and Hussain (1986), the key components of the computer were vacuum tubes which controlled internal machine operations, and Capron (1998) claimed that it used magnetic cores for memory. The UNIVAC filled a very large room with thousands of tubes which required special air conditioning because of the considerable heat they generated which frequently caused the tubes to fail making the reliability of the computer poor (Hussain and Hussain, 1986). On June 14, 1951, Mauchly and Eckert installed the UNIVAC computer at the U.S. Census Bureau which used it for over 12 years; in 1952, CBS borrowed one to accurately predict the winner of the presidential election; and in 1954, the General Electric Company in Louisville, Kentucky, used one to process the first computerized payroll (Capron, 1998; Cowan, 1997; Hussain and Hussain, 1986;

Szymanski, et al., 1995). In the meantime, Maurice V. Wilkes of England incorporated the stored-program concept into the Electric Delay Storage Automatic Computer (EDSAC). In 1949, Ann Wang created magnetic-core memories which is magnetized in different directions when the current flows through the wires inside it (Szymanski, et al., 1995).

Development of Computer Languages

John Backus and several IBM engineers developed FORmula TRANslator (FORTRAN) which was the first problem-oriented algebraic programming language. Mathematicians and scientists were more likely to use it than computer specialists were. In the late 1950s, Jack Kilby of Texas Instruments and Robert Noyce of Fairchild Semiconductors discovered that resistors, capacitors, and transistors could be made from or etched on silicon; therefore, the integrated circuit was developed and refined. In the 1960s, Gene Amdahl introduced the IMB system/360 series of mainframe computers which were the first general-purpose digital computers that used integrated-circuit technology (Szymanski, et al., 1995). The IBM system/360 was a group of computers that made it possible for small, growing companies to start with relatively inexpensive, small computer systems than larger, more powerful computers. Since all the computers were from the same family tree, software programs were compatible with all of them. This made the unbundling of software possible and led to the creation of today's software industry (Capron, 1998; Szymanski, et al., 1995). Rear Admiral Grace Murray Hopper developed Common Business-Oriented Language (COBOL) which was the first programming language designed for business data processing. Ken Olsen, the founder of the Digital Equipment Corporation (DEC), was one of the students who helped develop the Whirlwind computer at MIT during the early 1950s for the U.S. Navy and the Digital Computer Lab. The Whirlwind was about 85 percent accurate, performed 50,000 operations per second, simulated high-performance trainer aircraft, and contained self-diagnostics. In 1963, miniaturization led Ken Olsen and DEC to build the PDP-I, the first minicomputer, and the PDP-8, its successor, was the first commercial minicomputer which was less expensive for small companies. In the mid-1960s, Dr. John Kemeny, a mathematics professor and president of Dartmouth, and Dr. Thomas Kurtz developed Beginner's All-purpose Symbolic Instruction Code (BASIC), and later, they developed True BASIC which used structured programming tools to make programs easier to read, debug, and update. Later, Steve Jobs and Stephen Wozniak built the first Apple computer in a garage with $1,300, and founded the Apple Computer in 1977. The Apple became a successful manufacture in the market because it was designed for home use with an easy-to-use keyboard and screen (Capron, 1998). In the meantime, Szymanski, et al. (1995) claimed that Jobs and Wozniak, the technical expert, made microcomputers affordable for individuals and small business people while Jobs provided the marketing impetus for the company. The Apple I was not compellingly a commercial success; but the Apple II was because of the spread sheet software; VisiCalc was successful when it caught the attention of the business community which propelled personal computers into the workplace (Capron, 1998). The Apple was also the first PC which was able to generate color graphics.

Today, people can use voice input on computers by talking to them through microphones and the computer then converts the information into binary code (Capron, 1998; Hussain and Hussain, 1986). Speech synthesis, the process of machines talking to people, is now available to people who buy computers with speakers and additional equipment required (Capron, 1998; Szymanski, et al., 1995). Additionally, two- and three-dimensional pictures of anything can be designed with the computer-aided design/computer-aided manufacturing system (CAD/CAM) (Capron, 1998; Hussain and Hussain, 1986; Szymanski, et al., 1995). Such businesses as libraries, hospitals, factories, and retail stores use handheld word readers for reading optical characters (OCR-A) (Capron, 1998; Hussain and Hussain, 1986). Some businesses use magnetic-ink character recognition which involves using a machine to read characters made of magnetized particles (Capron, 1998; Hussain and Hussain, 1986; Szymanski, et al., 1995). Business or presentation graphics, symbols and clip art for sophisticated presentations, and video graphics, animated pictures produced by computers, have become quite popular (Capron, 1998; Szymanski, et al., 1995).

As computers changed in size, shape, capacity, and complexity, so did the software and how it was used. The internet which began around 1957 has evolved as computer technology and this evolution has made it what it is today. In 1957, the internet was made of thousands of computer networks that were connected to each other and used the Transmission Control Protocol/Internet Protocol communication method. When the Soviet Union launched the first spacecraft satellite, Sputnik, into orbit on October 4, 1957, the United States Department of Defense made research in science and technology a high priority and created the advanced Research Projects Agency (http://aivoo.com/info.html). In 1962, Paul Baran of the Rand

Corporation worked on a project commissioned by the United States Air Force in which he created the idea of dividing information into packets, marking the origin and the destination, and sending them individually from computer to computer until they reached their destination. The information continued to be transmitted between computers. In case of a nuclear attack during the Cold War, it could have caused all data to be destroyed (Capron, 1998; http://aivoo.com/info.html). Between 1969 and 1971, the Advanced Research Projects Agency Network (ARPANET), the original precursor to the internet, was created, and it connected 23 mini-computers in universities and institutions using the network control protocol to transfer data (Capron, 1998; *The Chronicles of Higher Education,* March 1, 1996; http://aivoo.com/info.html). In 1973, Vint Cerf and Bob Kohn began Transmission-Control Protocol (TCP) while the ARPANET went international by connecting to England and Norway. In 1979, Steve Bellovin, Tom Truscott, and Jim Ellis used UUCP to create Usenet. In 1981, the National Science Foundation created CSNET, a separate Internet for institutions without access to ARPANET; Vinton Cerf later established a connection between ARPANET and CSNET. In January 1983, TCP/IP became the standard communication method and replaced network control protocol which was created to oversee web research. The development of the internet was called the Internet Activities Board. In addition, the University of Wisconsin developed the Domain Name System in 1983, and about 500 hosts were connected to ARPANET. In 1984, MILNET, a division of ARPANET, was used by the military, and ARPANET was used for research and educational purposes with 1000 hosts connected to it (http://aivoo.com/info/html). In 1985, the National Science Foundation (NSF) began funding universities and institutions with supercomputer systems around the country. The universities were linked to the NSF network for research, education, e-mail file transfer, and newsgroup (*The Chronicles of Higher Education,* March 1, 1996; http://aivoo.com/info.html). Between 1986 and 1989, the NSF continued making its own networks for education. It made faster connections when it hired Merit Networks to help (http://aivoo.com/info.html). In 1989, Tim Barnes-Lee the CERN Laboratory created the World Wide Web (Capron, 1998; http://aivoo.com/info.html).

In the past several years, there have been many advances in the internet making life easier for people to find and understand important information. One new advancement is the Virtual Reality Modeling Language (VRML) which allows programmers to create three-dimensional images that can be quickly transmitted over the internet into ordinary computer screens and manipulated by users. Some people are afraid that new language, the hardware, and the knowledge required to program it, will create barriers between experts and amateurs. The world-wide web helped break them down, but others believe adding a third dimension to the internet will make it easier to work, learn, and communicate. One man experimented with VRML models that allowed students to fly through models of molecules such as carbon 60. VRML builds three-dimensional spaces within the world-wide web which can be examined by any user with access to a computer which has internet connection. With the use of a mouse, a user can zoom in close, pass through the image, zoom backward, move right and left, and by holding down the shift key, can tilt the images (DeLoughry, 1996).

The Standards and Politics of Computer Usage

The term technology can organizationally be defined as follows: (1) "the characteristics of the inputs utilized by the organization; (2) the characteristics of the transformation processes employed by the organization; and (3) the characteristics of the outputs produced by the organization" (Scott, 1981, p. 209).

In other words, approaches to technology differ when scholars and scientists place emphasis on the nature of materials used for doing work, on the attributes of operations and methods used to do the work, and on the theoretical or abstract knowledge which productively underpins the transformation process. The three general variables that underlie specific technological measures that can be used to predict the structure of organizational features are complexity (diversity), uncertainty or unpredictability and interdependence (Scott, 1981). First, complex or diverse organizational elements and items need to be dealt with simultaneously. For instance, the multiplicity and customization of organizational inputs and outputs reflect the use of this approach. The greater the technical complexity of the organization, the greater is its structural complexity. Naturally enough, "the structural response to technical diversity is organizational differentiation" (p. 212). Second, uncertainty or unpredictability is the "variability of the items and elements upon which work is performed or the extent to which it is possible to predict their behavior in advance. Specific measures of uncertainty include uniformity or encountered in the work process, and the number of major product changes experienced" (p. 211). When technical uncertainty or technical unpredictability is high, the degree of organizational formalization and centralization is low. Organizational formalization and centralization are low attributes because the organization is incapable of resolving or explaining the inevitable contradictions and consequences associated with the technicality. Third, interdependence is the extent to which items or elements "upon which work is performed or the work processes themselves are interrelated so that changes in the state of one element affect the state of the other" (Thomson, 1967, pp. 54-55). According to Thomson (1967), interdependence is typologizable into pooled interdependence (process is overall goal oriented), sequential interdependence (activities performed in steps), and reciprocal interdependence (e.g., "design decisions regarding the weight and thrust of a jet engine and the aerodynamic design of the fuselage and wings must be made taking each other into account") (p. 212).

The higher the degree of technical interdependence, the more resources must be given for coordination. Thompson (1967) asserts that pooled interdependence can be managed by the processes of

> standardization, the development of rules or routines; sequential interdependence requires the development of plans or schedules, which specify timing and order in the work processes; and reciprocal interdependence requires the use of mutual adjustment or coordination of feedback, in which the interrelated parties must communicate their own requirements and be responsive to the needs of the other group. Each coordination strategy is increasingly costly in terms of resources expended (Scott, 1981, pp. 212-213).

Rules, schedules, programs, departmentalization, hierarchy, delegation, project teams, task forces and liaison roles are substantive elements of the matrix organization. This organization has both the "bureaucracy and an ad-hocracy" (p. 220).

In general, it is expected that the phases of the organization are the work processes of inputs, throughputs and outputs. The technical complexity of an organization is associated with structural complexity (professionalization). Technical uncertainty is likewise associated with lower formalization and decentralization of decision making; and "interdependence with higher levels of coordination" (p. 233). Complexity, uncertainty and interdependence are all similar in the sense that each has the capacity to increase the amount of information processable in the course of task performance. Given this light, the

> complexity, uncertainty, and interdependence increase structural modifications needed to be made that will either ... reduce the need for information processing ... by lowering the level of interdependence or by

lowering performance standards ... increase the capacity of the information processing system, by increasing the channel and node capacity of the hierarchy or by legitimating lateral connections among participants (p. 233).

Contemporary organizational analysts argue that effective organizations are challenged by the need for "technological imperative" (Gortner, Mahler, and Nicholson, 1997, p. 103). That is to say, these organizations' structure use and technology to transform raw materials into finished products. In other words, bureaus or organizations are designed to use programs and procedures whose results articulate legally established public policy objectives and initiatives. In this case, technology refers to the use of scientifically designed advanced machines that are used to run or operationalize the programs and performance routines of the bureaus. Hage and Aiken (1969) have established that organizational routine technologies reflect highly "developed rules and procedures manuals, centralized decision making, and a high degree of specialization" (p. 104). Likewise, Woodward (1980) found that effective organizations (firms) are associated with the organization's technology, structure and success. Routine technologies have centralized and traditional bureaucratic structures while less routine technologies have discretionary, i.e., flexible and decentralized structures. Also, Perrow (1967) has classified the organization's technology into four forms. These forms range from "high routine, rule-governed technology to a highly nonroutine, problem-solving technology" (Gortner, Mahler, and Nicholson, 1997, p. 105).

High-Technology and Politics of Dependency

Recently, economic and political restructuring processes have been taking place around the world. These processes of change have been associated with activities that have taken place or are taking place in the microelectronic, semiconductor and telecommunication industries. Computers and software are manufactured in industries which have become the sources of technologies and other products that factories, offices, schools, organizations, businesses and churches use. The progressive development and advancement of the telecommunication and computer industries have allowed transnational corporations to reorganize, coordinate and control global business activities around the world. The economic growth and functions of these industries have influenced many governments to encourage growth, development, and commercialization of such high-tech products (Schoonmaker, 1995; and Schutte, 1988). As Schoonmaker has indicated:

> information policy debates have converged with conflicts over trade and development in the global economy. In the 1970s, Third World demands for a New World Information Order were rooted in an analysis of information flows as a key facet of economic power. Information was understood in a historical context, where it was structured, used, and disseminated by transnational corporations in a global capitalist market. News, film, television and other media purveyed commodified images of reality, imbued with the values of the former colonial powers. In addition, flows of computerized data between subsidiaries of transnational corporations allowed firms to manage production operations in distant parts of the globe from central corporate headquarters (p. 369).

Though debates concerning the transborder data flows were the main part of the wider struggle for a New World Information Order (NWIO), industrializing countries like Brazil, and some East Asian countries feel that these information flows are a new form of information dependency which strengthens the "historical structure of inequality between countries in global capitalism" (p. 370). Information dependency is influenced by "a lack of technologies, skills, research facilities and industries involved with the computer manufacturing and software" (p. 370). The use of technology has become not only global, but it has also become competitive in its production, distribution and consumption patterns. Computers have become a growing economic sector on their own. The issues, activities and opportunities associated with the information revolution have technically, politically and economically evolved with new structural inequalities and other problems that challenge the wisdom of decision-makers everywhere. For instance, Brazil's attempt to become self-sufficient and autonomous in the development of its informatic industry seems to come into conflict with its U.S. economic and the technological mentors in terms of "policy choices and outcomes: trade ... rapidly changing international product market, and trade dependence" (p. 369).

The Information Revolution triggered inestimable technological progress. The technological progress has globally and socially sparked an attractive wave of politically and economically attractive and interdependent forms of inequality at the international, national, corporate, institutional, organizational and individual levels. Currently, a majority of the developed world's citizen's benefit from the influences of technology while the reverse is true in most developing and industrializing countries.

Threat or Opportunity

Information technology can be both a threat and an opportunity. As a threat, information technology could be used for recolonization, dependence, and overdependence in many places around the world. The weaknesses of economic, financial, and technological backwardness of Third World nations makes them incapable of effectively competing with traditionally well-established industrial and high-tech manufacturers. These southern nations whose political institutions are at infancy in terms of stability, democracy and bureaucratic red-tape, waste, and accountability (McKeanna, 1994) may find it increasingly difficult, as it was during the colonial and post-colonial periods, to try to compete and catch up with their northern neighbors. Even when small and powerful elites in organizations control technology, it is likely to be of little value for urban, local, national, or regional development if it is not equitably shared with the populace. In other words, poverty and inability to possess and use technological skills is a threat to the technological and economic progress of Third World nations and their peoples. Even in the U.S.A.,

> Analyses of the deployment of technology in schools have tended to note its failure to affect the day-to-day values and practices of teachers, administrators, and students. This absence of trace is generally regarded as an implementation failure, or as resulting from some temperamental shortcoming on the part of teachers or technologists. Such a construction is predicated on the frequently tacit assumption that the refused technology is value-free and its implementation therefore not a field of struggle ... no technology is ever neutral: that its values and practices must always either support or subvert those of the organization into which it is placed; and that the failures of technology to alter and look – and – feel of the schools frequently result from a mismatch between the values of school organization and those values that are embedded within the contested technology itself (Hodas, 1996, p. 1).

The Politics and Standards of Usage

Technologically, the internet has also improved people's abilities to do research and gain more education. Many professors, students, and librarians believe placing scholarly journals in electronic format on the internet will increase interest in the internet, journals, and scholarly concepts and theories because it will make more than one million pages from as far back as 1886 easily accessible (*The Journal of Politics*, August 1996; *The Chronicle of Higher Education*, December 6, 1996).

Many librarians believe the digitized collection will give easy access to articles not on the shelves and that would otherwise be difficult to obtain from other libraries. Just on time publishing offers licensed subscribers the full text of 17 journals dating from the first publications and has permission from 45 journals to put editions of their publications on-line excluding the last three years with plans to have hundreds of publications in a dozen fields. An example is students enrolled in a course of the history of economic thought who may be wrestling with the question of whether business leaders behave according to the predictions of economic models, may read papers from the 1930s by noted economists such as Fritz Maclup (*The Chronicle of Higher Education,* December 6, 1996). Unrefereed servers on the internet provide a place for scholars to make their research and ideas available to the scholarly community and anyone else interested in the information. On a refereed server manuscripts are reviewed and then accepted or rejected for placement on a server. The internet improves the accuracy and speed of publications of important yet up-to-date information. The internet will be more efficient for research, speed up scholarly exchange, and be more open for scholarly debate (*The Journal of Politics,* August 1996). On the other hand, the Humanities and Social Sciences On-line, H-NET, is seen as an example of how the internet has helped academics with e-mails reaching more than 51,000 scholars in 70 countries with more than five million pieces of e-mail going through the network each month covering various topics such as film history and African affairs. Dr. Richard Jensen saw H-NET as a way e-mail could help scholars share ideas, solve problems, and work together. When Dr. Jensen began using e-mail, he felt an urge to create a network of e-mail lists that would connect his contacts and scholars interested in the humanities and social sciences, and he made his dream a reality. The H-NET began as a handful of e-mail lists with each beginning with "H" which stood for history, but eventually became a network of many lists devoted to the humanities and social sciences (*The Chronicle of Higher Education,* January 24, 1997). According to Weingarten of *The Chronicle of Higher Education,* October 11, 1996, the internet is used constantly by scholars, makes on-line journals available, provides researchers access to data bases, allows experimenting with on-line "chat rooms" and virtual laboratories, and helps literate scholars to create complete digital sets of texts.

Computers for the New Millennium

With all the new advances in telecommunications, people are trying to create a wireless internet that will be convenient for almost everyone. Wireless communications and internet use are spreading rapidly and are expected to converge into the development of wireless internet and e-mail applications. In the next millennium, wireless internet and e-mail are predicted to be very popular with a projected 29.6 million users by the year 2003. Wireless Internet and E-mail Markets found that 30 percent of people surveyed were interested in wireless devices that can send and receive e-mail. More than 35 percent showed interest in receiving two-way e-mail over a wireless device like a cellular phone or pager while 25 percent were only interested in using a portable PC for a wireless e-mail platform (http://www.gii.co.jp/cnglish/sg3056_wireless_internet.html). On February 23, 1998, w-Trade Technologies provided the solution to wireless internet securities trading. The new system's software has the ability to support various internet-enabled handheld, wireless devices such as cell phones, personal digital assistants, and handheld PC devices which allow financial organizations to offer wireless, handheld on-line trading capabilities to customers and employees. The solution provides individuals and financial professionals with a customizable, portable on-line trading environment where they can receive alerts on market fluctuations, obtain real-time price quotes, manage their portfolios, execute trades, and receive immediate confirmation of trades with just the press of a few buttons. The solution is fully-customizable to make trading of most financial instruments easier, and can be linked to any real-time price feed, proprietary database and trade execution system using internet-capable cell phones and other wireless devices. People can perform direct, cost-effective trade requests when they are near a desktop PC because of wireless, handheld on-line trading. User screens can be produced in Handheld Device Markup Language and HyperText Markup Language to work with a variety of wireless internet devices and networked computers on corporate intranets or web sites (http://www.att.com/press/0298/9823.pcc.html). In Chicago, the Motorola Corporation and Cisco Systems Inc. were expected to announce their plans to form an alliance to create the world's largest wireless internet system on February 15, 1999. These plans are considered to be the next giant step in the internet revolution. This project is expected to enable businesses and consumers to have access to high speed internet, e-mail, and faxes without wires, cables, and walls. The AT&T Corporation already offers wireless service for electronic mail and internet information. Several giant mergers such as Northern Telecom Ltd. and Bay Networks Inc, have formed in order to compete to become the ones to improve the internet which may result in better wireless access. Motorola and Cisco plan to spend over a billion dollars in the next four or five years to form a system that will transmit voice, data, and video over cellular telephones stations directly to wireless phones and laptop computers. Motorola and Cisco also plan for wireless transmissions to be delivered using the Internet Protocol platform which will be compatible with all wireless formats (*The Edmond Evening Sun,* February 14, 1999).

General Technological Trends

Technology is the totality of the means employed to provide objects necessary for human sustenance and comfort. In other words, technology is "a technical method for achieving practical" ends (Clifton, et al., 1989). The term technology itself has different meanings based on how it is used and defined. Historians and philosophers of technology define technology as an "autonomous and out of control force driving civilization to social or literal doom" (Constant, 1989, p. 531) or as "the culture of extermination" (Jamison, 1989). These perspectives are neo-Marxist in sentimental orientation. They view technology as a pernicious instrument used to oppress lower classes in some cases, destroy life enmasse; the same technology is viewed as a creative social construct with potential for transient (temporary) social relations.

Other scholars view technology to be a powerful factor for the revolutionary transformation of social relations. Viewed in this light, technology is an integral part of society's "social, political, and economic life that is inextricably interwoven with other social fabric" (p. 426). In this social fabric, technology revolutionizes technology too. Technological innovations, especially those which have evolved with the use of "mini methods" (p. 503) help management to deal effectively with false analogies, incorrect assumptions, and defective planning strategies. By so doing, decisions generated with the use of technology prove that they are quality decisions which executives can use for policy formulation, policy analysis (policy making), policy implementation, and policy evaluation.

Viewed from positively social, intellectual, and economic traditions, technology contains great strategic importance. This strategic importance involves what happens in military, commerce, domestic and international markets and innovation processes—such as scientific research, laboratory investigation, and the diverse structures of our institutional organizations (Jamison, 1989).

Although technological theory and policy change technological practice, science and technology are continuously related to "energy, economic, and environmental crises" (p. 531) and risks of the past industrial society. The creativity and revitalization of this society will depend on how new entrepreneurs will use building blocks of the future (high-tech society, information, and know how) to keep society running, to reindustrialize and modernize America and the Third World, to create jobs that will enable workers, graduates, and families to have a hope, believe in the future, and rearm themselves for action. According to Jamison, new entrepreneurs are technologically pregnant because they live in a society whose culture is technologically vibrant. Technological vibrancy is technological culture which is identified with consensual elitism or corporatism (Jamison, 1989) of the Japanese Model through which the elite (bureaucrats and corporate industrialists) are enthused by societal ethos of creativity and innovation to translate technology and policy into development reality. Japanese revolutionary transformation of cultural and technological ideas into development has not only demonstrated that human relations, group psychology, and organizational culture are dynamic forces underlying the transformation, but also that this transformation is not an historical accident; it is the result of hard work, grand dreams, superior management strategy, and clear and well integrated national, educational, economic, and political objectives.

As an importance resource, technological culture is a national heritage essential for the security of national survival on the domestic and international plane particularly in the cases connected with AIDS research, and cancer research, plastic bomb control, cardiac arrest and pollution control, toxic chemicals, and waste and energy crisis management (Hatsopoulos, 1989) and trade and development research. Associated with these security measures are five trends which will shape the new age of technology in the new millenium. These five trends include: (1) the global dissemination of expanding scientific knowledge, (2) a striking growth in the number of global competitors, (3) fragmented markets and shifting customer preferences, (4) diverse and transforming process technologies leading to greater flexibility and responsiveness, and (5) proliferation in the number of technologies relevant to any given product (Clark, 1988).

The most important new technologies of the new age in which these trends will be dominant are biotechnology, artificial intelligence (computers), and advanced materials. The technologies are critical for every corporation's and company's struggle for existence. However, notwithstanding, the challenges of technological competition, technology cannot be management's primary solution to strategic problems because every competitor uses technology to solve those problems. Because of that kind of managerial dilemma, top management has to use superior strategy and execution (Clark, 1988) in order to be competitive.

Top management in the business world needs to succeed by revitalizing their technological, productive, and competitive position. What they need is to link the technological world with the world of business. New technology must create new products. New products can be created if scientists, engineers, and top management collaborate to identify the nature of their competitors, the technical alternatives, improvable capabilities, where to concentrate their resources, where they are coming from, and where they expect to be at a given time in the future.

In the new global economy, technical, technological and scientific competence will strategically be utilized by a new wave of market place competitors in the form of partnerships, consortia, or companies of which allied companies, corporations, major universities and governments will be dominant. Traditional competition which was based on product against product, or company against company is being or has been overshadowed by this new wave of regional and global, consortia, and partnership rivalry whose global view will dwarf the parochialism of traditional firm, corporate, and company competition against each other.

Within this new economic and global order, the essence of time and productivity will be measured by parameters of environmental efficiency and effectiveness. In other words, the need for integration of scientific understanding and information systems with factors of competitive advantage need to be fully conceptualized and utilized to build the corporation's or organization's or institution's technical core, hold the levers and processes for change, determine the rate, quality, and direction of learning in the organization, organize the force of technology in the competitive environment, and integrate human imagination and creativity, to enhance productivity.

A comparison between contemporary Japanese and American technological performance and creativity is purposefully instructive. The United States is superior to Japan in science while Japan is superior to the United States and the world in engineering. Japan's engineering culture makes Japanese engineers so flexible that they cannot like the status quo in their factories (Avishai, 1988). Because of

Japan's anti-status quo attitude and superior work-management ethic, she has superiority in manufacturing technology over the United States. Whenever Japanese and American manufacturers concentrate on small and doable productive processes, i.e., design for manufacture, getting the product into the customer's hand on time, in the right know how (not the first but the best in the market), satisfying the customer's needs, etc., the sale of such technological products is quite attractively high (Gomory, 1889).

Technologically, innovations are created, usable know how and things result from the culmination of cumulative scientific research especially in nuclear physics and organic chemistry. Production in manufacturing plants incrementally and increasingly becomes like a race rather than a collegiate problem. Company workers refine the product, customize it for more and more consumer publics, make it more reliable, and market it more cheaply (Gomory, 1989).

Generally speaking, Americans have fallen behind in the technological race. Our products and marketing strategies are relatively inferior to those of Japan. We have lost our competitive technological edge because we use fewer dollars and spend less time in engineering research, quality design, and careful manufacturing. Japanese products, especially those in automotive and electronic fields are high quality manufactures because they are durable and reliable, provide comfort and convenience; and in the case of autos, they are designed to provide more mileage per gallon of gas. Such products command a higher demand which correspondingly and increasingly attracts larger supply. For instance, in 1989, "Honda rather than Chevrolet became the heartbeat of America" (Adams, in *Lansing State Journal,* January 11, 1990).

Some of the main reasons for America's relatively poor technological performance can be attributed to poor management, production, and marketing techniques. For instance, American manufacturers are short-term rather than long-term strategic entrepreneurs. Their prime motive for production is a short-term and fast profit-making orientation whose purpose is specialization in quantity rather than environmentally sound and quality manufacturing. Such a producing market climate discourages customers from buying our own products; it makes labor costs extremely unbearable; and projects management to be redundant (Mosbacher, CNN, 5:30 p.m., January 7, 1990).

Clearly, America's technological lag and comparatively low quality manufacturing has not only made it to lose its competitive edge, but the nation's increasing "technological slumber" has significantly contributed to the decline of our domestic and international social prestige, economic, technological and diplomatic power. American leadership is weak and interdependent rather than decisive and dominant in the global competition for strategic markets and geopolitical influence.

Further comparison between Japanese and American technological and industrial behavior reveals interesting and striking observations. In this regard, there are two major reasons showing why Japan is ahead. First, the Japanese Ministry of International Trade and Industry (MITI) is a national agency which coordinates the research effort of corporations to start and concentrate on superconductivity research; acquires, uses, and modifies western technology; and which funds and coordinates other national research programs. In recent years, corporations have become dominant in playing that role. Second, Japan is also technologically ahead of the United States because Americans rely on archaic or traditional technology while Japanese keep on renewing their products (Gomory, 1989). Americans have strategically learned about their weaknesses and have moved ahead to rectify them.

In addition, U.S. company engineers do not like to use foreign or outside ideas because they are intellectually, culturally and psychologically prejudiced to new, foreign, and creative ideas. They rightly behave so because of sensitivity associated with the use of classified information. Japanese design specialists and manufacturing teams work side by side for cost effectiveness and manufacturing simplicity. Corporation management motivates engineers to keep up to date in new global technology, attending conferences, reading technical and professional literature, actively participating in engineering and scholarly communities, and facilitating communication within the scientific community (Gomory, 1989). Unlike their Japanese counterparts, and because of their theoretical rather than practical orientation, American scientists do not easily share their scientific knowledge with corporate executives and manufacturing companies for product design, product creation, product refinement, product modification, and product competition. As a result, the Japanese have an advantage over us.

A large portion of the U.S. economy, apart from manufacturing, is a service sector. Policies supporting technology in services need to be an important component of the ongoing debate about the government's proper role in supporting technology for both public and private purposes, especially, policies that are necessary for improving U.S. industrial and international competitiveness. Evidently, it should be made clear that the services sector is not independent of the manufacturing sector. The U.S. services and manufacturing industries are effectively and mutually intertwined and interdependent. For instance, some services activities create new markets for manufactures goods. Manufacturers produce at low costs that are central to the value gained by manufactured products. Likewise, manufacturers are important suppliers, customers, and innovators for services activities. Not only are services and manufacturing mutually complementary, but, the same policy approaches that stimulate or retard one sector will generally affect the other in similar ways. It should also be made clear that the "services industries provide 75 percent of all jobs and 71 percent of all U.S. gross national product (GNP)" (Guile and Quinn, 1988, pp. 211-212). Critical factors affecting both include the high relative cost of U.S. capital (which may benefit from a general leveling of such costs worldwide induced by the global integration of capital markets), the skill and literacy levels of the work technologies (especially those related to communications), health care, information handling, and public transport).

Technologies in the services sector are used to restructure many manufacturing and services industries as well as the entire U.S. economy and its international trade patterns. "The dynamics of technology, combined with deregulation, have broken down barriers among industries such as transportation, communications, finance, distribution, education, and health care, and have created a degree of cross-industry interaction and competition that calls for new regulatory philosophies and institutions across a wide spectrum" (Guile and Quinn, 1988, p. 214).

For educational purposes, an emphasis on retraining, adapting and cushioning the personal costs for those displaced because of the loss of certain manufacturing jobs or because of changes in occupational mix would be more appropriate. Producing a literate and numerate work force would be more instructive and adaptive in changing economic conditions. Within the academic environment basic education remains a high priority especially if educators could learn to prepare people for life-long learning in a constantly changing job market whose demand is elastic (Guile and Quinn, 1988). In this environment, Plutzer, Maney, and O'Connor (1998) argue that journalists, policy makers and scientists are the elite from different intellectual traditions whose opinion about nuclear energy, genetic engineering and other new technologies emanate from culturally biased political ideology. As a result, environmental and technological issues are not, paradoxically speaking, "technical policy issues, but proxies for older conflicts between left egalitarians and the corporate establishment" (p. 190).

The expansionary use of the internet has created a complex and thorny patchwork of issues concerning defamatory postings, spamming (unwanted e-mail) and the invasion of the rights of privacy. Without resolving these conflicts, there will be no information on the information superhighway.

Case Study of Prosolvia

Between January and May 1999, I conducted an unstructured telephone interview with Paul M. Sagini concerning strategic, technical and operational efficiency of the failed Prosolvia Company that was based in Gothenburg, Sweden. On the verge of the Company's collapse, Paul resigned from Prosolvia and was employed by the GM where he is a software engineer. With a comparative perspective, he has analytically reflected on the causes of Prosolvia's collapse and what the company could have done to survive. It is interesting to read the paraphrasiology.

This is a document summarizing the observed events of the failure of a high-tech computer software company specializing in virtual reality technology from an engineer's point of view. May 5 1997 I had graduated from the University of Michigan in Ann Arbor with a degree in Computer Visualization. This was my first degree. With a degree like that I had anticipated and pursued a number of computer/info tech firms. At that time anyone who could spell the word computer in his or her resume was assured an interview. After a number of interviews I accepted a job as instructor and application engineer for a Swedish based company, headquartered in Gothenburg, virtual reality and interactive visual simulation company. In October 1997, I began in one of the US branches which also acted as US headquarters.

At that time of my beginning there were roughly 300 employees in the company. During that year Prosolvia was hailed as the number one service company in Sweden. Prosolvia exercised an initial public opening in the Stockholm Stock Exchange in that same year rapidly expanded worldwide to capture new markets. As exciting, new, and impressive had Prosolvia risen to the top, equally as incredible was the sudden plunge that brought Prosolvia to its crumbling knees.

The fall of the company began that year. In October 1997, the company had about 300 employees. Six months later the company its workforce 100%. First mistake!

Workforce Increase From 300 to 600 in Six Months

In about 5 to 6 months the company had hired roughly 300 people. This is an indication that the company is completely out of control. No major sales and/or contracts had been signed to justify such a drastic increase in personnel. Furthermore with this large increase of resources a management strategy had not been put in place to facilitate, maintain, and assign responsibility. Prosolvia had been set up as a matrix organization where resources could be pulled from any level of management. The problem with this method is that responsibility is compromised. If a director can pull a manager's engineer from a specific task, how and by whom is that task completed? If a director can pull resources at any time in conflict with a manager's plan.

Employee Growth without Sales/Income to Support Growth

The company had hired employees in hopes of landing huge contracts. The method was to bring in as much of a sales force as possible to infiltrate new markets. In addition to the new force these sales people were salaried so high that there was almost no drive to sell products. Why does a sales person need to sell if his/her salary is as high as a manager's salary—not including commission?

Selling of Visions or Promises as Opposed to Products

With a new and sophisticated technology such as virtual reality, simulation and digital plant technology, there is a tendency of over inflating the realities of the technology and even the science of the technology. On many occasions the customer does not know enough about the technology's science and limitations. Because of this fact miscommunication about the product, and its limitations cause enormous fabrications compromising the confidence of the sales process and the confidence of the company. For instance, a question, can you do CFD, crash analysis, in VR? Miscommunication gives the company a bad image.

Lack of Business Plan

Prosolvia had three product lines. One for industrial strength simulation, the second was consumer strength simulation, and the third was for industrial strength plant layout, analysis, design, and robot offline programming. The company was divided into three divisions.

Research and Technology, Systems, and Clarus. R&T did consulting work in the area of Finite Element Analysis, Computational Fluid Dynamics, Crash Analysis, and also developed some of the tessellation algorithms intended or the VR and plant design applications. Systems developed the plant design and analysis product line. Clarus developed the industrial and consumer VR products. All three-product lines and the two divisions Clarus and Systems competed in the same market segments and in many cases approached the same customer. The company never gave a clear message what strategy to use in selling the products and which customers to pursue with which product. Some instances include sales persons from Sweden selling in the U.S. market when a U.S. branch and market director had no knowledge of both Swedish and American sales activity, environment and climate.

Based on his on-site observation, Sagini reported that Prosolvia declined and vanished largely due to a variety of problems of which the following were paramount. There was lack of a management structure change in critical time. The same management used new and unproven technology requiring expensive hardware which the corporation was unable to provide. The absence of effective managerial leadership contributed to rapid expansion into the world market without business plans for success with strategic overtones. Poor technology transfer to new business areas in the U.S., Canada, Japan, Europe and the Third World made the sale of "oxygen" problematic. Overconfidence in projecting sales forecasts and ignorance of American culture and market became entrepreneurial obstacles. Absence of efficient customer service, total quality management, and "just ontime manufacturing" discouraged and confused customers. Failure to produce products based on research and development, inconsistent product intercommunication, use of an extremely broad rather than narrow product line, extraneous and uncontrolled expenses and the corporation's inability to adequately position new technology contributed to the rapid "death" of Prosolvia.

To succeed in a foreign cultural, technological and political climate Prosolvia needed to create a product the customer wanted. Management needed to be familiarized with the determinants of successful sales, marketing, and accounting techniques that are in demand in the American and other markets. It needed to tailor the product to customer specifications and preferences. Before introducing the product, they should set up a pilot project on site and approve the product based on market response in terms of demand and supply. They needed to communicate a clear vision (mission) of the organization by articulating the strategic, technical and operational goals of the business plan. The plan required simple intuitive user interface, user-friendly diplomatic networking, and multiple platform OS support. Management needed to hire employees based on sales and profits rather than on premium and inaccurate forecasts. Prosolvia needed to acquire complimentary technologies from other companies in order to remain competitive. Lowering hardware requirements for running software would have enhanced the company's performance.

Conclusion

In this chapter, the author has analyzed the historical overview of the evolution, meaning and politics of computer technology. In discussing about the invention, usage and commercialization of the computer, critical First Amendment right issues and other legal, political, moral, ethical and academic concerns have been raised. Though these issues have emerged with the recent growth and expansion of the computer industry, earlier evolutionary developments of artificial intelligence appear to have escaped, in comparative perspective, a plethora of contemporary issues and concerns. Computer technology is information age revolutionary dynamics whose market has profoundly influenced global organizations in finance and trade patterns, education, business, labor, law, crime, industry, media and government.

Within the democratic world and free enterprise and capitalistic economies, market forces have animated the computer industry whose aim is the maximization of profits rather than the welfare of stakeholders. The forces have a vested interest for replicating colonial inequality in a post-colonial environment. These forces use corporate efficiency, media communications and consumer entertainment rather than electoral efficiency, civic communication, and political education to supplant rather than to foster the cultural economic and social interests of the poorer classes within the global village. Globally, the use and promotion of technological inequality particularly when the media dominates it is not only a form of electronic colonialism, but it also promotes an economically inegalitarian ideology.

Computer technology could be an effective instrument for standardization, control and repression. This new technology is used for centralization of information, control over information, and retention of files and "taps." It can be a powerful instrument of control by the powerful economic and political elite (Barber, 1998/99). On the other hand, the fact that insurance companies, legal, law enforcement agencies, businesses, and professional and medical organizations can store information about every individual in "infobanks," lends its possible abuse of the Bill of Rights including the privacy issues. In this regard, computer technology could inadvertently become a destructive facilitator of tyranny. If it is monopolistically used, "absence of conscious government abuse, this potential can constrict our freedom, encroach on our privacy, and damage our political equality. There is no tyranny more dangerous than an invisible and benign tyranny, one in which subjects are complicit in their victimization and in which enslavement is a product of circumstance rather than intention" (pp. 581-582).

In spite of the potential for the abuse of computer technology, the computer can be the source of power and hope if it is positively used to enhance and promote social institutions of democratic governance. For instance, the "tool" can be used to keep citizens informed provided communication is openly maintained. Democracy is a government which relies on information and communication...new technologies of information and communications can be nurturing to democracy. They can challenge passivity...enhance information equality...overcome sectarianism and prejudice, and they can facilitate participation in deliberative political processes" (p. 282).

Mediawise, the past emphasized active programming and passive viewing. New technology places emphasis in interactive viewing in which customers are actively involved in watching and responding to programs that are harnessed to "interactive television, information network hookups, and public access cable channels" (p. 582). The users of "complex computer/telephone/video set-up" (p. 582) have been so electronically and communicatively modernized that technology has changed their public and private perceptions of reality. Therefore, "linked together horizontally by a point–to-point medium like the internet, citizens can subvert political hierarchy and nurture an unmediated civic communication" (p. 582). For instance, if computer terminals that are equipped with user friendly programs and technicians in public places like town or city halls, libraries, stadia, clubs and other public places, the general public will easily be accessible to information on employment, housing, zoning regulations, welfare, etc. Such interactive capabilities from television and the internet technology will educate the civilian populace to overcome "regional parochialism, local prejudice and national chauvinism" (p. 583) for the purpose of enhancing globalism, educated and less biased citizenship and antiluddism.

Finally, in education and in other organizations, computer technology can be used for long-distance learning, influencing voter opinions on issues and candidates, and for tracking criminals and terrorists

(Muraskin and Roberts, 1998). In doing this, democracy in its participatory representation and deliberative and plebiscitary forms will be enhanced.

Bill Gates (1999), the CEO of Microsoft, has expressed himself concerning how technology will help people to better manage and transform their businesses and organizations. These companies, firms and other organizations use digital tools for monitoring basic operations, for running their production processes and systems, for producing customer invoices and providing accounting procedures. This flow of digital information was used to provide organizations with quality in the 1980s and reengineering in the 1990s. However, in the 2000s, the flow of digital information will produce velocity (speed). "For the first time, all kinds of information—numbers, text, sound, video—can be put into a digital form that any computer can store, process, and forward" (p. xv). Standard hardware has been combined with standard software platforms to create enormous economies of scale. Personal digital companions like handhelds, Auto PCs, smart cards, etc. have made the pervasive digital information to activate internet technologies, resulting in worldwide connectivity.

Electronic-based intelligence system is used to connect people taking care of sales, organizational activities and customer needs. In the digital age, the digital infrastructure which works like the human nervous system, will function as the "digital nervous system" (p. xvii). The goal of the digital nervous system is to ensure that organizations adapt strategically and continuously. In reality then:

> A digital nervous system consists of the digital processes that enable a company to perceive and react to its environment, to sense competitor challenges and customer needs, and to organize timely responses. A digital nervous system requires a combination of hardware and software; it's distinguished from a mere network of computers by the accuracy, immediacy, and richness of the information it brings to knowledge workers and the insight and collaboration made possible by the information" (p. xviii).

The digital approach will enable people and organizations to conduct business instantaneously. This will happen when different systems like knowledge management, business operations and commerce will be interlinked. The interlinked infrastructure of the digital nervous system will eliminate the middleman by creating worldwide virtual teams. These knowledgeable teams will eliminate unnecessary administrative positions, exchange information on time, use digital transactions with suppliers, partners and employees in order to transform business into "just-in-time delivery" (xxi).

References

Adams, W. 1990. MSU Economists: Short-term gains in U.S. economy. *Lansing State Journal,* January 11: 6.

Almon, C., Jr., et al. 1985. *Interindustry Forecasts of the American Economy.* Lexington, MA: D.C. Heath Company.

Avishai, B., and W. Taylor. 1989. Customers drive a technology-driven company: An interview with George Fisher. *Harvard Business Review.* November/December.

Barber, B.R. 1998/99. Three scenarios for the future of technology and strong democracy. *Political Science Quarterly* 13, 4: 573-589.

Barboza, D. 1999. Venture aims to create internet world without wires. *The Edmond Evening Sun.* February 14: 21.

Bowles, P. 1989. Peripheral capitalist development revisited. *Studies in Political Economy: A Socialist Review,* 28, Spring.

Capron, H.L. 1998. *Computers Tools for an Information Age. 5th Ed.* Reading: Addison Wesley Longman.

Cetron, J.M., W. Rocha, and R. Luckins. 1988. Into the 21st century: Long-term trends affecting the United States. *The Futurist,* July to August.

Clark, K.B. 1989. What strategy can do for technology. *Harvard Business Review,* November/December.

Clifton, D.S., Jr. et al. 1989. Elements of an effective technology assistance policy to stimulate economic development. *Economic Development Quarterly* 3, 1, February.

Commission on the Future of Community Colleges. 1990. *Building Communities: A Vision for a New Century.* Washington, D.C.: American Association of Community and Junior Colleges.

Constant, E.W., II. 1989. Cause or consequence: Science, technology, and regulatory change in the oil business in Texas, 1930-1975. *Technology and Culture* 30, 2 and 3, July: 426-455.

Cowan, R.S. 1997. *A Social History of American Technology.* New York: Oxford University Press.

DeLoughry, T.J. 1996. Journal articles dating back as a century are being put online. *The Chronicles of Higher Education,* December 6, pp. A30, A32.

DeLoughry, T.J. 1996. Computing officials at 34 universities seek to create a network for higher education. *The Chronicles of Higher Education,* October 11, pp. A29-A30.

DeLoughry, T.J. 1996. Judge blocks enforcement of one internet restriction, allows another to stand. *The Chronicles of Higher Education,* February 23, p. 22.

Detweiler, R.A. 1996. Democracy and dependency on the internet. *The Chronicles of Higher Education,* June 28.

DiFazio, W. and S. Aronowitz. 1994. The jobless future: Sci-tech and the dogma of *work.* Minneapolis: University of Minnesota Press.

Fountain, M., ed. 1989. *Occupational Outlook Quarterly,* 33, 3, Fall.

Giles, M.W. 1996. Presidential address from Gutenberg to gigabytes: Scholarly communication in the age of cyberspace. *The Journal of Politics* 58, 3: 613-626.

Glover, J.E., and R.W. Gibson. 1997. *The Millenium Dilemma: Month Modification - A File Interface Solution which Retains Files,.* A Paper for Domestic – Local Consumption, September. Stillwater.

Gomory, R.E. 1989. From the ladder of science to the product development cycle. *Harvard Business Review* November/December.

Gortner, H.F., J. Mahler, and J.B. Nicholson. 1997. *Organization Theory: A Public Perspective.* Fort Worth: Harcourt Brace College Publishers.

Governor's Cabinet Council on Human Investment. 1988. *Countdown 2000.* Lansing: Adult Literacy Task Force.

Guernsey, L. 1997. A humanities network considers what lies beyond e-mail. *The Chronicles of Higher Education,* January 24, pp. A23-A24.

Guile, B.R., and Quinn, J.B. 1988. *Technology in Services: Policies for Growth, Trade, and Employment.* Washington, D.C.: National Academy Press.

Herbeck, D.A., and C.D. Hunter. 1998. Intellectual property in cyberspace: The use of protected images on the world wide web. *Communications Research Reports,* 15, 1: 57-63.

Hodas, Steven. 1996. *Technology Refusal and the Organizational Culture of Schools.* http://homepage.seas.upenn.edu/~cpage/techref.html. 10/3/1996 4:25.

Hoveland, H., P. McInturff, and T.C.E. Rohn. 1986. Editor's notes. *New Directions for Higher Education,* 55: 1-3.

Hussain, D.S., and K.M. Hussain. 1986. *The Computer Challenge: Technology, Applications, and Social Implications.* Edina: Burgess Communications.

Ignatovich, F.R., and S.E. Hecker. 1989. *Summary of Enrollments and Projections United States Public and Michigan Public.* East Lansing, February 15.

Jackson, B.W., et al., 1987. *Conditions in Postsecondary Education in Michigan.* East Lansing: State Board of Education.

Kaul, M., G. Walsham, and V. Symons. 1989. Management of technological change: Themes and issues. *Information Technology and Development: An International Journal,* 4, 2, June.

Lybrand and Coopers. 1989. *Made in America II. A Survey of Manufacturing's Future.* Solutions for Business.

MacEwan, A. and W.K. Tabb. 1989. The economy in crisis: National power and international instability. *Body Politics: Engineering Reproduction in Anxious Times – U.S. Power and Global Economic Disorder TV Culture,* 19, 3, July/September.

Muraskin, R. and A.R. Roberts. 1996. *Visions for Change: Crime and Justice in the Twenty-first Century.* Upper Saddle River, N.J.: Prentice Hall.

Norton, R.D. 1989. Reindustrialization and economic development strategy. *Economic Development Quarterly* 3, 3, August.

Pestillo, P.J., and S.P. Yokich 1989. *Jobs: Governor's Commission on Jobs and Economic Development.* Lansing: Employment Skills Task Force.

Plutzer, E., A. Maney, and R.E. O'Connor. 1998. Ideology and elites' perceptions of the safety of new technologies. *American Journal of Political Science,* 42, 1: 190-209.

Poe, C.A. 1989. *The New Work Force.* New York.

Schoonmaker, S. 1995. High-Tech development politics: New strategies and persistent structures in Brazilian informatics. *The Sociological Quarterly* 36, 2: 369-395.

Scott, W.R. 1981. *Organizations. Rational, Natural, and Open Systems.* Englewood Cliffs, N.J.: Prentice Hall, Inc.

Schutte, H. 1988. *Strategic Issues in Information Technology: International Implications for Decision Makers.* Pergamon Infotech Ltd.

Secretary-General of UNCTAD. 1989. *Trade and Development Report 1989. Report by the Secretariat of the United Nations Conference on Trade and Development.* New York. United Nations.

Simpson, L.C. 1995. *Technology, Time and the Conversations of Modernity.* New York: Routledge.

Spinetta, K. 1990. Part-time instructors in the California community colleges: A need to revise current policies. *Community College Review,* 18, 1.

Szymanski, R.A., D.P. Szymanski, and D.M. Pulschen. 1995. *Computers and Information Systems.* Upper Saddle River: Prentice Hall.

Thibodeau, P. 1998. Intel evidence paint 'arrogant' Gates. *Computerworld,* November 16, p. 8.

U.S. Industrial Outlook. 1989. *30th Annual Edition.* U.S. Department of Commerce, U.S. Department of Labor, and International Monetary Fund.

Weingarten, F.W. 1996. Uncle Sam as internet Nanny. *The Chronicles of Higher Education,* March 1, pp. A56.

Wilson, D.L. 1996. Clinton's new internet proposal could involve half a dozen agencies. *The Chronicles of Higher Education,* October 25, pp. A29-A30.

Wilson, D.L. 1996. The internet takes a journey into 3rd dimension. *The Chronicles of Higher Education,* February 23, pp. A21-A22.

Young, J.R. 1999. Presidential panel seeks spending increases on computing research. *The Chronicles of Higher Education,* March 5, p. A27.

Chapter 13

Organizational Work Motivation

Definitively, "work motivation is the sum of processes which influence the arousal, direction and maintenance of behaviors relevant to work settings" (Steers and Porter, 1975 and Siegel and Lane, 1987, p. 373). Definitions of organizations discuss structures, "positions" and "competencies" in a very mechanistic way; however, organizations are ultimately social and human systems. As human beings fill the structures and positions, this indicates that human behavior is central to the functioning and effectiveness of competencies. Human motivation is of special consequence in public organizations because of the political environment and the limitation placed on actions by managers in bureaus. Private organizations value human motivation likewise though they are not accountable to public and elected officials. Instead, they are accountable to boards of directors.

The term motivation comes from the Latin word "to move." Psychologically, human motivation pertains to internal conditions or states; it is not intangible. Motivation, then, is a hypothetical or theoretical construct. It is based on what we infer about internal needs and the activity or behavior consequent to them. Bernard Berelson and Gary Steiner (1964) have given a well-stated definition. "A motive is an inner state that energizes, activates, or moves (hence 'motivation'), and that directs or channels behavior toward goals" (p. 240).

The individual, for need satisfaction, desires these goals, incentives, or rewards toward which motivation and activity are directed. Needs are internal incentives while goals are more external or environmentally based ends. For example, hunger is a need, and food is the goal. An organization that appropriately provides goals, rewards, or incentives for members' need satisfaction will be more successful in motivating workers than the one which doesn't.

A good administrator does not work alone. No manager can single handedly maintain a high level organizational functioning. To achieve organizational goals, the energies and actions of others must be brought forth or drawn from them and directed toward productive ends. Because administrators must delegate to others to get things done, understanding the motivation processes and needs of these individuals contributes to organizational and managerial effectiveness.

Motivation is an important organizational concern for several reasons. It is a factor in determining why people participate in an organization; it determines the extent to which they will allow others to direct and control their behavior; and it matters whether they strive to accomplish personal or organizational goals, or both.

Daniel Katz and Robert Kahn (1982) have identified the patterns of individual behavior that the organization needs for effective functioning. First, the organization requires that sufficient personnel join and stay in the system. Second, the dependable performance of assigned roles is necessary. A third and more subtle set of organizational requirements is for actions to be carried out that are not specified by role prescriptions but are needed to meet unanticipated changes and consequences. Spontaneous innovation, cooperation with other members, and behaviors that protect and create a favorable external climate for the organization are activities of this type. Each of these organizational requirements depends on somewhat different theoretical persuasions and motivational patterns.

Specifically, Katz and Kahn (1982) have looked at organizationally designed work motivation from both individual and organizational perspectives and identified four types of reward systems that normatively affect different motivation patterns. First, legal compliance form of motivation is rooted in the individual authority and rule structure that are legitimate. Such an internalized acceptance of this structure influences the individual's motivational and behavioral focus. Second, motivation is characterized by instrumental satisfaction because individuals are rewarded by the organization, other individuals, and they also get approval from leaders and peers. For instance, the organization as a general system may incentively reward senior employees with a variety of "retirement systems, sick leave, cost-of-living increases" (Gortner, et al., 1997; p. 277). Though these rewards may reduce turnover, they are not likely to increase the quality and quantity of work. However, generally speaking, performance (productivity) is likely to be higher.

Rewards in the form of pay increase and promotion are given on the basis of "merit or performance" (p. 277). Such rewards are effective in motivating individuals to exercise high standards, reduce turnover and lower absenteeism.

Third, internalized self-expressioned motivation is a form of self-determination, self-organization and intrinsic job satisfaction that is reached with a positive self-outlook. When work provides sufficient variety, complexity, challenge and rigor, self-expression is aroused to enhance the values of job enrichment in terms of engaging skills and untapped abilities (Katz and Kahn, 1982).

Finally, motivation as self-expression is the process of internalization of the goals of the organization. Individuals who internalize organizational goals are those who display "a sense of mission, direction, or commitment" (p. 362). It is difficult to internalize goals of the organization because they clash with individual goals and preferences. The three conditions which foster organizational internalization of goals are: "participating in decisions, contributing ... to organization performance and sharing rewards for group accomplishment" (Gortner, et al., 1997, p. 279).

The theory of motivation is characterized by a diversity of models and theoretical frameworks. Since motivation is a multifaceted concept, its diversity provides the researcher, practitioner, and student with a variety of insights and perspectives from which to choose and combine or separate. There are many possible ways of grouping the numerous motivation theories, ideas, and models. In this chapter, it is instructive to organize them according to four major types; content models, cognitive processes, behaviorist theories, and bureau-based perspectives (Gortner, et al., 1997). In addition to describing the conceptual frameworks of various theories, elements allied to application, satisfaction, and performance appraisal will be included where appropriate.

Content models of motivation focus on identifying the substantive nature of individual needs; in other words, they attempt to determine what motivates individuals. Cognitive process theories attempt to explain how and why people are motivated. Motivation is presented here as a complex process in which cognition especially perception, thinking, memory, reasoning, chunking and expectation are important.

It is the interaction of these psychological variables with other factors related to the situation or environment that distinguish process models. By contrast, internal psychological variables are excluded from the behaviorist perspective because of their introspective nature. External factors count as behavioral and environmental response to behavior.

After examining these approaches, their implications on public organizations will be examined. Anthony Downs, whose model of motivation relates directly to bureau settings and opportunity structures, has discussed this fourth perspective (Self-interest and personalistic goals characteristic of other theories are also included in Downs' Model). This model adds to our understanding of individual motivation in bureaus by including policy and public interest goals as well. This additional insight will allow us to consider the traditional motivational theories, and their application in the new management models like total quality management to public bureaus. As it was inferred earlier, there are eight theories of motivation that can be grouped into three sections, i.e., content, cognitive, and behaviorist theories. Of the eight, four are content theories. These include need-hierarchy, EGR, two-factor and need-achievement.

Content Theories

Maslow's positive psychology is a theory of value that is scientifically descriptive and naturalistic. The theory advances the notion that humans have "instinctoid" needs that are neither conscious nor unconscious. The needs are hierarchically integrated and are part and parcel of the human personality structure. The study of human needs and how their satisfaction impels self-actualization is not only an inclusive and anticlassical, but this theory of human value is an analytical, critical and metaethical inquiry (McDonald, 1969 and Maslow, 1954). The satisfaction of the needs influences behavior. In reality behavior is multimotivated. In other words, the determinants of motivation of which self-actualization is a component are multivarious. Intrinsic and extrinsic forces motivate a person toward growth and maturation. According to Maslow, this view of positive psychology is antiFreudians who tend to pathologize the scientific and humanistic science of positive psychology and human development (Kolberg). The values acquired during the developmental process tend to influence the personality and the methodological posture of the researcher's scientific inquiry.

Figure 13.1. Maslow's Hierarchy of Needs

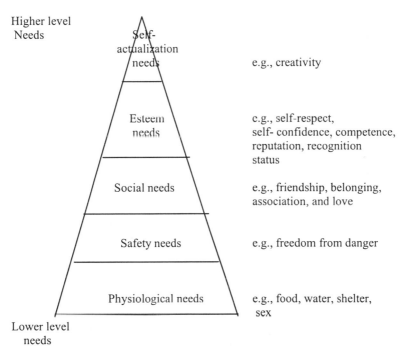

Higher level
Needs

e.g., creativity

e.g., self-respect,
self- confidence, competence,
reputation, recognition
status

e.g., friendship, belonging,
association, and love

e.g., freedom from danger

e.g., food, water, shelter,
sex

Lower level
needs

"Self-actualizing persons have been characterized very generally as those who have sufficiently gratified their basic needs for safety, belongingness, love, respect, and self-esteem so that they are motivated primarily by growth needs, including the need to actualize their potentials" (McDonald, 1969, p. 43). These self-actualizing persons have the following characteristics:

1. They efficiently see themselves and others realistically and are not frightened by the unknown. They think and reason scientifically (use facts pragmatically).

2. They accept their own human nature irrespective of its flaws and strengths. They live without posing, or without feeling unnecessary guilt, and without exaggerating their own goodness and the weaknesses of others.

3. They are spontaneous and tend to avoid to buttress themselves unconventionally.

4. They are more problem centered rather than ego centered because they deal with broad rather than petty, universal rather than local and long-range (century) rather than momentary issues.

5. They are detached rather than intensely involved in their own problems and the problems of other people without being different or indifferent. They are alone, stand alone without others' "reassurance and compliments" (p. 48).

6. They are culturally and environmentally autonomous because they exercise independent judgment as they develop and grow. Because they are not motivationally deficient, they do not think of other people as the "source of their needs for safety, love, respect and prestige" (p. 48). "They are growth motivated" and "self-contained" (p. 48), i.e., they are stable and serene.

7. Because they were given love and respect in the past, they are unique in "thought, impulse, behavior, and motions" (p. 49). "They have a family feeling toward their weaker, foolish, and sometimes nasty and unsympathetic fellowmen" (p. 49). They are not condescending even though they are knowledgeable about the limits and appreciations of other people.

8. They choose friends selectively and their ties "are more obliterating of ego boundaries" (p. 49). When they become hostile, their hostility is directed for the protection of others rather than for self-defense.

9. They are democratic rather than authoritarian and they tend to be friendly to all people "regardless of class, education, political belief, race or color" (p. 49).

10. They experience things uniquely; whenever "they experience events, beauty, sex, or knowledge, there is a creative quality of wholesomeness and freshness. Their strength lies in this quality. Such creativity gives them a sense of originality for viewing the world with "awe, pleasure, wonder and even ecstasy" (p. 50) regardless of how stale others may see it.

The following quotation is used to summarize the character of self-actualizing people: "Such people, when they feel strong, if really free choice is possible, tend spontaneously to choose the true rather than the false, good rather than evil, beauty rather than ugliness, integration rather than dissociation, joy rather than sorrow, aliveness rather than deadness, uniqueness rather than stereotype, etc." (p. 57).

According to Maslow (1954, 1966, and 1970), the "physiological, safety, social, esteem and self-actualization needs are hierarchically arranged" (Siegel and Lane, 1987, p. 375) and integrated in the human personality structure. Individuals are motivated by the lowest or basic or fundamental and unsatisfied needs in the hierarchy. If one level of needs is satisfied, it ceases to motivate behavior. The next level in the hierarchy tends to dominate. The higher the level of a need, the less likely it is used for survival purposes for it will be satisfied and diminish ex-posto facto. Motivation is a construct for understanding and predicting behavior. It is individually or environmentally determined. That is to say that it is both intrinsic and extrinsic. In organizational settings, managers who feel that social needs conflict with organizational needs tend to incorrectly stop the satisfaction of those needs (McGregor, 1960).

Unlike the lower level needs, most esteem needs remain unsatisfied particularly with lower level employees in certain organizational settings. Needs cannot be completely satisfied because those who experience self-actualization in one area exert more pressure for self-actualization in another. Evidently, Maslow's clinical observations from which he drew conclusions may be subject to criticism and challenge by empirical observers and analysts. For instance, needs that are satisfied may not necessarily be extinguished, they may personally be regarded as important and valuable. This implies that people cannot be motivated in the same way because they have individual differences. As a result, managers should be flexible enough to tailor incentives in such a way that they can motivate employees to maximize productively. In addition, most employees are motivated by higher-level needs. Given this reality, job design and placement should be structured to facilitate the satisfaction of these higher-level needs.

EGR Theory

In 1969 and 1972, Alderfer advanced ERG Theory which comprises the existence needs, relatedness needs and growth needs; that is to say ERG. Individuals have these three types of needs. Existence needs are by nature, and to a large extent, materialistic. They consist of "food, water, housing, money, furniture and automobiles. From the Masloic perspective, these needs are physiological and safety concerns. Second, relatedness needs dictate the sharing of one's thoughts, feelings and, sometimes, attitudes. The needs are comparable to the Masloistic school of social and esteem needs. These social and esteem needs are rooted in traditions of meaningful relationships within familial, social and organizational settings.

Third, growth needs are those abilities and capabilities individuals have to cultivate in order to experience Masloic self-actualization. The concreteness of EGR needs lies in a hierarchical continuum. The fundamental teaching in EGR theory is that "the more completely a more concrete need is satisfied, the greater is the desire to satisfy the less concrete needs and ... the less completely a need is satisfied, the greater is the desire to have it satisfied" (Siegel and Lane, 1987, p. 378).

The main difference between Maslow's and Alderfer's approaches is "how an individual is theorized to move from one level of needs to another" (p. 378). In Masloic conception, "an individual moves up the need hierarchy when a lower-level need is satisfied" (p. 378). This process is called 'fulfillment-progression.' Alderfer also argues that when higher level needs are satisfied, the individual regresses and tries to procure more pleasure by operating at the lower level needs. This process is called "frustration-regression" (p. 378) and it operates in a dialectical relationship with the fulfillment-progression. Figure 13.2 graphically illustrates this phenomenon.

From his studies of 800 people, Alderfer's (1969 and 1972) ERG theory confirmed the "predicted positive correlation between satisfaction with growth needs and the perceived importance of these needs in ... fraternity houses (Gortner, et al., 1997, p. 378) but not in "a bank and a manufacturing company" (p. 378). This understanding is essential for managerial employers who deal with employee motivation in unmotivating work situations. Due to the fact that the need concept is tough to empirically operationalize, the ERG theory has recently not attracted much scholarly research in the field.

Herzberg's Two-Factor Theory

The two-factor theory of Frederick Herzberg has considerably expanded Maslow's work on motivation. In this study, respondents were asked to "Think of a time when you felt exceptionally good or exceptionally bad about your job, either your present job or any other job you have had. This can be either the 'long range' or 'short range' kind situations, as I have just described it. Tell me what happened" (Herzberg, Mausner, and Snyderman, 1959, p. 141; and Gortner, Mahler, and Nicholson, 1997, p. 272).

Figure 13.2 Relationship Among Alderfer's ERG Needs, Maslow's Hierarchy of Needs, and Herzberg's Two Factors

Herzberg's Two Factors	Maslow's Hierarchy of Needs	Alderfer's ERG Needs

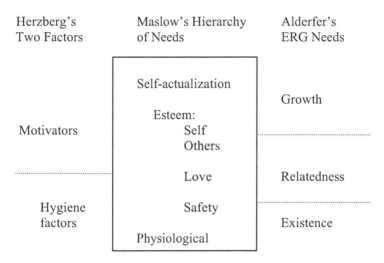

Source: Luthans, F. (1985). *Organizational Behavior, 4th Ed.* New York: McGraw-Hill: 204

Initially, two hundred engineers and accountants in Pennsylvanian firms responded. Later, many interviews involving hundreds of interviewees in a variety of occupational, organizational and cultural millieux were conducted for data analysis and reflection.

The results of the study were Masloically very revealing. The respondents were wholistically consistent when they associated bad feelings with factors influenced by and related to the job environment. These factors included but were not limited to "working conditions, interpersonal relations, supervision, company policy and administration, salary and wages" (p. 272). The source of good feelings was rooted in extra-environmental (inside the job context). Specifically, the good feelings stemmed from "growth, advancement, responsibility, the work itself, recognition and achievement" (p. 272). According to Herzberg, factors intrinsic to work contributed to job satisfaction. These were called motivator factors. The extrinsic factors were called hygiene factors (see Figure 13.3).

Figure 13.3. Herzberg's Two-Factor Theory

Job Environment (Context) Hygiene Factors	Environment Content Motivator Factors
1. Policies and administration	Achievement
2. Supervision	Recognition
3. Working conditions	Challenging work
4. Interpersonal relations	Responsibility
5. Money, status, security	Growth and development

One of the things Herzberg learned is that "job dissatisfaction and the factors that cause it are different from, rather than opposites of, those factors causing satisfaction" (p. 273). Herzberg concluded that "satisfaction and dissatisfaction are separate concepts and do not oppose ends of the same continuum" (p. 273).

The motivator factors are analogous to Masloic higher-level needs which, in the case of Herzberg's motivators, promote worker satisfaction and job performance. On the contrary, hygiene factors are analogous to Maslow's lower-level needs which may contribute to dissatisfaction without, according to Herzberg, bringing or contributing to satisfaction. Though they can symptomatically reduce dissatisfaction in the area of absenteeism and higher turnover, these hygienic influences are not causative agents of productivity. "Where dissatisfaction has been prevented, people work at minimally acceptable levels to avoid job or pay loss; but motivators are needed to boost satisfaction and motivate performance" (p. 273).

Several scholars particularly Herzberg (1966), Bockman (1971) and Grigaliunas and Herzberg (1971) have positively popularized Herzberg's two-factor theory. Others including Vroom (1964) and Schwab, Devitt and Cummings (1971) do not think that Herzberg made any scientific breakthrough. In a sense, Herzberg's contributions motivationally promote Maslow's hierarchy of needs by making the content of needs to be more specific. The fact that managerial leaders have gained insights into Herzberg's ideas has contributed to the creation of flexible work climates in terms of job enrichment, workshop design and participative management. Alternatively, and by motivating individuals to be challenged for effective service, recognition, growth and respectability (Figure 13.2).

McClelland's Social Motives Theory

By criticizing Maslow's concept of self-actualization, McClelland argues that most human needs that are analyzed in Maslow's hierarchy are a product of human socialization rather than biological determinism. If this is true, then various individuals in different cultural settings perceive self-actualization to be differentially constructed to enhance productivity and cohesion and to reduce conflict in order to create a suitable climate for facilitating leader-follower relationships. This study revealed that persons who have high affiliation needs like to interact socially. Because these individuals want to be liked, they tend to be helpful and supportive. Organizationally, they informally promote positive and productive social climates that enhance group and interpersonal relations. Their interaction experience and results indicate that humans are motivated by the need to belong (Baumeister and Leary, 1995). Belongingness promotes group cohesion and norms that control member behavior (Cartwright, 1968) that is effectively fashioned to enhance collective and collaborative activities within the organization (Likert, 1961).

Second, people who have an excellence standard or criteria for rigor that they persistently and consistently pursue, are competently motivated by high-achievement needs. These people are creative and responsible problem solvers. They set challenging goals, like to risk and dislike lengthy and fruitless gambles. These creative risk takers like to see concrete feedback of their activities (McClelland, 1961). These higher-achievement individuals may not be necessarily motivated by managerially established high standards. They are only motivated when their goals are attainable. Lowly set goals do not motivate these people either. Creative and flexible organizational climates tend to enable these people to excel and become productive while managerially uncreative and inflexible organizational climates demotivate them for unproductivity, frustration and resentment.

According to McClelland and Winter (1971), highly bureaucratized organizations discourage the effective functioning of high-achievement behavior while less bureaucratized organizations encourages it. Lonely and high-achievement managers are interpersonally ineffective while interactive and optimistic high-achievement managers who use participative strategies are effective in managing people and raising productivity. However, moderate managerial achievers are concerned with symbols of prestige "while managers with low-achievement motivation are largely interested in safety and security.

Third, people who have a strong influence over others have a need for power (Veroff, 1957). People are motivated by different visions of the need for power acquisition. There are two ways of striving for power. First, people have to compete in terms of a "zero-sum game" (Gortner, et al., 1997, p. 276) where one person wins and another loses. This is "personalized power" (p. 276). Second, socialized power is exercised by an individual for the common good of the community or group or nation (McClelland, 1970). According to McClelland, personalized power makes the leader to "overwhelm others, to compel their submission through dominance. This behavior may evoke follower obedience, but their passivity or conversely, desire to resist may be the price" (Gortner, et al., 1997, p. 276). Personalized power is effective in small rather than large organizations and groups where socialized elements of motivation are imperative.

Leaders who exemplify socialized power needs do not force others to submit. They are interested in group goals and the promotion of them. Socialized power agents inspire confidence in their followers. The followers are empowered to excel. In the United States, most leaders practice dominance, manipulation, and authoritarianism (McClelland, 1970).

It is normally natural to think about motivation in terms of theoretical models. What motivates humans? Motivational forces are as many as there are intrinsic and extrinsic drives. The Greek philosophers believed that since humans are hedonistic in character, they seek pleasure in order to avoid pain, deprivation and loss. These classical assumptions are repeated in modern and contemporary social and economic theories of John Locke, Jeremy Bentham, John Stuart Mill and Adam Smith (Gortner, et al., 1997).

At a later time, the ideas of motivation were conceived to be instinctual. As it was introduced, and Freud and other pessimistic psychologists proposed that unconscious desires are what motivate behavior. The modern study of work motivation is widely agreed to have begun with need or content theories. After Bentham grew benthamism, the utilitarian philosophy which holds that pleasure is the chief end of life and that the greatest happiness for the greatest number should be the ultimate goal of people.

Content theory is based on individual needs, but its development has been marked by greater inclusion of situational variables and their applicability to work organizations. The content approach has branched out considerably from Maslow's hierarchy of needs. The movement of content theory is toward a larger conceptual scope and greater usefulness for managers. A major contribution of the content approach is that its explicit treatment of needs serves to bridge the gap between individual needs and organizationally based incentives. Efforts to discover the links between individual satisfaction and productivity and even organizational effectiveness also add to the development of work motivation theory and its organizational application.

Effectively, linking incentives to motivation requires an understanding of worker needs and goals. Moreover, the organization must have access to appropriate resources and managers need to have sufficient discretion or authority to make appropriate changes in reward systems – conditions that are more likely to be unmet in public rather than private organizations.

Government bureaus which do not make profits, in all likelihood, do not compare favorably with private firms in tangible rewards such as salaries, bonuses, advancement, and promotion. Moreover, tangible rewards are dispensed on a system basis—that is, for being a member or employee and having seniority—rather than for an individual's above average work performance. Promotion opportunities are often limited both by freezes on hiring and advancement, and by time-in-grade rules and policies.

Since tangible rewards in bureaus are in short supply and management control over them is limited, it is common practice to substitute intrinsic and recognition-type rewards such as honor boards, office or employee-of-the-month awards, and the like. Other opportunities for intrinsic and self-actualizing rewards are more promising. For example, members of bureaus like the Environmental Protection Agency can see themselves as part of a movement for a cleaner and more beautiful environment. Internalized goals of community service can be rewarding to bureau members, especially at the local level where community needs and results are more proximate and visible.

Content theory has normative significance as well. Implicit in this perspective is that organizations do not have to be hateful, punitive places to be productive. A worker's motivation cannot be reduced to money as the sole motivator coupled with an inherent dislike for work. Potentially and empirically, the substance of worker motivation encompasses a far greater range of needs and incentives that are more socially and organizationally constructive. Content theory adds a scientific basis to the belief that work organizations can be invested with humanistic values. Humanistic values place emphasis on the wholistic awareness of the workers' needs and their potential for self-actualization.

Cognitive Process Theories of Work Motivation

Cognitive process models and operant conditioning dominate motivation theory and research. They concentrate on identifying the factors, especially cognitive variables, that compose the motivation process and, on determining how and why these factors result in motivation. Their complexity results not merely from the inclusion of actions among variables. It is this ideal of process in formulating models that represents a significant advance in work motivation theory. The basic assumption of process theory is that internal cognitive states and situational variables interact in the motivational process. The individual is an active factor, selecting behaviors based on his or her needs and based on expectations about what kind of behavior will lead to a desired reward. This perspective has greatly expanded our understanding of human motivation and its complexities. Process theories provide a good conceptual grasp of how elements of internal states and behavior are related. They offer diagnostic and operational alternatives that can be applied to motivation, but they are difficult for managers to apply on a daily basis.

Part of the difficulty is that process theories are far more abstract than content models. This makes it difficult to identify specific and appropriate incentives. Further, process models do not only deal with differences in individual needs, but with differences among individuals' perceptions of important elements of the situation, such as rewards, opportunity, equity, and control over outcomes. Linking the effect of specific rewards to an individual's work motivation (or satisfaction or performance) is exceedingly difficult when the effect of actual rewards is mediated by a number of subtle and internal processes of perception and expectancy. It is impractical and time consuming for managers to attempt such an assessment of employees and organizational incentives on a one by one basis.

For government agencies, the application of process models is difficult in other ways as well. For example, Chester Newland (1984) identified several problems with the politically popular merit system. Newland (1984, p. 39) pointed out that "Unless performance can be appraised well, it is impossible to relate pay to it." In addition, he notes that using pay to motivate performance is probably not an effective technique unless relatively large pay increases are available. Newland also cautions in a statement prescient of later developments in total quality management and other participative methods, that individual rewards such as merit pay that focus on individually competitive behaviors "may frustrate modular and team management approaches" (p. 39).

The two problem-rewards (their adequacy and appropriateness) and performance (its definition and appraisal)—are crucial to forging the principal link in process models: High performance results in desired and equitable rewards. The utility of rewards in bureaus is limited by constraints already discussed. Defining performance targets or goals and appraising performance are equally challenging. The link between effort and performance is stronger when performance standards or goals are clear and relatively specific and comprehensive rather than general.

Performance targets and their measurement are an increasing part of programs such as the National Performance Review (1993) where total organizations are being rewarded for the "use of such tools is given mixed reviews when dealing with individuals" (Deming, 1986, p. 110). In spite of debate by scholars, the use of techniques such as MBO, employee appraisal processes, and work standards seems to be increasing in government. In such cases, there is a danger that workload rather than efficiency or effectiveness criteria may be used because of the difficulty in setting specific organization goals and breaking these into objective specific performance measures for individuals (Greiner, et al., 1981). Compared to the more specific and tangible goals of firms, bureaus pursue goals that are diffuse and conflicting because their performance criteria are less clearly defined. The link between effort and performance, and thus the expectation that given performances will produce specific rewards, is weakened by the lack of goal clarity as well as by conflicting demands. Thus the cognitive process models assume a flexibility and control over rewards. This is somewhat unrealistic when applied to public managers. The next approach, behaviorism and operant conditioning, offers an alternative perspective on directly linking individual behavior and organizational incentives or rewards (Katz and Kahn, 1982).

The term cognition comes from the Latin name *cognicioun* or *cognito* which means mental faculty or process by which knowledge is acquired through perception, reasoning, thinking, memory, and intuition (Posner, 1989, and Siegel and Lane, 1987). This mental faculty is intellectual awareness associated with ability to learn and apply what has been learnt. Unlike content theories which are rooted in humanistic Masloism, cognitive process theories dominate current theorizing about work motivation. The three cognitive theories which place emphasis on the underpinning decision making processes are expectancy theory, equity theory and goal theory (Siegel and Lane, 1987). These cognitive theories are also influenced by operant conditioning, information processing, situation and job environment (Gortner, et al., 1997).

Expectancy Theory

The major authorities in expectancy theory are Georgopolous, Mahoney, and Jones (9157), Graen (1969), Porter and Lawler (1968), and Vroom (1964). A variety of expectancy theories are essentially cognitive and hedonistic. Persons are seen as "rational calculating, and thoughtful entities who decide on which course of action to pursue and how much effort to expend. Peoples' decisions ... based on their expectancies about the relative degree of pleasure and discomfort resulting from alternative courses of action" (Siegel and Lane, 1987, p. 390). These theories conclude that individuals "will select the course of action that they feel will maximize pleasure and minimize discomfort" (p. 390). A major characteristic inherent in expectancy theories emphasizes that "the selection of a course of action reflects the anticipated consequences of that action" (p. 390).

Lawler's model has been used for its simplistic sophistication and illustrative essence in contemporary theorizing. The model has four basic assumptions that are rationally and scientifically valid. The assumptions state that

1. People have preferences among the various outcomes that are potentially available to them. In other words, each alternative outcome has a valence (V), which refers to its attractiveness to the individual.
2. People have expectancies about the likelihood that their efforts (E) will lead to the intended behavioral performance (P). this is referred to as the E ⟶ P expectancy.
3. People have expectancies about the likelihood that certain outcomes (O) will follow their performance (P). This is referred to as the P ⟶ O expectancy and will also be described in greater detail.
4. In any situation, the actions and efforts associated with them that a person chooses to take are determined by the

expectancies (E ⟶ P, and P ⟶ O) and are the preferences that a person has at that time (Siegel and Lane, 1987, pp. 390-391).

For illustrative purposes, Figure 13.4 and Figure 13.5 are Lawler's and Porter-Lawler examples of what factors motivate employees to exert their efforts and perform in order to experience intrinsic and extrinsic rewards which bring satisfaction. Rewards, motivation and satisfaction are dependent on performance. When organizations provide automatic pay raises and especially if they are across-the-board for each person in a variety of job categories, the link between performance and rewards is weakened "because the rewards are not contingent on individual performance" (Gortner, et al., 1997, p. 284). It is weakened because it does not become a motivator for high or greater performance.

Figure 13.4. Lawler's Expectancies Refinement

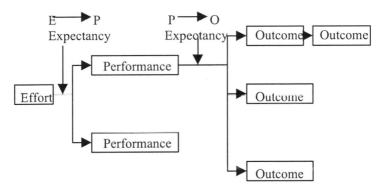

Source: Gortner, H.F, J. Mahler, and J.B. Nicholson. (1997). *Organization Theory: A Public Perspective.* Fort Worth: Harcourt Brace College Publishers: 283

Figure 13.5. Porter-Lawler Motivation Model

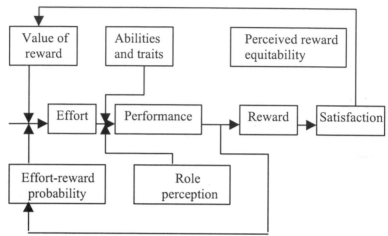

Source: Gortner, H.F, J. Mahler, and J.B. Nicholson. (1997). *Organization Theory: A Public Perspective.* Fort Worth: Harcourt Brace College Publishers: 283

Rewards are intrinsic when they positively generate internal states and feelings that become the base for radiant performance and behavior. Such performance and behavior are empirically demonstrable and scientifically observable because employees use their capacity in a crafty and professional way to complete challenging and intrinsically rewarding tasks. For instance, job enrichment can technically become the genesis for intrinsic rewards of which satisfaction is a classic internal norm. Alternatively, extrinsic rewards are influenced by external forces of which money, promotion become the essence of work motivation. On the other hand, in the case of scholars, writing a book for publication may be viewed as both intrinsic and extrinsic forms of motivation because the former concerns their contribution to the advancement of knowledge in a given field while the latter may concern the possible amount of money the book will generate from the sales. In public agencies, there are many constraints put on monetary incentives. These include but are not limited to "legal and statutory prohibitions; civil service restrictions and uniformity requirements;

unavailability of funds; public opposition; and legislative reluctance to surrender control of wage increases and give supervisors and managers wide discretion" (p. 284).

Given the nature of the rewards, satisfaction or dissatisfaction takes place when rewards are perceived to be equitable or inadequate or inappropriate respectively. In essence, the import of Porter-Lawler theory rests on the understanding that performance causes satisfaction and satisfaction depends on it. This model is heuristically more functionalistic than the simpler content theories. It shows that workers, employees and in some cases managers, are "active participants in the motivation process; they make decisions about their behavior on the basis of their expectancies about outcomes, and they choose those behaviors that they perceive they can perform" (p. 285). This theory has generated a lot of scholarly work that is empirical in character. Though expectancy theory was initially popular with industrial organization psychologists, other social scientists have started to use it in a variety of organizational and institutional settings.

Equity Theory

The theoretical model of equity is cognitive and it evolved at the time expectancy models came into existence. Motivationally speaking, equity theory is rooted in "cognitive dissonance and exchange theories" (Gortner, ct al., 1997, p. 285). According to Stacy Adams (1975), "inequity exists for Person whenever he perceives that the ratio of his outcomes to inputs and the ratio of Other's outcomes to input are unequal" (p. 141). Parenthetically, equity exists if the ratios of outcomes to inputs are perceived to be equal. To formularize this perceptual situation, the following formula has been offered for clarification:

$$\frac{\text{Person's outcomes}}{\text{Person's inputs}} = \frac{\text{Other's outcomes}}{\text{Other's inputs}}$$

The terms person and other apply to any person who views his or her role to be "in exchange relationship with some other individual or group, and to other individuals or groups with whom the individual feels that equity comparisons are relevant" (p. 285). If individuals perceive an element of inequity in their dealings with an organization, they get motivated to seek or articulate equity issues. To seek equity, people can change their outputs, increase or decrease "the quantity or quality of their work, or change their outcomes" (p. 285). Sometimes when people ask for a raise and they receive it, or when noticeably try to make their contributions to be viewed from a higher profile, this may "change outcomes without increasing input" (p. 285). Some people can "increase input by turning out high-volume but low-quality products" (Gortner, et al., 1997, p. 285 and Goodman and Friedman, 1971).

Attribution (Locus of Control Theory)

The theory of attribution deals with cause and effect perceptions of behavior. Based on attribution theory, "human behavior is shaped by the perceptions or attributions of causality that an individual ascribes to" (p. 286) causative agencies in his or her environment (Kelley, 1972). These causative agencies (attributes) are internal (e.g., competence or effort) or external (e.g., policies, procedures, expectations, rules, and leader-attitudes). If individuals feel that the outcomes of their work are internally controlled, they attribute that to personal skill, competence or effort. If they feel that the outcomes are externally controlled, they have no influence over them. In other words, the locus of control is based on perceptions rather than the real causes which determine human behavior and performance. If perceptions rather than actual reality influence behavior and performance, then the causes of behavior and performance are humanistically elusive. This elusiveness should be the subject of further scholarly inquiry.

Evidence has demonstrated that attribution and locus of control theory tend to influence worker satisfaction and styles of management. Individuals who are internally controlled experience job satisfaction more than those who are externally controlled did. These two categories of employees respond differently to different leadership styles. The internally controlled persons are satisfied when the participative leadership style is employed (Mitchell, Smyser, and Weed, 1975).

When poor performance is attributed to internal (insufficient ability less effort or lack of enough attentiveness) factors, leadership tends to respond punitively. However, if poor performance is attributed to external forces which the employee or worker has no control over, leadership responds sympathetically (Mitchell and Wood, 1979; and Green and Mitchell, 1979).

Though externally controlling forces may be used to blame or criticize bureaus for failure, incompetence, red-tape rigidity and waste (McKenna, 1994) some of these problems happen because externally (Congressionally) influenced factors such as "conflicting goals, inadequate resources, insufficient time for results," and "reliance on system rather than on individual rewards" (Gortner, et al., 1997, pp. 286 and 287) can be attributed to be the real courses.

Behavior and Work Motivation

Behaviorist theory of work motivation explores a broad range of inner psychological states such as needs, expectancies and perceptions that are unobservable and irrelevant to the behaviorist scientific enterprise. However, this section provides a historical perspective of some of the key theorists who have contributed to the behaviorist movement. It also discusses some general applications of behaviorist theories to educational and work motivation settings.

Assumptions

Before behaviorism became a prominent psychological theory at the end of the last century, the two dominant psychological schools of thought were *structuralism* (started by Wundt) and *functionalism* (which was started by William James and advanced by Dewey). Although the two schools differed in many ways, structuralist and functionalist commonalities were based on their lack of research methodology needed to advance them scientifically. As a result, they, especially the structuralists, started to rely on *introspection* (method of collecting data through feelings and thoughts). Introspection was "prescientific" foundation for cognitive theories of learning and motivation. However, with the development of Pavlovian theoretical classical conditioning theory, and Thorndike's observational objectivity, behaviorism as a theory was further advanced as a public, objective, and a deductively observational research theory. With the emergence of methodologies that emphasized stimuli and responses in learning, the behaviorist school was born. The common basic assumptions behaviorists share are equipotentiality, tabula rasa, observation.

1. *Equipotentiality:*- principles of learning apply equally to different behaviors and to different species of animals, including human beings. Behaviorists use the term organism to refer to both animals and humans.

    Because of equipotentiality of organisms a cross species, principles of learning developed from research with one (animal) species should apply to other species within the animal kingdom as well.

2. Organisms are born with "blank slates" (tabula rasa). Apart from certain species which use specific instincts, people and animals are not born predisposed to particular behaviors. They learn about these behaviors.
3. The study of learning is a scientifically measurable and observable phenomenon comparable to the physical sciences. The criteria of measurement are based on S-R (stimuli-response) theory.

   Most behaviorists believe that internal processes (thoughts, motives, and linotions, etc) cannot be directly observed or measured, and therefore should not be considered in the scientific study of learning.
4. Principles of learning are based on the relationship between stimuli and response—behaviorism (S-R psychology).
5. Behaviorists use the name conditioning to mean learning (past or present).
6. When change in relatively permanent behavior is involved and learning is said to have occurred, simple and complex learning behaviors should be explained by very few and concise principles.

The behaviorist scientific tradition is not interested in whether or not a person experiences motivation; instead, behaviorists are interested in publicly observable and measurable behavior and its consequences. Though behaviorist theories are not strictly motivational and comparable in character, their operant and expectancy elements (noncognitive vs cognitive) unite them in three major aspects. First, rewards may be closely related to behavior. Second, for motivation to be consequential or inconsequential, rewards must be administered frequently and consistently. This means that behavior is based on cause and effect phenomena. Since it is caused by contingent consequences, the consequences are contingent upon the occurrence of specific behavior (Gortner, et al., 1997). Third, evidence has shown that individuals are motivated by past or future outcomes (Mitchell, 1982). In spite of theoretical differences of the terms in question, they have similarities in terms of how their policy applications in organizational settings are rationalized.

Environmental behavior is called operant conditioning because it is learned within a specific environment which has mechanisms to reinforce the display of behavior (Skinner, 1976). The four types of consequences which determine operant conditioning are "positive reinforcement...negative reinforcement...extinction, and ... punishment" (Gortner, et al., 1997, p. 288). Observable effects are used to functionally define reinforcers. A reinforcer strengthens by increasing specific behavior while reward is that which is perceived to be desirable. Reinforcement is influenced by external, observable and objective factors while reward is influenced by internal and subjective experience. This distinction is behaviorally essential for clarifying the theory of operant conditioning.

If reinforcement is positive, it enhances satisfying consequences which are essential for work motivation which iteratively subsequently and participatively leads to higher productivity in organizational settings. Alternatively, negative reinforcement produces unsatisfying or noxious consequences. However, both forms of reinforcement tend to strengthen or increase a given behavior. Any behavior that is not reinforced either negatively or positively is weakened for extinction. "The effects of extinction and punishment on behavior are dialectically opposed to reinforcers because they weaken or decrease a given behavior. Humans are easily discouraged by unrewarding behavior while the opposite is also true.

Punishment, is a form of negative reinforcement that is aversive in stimuli. The effects of punishment weakens and extinguishes given behaviors. Punishment breeds defects and negative side effects because it tends to suppress undesirable behavior being solvent or without eliminating it. "When the aversive agent is removed or discontinued, the behavior recurs" (p. 289). Managers who use punishment and negative reinforcement instead of reward or positive reinforcement (e.g., praise or participative involvement) fail to motivate employees. Similarly, teachers and professors who do not frequently and consistently reward or reinforce student performance because they are pessimistic facilitators of learning teach their learners how to be demotivated and fail.

Although Pavlov and Thorndike are among the earliest contributors to the behaviorist movement, John Watson (1913) coined the term behaviorism by popularizing it at the beginning of the 20th century. By using Pavlovian classical conditioning of S-R theory, the stimulus-response phenomenon became the basic unit of learning and behavior modification. According to Watson, past experience and environmental effects rather than genetic heredity are accountable for a variety aspects of human ability and behavior.

Theory of Motivation in Bureaus and Organizations

Bureaus are government agencies which differ in certain constraints, values and motivation structure. Though the merit system enforces bureaucratic competence, equal pay for equal work, etc., (overseers

Congressional committees and executive requirements) can externally manipulate them. As a result, in spite of "sticking" to job descriptions, external manipulation may influence them to become overspecialized and have narrow rather than broad job descriptions. In addition, it is difficult to implement job enrichment due to human incapacity and violation of professional ethics. In the U.S., Federal jobs have been reduced to 16 categories each of which has a salary attachment. System rewards and retirement are based on seniority and/or membership. Retrenchment demoralizes individuals (Perry and Porter, 1982).

Committed bureaucrats perform at a higher level and accept organizational goals and values. Those who have been successful through organizational commitment perceive that they have contributed significant impact (Buchanan, 1974). Comparatively, individuals need satisfaction and commitment to organizational goals which are higher in the private rather than public sector (Rainey, 1979). In addition, "job content and job challenge satisfy needs of public employees" (Gortner, et al., 1997, p. 293). "Job content satisfaction was indicated by 84% of managers and 64% of nonmanagers; job challenge satisfaction was indicated by 86% of managers and 77% of nonmanagers" (p. 293). If the mission of the agency is clear, distinctive and exciting, it contributes to a higher degree of employee commitment.

As far as bureaus are concerned, motivation and behavior are influence by the public nature of the organization. Alternatively, bureaucrats motivationally and behavioristically influence public organizations. Anthony Downs has constructed a motivational typology of bureaus which shows that bureaucratic context is an integral part of the symbiotic "interplay between individual motivation and policy preferences" (Gortner, et al, 1997, p. 293). Downs' typology is grounded in observationally realistic and individual personality types that are rational, their behavior is goal directed. The same people are motivationally self-interested to the extent of pursuing personal interests. Although these bureaucratic officials consider other people's interests, the officials have a variety of altruistic goals some of which are reflective of their clients' interests too. Other bureaucratic goals may be both a product of the bureaucrats' self-interest or altruism.

Downs (1967) argues further that the five types of bureaucratic officials that reflect the "ideal types" Weber's notion include climbers, conservers, zealots, advocates and statesmen. Although these officials are not behaviorally and motivationally influenced by similar motives in similar ways, a variant mixture of motives motivates each individual bureaucratic official.

Downs says that all bureau officials have multiple goals that derive from a set of general motives: power, money, income, prestige, convenience, and security. Pride in work proficiency, personal loyalty" (to the team, bureau, or state) "desire to serve the public interest, and commitment to a specific program of action are also sources of motivation (Downs, 1994, pp. 60 – 84).

Comparing to content models, Downs' theory of behavior is a product of human needs, goals and motivations. Both motivational and behavioral phenomena are deterministic elements of environmental forces (variables and expectancies). In addition, the characteristics of the bureaus and the officials who occupy specific ranks in them tend to influence behavior and the mission of the organization in specific ways.

Climbers tend to strike in order to attain power, income and prestige in the bureau. Their greatest rewards are promotion which they tend to use to control others for self-aggrandizement. They can use subordinates as pawns for their own advantage. They are receptive to change because they can manipulate their rise to power within or without the organization. Unlike climbers who seek power and influence, conservers are motivated to maximize their security and convenience. Since they avoid taking risks, they resist change in order to protect the status quo. "Only changes that head off threats to their security or that make their lives easier because less effort will be required of them, are welcomed by conservers" (Gortner, et al, 1997, p. 296). They use minimal and acceptable performance standards and tend to evade actions and practices that invite risk and potential failure. Organizational climate in terms of rules, procedures, red tape and personal practices reinforce their security. Aspects of neutrality and status-quo related accountability legitimize their behavior. Such behavior is a product of organizational expectancies. Public organizations which have wise, older, slow-paced and rigid practices have more conservers. All public organizations have the tendency to become "conservative" in the long run (Downs, 1967). In terms of attribution and locus of control, and in respect to opportunity structure, climbers are externally rather than internally controlled (rewardwise) while conservers are internally rather than externally controlled. Most conservers are found in the middle level rather than at the top or lower levels of the organizations.

Like advocates and statesmen, zealots are motivated by higher level needs rather than self-interest (Maslow, 1969; Herzberg, 1966; and Katz and Kahn, 1982). Zealots narrowly conceptualize goals and public interest of the organization from which they draw "sacred or special policy" (Gortner, et al., 1997, p. 297). Zealots use a lot of energy and pressure to break through inertia and bring about change. Although zealots are vigorous and catalytic innovators of change, their efforts generate a lot of conflict and resentment due to the fact that their policies attack the status quo. Though their attack is directed at conservers, it is paradoxical that the latter, rather than the former, are the ones who cause effective change particularly in organizations dominated by climbers and advocates. Most of the time, zealots are found at the top of the agencies.

Unlike the selfish climbers, "static" conservers and narrow-minded zealots, advocates are motivated to advance the best interests of the office(s) they hold. They focus on the overall variety of conditions in the organization rather than on just a few of them. Internally, they are impartial organizational "judges." Externally, "advocates create conflict because they are aggressively competitive. Such behavior helps to solidify internal groups because their morale is heightened. Organizational members are loyal to the advocates because they articulate their interests. They persistently support the policies that matter. As a result, and unlike climbers, advocates' aggressiveness and persistence significantly contributes to the evolution of "bureaucratic imperialism" (p. 299). They believe in organizational innovation, expansion and strategic adaptation. In addition, they use processes rather than structures for channeling critical and specialized information that is essential for effective organizational performance.

Statesmen are broadminded in terms of their loyalty to the public interest. This interest is philosophically and rhetorically rooted in their focus on social and national or international issues. However, given the external and internal structures which determine the bureau's contextual behavior, consistent statesmanlike behavior is open to a variety of challenges and constraints. "Statesmen or stateswomen" become captives of hostile forces in their organizations, are rarely promoted although they tend to hold lower rather than higher positions in the structural hierarchy of the organizations. However, their "statesmanship" is an operational rather than tactical or strategic posture.

Based on Blau's and Scott's (1962) conclusions, there are only four types of organizations. These organizations include "mutual-benefit associations—where the primary beneficiary is the membership; ... business concerns—where the owners are prime beneficiaries; ... service organizations—where the client group is the prime beneficiary; and ... commonwealth organizations—where the primary beneficiary is the public at large" (Gortner, et al., 1997, pp. 293-294). Within this framework, nonprofit organizations are treated as service organizations while bureaus are regarded as an element of commonwealth organizations. In all these organizations, the keys that motivate people to succeed are rooted in clear goals, a reward system that encourages commitment and effort, and devotion to serving clients in the name of public interest (Blau and Scott, 1962).

Conclusion

Motivation is a need-driven natural force that is internally and externally controlled by factors of human socialization and personality structure. The three major perspectives through which motivation is defined and rationalized are the content theories, the cognitive orientation and behaviorism. Motivationally, whenever certain needs are satisfied, the person is no longer motivated to pursue original goals.

Content theoretical blueprints are centered on specific factors in a person which drive, sustain or stop behavior. The content theories show how specific needs motivate people to act, perform and self-actualize. Of the most classic content models available, Maslow's Alderfer's, McClelland's, and Herzberg's theories have striking and derivative similarities and obvious differences. Maslow believes that five types of basic needs all humans have are physiological, security, affiliation, esteem and self-actualization. Like Maslow, Alderfer agrees that needs motivate people but the latter differ by saying that these needs are existence, relatedness and growth. Also, with the exception of relatedness needs, a person's growth needs are naturally unsatisfiable. Unlike Maslow and Alderfer, McClelland assumes that people have three learned needs (achievement, affiliation and power) which are rooted and inherited from their social culture. Unlike the three previously discussed "humanistic psychologists," Herzberg and others argue that two complex factors (motivators and hygiene) influence a person's motivation. Motivators, e.g., job challenge may result in job satisfaction rather than job dissatisfaction. Alternatively, hygiene factors such as job or work conditions can prevent job dissatisfaction and have no influence on job satisfaction.

Though individual needs and situational variables account for the various ways in which content theories are applied, one of the major contributions of content theories has been their use in the explicit treatment of needs which serves as a base for meeting individual needs and organizationally-based and goal-directed incentives.

Cognitively, internal and cognitive situations and external variables interact in the motivation process. As active and motivationally participative agents, the individuals select behaviors that are based on their needs, desires and expectations for which reward is expected. The process is called expectancy because individuals know what they want from work. They choose or select activities after they have decided that they will satisfy their needs. The "primary components of this model are first- and second-level outcomes, expectancy, instrumentality, and valance" (Hellriegel, Slocum, and Woodman, 1998, p. 65). The individual believes that effort used leads to expectancy of the desired level of performance. This level of performance is instrumental (leads to desired rewards). Otherwise, unless the individual expects rewards that accrue with increased performance (qualitywise), individuals will not be motivated to use effort that is essential for necessary productivity. It is ironic that inequity rather than equity motivates individuals to perform based on specific rewards and incentives.

Behavioristically, organizational members and managers frequently use operant conditioning without formal theoretical and practical training in the behavioral movement. Though the results may be favorable, inappropriate behavior may be reinforced (Nord, 1970). Obviously, the reinforcement of such dysfunctional behavior particularly in public agencies that are expected to be models for emulation could create lasting and negative implications for both individuals and the bureaus at large. Given the fact that these bureaus are externally controlled by legislation, executive and judicial authority, their public image is likely to suffer if implemented inappropriate and operant behaviors are publicized, professionalized or used to determine or influence organizational performance. For instance, bureaus are not expected to "save" or keep surplus funds that accrue from the previous year's authorizations and appropriations. Since "saving and keeping" the surplus will be an illegal affair, returning the funds to the public or general treasury is the legal and legitimate thing. In addition, hurried expenditures and unnecessarily approved funds for equipment, services or travel are not desirable actions worth of bureaucratic practice that is dominated by external "supervisors." However, if the bureaus spend "leftovers," they reinforce the obviously undesirable and publicly questionable behaviors. Regardless of the rationality for bureaucratic malaise, the triangular theoretical origin of issues resonate with interesting complexity and challenge for work motivation.

References

Adams, J.S. 1975. Inequity in social exchange. In *Motivation and Work Behavior,* eds. R.M. Steers and L.W. Porter, 138-154. New York: McGraw-Hill.

Alderfer, C.P. 1972. *Existence, relatedness, and growth: Human needs in organizational settings.* New York: Free Press.

Alderfer, C.P. 1969. An empirical test of a new theory of human needs. *Organizational Behavior and Human Performance* 4: 142-175.

Baumeister, R.F., and M.R. Leary. 1995. The need to belong: Desire for interpersonal attachments as a fundamental human motivation. *Psychological Bulletin* 117, 3: 497-529.

Berelson, B., and G.A. Steiner. 1964. *Human Behavior: An Inventory of Scientific Findings.* New York: Harcourt Brace Jovanovich.

Blau, P.M. and W.R. Scott. 1962. *Formal Organizations: A Comparative Approach.* San Francisco: Chandler.

Bransford, J., et al. 1986. Teaching thinking and problem solving: Research foundations. *American Psychologist* 41, 10: 1078-1089.

Buchanan, II, B. 1974. Government managers, business executives and organizational commitment. *Public Administration Review* 34, 4: 339-347.

Cartwright, D. 1968. The nature of group cohesiveness. In *Group Dynamics: Research and Theory,* eds. D. Cartwright and A. Zander, 91-109. New York: Harper and Row.

Deming, W.E. 1986. *Out of Crisis.* Cambridge, MA: MIT Center for Advanced Engineering Study.

Downs, A. 1994. *Inside Bureaucracy.* Prospect Heights III: Waveland Press.

Fromm, E. 1941. *Escape from Freedom.* New York: Avon Books.

Georgopolous, B.S., G.M. Mahoney, and N.W. Jones. 1957. A path-goal approach to productivity. *Journal of Applied Psychology* 41: 345-353.

Goodman, P.S. and A. Friedman. 1971. An examination of Adam's theory of inequity. *Administrative Science Quarterly,* 16, 3: 271-288.

Gortner, H.F, J. Mahler, and J.B. Nicholson. 1997. *Organization Theory: A Public Perspective.* Fort Worth: Harcourt Brace College Publishers.

Graen, G. 1969. Instrumentality theory of work motivation: Some experimental results and suggested modifications. *Journal of Applied Psychology Monograph* 53: 1-25.

Green, S.G., and T.R. Mitchell. 1979. Attributional processes of leaders in leader-member interactions. *Organizational Behavior and Human Performance* 23: 429-458.

Greiner, J.M., and R.E. Wood. 1979. An empirical test of attributional model of leaders' responses to poor performance. In *Academy of Management Proceeding,* ed. R.C. Huseman.

Greiner, J.M., H.P. Hatry, M.P. Koss, A.P. Miller, and J.P. Woodward. 1981. *Productivity and Motivation: A Review of State and Local Government Initiatives.* Washington, D.C.: The Urban Institute Press.

Grigaliunas, B.S., and F. Herzberg. 1971. Relevancy in the test of motivation-hygiene theory. *Journal of Applied Psychology,* 55, 1: 73-79.

Hellriegel, D., J.W. Slocum, Jr., and R.W. Woodman. 1998. *Organizational Behavior.* Cincinnati, OH: South-Western College Publishing.

Hersey, P., and K.H. Blanchard. 1993. *Management of the Organizational Behavior: Utilizing Human Resources.* Englewood Cliffs, N.J.: Prentice-Hall.

Herzberg, F. 1966. *Work and the Nature of Man.* Cleveland: World Press.

Herzberg, F., B. Mausner, and B. Snyderman. 1959. *The Motivation to Work.* New York: Wiley.

Holden, Jr. M. 1966. Imperialism in bureaucracy. *The American Political Science Review* 60: 943-951.

Katz, D. and R.L. Kahn. 1982. *The Social Psychology of Organizations.* New York: John Wiley and Sons.

Kelley, H.H. 1972. Attribution in social interaction. In *Attribution: Perceiving Causes of Behavior,* eds. E.E. Jones, et al., 1-26. Morristown, N.J.: General Learning Press.

Kolberg, L. 1980. *Moral Development, Moral Education and Kolberg: Basic Issues in Philosophy, Religion, and Education.* Birmingham, AL: Religious Education Press.

Lawler, III, E.E. 1994. *Motivation in Work Organizations.* San Francisco: Jossey-Bass.

Likert, R. 1961. *New Patterns of Management.* New York: McGraw-Hill.

Luthans, F. 1985. *Organizational Behavior.* 4th ed. New York: McGraw-Hill.

Maslow, A. H. 1969. Some educational implications of the humanistic psychologies. *Harvard Educational Review* 38, 4.

Maslow, A.H. 1966. *The Psychology of Science.* New York: Harper and Row.

Maslow, A.H. 1959. Psychological data and value theory. In *New Knowledge in Human Values.* New York: Harper.

Maslow, A.H. 1957. A philosophy of psychology. In *Personal Problems and Psychological Frontiers,* ed. J. Fairchild. Chicago: Sheridan.

Maslow, A. H. 1954. *Motivation and Personality.* New York: Harper and Row.

McClelland, D.C. 1970. The two faces of power. *Journal of International Affair,* 24, 1: 29-47.

McClelland, D.C. 1961. *The Achieving Society.* Princeton, N.J.: Van Nostrand Reinhold.

McClelland, D.C., and D.G. Winter. 1971. *Motivating Economic Achievement.* New York: Free Press.

McGregor, D. 1960. *The Human Side of Enterprise.* New York: McGraw-Hill.

McKenna, G. 1994. *The Drama of Democracy: American Government and Politics.* Guilford: The Dushkin Publishing Group, Inc.

Mitchell, T.R. 1982. Motivation. New directions for theory. *Academy of Management Review* 7, 1: 80-81.

Mitchell, T.R., and R.E. Wood. 1979. An empirical test of an attributional model of leader's responses to poor performance. *Academy of Management Proceeding:* 94-98.

Mitchell, T.R., C.M. Smyser, and S.E. Weed. 1975. Locus control: Supervision and work satisfaction. *Academy of Management Journal* 18, 3: 623-631.

National Performance Review (U.S.). 1993. *From Red-Tape to Results: Creating a Government that Works Better and Costs Less: Report of the National Performance Review.* New York: Times Books.

Newland, C. 1984. Crucial issues for public personnel. *Public Personnel Management* 13, 1: 15-46.

Nord, W.R. 1970. Improving attendance through rewards. *Personnel Administration,* 33: 37-41.

Perry, J., and L.W. Porter. 1982. Factors affecting the context for motivation in public organizations. *Academy of Management Review* 7, 1: 89-98.

Porter, L.W., and E.E. Lawler. 1968. *Managerial Attitudes and Performance.* Homewood, IL: Richard D. Irwin.

Posner, M.I. 1989. *Foundations of Cognitive Science.* Cambridge, MA: The MIT Press.

Skinner, B.F. 1976. *About behaviorism.* New York: Vintage Books.

Skinner, B.F. 1971. *Beyond Freedom and Dignity.* New York: Alfred A. Knopf.

Skinner, B.F. 1953. *Science and Human Behavior.* New York: The Macmillan Co.

Skinner, B.F. 1948. *Walden Two.* New York: The Macmillan Co.

Veroff, J. 1957. Development and Validation of a Projective Measure of Power Motivation. *Journal of Abnormal and Social Psychology* 54, 1: 1-8.

Vroom, V.H. 1964. *Work and Motivation.* New York: John Wiley and Sons.

Zemke, R. 1979. What Are High-Achieving Managers Really Like? *Training: The Magazine of Human Resource Development*: 35-36.

Chapter 14

Organizational Control: The Bureaucracy

This chapter is a synoptic analysis of organizational control which is a system of checks and balances used to ensure operational efficiency and empirical accountability. The theory of control, control systems and organizationally controlled models are exposed in a sea of controversies that are the dynamics that propel bureaucratic rationality and its mechanomorphic essence. Specifically, this chapter deals with the interdependent nature of bureaucratic control. The organization's intelligence system of control, and communication and decision making. The control system depends on the communication structure for the gathering and processing of information. This means that the problems in one part of the system affect the other parts. Various forms of control that use quantitative, behavioral, and socio-psychological approaches are discussed. Etzioni (1965) has emphasized that organization or agency control is the "means used by an organization to elicit the performance it needs and to check whether the quantities and qualities of such performance are in accord with organizational specifications" (p. 650). Downs (1967) has identified a variety of control systems characteristic of large complex organizations. He says that direct supervision is done through the "hierarchy, time clocks, personnel evaluations, program evaluations, 'spies', quality circles, statistical quality control, and many types of management information systems (MIS) which are all designed to provide upper management with qualitative and quantitative information on performance" (Gortner, et al., 1997, p. 185).

The indirect methods of control of the bureaus include:

1. Socialization to professional values in graduate schools and socialization within the mission, norms and the bureau's sense of identity. These socialization forms are also management theories.
2. Theory Z (Ouchi, 1981) Japanese management and cultural system which some organizations have adopted in the West and elsewhere.
3. The "excellent" organization (Peters and Waterman, 1982).
4. Quality control in total quality management (Creech, 1994; and Deming, 1986).
5. Downs' (1967) Law of Counter Control which states that "The greater the effort made by a sovereign or top-level official to control the behavior of subordinate officials, the greater the effort made by those subordinates to evade or counteract such control" (Gortner, et al., 1997, p. 1470).

The purpose of organizational control is to monitor the bureau's internal and external state and correct its course. Monitoring the system can rely on formal or informal structure of the organization. Each system relies on different aspects of the communication system. Any inaccuracies or distortions in communication, decision-making and information processing make effective monitoring almost impossible and as a result tends to neutralize the control function of bureaus and other organizations.

Layers of Control Systems

Public bureaus function within a complexity of layers of control systems. The most commonly discussed and acknowledged system is oriented toward control within the organization. However, the bureau is also subject to control by the larger environment of external government policymakers, including elected officials, legislative bodies, courts, and client and interest groups. These bodies closely monitor and enforce their standards on the bureau; control is a matter of politics and public agenda setting rather than philosophical intrigue and speculation. External critics, supporters and interest groups may organize and press for the imposition of standards that they believe are needed as part of the broader struggle to control policy goals. Generally, external policymakers, preparing for an election, may impose tougher performance standards on a bureau, which in turn leads to changes in internal control systems. Bureaus may also establish control systems over the organizations. For instance, regulatory agencies can implement policy by administering grants and contracts in conjunction with other units of government or firms. Outside bodies create demand on the bureau's internal control system. For instance, antinuclear groups and consumer groups demand strict monitoring and enforcement of regulatory standards for industries, firms and multinational organizations. This happens in specific contexts and theoretically observable frameworks that are concerned with the quality of preserving and maintaining environmentally sound ecological equilibrium..

The Theory of Control

The theory of organization control for public agencies has two forms: a systems theory (cybernetics) and a political theory. These theories are not necessarily incompatible though they are differentiated by the different values and phenomena they attend to. The cybernetic theory of control is based on an analogy between the organization and the idea of an automatically self-correcting system. The system maintains itself at a point of equilibrium of activities and resources which are conducive to its survival. The point of equilibrium changes over time if the system's various components can jointly and smoothly adapt to changes. For instance, an agency can survive and continue to be effective even if its size, funding levels, or the scope of its mission and programs were to change from year to year. The cybernetic model is essentially concerned with the operation of the self-controlling mechanisms that evaluate information on the state of the system and its environment, and adjust the system's activities to achieve equilibrium. In "a cybernetic system, mechanisms for monitoring feedback and feedforward and routines for taking corrective action are automatic, as in a thermostat, so that the system is self-maintaining." The bureaucracy is cybernetical in character.

The political theory of hierarchy is an important base of control. Weber considered professional training to be the backbone of a disciplined professional bureaucracy. The new or emerging typological techniques of participative control, such as workers' councils of Europe or quality cycles like TQM constitute theory of control.

The full range of contemporary typologies or methods of control are as follows:

1. Controls that use quantitative measures of work outputs for review.
2. Controls based on quantitative and qualitative reports of activities and behaviors.
3. Controls that rely on the active participation of the workers themselves for monitoring and, in some cases, corrective action.
4. Controls based on a worker's identification with the organization, its mission, or profession within it (Gortner, et al., 1997, p. 190).

During the past decade, quantitative measures for control, such as management information systems and program evaluation, have received the greatest attention. Other important techniques of bureau control include mentoring relationships, participatory management of control is concerned with the bureau's accountability to policymakers. Weber's "ideal type" is accountable to democratic as well as socialist regimes which use rational strategies for controlling the behavior of their organizations. Normally a bureau is subject to control by outside authorities and internal control is maintained by the chain of command leading to a politically accountable executive. Both cybernetic and political theories of control guide the design of control systems in bureaus.

Several typologies for distinguishing among internal control systems are offered in the organizational literature. Etzioni's (1965) theory of organizations rests on the sources of control in organizations. The sources include "physical, material, and symbolic bases in which coercion, self-interest, or identification with certain values motivate compliance. Robey (1994) contrasts control based on measured work outputs with that based on behavior or activity levels that are only indirectly or indeterminately linked to organizational outputs. As substitutes for control, Robey considers those compliance techniques based on identification that Etzioni describes. These techniques, such as selection and socialization, management and unionization are types of control.

Controls Based on Quantitative Measures of Output

The control system is based on measures of program output or project milestones that are currently receiving a great deal of attention and have become increasingly sophisticated and accessible. Some of the techniques used include a variety of work output data (often called efficiency or productivity measurement). The strength of these techniques depends on their concreteness and clarity in terms of the linkage between the measures and the presumption of organizational effectiveness. Less positively, this approach to control is generally difficult, costly and time consuming to administer. It may suffer from problems of inaccuracy and invalidity and from ambiguous or conflicting standards for evaluating results. The accuracy of the output measurements may be compromised by the kinds of intentional and unintentional distortion common to organizational communications of all kinds, such as the filtering that results from messages passing through a long chain of command, the intentional alteration of emphasis and content to further the political and personal interests of the senders, and the misinterpretations that result from information overload or too much jargon. The validity of control measures refers to the degree to which they measure what they purpose to measure.

Control Through Behavior Monitoring

Monitoring the behavior, process, or activities within a bureau to determine compliance is markedly different from output monitoring both in the techniques used and in the standards against which the information is evaluated. Both quantitative and qualitative observations are made on the basis of behavior and actions of the bureau's workers. Some of the measures of behavior or activity may include simple tracking of work, personnel evaluations, more elaborate and exotic lic-detector tests, or the medical tests designed to monitor undesirable behavior such as drug use. Activity reports describing efforts, successes, and problems the officers and individuals have are common. Direct observation by "supervisors and indirect observation of behaviors through time clocks, information monitoring agencies, or the grapevine are other methods that are commonly used. Monitoring activities and behaviors has limits and advantages" (Gortner, et al, 1997, pp. 199-202).

Participative Control Systems

Generally speaking, participatory control refers to an organizational program in which members, directly or through representatives, take an active role in monitoring and establishing standards for their work. Work processes, personnel matters, and decisions about price may come under review by the participatory body. Participation adds quality management characterized by teams that analyze and solve production problems while the bureaucratic hierarchy coordinates and sets goals.

The workers' councils of Western Europe rely on a mixture of trade unionist, egalitarian, and socialist perspectives. In the U.S., humanistic psychology of Maslow egalitarian and the human relations theory of Mayo and others are used to promote participation as a way to increase motivation and commitment to the organization, eschewing and political reasons for fostering participation as a means of real power sharing (Strauss, 1993). In Japan, theory Z tends to humanize participatory management through "cultural lenses" that are perceptually established and habitually conditioned.

In addition, quality control circles which are generally considered to be an element of Japanese management and the monitoring and analysis of teams established in TQM. Quality control circles stress group-based control systems that stem from a cultural commitment to group psychology responsibility, and decision making (Ouchi, 1981; and Walton, 1986). Evidently, the quality circles are an example of participatory controls. These voluntary groups of employees who meet regularly to enhance "the quality of goods and services ... solve work place problems; develop a closer identification with the goals of the organization; and improve communication between supervisors and workers" (Bryant and Kearns, 1982, p. 144).

Intrinsic Control

Control can be intrinsic or external. The bureau, as an agent of society, tends to inculcate conformance with goals, rules and performance expectations. Intrinsic controls produce conformance with monitoring and correction of work by relying on the fact that the goals of the individual and the goals of the organization have become the same. "Whether based on personal loyalty, professional socialization, socialization to the norms of a particular organization, careful screening of job applicants, self-selection, or strong ideological beliefs in the bureau's mission, intrinsic controls fulfill many of the functions of the control system" (Gortner, et al., 1997, p. 204).

In relation to intrinsic controls, Weber's ideal-type of bureaucracy recognized the importance of socialization to "professional norms of impartiality, competence, and career commitment to the bureau" (Weber, 1947, pp. 329-341). Even Gulick (1937 and 1973) talked about it in terms of "leading through an idea." Burns and Stalker's (1994) model of "organismic" (p. 24) form of organization relies largely on technology used in an organization though not necessarily to the specific organization. Etzioni's (1965) analysis of reasons for compliance with orders of organizations includes norms or the "identitative" (Gortner, et al, 1997, p. 204) power of the organization. Identitative power "is shared beliefs in the organization, goals, as one finds in voluntary religions or "ideological-political" (p. 204) behavior. The greater the basis of identitative power in the organization, the greater the likelihood that an individual's loyalty and compliance will be strong enough to reduce the need for overt forms of control (see pages 205-206). Max Weber characterized the ideal or identitative bureaucracy in the following manner:

1. They are personally free and subject to authority only with respect to their impersonal official obligations.
2. They are organized in clearly defined hierarchy of offices.
3. Each office has a clearly defined sphere of competence in the legal sense.
4. The office is filled by a free contractual relationship. Thus, in principle, there is free selection.
5. Candidates are selected on the basis of technical qualifications. In the most rational case, this is tested by examination or guaranteed by diplomas certifying technical training, or both. They are appointed, not elected.
6. They are renumerated by fixed salaries in money, for the most part with a right to pensions. Only under certain circumstances does the employing authority ... have a right to terminate the appointment, but the official is always free to resign. The salary scale is primarily graded according to rank in the hierarchy; but in addition to this criterion, the responsibility of the position and the requirements of the incumbent's social status may be taken into account.
7. The office is treated as the sole, or at least the primary occupation of the incumbent.
8. It constitutes a career. There is a system of "promotion" according to seniority or to achievement, or both. Promotion is dependent on the judgment of superiors.
9. The official works entirely separated from ownership of the means of administration and without appropriation of his position.
10. He is subject to strict and systematic discipline and control in the conduct of the offices (Weber, 1947, pp. 333-334, and Gortner, et al., 1997, pp. 53-54).

External Controls. The bureau may control other bureaus and firms. It may also be controlled by external policymakers, interest groups, and other agencies especially the iron triangles (Volkomer, 1998). Controls from these groups influence its internal control systems. The bureau is a regulatory agency, and an implementer and enforcer of policies and regulations. Captive theory argues that a regulatory agency is dependent on regulated firms for political support and private decision makers conspire to use a public agency as a tool for their own personal interest (Garvey, 1993; and Brandl, 1989).

The previous section has highlighted various techniques of bureaucratic and organizational control. Some control techniques such as MIS and program evaluation tend to distort the role of management and thereby make it more difficult for organizations to function effectively. Though recent developments in science have helped to make control more sophisticated, and since the sophistication makes management a more automatic process, control, which is a function of knowledge, does not exist in certain environments. Program managers who overly on control systems may focus too much on reestablishing controls and restoring previous levels of outputs, without considering alternative program ideas, or even more importantly, without encouraging the political and professional debates and negotiations that will constitute reformed public management. Techniques of system control are used for their neutrality in order for the political regime or policymakers, to achieve their stated goals in the liberal, conservative, democratic or autocratic environments. Such environments use a variety of other control techniques of which subsidies, contracting, redistributive or macroeconomic techniques (e.g., Keynesianism with flexible tax policy) credit insurance and social security are classic (Lowi and Ginsberg, 1996).

Before World War II, university training in public administration reflected Luther Gulick's POSDCORB rational model of the classical type which dominated management. However, like textbooks, a variety of American higher education teaching practices in the field today reflect a broad diversity of specialized options. In-servicing institutions provide programs, and curricula orientations which fit "on-the-job experience" (p. 164). Online supervisors and managers receive such fragmentary and ad hoc education. The federal government, states, as well as the cities provide specific skills demanded by agencies. Each agency candidates and utilizes internship opportunities availed by training institutions. Each candidate or student is supervised or critiqued by a mentor in a series of rotations.

In other cases, in-service training is conducted formally in classroom settings. Students may take degree courses and earn degrees. Examples of well known in-service public administration programs include International City Management Association "Green Book Series" (p.

165) and the Naval Postgraduate School. In the U.S. National Association of Schools of Public Affairs and Administration (NAS PAA) accredits MPA programs.

Notwithstanding the fact that America was created stateless, the gradual growth and expansion of its bureaucratic, and more recent, technocratic demands have necessitated the evolution of its "Inventive power of the mind." The inventive mind has produced experts, who have become the state's machinery for managing public administration. But, because the state is still weak or relatively absent, "technology, professionals, and globalism" (p. 170) are used to define the American state. Analogically the relatively historic statelessness of the American state is like a body which has an artificial heart attachment that enables it to function in a variety of dynamic but diagnostically and medically questionable ways.

Ingersoll (1994) is an education policy analyst who has advanced two points concerning organizational control in secondary schools. First, Ingersoll asserts that "Schools are highly decentralized organizations in which teachers have workplace autonomy and discretion." Second, "Schools are top-down bureaucracies in which teachers have little influence over school operations" (p. 150). Though both positions are empirically true, they also are inherently contradictory because it is difficult to assess organizational control of schools. By examining the control issue particularly in major "social, sorting and behavioral activities and decisions" (p. 150), he conclusively recognized that faculties, principles and central boards differentially and jurisdictionally exercise control across the schools. Though such control is further exercised by teachers' unions and ministries of education in Western Europe and Third World nations, the general principles of control in terms of qualifications, discipline, training, competitiveness and values are universally applicable.

In his book, *The Ideology and Educational Reform,* David C. Paris (1995) has pointed out two questions: the contemporary controversy over public education in the United States and the question of how political theory or political philosophy should be related to political practice. One hidden reason educational reform has been so difficult to achieve, he argues, is that as citizens and as policy analysts, we do not sufficiently recognize that we want a number of different and often incompatible things from schools. As a result of this plurality of views, solving problems of schools cannot be simply a matter of finding the right means to an end we all share, as most nonphilosophical policy analysts imagine. The fact that different citizens understand the goals of education differently is not a perplexity peculiar to education policy, it is a difficulty, but not a pathological one, since it is an inevitable condition of genuinely liberal democratic politics.

To solve the problem, he says, "Instead of attempting to avoid the plurality and conflict of goals," the suggestion here is to expect them to clearly display and examine the ways the institutions deal with them. Reforms need to articulate the inculcation of intellectual and moral values that will transform human capital to be agents for a dynamic economy. Public schools should serve the needs of their clients regardless of their liberal or conservative ideological variants. Logically, the individualistic goals of education demand the pragmatic and pluralistic applications for the solution. Solutions are locally rather than nationally based. Like Aristotle's day, schools should teach virtue and wisdom (phronesis).

The Pivotal Controversies Affecting Control

Gortner, et al (1997) have discussed some of the pivotal areas of interest to public administration and how a variety of global theories of the organization address or fail to address these issues. In respect to the organization, Waldo (1978) has described organization theory as "a disorderly and fascinating field." The public debate which organization analysis or theorists rationalize concerns four major controversial perspectives in organization theory. First, in the context of law and legal authority, the bureaus are legally established to administer the law within the nation as a whole. As a result, questions concerning the interpretation and implementation of the law and its mandatory applicability in public organizations is centrally critical and debatable. Second, it is expected that the public's material resources can be used by public organizations. How effectively and rationally the resources are put into use is of paramount importance for those inside and outside the bureaus.

Third, since bureaucrats, i.e., civil servants are humans, public managers need to understand the humanistic (psychological and sociological) imperative of the organization in order to be successful as they wisely apply human relations theory. The theory should be applied with a sense of maintaining individual motivation, neutrality and participation or involvement. Psychological and social principles that apply to individuals and groups in organizations must be understood and then interpreted to fit the public milieu.

Fourth, in terms of politics and its relations to power, public organizations conduct their activities and actions in a politically charged environment. Hence, decisions and actions of the main actors on the organization need to be viewed from a political perspective. The second (rationality and efficiency) and third (psychological and social relations) controversies are universally applicable to the context of the public sector and organization theory in general. With respect to the fourth controversy (politics and power relations), students or scholars of public bureaucracy need to understand that there are culturally embedded assumptions and thoughts which underpin organizations and organization theory. For instance, in page 75 of Gortner, et al., (1997), the public choice theory's assumptions of individuals and organizations in the democracy are as follows:

1. They are mainly motivated due to self-interest.
2. They rationally rank alternative choices known by them.
3. They are reasonably informed concerning the probable consequences of pursuing the alternative.
4. They prefer a well ordered environment in which to engage in the pursuits.
5. They select "right" strategies that will enable them to maximize their interests.

The assumptions in which organization theory is infused raise questions and answers that are implicit or explicit expressions of the organization. These questions and answers may be "criticism of the political system and the predominant culture, and agendas for change" (Gortner, et al., 1997, p. 52). The assumptions, questions, answers or criticisms may concern a "particular authority, conflict, power, and the proper criteria for choice within organizations" (p. 52).

Models of Organizations
Gortner, et al. (1997) highlight four classic models of organization theory. The first one is the classical "ideal type" (pp. 53-54), bureaucratic, conviviality and "Universal" Weberian blueprint used for the analysis of complex organizations. The second model is Deming's (1986) 14 point total quality management (TQM) which is popular in the private sector. The international threat to American economic competitiveness influenced U.S. corporate executives and management and organization intellectual elite to device TQM and use it for the revitalization of American business and public and academic administration. Even government has been attracted to adopt it by using Gaebler's (1992) *Reinventing Government* and the report on the *National Performance Review, Creating a Government that Works Better and Costs Less* (1993). The principles of Deming's model were

originally developed for manufacturing companies. If the bureaus are going to use them, as it appears, they may need to modify them for adaptation of the public sector. These principles include:

1. Create constancy of purpose toward improvement of product and service, with the aim to become competitive and to stay in business, and to provide jobs.
2. Adopt the new philosophy. We are in a new economic age. Western management must awaken to the challenge, must learn their responsibilities, and take on leadership for change.
3. Cease dependence on inspection to achieve quality. Eliminate the need for inspection on mass basis by building quality into the product in the first place.
4. End the practice of awarding business on the basis of price tag. Instead, minimize total cost. Move toward the single supplier for any one item, on a long-term relationship of loyalty and trust.
5. Improve constantly and forever the system of production and service, to improve quality and productivity, and thus constantly decrease costs.
6. Institute training on the job.
7. Institute leadership. The aim of supervision should be to help people and machines and gadgets to do a better job. Supervision of management is in need of overhaul, as well as supervision of production workers.
8. Drive out fear, so that everyone may work effectively for the company.
9. Break down barriers between departments. People in research, design, sales, and production must work as a team, to foresee problems of production and in use that may be encountered with the product or service.
10. Eliminate slogans, exhortations, and targets for the work force asking for zero defects and new levels of productivity. Such exhortations only create adversarial relationships, as the bulk of the causes of low quality and low productivity belong to the system and thus lie beyond the power of the work force.
11. a. Eliminate work standards (quotas) on the factory floor. Substitute leadership.
    b. Eliminate management by objective. Eliminate management by numbers, numerical goals. Substitute leadership.
12. a. Remove barriers that rob the hourly worker of his right to pride of workmanship. The responsibility of supervisors must be changed from sheer number to quality.

b. Remove barriers that rob people in management and in engineering of their right to pride of workmanship. This means, *inter alia,* abolishment of the annual or merit rating and of management by objective.

13. Institute a vigorous program of education and self-improvement.

14. Put everybody in the company to work to accomplish the transformation. The transformation is everybody's job (Deming, 1986, p. 23; Gortner, et al., 1997, p. 55).

The third model is James E. Swiss (1992). TQM model for successful management of (p. 55) government organizations. The model places emphasis in managing people (customers) in industry or in service areas for building up quality "in the production process (upstream) rather than at the end (downstream). TQM opposes mass inspections since quality is everybody's endproduct in the process. The model emphasizes that variability reduces quality which is a product of well coordinated systems rather than individuals. Quality requires fearless, cooperative and active workers who continually improve inputs and processes. Managerially initiated organizational climates and cultures enhance high quality productivity and organizational commitment. Swiss's (1992) seven primary tenets are for improving quality state that:

1. The customer is the ultimate determiner of quality. If the product does not meet the desires of the customers, it is bad quality, no matter how "perfectly" made.

2. Quality should be built into the product early in the production process (upstream) rather than being added on at the end (downstream). Proper early, upstream design saves later redesigning or reworking and makes customers happier. TQM opposes inspections—quality is everyone's task, not someone's at the end of the process.

3. Preventing variability is the key to producing high quality. Quality slips when variation occurs. Therefore, process control charts that track deviation from the optimum are analyzed to prevent deviation in product or service.

4. Quality results from people working within systems, not individual efforts. The system usually creates quality slips, not individual. With committed people working together, it is a mistake to focus on individuals. The system should create intrinsic motivators that lead all workers to perform well.

5. Quality requires continuous improvement of inputs and processes. This continuous improvement should be in processes and inputs—not in outputs (defined as profits).
6. Quality improvement requires strong worker participation. The workers must do it right the first time, so managers and workers must work together "without fear."
7. Quality requires total organizational commitment. Managers must create an organizational culture where everyone focuses on consistently producing quality products and improving them constantly (Swiss, 1992, pp. 357-358; and Gortner, et al., 1997, p. 56).

Through the TQM model has arisen "a universal organizational and managerial model that the authors argue is the structure necessary for success in the competitive" (p. 56) and free enterprise capitalist domain. Like Weber's model, TQM "operates from a set of assumptions about the functions of organizations within the larger society, the goals of the organization and where they are established, and the individuals within the organization and how they think and act" (Gortner, et al., 1997, p. 56). In miniature, the TQM technique may be a new form of mechanistic and classical Taylorism. Both entrepreneurial universities and business firms use TQM strategy for ensuring the realization of institutional excellence. As universities face budget problems, external pressures for dealing with government and industry, their internal demands for thin bureaucratic hierarchy, and operational efficiency, many administrators have incorporated the TQM paradigm into the reservoir of their managerial theories (Smilor, Dietrich, and Gibson, 1993).

Principally, TQM advocates organizational commitment to the improvement of quality organizationwide. TQM tries to identify customers and satisfy their needs. Organizational employees should attack processes rather than employees. Organizations should try to eliminate organizational climates that diminish or lessen quality by socializing them to install teamwork, creativity and innovation (Oberle, 1990). At university level, a variety of institutional units especially finance, administration, business affairs, budgeting and planning, physical plant operations and human resources have implemented TQM.

In spite of the uniqueness of the TQM paradigm in higher education, its processes tend to save time, reduce costs, motivate people for action and satisfies the internal and external needs of the organizations. It helps employers and employees to improve their problem-solving skills. Employee morale is enhanced. Though TQM places emphasis in the creation of customer-driven rather than management-driven opportunities in the organization, its theoretical and empirically-laden practical essence is rooted in mechanistic classicalism of Frederick Taylor's theory of principles of management and its articulation in a free-enterprise and capitalistic economy. The paradigm rationalizes the commercialization of research results, proactive organizational involvement to regional, rural and national economic development, problem-solving and data-driven approach to curriculum improvement, and the use of TQM in managerial operations. While the articulation of this new paradigm is broader compared to the traditional concept of the university's mission (teaching, research and service), this new paradigm should be applied with caution in order to preserve institutional integrity and autonomy. Both Weberian and TQM models address some and de-emphasize some of the four perspectives we started with in this chapter. All these perspectives, as opposed to one, are central for meaningful organizational and theoretically integrative operations.

The fourth theory is the seven point, elitist theory (Gortner, et al., 1997, pp. 73-74) which divides society into the few who have power and the masses who do not. The elitist theory of politics is as old as the history of the human race (Dye and Ziegler, 1993). The theoretical counterpart of the elitist theory is the pluralist school which was started by Bentley (1908). The subsequent contributors to the pluralist school include Truman (1951), Dahl (1961), and Dahl and Lindblom (1953).

In relation to the elitist model, it can be argued that elites control politics and government as it is known. In other words, "theories about individuals, groups, and formal organizations in the public sector must reflect the realities of the situation" (Gortner, et al., 1997, p. 74). Public agencies will fall into a hierarchical arrangement based on such factors as which bureaus serve members of the elite, receive and serve members of the elite, receive the elite's attention and accolades, or in some other way gain the support or fulfill the programmatic desires of those who control the political environment. The tactics used, even the goals perceived as feasible and appropriate, will match the perceptions if there is agreement that power rests in gaining the ear and influencing the decision of an elite rather than in coalition and majority building. Elitist theory asserts that:

1. Society is divided into the few who have power and the many who do not. Only a small number of persons allocate values for society; the masses do not decide public policy.

2. The few who govern are not typical of the masses who are governed. Elites are drawn disproportionately from the upper socioeconomic strata of society.

3. The movement of nonelites to elite positions must be slow and continuous to maintain stability and avoid revolution. Only nonelites who have accepted the basic elite consensus enter governing circles.

4. Elites share a consensus on the basic values of the social system and the preservation of the system. They disagree only on a narrow range of issues.

5. Public policy does not reflect demands of masses but the prevailing values of the elite. Changes in public policy will be incremental rather than revolutionary.

6. Elites may act out of narrow self-serving motives and risk undermining mass support, or they may initiate reforms, curb abuse, and undertake public-regarding programs to preserve the system and their place in it.

7. Active elites are subject to relatively little direct influence from the apathetic masses. Elites influence the masses more than the masses influence elites (Dye and Ziegler, 1993, p. 5; and Gortner, et al., pp. 73-74).

According to Fischer (1990), technocratic theory has undercut the pre-eminence of elitist theory of public and private organizations. Technocracy assets that "technocrats use their expertise and positions of power to dominate in the policy formulation and implementation process" (Gortner, et al., 1997, p. 75). They have become dominant in policy arena because of "(1) the increase in complexity and interdependence of society (technologically and economically, nationally and internationally) to create a need for expertise and attention to both broad and specific effects that are beyond the time and perhaps intellectual capacity of much of society; and (2) at the same time, technocrats are aware of their monopoly on information and use this very powerful tool to make their positions secure"(p. 74).

Garvey (1993) has argued that in matters affecting public interest, self-interest (which is private and individual interest in the context of public choice theory), is dangerous because private interest is inconsistent with the values and culture of the larger society whose human experience and democratic underpinnings are reflections of a collectivity whose group goals are inconsistent with the "egoistic model of public choice" (Gortner, et al., 1997, p. 75).

A variety of forces have influenced the evolution of organization theory as it particularly concerns the public sector. Although many perspectives and theories underpin the sector in question, none of these theories and perspectives in itself gives a full explanation of the organizations or bureaus. All of the theories and perspectives contribute to a multi-theoretical and interdisciplinary explanation of what a public organization is. The political environment of public management is imperatively essential. Although *rationality* and *efficiency* are recognizable, managerial, political, and economic definitions, the two italicized terms are semantically vague, varied, conflictual or confusing. Though public managers may know about the psychological and sociological theories of complex organizations, it is equally or more important to know how these theories apply in the legal and political environment in which they develop. Such knowledge and understanding will be beneficial because it portrays a real picture concerning how the bureau works.

The Bureaucracy and Public Policy

It is self-evident that political science and administration have in recent memory drifted apart and become uniquely distinguishable. Yet, the character and quality of the public service continuously influences governmental efficiency and responsiveness both of which are the analytic province of political scientists (Ingraham, 1995). In *The Foundation of Merit,* Ingraham has ambitiously analyzed, in a general way, the values and political goals that shaped the development of the federal public service. He examined changing personnel policies and detailed how political executives control them. Irrespective of the bureaucratic control, he has proposed reforms in the changing work force, changing citizen expectations, and changing public policy domains.

Frederick C. Mosher's (1968) *Democracy and the Public Service* is comparable to Ingraham's *The Foundation of Merit.* However, the latter's glaring assertion that the problems of the bureaucracy and their service result not from separation of merit from politics, but instead, they "result from the association of merit and politics in the American experience." There is a schizoid quality to the idea and practice of merit in federal employment. It began with the rejection by right thinking citizens of politics as the criterion of public employment. Even though Americans generally have always distrusted any government that tries to extricate itself from political responsibility.

With the assassination of President Garfield in 1881, the spoils system was replaced with the merit system which the Pendleton Act of 1883 affirmed. This relatively more elitist system was professionalized with its participation in standardized public examinations. The examinations were used to screen the competent and experienced from the less competent and inexperienced public employees. The expansion of the merit system depended upon president's political incentives for expansion or for temporary or occasional exemption of positions from protection. For instance, FDR excluded the employees of New Deal agencies from merit protection. This action enabled him to use those agencies for patronage. However, at the end of the 1930s, and with the new agencies fully staffed by FDR loyalists, the President incorporated the positions into the merit system.

The main theme of the merit system from 1883 through World War II is its expansion across the breadth of federal employment. Two main themes that cover both postwar and current periods have emerged. First, the relationship of high-level career administrators to political officials has become increasingly tangled. Contemporary political regimes depend on careerists who are specialized and who have career-long associations with agencies. Yet, political responsiveness dictates government by political appointees. For instance, nowadays, a president fills almost 3,000-4,000 appointive positions in the executive branch. These political executives are top civil servants whose role in the iron triangles contributes to their empirical professional effectiveness. For about a half a century, reformers and participants have been searching for a machinery for rationalizing the relationships of upper-level careerists and political appointees. In other words, the "super-grade" ranks of the bureaucracy were established in 1949. President Eisenhower designated schedule C-exempted positions to accommodate policy-sensitive roles within the career oriented bureaucratic system. The second Hoover Commission proposed a senior civil service as a way of bringing careerists into the upper levels of the executive branch. Finally, the senior executive service was created in 1978 to provide the flexibility and incentives thought to be necessary for creating stable relationships between senior careerists and political executives. In Ingrahamian analysis, the reality of governance within the contemporary executive branch is motivated by the presidential agenda. This type of bureaucratic politicization does not only erode the reforms that are intended to stabilize the system, but it also questions the validity of the 1939 Hatch Act which requires bureaucrats to be politically neutral if they are supposed to perform efficiently, responsibly, effectively and accountably.

The second major bureaucratic theme is viewed to be the inability of the old classification system to meet new challenges, ranging from expanded and more complicated job roles to the "demands of a changing society for fairness and equality in hiring, evaluation, and promotion. In the federal merit system, job dictates rank, and the civil understanding that a deeper cause for bureaucratic malaise lies in "The fit between values that the polity deems it desirable to pursue and those reflected in its public service is critically important" (Ingraham, 1995, p. 140).

Rochefort and Cobb (1994) have been involved in policy research and have indicated that the bureaucracy has difficulty with defining what the problems of the public service are. The text, *The Politics of Problem Definition: Shaping the Policy Agenda,* argues that problems can be defined by examining detailed policymaking case histories of issues that center around plant closings, air transportation, sexual harassment, drug use, tax policy, agricultural policy, traffic congestion, AIDS, and culture and structure. In political discourse, the role of problem definition is to explain, describe, recommend and persuade. The authors view problem definition in public service consumer market to be importantly associated with social conflict and politics, social construction of reality, postmodernism and policy analysis. Language can be used in malleable and extraordinary ways to define the dynamics of public policymaking. In a capitalistic and individualistic society where communitarian values compete with individualistic concerns, and in which both types of value structures are dominant in society, American political conflict is used to determine or resolve problem definition. In other words, societal characteristics and cultural values do frequently converge with the existing structural and political conditions to create the contexts through "which political actors jockey to promote competing problem definitions and formulate public policy" (p. 200).

Such performance requires bureaucrats who are public entrepreneurs in terms of being change agents, who do not only command power, celebrity, personal achievement and plenty of financial gain, but, these social engineers must risk or sacrifice reputation, time, energy, credibility, and careers in order to effectively motivate and coordinate networks of opportunity for individuals and organizations (Schneider, Teske, and Mintron, 1995). In other words, as Lawrence Brown has pointed out, bureaucrats serve politicians who are involved in practical politics. "Politics is how society manages conflicts about values and interests. On the other hand, a prominent political philosopher has argued that "Politics is the authoritative allocation of values." For instance, Clark (1995) has shown that the influence of race and class in urban areas has declined during the last quarter of a century. Though rival class and race issues are among the forces that shape urban political issues, recent conclusions from his *New Political Culture* indicate that politics of the environment, growth management, gay rights, and abortion have overtaken the concerns associated with work space, jobs, and issues of class politics.

The political theory of bureaucratic control enhances the efficiency and effective accountability of the bureaus. The ideas discussed elsewhere in this volume concerning reinventing government for quality and quantity control are real. Downs (1967) indicated that a variety of control systems (time clocks, personnel evaluations, program evaluations, MBO, etc.) are used by the bureaucratic hierarchy to enhance the efficiency and effectiveness of bureau operations. Further still, inner checks such as professional behavior and self-actualization aspects explained in humanistic psychology are measures of bureaucratic and organizational control purposed to enhance discipline, quality and productivity.

Cybernetic organizations behave thermostatically because they are self-regulated in terms of making social, economic, and structural adjustments that are essential for their competitive survival. The same organizations provide information feedback mechanisms of which customer complaints, survey results, workload measures, and change procedures culminate in summative goals, processes and procedures. Such an evaluative procedure is an internal or external corrective device intended to promote individual, personnel and organizational performance.

Emit Redford has argued that the bureaucracy should be politically controlled because it is an overhead democracy. Political control of the bureaus is external rather than internal. Since the bureaucracy is not elected, because its recruitment is largely based on political or professional appointment, it is an overhead democracy which deserves external (legislative, judicial and executive) control. As a result, elected officials who are part and parcel of the bureaucratic machinery, and who supervise the bureaucracy, are held accountable through elections. Good performance is rewarded at the ballot box. Poor performance is equally punished at the ballot box. These elected officials, in turn, hold the bureaucrats accountable. Good bureaucratic behavior (performance) is rewarded with raises, bonuses, promotions and tenure. Ineffective bureaucratic behavior is rendered the opposite view including dismissal, demotions and denial of benefits.

The Legislature

The accountability of bureaucrats is sanctioned through legislative, judicial and executive authority. Legislatively, financial appropriations are legislatively enacted and supervised in terms of expenditure. If the legislature feels that the bureaus are unaccountable in their handling of finances, it vetoes policies, programs and financial requests needed for the programs and projects in question. If the programs and projects in question are essential for the vitality of the group, organizational and social interests of the community or nation, ineffective bureaucrats may be replaced in order to protect bureaus that are essential for the local and national interest of the community. In other words, bureaus are agencies which can be legislatively made an unmade based on a variety of behavioral, economic, political and ecological circumstances. For instance, Congress exercises oversight supervisory responsibility by using its committee and subcommittee structure. Congressional members can use legislative "vetoes", if their constitutionality is not questionable, for the purpose of rejecting certain rules, regulations, procedures and other standards for controlling the bureaucracy. Before they arrive at such conclusion, thorough inquiry concerning bureaucratic behavior must be conducted in advance. Further consultations from legal and consultative authority may help to reinforce Congressionally and empirically assessed conclusive observations. Such scrupulous examinations of bureaucratic performance are necessary for the purpose of protecting the strength and viability of American democratic federalism and its essential institutions.

The Judiciary

The judicial branch of the American bureaucratic machinery has three checks through which its operations are professionally and politically scrutinized for efficiency and effectiveness. First, the courts have power to authorize the stoppage of anything from happening if such happening is considered to be detrimental to the well being of the family, group, organization, community, nation or world. When courts do so, they know that their actions can be challenged in a comparative court of law for the opposite effect. Such understanding enables them to exercise judicial restraint textually and contextually. Relevant textual and legal theory will enable them to contextualize stoppage legitimately, authoritatively and contextually. Stoppage is control injunction used to check the bureaucracy.

Second, the judicial branch awards individuals with money as a form of compensation for what the government, through its bureaucratic machinery, and in its rational dispensation of distributive and other forms of justice, inadvertently injures, or does actions that are economically, morally and legally harmful to the welfare of its citizens. If the offended party takes the government to court, or if the government recognizes the wrong and tries to remedy it, the judiciary system, under the constitution and in protection of the First and 14th Amendments, can provide damage awards to vindicate the suits against it. Doing that is consistent with American democratic principles of fairness, protection of "life, liberty and the pursuit of happiness" (Volkomer, 1998, p. 9) and the legitimate veracity of American legal jurisprudence. Failure to provide citizens with damage awards for injury or any wrongdoing will be tantamount to tyranny, dictatorship and unfairness on the part of Uncle Sam. Such a failure will make many to question the logic of their government and what types of legal and political system they live under. Such conflict may not only intensify the bipartisan rivalry for interpretations and ideological logics that help to justify the actions in question, but, the actions may provoke further litigation, futuristic electoral issues and even violent retaliation that will complicate the complexity of suits against the government.

Third, the judicial branch is a check on the bureaucracy when the former exercises judicial review. Judicial review is the process through which the federal courts can legally and constitutionally review federal law and statutes and declare them unconstitutional. Since most administrative law rather than common, statutory, and constitutional law is by nature the one that is reviewed constantly for relevance with the times and for legal and constitutional constitutionality, its revisory constitutionalism is bureaucratically vindicated as good public policy which enhances the legitimacy of legal and political practice in a democratic society.

The Executive

The executive branch can be a check on the bureaucracy. Within the U.S. case, more than 4,000 political executives are appointed by the President to senior managerial positions in the Federal government. This is a patronage system. In turn, these people also appoint their immediate subordinates. In most countries of the world, the bureaucracy is appointed by boards of directors, political executives, board of regents or civil service commissions. Including the power to appoint, these top policymaking bodies, particularly the U.S. president, have the power to persuade bureaucracies to accept new programs, structures, mandates and reorganization of the public agencies. Newly established structures, programs or agencies can be approved legislatively if the president uses persuasive rather then vindictive and autocratic influence. Though the media, interest groups, Congress and the Ombudsperson can also exert the checking influence on the bureaucracy, executive influence, which has the legal, moral and constitutional power to make and unmake the bureaucracy, in spite of the bureaucracy's power to resist and isolate the president, his power of persuasion is a catalyst (McKenna, 1994).

Writing on the organizational rules and the bureaucratic personality (Bozeman and Rainey, 1998) have conclusively argued that certain personal characteristics of burcaucrats influence them to incorporate many rules and regulations for their organizations. In other words, the unique characteristics of bureaucratic organizations help to determine "members' preferences for rules" (p. 182; Thompson, 1961; and Merton, 1940). The study by Bozeman and Rainey (1998) shows that:

> the perceived need for more rules relates closely to the individual's sense of alienation. This generalized alienation and sense of personal powerlessness seems more important than satisfaction with one's job or organization, and with reward and pay expectancies (p. 182).

In addition, the sense of alienation is more highly pronounced with corporate rather than public sector managers and executives. As a result, managers especially those in the private sector, create more rules to satisfy themselves for the alienation element they suffer. Further still, the public sector especially in the U.S. provides more opportunity for employees to be rated higher for workforce quality (Crewson, 1995).

Also, a national sample conducted by Kanter and Mirvis (1989) found that 40 percent of the respondents expressed cynicism and skepticism about their organizations. Employees distrusted their organizations and how they were managed. Given these weakening organizational trends, it can be argued that the processes of downsizing and contracting out the functions, which might result in further discouragement, distrust and alienation might have far reaching implications. Evidently, alienation is linked to layoffs and downsizing. To rectify the situation, organizations need to resocialize and retrain their managers and employees by articulating "organizational characteristics and individual characteristics and attitudes" (Bozeman and Rainey, 1998, pp. 186-187; and Hilton and Testa, 1998).

Clayton (1995), in viewing the role of government lawyers within the federal bureaucracy, argues that high level bureaucratic lawyers who contribute to the construction of public policy could dialectically be contradictory. Some of these lawyers include the attorney general, the solicitor general, independent counsel, agency general counsel offices, independent agency legal officials, the Justice Department's Office of legal counsel, and the White House Office of the Counsel to the President. Though lawyers attempt to deal with the principle of separation of powers, which they find very contradictory in practice, they also try to control partisan abuse. These two themes are dichotomous and professionally full of tension in terms of detachment and maintenance of client patron interest in litigation. For instance, as Nelson Lund and Antonio Scalia have maintained, there is too much likelihood for abuse of power by the independent counsel and other special prosecutors. This abuse does not emanate from "the independence of the office but rather in the nature of prosecutorial discretion possessed by all prosecutors, independent or not" (Clayton, 1995, p. 85). In addition, ethically, lawyers who work in the White House play a role of protecting the president. The action of protecting is both legal and political. An effective White House Counsel must have knowledge to balance spasmodic conflicts that evolve from the political and legal provinces. In addition, the Justice Department's Office of Legal Counsel tends to come into conflict with the White House's Office of Counsel to the President. The conflictual tensions between the two bureaucratic legal agencies are inevitable because the tensions are a product of the inherent rise of the evolutionary and expansionary administrative state. In this case, the occupant of the Oval Office must be astutely political in acumen to be able to wisely control his advisors.

Sometimes the government hires outside lawyers for litigation particularly the one associated with securities litigation, anti-trust litigation, civil rights litigation, tax litigation, personal injury litigation and medical malpractice litigation. Private corporations use inhouse lawyers who are substantively specialized in litigation matters. If firms hire lawyers from outside, that action is influenced by location of litigation rather than anything else. In other words, both the White House and corporations tend to rely on inhouse lawyers more often than otherwise. This approach is economically and logistically deterministic and solvent.

Legislatively, viewing the dynamics which control parliamentary governments universally, Baron (1998), who is a professor of business economics and the environment at Stanford University, has advanced

A dynamic theory of parliamentary governments that incorporates attributes of the institutional system in a country, exogenous events that shape parliamentary and electoral opportunities, and the strategies of the government and the opposition as structured by institutions and preferences. The dynamics are investigated in an infinitely repeated game in which events in the form of shocks to income or government resources occur and the government responds with a legislative proposal that is subject to a confidence or censure procedure and may lead to government continuation, reorganization, or dissolution. With a majority confidence procedure, governments are stable, and if parties are politically patient, voting cohesion within the government is high. A censure motion initiated by the opposition can result in voluntary dissolution of government, and the approach of required elections increases the likelihood of dissolution. If events represent fluctuations in aggregate income, government dissolution occurs in good times for the government leader and bad times for the other parties (p. 593).

Baron's comparative model of the dynamics of political governance reinforces and complements scholarly analysis which focuses on differences in "voter preferences, history, and culture" (p. 608). This model articulates how government is formed, legislatively rationalized, and restructured or dissolved. These aspects depend on the character of distributive politics constituted in government spending and income redistribution. The model makes government stability, as a bureaucracy, difficult since it relies on coalitions from which both stability and instability originate. Only when the majority of parliamentarians set or control the agenda through its coalitions will voting cohesively become inerodable in spite of a variety of implications to the contrary.

The United Nations

Unlike legislative, executive and judicial bureaucracies of various nations, the UN bureaucracy is a supranational and confederate agency whose specialized units exercise power in the light of neorealist and neoliberalist perspectives. Neorealist and neoliberal institutional conceptions of the league promote the belief that "international order is founded on force coupled with institutional restraints that are supported by a convergence of state interests" (Barnett, 1997, p. 528). Further still, international order is not only the product of the use of force and institutional restraint, but, it is legitimately constructed. This classical realist perspective of international relations theory and political behavior argues that (1) "international orders must be legitimated if they are to have any staying power; (2) .. legitimation principles of a particular order can shape state practices; (3) ... UN can be the site for the legitimation of a particular order and for holding states accountable to its norms" (p. 529). Given this scenario, the UN then, is an agent of normative integration of which the principles of legitimacy, universality of protection of certain values and mutual interdependence are fundamental to global stability, peaceful coexistence and economic and technological progress.

This universal and international body and logic of survival discourages disintegration of states by securely endorsing the principle of multilateralism for the security of international order. From this perspective, the UN is a neutral forum where "state and nonstate actors can voice their grievances, communicate their preferences, and coordinate their policies" (p. 535). Also, this encourages states to concentrate on "building agreements and fostering transparency so as to encourage states to adopt a more defensive and less militarized security posture" (p. 535). By monitoring and overseeing the enforcement of domestic and international agreements the UN helps to solve conflicts through enhancing global democracy.

Since most conflicts are domestic rather than global, domestic violence should be reduced by emphasizing the importance of human rights. This is an issue that resonates with domestic and international implications in terms of civilization, democracy, respect, accountability and peace and security. As individual states enhance these mechanisms for peace and stability, the state as the main actor in global politics enhances the property of NGOs, "identity-based groups ... nations, indigenous peoples, women, ethnicities and individuals" (p. 535). Peace and social stability promote the rule of law, democracy and free enterprise. These in turn become the base for the new superstructure (political, economic opportunity and freedom). These are the blueprint for long lasting, stable and substantive and procedurally legitimate international order.

The UN is the forum for collective security, legitimation and normative integration of universal values. Here in, international order is crowned or dethroned in order to legitimately enhance the interdependence, nationhood, sovereignty and collective personality of its member states (Perez de Cuellar, 1988; and Durkheim, 1964). As an isomorphic cathedral of universality, the organization is a legitimate repository of the collective beliefs and practices of its personality. The most efficient way of ensuring compliance is through "direct contact, publicity, deterrence, and the mobilization of same" (Chayes and

Chayes, 1993, p. 328). Legitimate power is limited power because it is exercised judiciously and contextually.

The UN Charter and the UN itself are cosmopolitan in structure and rhetoric rather than in normative design. The violation of its fundamental and universally accepted humanitarian principles demands justifiable intervention in order to bring an end to injustice. Third World nations which question its normatively exclusionary definition of autonomy and authentic and contextual historicity and the jurisprudence of its dispensation of justice is sometimes contradictory. Such contradiction is the essence of the underlying ideological and neorealist polemics within its legislative proceedings and rationalized disagreements.

Weak states accept the ideas of the New World Order drafted by stronger states when principles are linguistically and legally constructed in universal rather than in particularistic fashions. Such a form of construction tends to enhance legitimation. Second, such legitimation is reinforced when a structure is formalized for the state identity, articulation of state interests and interstate interaction. Third, affordable interaction of UN member states is a socialization process intended to empower, supervise and integrate new member states in spite of the drain of brain power in these states.

Deliberatively, UN decisions, proceedings and normative sanctions profoundly influence the foreign and domestic politics of each member state particularly that of the U.S. Such influence is the essence of bureaucratic behavior and its controlling and inherently normative, global, and universally internationalist duty.

Political appointment, as a means of selecting top management and policy positions in the executive branch of the U.S. government, is a familiar target for reformers. The failure to develop a cadre of permanent civil servants modeled on the European and Japanese experiences, for managing federal employees, organizations, and programs has been cited frequently as one of the failing of the system and its allegedly poor performance. Huddleston and Boyer (1996) performed an admirable service in detailing the history of the senior civil service in the U.S. from the early twentieth century until the mid-1990s. The passage of the Civil Service Reform Act of 1978 and the creation of the Senior Executive Service during the Carter administration were the culmination of a long struggle to create a leadership group in the civil service that would be independent of particular organizations and that could function as groups did in Europe. This history points to the complexities of "the separated system" in the management of the civil service and to the consequent difficulties faced by the chief executive in managing his own branch of government (checks and balances). Almost every president has sought to gain greater control over the civil service, but significant legislation has been far from successful in solving the policy and management problems in the federal government and the pursuit of an improved system continues. Although the U.S. bureaucratic system has been called many bad names including weakness, it is paradoxical that other democratic countries like the United Kingdom, New Zealand, Germany, France and lately Russia are "drifting" towards the U.S. model whose weakness politicizes appointments.

Conclusion

Every good organization exercises control on its operations. Within the bureaucracy, the organization's intelligence system of control, communication and decision making are controllably interdependent. The effectiveness of the control system depends on the communication structure for collecting data, analyzing results or processing information. A variety of control agents employ quantitative, behavioral and socio-psychological techniques to ensure the efficiency, effectiveness and accountability of organizational operations. Some of these techniques are acquired through well managed and formalized philosophical and theoretical empiricism in academic training.

Public organizations and some private organizations operate in a controversial theoretical, empirical and temporal terrain. Such controversies, though time-consuming and expensive, could be rational intricacies that determine the latent and inherent dynamics of organizational reality. Though rationality and efficiency are organizationally and rhetorically valued operational and abstract terms, their managerial, political and economic meanings and applicability tend to create vagueness, conflict and confusion in public agencies. These problems can be solved through organizational restructuring, socialization of employees and innovation.

Organizational control is the management, supervision and design of agencies. The focus of this scientific study of public organizations largely falls within the realm of political science, public administration and higher education administration and management. Though there is an inseparable dichotomy between political science and public administration, both sciences are separate and complement each other in unique realms of theory and practice. For instance, while organizational control is an executive practice, this practice is philosophically and intellectually rationalized by the use of scientific and theoretical discourse of social and behavioral scientists who act as analysts, consultants, advisors and professors. Legal scholars who have been "beaten by the intellectual political bug" tend to view their scholarly writings through the "lenses" of political scientists in order to legitimize their scholarly productivity. Abstract, empirical, theoretical and philosophical productions of all these scholars inform the structural and cultural regimes of organizational repertoire.

The bureaucracy is incapable of defining the problems of the public service (public administration). With the help of political scientists, they are able to show that explanation, description, recommendation and persuasion are paramount analytic dynamics of public policymaking. In this arena, communitarian and ideologically individualistic goals and values tend to clash as political actors and policy analysts "probe" for politically correct linguistic jargons suitable for constructing such policy. For instance, such linguistic jargon may be called reinventing government. When government is reinvented, reinvention becomes a form of checks and balances for qualitatively and quantitatively maintaining control. More checks like professional socialization, self-actualization and cybernetic systems are put in place to controllably enhance bureaucratic efficiency and accountability. Bureaucratic efficiency and accountability are further sanctioned through supervisory, legislative, judicial and executive authority.

The supervisory nature of public policy by executive, legislative and judicial systems of authority is a legal, descriptive and normative endeavor (Sills, 1968). The three branches of government exercise their legality on public policy. The detailed and comprehensive nature of its analysis is descriptive. The normative state of the policy deals with how it is judged in terms of values and evaluative processes in order to determine its merits and demerits. The legal, descriptive and meritorious character of public policy is enhanced by its own problem and action oriented research agenda. For instance, the case studies by which it is characterized are conclusively useful for theory development, explanation, prediction and control.

References

Alger, C. 1963. United Nations participation as a learning process. *Public Opinion Quarterly* 27, 3: 425.

Barnett, M.N. 1997. Bringing in the new world order: Liberalism, legitimacy, and the United Nations. *World Politic,* 49: 526-551.

Baron, D.P. 1998. Comparative dynamics of parliamentary governments. *American Political Science Review* 92, 3: 593-609.

Bentley, A.F. 1908. *The Process of Government: A Study of Social Pressures.* Chicago: University of Chicago Press.

Bozeman, B., and H.G. Rainey. 1998. Organizational rules and the bureaucratic personality. *American Journal Political Science* 42, 1: 163-189.

Brandl, J. 1989. How organization counts: Incentives and inspiration. *Journal of Policy Analysis and Management* 8: 489-493.

Bryant, S., and J. Kearns. 1982. Workers' brains as well as their bodies: Quality circles in a federal facility. *Public Administration Review* 42: 144-150.

Bukey, E.B. 1996. Great men and the twentieth century. *The Historical Journal* 39, 1: 277-283.

Burns, T., and G. Stalker. 1994. *The Management of Innovation.* Oxford: Oxford University Press.

Carnevale, D.G. 1995. *Trustworthy Government: Leadership and Management Strategies for Building Trust and High Performance.* San Francisco: Jossey-Bass.

Chayes, A., and A.H. Chayes. 1993. *International Organizations.* Spring.

Clark, T.N. 1995. *Urban Innovation: Creative Strategies for Turbulent Times.* Bervely Hills, CA: Sage Publications.

Clayton, C.C. 1995. *Government Lawyers: The Federal Legal Bureaucracy and Presidential Politics.* Lawrence: University of Kansas.

Creech, B. 1994. *The Five Pillars for TQM: How to Make Total Quality Management Work for You.* New York: Truman Talley Books/Dutton.

Crewson, P.E. 1995. A comparative analysis of public and private sector entrant quality. *American Journal of Political Science* 39: 628-639.

Dahl, R. 1951. *Who Governs? Democracy and Power in the American City.* New Haven: Yale University press.

Deming, W.E. 1986. *Out of the Crisis.* Cambridge, MA: MIT Center for Advanced Engineering Study, 23.

Downs, A. 1967. *Inside Bureaucracy.* Boston: Little Brown. (Reissued, Prospect Heights, IL: Waveland Press.)

Durkheim, E. 1964. *The Division of Labor in Society.* New York: Free Press.

Dye, T.R., and H. Ziegler. 1993. *The Irony of Democracy: An Uncommon Introduction to American Politics.* Belmont, CA: Wadsworth.

Etzioni, A. 1965. Organizational control structure. In *Handbook of Organizations,* ed. James March. Chicago: Randy McNally.

Finnermore, M. 1996. *National Interests in International Security.* Ithaca, N.Y.: Cornell University Press.

Fischer, F., Ed. 1990. *Technocracy and the Politics of Expertise.* Newbury Park, CA: Sage Publications.

Garvey, G. 1992. *Facing the Bureaucracy: Living and Dying in a Public Agency.* San Francisco: Jossey-Bass.

Goodsell, C.T. 1994. *The Case for Bureaucracy: A Public Administration Polemic.* Chatham, N.J.: Chatham House Publishers, Inc.

Gortner, H.F., J. Mahler, and J.B. Nicholson. 1997. *Organization Theory: A Public Perspective.* Fort Worth, TX: Harcourt Brace College Publishers.

Gulick, L. (1973). Notes on the theory of organization. In *Papers on the Science of Administration,* eds. Luther Gulick and Lyndall Urwick. Clifton, N.J.: Augustus Kelley.

Hilton, S.G., and A.R. Testa. 1998. *Glass Houses: Shocking Profiles of Congressional Sex Scandals and Other Unofficial Misconduct.* New York: St. Martin's Paperbacks.

Huddleston, M.W., and W.W. Boyer. 1996. *The Higher Civil Service in the United States: Quest for reform.* Pittsburgh, PA: University of Pittsburgh Press.

Ingersoll, R.M. 1994. Organizational control in secondary schools. *Harvard Educational Review* 4, 2: 150-172.

Ingraham, P.W. 1995. *The Foundation of Merit: Public Service in American Democracy.* Baltimore: Johns Hopkins University Press.

Kanter, D.L., and P.H. Mirvis. 1989. *The Cynical Americans: Living and Working in an Age of Discontent and Disillusion.* San Francisco: Jossey-Bass.

Kay, W.D. 1995. *Can Democracies Fly in Space? The Challenge of Revitalizing the U.S. Space Program.* Westport, CT: Praeger.

McKenna, G. 1994. *The Drama of Democracy: American Government and Politics.* Gilford, CT: The Dushkin Publishing Group, Inc.

McNeely, C. 1995. *Constructing the Nation-State: International Organization and Prescriptive Action.* Westport, CT: Greenwood Press.

Merton, R. 1940. Bureaucratic structure and personality. *Social Forces,* 18: 560-568.

Oberle, J. 1990. Quality gurus: The men and their message. *Training Magazine,* p. 47.

Osborne, D., and T. Gaebler. 1992/93. *Reinventing Government: How the Entrepreneurial Spirit is Transforming the Public Sector.* Reading, MA: Addison.

Osborne, D., and T. Gaebler. 1992. *Reinventing Government: How the Entrepreneurial Spirit is Transforming the Public Sector.* Washington, DC: Plume-Penguin Group.

Ouchi, W. 1981. *Theory Z.* Reading, MA: Addison-Wesley.

Paris, D.C. 1995. *Ideology and Educational Reform: Themes and Theories in Public Education.* Boulder, CO: Westview.

Patel, K., and M.E. Rushefsky. 1995. *Health Care Politics and Policy in America.* Armonk, N.Y.: M.E. Sharpe.

Perez de Cuellar, J. 1988. The United Nations and the United States. An Address at the Fiftieth Anniversary Celebration, Dartmouth College, May.

Peters, T., and R. Waterman. Jr. 1982. *In Search of Excellence.* New York: Warner Books.

Peterson, P.E. 1995. *The Price of Federalism.* Washington, D.C.: The Brookings Institution.

Robey, D. 1994. *Designing Organizations.* Burr Ridge, IL: Richard D. Irwin.

Rochefort, D.A., and R.W. Cobb. 1994. *The Politics of Problem Definition: Shaping the Policy Agenda.* Lawrence: University of Kansas Press.

Schneider, M., P. Teske, and M. Mintrom. 1995. *Public Entrepreneurs: Agents for Change in American Government.* Princeton: Princeton University Press.

Scott, G.M., and S.M. Garrison. 1998. *The Political Science Student Writer's Manual.* Upper Saddle River, N.J.: Prentice-Hall.

Sills, D.L. 1968. *International Encyclopedia of the Social Sciences, 13.* New York: The Macmillan Company and the Free Press.

Smilor, R.W., G.B. Dietrich, and D.V. Gibson. 1993. The Entrepreneurial University: The Role of Higher Education in the United States in Technology Commercialization and Economic Development. *International Social Science Journal* 135: 1-11.

Stillman, R.J., II. 1991. *Public Administration: Preface to a Search for Themes and Direction.* New York: St. Martin's Press.

Strauss, G. 1963. Some notes on power equalization. In *The Social Science of Organizations,* ed. Harold Leavitt. Englewood Cliffs, N.J.: Prentice Hall.

Swiss, J.E. 1992. Adapting total quality management (TQM) to government. *Public Administration Review,* 52: 356-362.

Thompson, V. 1961. *Modern Organization.* New York: Knopf.

Truman, D. 1951. *The Government Process; Political Interests and Public Opinion.* New York: Alfred A. Knopf.

Volkomer, W.E. 1998. *American Government.* Upper Saddle River, N.J.: Prentice Hall.

Waldo, D. 1978. Organization theory: Revisiting the elephant. *Public Administration Review*, 38: 589-597.

Walker, D.B. 1995. *The Rebirth of Federalism: Slouching Toward Washington.* Chatham, N.J.: Chatham House.

Walton, M. 1986. *The Deming Management Method.* New York: Praeger.

Weber, M. 1947. *The Theory of Social and Economic Organization.* Edited and translated by A.M. Anderson and Talcott Parsons. New York: Free Press.

Chapter 15

Organizational Change

Organizational change is a complex, planned or unplanned process that is influenced by the synergistic interplay of conflicting technological, historical, human relations, behavioral research, and other socioeconomic and political forces (Gortner, Mahler, and Nicholson, 1997, and Wallerstein, 1979). Organizational change "is an empirical observation of difference in form, quality, or state over time in an organizational entity. The entity may be an individual's job, a work-group, an organizational strategy, a program, a product, or the overall organization" (Van de Ven and Poole, 1995, p. 512, and Dunford, 1996, p. 692). Though change means "alteration, alternation, innovation, substitution, transition, variation" (*New Webster's Dictionary and Thesaurus of the English Language*, 1992, T-5), the change which organizations experience may be or may not be elements of growth in size or measurement, in quality or axiological and ethical development, or in physical, economic, or numerical dimensions, and in technological or functional, mechanistic or electronic efficiency.

There are more than one million articles on the subject of change within organizations. Attempts to explain when, how and why organizations change have been a central and an unending quest of scientific inquiry in management and a variety of other disciplines. The processes and sequential stages of change involve "transitions in individuals' jobs and careers, group formation and development, and organizational innovation, growth, reorganization and decline" (Van de Ven and Poole, 1995, p. 510). Organizations change within the framework of conceptually and normatively established analytical contexts in terms of concepts, metaphors and theories, that evolve with a wealth of disciplinary and interdisciplinary millieux. Thematically, the multidisciplinary millieux from which concepts, metaphors, and theories emanate include but are not limited to "punctuated equilibrium, stages of growth, processes of decay and death, population ecology, functional models of change and development, and chaos theory" (p.510). Development is the process or progression of change which may be regressive in terms of decline or progressive in terms of growth in size, value, form and dimension.

Viewing the concept of change through the Foucaultian (French history professor of systems of thought at the College of de France, Paris) analysis of HRM, organizational elements is not only part of the familiar landscape that is not 'natural' (Townley, 1993, p. 519) or "part of the naturally existing order" (p. 519) but what is regarded as truth is largely based on or determined and influenced by "the conceptual system in operation" (p. 519). In other words, this philosopher who died in 1984 produced work that dispels self-evidences by clarifying that "established ways of ordering limit our analysis and therefore impoverishes our analytical imagination." Michael Foucault's understanding of the use of power and knowledge in relation to the sanctioning of change can be understood as a relational proposition. Foucault persuasively argues that the exercise of power which is knowledge, is relational rather than belonging to the individual, managers, employers, group and organization or institution. Individual, group and organization or institution, etc are sociological categories to which, for which, and with which knowledge, which is power, and vice versa, can be the subject and object of discovery. The application of knowledge—power—sociological categories nexus is a relational rather than a functional or theoretically mechanistic and empirical practice.

The relational or sociological nature of organizational change can metaphorically be reconceptualized for the purpose of understanding organizational situations and difficulties (Palmer and Dunford, 1996; Bolman and Deal, 1991; Frost, Moore, Louis, Lundberg and Martin, 1991). Of these, machine and organism metaphors of the organization were initially dominant (Morgan, 1980). Other metaphors include cultures, political systems, brains and psychic prisons (Morgan, 1986), jazz bands and missionaries (Akin and Schultheiss, 1990), clouds and songs (Gergen, 1992), soap bubbles (Tsoukas, 1993), and strategic termites and spider plants (Morgan, 1993). For instance, nations are culturally, in terms of behavior, viewed as follows: Italian opera, German symphony, French wine, Russian ballet, Japanese garden, Spanish bullfight, British house, Nigerian market rings (Gannon, 1994).

Scholars have used metaphors to analyze organizational behavior and practice in the area of decision making (Connolly, 1988), leadership (Bensimon, 1989), organizational change (Lundberg, 1990), organizational development (Marx and Hamilton, 1991), policy (Dobuzinskis, 1992), strategy (Peters, 1992), information technology (Kendall and Kendall, 1993), organizational culture (Brink, 1993), organizational design (Tsoukas, 1993), production management (Garud and Kotha, 1994; and Palmer and Dunford, 1996).

Metaphors are used

as guiding images as of the future, as ways of increasing organizational effectiveness, as tools for organizational diagnosis, and as methods for simplifying the complexities of organizational life...also have been used to understand individual perceptions toward change, identify resistance to change, unearth emotions associated with change...and establish 'gaps' in individual acceptance of proposed changes (Palmer and Dunford, 1996, p. 692).

For instance, the metaphor of organizational mudhouse connotes the organization as needing a lot of professional, technical and scientific management support in order to dispel its disorderliness, incompetence, and cultural inertia which undercut its performance. Metaphors emphasize the need for organizational learning and adaptation. They point a "finger" at the existing problems in the arena of management of change. Metaphors are original ways of evocative and suggestive elements that reflect major organizational interests. According to Koch and Deetz (1981, p. 13), metaphors of organizational change emerge because they "bring more productive or interesting possibilities to conceptualization" (Palmer and Dunford, 1996, p. 693). Metaphors of organizational change can stimulate creativity and imagination. They liberate because they provide new choices, alternatives and ideas. They can be used as a tool for directing employees in certain ways. Managers use metaphors to get employees motivated and excited as they embrace new changes. Metaphors can be used to "influence employees' thinking, feelings, and their construction of reality in ways which facilitate organizational transformation...trigger a perceptual shift" (Sackmann, 1989, p. 468; and Palmer and Dunford, 1996, p. 694). Metaphors are superior to literal linguistic usage because they capture "experience and emotions better and because" they "can communicate meaning in complex, ambiguous situations where literal language is inadequate" (Palmer and Dunford, 1996, p. 694). Change agents need to use more metaphors rather than single ones because many metaphors will help to generate more literal as well as metaphorical meanings of situations that are, more often than not, very complex. Organizational analysts can use a reflexive approach to ontologically and epistemologically represent, enunciate, separate and routinize the structure, architecture, and infrastructure of organizational dynamics. Organizational change metaphors that are ontologically and epistemologically loaded should be contextualized realistically. Realistic and reflexive analysis of how semantics, ontology and epistemology are the bases for metaphorically constructed and conceptualized organizational change generates credible and plausible scientific theorizing.

The Change Paradigm

Organizations do not experience innovative change in the context of the their humanistically relational, sociologically interactive aspects of their identity and the use of metaphors, instead, there are more complex theoretical issues involved in the change paradigm. Theoretically, there are six major theories through which the change paradigm is rationalized. The theories are a product of more than a million scholarly articles and books which have been reviewed or studied extensively. The interdisciplinary nature of these sources is of great interest as it particularly reflects their dominant psychological, sociological, biological, educational, physical, medical, meteorological, geographical, and economics sciences (Kaplan, 1964). These major theories of change include but are not exclusionary to life-cycle, teleology, dialectics, evolution, chaos, and sectoral borrowing (synergism) (Van de Ven and Poole, 1995; and Osborne and Gaebler, 1992).

The Life-Cycle Theory

Most management scholars use the metaphor of organic growth to heuristically explain development in any organization as a process that starts with conception and ends with death. For instance, in real life situations, this concept is reflected in the "life-cycle of organizations, products, and ventures, as well as stages in the development of individual careers, groups, and organizations: startup births, adolescent growth, maturity, and decline or death. Some of the life-cycle theories are developmentalism (Nisbet, 1970), biogenesis (Featherman, 1986), ontogenesis (Baltes, Dittman-Kohli, and Dixon, 1986), stage theories of child development (Piaget, 1975), human development (Levinson, 1978), moral development (Kohlberg, 1969), organizational development (Kimberly and Miles, 1980), group decision-making stages (Bales and Strodtbeck, 1951; and Van de Ven and Poole, 1995, p. 513). Life-cycle theory is the dominant explanation of change as development in management scholarship.

Within the framework of life-cycle's theoretical domain, change is imperative; it is a developing entity which has "within it an underlying form, logic, program, or code that regulates the process of change and moves the entity from a given point of departure toward a subsequent end that is prefigured in the present state" (p. 515). The form that "lies latent, premature, or homogeneous in the embryo or primitive state becomes progressively more realized, mature, and differentiated. External environmental events and processes can influence how the entity expresses itself, but they are always mediated by immanent logic, rules, or programs that govern the entity's development" (Van de Ven and Poole, 1988, p. 37).

Naturally enough, the progression of change events in a life-cycle model is a unitary sequence. The sequential unit follows a single step by step phasal process. The process of unitary development is cumulative because the developmental characteristics acquired during earlier and rudimentary stages are retained in later stages. These stages of development are conjunctive because they are relatedly derivative from a common underlying process of development. This progressive development is a trajectory "to the final end state" which is "prefigured and requires a specific historical sequence of events. Each of these events contributes a piece to the final product, and they must occur in a prescribed order, because each piece sets the stage for the next. Each stage of development is seen as a necessary precursor of succeeding stages" (Van de Ven and Poole, 1995, p. 515).

Analogically, life-cycle theory does not only parallel gross anatomist biological studies, but the biological studies are used for the sequential observation in the development of the human animal fetus in which each successive stage evolves from the preceding one. In a sense, organizational development, i.e., change is driven by "some genetic code or prefigured program within the developing entity" (p. 515; and Nisbet, 1970). In addition, cognitive psychology of Piaget and other developmental and cognitive psychologists have demonstrated that different tasks of the learning process take place at different and logically sequential stages of mental and physical evolution of young children (Flavell, 1982). As embryonic and cognitive development in stages from infancy to maturity take place, organizational development parallels them. Rogers (1983) has demonstrated that the five stages of evolutionary social innovation change are "need recognition, research on problem, development of idea into useful form, commercialization, and diffusion and adoption" (Van de Ven and Poole, 1995, p. 515; Bentley, 1996; and Manning, 1996).

The Theory of Teleology

Teleology is the philosophical study of design or purpose in natural phenomena. It is the ultimate purpose to explain phenomena. This philosophical doctrine asserts that purpose or goal is the final cause which guides the developmental movement of an entity. This notion does not only underlie a variety of organizational theories of change, but some of those theories include functionalism (Merton, 1968, 1968), decision making (March and Simon, 1958), epigenesis (Etzioni, 1963), voluntarism (Parsons, 1951), social construction (Berger and Luckmann, 1966), and adaptive learning (March and Olsen (1976), and a variety of strategic planning models in which goals are infused (Chakravarthy and Lorange, 1991, 1991). Commons (1970) who argues that society is a complex social organization rather than an organism or mechanism that is driven by natural forces or cybernetic machine; the "organization" and its institutions are mechanisms for accomplishing its purposes. For instance, the goals of an organization can naturally be activated as follows:

> The sheer number of organizations adopting an innovation can cause a bandwagon , prompting other organizations to adopt this innovation. Institutional bandwagon pressures occur because nonadopters fear appearing different from many adopters. Competitive bandwagon pressures occur because nonadopters fear below-average performance if many competitors profit from adopting. Our mathematical model of bandwagons examines how organizational collectivities' characteristics determine (a) whether a bandwagon will occur, (b) how many organizations jump on it, and (c) how many retain the innovation it diffuses. Simulating the model suggests, first, that any technological, organizational, or strategic innovation with ambiguous returns can diffuse in a bandwagon manner; second, that minor differences in organizational collectivities can have major effects on bandwagons' occurrence, extent, and persistence; and third, that bandwagons can prompt most organizations in a collectivity to adopt an innovation, even when most of

them expect that this adoption will yield negative returns (Abrahamson and Rosenkopf, 1993, p. 487).

The bandwagon metaphor has two interesting observations and several implications. First, "less ambiguity exists in the assessment of nonadministrative innovations' technical efficiency... Second, for profit organizations it has less ambiguous goals because they pay greater attention to the impact of innovations on the bottom line" (p. 512). As a consequence, independent, rational choices based on innovations' efficiency, rather than bandwagons, determine whether nonadministrative innovations diffuse, persist, or disappear in for-profit sectors. In this situation, independent and rational choices can trigger bandwagons. In addition, "competitive bandwagon pressures are capable of impelling bandwagons. These can analytically be reinforced with the use of research and technology.

In some cases, technically inefficient innovations can diffuse while technically efficient innovations can be rejected. According to bandwagon theories, organizations adopt innovations because of the sheer number of adopter pressures and not because of their analysis of "innovations' technical efficiency and returns. Again if "bandwagons cause diffusions and rejections of innovations, regardless of their efficiency and returns, then bandwagons do not only diffuse technically inefficient innovations or reject technically efficient ones, but, bandwagons also may diffuse technically efficient innovations or reject technically inefficient ones" (p. 513). As a result, it is not wise to conclude that bandwagon theories suffer from anti-innovation bias. In essence, bandwagons are important processes that animate the random variations from which knowledge for improving organizational and technological forms emanate (Anderson and Tushman, 1990; and Hannan and Freeman, 1977). Bandwagons are a teleological element.

Teleologically, the development of an organizational entity progresses toward a goal or an end state in itself. The entity is purposeful, adaptive and interactive. The same entity tends to construct an envisioned end state for which it prepares to reach or attain. It also monitors progress. The proponents of the teleological theory envision "development as a repetitive sequence of goal formulation, implementation, evaluation and modification of goals" (Van de Ven and Poole, 1995, p. 516). The goals are handled this way based of learned or intended experience. This theory can be used for individual, group or organizational purposes particularly in the context of "group-think." Since individuals and groups in organizations can exercise their freedom to be creative, group-think may not necessarily thwart developmental goals particularly in public policy arena.

Contrary to life-cycle theory, "teleology does not prescribe a necessary sequence of events or specify which trajectory development of the organizational entity will follow" (p. 516). In any case, the development trajectory is a yardstick for "measuring" change which is expected to move towards a final stage of development. In some cases, other teleological models are symbolic of systems theory assumption of equifinality. Equifinality asserts that there are more and equally effective ways for achieving a goal. According to equifinality, there is no prefigured rule or logically necessary direction of development or sequential stages within a teleological progression. Supporters or proponents of teleology concentrate on the basics or prerequisites for reaching the goal which is the end state. They also focus on "the functions that must be fulfilled, the accomplishments that must be built or obtained for the end state to be realized" (p. 516). The prerequisites are used to judge if the entity is developing, growing in a more complex and integrated way, or functionally fulfilling certain expectations.

In spite of the fact that teleology places emphasis on purposiveness of the actor or unit as the logical motor for change, there are recognized limits on action. The organization's environment and resources constrain what it can accomplish. Some of the constraints are embedded in institutional and organizational prerequisites. Obviously, individuals do not control natural laws or environmental constraints. However, they can plan in the light of the laws and constraints for the purpose of accomplishing their teleological goals and purposes (Commons, 1950; and Gibson, 1988).

When the entity has achieved its goal, it does not permanently equilibrate. Its goals are socially reconstructed and enacted on the basis of past experience and actions (Weick, 1979). Internal and external environmental forces may cause instabilities that propel it to a new developmental path. Though theories that depend on teleological process cannot be specific concerning what trajectory development of an organizational entity will take, proponents of the theories in question can formulate a variety of possible paths and then depend on the norms of decision or rationality and action rationality to provide specific paths (Brunsson, 1982).

The Dialectical Theory

The third major school of organizational change is the dialectical theory. Dialectics is the science of revolutionary conflict which Marxists call historical materialism. Russians used it to transform their feudal past into scientific and socialist system in 1917. However, dialectical theory began with Hegel's assumption that the organization as an entity exists in a pluralistic environment characterized by "colliding events, forces or contradictory values that compete against each other for mastery, domination and control. Opposition may be internal to the organization. If it has several conflicting goals or interest groups which rival each other for priority. Opposition may be external to the organization as it tries to chart new directions that collide with the direction of other organizations in the system or suprasystem. Evidently, a dialectical theory needs two or several clear entities whose interplay generates opposition for confronting and engaging one another in conflict.

Dialectically, stability and change are explained by reference to the balance of power between opposing entities. The struggles and accommodations that perpetuate the status quo in the midst of oppositions produce stability or equilibrium. Change occurs when these opposing values, forces or events attain enough power for confronting and engaging the status quo. The relative power of an antithesis can mobilize an organizational entity to the extent that the prevailing thesis (status quo) is challenged to set the stage for producing a synthesis. In the long run, the synthesis can become a new thesis in order to keep the dialectical process continuous. By its true colors, the synthesis is an innovation or new invention which is diametrically opposed to the thesis and antithesis. Both the antithesis and synthesis symbolize positive or negative results of change. Change is either promoted or suppressed by either the adopters or nonadopters respectively.

Exploring the limits of new institutionalism in the light of the causes and consequences of illegitimate (not according to the traditional mission) organizational change, 631 private elite and nonelite colleges were investigated between 1971 and 1986 (Kraatz and Zajac, 1996). The purpose of the study was to determine under what circumstances neoinstitutional (DiMaggio and Powell, 1991; and Perrow, 1986) predictions concerning organizational inertia, institutional isomorphism, the legitimacy imperative and other fundamental beliefs can be overshadowed by more traditional sociological theories (Pfeffer and Salancik, 1978; Selznick, 1948; and Thompson, 1967) which accentuate organizational adaptation, variation and the role of specific and technically oriented global and local demands of the environment to be changed. The findings show little support for neoinstitutional interpretations and predictions. First, most liberal arts colleges underwent change contrary to institutional demands. The change was largely attributed to their professionalization and vocationalization of their curricula. Second, technically global and local conditions of the environment, i.e., changes in consumers' preferences and local economic and demographic differences were strong and indicative predictors of the observed changes. Third, over time, the schools became less rather than more homogeneous. In other words, significant elements of heterogeneity colored their populations. Fourth, in general terms, schools did not "mimic" other colleges that are more prestigious than they were. Finally, the illegitimate changes had positive rather than negative consequences which will enhance their enrollment and survival in a competitive environment. These results dialectically indicate that current research on "organization-environment relations may underestimate the power of traditional adaptation-based explanations in organizational sociology" (p. 812). Such adaptations are reflections of strategic restructuring that has been going on in higher education and private arena to accommodate diversity, globalism, quality, competition and survival (Zajac and Kraatz, 1993).

It is instructive to differentiate the relationship of traditional theories concerning organizations (Pfeffer and Salancik, 1978; Selznick, 1948; and Thompson, 1967) and their neoinstitutional perspective (DiMaggio and Powell, 1991; Meyer and Rowan, 1977; and Perrow, 1986). Meyer and Rowan and DiMaggio and Powell advanced a neoinstitutionalist idea that organizations dialectically exist in fields of other organizations that influence their behavior. When the organizational fields become 'structured' in terms of definition and maturity, they

> exert powerful influences on the behavior of the organizations within them. As fields undergo increasing structuration, the organizations ... become increasingly homogeneous. The collective rationality of organizations, along with their collective striving for legitimacy and social fitness, leads them to adopt uniform, institutionalized structures and practices that conform to the mandate of the institutional environment (Kraatz and Zajac, 1996, p. 814).

This notion stands in dialectical contrast to an adaptation perspective which views organizations as fundamentally altering their structures and practices in order to coalign with the technologically changing general and local environments (Thompson, 1967). While neoinstitutionalists regard organizational change as constrained, and tending toward conformity (DiMaggio and Powell, 1983; Meyer and Rowan, 1977; and Scott, 1987) and organizational inertia, old traditional institutional theorists argue that organizations are continually adapting and changing (Selznick, 1948). Both neoinstitutionalism and old institutional theory of organization show, regardless of their differential perceptions in terms of organizational change, concur that organizations are among other things, rational actors (Tolbert and Zucker, 1983).

Miller (1994) of Montreal and McGill Universities examined how past performance has influenced organizational evolution, decision making and adaptation to environment. By studying 36 companies, he has demonstrated that after they have attained excellence in terms of success, these companies "exhibit inertia in many aspects of structure and strategy-making process; ... pursue immoderation, i.e., adopt extreme process orientations; ... manifest inattention i.e., reduce intelligence gathering and information processing activity; and ... demonstrate insularity by failing to adapt to changes in the environment" (p. 325). Past organizational successes give rise to periods of creativity and productivity which Tushman and Romanelli (1985) call "convergence" and "momentum" (Miller and Friesen, 1980a, 1984) respectively. Such past success encourages ideological and strategic continuity which strengthen the structures and processes which support it. Dialectically, poor performance is likely to provoke the self-evaluation of existing values and strategies. Such an evaluation will highlight existing strengths, weaknesses and possibilities. Analytical self-evaluation can pave the way for "revival, restraint, reawakening, and realignment with the environment" (Miller, 1994, p. 345). Ideally, there is a dialectical process in the making in organizations that emanates from the effects of past experience, practice and performance.

If the dialectic of change negatively drifts into a crisis, the intervention of crisis management can mean the difference between life and death to the organization, the production system and employees. In other words, an organizational crisis is

a low probability, high-impact situation that is perceived by critical stakeholders to threaten the viability of the organization and that is subjectively experienced by these individuals as personally and socially threatening. Ambiguity of cause, effect, and means of resolution of the organizational crisis will lead to disillusionment or loss of psychic and shared meaning, as well as to the shattering of commonly held beliefs and values and individuals' basic assumptions. During the crisis, decision making is pressed by perceived time constraints and colored by cognitive limitations. Effective crisis management involves minimizing potential risk before a triggering event. In response to a triggering event, effective crisis management involves improving and interacting by key stakeholders so that individual and collective sense making, shared meaning, and roles are reconstructed. Following a triggering event, effective crisis management entails individual and organizational readjustment of basic assumptions, as well as behavioral and emotional responses aimed at recovery and readjustment (Pearson and Clair, 1998, p. 59).

The crisis can be minimized or eliminated by initiating a successful project, planning, modeling, rapid learning, vision, integration of information and resources, ownership and commitment, and free team spirit (Bowman, 1994). The crisis can be a profound status quo rather than violence. To challenge it, change agents need to be fully informed on four arenas: cost and quality, timing and know-how, strongholds and deep pockets (D'Aveni, 1994). They can disrupt the status-quo by exploiting superior stakeholder satisfaction, strategic soothsaying, capabilities for speed, capabilities for surprise, shifting the rules, signaling strategic intent and simultaneous and sequential strategic thrusts. In addition, organizations for which change is intended can be viewed as a form of scientific specialties. The specialties are the organizations in which labor deals with a variety of degrees of task uncertainty and mutual dependence. Given this scenario, the "sociological theory of change suggests that scientific change is generally triggered by competition, but that various types of change depend on the social organization and status of scientific groups. Some fields change through permanent discoveries, some through specialization and cumulation, yet others change through cognitive fragmentation" (Fuchs, 1993, p. 993). This theoretical proposition can create a dialectic both within the social sciences and the physical sciences or within a variety of interdisciplinary and multidisciplinary intellectual dynamics that are an essential tension for change in organizations.

As part of the dialectical discourse of change, Wall and Callister (1995) have discussed the causes and effects of the escalation and de-escalation of conflict in interpersonal, intergroup, interorganizational and indirectly, in international settings. This situation of person-role conflict, inter-sender variety and inter-role conflict is a "process in which one party perceives that its interests are being opposed or negatively affected by another party" (p. 517). The opposed interests can be concerns (Thomas, 1992), goods, aims and values (Putman and Poole, 1987), or aspirations (Pruitt and Rubin, 1986) and activities (Deutsch, 1980). Conflict can be managed by the disputants themselves, by managers or by third party influences (Wall and Callister, 1995). Both conflict and conflict resolution are aspects of change.

The Theory of Evolution

At times, the term evolution is synonymous with change. Restrictively enough, evolution, organizationally speaking, concerns the "cumulative changes in structural forms of populations of organizational entities across communities, industries, or society at large" (Van de Ven and Poole, 1995, p. 517; Aldrich, 1979; Campbell, 1969; and Hannan and Freeman, 1977). Parallel to evolution in biology, change happens in a continuous cycle of variation, selection, and retention. The variations are creative and novel forms of organizational entities that stochastically emerge at random (Aldrich, 1979 and Campbell, 1969). Selection of the organization largely occurs due to competition for resources. The environment in which the organization exists selects organizational entities whose resource base is environmentally conducive to the organization's niche (Hannan and Freeman, 1977). Retention involves forces of which inertia and persistence do perpetuate and maintain certain organizational forms. The functional purpose of retention is to "counteract the self-reinforcing loop between variations and selection" (Van de Ven and Poole, 1995, p. 518). According to Weick (1979) the function of variations is to stimulate the selection of new organizational forms. However, retention maintains previous forms and practices. In other words, while variation enhances change, retention maintains the status quo of organizational entities. Therefore, "evolution explains change as a recurrent, cumulative, and probabilistic progression of variation, selection, and retention of organizational entities" (p. 518). This motor or logic of change has been given to enable us to "specify actuarial probabilities of the changing demographic characteristics of the population of entities inhabiting a niche. Although one cannot predict which entity will survive or fail, the overall population persists and evolves through time, according to the specified population dynamics" (p. 518).

A variety of scholars think that organizational evolution has many meanings. These meanings emanate from their conceptions concerning how traits are inherited, the speed of change, and the unit of analysis.

For instance, Hannan and Freeman (1977, 1989) and McKelvey (1982) assert that traits are inherited through the processes of intergenerational evolution. Lamarckians like Boyd and Richerson (1985), Burgelman (1991), Sigh and Lumsden (1990) and Weick (1979) believe that traits are generationally acquired as species or as entities learn and imitate. It seems that this form of Lamarckism is more appropriately acceptable than rigid Darwinism as a model for organizational evolution and management practice. Rigid Darwinists lack adequate solutions for operationally identifying an organizational generation (McKelvey, 1982).

Darwinist popularizers argue that organizational change is gradual and continuous while other evolutionists support the saltation process. Also, Gould's (1989) punctuated equilibrium model adds a hierarchical dimension to evolutionary theory by distinguishing this sorting. The sorting is comprised of the development or "decline of organisms of a given species through differential birth and death rate" "from speciation." Speciation is the process through which new species and subgenus are formed. While speciation is a property of populations, adaptation is a property of organisms that exist within a population. Extinction, which is a sorting process, is characterized by a simplified "concatenation of deaths among organisms" (Gould, 1989, p. 122).

In the field of scientific scholarship, a variety of theories of evolution exists. Some theorists such as March (1994) view evolutionary theory as development or gradual, dynamic and sequential change. As it applies here, that is in leadership and management social science literature, evolutionary theory is exclusive from its historically defined sociological and biological evolutionism. Comtian and Spenserian metaphoric idea of organic evolution rather than Darwinian and biological evolution which deal with society's lifespan from its rudimentary origins to its more advanced and differentiated forms do not apply either (Sztompka, 1993). The early sociological evolutionism relatively parallels life-cycle theory than biological evolutionary theory. In a profound way, though a large number of current social scientists espouse Darwinian, Lamarckian, Gouldian and Mendellian evolutionary theories, this scholarly endeavor places emphasis on biological evolution by clarifying its current interpretation in organizational theory, i.e., organizational science and practice.

Typologically, the change process theories of life-cycle, teleology, dialectics and evolution are characterized by four consistent elements. First, in each theory, the process of change is seen as a different cycle of events. Second, the events are controlled and dominated by a different motor or logic generating mechanism of change. Third, the change process "operates on different unit of analysis" (Van de Ven and Poole, 1995, p. 520). Fourth, each "unit of analysis represents a different mode of change" (p. 520). Figure 15.1 is a metatheoretical design illustrative of the four dominant theories in question.

Unit of Change

The processes of change and development continue to happen at many organizational levels including the individual, group, organization, population and larger organizational communities. This nesting of entities is systematically hierarchical. This nested element of organizational classification is used to focus organizational change in two ways: "(a) the internal development of a simple organizational entity by examining its historical processes of change, adaptation, and replication, and (b) the relationships between numerous entities to understand ecological processes of competition, cooperation, conflict, and other forms of interaction" (p. 521).

Logically, the theories of evolution and dialectics operate on multiple entities. For instance while evolutionary forces are analytically simplified in terms of the impact they have on populations and their lack of meaning at the level of the individual entity, dialectical theories require two or three entities (thesis, antithesis, and synthesis, etc.) in order to cause change. Also, for further exemplification, and as Riegel (1975) has demonstrated, child development is a dialectical process. In this process, the motor or logic of change focuses on the interaction between two entities (the child and the environment). The entities can be distinguished in the child's mind and world. Riegel's case for entities that are involved in the child's dialectic of change is classic.

Contrary to the dynamics of change in evolutionary and dialectical realm, life cycle and teleological theories operate in a single entity. Life-cycle theory explains development as a function of potentials immanent within the entity regardless of environmental impact on it. The force that drives development comes from within the single and whole developing entity. Likewise, teleological theories "require only a single entity's goals to explain development" (p. 522). In other words, a "teleological motor drives individual entities to enact an envisioned end state" (p. 522). Whenever research scholars and scientists try to examine the processes of change within, among, and between specific organizational entities, they use dialectical or evolutionary theories

Figure 15.1. Process Theories of Organizational Development and Change

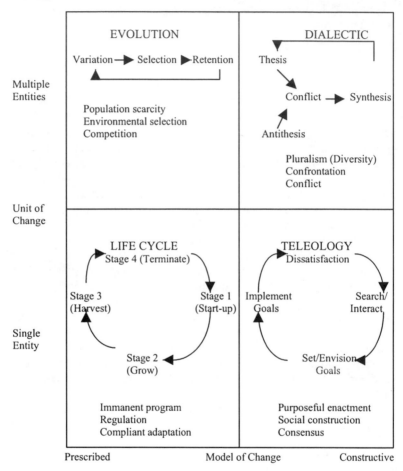

[a]Arrows on lines represent likely sequences among events, not causation between events.

Source: Van de Ven, A.H. and Poole, M.S. (1995). Explaining Development and Change in Organizations. *Academy of Management Review,* 20, 3, p. 520.

rather than life-cycle and teleological ones due to the fact that the former theoretical pair tends to specify the laws, rules and processes which govern the entities.

Mode of Change

Four motors of change are distinguishable on the following conditions:

Whether the sequence of change events is prescribed prior to either deterministic or probabilistic laws, or whether the progression is constructed and emerges as the change process unfolds. A prescribed mode of change channels the development of entities in prespecified direction, typically of maintaining and incrementally adapting their forms in a stable, predictable way. Unprecedented novel forms that, in retrospect, often are discontinuous and unpredictable departures from the past. A prescribed mode evokes a sequence of change events in accord with a preestablished program or action routine. A constructive mode, in contrast, produces new action routines that may or may not create an original (re)formulation of the entity. Life-cycle and evolutionary theories operate in a prescribed modality, while teleological and dialectical theories operate in a constructive modality (p. 522).

The prescribed mode of change is patterned on the original state, changes are small, gradual, cumulative and less disruptive because of low levels of uncertainty. Biologically, such changes are ontogenetic (DeRosney, 1970). Ontogenesis is the process of the reproduction of entities that are the same as the original ones.

Life-cycle and evolutionary theories "incorporate a prescribed mode of change. ..the immanent form is realized by steps, and although some steps may seem like a radical morphogenetic change, there is an underlying continuity due to the immanent form, logic, program, or code that drives development" (Van de Ven and Poole, 1995, p. 523). Because life-cycle models have an immanent motor frame-braking changes and mutations hardly happen though their cumulative accounts are an intellectual exercise of researchers and statisticians who use such data to manipulate the gradual change of larger populations. Mutations are neither sudden nor dramatic. Mutations happen in the context of "punctuated equilibrium" (Gould and Eldridge, 1977). The punctuated equilibrium mode of biological evolution allows the sudden emergence of species at the microlevel of an entity. However, the diffusion of species which transforms the nature of the population (to cause to change) takes place gradually, sequentially and over millions of years (Gould, 1989). This kind of punctuated equilibrium model of organizational change is different from the one discussed elsewhere by Tushman and Romanelli (1985) in organizational science literature. Though teleological and dialectical motors have a constructive mode of development, the former's goal is to preserve the status quo. For instance, while the theory of statistics preserves that status quo, the theory of dynamics doesn't. Teleological theories are unpredictable and discontinuous (Von Wright, 1971). Dialectical theory is constitutive of the constructive second order mode of change. It "produces a revolutionary change, resulting in a new entity that is an original rather than the reproduction of some prior state or entity" (Van de Ven and Poole, 1995, p. 524).

The double dimensions of unit and mode of change codify the four theories, which are also motors of change/logics of change, in terms of their behavior and processes. These dimensions differ from others that are used to classify theories of organizational change, e.g., "incremental versus radical change" (p. 524), continuous versus discontinuous change (Meyer, Goes, and Brooks, 1993), first-order versus second-order change (Meyer et al., 1993) and competence-enhancing versus competence-destroying change (Abernathy and Clark, 1985). These "dimensions classify organizational change by their consequences or outcomes rather than by their starting or process conditions" (Van de ven and Poole, 1995, p. 524). Statistically, large "incremental, continuous and competence-enhancing changes follow the operations of a prescribed mode, just as radical, discontinuous, and competence-destroying changes" (p. 524) tend to "follow from a constructive mode" (p. 524).

Most known theories of organizational change and development are more complex that the four mentioned ideal types. First, their complexity can be attributed to the fact the organizational context of development and change continuous for millions of years. As a result, more than one motor of change can influence the organization to develop or change particularly when diverse units and actors, both from inside and outside the organization disperse their influence simultaneously. This influence may impart its momentum to the developmental process. As a result, more than one motor of change may affect development and change processes. Given the time taken to change, and given the complex variety of the forces, units, modes and motors of change, the byproduct of change and development could be multilayered and complex. It cannot be simplified. Second, the complexity of organizational change and development theories is the inherent incompleteness of any single motor. Each motor of change has one or more components whose values and rhetoric of change are exogeneously rather than endogeneously determined. For instance, in the context of the theory of evolution, the assumption is that variations come at random, "but the process that gives rise to variations remains unspecified. In the dialectical model, the origin of the antithesis is obscure, as is the source of dissatisfaction in the teleological model, and the processes that trigger start-up and termination in the life-cycle model" (p. 526). Further still, combinations of these theories can make hybrid or composite theories to become dual-motor or tri-motor or quad-motor rather than single motor theories which contribute to prolific forms of change. For illustrative purposes, the four examples of composite hybridization include Clark's (1975) life-cycle teleological motors; Greiner's (1972) interaction of life-cycle and dialectical motors; Tushman's and Romanelli's (1985) teleological and evolutionary motors; and the life-cycle, teleological and evolutionary theoretical hybridization model of Weick (1979).

Leaders of change need to understand that the management of change is a challenging and complex function. They need to identify and sensitize the sources of individual and organizational resistance to change and provide solutions to overcome resistance (Hellriegel, Slocum and Woodman, 1998). Some of the major barriers to organizational change and innovation include the "lack of specificity concerning the innovation stage upon which investigations focus, ... minimal consideration given to innovation characteristics; ... research being limited to single-organizational type studies, and ... researchers limiting their scope of inquiry by working within single theoretical perspective (Wolfe, 1994, p. 414). In addition, other sources of individual resistance to change are perceptions, personality, habit, threats to power and influence, fear of unknown and economic reasons. Organizationally, resistance to change comes from organizational design, organizational culture, resource limitations, fixed investments, and interorganizational agreements (Hellriegel, Slocum, and Woodman, 1998).

Organizational change is a form of organizational development (OD). Organizational development is a planned and systematic process of organizational change that is rooted in empirical and behavioral science research theory. Some of the major disciplines by which it is consisted of include sociology, psychology, cybernetics, political science, and anthropology (Gortner, Mahler, and Nicholson, 1997; and Hellriegel, Slocum, and Woodman, 1998). While it is multidisciplinary in perspective, it relies on data from personality, learning and motivation theories. It is strengthened with research on group dynamics, power, leadership and organization design which are elements of group and organizational behavior.

Organizational development is a collectivity of philosophical techniques which seek to create self-directed change to which people are committed. The problems and issues to be solved are those identified by the organization's members who are directly concerned with and are affected by them. OD is an organizationwide change effort (Hellriegel, Slocum, and Woodman, 1998, p. 591). For the changes to last, change agents must understand how, when, where, and why they need to involve the entire organization. The agents see the organization as an adaptive institution whose members are prepared to solve problems now and in future. To be able to do that, the organization collaboratively gathers data, digests it analytically and attempts to arrive at conclusive solutions. This approach tends to actively emphasize the satisfaction of human needs as effective organizational performance. This is accomplished through a team effort in cultural analysis. Agents use technology and structural "tentacles" to change the complex and holistic organization (Gortner, Mahler, and Nicholson, 1997). (See Table 15.1.)

Chaos Theory

The contemporary semantic theory of chaos indicates that it means "anarchy, confusion, disorder, disorganization, jumble, muddle, shambles and snarl" (*New Webster's Dictionary and Thesaurus of the English Language*, 1992, T5). However, contrary to the apparent and contemporary shallowness of its semantics, chaos, viewed from the standpoint of its original universality means more than what the thesaurus has prescribed above. Since the goal of science is a search for order rather than chaos, paradoxically there is order in chaos too. Both mythic and scientific world views indicate that chaos has structure and order. The fact that there is order in chaos indicates that even science has limits that are set by "quantum theory, mathematics and chaos theory" (Braunschweig, 1992, p. 256).

In Greek, chaos (xaivw) means to gape, open up or yawn. It does not mean lack of order. The possibility for its negation is nonexistent in Greek linguistic theoretical structure and semantics. However, in Hesiod's cosmogony, there was chaos before the earth, night and darkness came into existence. In addition, Babylonian "Enuma elish"

Table 15.1. Families of Ideal-Type Theories of Social Change and Their Proponents

Family	Life Cycle	Evolution	Dialectic	Teleology
Members	Developmentalism Ontogenesis Metamorphosis	Darwinian evolution Mendelian genetics Saltationism	Conflict theory Dialectical materialism Pluralism	Goal setting, planning Functionalism Social construction
Pioneers	Comte (1798-1857) Spencer (1820-1903) Piaget (1896-1980)	Lamarck (1744-1829) Darwin (1809-1882) Mendel (1822-1884) Gould & Eldridge (1977)	Hegel (1770-1831) Marx (1818-1883) Freud (1856-1959)	Mead (1863-1931) Weber (1864-1920) Simon (1916--)
Key Metaphor	Organic growth	Competitive survival	Opposition, conflict	Purposeful cooperation
Logic	Imminent program Prefigured sequence Compliant adaptation	Natural selection among competitors in a population	Contradictory forces Thesis, antithesis, synthesis	Envisioned end state Social construction Equifinality
Event Progression	Linear & irreversible sequence of prescribed stages in unfolding of immanent potentials present at the beginning	Recurrent, cumulative, & probabilistic sequence of variation, selection, & retention events	Recurrent, discontinuous sequence of confrontation, conflict, and synthesis between contradictory values or events	Recurrent, discontinuous sequence of goal setting, implementation, and adaptation of means to reach desired end state
Generating Force	Prefigured program/rule Regulated by nature, Logic, or institutions	Population scarcity Competition Commensalism	Conflict & confrontation between opposing forces forces, interests, or classes	Goal enactment consensus on means cooperation/symbiosis

Source: Van de Ven, A.H. and M.S. Poole. (1995). Explaining Development and Change in Organizations, *Academy of Management Review*, 20, 3, p. 514.

and Nordic world view show a "structureless" cosmic reality. In German, chaos means "yawning, charm, gap ... opening ... or cleft" (p. 257). Christian thinkers understand chaos to mean lack of order comparable to Biblical "Tahubohu" (p. 257). Such lack of order has important roles to play in cosmogenic mythologies which place emphasis in vacuum or nothingness and which "lead from chaos to cosmos" (p. 257).

In the short run, chaotic situations appear to be unpredictable. But, in the long run, they predict the future with reasonable accuracy, with some imperfections, and with a sense of impossibility (Aley, 1996, p. 1). For instance, "Building on chaos theory, ... complexity theory argues that groups of randomly operating independent units – amino acids floating in primordial seas, humans acting in their own interests, populations of animals – can spontaneously and without outside direction organize themselves into complex systems – self-reproducing DNA molecules, functioning economies, and social groups (Lemonick, 1995, p. 1). The paradox is that such complex and stable systems can, without much difficulty, become unstable given the slightest provocation. In other words, in stability there is instability, conversely, in instability there is stability. This means that order and chaos are spontaneous simultaneities occurring in the rational irrationality of our cosmic, functionalist, mechanistic, and behavioral environment of post-Soviet and totalitarian organizations.

Sectional Borrowing: Case Study and Critique on Reinventing Government

Osborne's and Gaebler's text on *Reinventing Government* (1992) has been constructed by observing how three mayors (Stephen Goldsmith of Indianapolis, Edward Rendell of Philadelphia, and Brett Schundler of Jersey City) and other state governors are using innovative strategies to make government "more efficient if it acts more entrepreneurial and less bureaucratic" (Buckkstein, 1995, p. 1). The evolution of *Reinventing Government* has become the blueprint for *From Red Tape to results: Creating a Government that Works Better and Costs Less* (1993). The latter document has been composed by *National Performance Review*, which Vice President Al Gore coordinated. Both books assertively argue that "government can be transformed in much the same way that many corporations have been transformed. Transforming it will make it to become more attuned to customer needs, less bureaucratic, more flexible, more innovative, more entrepreneurial, and more effective" (Weiss, 1995, p. 229). This quote is not only the thesis of *Reinventing Government*, but the quotation's import has been ratified by other management experts or specialists such as Peter Druker and Tom Peters whose works are reflected in *American Management Review*. Osborne and Gaebler have suggested ten principles suitable for reinventing government. These are:

1. Steer rather than row to get catalytic government. An effective government steers but doesn't row. If services are cheaper and effective in the private sector, they should be used.
2. Leaders should empower their government by placing emphasis on participatory decision making processes.
3. They should introduce competition into service delivery in order to procure competitive government. For instance, they need to use abiding process to deliver all services.
4. Change rule-driven organization eliminates bureaucratic rules in order to establish mission-driven government.
5. Bureaus should fund outcomes rather than inputs in order to obtain results-oriented government. For example, it is good to fund successful schools rather than their enrollments.
6. Organizations should meet the needs of the customer rather than the bureaucracy in order to enhance customer-driven government.
7. Organizations should earn rather than spend to get enterprising government.
8. They should prevent rather than cure in order to get participatory government.
9. They should move from the culture of hierarchy to the one of participation and teamwork in order to procure decentralized government.
10. They should leverage change through the market in order to obtain market oriented government which gives incentives.

These ten principles on *Reinventing Government* put people first by "serving customers, empowering its employees, fostering excellence, creating a clear sense of mission, delegating responsibility, replacing regulations with incentives, developing budget-based outcomes, "and measuring our success by customer satisfaction" (Moe, 1994, p. 111). In addition, Moe asserts that this process of reinventing government has not become the unshackling of an outdated bureaucratic paradigm and its replacement with the entrepreneurial one, but through this shift, the process has attained "theological immunity" that "discourages discussion within the public administration community""(p. 113). How long this model will be used will depend on the personalities of political leaders and their ideological inclinations.

Weakness of the Document

Though *Reinventing Government* is a blueprint for effective and efficient government, it has several weaknesses that warrant its criticism. Notwithstanding its presentation, noteworthy concepts for total quality management (TQM), "it takes liberties with historical fact, makes unsupported assumptions and demonstrates little respect for the country's conscientious, hard-working and productive public sector employee" (Masden, 1995, p. 113). Consequently, the book and most of its recommendations, while being useful discourse, "can not be considered a serious piece of scholarly" literature (p. 113). For instance, the text does not spell out its theoretical stance. Lack of scientific theory makes it less academic. The use of stories for its documentation and personal interviews and press accounts are untraditional modes of organizing it that fail to comprehensively and realistically rationalize its scientific rhetoric. Undoubtedly, the authors emphasize the benefits of efficient government, they show the willingness to consider alternative and innovative managerial approaches that can produce better policy results. They also talk about the virtues of or essence of small (conservative) government and big (liberal) alternative without focusing on how government agencies can work smarter and better or can work more efficiently and effectively. A smarter, better, effective and efficient government must deal with the problems of illiteracy, drug culture, national and federal debt, pollution of the environment, crime, health care, campaign financing reforms, and standards of living for all Americans. Downsizing government may result in saving but those savings must be managed with a sense of responsibility and accountability. Bureaucratic "red tape, waste, incompetence, and mediocrity (McKenna, 1994) should be dealt with by reforming the 1883 Pedleton Act which professionalized the bureaucracy by protecting the interests of politicians and the government without protecting efficiency, accountability and effectiveness of employees (Masden, 1995) and without being effectively responsive to societal needs.

Again, both books, *Reinventing Government* and the *National Performance Review* argue that the industrial-era bureaucracies must be restricted so that they can minimize risk and handle the problems of information age' (Posner and Rothstein, 1994, p. 133). The couple argue that the three barriers to reinventing government, which make reforms more difficult include the fact that reforms lack an external or extrinsic force; Congress tries to advance its interest in accountability and by doing so, it tends to prevent the executive branch from achieving its goals; and finally, federal employee unions which help to decide the number and classification of the workforce have no legislative power which is essential for vetoing and protecting the workers.

Though these reformatory documents combine total quality management with preferences for lean and flexible structures for competition, entrepreneurship, and decentralization, their motif is based on private as opposed to public theoretical orientation. The extent to which management theories can be couched, interpretively understood and implemented at every level of government, in order to produce accountably efficient and effective results for public consumption could be an interesting and revealing performance. Some of the expected results include, "eliminating waste, reducing the number of federal employees, saving costs of procurement, and enacting savings that are attributable to information technology" (Weiss, 1995, p. 230).

Between 1979 and 1994, 'new capitalism,' which is to say, downsizing, eliminated more than ten million jobs in American industry. The elimination of these jobs has had negative human and organizational impact. Having examined the causes of downsizing in 100 of the Fortune companies, Budros (1997) found that the reasons were attributed to "shareholder values, foreign consolidations, market share, productivity, employee compensation, deregulation, and business peaks; by innovational forces—the adoption effect and industry culture; and by firm traits—ownership status and firm size" (p. 229). Rationally, the downsizers made these cuts for economic and social reasons.

Although the techno-economic benefits of downsizing are economically and negatively negligible, downsizers receive noneconomic rewards for downsizing. Social acceptance and favorable reputation for these actions are craved for. In a global economy in which downsizing is a psychologically catchy word, downsizing is well received by "the business, media, consultants, financial analysts, politicians and shareholders" (p. 245). In spite of the effects caused by these 'corporate killers,' the economic and social rationality of downsizing is a popular game that has been universalized in the global arena.

Implications

The successes and failures of this type of idealistic sectional borrowing shades management light on the difference between private and public sectors. In the first place, important ideas from one sector may be the nucleus for creative and insightful change in another sector. For instance, the managers of large, sprawling, heterogeneous structures in the private sector may discover that solutions and insightful experiences are rooted in public administration sector. Making these ideas visibly tangible for public managers breaks through habitual thinking and can stimulate genuine creativity and inspiration. Osborne and Gaebler's book and the NPR report provide clear and exciting cases of public managers who have translated these ideals into new reality. The ideas persuasively show that alternative ways of management can succeed in public settings. Particularly useful applications may involve getting better results at less cost by reducing layers of overhead and approval, capitalizing on information technology, and placing more trust in better trained and equipped front line employees.

Second, sectional borrowing may be a failure which can liberate the reader's views concerning possible difficulties in the management know how or lessons that are being generalized. A classic example is the role of customer orientation. Both documents are persuasive in explaining that public managers can sometimes benefit from identifying and serving their citizen customers. The text and the report offer great anecdotes concerning the shift in the attitude of public officials and leaps in service quality that follow from defining "visitors at parks, recipients of social security checks, applicants for drivers licenses, taxpayers, builders, and other customers of cities, states, and national governments" (p., 231).

In most or some cases, bureaus do not fit neatly into a customer-service model. Some provide service on an involuntary or irregular basis. Agencies like public regulatory and criminal justice bureaus 'could treat polluters, stock price manipulators, civil rights violators, burglars, child abusers, and drug dealers as customers." Such a form of interaction with people or groups that violate the law may not enable agencies to change the behaviors of violators. The target of the agencies is not to satisfy the "customers" who violate the law. It is to stop the negative or disruptive or criminal behavior common in their practice. Public managers can and do identify their customers as the law abiding citizens and innovators of society. However, agencies do not have close or any regular or direct contact with the 'customers.'

The former assess the satisfaction of the latter through the feedback mechanisms of electoral political representation and similar processes. Further still, in the private sector, customers are those who receive service by buying a product whose price is determined by the open and impersonal market. Those who serve customers are profit making centered rather than public service oriented. In other words, the private sector has autonomy in defining its mission which is profit maximization. On the other hand, the bureau has no autonomy or power to independently make decisions concerning programs, performance, coordination, evaluation, and funding without support from executive, judicial, legislative, and supervisory authority. Given this scenario, it is interesting that the "NPR Report hardly or barely recognizes the difficulty of federal managers' clarifying their objective in ways that explicitly reject or de-emphasize some of the goals that Congress expects them to carry out.

Any successes reinventing the government might realize will be an accomplishment in the right direction. Reinventing the government with the use of sectional and sectoral ideas' is in an experimental condition. Will this experiment unleash the force, motivation and creativity in this complex, dynamic and contradictory domestic and global environment that will chart new directions? Will the new directions be positive or negative? Who will manage the realization of the new state of affairs? Is it aliens from "Mars"? The earthly? The earthly "saints" are no longer saints any more—only time will tell. Osborne's and Gaetler's *Reinventing Government* is a prescriptive of the "ten commandments" of reinventing government in the post industrialized, post-Cold War and post-Soviet era. The ten commandments or principles it prescribes are not only an analytic extrapolation of the works of prominent American management gurus like Drucker, Tom Peters, and Waterman and others, but the document's untheoreticalness, simplicity and narrative are solvent expressions for bureaucratic malaise. While it may not be too late yet to cry for the spilt milk—our golden age, the "boom and bust" of the East particularly China and Japan may have contributed to our less competitiveness because we prejudicially do not want to integrate or borrow their culture of the market in order to strengthen our own. Conceptually, though reinventing the government is a form of sectoral borrowing, this borrowing needs to be done in the context of our narrow Eurocentric cultural presuppositions which could minimize our potential for theoretical inclusion, efficiency, superior innovation, creativity comprehensiveness and accountability.

Unlike *Reinventing Government, Organization Theory* (1997), whose main purpose is literary public organization theory of the industrialized world, argues that effective management of bureaus radically differs from the management of private organizations. The bureaus function in a climate of open systems that produce feelings of uncertainty, hostility risk, and inefficiency. On the contrary, private organizations operate under a "closed" system which strengthens the vales of stability, rationality and efficiency. In spite of the fact that these values of the "closed" system are highly being craved for in the public sector as indicated in *Reinventing Government*, both sectors, as Gortner et al. (1997) assert are characterized by theoretical interdependence and structural bureaucratic similarity.

Above all, while *Reinventing Government* is untheoretical and therefore less scientific, *Organization Theory* is theoretically multitheoretical and interdisciplinary in scientific scholarship. Its multitheoreticalness does not necessarily make it more effective and efficient in addressing the solutions of "bureaucratic morass" as *Reinventing Government* does; however, Gortner et al. (1997) show how theories, processes and structures of the public organization can be used conflictually in order to bring change. These theories, processes and structures are applicable in a dialectically Marxist, and Hegelian sense of organizational dialectics. Of the most important among the theories are "systems theory, theories of group politics and influence, theories of political economy, personality and attitude formation, theories of psychological humanism, public choice theory, theories of culture and interpretation, and theories of social change"(pg. 4).

While the gamut of theoretical text speaks to academic and advanced students in undergraduate and graduate levels, its readership may include the larger and literate but intelligent public. Unlike Gortner et al., *Reinventing Government* is written for the layperson and the public intellectual alike. Its popular appeal concerning how government can be made more efficient, effective, accountable and entrepreneurial has made it to be one of the best sellers. More than 400,000 copies have been sold. Its simple layout in terms of the ten clear steps (principles or commandments) for bureaucratic reform has made its bureaucratic "theology" quite appealing. In spite of its proselytizing influence, it is hoped that its converts will make government better, stronger, innovative, productive, and acceptable. Since the themes of its logic are not new in American history, and since what is new is the focus rather than the content or substance, it is unlikely for *Reinventing Government* to provoke general, massive, or systematic reforms of any kind unless theories and agents of change have fizzled from the "new heaven" to implement the reforms. When change agents persuasively interact, especially when that interaction is social, military, economic, political, or technological (Manning, 1996; and Bentley, 1996), the diffusion and fusion of ideas generate more effective aspects of innovative change in a macro rather than micro scale.

Conclusion

The charge for sectoral borrowing has strengths and weaknesses. Both books *(Reinventing Government and NPR Report)* make a convincing case that some borrowing can be valuable. The promise and value of trying this experiment has influenced the authors to become overly optimistic about the benefits of incorporating business practices into the public sector. The same authors are reasonably concerned with the ways these practices should be modified to warrant the functioning, expression, and productive containment of the sectoral differences. Sectoral borrowing is not only an old American tradition, but in abstract, it is theoretically and intellectually a form of theoretical syncretism whose synergistic practice is likely to eliminate political and bureaucratic pathologies whose misapplication or misimplementation might cause the system to decline, decay and go under or experience "a big bang." Regardless of the unscholarly and conflicting assertions of the *Reinventing Government*, the values and promises to be gained are worth using the effort to try than never. Though the book is essentially simple, clear, and principally a step by step prescription of the ten commandments for public entrepreneurship, the steps it enunciates can be well explained with the structural theoretical and functional process through which change is addressed in *Organization Theory* (Gortner, et al., 1997).

Organizational change is ubiquitous. Ecological, demographic and cultural changes are external forces of social change that can have an impact on political, economic, and technological aspects of organizational change in space over time. For instance and historically speaking, great changes in social structure are those which were brought about by the technological revolution in ancient antiquity. This revolution which changed the lives and times of sedentary agriculturalists from hunters, gatherers, herders and fishermen to developed and elaborate political and social systems of palaces, temples and cities was accompanied with the rise of states. With the use of more advanced technology and philosophical, religious and political systems, these states improved their economies and standards of living that have progressively become to be known elements of modernization. When the influences of the above mentioned macro forces of change have "touched" every facet of organizational reality, organizational concepts, ideas, metaphors and theories are constructed, reconstructed and applied in specific situations for the purpose of enhancing organizational learning, organizational goals, and organizational productivity in the midst of conflict, doubt, and a variety of struggles within and without the organizational field that constitute change.

Change agents will do a better job to diagnose the prerequisites for change. They need to recognize and interpret the problem and assess the need for change. They must ascertain the organization's readiness and capability for change. They should identify managerial, leadership and on line resources and motivations for change before they prioritize the goals of productivity.

The driving micro forces of organizational change, irrespective of the external and macro forces talked about earlier, include "high performance goals, new equipment, competition, employees with new skills and desire for increased influence and rewards." Likewise, the micro resisting forces of change include but are not limited to "group norms for output, familiarity with present equipment, complacency, need to learn new skills, fear of reduced influence and rewards" (Zand, 1995, p. 181; and Hellriegel, Slocum, and Woodman, 1998, p. 590). These two micro and macro dialectically antagonistic forces tend to determine the current and desired level of performance in organizations.

Theoretically, this chapter has largely defined the meaning of organizational change and the wealth of theoretical and intellectual traditions which explain how change happens and how it is animated. Change that is observed in conjunction with development are complex organizational processes. At times, given the diversity of the major theories (life-cycle, teleology, dialectics, evolution, chaos and sectoral borrowing) prevailing conditions may trigger the interplay of several change motors and produce interdependent cycles of change. Though each of these changes may have its own internal logic, complexity and potential for theoretical confusion, it may arise from the interplay of diverse and nested motors. These theories are rampart in the management and public organization literature that herein form the parlance for a synergistic conclusion and theoretical elegance. Motors may compliment or contradict each other. Some may operate simultaneously while others may operate at different times and different 'wavelengths." They also may alternate. As they behave differentially rather than uniformly, they determine the "vertical and horizontal relationships between ecological and genealogical hierarchies in the levels of organizational systems" (Van de Ven and Poole, 1995, p. 534). These relationships indicate that the relative balance between the constructive and prescribed motors operate at different levels of analysis. This helps to explain the nature of patterns of stability and change in organizations.

For instance, whenever an institutionally prescribed motor dominates organizational growth and development, it may "suppress or dampen internally generated variety" (p. 534) to a point where the organization will begin to remain rigid and predictable.

If a constructive motor dominates through either the teleologically or dialectically oriented avenues, the organization is likely to have difficulty to "suppress rival subsystems that rise up from within, creating too much variety to integrate into one system" (p. 534). To say it in another way, "positive and negative feedback between constructive and prescribed motors reinforces" complex change while negative feedback is "likely to produce a moving equilibrium in organizational development" (p. 534).

When positive and negative feedback loops operate in different motors, the organization may be pushed into four developmental "gears." First, it can flow toward a fixed point equilibrium. Second, it may periodically oscillate between two fixed points. Third, it may bifurcate far from equilibrium by creating new structures, and fourth, it may behave randomly. Obviously, the interplay of interdisciplinary, multimotor and the positive and negative feedback loops may result in chaos that may be resolved through intersectional and intrasectional borrowing. Organizationally, change is a product of the borrowing interplay of conflicting forces whose mutation of ideas, structures and processes tend to continually enhance it.

References

Abernathy, W.J., and K.B. Clark. 1985. Innovation: Mapping the winds of creative destruction. *Research Policy* 14:3-22.

Abrahamson, E., and L. Rosenkopf. 1993. *Simulating the Bandwagon Diffusion of Innovations through Interorganizational Networks.* New York: Working Paper, Columbia University Graduate School of Business.

Abrahamson, E., and L. Rosenkopf. 1993. Institutional and competitive bandwagons: Using mathematical modeling as a tool to explore innovation diffusion. *Academy of Management Review* 18, 3:487-517.

Akin, G., and E. Schultheiss. 1990. Jazz bands and missionaries: OD through stories and metaphor. *Journal of Managerial Psychology* 5, 4:12-18.

Aldrich, H. (1979). *Organizations and Environments.* Englewood Cliffs, N.J.: Prentice Hall.

Aley,   J.   (1996). http://www.Pathfinder.com/fortune/magazine/1996/960205/wallstr eet.html, 1-4.

Anderson, P.W., and M.L. Tushman 1990. Technological discontinuities and dominant designs. *Administrative Science Quarterly* 35: 604-633.

Bales, R.F., and F.L. Strodtbeck. 1951. Phases in group problem-solving. *Journal of Abnormal and Social Psychology* 46: 485-495.

Baltes, P.B., F. Dittman-Kohli, and R.A. Dixon. 1986. Multidisciplinary propositions on the development of intelligence during adulthood and old age. In *Human Development and the Life Course: Multidisciplinary Perspectives,* eds. A.B. Soresnen, F.E. Weinert, and LR. Sherrod, 467-507. Hillsdale, NJ.: Erlbaum.

Benitez, Ben. 1995. Reinvention battle must continue and must be won. *The Public Manage: The New Bureaucrat* (Summer): 27-31.

Bensimon, E.A. 1989. The meaning of 'good presidential leadership.' a frame analysis. *Review of Higher Education* 12, 1:107-123.

Bentley, Jerry H. 1996. Cross-cultural interaction and periodization in world history. *American Historical Review* (June): 749-770.

Berger, P.L., and T. Luckmann, 1966. *The Social Construction of Reality.* Garden City, N.Y.: Doubleday.

Bolman, L.G., and T.E. Deal. 1991. *Reframing Organizations: Artistry, Choice and Leadership.* San Francisco: Jossey-Bass.

Bowman, K. 1994. *The Perpetual Enterprise Machine: Seven Keys to Corporate Renewal through Successful Product and Process Development.* New York: Oxford University Press.

Boyd, R., and P.J. Richerson. 1985. *Culture and Evolutionary Process.* Chicago: University of Chicago Press.

Braunschweig, G.V. 1992. *Universitas: An Interdisciplinary Journal for the Sciences and Humanities* 34:256-267.

Brink, T.L. 1993. Metaphors as data in the study of organizations. *Journal of Management Inquiry* 2:366-371.

Brunsson, N. 1982. The irrationality of action and action rationality: decisions, ideologies, and organizational actions. *Journal of Management Studies* 19:29-34.

Budros, A. 1997. The new capitalism and organizational rationality: The adoption of downsizing programs, 1979-1994. *Social Forces* 76, 1:229-250.

Buckestein, Steve. 1995. Reinventing government, sounds good, but does it work? *Portland Business Journal.* Http://WWW.Catalog.com/cascade/bjreason.html-2.

Burgelman, R.A. 1991. Intraorganizational ecology of strategy making and organizational adaptation: Theory and field research. *Organization Science* 2:239-262.

Campbell, D. 1974. Evolutionary epistemology. In *The Philosophy of Karl Popper,* ed. P.A. Schilpp, 413-463. LaSalle, IL: Open Court Press.

Campbell, D. 1969. Variation and selective retention in socio-cultural evolution. *General Systems* 16:69-85.

Chakracarthy, B.S., and P. Lorange. 1991. *Managing the Strategy Process.* Englewood Cliffs, N.J.: Prentice Hall.

Clark, K.B. 1985. The interaction of design hierarchies and market concept in technological evolution. *Research Policy* 14:235-251.

Clark, Terry N. 1995. *Urban Innovation: Creative Strategies for Turbulent Times.* Beverly Hills, CA: Sage Publications.

Commons, J.R. 1950. *The Economics of Collective Action.* Madison: University of Wisconsin Press, 1970.

Connolly, T. 1988. Hedge-clipping, tree-felling and management of ambiguity: The need for new images of decision making. In *Managing Ambiguity and Change,* eds. L.R. Pondy, J.R. Boland, Jr., and Thomas, 37-50. Chichester, England: Wiley.

D'Aveni, A.R. 1994. *Hypercompetition: Managing the Dynamics of Strategic Maneuvering.* New York: Free Press.

De Rosnay, J. 1970. Evolution and time. *Main Currents* 27:35-47.

Dean, J.W., Jr., and M.P. Sharman. 1993. Procedural rationality in the strategic decision making process. *Journal of Management Studies* 30, 4:587-610.

Dobuzinskis, L. 1992. Modernist and postmodernist metaphors of the policy process: Control and stability versus chaos and reflexive understanding. *Policy Sciences* 25:355-380.

Etzioni, A. 1963. The epigenesis of political communities at international level. *American Journal of Sociology* LXVII: 407-443.

Farnun, R. 1997. Elite college discrimination and the limits of conflict theory. *Harvard Educational Review.*

Featherman, D.L. 1986. Biography, society and history: individual development as a population process. In *Human Development and* the Life Course: Multidisciplinary Perspectives, eds. A.B. Sorensen, F.E. Weinert, and L.R. Sherrod, 99-149. Hillsdale, N.J.: Erlbaum.

Flavell, J.H. (1982). Structures, stages, and sequences in cognitive development. In *The Concept of Development: The Minnesota Symposia on Child Psychology,* ed. W.A. Collins, 1-28. Hillsdale, NJ.: Erlbaum.

Frost, P.J., et al., eds. 1991. *Reframing Organizational Culture.* Newbury, CA: Sage.

Fuchs, S. 1993. A sociological theory of scientific change. *Social Forces* 71, 4:933-953.

Gannon, M.J. 1994. *Understanding Global Cultures: Metaphorical Journeys through 17 Countries.* Thousand Oaks, CA: Sage.

Garnavale, David G. 1995. *Trustworthy Government: Leadership and Management Strategies for Building Trust and High Performance.* San Francisco: Jossey-Bass.

Garud, R., and S. Kotha. 1994. Using the brain as a metaphor to model flexible production systems. *Academy of Management Review* 19:671-698.

Gergen, K.J. 1992. Organization theory in the postmodern era. In *Rethinking Organization,* eds. M. Reed and M. Hughes, 207-226. London: Sage.

Gibson, E.J. 1988. Exploratory behavior in the development of perceiving, acting and the acquiring of knowledge. *Annual Review of Psychology* 39:1-41.

Gore, Al. 1993. *National Performance Review (U.S.). Creating Government: How the Entrepreneurial Spirit is Transforming the Performance Review.* New York: Plum/Penguin.

Gortner, H.F., et al. 1997. *Organization Theory: A Public Perspective.* Fort Worth, TX: Harcourt Brace College Publishers.

Gould, S.J. 1989. Punctuated equilibrium in fact and theory. *Journal of Social and Biological Structures* 12:117-136.

Gould, S.J., and N. Eldridge 1977. Punctuated equilibria: The tempo and model of evolution reconsidered. *Paleobiology* 3:115, 151.

Gray, C.S. 1994. *The Navy in the Post-Cold War World: The Uses and Values of Strategic Sea Power.* University Park: Pennsylvania State University Press.

Greiner, L. 1922. Evolution and revolution as organizations grow. *Harvard Business Review* 50, 4:37-46.

Hannan, M., and F. Freeman. 1989. *Organizational Ecology.* Cambridge, MA: Harvard University Press.

Hannan, M., and F. Freeman. 1977. The population ecology of organizations. *American Journal of Sociology* 82: 929-940.

Hellriegel, D., J.M. Slocum, and R.W. Woodman. 1998. *Organization Behavior.* Cincinnati, OH: South-Western College Publishing.

Huddleston, Mark W., and William W. Boyer. 1996. *The Higher Civil Service in the United States: Quest to Reform.* Pittsburgh: University of Pittsburgh Press.

Inbar, E. 1996. Contours of Israel's new strategic thinking. *Political Science Quarterly 111, 1:41-64.*

Ingraham, Patricia W. 1995. *The Foundation of Merit: Public Services in American Democracy.* Baltimore: Johns Hopkins University Press.

Jackson, S.E., et al., eds. 1996. *The Academy of Management Review* 21, 4.

Kaplan, A. 1964. *The Conduct of Inquiry: Methodology for Behavioral Science.* New York: Chandler.

Kay, W.D. (1995). *Can Democracy Fly in Space? The Challenge of Revitalizing the U.S. Space Programs.* Westport, CT: Praeger.

Kendall, J.E., and K.E. Kendall. 1993. Metaphors and methodologies: Living beyond the systems machine. *MIS Quarterly* 17:149-171.

Kimberly, J., and R. Miles. 1980. *The Organizational Life-Cycle.* San Francisco: Jossey-Bass.

Koch, S., and S. Deetz. 1981. Metaphor analysis of social reality in organizations. *Journal of Applied Communication Research* 9: 1-15.

Kohlberg, L. 1969. Stage and sequence: The cognitive-developmental approach to socialization. In *Handbook of Socialization Theory and Research,* ed. D.A. Goslin, 347-480. Chicago: Rand McNally.

Kraatz, M.S., and E.J. Zajac. 1996. Exploring the Limits of the New Institutionalism: The causes and consequences of illegitimate organizational change. *American Sociological Review* 61: 812-836.

Lemonick,   M.D.   (1995). http://WWW.Pathfinder.com/time/magazine/archive/1995/950925. cover.box.html, 146, 13 (September 25, 1-2.

Levinson, D.J. 1978. *The Seasons of a Man's Life.* New York. Wiley.

Lundberg, C.C. 1990. Towards mapping the communication targets of organizational change. *Journal of Organizational Change Management* 3:6-13.

Manning, P. 1996. The problem of interactions in world history. *American Historical Review:* 771-782.

March, J.G. 1994. The evolution of evolution. In *Evolutionary Dynamics of Organizations,* eds. J. Baum and J. Singh, 39-49. New York: Oxford University Press:.

March, J.G., and J.P. Olsen. 1976. *Ambiguity and Choice in Organizations.* Bergen, Norway: Universitetsforlaget.

March, J.G., and H.A. Simon. 1958. *Organizations.* New York: Wiley.

Marx, R.D., and E.E. Hamilton. 1991. Beyond skill building. a multiple perspectives view of personnel. *Issues and Trends in Business and Economics 3:1-4.*

Masden, D. 1995. Reinvention battle must continue and must be won. *Public Personnel Management* 24, 1: 27-31.

McKelvey, B. 1982. *Organizational Systematics: Taxonomy, Evolution, Classification.* Berkeley: University of California Press.

McKenna, G. 1994. *The Drama of Democracy: American Government and Politics.* Guilford, CT: The Dushkin Publishing Group, Inc.

Merton, R. 1968. *Social Theory and Social Structure.* New York: Free Press.

Meyer, A.D., J.B. Goes, and G.R. Brooks. 1993. Organizations reacting to hyperturbulence. In *Organizational Change and Redesign,* eds. G.P. Huber and W.H. Glick, 66-111. New York: Oxford University Press.

Meyer, J., and B. Rowan. 1977. Institutionalized organizations: Formal structure as myth and ceremony. *American Journal of Sociology* 83:340-363.

Midlarsky, M.I. 1996. Analyzing political conflict. *The Journal of Politics* 58, 3:863-869.

Miller, D. 1994. What happens after success: The perils of excellence. *Journal of Management Studies* 31, 3:325-358.

Miller, D., et al. 1996. The evolution of strategic simplicity: Exploring two models of organizational adaptation. *Journal of Management* 22, 6:863-887.

Mintzberg, H. 1994. *The Rise and Fall of Strategic Planning: Reconceiving Roles for Planning, Plans, Planners.* New York: Free Press.

Moe, R.C. 1994. Observation and comments on reinventing government. *Public Administrative Review* 52, 2:111-119.

Morgan, G. 1993. *Imagination: The Art of Creative Management.* Newbury Park, CA: Sage.

Morgan, G. 1986. *Images of Organization.* Beverly Hills, CA: Sage.

Morgan, G. 1980. Paradigms, metaphors, and puzzle solving in organization theory. *Administrative Science Quarterly* 25:605-622.

New Webster's Dictionary and Thesaurus of the English Language. 1992. T-5. Dunbury, CT.

Nisbet, R.A. 1970. Developmentalism: A critical analysis. In *Theoretical Sociology: Perspectives and Developments,* eds. J. McKinney and E. Tiryakin, 167-206. New York: Meredith.

Osborne, D., and Gaebler. T. 1992. *Reinventing Government: How the Entrepreneurial Spirit is Transforming the Public Sector.* Reading, MA: Addison-Wesley.

Palmer, I., And R. Dunford. 1996. Conflicting uses of metaphors: Reconceptualizing their use in the field of organizational change. *Academy of Management Review* 21, 3:691-717.

Paris, D.C. 1995. *Ideology and Educational Reform Theme and Theories in Public Education's.* Boulder, CO: Westview.

Parsons, R. 1951. *The Social System.* New York: Free Press.

Patel, K., and Rushefsky, M.E. 1995. *Health Care Politics and Policy in America.* Armonk, N.Y.: M.E. Sharpe.

Pearson, C.M., and J.A. Clair. 1998. Reframing crisis management. *Academy of Management Review* 23, 1:59-76.

Peters, T. 1992. *Liberation Management: Necessary Disorganization for the Nonsecond Nineties.* New York: Knopf.

Peterson, P.E. 1995. *The Price of Federalism.* Washington, DC.: The Brookings Institution.

Pfeffer, J. 1982. *Organizations and Organization Theory.* Boston: Pitman.

Piaget, J. 1975. *The Child's Conception of the World.* Totowa, NJ.: Littlefield, Adams.

Posner, B.G., and Rothstein, L.R. 1994. Reinventing the business of government: An interview with change catalyst David Osborne. *Harvard Business Review* (May-June): 133-143.

Riegel, K.F. 1975. From Traits and Equilibrium toward Developmental Dialects. In *Nebraska Symposium on Motivation,* eds. Cole and W.S. Arnold, 349-407. Lincoln: University of Nebraska Press.

Rocherfort, D.A., and Cobb, R.W. 1994. *The Politics of Problem Definition: Shaping the Policy Agenda.* Lawrence: University Press Kansas.

Rogers, E. 1983. *Diffusion of Innovations.* New York: Free Press.

Sackmann, S. 1989. The role of metaphors in organization transformation. *Human Relations* 42:463-485.

Schneider, M., et al. (1995). *Public Entrepreneurs: Agents for Change in American Government.* Princeton: Princeton University Press.

Shrivastava, P. 1995. Economic management for a risk society. *Academy of Management Review* 20, 1:118-137.

Singh, J.V., and C.J. Lumsden. 1990. Theory and research in organizational ecology. *Annual Review of Sociology* 16:161-195.

Sztompka, P. 1993. *The Sociology of Social Change.* London: Basil Blackwell.

Tolbert, P., and L. Zucher. 1983. Institutional sources of change in the formal structure of organizations. *Administrative Science Quarterly* 28:22-39.

Townley, B. 1993. Performance appraisal and the emergence of management. *Journal of Management Studies* 32, 2:27-44.

Townley, B. 1993. Foucault, power/knowledge, and its relevance for human resource management. *Academy of Management Review* 18:518-545.

Training (U.S.) 1994. An interview with Ted Gaebler (January): 107-111.

Tsoukas, H. 1991. The missing link: A transformational view of metaphors in organizational science. *Academy of Management Review* 16:566-585.

Tushman, M.L., and E. Romanelli. 1985. Organizational evolution: A metamorphosis model of convergence and reorientation. In *Research in Organizational Behavior,* ed. L. Cummings and B. Slaw. Greenwich, CT: JAI Press.

Van de Ven, A.H., and M.S. Poole. 1995. Explaining development and change in organizations. *Academy of Management Review* 20, 3:510-540.

Von Wright, G.H. 1971. *Explanation and Understanding.* Ithaca, N.Y.: Cornell University Press.

Walker, D.B. 1995. *The Rebirth of Federalism: Slouching toward Washington.* Chatham, NJ.: Chatham House.

Wall, J.A., Jr., and R.R. Callister. 1995. Conflict and Its Management. *Journal of Management* 21, 3:515-558.

Wallerstein, I. 1979. *The Capitalist World Economy.* Cambridge: Harvard University Press.

Weick, K.E. 1979. *The Social Psychology of Organizing.* Reading, MA: Addison-Wesley.

Wiebe, R.H. 1995. *Self-Rule: A Cultural History of American Democracy.* Chicago: University of Chicago Press.

Wolfe, R.A. 1994. Organizational innovation: Review, critique and suggested research directions. *Journal of Management Studies* 31, 3: 405-431.

Zajac, E.J., and M.S. Kraatz. (1993). A diametric forces model of strategic change: Assessing the antecedents and consequences of restructuring in the higher education industry. *Strategic Management Journal* 14:83-102.

Zand, D.E. 1995. Force field analysis. In *Blackwell Encyclopedic Dictionary of Organizational Behavior,* ed. N. Nicholson, 181. Oxford, England: Blackwell:.

Zucker, L. 1977. The role of institutionalization in cultural persistence. *American Sociological Review* 42:726-743.

Section Four: Political Economy

Section Four is about political economy. The term political economy is derived from politics and economics. Economics is acting in certain ways. Politics is a platform from which action takes place. Economics rationalizes what is done and why. Politics is a context for doing and acting. Sometimes economics is about an existing activity excluding market institutions though such exclusion may not fully define the term without the latter. Economically, market institutions tend to satisfy human wants better than any others that are known and thereby making them more dominant than politics which is subordinate to them—economics. Politics means "who gets what, when, and how" (Lasswell, 1936). It is "the struggle for power" (Morgenthau, 1948). Politics is "the art and science of government" and "the socialization of conflict" (Schattschneider, 1960). Politics is "the authoritative allocation of values" (Easton, 1953). Evidently, it is "pure conflict" (Schmitt, 1976) and "the conciliation of conflicting interests through public policy" (Crick, 1962; and Caporaso and Levine, 1997, p. 8).

There are seven major theoretical approaches to the study and application of political economy whose diverse views influence organization theory and practice and vice versa. The theoretical approaches have a variety of assumptions, stage actors, and different explanatory, interpretive and inferential issues. As a structure of national and international dependence in terms of division of labor, political economy is a system held together by exchange contracts between legally independent property owners (the market economy).

These property owners have property rights, which the political system, in its legal nature, protects.

Classical economists associate the term political economy to the unlimited but satisfied wants that exist in a world of scarcity and competition. To satisfy peoples' wants, society is depoliticized because politics is eroded with the rising dominance of the autonomous and self-interested primitive capitalists. The state defines how production and distribution of wealth among classes is to be conducted. The economy is mercantilist in character. Second, Marxists argue that politics and economics can be connected by using revolutionary activity to transform political structure, social democratic politics and the Marxian state model whose radicalism is anti-competitive market, anti-democracy and anti-free enterprise. Their production goals are based on satisfying needs, rather than wants. Planning is centralized and production and distribution are collectivized. The theory emphasizes partial rather than holistic inclusion of the state. The state coercively emerges to resolve the irreconcilable contradictions in society, which the pre-capitalist and capitalist classes fail to deal with. Though the theory contributed to the collapse of the Soviet Union largely due to the latter's lack of creativity and destruction of genius. It is a living intellectual reservoir that exists as a radical critique of the organizing principle of the capitalist system and its liberal and conservative values including that of the market. Evidently, there is inevitable and irreconcilable tension between economics and politics in classical Marxism.

Third, the end of the classical period which was characterized by the classical and Marxian theoretical models, was replaced by the neoclassical economic theory of marginalism during the 1870s. Neoclassical economic theory was a shift from the fascination with class categories to the concern with individualism through which the individual selfishly sought productive utility in the areas of consumption and profit maximization. The individual's self-seeking behavior was manifested in both perfect and imperfect competitive setting of the market. In itself, individualism has been viewed as a form of liberal philosophy where the individual has "a commitment to personal initiative, self-sufficiency, and material accumulation. This principle upholds the superiority of private-enterprise economic system and includes the idea of the individual as the foundation of society" (Patterson, 2000, p. 4). Within neoclassical political economy, politics becomes deterministic when market failure prevails. In other words, in such an arena, self-seeking, particularly that of the state, can enter non-market institutional and organizational domains in order to "provide public goods, correct externalities, and solve collective action problems through coercion" (Caporaso and Levine, 1997, p. 219). Within neoclassical economic realm, the market economies lack the full potential for productive exploitation. As a result, the economies fail to reconcile the relationship between wants and means. Such failure caused the Great Depression of the 1930s when FDR used keynesianism to involve political leadership in the circular flow including the securing of incomes and investment to challenge the failed creativity of specialization and capital markets.

Fourth, neoclassical economic ideas, in the form of rational self-interest, have been extended into the political arena. Rational self-interest is used to analyze politics. "Neoclassical political economy, with its focus on the states role in market failure, offers a way to complete the liberal project in one direction" (p. 220). In other words, rationality is used to analyze the market in order to enhance the political economy and uplift the state's interest and stake in it.

The last three theoretical models of political economy are power-centered, state-centered and justice-centered. The first one sees relations of power and domination in the market to be existing between the market and the state and within the state itself. Economic agents who include firms and pressure groups may challenge the state by voting and lobbying over the political process, economic agencies and consumers. Since power is almost everywhere within the political and nonpolitical spheres of the state, to address the states' interest and the interest of citizens, policy analysis should be more focused rather than broad and generalized. State-centered theoretical models of central political institutions can define politics decisively. Since politics is what the state does in and with society, this may involve the "regulation of the economy and economic actors, the effect of the economic actors on the state policy, distributional effects of policy on economic resources, and traditional macroeconomic policy along Keynesian lines" (p. 220). Finally the justice-centered approach concentrates on fairness and rights instead of concentrating on individualistic efficiency. Justice is not an historical accident; it is politically, legally, and morally definitive state policy for reconstructive economic and political practice. In the light of such theoretical practical conceptualization, political economy becomes a political process for sound economic planning. The term political economy has been used for the last 300 years in which it has always meant the interrelationship between political and economic affairs in the light of state policy. All modern organizations exist as "island" blueprints of the structure of political economy.

References

Caporaso, J.A., and D.P. Levine. 1997. *Theories of Political Economy.* London: Cambridge University Press.

Crick, B. 1962. *In Defense of Politics.* London: Penguin Books.

Easton, D. 1953. *The Political System: An Inquiry into the State of Political Science.* Chicago: University of Chicago Press.

Lasswell, H.D. 1936. *Politics: Who gets What, When and How?* New York: Whittlesey House.

Morgenthau, H.J. 1948. *Politics among Nations.* New York: Alfred Knopf.

Patterson, T.E. 2000. *We the People: A Concise Introduction to American Politics.* Boston: McGraw-Hill.

Schattschneider, E.E. 1960. *The Semisovereign People: A Realistic View of Democracy in America.* New York: Holt, Reinhart, and Winston.

Schmitt, C. 1976. *The Concept of the Political.* New Brunswick, N.J.: Rutgers University Press.

Chapter 16

Political Economy: Its Effects on Nations and their Organizations

The world's economic system is stratified (Nemeth and Smith, 1985 and Schott, 1986) in terms of core, semi-periphery and periphery. It also makes the strata to be seen as discrete clusters (Wallerstein, 1974) or structural continuum (Chase-Dunn, 1989). Some of the strata within the world-system play certain roles which serve hegemonic, regional and spatial interests of these clusters and trade partners (Bollen, 1983; Evans, 1979a; Snyder and Kick, 1979; and Steiber, 1979). In other words, the role of each country or cluster within the stratified world's economic system is either different or unique to each country or mutually reciprocal. The positions of the continual strata members have unequal trade exchange relationships whose theoretical and philosophical underpinnings exacerbate dependency (Bunker, 1984; Mandel, 1975; and Firebaugh and Bullock, 1987). In recent history, traditional hegemonic powers have been relatively neutralized by the emergence of a multicentric core stratum whose network, block or subblocks has not only produced a new international division of labor, but the new division of labor has been reinforced by the character of "currency flight" to Third World areas where the cost of production of goods, services and labor are comparatively lower than those in the core countries (Caporaso, 1981 and Arrighi, 1982). The dramatic and historic collapse of the ex-Soviet Empire and the current financial mismanagement and fiscal instability in southeast Asia may have threatened investors to return their currency back to the United States and Western Europe. In the wake of Asian decline, this behavioral phenomenon may not only help to explain the apparent resurgence of these Western economies, but the previous use of these currencies for the geo-strategic containment of the empire in question, may have helped the West to formidably eclipse the rival empire while hegemonically reasserting itself anew on the global plane of international relations and political economy. That reassertion is accomplished through international economic cooperation, mobility of capital, and imposition of fixed rather than flexible exchange rates (Webb, 1995). Cooperative mobility of capital may cause regional or global economic turbulence.

In the light of the structure of international political economy, 15 major trade variables have been selected to represent the structure (in terms of blocks and subblocks) of the major types of global commodity exchange goods. These blocks and their respective subblocks, as Smith and White (1992, p. 886) have noted, include:

1. High technology heavy manufacture
    - machinery
    - nonelectrical
    - artificial resins, plastics, cellulose, esters, and ethers
    - manufactures of metal, not elsewhere specified
2. Sophisticated extractive
    - paper, paperboard, and articles of paper pulp
    - pulp and waste paper
    - gas, natural and manufactured
3. Simple extractive
    - oil seeds and oleaginous fruit
    - animal oils and fats
    - cereals and cereal preparations
4. Low wage/light manufacture
    - articles of apparel and clothing accessories
    - footwear
    - travel goods, handbags, and similar containers
5. Food products and byproducts
    - meat and meat preparations
    - dairy products and birds' eggs
    - crude animal and vegetable material, not elsewhere specified.

The structure of the global economic system is hierarchical, competitive, hegemonic, and reciprocal. Countries in the core strata are richer and more economically and geostrategically competitive than those in the semi-periphery. Likewise, countries in the semi-periphery are wealthier and more economically and geostrategically competitive than those in the periphery of marginalization. Both the semi-periphery and the periphery are the middle and lower socioeconomic and global strata of blocks, each of which is further, subdivided into two subblocks. The subblock is the fifth stratum which has been more recently described as the Fourth World or the "underclass." For instance, Table 16.1 shows five countries that represent each of the five strata into which the global economic system (calculated in terms of GNP per capita income) is categorized (Smith and White, 1992).

Table 16.1. Selected Countries Representing Five Strata: Core to Periphery

GNP (1979)	Core	Semi-Periphery 1	Semi-Periphery 2	Periphery 1	Periphery 2
$10,610	U.S.A.				
$8,870		Australia			
1,380			Turkey		
$1,200				Morocco	
$300					Niger

Table 16.1 further illustrates the simplified and tabular construction mentioned above. Theoretically, network analysis which explains and validates the morphological hierarchy and structural stratification of the global economic system has been used to demonstrate that "massive

intracore trade is one of the defining features of this strata's global dominance" (Smith and White, 1992, p. 886). These global trade patterns are asymmetrical. They tend to promote unequal exchange which continually reproduces, perpetuates and rationalizes the expressed inequality and hierarchy. Given this understanding:

> results support world-system and dependency arguments about asymmetrical flows of raw materials versus processed goods. Exports of high-technology heavy manufacturing goods flow primarily within the core and from the core to the lower blocks. While the lion's share of these commodities circulates within the core, the interblock exchanges follow a cascade pattern: all through the international system it is more likely to move from higher to lower strata. The standard image of core advantage in high levels of processing and capital intensiveness implies precisely this pattern ... The reciprocal pattern of exporting agricultural goods (crude animal and vegetable material, meat products) also fits this model: while intracore exchange is still very large, we find that interstrata exchange is more likely to move from the periphery to higher blocks, including the core. Highly industrialized capital-intensive agriculture is the exception in that it is mostly exported from higher to lower blocks.

Some countries in the core stratum are dependent on others. Canada is a classic example of a core country which depends on the U.S. Other countries like Libya which enjoys core and semi-periphery economic status is not treated so by economists largely because of its geopolitical, technological and ideological uniqueness. Though some semi-periphery countries like Brazil and South Korea tend to triangulate in the core areas very aggressively, their progressive ascendance toward the core area tends to be arrested by their own technological and socioeconomic relativity. In other words, with the use of specific trade nets, all blocks and subblocks display the tendency to move toward the core rather than moving away from it. Since the global economic system is structurally stratified and hierarchically arranged, and since intrastrata mobility is more easily facilitated than interstrata mobility, lower case mobility of the periphery and semi-periphery to the core is not only difficult, but such difficulty is associated with the forces of global and geostrategic rationality which tend to thwart such a form of mobility. By thwarting rapid or frequent attempts to ascend toward the core, which is the center of world civilization, the core area countries protect themselves against such forceful and carefully calculated "penetrating projectiles" from the outer periphery and "alien" lands. In other words, the dynamics of global centripetal forces (which undermine autonomy) and centrifugal (disruptive) economic and geostrategic forces of the world economic system tend to reproduce its antagonistic equilibrium. The dichotomy of these negative and positive forces tends to gravitate around issues which equilibrate and rationalize global stability and interinstitutional and interorganizational coexistence and reciprocity. Whether reciprocity is reached at through coercive diplomacy, the use of the stick and the carrot, or through design or accident could be a matter of theoretical controversy rather than conjecture (Etzioni, 1996).

Evidently, quantitative analysis of global exchange is a powerful tool to analyze the stricture, structure, and dynamics of the world's system and its constituent countries. Regardless of its dialectical components, global and state politics stimulate block, intra and interblock politico-economic strategies for development that reproduce international economic dependency. Explicit and implicit state policies are constructed by economically and politically pressured elites. Such exerted and external pressure influences the development of industrial and export strategies (Gereffi and Wyman, 1990). The development strategies and the extent of their implementation helps to influence changes in the composition and structure of exports and each country's structural level within the international political economy. Therefore, in order to understand how national mobility in the world system takes place, it requires the linkage of the global external analysis similar to this one, in order to articulate, rationalize, and reconstruct research agenda that focuses on internal, regional, national and historico-political economies. According to a critique of the neoliberal institutionalist thesis (Mansfield and Milner, 1997) regionalism is rationalized as the solution to the collective dilemmas and high transaction costs associated with multilateral institutions which are more highly institutionalized in the Americas than in Asia. These institutions serve functionalist and hegemonic values of the countries in question. These countries are dominated by self-interested actors who initiate the formation of the institutions.

Domestic and Foreign Corporate Political Activity

In the United States, the elites and their corporations have tremendous influence on the culture, politics and economics of the country at large. They massively contribute large sums of money through PACs in order to support the electoral campaigns of senators, members and even the president. Other elites become trustees in university and college boards where they help to formulate institutional and organizational policy. Some of these corporate elites have multiple directorships in business and industry (Burris, 1991).

Most of these capitalistic and profit minded corporate elites are politically conservative rather than liberal. These capitalists are highly connected and have control at the pinnacle of the elite kinship of intercorporate networks. The influence of their corporations and their political behavior is interlocked. This influence varies with the "level of government regulation, defense contracts, and geographic location" (Burris, 1991, p. 543). In other words, the attempt to control the political system is purposefully grounded on electing political "officials whose ideological position is sympathetic to the general interests of their class" (p. 547). In addition to the "partisan interest in electing candidates sympathetic to business, corporations have a pragmatic interest in maintaining access to and influence over elected officials of both parties" (p. 547). Practically, this tends to translate into a "strong temptation to support incumbents, regardless of party ideology" (p. 547). In the wake of specific legislative and administrative action, there is no doubt that lobbying, director interlock networks, and political behavior become the payoffs of the system derived from such actions. Corporations that are marginalized into the periphery by the interlockage of the "over-class," tend to behave like most individual capitalists. Since they are ideologically conservative, the only way available to them for reaching the incumbents is that of making large donations to conservative, liberal and moderate incumbents. This behavioral attitude helps to explain why most incumbents are elected more often times than nonincumbents. By making contributions for the election of public officials, lobbyists or individual capitalists indirectly become conservative elements of the elite class which is represented at the highest level of policy planning arena. For instance, PACs have become an extended arm of the corporate sector for "government regulation and defense contracts" (p. 548). As far as this is concerned, there is no need to hypothesize a tendency toward ideological liberalism within the inner circle of the business community. As individual citizens, members of the inner circle exhibit political behavior that is more consistently conservative than other capitalists. As corporate decision makers, they are involved in interorganizational networks that allow and encourage efforts to coopt potential political opponents. The reduced support they give to right-wing candidates in this context is not a sign of ideological liberalism, but of a conservatism that assumes a more pragmatic stance when confronted with a different structure of political opportunities (p. 548).

Both Smith and White (1992) and Burris (1991) used the methodology of social network analysis to conduct research on two different types of problems, namely, the structure of international political economy and the cohesive mechanisms for regulating its geopolitical and strategic dynamics; and the political behavior of U.S. corporations and corporate elites whose intercorporate strategic networks form interlocking directorships that are class networks and structures for political cohesion and bases of political action in the capitalist society. Since all capitalist elites in capitalist societies have the same psychology, lifestyle and socioeconomic entrenchment, it is not surprising that the internal needs for social cohesion, decision-making (policy planning and formulation) and survival (both as individuals and as a nation) extend beyond their national frontiers in the structuration, regulation and control of the "international other" particularly those in the semi-periphery and the periphery of marginalization. In a sense, they can profitably use their domestic (U.S.) experience to replicate the behavior of the political and economic elites in the global strata in order to dispel political instability and help create favorable economic markets for the supply of raw materials and demand of corecentric manufactured products, investments and repatriation of capital. In general, such behavior of class networks and corporate networks or inter and intrastrata networks may be viewed as structures of cohesion and bases for internal and external political control and action. Viewed from a corecentric perspective, these intercorporate, intraclass and intracore multinationals which radiate from metropoles and megalopolises have used, through dependency, suckling tentacles (*milija ya unyonyanji*) to control, impoverish and marginalize the Third and Fourth Worlds.

Eichner (1991) has used a post-Keynesian perspective to comment on the macrodynamics (money, finance, inflation, income distribution and the labor market) of advanced market economies most of which are the core countries of the global economic system. At the center of these market economies is the megacorp which is the archetypical oligopolistic industrial sector that is dominant in modern economic investment, production and pricing. While post-Keynesianism rejected neoclassical orthodoxy for its "idealized, timeless, institutionless, nonmonetary and barter framework" (Eichner, 1991, p. 416), of the neo-Walrasian model, the former argued that post-Keynesian macroeconomic model is relevant because it is methodologically empirical and predictive rather than descriptive. As a subset of human activity post-Keynesianism is both institutionalist and cybernetic rather than dialectical and an unspecific historical explanation.

The megacorp is the dominant form of the modern corporation that strives for growth and survival. Its investment decisions are strategic (long-term) while its pricing ones are tactical (short-term). The neoclassical profit maximizing firm's pricing decision is made independent of its fixed costs or its investment decisions. When pricing and investment decisions are incorporated the megacorp makes short-term profit (Eichner, 1976). The megacorp makes profits because it acquires and maintains market share which it controls because of its investment expenditures. Intertwined with its market power, production structure, and pricing mechanism, the megacorp operates productively. In the light of classical thinking, prices are determined by the reproduction requirements of the economy in the face of factors of scarcity.

In the private enterprise economy, the three basic types of cyclical effects around the long-term trend include "(1) the multiplier effect, (2) the accelerator effect, and (3) the cash-flow feedback effect" (Eichner, 1991, p. 422). The first two effects are common to many macroeconomic models. However, the cash-flow feedback effect comprises "the actions of different economic sectors (megacorp, nonmegacorp firm, household, government, and foreign) and their component units to imbalances between their income and expenditure flows" (Eichner, 1987, pp. 98-106; Eichner, 1991, p. 422). In the megacorp sector, higher profits generate higher investment returns and cause booms. Lower profits lead to lower investment which causes recessions. The megacorp generates demand and enhances capacity.

In a neoclassical way money that is saved by households and firms make profits that are spent in future. The modern economy is based on credit rather than on commodity or fiat money. Money is put outside the scarcity realm of neoclassical economics. It is regulated by the central banks or Federal Reserve Bank which determines the discount rate (interest rate) for the banks.

While inflation may be caused by increases in wage rate and markup above technological progress (increase in productivity), income is distributed mechanistically due to its determination by technical production and innate intelligence. This is a neoclassical position, on the contrary, post-Keynesianism humanistically argues that income is socially distributed in segmented labor markets that are stratified and substratified along class lines. Competitive firms within the industry evolve with changes in structure. The changes influence the "development of new technologies, new products, and new industries and the elimination of old technologies, products and industries" (Eichner, 1991, p. 427).

Studies done by political scientists, economists, and sociologists have demonstrated that corporate political action committees (PACs) are financially heavily subsidized by corporations, industries and Japan at state and national levels. The 270/500 Fortune and other 1,000 companies were analyzed. The purpose of making such financial contributions to electoral candidates was to gunner legislative support for securing sales and avoiding regulation costs. Evidence indicates that corporate officials are extremely sensitive to press releases on their connections. They become nervous about negative aggressive and potentially prosecutorial news reporting. Such involvement of the corporate sector in political affairs indicates that the corporation is a political as well as an economic institution which tends to capitalize on "free-rider incentives" which are used as models for "organizationally constrained profit-maximizing behavior" (Mitchell, Hansen, and Jepsen, 1997, p. 1018). Foreign political activity, especially the Japanese corporations have been observed to be disproportionately active in American political system (Choate, 1990; Prestowitz, 1988; and Tolchin and Tolchin, 1988). In doing that, the corporate sector, which influences the regulation of industries, government procurement, social connections, corporate culture, secures its place in the "sun." Consequently, "elected" government learns and understands how, when and where to facilitate government regulation, corporate visibility, legitimacy and countermobilization. In doing that this business-antibusiness dynamic is politically and legally rationalized in the face of political complexity, economic interests and social and legal expediency.

International Perspectives on Corporate Political Behavior

Unlike in their home countries, international business corporations behave differently in order to maximize their own business interests.

The corporations advance different "assumptions concerning the political nature of international business and the role of government as a factor of production, which firms manage ... (Boddewyn and Brewer, 1994, p. 119) through a chain-nexus of contingencies. These corporations use business principles to interact with firms, industry and nonmarket factors to influence political behavior for the successful implementation of their resource-based strategic objectives. The corporations view government as a variable rather than constant that has to deal with international firms particularly the "exporters, importers, licensors, and foreign direct investors" (p. 119) that need to politically negotiate the terms for their "entry, operation and exit" (p. 119).

According to Fayerweather (1969), international business deals with policy-oriented research that stresses 'the accumulation of interests and resolution of conflict' "between international firms and political actors at home and abroad" (Boddewyn and Brewer, 1994, p. 119).

Based on resource dependence, institutionalization, and interorganization theories, business-government relations tend to be conflictual, isomorphic and relational (Pfeffer and Salancik, 1978; DiMaggio and Powell, 1983; and Benson, 1975). In addition, resource-based theory of strategic advantage (Barney, 1986; Collis, 1991; Conner, 1991; Grant, 1991; and Peteraf, 1993) shows that international firms have competence to deploy economic and organizational rather than political capabilities. Under normal circumstances, political factors act as constraints (Conner, 1991). Even though, in respect to the tradeability of resources, economic rather than political markets are important. These economic markets are "means acquired and used to gain rents ... aim of strategic behavior ... purely" 'economic' (Boddewyn and Brewer, 1994, p. 120; and Etzioni, 1988, pp. 218-220).

In a business environment, business political behavior is a required component. Political behavior is the "acquisition, development, securing and use of power ... where power is viewed as the capacity of social actors to overcome the resistance of other actors" (Boddewyn and Brewer, 1994, p. 120). These social actors exist in nonmarket settings. The actors include governments, interest groups, the intelligentsia, media and public opinion. The interaction between business corporations and the nonmarket sector involves various actions such as "compliance, evasion, negotiation, cooperation, coalition building, and co-optation" (pp. 120-121).

Political behavior creates winners and losers in the marketplace (Leone, 1986). Although political behavior does not necessarily require wealth, it may be the product of other resources such as used "time,

organizing ability, legitimacy, privileged information and access"
(Boddewyn and Brewer, 1994, p. 121). Political behavior may be a
form of collusion (collective action) that is legally sanctionable.
Political power may be retained longer than economic power for the
purpose of sustaining competitive advantage (Hayes, 1981). Although
actors may not benefit from their actions, they may gain through
"political externalities" (Perrow, 1986, p. 234) such as protectionism
which benefits a few at the expense of millions of people. In other
words, there are more losers than winners in the marketplace of
competition.

An integrated model of business political behavior may be
triangularized to show its interactive, strategic, and dynamic
infrastructure as in Figure 16.1.

Figure 16.1. Model of Business and Political Behavior

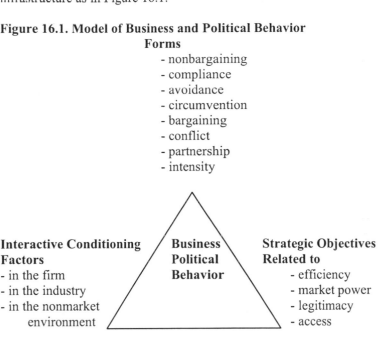

In the light of the essence of corporate political behavior, the political
behavior of international firms can be affected simultaneously by
differences in (a) the task-based nature in which the firms operate.
These firms comply when government actions have a low level of
strategic salience and are favorable to them. Moreover, due to their
narrow political base, the firms suffer from inadequacy of resources for

challenging governmental actions. The firms tend to evade or circumvent government policies as long as the gains of such behavior exceed their legitimacy costs. At times, conflictual political behavior prevails under three conditions: (a) when actions of international firms and governments have high strategic salience for the other party, (b) when both sides perceive the situation as zero-sum game, and (c) when they have enough power to influence, through bargaining, the uncertain outcomes concerning winners and losers.

In other situations, political partnership between international business firms and governments may prevail if three conditions are met: (a) when states are willing to correct for natural market failures or to generate unnatural market imperfections, (b) when both parties to the conflict (deal) perceive the situation to be strategically beneficial to them—parties, and (c) when both parties have enough power to influence uncertain outcomes of their bargaining processes that may result in mutual gains. The intensity of political behavior on the part of the international business firms is greater when the stakes are not only higher, but also when opportunities to leverage and arbitrate governmental policies are plentiful. In addition, intense political behavior is displayed when the international businesses' political competencies are advanced and enhanceable.

Since international business firms are strategic thinkers and operators, they make choices on resources, competitive methods and geographic zones and areas (Morrison and Roth, 1989). Strategic planning literature emphasizes profitability, population ecology, resource dependence, transaction cost analysis (emphasizes survival), various strands or resource dependence, industrial organization and political economy theory. These strategic elements are collectively viewed as aspects of international dominance, monopoly, and hegemony (Perrow, 1981). The sources of profits are efficiency and are congruent with the values that are dominant in the nonmarket environment, legitimacy becomes a political resource firms want to secure. This behavior helps firms to have access to policy makers, influence public policy making, and reduce opposition from other competitors and stakeholders. Both governments (at home and abroad) expect these firms to treat local political imperatives as goals and private economic imperatives, e.g., flexibility and profitability as constraints (Doz, 1986). The firms' legitimacy is enhanced when they contribute to national goals of development such as employment, technological development, and balance of payments surplus. Further still, firms enhance their legitimacy when they abide by local laws, customs, symbols, and loyalty during interstate conflicts (Kindleberger, 1969).

Consistent with conceptions of efficiency, firms can act politically to reduce their own production and transaction costs for the purpose of providing cheaper, better or unique products to their customers. They can do this while raising the costs of production for their rivals at home and abroad. This is called protectionism or 'sheltering' (Rugman and Verbeke, 1990, p. 8, and 1992, p. 206). This is a resource-based model of strategic management. These same firms have market power. The struggle to obtain market power is based on a dialectic of ideological and empirical beliefs regarding whether profits are more readily secured through efficiency and competitiveness as opposed to through anticompetitive market power. In a sense, a firm's "ability to raise prices, eliminate competitors or collude with them, to obtain favorable regulations, and to deny such benefits to others by raising barriers of entry and mobility is a real source of competitive advantage in the domestic and international markets" (Boddewyn and Brewer, 1994, p. 134).

To meet their strategic objectives, international corporations and firms use resource strategy, competitive methods and political markets to strike deals for profit maximization. Politically, the international businesses have to use better intelligence and cognitive maps in order to penetrate nonmarket climates and environments. These nonmarket areas have better access to decision makers and opinion leaders and secure better bargaining or nonbargaining influence. To be effective in generating sustainable rents, their bargaining and nonbargaining skills should be competencies that are nonimitatible and nonsubstitutable. For instance, their strongest "weapons" should be "reason, argument, persuasion and diplomacy" (p. 136) rather than bribery, evasion and circumvention. However, they must be aware that since they have a lot of power, they should use it carefully and wisely, lest it "corrupts people, organizations and society" (p. 136) in general.

Political Economy in the Third World

With the recent decline and total collapse of the communist economic and political system, most countries, especially those in the Third World, view reformatory economic transitions to be associated with democratization of their political systems. In some cases, inconclusive evidence seems to suggest that economic growth tends to be conducted better and faster in authoritarian rather then in democratic countries. In other words, democracies are less capable of imposing economic reforms than authoritarian regimes. On the other hand, it is easier for democracies to legitimate economic reforms if their policy processes are more transparent, and accountable than when decision making is conducted secretively and corruptly. Successful economic reforms largely depend not only on the policy design, but they also depend on the state's implementation machinery. Given these arguments, it may be argued that regime type may not necessarily be an objective indicator or determinant of economic performance (Diamond and Plattner, 1995). Of importance, it is observationally important to say that the politics of authoritarian structures and democratic consolidation cannot be understood in isolation from the economic choices and constraints associated with the transition.

What are the proper governmental strategies for operationalizing economic reforms? In a political, competitive and global or open environment, this question's answer could have a lot of dialectics. However, in accordance with the wisdom of eminent and scholarly analysts, several may be mentioned. First, based on the shock-therapy school of thought, rapid and radical reforms are essential for forestalling countermobilization by previous elites who might be attempting to build popular confidence which indicates that economic changes do last. In addition, economic development gradualists argue that shock-therapy is invalid in many democratizing societies where the president lacks political insulation and predominance for imposing economic policy by decree.

Second, different political strategies are more effective than one that is used for various economic development reforms. The involvement of relatively simple and straightforward administratively guided economic reforms in which liberalization and stabilization measures can be accomplished through presidential leadership is a possibility. Third, complex and all drawn-out structural and institutional transformations require different political approaches that involve broad mobilization of social support from constituencies. Social support for economic reforms should be conducted wisely because, politically, the winners are fewer than the losers. These short-term winners of economic reforms are fewer and difficult to organize politically. The losers, who are the majority, are members of the "ancient regime." To strike a compromise in this dichotomous conundrum, it might be wise "to co-opt critical segments of the electorate by providing government benefits to compensate for the effects of economic austerity" (Henderson, 1996, p. 448). Fourth, reductions in government revenues in addition to spending cuts can collectively be reconciled with compensatory schemes in order to placate politically relevant losers who could become potential and socially disruptive malcontents. One of the problems of this strategy is that most Third World political regimes are too poor to afford buying off both the middle and lower income voters. This difficulty makes it almost impossible to build broad-based coalition support and reform the movement. Even neocorporatist solutions are not more solvent than social coalitions. In a large number of new democracies "corporatism (which depends on the state-mediated cooperation of organized business and labor interests) is rendered infeasible by fragmentation and differences of interest within the labor movement and employer's groups. Given the difficulties of mobilizing new social coalitions, many democratizing states may be tempted to seek support among the beneficiaries of the old regime—with possible negative consequences for democratic consolidation and economic reform.

Haggard and Kaufman (1995) have attempted to construct a comprehensive theory of democratic transition. In this attempt, they have tried to identify critical factors whose propensity destroys authoritarian regimes. They have also tried to identify reasons that enable the newly elected governments to strengthen democracy and pursue economic reforms. They indicate that most political actors "overlook the socioeconomic and institutional factors that shape" these "actors' preferences" (Henderson, 1996, p. 449). While this argument sounds convincing, it becomes more contradictory and less convincing when the authors try to tabulate specific socioeconomic and institutional factors accountable for democratic transition.

Haggard and Kaufman have strongly proposed a simple model of authoritarian structure based on economic performance and elite cohesion. They argue that authoritarian regimes tend to collapse "when poor economic performance undermines their ability to purchase social compliance and when elite fragmentation weakens their ability to manage economic and political problems" (p. 449). Recent examples include Indonesia, Marcos Philippines, Thailand and Mobutu's Zaire. On the contrary, cohesive elites can effectively prevent economic crises and withstand political pressures. When cohesive elites operate under noncrisis economic conditions, even when they come under pressure to democratize, they positively impose and enforce a political solution which protects their future access to power by limiting the options of their potential successors. Gradually and subsequently, bargains worked out during the transition are revised later in order to balance power at different intervals. Consequently, predictions based on the terms of pacts of the exercise of power lose their significance over time. To use political consolidation for the improvement of economic performance in the new democracies, Haggard and Kaufman (1995) have prescribed a theoretical model of institutional structure. First, "the organization of executive authority and the structure of the party system—are important in determining the success of economic reform and political transition" (Henderson, 1996, p. 449). A centralized executive authority is essential for initiating economic reforms. That forum of consolidation of economic reform and political democracy requires creative assemblage of coalition of interests—supporters and beneficiaries. The most effective machinery for effecting such support base is the utilization of a cohesive nonpolarized political system. In the era of democratization, technology and ethnicism, it is difficult to realize such a uniform structure on a grand scale. Democratization and ethnicism in themselves are dialectically problematic because they are the sources of polarization and fragmentation particularly when they are not well managed. In other words, the ultimate causes of political outcomes may not lie in the characteristics of particular party systems, but in the "social and economic forces which gave rise to them" (p. 449).

Haggard and Kaufman have used a minimalist rather than maximalist explanatory model by using examples from South America and Asia and by avoiding to include European and African cases in their study. Doing so does make the study less generalizable and less international (global). It should be made clear that economic and political reforms for democratic consolidation requires a strategic institutional shift. Democratizing states need to move from reliance on broad discretionary powers to reformist executives and be invested in newly constructed institutional mechanisms for governmental consultation with the interests of society. In a world that has a diversity of presidential versus parliamentary structures, two versus multiparty systems, and a variety of electoral systems and mechanisms for representation, the political economy of democratic consolidation can hardly be regulated by the perceptually visualized perfect and reformist state which Haggard and Kaufman have proposed.

Moreover, paradigmatically speaking, the political ideologies upon which the economic foundation of these nations is based have profound Western theoretical and empirical underpinnings that make them difficult if not impossible to productively implement in the Third World. These political ideologies are conservative, liberal and radical (Gondwe, 1992). The hegemonic character of their use in the market does not only ignore the "balance between individual rights and social obligations and responsibilities, as well as the role of culture and traditions in human behavior" (pp. 8-9), but these paradigms place emphasis on the employment of capital investment that mimics the path of historical development structure of more advanced and well established capitalist nations. Because this is ill-advised and destructive, many poor nations suffer from regressive development. Use of appropriate technology, well trained and well placed human capital should complement existing or reformed power structures in a 'people-centered theory of value' (Chapter 7) to enhance development. Given the fact that most state-driven economic programs have failed in many countries, the World Bank has confirmed that more than 3,000 private firms and transactions have been established in the Third World since 1980. The reasons for privatization include attempts to solve "macroeconomic problems, particularly in reducing budget deficits and public debt" (Ramamurti, 1996, p. 10). Further still, privatization was driven by structural conditions in each Latin American country particularly the cost of government ownership and management and external pressure from international organizations (DeCastro, 1997). Ramamurti (1996) has made a compelling argument that privatization results in important improvements in the "quality of services, capital expenditures, labor productivity, and financial performance of the firms involved" (p. 998). Other types of mergers/acquisitions, and privatization transactions invariably require paramount changes in systems, structure, and culture.

Privatization introduces competition which lowers prices for customers, consumers and government. The firms that were privatized in Latin America included those in telecommunications, transportation industries, roads, airports, ports, prisons, educational systems, tax collection, and duty assessment. Also, telephone companies and airlines were privatized.

Though privatization has its merits, it is not without profound demerits which also are constraints on the effective functioning of the state's autonomy. Privatization diminishes the power of the state because the global financial markets enforce the dictates of the IMF particularly in Africa, Asia, Latin America and even in Britain and France. Indeed, the power to overrule majority governments that is wielded by international capital markets and by the IMF constitutes the greatest contemporary threat to substantive democracy in this era, when, paradoxically," liberal democratic political systems have flourished" (Pauly, 1997, p. 427). In other words, majority governments in Poland, South Africa, Philippines, Haiti and Bosnia control their political systems without the capacity to determine their nations' economic destiny or rule over most of the things that matter. International financial markets and multilateral institutions have considerably narrowed state power. In doing that the states, particularly the ones in Third World countries, have become "toothless extensions" of the institutions (IMF, World Bank) which have become the regulators of the unregulated economies. Since the need and interests of these financial institutions are inconsistent with those of the people and nations of the Third World, international institutions may be addressing the needs of these nations exploitatively and criminologically. In other words, "the bankers, both the private ones operating in the global financial markets and the public ones—the international public servants, central bankers, and finance ministers who operate the IMF" (Pauly, 1997, p. 427) as well as those who operated its predecessor agencies of the League of Nations should reexamine their policies which constrain governments, isolate them from their peoples and marginalize them in matters of decision making, policy initiative, implementation and nonmarket influence of the iron triangles (Volkomer, 1998). Paradoxically, the national governments suffering from the constraints of the global markets and intergovernmental obligations were responsible for either strengthening or mismanaging the affairs of their state systems that have now become vassal elements of the international capitalist economy. This form of "casino capitalism" (Pauly, 1997, p. 428) has been existing since the 1920s though it became more highly pronounced since the 1970s. Pauly makes a strong and persuasive argument by encouraging states to promote democratic decision making while demonstrating their accountability to their domestic and international obligations. Decisions should not be secretly carried out by central bankers, finance ministers and political executives. Instead governments should mobilize their citizens to make decisions that open global markets and provide viable and necessary coordination of national economic policies. If that happens, development and democratization will actively become legitimate and meaningful elements of the new world order.

Since the end of the Cold War, Western Europe's relations with Africa have contributed to the marginalization of the latter. For instance, during the 1960s, Black Africa's share of the world trade was 3.8 percent. In 1989, it had declined as low as 1.05 percent. Also, the whole continent's share had declined from 11 percent during the 1980s to 4 percent in 1994 (Olsen, 1997). Marginalization is a dependency theory of development because African nations view foreign aid as the only main external source of funding for development projects and foreign exchange for most African regimes. These former colonial masters buy nearly 50 percent of the continent's exports (raw materials and minerals) while importing 60 percent of what the continent consumes—resulting in an imbalanced balance of payments. In spite of the trade concessions contained in the Lome Convention, the African,

Caribbean and Pacific countries have failed to increase and maintain their market share in the EU.

African countries are dealt with as a "collective clientelism" (Ravenhill, 1985, pp. 22-23). This interdependent relationship is asymmetrical, has emotional ties, is noncomparable and paternalistic form of neocolonialism which has transformed Lome's decolonization principles into aspects of stagnation. Democracy as a capitalist ideology has replaced development. This is comparable to when the communist ideology and its long awaited results, became comparable to development too. The outcome of ideologically rather than rationally and realistically guided socioeconomic system is chaos, bankruptcies, political repression, and worst forms of statecentric authoritarianism.

The South American, Asian and Eastern European regions have received greater amount of assistance than Africa which used to get such comparable assistance from the Western World when it faced the threat of communism during the Cold War. The African, Caribbean and Pacific countries (ACPs), irrespective of the principles enunciated in Lome I and II, have not only been progressively denied the requests they demand, but compensation for the losses entailed by the General Agreement on Tariffs and Trade (GATT)—the equivalent of WTO, have heavily curtailed their protection of favored access to the European market. Further still, recent political crises in Somalia (1992-1996), Rwanda (1994-1996), and Eastern Zaire (1996-1998) have demonstrated EU's lack of economic and political interest in the region. Moreover, France, may have conspired against the central African nations for their rejection of its neocolonial and paternalistic attitude. Without the formidable U.S. humanitarian intervention for the normalization of relations, a greater catastrophe in terms of loss of human life and farther political destabilization of the interlucastrine region could take place. The task would have been impossible without U.S. supplies and transport planes which delivered food, medicine and shelter to the refugees.

Conclusion

Political economy is greatly associated with globalism. The global idea is the electronic and telecommunication movement of the world community and its resources. The movement is futuristically realized in the global vision of the village. Some of the challenges of globalism in the next century will arise from the notion that technology will be the dominant force in human history that will influence society for good or for worse.

Castells (1992) argues that the global economy is different from the world economy. The global is

an economy that works as a unit on real time on a planetary scale. It is an economy where capital flows, labour markets, commodity markets, information, raw materials, management and organization are internationalized and fully interdependent throughout the planet, although in asymmetrical form, characterized by the uneven integration to the global system of different areas of the planet (p. 5).

This global economy is witnessing the emergence of global cities that coordinate the economy. The characteristics of the global cities are duality of life (economic restructuring characterized by "decline of manufacturing industry, loss of skilled manual middle-income jobs, growth of highly skilled and highly paid and managerial stratum which will manage the new global economy and financial system" (Dieleman and Hamnett, 1994, p. 358). This global city will be paralleled by the emergence of "low-skilled and low-paid service jobs to 'service' the service sector, is said to be accompanied by a growing polarization or dualization in the occupational and income structure, which is paralleled by high levels of spatial and ethnic segregation" (p. 358).

The cities will be the hub for the control, coordination, and regulation of global finance (Thrift, 1987; Sassen, 1991), producers of business services (Daniels, 1991), experiencing control and coordination of new international division of labor (Friedman, 1986), key nodes of the international urban system (Mollenkopf, 1993) and cotter pins of global capitalism (Smith and Feagin, 1987). These cities have been infrastructured with telecommunications which allows control and coordination to be managed from remote centers by phone, fax and computer networks that utilize satellites and fiber optics. This technology is used by multinational corporations, companies, firms, financial markets and political executives and diplomats. Banks, accountants, lawyers, managers and consultants use the same telecommunication infrastructure.

Cities are polycentric, multimodal or monocentric. The monocentric city has high levels of congestion. Religious, ideological, economic, racial, housing and political issues divide cities into zones of quartered, nucleated, or spatial settlements.

Connected to control functions and global functions, global cities are physically and socially rich in infrastructure. Their office buildings are distinctly and architecturally designed to symbolize an image of power and prestige (Zukin, 1992). Main international airports, superfast trains and telecommunications networks are global elements of a world city. Their social networks are strengthened by a rich variety of cultural and entertainment industry.

Viewed in this light then, the world city does not only coordinate the free flow of the global economy, but this new, dynamic, and high-income growth city seems to be coveted and highly valued in spite of its inherent hegemonic and segmented inequality (Dieleman and Hamnett, 1994). Cities have grown with rapidity and spectacle during the 20th century. Shanghai has 15 million people, Sao Paulo has 17 million, New Delhi has 10 million, Cairo has 10 million, Tokyo and Yokohama have 27 million, Mexico City has 22 million. There are more than 2,500 metropolises each of which has 1-4 million people. More than 40 cities are 'supercities' which have between 4 million and 10 million people. Twenty-four 'super giants' have more than 10 million each. Predictions indicate that by the year 2050, the world will have 80 super giants (Moyer, 1998).

Historiographically, these developments, many of which are taking place in the Third World, have challenged mainstream academic scholars and researchers to change their analytical traditions in terms of their intellectual universe. Their loaded concepts of race, identity, nation, and tradition have been unbundled. They have theoretically and empirically lost their notions of colonized and colonizer or center and periphery or empire and its others. Academic disciplinarians are negotiating the relationship between local and global. Their academic debate and agenda particularly in the social sciences, focuses on problematics of displacement and relocation, national literatures, transnationality and the challenges of creating and preserving localisms in the context of modernization and globalization.

Politically, the territorial nation-state and its inhabitants are likely to be affected by the technological revolution's impact on the world's political economy and culture. Floods of money, goods and services (labor) and information will be relocated once or several times. Evidently, rational choice which will enable these happenings to take place need to be managed to avoid anarchy (Elkind, 1995). In other words, extraordinary effects of contemporary technological and economic processes are likely to overwhelm the traditional controls known by territorial states. If the newly globalized resources will have been decoupled from their territorial roots, then new forms of governance structures will be needed to foster and necessitate "new nonterritorrial political and social configurations throughout the globe" (Mendlovitz, 1997, p. 229). Corporations, firms, religious institutions, professional organizations, parliamentary and congressional political institutions, NGOs, and other organizations will require new forms of governance structures, values and norms in order to formalize and rationalize their informal and new existence. Formalization of their existence will include but will not be limited to the regulation and control of nuclear proliferation, reduction of global differences that arise from economic inequality and market competition (trade wars); there should be rigorous processes for regulating information technology in order to enable competitors to practice fair competition in the market, such as the split decision issued by the courts to reduce Microsoft's monopoly. As usual, some noncompetitive, unreformed, and mechanistically dominated organizations will disappear because their humanistic and behavioral existence will be inconsistent with the technologically and organizationally reformed ways of managing things.

Unlike the unreformed decline and extinction of the medieval institutions and organizations (lords, knights, vassals, serfs, fiefdom, church, commerce, or the city and town), whose system undermined land commodification, commerce and scientific exploration, to survive and flourish, the modern society of the future should establish strong structures for self-reconceptualization, self-reconstruction, new citizenship, and collective global and moral rearmament all of which become the framework and springboard for production, recreation, self-realization, and self-actualization.

In the New Millennium, each individual will inherit a new sense of multiple identity which will continue to transform him/her. They will not only be very multicultural, but they will also be reflective of a plurality of cultural elements of nation-state citizenship. This global society, to practice its civilian and vocational life, will select to participate by seeking membership among a wide variety of "electronic communication groups, international groupings, new political processes and organizations, citizenships" (Mendlovitz, 1995, p. 229).

The new inhabitants will exercise individual choice more assertively in order to keep up with the electronically governed communication structure in order to reaffirm their new identities. Social arrangements and self-conceptions will be shaped exclusively by and through existing societal structures rather than the family, kinship group, or one's own culture. Current societal structures are radically preparing people for globalization. They have become consciously aware that new global interactions have enabled the evolution of these formally nonexistent interactional relations to exist. The "old citizen" is being 'unbundled' (p. 229).

The socioeconomic evolution of the global and post-Cold War society has produced a global mind in terms of transnational corporations, global social movements, world religions, and the growth of regional and global supranational economic and political organizations. Elkind calls them 'anarchy.' These new social and economic organizations are an articulated, self-conscious transnational civil society that is being analyzed, socialized, and transformed to produce supranational global political institutions like UN, NAFTA, EU, APEC, NATO, and the Third World which will function as centralizing rather than decentralizing forces. Since 1992, more than 30 UN global conferences including those of the NGOs have tried to agree on the construction of the global formative order. NAFTA in itself is a regional rather than multilateral instrument of U.S. economic and foreign policy (Bhagwati, 1992/93).

For instance, the environmental movement is a stimulus for nonterritorial political organization which articulates it in the fashion of unbiblical and unspiritual way. With the impetus for their ideological spiritual union, environmentalists, feminists, and peace and human rights activists, and civil rights or social justice advocates are recognized elements of the new global society which has no territorial boundaries or cultural norms of a traditional type. These groups advocate the promotion of decentralized governance (small is beautiful). They are assertively contributing to the formulation and institutionalization of global political standards. In the era of global communications, economics, technology and culture, historically and culturally established notions of Western culture and civilization are being questioned. A new paradigm of global hegemony is arising in the East to which region power has significantly shifted. This power is being exercised by nongovernmental and nonprivate entities which Drucker calls the 'third force' (p. 230). This force whose influence of cities and world religions are characterized by vibrant and revolutionary world spirituality which is galvanizingly unparalleled in world history.

What role should the state play in such a climate of economic and sociotechnical change? This question has been central to political economists since the time of Adam Smith's classical era of the *Wealth of Nations*. Neoclassical economists see that perceived role to be both laissez-faire and neoliberal rather than radical. Neoliberal economists view the role of the state to be central in moving planned economies to a market orientation and in maintaining macroeconomic stability where prices are freely determined by competitive markets. As an agent of economic change, the state should play the dual role of entrepreneur and conflict manager (Chang and Rowthorn, 1995). This has happened in European and East Asian countries in which industrial policy, entrepreneurial vision and bureaucratic involvement have used a gradualist and incremental perspective rather than the "big bang" or shock-therapy for growth through global, institutional, and organizational interdependence.

The methodology of the new political economy rejects the old dichotomy between agency and structure which fragmented classical political economy into separate disciplines that were based on ideological rather than rational reality. The new thinking in political economy seeks instead, to build on those approaches in social science, such as the structuration theory, institutional economics, new public choice theory and critical theory, which have tried to develop an integrated analysis, thereby combining parsimonious theories which analyze agency in terms of instrumental rationality with contextual theories which analyze structures institutionally and historically. The aim of the *New Political Economy Journal* is to create a forum for work which seeks to bridge past empirical and conceptual divides. The emphasis will be based upon explanatory and innovative work which draws on different disciplines and which addresses core issues in the emerging research agenda in the field of political economy which is a subparadigm of organizational theory. In totality, this paradigmatic discipline is a sound framework for interweaving social, political, and economic history.

References

Aggarwal, V.K. 1996. *Debt Games: Strategic Interaction in International Debt Rescheduling.* New York: Cambridge University Press.

Amin, S. 1974. *Accumulation on a World Scale.* New York: Monthly Review.

Arrighi, G. 1982. A crisis of hegemony. In *The Dynamics of Global Crisis,* eds. S. Amin, G. Arrighi, A.G. Frank, and I. Wallerstein, 55-108. New York: Monthly Review.

Benson, J.K. 1975 The interorganizational network as a political economy. *Administrative Science Quarterly* 20: 229-248.

Berger, S., and R. Dore, eds. 1980. *National Diversity and Global Capitalism.* Ithaca: Cornell University Press.

Bhagwati, J. 1992/93. Beyond NAPHTHA: Clinton's trading choices. *Foreign Policy* 89: 155-162.

Blake, D.H. 1977. *Managing the External Relations of Multinational Corporations.* New York: Fund for Multinational Management.

Boddewyn, J.J. 1986. *International Political Strategy: A Fourth "Generic" Strategy?* Working Paper. New York: Baruch College.

Boddewyn, J.J., and T.L. Brewer. 1994. International business political behavior: New theoretical directions. *Academy of Management Review* 19, 1: 119-143.

Boesche, R. 1996. *Theories of Tyranny from Plato to Arendt.* University Park: Pennsylvania State University Press

Bollen, K.A. 1983. World system position, dependency and democracy. *American Sociological Review* 48: 468-497.

Brewer, T.L. 1993. Government policies, market imperfections, and foreign direct investment. *Journal of International Business Studies* 24: 101-120.

Brewer, T.L. 1992a. An issue-area approach to the analysis of MNC-government relations. *Journal of International Business Studies* 23: 295-309.

Brewer, T.L. 1992b. MNC-government relations: Strategic networks and foreign direct investment in the United States in the automotive industry. *The International Executive* 34: 113-129.

Bunker, S.C. 1984. Modes of extraction, unequal exchange, and progressive underdevelopment of an extreme periphery: The Brazilian Amazon, 1960-1980. *American Journal of Sociology.*

Burris, V. 1991. Director interlocks and political behavior of corporations and corporate elites. *Social Science Quarterly* 72, 3: 537-551.

Caporaso, J.A. 1981. Industrialization at the periphery: The evolving division of labor. *International Studies Quarterly,* 25: 347-384.

Cardoso, F.H. 1973. Associated-dependent development. In *Authoritarian Brazil: Origins, Policies and Future,* ed. A. Stephen, 142-176. Yale University Press.

Castells, M. 1992. *European Cities, the Informational Society, and the Global Economy.* Amsterdam: Centre for Metropolitan Research, Amsterdam University.

Chang, H.G., and R. Rowthorn. 1995. *The Role of the State in Economic Change.* Oxford: Clarendon Press.

Chase-Dunn, C., and R. Rubinson. 1977. Toward a structural perspective on the world system. *Politics and Society.*

Chen, F. 1995. *Economic Transition and Political Legitimacy in Post-Mao China.* Albany: State University of New York Press.

Choate, P. 1990. *Agents of Influence: How Japan's Lobbyists in the United States Manipulate America's Political and Economic System*. New York: Alfred A. Knopf.

Collis, D.J. 1991. A resource-based analysis of global competition: The case of the bearings industry. *Strategic Management Journal* 12: 49-68.

Conner, K.R. 1991. A historical comparison of resource-based theory and five schools of thought within industrial organization economics. *Journal of Management* 17: 121-154.

Croft, S. 1997. International relations and Africa: Review article. *African Affairs* 96, 385: 607-615.

Daniels, P.L.D. 1991. *Services and Metropolitan Development: International Perspectives*. London: Routledge.

Deane, P. 1978. *The Evolution of Economic Ideas: Modern Economics*. Cambridge: Cambridge University Press.

DeCastro, J.O. ed. 1997. Privatizing monopolies: Lessons from the telecommunications and transport sectors in Latin America. *Academy of Management Review*, 22, 4: 997-1010.

Deprez, J. 1991. The Macrodynamics of Advanced Market Economies: The Post-Keynesian Perspective of Alfred Eichner. *Social Science Quarterly* 72, 3: 415-430.

Diamond, L., and M.F. Plattner., eds. 1995. *Economic Reform and Democracy*. Baltimore: Johns Hopkins University Press.

Dieleman, F.M., and C. Hamnett. 1994. Globalization, regulation and urban system: Editor's introduction to the special issue. *Urban Studies*, 31, 3: 357-364.

DiMaggio, P.J., and W.W. Powell. 1983. The iron cage revisited: Institutional isomorphism and collective rationality in organizational fields. *American Sociological Review* 48: 147-160.

Doz, Y. 1986. *Strategic Management in Multinational Companies*. New York: Pergamon Press.

Eichner, A. 1987. *The Macrodynamics of Advanced Market Economies*. Armonk, N.Y.: M.E. Sharpe.

Eichner, A. 1976. *The Megacorp and Oligopoly: Micro Foundations of Macro Dynamics*. New York: Cambridge University Press.

Elkind, D. 1995. *Beyond Sovereignty: Territory and Political Economy in the Twenty-First Century*. Toronto: Toronto University Press.

Etzioni, A. 1996. The responsive community: A communication perspective. *American Sociological Review* 61: 1-11.

Etzioni, A. 1988. *The Moral Dimension: Toward a New Economics*. New York: Free Press.

Evans, P. 1979a. Beyond center and periphery a comment on the world system approach to the study of development. *Sociological Inquiry* 49: 15-20.

Evans, P. 1979b. *Dependent Development.* Princeton: Princeton University Press.

Fayerweather, J. 1969. *International Business Management.* New York: McGraw-Hill.

Feagin, J.R. 1985. The social costs of Houston's growth. *International Journal of Urban and Regional Research* 9: 164-185.

Firebaugh, G., and B. Bullock. 1987. Level of processing of exports: Estimates for developing nations. *International Studies Quarterly* 30: 333-350.

Fox, A.B. 1995. Environment and trade: The NAFTA case. *Political Science Quarterly* 110, 1: 49-68.

Frank, A.G. 1969 *Latin America. Underdevelopment of Revolution?* New York: Monthly Review.

Friedmann, J. 1986. The world city hypothesis. *Development and Change,* 17: 69-84.

Gamble, A. 1996. *The New Political Economy Journal.* File: ///C\/Iconovex/EchoSearch/Work/Views/5.html#ICVX8000C.

Gereffi, G. and D. Wyman. 1990. *Manufacturing Miracles: Paths of Industrialization in Latin America and East Asia.* Princeton: Princeton University Press.

Gondwe, D.K. 1992. *Political Economy, Ideology, and the Impact of Economics on the Third World.* New York: Praeger.

Grant, R.M. 1991. The resource-based theory of competitive advantage: Implications for strategy formulations. *California Management Review* 33, 3: 14-135.

Haggard, S., and R.R. Kaufman. 1995. *The Political Economy of Democratic Transitions.* Princeton: Princeton University Press.

Hayes, M.T. 1981. *Lobbyists and Legislators: A Theory of Political Market.* New Brunswick, N.J.: Rutgers University Press.

Henderson, A.E. ed. 1997. Afrocentrism and world politics: Towards a new paradigm. *American Political Science Review* 91: 448.

Jacoby, S. 1995. *The Workers of Nations: Industrial Relations in a Global Economy.* New York: Oxford University Press.

Keohane, R. 1984. *After Hegemony: Cooperation and Discord in World Political Economy.* Princeton: Princeton University Press.

Kindleberger, C.P. 1970. *Power and Money.* New York: Basic Books.

Kindleberger, C.P. 1969. *American Business Abroad.* New Haven, CT.: Yale University Press.

Klein, L.R., R. Pauly, and P. Voisin. 1982. The world economy—a global model. *Perspectives in Computing* 2: 4-17.

Korzeniewicz, R.P., and T.P. Moran. 1997. World economic trends in the distribution of income, 1965-1992. *American Journal of Sociology* 102, 4: 1000-1039.

Leone, R.A. 1986. *Who Profits: Winners, Losers and Government Regulations.* New York: Basic Books.

Linnemann, H. 1966. *An Econometric Study of World Trade Flows.* Amsterdam: North Holland.

Mandel, E. 1975. *Late Capitalism.* London: Mew Left Review.

Mansfield, E.A., and H.V. Milner, eds. 1997. *The Political Economy of Regionalism.* New York: Columbia University Press.

Marklew, V. 1995. *Cash, Crisis, and Corporate Governance: The Role of National Financial Systems in Industrial Restructuring.* Ann Arbor, MI: University of Michigan Press.

Mendlovitz, S.H. ed. 1997. Beyond sovereignty: Territory and political economy in the twenty-first century. *American Political Science Review,* March: 229-230.

Mitchell, N., W.L. Hansen, and E.M. Jepsen. 1997. The determinants of domestic and foreign corporate political activity. *The Journal of Politics* 59, 4: 1096-1113.

Mollenkopf, J.E. 1993. *Key Urban Nodes in the Global System.* New York: Social Science Research Council.

Morrison, A.J., and K. Roth. 1989. International business-level strategy: The development of holistic model. In *International Strategic Management,* eds. A.R. Negandi and A. Savara. 29-49. Lexington, MA. Lexington Books.

Moyer, B.C. 1998. Surrounded? Thank God! The urban paradox. *Adventist Review* June: 12-15.

Nemeth, R., and D. A. Smith. 1985. International Trade and World System Structure: A Multiple Network Analysis. *Review,* by Ferdinand Braudel Center, 8: 517-560.

Naughton, B. 1995. *Growing Out of the Plan: Chinese Economic Reform, 1978-1993.* Cambridge: Cambridge University Press.

Olsen, G.R. 1997. Western Europe's relation with Africa since the end of the cold war. *The Journal of Modern African Studies* 35, 2: 299-319.

Pauly, L.W. 1997. *Who Elected the Bankers? Surveillance and Control in the World Economy.* Ithaca: Cornell University Press.

Perrow, C. 1986. *Complex Organizations.* New York: McGraw-Hill.

Perrow, C. 1981. Markets, hierarchies and hegemony. In *Perspectives on Organization Design and Behavior*, eds. A.H. Van de Ven and W. Joyce, 317-386. New York: Wiley.

Peteraf, M.A. 1990. The cornerstones of competitive advantage: A resource-based view. *Strategic Management Journal* 14: 179-191.

Pfeffer, J., and G.R. Salancik. 1978. *The External Control of Organizations: A Resource Dependent Perspective.* New York: Harper and Row.

Prestowitz, C. 1988. *Trading Places.* New York: Basic Books.

Ramamurti, R., ed. 1996. *Privatizing Monopolies: Lessons from the Telecommunications and Transport Sectors in Latin America.* Baltimore: The Johns Hopkins University Press.

Ravenhill, J. 1985. *Collective Clientelism: The Lome Conventions and the North-South Relations.* New York.

Rugman, A.M., and A. Verbeke. 1992. Multinational Enterprise and National Economic Policy. In *Multinational Enterprise in the World Economy,* eds. P.J. Buckley and M. Casson, 194-211. Aldershot, England: Elgar.

Sassen, S. 1991. *The Global City.* Princeton: Princeton University Press.

Schott, T. 1986. Models of dyadic and individual components of a social relation: Applications to international trade. *Journal of Mathematical Sociology* 12: 225-249.

Sethi, S.P. 1994. *Multinational Corporations and the Impact of Public Advocacy on Corporate Strategy: Nestle and the Infant Formula Controversy.* Boston: Kluwer Academic.

Smith, D.A., and D.R. White. 1992. Structure and dynamics of the global economy: Network analysis of international trade 1965-1980. *Social Forces* 70, 4: 857-893.

Smith, M.P., and J.R. Feagin, eds. 1987. *The Capitalist City.* Oxford: Blackwell.

Snyder, D., and E. Kick. 1970. Structural position in the world system and economic growth: A multiple network analysis of transnational interactions. *American Journal of Sociology* 84: 1096-1126.

Steiber, S. 1979. The world system and world trade: An empirical explanation of conceptual conflicts. *The Sociological Quarterly* 20: 23-36.

Thompson, W.R. 1983. Uneven economic growth, system challenges, and global wars. *International Studies Quarterly* 27: 341-355.

Thrift, N. 1987. The fixers: The urban geography of international commercial capital. In *Global Restructuring and Territorial*

Development, eds. J. Henderson and M. Castells. Newbury Park: Sage.

Tolchin, M. and S. Tolchin. 1988. *Buying into America: How Foreign Money is Changing the Face of Our Nation.* New York: Times Books.

Wallerstein, I. 1980. *The Modern World System.* New York: Academic Press.

Wallerstein, I. 1979. *The Capitalist World Economy.* New York: Academic Press.

Wallerstein, I. 1974. *The Model of World System.* New York: Academic Press.

Webb, M.C. 1995. *The Political Economy of Policy: International Adjustment Since 1945.* Ithaca: Cornell University Press.

Yan, S. 1995. *The Chinese Reassessment of Socialism, 1979-1992.* Princeton: Princeton University Press.

Zukin, S. 1992. The city as a landscape of power: London and New York as global financial capitals. In *Global Finance and Urban Living: A Study of Metropolitan Change,* eds. L. Budd and S. Whimster, 195-223. London: Routledge.

Chapter 17

African Political Economy: The Global Context

Introduction

Scholars in the social sciences are trying to redefine the concept of political economy in order to overlap its classical, dialectical and ideological narrowness. Scholarly analysis of the subject indicates that political economy is interdisciplinary in orientation. On the global scene, its application shows evidences of hierarchical and continuous reproduction of dependency and reciprocity. On the African and Third World scene, the global structures through which political economy is facilitated, applied, and rationalized have created strategic and logistic mechanisms in the socioeconomic arena that have greatly contributed to the marginalization and paramount delinkage of Africa from the core and semi-periphery of the world civilization. In spite of the apparent marginalization and delinkage of the continent, the prospects for and contributions of its political economy could be promising. The differential character of delinkage and promise affects the way in which organizations operate.

The structure and dynamics of the global economy has been quantitatively investigated thrice (1965, 1970, and 1980). Methodologically, the investigation was centered on quantitative network analysis of the international commodity trade flows. The research was designed to measure the structure of the world's economic system. Second, the same research was designed to identify specific roles that are played by certain countries in the global division of labor. The structure of the world economy and how it changes are major elements of international political economy (Smith and White, 1992; Deane, 1978). Three major perspectives are substantively and analytically paramount. First, based on theoretical, global and neoclassical economic theories, global political economy is analyzable by use of comparative advantage perspective (Klein, Pauly and Vision, 1982 and Linnemann, 1966). Second, international relations perspectives of political economy puts a lot of emphasis on its strategic and geopolitical dynamics rather than on comparative advantage (Keohane, 1984 and Thompson, 1983). Third, the global system perspective which stresses regular inequality of exchange of goods and services (Amin, 1974 and Wallerstein, 1974 and 1980) tends to promote and perpetuate economic, political and technological domination of the core countries on those that are viewed as the periphery and semi-periphery. Through the social network analysis, five empirical components are addressed by several theories of international political economy, namely:

(1) the constituent economies of states (or cities, hinterlands, and regions) that produce, distribute, consume, and exchange exports and imports; (2) links or directed pairwise flows between these economies/polities, and country level and international policies that regulate these flows; (3) the political-economic networks which formed these links or pairwise flows; (4) the positions occupied by constituent economies/polities in these networks; and (5) the structure of these networks as patterns of flows between positions (Smith and White, 1992, 858).

Social network analysis is theoretically world-system based. It places emphasis on the importance of global economic exchange. In its origin, operation, and organization of the modern global economy, it exists to perpetuate structural dependency (Wallerstein, 1980; Frank, 1969 and Chilcote, 1974), global inequality (Amin, 1974 and Emmanuel, 1972) through international trade circuits and dependent development (Cardoso, 1973 and Evans 1979b).

The world's economic system is stratified (Nemeth and Smith, 1985 and Schott, 986) in terms of core, semi-periphery and periphery. It also makes the strata to be seen as discrete clusters (Wallerstein, 1974) or structural continuum (Chase-Dunn, 1989). Some of the strata within the world-system play certain roles which serve hegemonic, regional and spatial interests of these clusters and trade partners (Bollen, 1983; Evans, 1979a;

Snyder and Kick, 1979; and Steiber, 1979). In other words, the role of each country or cluster within the stratified world's economic system is either different and unique to each country or mutually reciprocal. The positions of the continual strata members have unequal trade exchange relationships whose theoretical and philosophical underpinnings exacerbate dependency (Bunker, 1984; Mandel, 1975; and Firebaugh and Bullock, 1987). In recent history, traditional hegemonic powers have been relatively neutralized by the emergence of a multicentric core stratum whose network, block or subblocks has not only produced a new international division of labor, but the new division of labor has been reinforced by the character of "currency flight" to Third World areas where the cost of production and of labor are comparatively lower than those in the core countries (Caporaso, 1981 and Arrighi, 1982). The dramatic and historic collapse of the ex-Soviet Empire and the current financial mismanagement and fiscal instability in southeast Asia may have threatened investors to return their currency back to the United States and Western Europe. In the wake of Asian decline, this behavioral phenomenon may not only help to explain the apparent resurgence of these economies, but the previous use of these currencies for the geo-strategic containment of the empire in question, may have helped the West to formidably eclipse the rival empire while hegemonically reasserting itself anew on the global plane of international relations and political economy. That reassertion is accomplished through international economic cooperation, mobility of capital, and imposition of fixed rather than flexible exchange rates (Webb, 1995). Cooperative mobility of capital may cause economic turbulence.

These global factors describe how and why Africa has been marginalized and peripheralized in and by the international politico-economic system. The marginalized and peripheralized condition has caused African political economies and their structures of production to remain perennially static. These structures of production have not only become obsolete, but, they have contributed to Africa's loss of comparative advantage particularly in the traditional raw material sector of its economies. Unsophisticated technology for mineral production has also affected their demand and supply on the world market. Domestic political intervention characterized by state-centric goals of production and mismanagement have no relevance to market dictates that are externally designed, politically rationalized, socioeconomically hegemonic, and intellectuo-technologically exclusive. Suggestions for restructuring and improving the political economy of the continent are likely to face the challenges of practice and praxis.

During the last two decades of the 20th century, Africa has been marginalized and peripheralized within the international political economy (Berg, 1981; *Lagos Plan of Action*, 1980; *World Development Report*, 1981). The tone for this debate was clearly set by the World Bank's *Accelerated Development in Sub-Saharan Africa: An Agenda for Action* (1980), otherwise known as the *Berg Report*. The report considers the stagnation and decline in agricultural production for export and domestic consumption; decline in national output; crisis in internal and external economic balance, and institutional crises of governance. Pessimism about Africa's future looms high in the horizon. According to the Development Committee of OECD (cited in Bogdanotwitz-Bindert, 1982, 282): "Africa in the year 2000 will not be in the ditch it is in now, it will be in the bottom of a deep black hole." Another observer, Higgot (1986, 295) has concluded: "Africa may well be more peripheral, more dependent and in greater economic crisis by the end of the current decade than it was in the 1960s."

The view that Africa faces a crisis is not in contention. However, significant debate surrounds the causes of Africa's difficulties and possible solutions for ameliorating the crisis. The *Berg Report* recommended integration into the world economy by focusing on the continent's comparative advantage of exporting agricultural raw materials. This solution has been criticized as lacking efficacy and questioned for relegating Africa to the status of "hewers of wood and drawers of water" (cited in Berg, 1986, 53). At best, the solution is viewed as a mere palliative. In the spirit of the recommendation, countries like Ivory Coast which did imbibe the precepts of "Big Push" and orthodox development paradigms have argued that "we are where we are because we did what you told us" (Green and Allison, 1986, 63). Africa, it can be argued, is caught in a paradox. Concern for Africa's problems has shifted from "development" to "adjustment." Adjustment "to democratization (Gilbert, 1994 and Croft, 1997). Democratization without development is the same thing as spreading an ideology which is economically bankrupt.

An alternative explanation, separate from both the standard thesis put forward by modernization and more radical globalist theorists will be offered. It is the thesis of this chapter that marginalization and peripheralization of Africa in the changing international political economy is due to the fact that the continent has been delinked. Delinkage in the context of this chapter means the severing of undermining of Africa's participation in the international political economy. The delinking of Africa has been brought about by the obsolescence of the "traditional trinity" in terms of the role that Africa played in the international division of labor when it was incorporated into the capitalist world system; the transformation of the international political economy and the forging of a new international division of labor (NIDL); the static structures of production of many African countries and their inability to meet the challenges of the NIDL; the impact of technological innovations on agriculture and mineral products offered for sale on the international market; and the failure of import substitution industrialization (IS) to integrate the economies of Africa into the international political economy. These problems are beyond the capacity of either orthodox or racial solutions (Boansi, 1997) to the African situation. I will mainly use Boansi's paraphrasiology to explain this case study.

Ghana, Cote d'Ivoire, Tanzania, and Zaire (Democratic Republic of Congo – DRC): Case Study

The thesis by Boansi examines the political economies of Ghana, Ivory Coast (Cote d'Ivoire), Tanzania, and Zaire. The four countries were selected on the basis of their ideological orientation and development strategy, governmental attitude toward private foreign investment, and the structure of production of each country's corpus of information. This study was informed by theoretical presuppositions of modernization and globalization thesis. The structure of production of the four countries also varies across the continent based on a classification scheme which shows that:

1. Countries with agriculture as the mainstay of the economy without a supporting export mineral sector, e.g., Cote d'Ivoire and Tanzania;
2. Countries with a combination of agriculture and mineral exports, but with agriculture as dominant, e.g. Ghana and Cote d'Ivoire;
3. Countries with a combination of agriculture and mineral exports, but minerals as dominant; and
4. Countries with minerals as the mainstay of the economy without a supporting agricultural sector, e.g., the rest of Africa.

This analysis will show that neither incorporation as advocated by modernization scholars nor delinking as proposed by the globalists is a panacea to Africa's development problematique even though popular arguments suggest that those pursuing integration into the international political economy are better off. It is contestable that countries that pursued integrationist policies are better off not because of the policies or development orientation per se, but they fare slightly better because of the class character of the ruling elite and their position vis-a-vis the means of production. Elites who came to power during independence such as Kenyatta's regime, had a close relationship with the means of production anchoring the economy. They were able to use state power to advance their economic interests while nurturing the economic system. Elites with no affinity to the means of production of which Moi's Kenya is an example, used state power to over-extract economic surplus thereby undermining the efficacy of the economic system. They control the state as a means of self-advancement. However, those exacted advantages lasted for only two decades because of the limitations of the structure of production bequeathed to African countries at independence. Similarly, the regimes played negative roles in the international division of labor (IDL) to the impact of technology on the commodities being offered for sale on the world economy. In other words, the structure of production limited the policy options of the ruling elite. This explains the widespread nature of Africa's development crisis. Traditional curatives are no longer tenable. The thesis that the structure of production and its diversification and how it is positioned to take advantage of the NIDL is a *sine qua non* to overcoming further economic peripheralization and marginalization of the continent.

Colonialism marked the normal integration of the four countries into the capitalist world economy. The British colonized Ghana, the French, Ivory Coast, the Germans, until the end of the First World War, Tanzania and Belgium Zaire. Tanzania became a mandated territory under the British. The four countries were colonized to serve metropolitan interests. In the process, their political economies were structured to play three important roles in the capitalist world system. The roles were to:
1. Supply industrial and agricultural raw materials;
2. Serve as a market for finished and semi-finished exports of manufactured products; and
3. Act as a field of investment, both public and private (Rood, 1975, 19-34; Leys, 1979, 315).

The four countries, like a variety of many African nations, emerged producing agricultural crops such as cocoa, coffee, cotton, sisal, timber, oil palm, quinine, tea, rubber and minerals such gold, diamonds, bauxite and copper (Shapiro and Tollens, 1992, 14). Ghana emerged as the world's leading producer of cocoa before and after independence (Killick, 1978, 3). Unlike Ghana and Cote d'Ivoire, the Germans introduced Tanzania to industrial crop production. Germany's interest at the time involved overcoming European protectionism. The introduction of sisal, cotton, coffee, cashew nuts, rubber and pyrethrum was intended to achieve that objective. Tanzania was therefore put at an international disadvantage competing with Mexico and the United States. In Tanzania, Cote d'Ivoire and Zaire, a dual mode of production emerged. A peasant mode of production supplanted settler efforts in the production of coffee, tea and cotton in al three countries (Rodney, 1979; Coulson, 1982). Agro-industrial companies dominated the agricultural sector (Lungunga, 1979, 64). Unlike Ghana, Tanzania and Cote d'Ivoire, it is mining which emerged as Zaire's dominant sector of the economy. Among the minerals produced by Zaire are copper, cobalt, zinc, manganese, tin, coal, iron ore, niobium, monazite, gold and industrial diamonds. Copper and its byproducts constitute approximately 60% of Zaire's exports and 75% of its foreign exchange earnings (Radman, 1978, 35).

In view of the role that colonies were supposed to play in the IDL, industrialization was not given serious attention anywhere on the continent or elsewhere in the periphery. Their role was to produce raw materials for metropolitan economies and consume the manufactured products of these countries which were and are advanced and free market capitalist economies. In Ghana, commissions of inquiry into industrialization prospects pointed out that the country was not ready. The backwater status of Ivory Coast also prevented industrialization from taking off. French West Africa imported more than 70% of its products from France (Alschuler, 1988, 78). In East Africa, ISI took hold because of production disruptions during the Second World War. Once again, the status of Tanganyika (Tanzania) as United Nations mandated or trustship territory created an ambivalent situation for the colony. Ideologically, the British supervised its administration paternalistically. The British government stifled all industrialization efforts including the processing of raw materials. Asians who attempted to establish industries were frustrated in their efforts (Coulson, 1982, 74-78). British colonialism destroyed existing domestic industries like iron work, basketry, weaving, spinning, sculpture and crafts. It has been documented extensively that imports displaced local production of textiles, iron and salt. The cotton weaving and dying industry could not withstand the flood of Indian textiles. Textile production declined in Bukoba and Nyamwezi in Tanganyika. Persian Gulf salt and Indian imports destroyed production of salt along the coast of East Africa. The iron ore industry in the areas of Sambuwanga also ceased production by 1920s.

The transfer of Belgium Congo to Leopold II made industrialization in Zaire inevitable. The Berlin Act and Saint German en-Laye Act had declared the Congo a free trading zone. By the 1920s, the state was experiencing difficulties in protecting the colonial economy from outside competition. The state therefore decided that import substitution industrialization in partnership with private capital could stem the tide of competition. Industrialization was therefore launched to deal with the problem of competition. Foreign dominated industrialization was also seen as having the potential capacity of increasing the purchasing power of the people and widening the tax base (Jewsiewicki, 1977). By the early 1950s, Belgium Congo was second only to South Africa in terms of industrial development. Agro-industries were established to process and export crops. The state barred Africans from processing agricultural crops under the pretext that African methods of processing resulted in inferior quality. The "rationale behind the policy was to prevent the growth of indigenous private capital and any competition which would have interfered with the flow of foreign investment" (Emoungu, 1983, 168; Lungunga, 1979, 93; Leslie, 1986, 162; 1993, 104).

From this analysis of the colonial political economies of Ghana, Ivory Coast, Tanzania and Zaire, it can be argued that the productive forces were better developed in Zaire than in the other three countries. The least developed was Tanganyika (Tanzania) because of its special status and the paternalistic ideology of guided British trustship. Tanganyika by all accounts exhibited the prognosis of Kay's (1975) underdeveloped economy where underdevelopment is ascribed to lack of investment resources. However, it is important to point out that if there was any commonality regarding colonialism on the continent, it is the structure of production bequeathed to the colonial people at independence. The economies of the four countries emerged peripheral within the capitalist world economy, dependent on imports and exports, with monocrop economy and little industry. The economies suffered from structural dislocation because of their dependence on the export of raw materials and lack of linkages. The countries bore all the characteristics of underdeveloped economies. Production and consumption were not integrated within the economy but through external trade. The countries exchanged commodities which they produced but did not consume or process their raw materials. Their economies were open to metropolitan exploitation and their success was dependent on favorable agricultural and mineral commodity exchange on the world market.

Post-Independence Economic Development Thought

The economic philosophy underlying the development efforts of African countries particularly those in this study can be described as eclectic. It was an amalgam of different ideas embraced by the ruling elite ranging from liberalism, statecentirc capitalism to African Socialism. It is important to point out that the policies which were implemented by African policymakers after independence, regardless of their names came under the influence of the dominant development paradigm of the "Big Push." Big Push emphasized the continuation of colonial economic policies while giving the state an active role in the economy. Proponents of Big Push argued that in underdeveloped economies, prices and markets were limited in their ability to coordinate economic decisions. To correct the deficiency, consensus emerged among mainstream economists that there was the need for centralized investment planning which would act as an additional communication system to supplement the pricing system. Factor and product markets were seen as imperfect in situations where entrepreneurial talents were scarce. In the words of Myrdal, "because of the various deficiencies in a backward country it is also accepted by everyone that the government will have to take over many functions which in most advanced countries in the Western world were left to private business" (Killick, 1978, 28).

Proponents of Big Push were also concerned with the role of developing countries in the international political economy. In his 1959 Wicksell Lectures, Nurske argued against export-led development in low-income countries. He posited that they face slow growth because of the structure of production and technological shift in the industrialized countries. These countries put a low price on commodities from LDCs. He further argued that underdeveloped countries face low income elasticity of demand for many agricultural products; development of synthetic substitutes and protectionism from industrialized states reduce the scope for low-income countries to switch to the exportation of manufactured goods. The observation of Nurkse was not new. A UN study a decade earlier showed that there was a downward trend in the export prices of primary products relative to manufactured products. Singer took up the theme when he wrote:

> It is a matter of historical fact that ever since the eighteen seventies the trend of prices has been heavily against sellers of food and raw materials and in favor of manufactured articles. The statistics are open to doubt and to objection in detail, but the general story which they tell is unmistakable" (Killick, 1978, 15).

The above position led to the rejection of the marginalist position that persistently argued that deteriorating terms of trade would result in adjustments of the pattern of production to take advantage of changing comparative advantage. Underdeveloped economies were deemed inflexible. This formed the basis of state intervention in the economy. "Some proponents however wanted state participation limited to provision of social overhead capital. Others limited state intervention to administrative control such as import restrictions as means of buttressing the balance of payments and stimulating domestic industrialization" (p. 23). Mainstream development economies of the 1950s through 1970s were highly interventionist in this arena.

In all the four countries studied, an affinity developed between development economics and the aspirations of nationalist leaders. The central role of the state followed Marxists. Liberalism, state-controlled capitalism and African socialism formed the basis of economic policy development in the Third World. Development economists like Arthur Lewis and Sir Robert Jackson found fertile ground in the Third World to implement policies they had been theorizing. Development in the Third World came to be predicated on the following precepts:

1. Economic development is a discontinuous rather than continuous process of structural transformation;
2. Above a certain critical level of per capita income, growth tends to become self-sustaining. This assumption is based on competitive Western and open market economic models of production rather than on Third World, less competitive and relatively closed market climates where it was applied;
3. To break out of the poverty trap and achieve self-sustaining growth, a "critical minimum effort" instead of critical maximum effort or "big push" was required;
4. While this push requires inputs, its single most important component is a massive increase in the ratio of investment to national income and repatriation of profits to sources of investment capital; and
5. Development entails industrialization, which by choice or from necessity, will concentrate on satisfying the home market for manufacturers rather than producers of raw materials. Manufacturers were, in essence, foreign corporations which controlled political climates in favor of their exploitation.

The chapter shows that the existing structure of production in the four countries limited what policymakers could do. It is therefore not surprising that all the countries ended up in economic crisis or some form of internal receivership in the 1980s and 1990s.

Solutions and Problems

Africa is marginalized, peripheralized and partially disconnected or delinked from and by international political economy. The problems which tend to alienate it from being a major and dynamic player in international affairs are deeply rooted in the structure of production and infrastructure of organizational management and technological know-how. The key to economic power and development rests in the ability of a nation or people to perceive and respond to the need for monopolies, technology and self-sufficiency all of which must be used for self-transformation brought about or instigated by the changes dictated by global economic environment of which comparative advantage and price fluctuations are paramount (Gilpin, 1987).

Currently, African countries do not have the capacity for effectively competing in the international global economy or for responding to the demands of a new (for Africa) international division of labor (IDL). Based on the differential and evolutionary development of the stage(s) and systems of capitalism, some countries particularly those in the core rather than those in the periphery, can effectively participate in IDL because they, early on in their history, experimented, at different stages of their economic development, the mercantilist and capitalist modes of production, distribution and consumption, and in the process, learned how to circumvent internal and exogenous problems, pathologies, and palliative traps in the realm of international political economy. Some of these problems which are well known by the international and financial, bilateral and multilateral institutions e.g., IMF and World Bank, are palliatively created by the same institutions.

Though some scholars argue that Africa's economic decline is caused by poorly constructed social policy, such intellectual allegations have not critically and realistically addressed the gist of African development problematique. In other words, their perception of it is not incisively and decisively well dissected. Nor, for that matter, properly and meaningfully well digested to warrant clarity and purposive, intentional and ameliorative action. At independence most African countries, including Cote d'Ivoire, Ghana, Tanzania, and Zaire experienced steady economic growth as demonstrated by their standards of living and the relatively positive balance of payments. These countries, with the exception of Marxist, Maoist, and centrally planned Tanzania, did better during the first decade of independence. This performance was attributed to the benign global market conditions that were created by the existing structure of production, distribution and consumption. The same structure was supported by the international division of labor. Cote d'Ivoire was successful because it capitalized on its growth-surplus and diversification of its agricultural industry (pineapples, coffee, oil palm, coconuts and sugar). However, in the short run, these crops have been affected by some of the changes in question. As a result, the ruling or political elite has failed to sustain the partnership between the peasantry (producers) and the state. Also, lower international prices of goods and services have influenced the African state to punitively appropriate more of the farmers' proceeds than its fair share. Farther still, the bureaucracy has institutionalized mismanagement and rent-seeking activities. Unlike

Ghana, Tanzania and Zaire which were not able to keep up with their production quarters, Cote d'Ivoire suspended its production goals during the 1980s because evidence indicated that commodity prices were increasingly decreasing rather than rising. African goods failed to command high prices because the demand for them was low. The low demand for the products and inability of African states to generate high demand has contributed to plague Africa.

Some of the problems could be related to what Denermark (1987) has said. Denmark has argued that the nature of the market (largely international) and the on-going product cycle makes the goods a country produces inferior although such goods are highly valued at the centers of production. This causes negative growth. When a country is incorporated into the world's economic system, production strings are attached by the system at large. Immediate demands of the industrialized countries have to be met. The world economy which determines the rules and conditions of international division of labor specifies zones that produce particular products; roles that are played by particular countries or blocks of countries, and determine the success or failure of each country based on production infrastructure and gains arising from the exchange of goods and services. In other words, the international market limits the role of "policy" initiatives of developing countries many of which are ill-informed concerning their place and role in the global political economy. Such a situation creates uneven growth in different countries. Uneven patterns of demand and the inability to control its creation continues to exacerbate the gap between the North and the South.

The intensity of demand for products strengthens the countries' participation and integration into the world system. When the product which led to the country's integration into the international system losses its demand, and when the same country fails to adjust its production structure in order to fit in and remain dynamically incorporated into the new structure, the same country does not only become noticeable, less integrated and less competitive, but it gradually, more often than not, tends to become marginalized. Its products are peripheralized. Its participation in the international political economy is sidelined. The fact that African countries specialize in less advanced products makes them so inflexible and unadaptable that they cannot incorporate technological changes by which advanced countries and their products are characterized. This situation duplicates an uneven pattern of development. Countries which experience these difficulties have been delinked because globalization treats them as outcasts that are without "pull" forces (Lughod, 1989, 368; and Boansi, 1997). These domestic and underlying market processes are problems which complicate adaptation and render the economy growthless by retarding it. Recessions, recoveries or booms in the OECD countries seem to have less influence in the economic performance of their poorer southern neighbors UNCTAD's (1990) *Trade and Development Report*. In other words, growth in the North is not a stimulating engine of comparable growth in the South. First, "low commodity prices and high interest rates" retard the growth of the southern neighbors. Second, weak or "collapsed financial flows, changed international cost relations" and the "supply rather than demand driven transnational mechanisms" (Pronk, 1992, 25) of the international market which is not "magnetically" attracted by the southern commodity market. A variety of possible solutions to the African economic crisis obtain and several have been registered and offered. First, the current major problem is to readjust the production structures of African political economies to meet the opportunities and challenges of the new international division of labor. This means foregoing specialization in basic raw materials as the major foreign exchange earning. Specialization in less advanced products does not allow for flexibility and adaptation in the face of changing demand. It is difficult if not impossible to be technologically innovative. It is equally difficult or impossible, regardless of their value, to trendfully improve the relative value of raw materials. The golden days are a dream of the future. The dependency theory, practice and praxis negates the possibility of using market strategies and tools to raise prices. Producers are in a dilemma as far as the art of influencing prices is concerned. The current market structures are impenetrable by producers who consume and who need to sell what they produce.

Worse still, the IMF's and the World Bank's minimalist vision of the state is visionless because these institutions know that the poor countries have limited adjustment capacity. In spite of this knowledge, these financial institutions perpetually impose exploitative structural adjustment programs on these societies which continually stagnate and see no end in sight in terms of the improvement of their standards of living. Given this scenario, the peasantry should be transformed economically, politically, and culturally. This transformation should be revolutionary in character.

First, the peasantry should be transformed by being mobilized and resocialized with the use of new technological and industrial values. They should be given a new political religion and work ethic that transcends their traditional conceptions of life. They should be taught that time is money and money is time. Their religious and spiritual experience should be used as a base for their empowerment and inculcation of the new values and work ethic. The peasantry should be taught how to earn and save money, how to budget and what to budget for. They should be helped to solve their most important needs including shelter, food, health, hygiene, love and the hatred of poverty, laziness and resource mismanagement. They should be helped to set goals that are operational, tactical and strategic in character. These goals should be constructed and adjusted periodically in order to streamline and validate them in the light of domestic and international production and marketing conditions of their produce. In other words, as producers, they have the right to know how, structure and infrastructure of production, distribution and consumption affects them. This first strategy is peaceful cultural revolution which transcends the shallowness of bloody peasant revolutions in history. This revolutionary transformation should be led by the intellectual wing of the ruling elite that is sympathetic with national development policy and the lot of the peasantry and the peasantry's patriotic, economic and social role in the political economy. Their traditional art, sculpture, portery, basketry, leather work, weaving and spinning should be celebrated and modernized to enhance its value and create consumer demand for it.

Second, using Boansi's (1997) analogy, peasant agriculture should be transformed by allowing the peasantry to be at the forefront of the agricultural revolution. They should be taught how to invest in social capital and how social capital will become a base for effective investment in family farms. The state should create a climate conducive to conditions that are producer incentives. Surplus productivity or extraction should be geared to the promotion of capital accumulation. Such restructuring of the economy will enable direct producers to dominate or to acquire power for influencing the state for rationalization of their interests. As producers, owners of property, citizens, voters, and parents, peasants should be more actively involved in their national economy rather than being sidelined to the economy of affection. Policy should be used to bring dynamic change in terms of laying a strong foundation for restructuring their national economy. The state should liberate itself of the myopism of seeing peasants as an exploitable and victimized class of parasites and empower them with freedom, leadership, skills and other resources that will enable them to be instrumental agents of capital accumulation. Since they are aware of their interests, expressive and instrumental resources should be given to them in order to use them as a base for channeling the tempo of development in the face of the internal and external forces of production. In other words the political regimes should make the relations of production the "shock absorbers" of the forces of production in order to effectively capitalize on the means of production.

Third, Mittelman (1989) has argued that if Africa has managed its economic path through a constellation of competing global and regional economic giants with which it is interwoven, it must wisely and realistically explore the available or designable alternative passages through which it can force openings for coming out at the end of the tunnel. A single country cannot create its own path of development just because it has eliminated externalities or intiated a centrally planned economy. If it went by this route, its own seclusion from the club of international political economy will farther alienate and marginalize it for failure to observe the principles of international relations and trade. This behavior is a form of autarky which by nature raises more problems than solutions. The country's responsibility is to actively participate in the global political economy while "simultaneously undercutting a contradictory world order" (p. 171) in international relations.

In relation to Africa's role in international relations, a disciplinary field from which Africa is scholastically or intellectually excluded largely due to its uniqueness, geostrategic and geopolitical significance, the continent needs to reexamine the essence of its place in the world community and evolve and chart new directions in order to be free from its marginalized peripheralism. For instance, the three paradigms which explain Africa's place in international relations are rationalist, realist and behavioralist (Croft, 1997). The rationalist paradigm was dominant during the 1920s. The paradigm prescribed global government, the institutionalization of international law that could be administered by a world police force, and collective security as a system for containing wars in future. The purpose of the rationalist perspective was to control global belligerence similar to the First World War.

Conceptions on the birth and fruition of the League of nations evolved during the 1930s. At this time the realist school (paradigm) emerged and argued that international relations (IR) concerned the definition of national interests by states which had the right to wield power and use force as an acceptable instrument for enforcing law, order and peace in the world. Those who opposed this school were viewed as expressive utopians. Though the realist paradigm was polemically dominant between 1940s and 1950s, its less scientific stance created avenues for it to be rivaled by the behaviorist school of thought. The behavioralists asserted that since behavioralism by nature is a scientifically quantifiable and predictive school, it was particularly well suited as an intellectual instrument for foreign policy agenda. This notion became equally debatable as well.

International relations paradigms of the 1960s excluded Africa from the scholarly debate in the field and concentrated on the "great power" East – West controversy during the height of the Cold War. During that time, debate centered on the prevention of war between them, the management of the relations between them and how or what they needed to do to advance their national interests. African and Third World issues were articulated in the light of trans-nationalism and dependency theories rather than in the context of IR theory. Transnationalists of which multinational corporations, religious organizations, and terrorist groups existed outside Africa as NGOs. The NGOs have become, in spite of their "rootlessness" on the continent, the most influential contributors to state and national policy planning at the detriment of the most intimate domestic and patriotic interests of the Third World peoples. The debate on dependency theory has centered on Latin America and East Asia but not on Africa. The knowledge on dependency theory popularized theoretical and practical marxism which became the third debate in IR during this period.

During the 1980s, the discipline of international relations became so fragmented, so much so that the discipline which was essentially American in character evolved a globalist perspective in which rationalism and realism became conflictual elements of the IR debate. Neo-realism whose theoretical proposition for IR was advanced by Kenneth Waltz. He argues that states hardly cooperate except in military alliances. These states cooperate because they are interested in relative gains for which they strive. Robert Keohanse suggests that neo-liberalism enables states to cooperate because these states are focused on absolute gains. However, the central issues that are not addressed in this debate on neo-liberalism are military security and international political economy. In long term strategic essence, the debates are characterized, none articulations of issues such as those related to the recent conflicts in Kosovo and East Timor. The inconclusive resolutions of the conflict in question seem to undercut neoliberal purposes. Further still, these issues deal with matters that affect Africa and other regions but that are not being addressed. The debate on Africa related issues is either psychologically suppressed and ignored or does not get included in the agenda, or it is automatically ruled out as a peripheral and less important or marginal topic in Europe and the West in general.

European social science intellectuals are predominantly either structuralists or Marxists. Their debates exclude African-related issues particularly in the area of international political economy. European post-positivists, post modernists, social constructivists and critical theorists have collectively attacked realism and neo-realism as reflections of palliative hegemonic conversation. Throughout the last seventy years of the 20th century, the many intellectual paradigms have a tendency to exclude Africa irrespective of the North-South dialogue that is spasmodically conducted. In addition, this unique exclusion is conducted while Middle East, North East Asia, South East Asia and South Asia and even Latin America have been given a place in the "sun".

The implications are that there exists intellectual poverty on African IR largely because major journals like *African Affairs* and the *Journal of Modern African Studies*, etc. lack competent scholars with interests on the region. If competent scholars are there, they may be involved in African IR when, and only when their nations' hegemonic and other interests have been provoked, or when they want younger scholars to earn a doctorate for their introduction into the world of scholarly and scientific learning, or when debt games have been written off to warrant strategic interaction in international debt rescheduling in which negotiating actors know each other and can be influenced to reschedule issuance of further loans in spite of their potential for a tour de force and exogenous shocks that are camouflaged beneath theoretical elegance and empirical robustness of the debt schemes (Aggarwal, 1996) and other dependency models.

During the 1990s, the rationalist-liberal theory of international relations concerned the preservation of ideals that affirm international law rather than pursuing world government. The state rather than the leader, was the unit of analysis and central player in international relations. States are expected to be legal regimes that enforce or guarantee responsible behavior (Deng, et al, 1996). Responsible behavior entails the respect of human rights, democratic governance, provision of basic needs to the populace and proper economic management which places emphasis in growth, and financial stability. Such a state should expect protection from the international system.

Currently, rationalists argue that though the state is necessary, it is not an end in itself. Rationalists indicate that the end is human dignity whose expression is "canonized" in terms of human rights and economic prosperity. However, in Africa, it seems, domestically speaking, that states are an end in themselves. Their sovereignty should be responsible in terms of serving the community's wider needs and interests. These needs and interests belong to the human family. In brief, realists view the state to be the means and the end. Rationalists see the same state as the means that are instrumental to the betterment of humanity. This then becomes the end of the rationalist conception of the state.

Within the IR sphere, few accept that colonialism was responsible for the underdevelopment of Africa as some scholars like Walter Rodney have vigorously asserted. In addition, the same school, the IR, which is interested in the positivist – rationalist intellectual tradition, does not believe that "there is structural inequality perpetuated by the international political and economic systems" (Croft, 1997, 612).

In his *Africa and the International System*, Clapham (1996) has analyzed the nature of IR in Africa between the 1960s and the 1990s. This period falls within the parameters of independence, the Cold War and post

Cold War era. Clapham has shown that African statehood is crisis ridden. The crisis originated in Africa, it was not caused by the Cold War although the latter exacerbated it and was heightened by the "collapse of the bi-polar structure" (Croft, 1997, 613). Though the African states are responsible for their foreign policies, the fact that the international system contributed to their creation, their continued survival has been dictated by their access to the system. The nature of access depends on the domestic structure of the state, its nature of links to the international political and economic system and the policy choices of leaders of particular countries.

Further still, in Africa, the NGOs have effectively used their influence to privatize diplomacy. The multinational corporations have also capitalized on such diplomacy to perpetuate dependency as it was argued in the chapter on political economy. Though topics on African international relations are largely concerned with the expression, defense and promotion of African statehood, the state is in a crisis – and has largely failed. The sovereignty of the people has become the sovereignty of the ruling elite or individual ruler. Autocratic leaders are supported through external patronage. Such leaders have contributed to the economic decay. This decay has been worsened by oil shortage, bureaucratic corruption and mismanagement. These problems have cumulatively become the genesis of rebellion and insurgency which farther weaken the structures of governance. Democratization and structural adjustment have replaced economic growth. These reform projects have given way, for being the nucleus for, to the privatization of the state. Though some delinkage problems cannot be avoided, African countries should reevaluate the policy of suppliers credit which is a means of financing development projects on the continent. The policy impacts Africa negatively.

Conclusion

Africa's political economy is a product of evolutionary and dependent global political economy. No single country is an economic island. In Tanzania, Nyerere's communal and socialist politico-economic experiment had no grassroots leadership of Nyerere's caliber which could wisely be used to implement his national villagization policy. The masses who collectively villagized used the village farms for entrepreneurship and private investment instead of making them collective farms. This became contradictory and contributed to the failure of the nation's socialist economic program, which was enshrined in the Arusha Declaration and canonized in the public press. In addition, negative reaction from Western markets and lending institutions contributed to this failure. Overall, socialist nations were too weak to do anything that could salvage Tanzania's political economy from the doldrums.

Ghana's economy was largely monocultural rather than diversified because it was dominated by cocoa production. Timber and minerals fetched less money compared to the cocoa industry. But disease and the disparity of exchange rate for cocoa in the world market caused prices to decline drastically. Cocoa smuggling to Cote d'Ivoire and Togo became a major problem because the exchange rate currencies for the product was good. Part of the reason for this failure was attributed to Nkrumah's leftist ideological stance which scared the free enterprise based lenders, buyers and consumers. The sophisticated invention of the technology of beverage production contributed to the further fall of the price of cocoa.

A decade after independence was characterized by growth and diversification of Cote d'Ivoire's economy. Though the country followed the right economic policies, it failed to identify prominent changes within the international political economy which were responsible for unleashing compulsive structural transformation. As a result, Cote d'Ivoire experienced the same problems as Ghana in spite of the formers' successes. Unlike Ghana, Cote d'Ivoire and Tanzania, Zaire's political leadership vacuum has continually contributed to the mismanagement of its economic and political affairs. Such mismanagement of the public trust has continued to result in spasmodic political and social instability that tends to engulf the Great Lakes region of Central and Eastern Africa, and thereby render its climate unsuitable for investment except in the foreign-owned mineral sector of the economy.

Overall, unlike Zaire, Cote d'Ivoire and even Tanzania in some respects, Ghana has three ideological tendencies – state socialist, populist and liberal whose competition for power results in periodic and intense social conflict. The present Rawlings' National Democratic Congress regime is radically populistic and ideologically capitalistic. Although the Party has weak social roots, its regime's current constitution provides excessive presidential powers. The Ghanaian military is so antidemocratic that its interventionist character tends to make the prospects for democracy, political culture, civil society and other political institutions unpredictable. Unlike Ghana, a single ideological terrain – socialism, has largely dominated Tanzania. This element including the Swahili culture, provided a unique form of single party political stability which limited internal competition for the evolution of liberal and popular forms of democracy (Pinkney, 1997). Compared to Ghana and Zaire, Tanzania's political culture is more pliant and egalitarian. In addition, though Tanzanian civil society is weaker, there is less conflict. Also, the ruling party, Chama cha Mapenduzi (CCM), the Revolutionary Party, in spite of its recent decline, is still better organized than the newly organized, class, and regionally disaffected elements of the fragmentary opposition. In Tanzania, civilian supremacy towers that of the military which is universally and deeply entrenched by continental (African) standards. The dominance of civil society in governance has enhanced the consolidation and centralization of political institutions, many of which are badly weakened on the continent. Such is the character of African political economy.

Political economy is the dialectical but dynamic relationship between the public and private sectors, labor and employers, the economic and the political elite, the professional classes and the political and economic establishment, the technologically industrialized North versus the developing and underdeveloped South, and above all, it is the technical, economic, social, political and moral relationship between professional social organizations and other institutions and organizations in society. On the global scale, the structure, morphology, and culture of political economy is hierarchically stratified and universally hegemonic. The hegemonic character of political economy socially suppresses and psycho-spiritually, politically, and economically tyrannizes the majority of the global population which it stratifies into classes the lowest of which are marginalized, "delinked," and alienated by a nexus-of-chains of global inequality. This produces the worst form of tyranny which is psychological because it may exist without real tyrants.

Recommendations

African governments should decentralize and diversify industrial or commercial policy in support of both corporate, state and regional economic development strategy.

They should harmonize the relationship between market policy and trade policy in order to strengthen agricultural incomes of domestic consumers who are also producers or potential investors.

They should create mechanisms for adaptation of convergent and divergent economic trends and establish a machinery for absorbing unproductive organizational resistance to change.

Economic planners should familiarize themselves with expansion of the international investments of multinational corporations and the new role of the World Trade Organization (WTO). They should examine how countries have changed their international trade and investment policies, and assess how these changes are affecting organizational operations in relation to corporate and national development policies.

Governments should create legal and commercial standards for the de facto rather than de jure integration of NGOs and other similar organizations.

References

Abu-Lughod, J.L. 1989. *Before European Hegemony: The World System A.D. 1250-1350.* New York: Oxford University Press.

Aggarwal, V.K. 1996. *Debt Games: Strategic Interaction in International Debt Rescheduling.* Cambridge and New York: Cambridge University Press.

Alden, C., and J.P. Daloz, eds. 1996. *Paris, Pretoria and the African Continent: The International Relations of States and Societies in Transition.* London: Macmillan

Alschuler, L.R. 1988. *Multinationals and Maldevelopment: Alternative Development Strategies in Argentina, the Ivory Coast and Korea.* New York: St. Martin's Press.

Amin, S. 1974. *Accumulation on a World Scale.* New York: Monthly Review.

Amin, S. 1970. Capitalism and development in the Ivory Coast. In *African Politics and Society: Basic Issues and Problems of Government and Development, eds.* Irving Markovitz and Leonard, 277-288. New York: The Free Press.

Arhin, K. 1985. The Ghana Cocoa Marketing Board and the farmer. In *Marketing Board in Tropical Africa, eds.* Kwame Arhin, et al., 37-52. London: KPI Ltd.

Arrighi, G. 1982. A crisis of hegemony. In *The Dynamics of Global Crisis,* eds. Amin, S., G. Arrighi, A.G. Frank, and I. Wallerstein, 55-108, New York: Monthly Review.

Beckman, B. 1981. Ghana, 1951-78: The agrarian basis of the post-colonial state. In *Rural Development in Tropical Africa,* eds. Judith Heyer et al., 143-167. New York: St. Martin's Press.

Berg, E. J. 1986. The World Bank's strategy. In *Africa in Economic Crisis,* ed. John Ravenhill, 44-59. New York: Columbia University Press.

Berg, E. J. 1971. Structural transformation versus gradualism: recent economic development in Ghana and the Ivory Coast. In *Ghana and the Ivory Coast: Perspectives on Modernization, eds.* Philip Foster and Aristide R. Zolberg. Chicago: The University of Chicago Press.

Boansi, K.O. 1997. Africa in the changing international political economy. Paper presented at the Annual Meeting of the New York State Political Science Association.

Bogdanowicz-Bindert, C.A. 1982. Sub-Saharan Africa: An agenda for action. *Journal of World Trade Law* 164: 283-291.

Bollen, K.A. 1983. World system position, dependency and democracy. *American Sociological Review,* 48, 468-497.

Brewer, T.L, and S. Young 1998. *Multilateral Investment System Rules and Multinational Enterprises.* New York: Oxford University Press.

Callaghy, T. M. 1986. The international commodity and Zaire's debt crisis. In *The Crisis in Zaire: Myths and Realities,* ed. Nzongola-Ntalaja, 221-244. Trenton, N.J.: Africa World Press.

Caporaso, J.A., ed. 1987. *A Changing International Division of Labor.* Boulder, Colorado: Lynne Rienner Publishers.

Caporaso, J.A. 1981. Industrialization at the periphery: the evolving division of labor. *International Studies Quarterly,* 25, 347-384.

Cardoso, F.H. 1973. Associated-dependent development. In *Authoritarian Brazil: Origins, Policies and Future.* ed. A. Stephen, 142-176. Yale University Press.

Chase-Dunn, C., and R. Rubinson. 1977. Toward a structural perspective on the world system. *Politics and Society.*

Chazan, N. 1983 *An Anatomy of Ghanaian Politics: Managing Political Recession, 1969-1982.* Boulder, Colorado: Westview Press.

Cheru, F. 1989 *The Silent Revolution in Africa: Debt, Development and Democracy.* London: Zed Book Ltd.

Chew, S.C., and R.A. Denemark 1996. On development and underdevelopment. In *The Underdevelopment of Development,* eds. Sing C. Chew and Robert A. Denemark, 1-16. Thousand Oaks: Sage Publications.

Clapham, C. 1996. *Africa and the International System: The Politics of State Survival.* London: Cambridge University Press.

Cline, W.R. 1982. Can East Asian model of development be generalized? *World Development* 10,2: 81-90.

Commodity Yearbook. 1995 and 1996. New York: John Wiley and Sons Inc.

Cook, P., and K. Morgan. 1998. *The Associational Economy: Firms, Regions and Innovation.* New York: Oxford University Press.

Coulson, A. 1982. *Tanzania: A Political Economy.* Oxford: Clarendon Press.

Coulson, A. 1979. *African Socialism in Practice: The Tanzanian Experience.* Nottingham: Russell Press Ltd.

Crane, G.T., and A. Amawi Eds. 1997. *The Theoretical Evolution of International Political Economy.* New York: Oxford University Press.

Croft, S. 1997. International relations and Africa: Review article. *African Affairs* 96, 385: 607- 615.

Crook, R. 1990. Politics, the cocoa crisis and administration in Cote d'Ivoire. *Journal of Modern African Studies* 28, 4: 649-669.

Crook, R. 1989. Patrimonialism, administrative effectiveness and economic development in Cote d'Ivoire. *African Affairs* 88, 351: 143-172.

Crook, R. 1988. State capacity and economic development: The case of Cote d'Ivoire, *IDS Bulletin* 4: 19-25.

Cunningham, G.L. 1973. Peasants and rural development in Tanzania. *Africa Today* 20, 4 : 3-18.

Deane, P. 1978. *The Evolution of Economic Ideas: Modern Cambridge Economics.*

Denemark, R.A. 1987. State Strength in the periphery of the capitalist world-system: A focused comparative critical case study analysis. Ph.D. dissertation. University of Minnesota.

Deng, F.M., et al. 1996. *Sovereignty as Responsibility. Conflict Management in Africa.* Washington, D.C.: The Brookings Institution.

Doern, G.B., and S. Wilks, eds. *Comparative Competition Policy: National Institutions in a Global Market.* New York: Oxford University Press.

Drucker, P.F. 1988. The changed world economy. *Foreign Affairs*: 769-791.

Dumont, R. 1998. *Stranglehold on Africa.* London: Andre Deutsch Ltd.

Ellis, F. 1984. Relative agricultural prices and the urban bias model: A comparative analysis of Tanzania and Fiji. *Journal of Development Studies* 20,3: 28-51.

Ellis, F. 1983. Agricultural marketing and peasant state transfers in Tanzania. *Journal of Peasant Studies* 1,10: 214-242.

Ellis, F. 1982. Agricultural price policy in Tanzania. *World Development* 10,4: 263-283.

Emmanuel, A. 1972. *Unequal Exchange: A Study of the Imperialism of Trade.* Monthly   Review.

Evans, P. 1979a. Beyond center and periphery a comment on the world system approach to the study of development. *Sociological Inquiry,* 49, 15-20.

Evans, P. 1979b. *Dependent Development.* Princeton: Princeton University Press.

Fieldhouse, D.K. 1986. *Black Africa, 1945-80: Economic Decolonization and Arrested Development.* Boston: Allen and Unwin.

Firebaugh, G., and B. Bullock. 1987. Level of processing of exports: estimates for developing nations. *International Studies Quarterly*, 30, 333-350.

Franco, R. 1981. The optimal producer price of cocoa in Ghana, *Journal*

Organizational Behavior

of Development Economies 8: 77-92.

Frank, A.G. 1969. *Latin America: Underdevelopment of Revolution?* New York: Monthly Review.

Frobel, F., J. Heinrichs, and O. Kreye. 1980. *The New International Division of Labor.* New York: Cambridge University Press.

Gbetibouo, M. 1983. Export Strategies for Ivory Coast. Ph.D. dissertation. University of Illinois.

Gbetibouo, M., and C.L. Delgado. 1984. Lessons and constraints of export crop-led growth: cocoa in Ivory Coast. In *The Political Economy of Ivory Coast,* eds. William I Zartman and Christopher L. Delgado, 115-148. New York: Praeger.

Ghosh, J. 1986. Foreign debt and economic development: The case of Zaire. *Development and Change* 17: 455-485.

Gilbert, A. 1994. Third World cities: Poverty, employment, gender roles and the environment during a time of restructuring. *Urban Studies* 31, 4/5: 605-633.

Gilpin, R. 1987 *The Political Economy of International Relations.* Princeton, N.J.: Princeton University Press.

Gould, D.J. 1979 The administration of underdevelopment. In *Zaire: The Political Economy of Underdevelopment,* ed. Guy Gran, 87-106. New York: Praeger.

Gran, G., ed. 1979. *Zaire: The Political Economy of Underdevelopment.* New York: Praeger.

Gran, G. 1979. An introduction to Zaire's permanent development crisis. In *Zaire: The Political Economy of Underdevelopment,* ed. Guy Gran, 1-22. New York: Praeger.

Gran, G. 1978. The ethical and intellectual bankruptcy of the world system. *Africa Today* 5: 5-23.

Green, R.H. 1971. Reflections on economic strategy, structure, implementation and necessity: Ghana and the Ivory Coast, 1957-67. In *Ghana and the Ivory Coast: Perspectives on Modernization,* eds. Philip Foster and Aristide R. Zolberg, 231-264. Chicago: The University of Chicago Press.

Green, R.H., and C. Allison. 1986. The World Bank's agenda for accelerated development: Dialectics, doubts and dialogues. In *Africa in Economic Crisis,* ed. John Ravenhill, 60-84. New York: Columbia University Press.

Green, R., et al. 1980. *Economic Shocks and National Policy Making: Tanzania in the 1970s.* Dar es Salaam: Tanzania Publishing House.

Grier, B. 1977. The peasantization of the Ghanaian cocoa farmer. University of Ghana. Mimeo.

Gyimah-Boadi, E. 1991. State enterprises divestiture: Recent Ghanaian experiences. In *Ghana: The Political Economy of Recovery,* ed. Donald Rothchild, 193-208.Boulder: Lynne Rienner.

Gyimah-Boadi, E. 1989. Policies and politics of export agriculture. In *The State, Development and Politics in Ghana,* eds. Emmanuel Hansen and Kwame A. Ninsin, 222-241. London: Codesria.

Hanisch, R. 1980. Cocoa policy: The struggle for control of a commodity market. *Economics* 22: 100-127.

Hanisch, R. 1976. *Ghana and the Cocoa World Market: The Scope of Action of a Raw Material Exporting Country of the Periphery in the World Market (Up to 1966.* Saarbrucken: Verlag der SSIP-Schiften.

Hayami, Y. 1997. *Development Economics: From the Poverty to the Wealth of Nations.* New York: Oxford University Press.

Hetch, R.M. 1983 The Ivory Coast economic 'miracle': What benefit for peasant farmers? *Journal of Modern African Studies* 21, 1: 25-53.

Higgott, R. 1986. Africa and the new international division of labor. In *Africa in Economic Crisis,* ed. John Ravenhill, 286-305. New York: Columbia.

Higgott, R. 1984. Export-oriented industrialization, the new international division of labor and corporate state in the Third World: An exploratory essay on conceptual linkage. *Australian Geographical Studies* 22: 58-71.

Higgott, R. 1983. Africa: The new international division of labor and the corporate state. Paper presented at 24th Annual Convention of International Studies Association, 5-9 April, Mexico City.

Hinderink, J., and G.J. Tempelman. 1979. Development policy and development practice in Ivory Coast: A miracle or a mirage? *Diskussiestuk* 4.

Howard, R. 1978. *Colonialism and Underdevelopment in Ghana.* New York: African Publishing Company.

Huq, M.M. 1989. *The Economy of Ghana: The First Twenty-Five Years Since Independence.* New York: St. Martin's Press.

Jeffries, R. 1982. Rawlings and the political economy of underdevelopment in Ghana, *African Affairs* 813, 24: 307-317.

Jenkins, R. 1984. Divisions over the international division. *Capital and Class* 22: 28-57.

Jewsiewicki, B. 1977. The Great Depression and the making of the colonial economic system in the Belgian Congo, *African Economic History* 4: 153-176.

Kabwit, G.C. 1979. Zaire: The roots of the continuing crisis. *The Journal of Modern African Studies* 17, 3: 381-407.

Kahama, G.C., et al. 1986 *The Challenge for Tanzania's Economy.* Portmouth, NH.: Heinemann.

Kay, G. 1975. *Development of Underdevelopment: A Marxist Analysis*. London: Macmillan.

Keohane, R. 1984. *After Hegemony: Cooperation and Discord in World Political Economy*. Princeton: Princeton University Press.

Klein, L.R., R. Pauly, and P. Voisin. 1982. The World Economy – A Global Model. *Perspectives in Computing*, 2, 4-17.

Killick, T. 1978. *Development Economics in Action: A Study of Economic Policies in Ghana*. New York: St. Martin's Press.

Krueger, A.O. 1990. Free trade is the best policy. In *An American Trade Strategy: Options for the 1990s*, eds. Robert Z. Lawrence and Charles L. Schultze, 68-133. Washington, D.C.: The Brookings Institution.

Krueger, A.O. 1984. Comparative advantage and development policy 20 years later. In *Economic Structure and Performance: Essays in Honor of Hollis B. Chenery*, eds. Moshe Syrquin et al, 135-177. New York: Academic Press, Inc.

Lee, E. 1980. Export-led rural development: The Ivory Coast. *Development and Change* 11: 607-642.

Leslie, W.J. 1993. *Zaire: Continuity and Political Change in an Oppressive State*. Boulder: Westview Press.

Leslie, W.J. 1987. *The World Bank and Structural Transformation in Developing Countries: The Case of Zaire*. Boulder: Lynne Reinner Publishers.

Leslie, W.J. 1986. The World Bank and Zaire. In *The Crisis in Zaire: Myths and Realities*, ed. Nzongola-Ntalaja, 254-264. Trenton, N.J.: Africa World Press, Inc.

Leys, C. 1979. Underdevelopment and dependency: Critical notes. *Journal of Contemporary Asia* 7, 1: 92-107.

Linnemann, H. 1966. *An Econometric Study of World Trade Flows*. Amsterdam: North Holland.

Lofchie, M.F. 1989. *The Policy Factor: Agricultural Performance in Kenya and Tanzania*. Boulder: Lynne Reinner Publishers.

Lumumba-Kasongo, T. 1992. Zaire's ties to Belgium: Persistence and future prospects in political economy. *Africa Today*: 23-47.

Lungunga, K.K.Y. 1979. Investment and Investment Policy in a Small Open Economy: The Zairian Case, 1965-75. Ph.D. dissertation, University of Pittsburgh.

MacGaffey, J. 1987. *Entrepreneurs and Parasites: The Struggle for Indigenous Capitalism in Zaire*. Cambridge: Cambridge University Press.

Mandel, E. 1975. *Late Capitalism*. London: Mew Left Review.

Mikesell, R.F. 1979. *The World Copper Industry*. Baltimore: The Johns Hopkins University Press.

Mikesell, R.F. 1974. The copper economy of Zaire. In *Commodity Exports and African Economic Development,* eds. Scott R. Pearson et al., 179-190. Lexington, Massachusetts: Lexington Books.

Mill, J.S. 1999. *Principles of Political Economy: And Chapters on Socialism.* New York: Oxford University Press.

Miracle, M.P. 1970. The Smallholder in agricultural policy and planning: Ghana and the Ivory Coast, 1960-1966. *The Journal of Developing Areas* 4: 321-332.

Miracle, M.P. 1969. The economy of the Ivory Coast. In *The Economies of Africa,* eds. P. Robinson and D.A. Lury, 194-235. Evanston: Northwestern University Press.

Mittelman, J.H. 1988. *Out from Underdevelopment: Prospects for the Third World.* New York: St. Martin's Press.

Mittelman, J.H. 1981. *Underdevelopment and the Transition to Socialism: Mozambique and Tanzania.* New York: Academic Press.

Mokoli, M.M. 1992. *State Against Development: The Experience of Post 1965 Zaire.* West Point, Connecticut: Greenwood Press.

Munoz, H. 1981 Introduction: The various roads to development. In *From Dependence to Development: Strategies to Overcome Underdevelopment and Inequality,* ed. Heraldo Munoz, 1-14. Boulder, Colorado: Westview Press.

Mwansasu, B.U., and C. Pratt, eds. 1979. *Towards Socialism in Tanzania.* Toronto: University of Toronto Press.

Mytelka, K.L. 1984. Foreign business and economic development. In *The Political Economy of Ivory Coast,* eds. William Zartman and Christopher Delgado. New York: Praeger.

Mytelka, K.L. 1983. The limits of export-led development: The Ivory Coast's experience with manufactures. In *The Antinomies of Interdependence: National Welfare and the International Division of Labor,* ed. John G. Ruggie, 239-272. New York: Colombia University Press.

Nemeth, R., and D.A.Smith. 1985. International trade and world system structure: A multiple network analysis. *Review,* by Fernand Braudel Center, 8, 517-560.

N'Guessan, T. 1987. The socioeconomic impact of the world and the African Development Bank on African countries: The case of Ivory Coast. In *Brazil and the Ivory Coast: The Impact of International Lending Investment and Aid,* eds. Werner Bauer and John F. Due, 57-71. London: Jai Press Inc.

Nyerere, J. 1970. *Ujamaa: Essays on Socialism.* New York: Oxford University Press.

Nyong'o, A.P. 1987. The development of agrarian capitalist classes in the

Ivory Coast: 1945-1975. In *The African Bourgeoisie: Capitalist Development in Nigeria, Kenya, and the Ivory Coast,* ed. Paul M. Lubeck, 185-248. Boulder, Colorado: Lynne Rienner Publishers.

Nyong'o, A.P. 1978. Liberal models of capitalist development in Africa: Ivory Coast. *African Development* 3, 3: 5-20.

Payer, C. 1983. Tanzania and the World Bank. *Third World Quarterly* 5, 4: 791-813.

Peemans, J.P. 1986. Accumulation and underdevelopment in Zaire: General aspects in relation to the evolution of the agrarian crisis. In *The Crisis in Zaire: Myths and Realities,* ed. Nzongola-Ntalaja. Trenton, 67-84. N.J.: Africa World Press, Inc.

Pellow, D., and N. Chazan. 1986. *Ghana: Coping with Uncertainty.* Boulder, Colorado: Westview Press.

Pinkney, R. 1997. *Democracy and Dictatorship in Ghana and Tanzania.* New York: St. Martin's Press.

Powelson, J.P. and Richard Stock. 1990. *The Peasant Betrayed: Agricultural and land Reform in the Third World.* Washington, D.C.: Cato Institute.

Price, R.M. 1984. Neocolonialism and Ghana's economic decline: A critical assessment. *Canadian Journal of African Studies* 18, 1: 163-193.

Pronk, J. 1992. The 1990s: From worlds apart to a different world. In *Change: Threat or Opportunity,* ed. Uner Kirder, 21-31. New York: United Nations.

Radman, W. 1987. The Nationalization of Zaire's Copper: From Union Miniere to Gecamines. *Africa Today*: 25-47.

Rado, E. 1986. Notes towards a political economy of Ghana today. *African Affairs* 85: 563-572.

Riddell, R.C. 1990. Cote d'Ivoire., In *Manufacturing Africa: Performance and Prospects of Seven Countries in Sub-Saharan Africa,* eds. Roger C. Riddell et al., 152-205. Portsmouth, NH.: Heinemann.

Ridler, N.B. 1985. Comparative advantage as a development model: The Ivory Coast. *Journal of Modern African Studies* 23, 1: 407-417.

Rimmer, D. 1992. *Staying Poor: Ghana's Political Economy, 1950-1990.* New York: Pergamon Press.

Rodney, W. 1979. The political economy of colonial Tanganyika: 1890-1930. In *Tanzania Under Colonial Rule,* ed. M.H.Y. Kaniki, 128-163. London: Longman.

Roe, A., and H. Schneider. 1992. *Adjustment and Equity in Ghana.* Paris: OECD Publications.

Rood, L.L. 1976. Nationalization and indigenization in Africa. *Journal of Modern African Studies* 14, 3: 427-447.

Ross, R.J.S., and K.C. Trachte. 1990. *Global Capitalism: The New Leviathan*. Albany: State University of New York Press.

Schott, T. 1986. Models of dyadic and individual components of a social relation: Applications to international trade. *Journal of Mathematical Sociology* 12, 225-249.

Sen, A., ed. 1997/98. *The Industrial Organization*. New York: Oxford University Press.

Shao, J. 1986. Politics and the food production crisis in Tanzania. In *Africa's Agrarian Crisis: The Roots of Famine,* eds. Stephen K. Commins et al., 84-102. Boulder, Colorado: Lynne Rienner Publishers.

Shapiro, D., and E. Tollens. 1992. *The Agricultural Development in Zaire*. Brookfield: Avebury.

Smith, D.A., and D.R. White. 1992. Structure and dynamics of the global economy: network analysis of international trade 1965-1980. *Social Forces* 70, 4, 857-893.

Snyder, D., and E. Kick. 1979. Structural position in the world system and economic growth: A multiple network analysis of transnational interactions. *American Journal of Sociology,* 84, 1096-1126.

Steiber, S. 1979. The world system and world trade: An empirical explanation of conceptual conflicts. *The Sociological Quarterly* 20, 23-36.

Takeuchi, K., et al. 1987. *The World Copper Industry: Its Changing Structure and Future Prospects*. World Bank Staff Commodity Working Paper No. 15. Washington, D.C.: World bank Publications.

Teal, F. 1986. The foreign exchange regime and growth: A comparison of Ghana and the Ivory Coast. *African Affairs* 85: 267-282.

Thomas, C. 1974. *Dependence and Transformation: The Economics of the Transition to Socialism*. New York: Monthly Review Press.

Thompson, W.R. 1983. Uneven economic growth, systemic challenges, and global wars. *International Studies Quarterly,* 27, 341-355.

Traore, A. 1990. Ivory Coast: Agricultural and industrial development. In *African Agriculture: The Critical Choices,* eds. Hamid Ait Amara and Bernard Fousnoe, 121-135. London: Zed Books Ltd.

Tshishimbi, B., et al. 1994. Missed opportunity for adjustment in a rent-seeking society: The case of Zaire. In *Adjusting to Policy Failure in African Economies,* ed. David E. Sahn, 96-130. Ithaca: Cornell University Press.

United Nations Economic Commission for Africa. 1983. *ECA and Africa's Development, 1983-2008*. Addis Ababa: ECA Publication.

Wallerstein, I. 1980. *The Modern World System*. 2, Academic Press.

Wallerstein, I. 1974. *The Model of World System*. Academic Press.

Webb, M.C. 1995. *The Political Economy of Policy Coordination: International Adjustment Since 1945.* Ithaca: Cornell University Press.

World Bank. 1990. *World Development Report: Poverty.* New York: Oxford University Press.

World Bank. 1984. *The Outlook for Primary Commodities, 1984-1995.* World Bank Staff Working Paper No. 11. Washington, D.C.: World Bank Publications.

World Bank. 1983a. *The Outlook for Primary Commodities.* Washington, D.C.: World Bank Publications.

World Bank. 1983b. *Tanzania: Agricultural Sector Report.* Washington, D.C.: World Bank Publications.

World Bank. 1981. *Accelerated Development in Sub-Saharan Africa.* Washington, D.C.: World Bank Publications.

World Bank. 1980. *Zaire: Current Economic Situation and Constraints.* Washington, D.C.: World Bank Publications.

World Bank. 1976. *Copper: Current Situation and Outlook for 1976.* Commodity Paper No. 18. Washington, D.C.: World Bank Publications.

Young, C., and T. Turner. 1985. *The Rise and Decline of the Zairian State.* Madison, Wisconsin: The University of Wisconsin Press.

Zartman, W.I., and C. Delgado, eds. 1984. *The Political Economy of Ivory Coast.* New York: Praeger.

Chapter 18

Organizational Development: Forces of Migration in Africa and Elsewhere

Introduction

The specific purpose of this chapter is to theoretically demonstrate that a variety rather than a scarcity of internal and external forces are attributed to the complex morphology of migratory experiences of Africans. Though such forms of migration are accountable for organizational and institutional instability, its significance lies beneath its theoretical and intellectual terrain. The same terrain signifies that organizational and institutional instability are negatively instrumental to elements of socially constructed and historicized constructive change. The chapter argues that there are many forces that cause people to politically migrate across national and cultural environments in Africa. Such political migration is a form of massive traffic caused by internal and external forces. While internal forces interpretively contradict the structural terrain of such migration, the external ones tend to greatly exacerbate the intensity, size, volume, and effects of migration. Though these legitimate forces which cause people to migrate could be attributed to modernizational, political, economic and psychological factors of depeasantization, such factors have also been responsible for intellectual traffic across environment and culture. The extraction of the brain-drain from their cultural and environmental roots may not only have reflected its negative continental side effects, but the influences of their being "uprooted up" from their environmental and cultural roots may have become global in character.

In this respect, migration assumes a considerable measure both of diversity and continuity in its causes, magnitude, and effects on African society and economy. Because the economic, social, cultural, demographic and colonial experiences of African societies are differently dissimilar, such varieties of experiences have helped to structure a complex morphology in terms of patterns and motivations of migration. In other words, migration is more heterogeneous than uniform. Internally, migratory movements within and across national borders have been influenced by commerce, pastoralism, natural and manmade disasters, and the search for jobs. In spite of its effects on the home front, the perpetuity of its causality makes migration a "permanently adopted child of its own circumstances" that affects all institutions and organizations.

A detailed analysis of slavery and slave institutions in the Western Hemisphere must address the migration of African people and the social and economic consequences involved. The Trans-Atlantic slave trade, from a historical perspective, was very crucial in the development of the vast economic complex that made up the south Atlantic system that eventually evolved into plantation slavery. In fact, the slave plantation systems that grew up in the American tropics and elsewhere in the world trace their origin from the Atlantic basin, specifically, in West Africa. As Stamp (1956) pointed out, slavery was a peculiar institution that deserves close study if only because its impact upon the continent was so disastrous. From a historical perspective then, slavery deserves to be closely studied. Also, because there is, according to Stamp, a peculiar urgency, "the American Negroes still await the full fruition of their emancipation a complete break from the caste barriers first imposed upon them in slavery days" (Stamp, 1956).

Why were Africans enslaved? There are three materialistic explanations. First, economics rather than racism was the first motive. Theoretically, they were "cheaper than any other available form of labor" (Northrup, 1994, p. 2). Second, rather than slavery causing prejudice or vice versa, these two value systems seem to have generated each other. Third, slavery was a universal human economic condition rather than a uniquely or exclusively African experience. It appears to be an element that was perpetuated in the context of laws of the jungle.

The Trans-Atlantic Slave Trade

The Atlantic slave trade was the largest intercontinental migration in the history of the world. Although the migration is important in understanding the evolution of slavery, it is often neglected by historians. Historically, such massive migration increased the New World population including that which came from Europe. Prior to that period, more Africans than Europeans crossed the Atlantic each year, and their migration was crucial not only for demographic reasons but also because it laid the groundwork for commerce and intercontinental trade that impacted all areas of the Atlantic basin. Ajayi (1971), in a comprehensive analysis of the history of West Africa, wrote that this complex South Atlantic economic system centered on the production of tropical staples in Brazil, the Caribbean islands, and southern North America. Ajayi notes that although the "South Atlantic system" was divided into competing international interests and under the rule of separate European powers, its various social paths had much in common. The system reached to Africa for its needed labor pool, to Europe for commercial direction and managerial staff, to North America for timber, fur, cotton, food, tobacco, and shipping, and to mainland South America for monetary silver and gold (Ajayi, 1971). Realistically, the pattern of the later South Atlantic slave plantation began in earnest as the European rulers and merchants began to use old institutions in new ways. In Europe, for instance, the peasants or the poor, whether free or bound, were forced to work on land according to village customs, culture and traditions.

According to Verlinden (1953), the landowners held a bundle of rights over the land and the people too, and thus they had a larger share of the total production. Worse still, these landlords were less interested in innovating new farming techniques, and as such if the peasants were to grow new crop for export, they had to innovate. Sugar was indeed one crop in higher demand both in Europe and the Americas. As a result, the demand for the product led to the increase in the number of agricultural and industrial elites and subsequent sugar plantations. In Europe and elsewhere, these feudal merchants and landowners found themselves in the position of early capitalists. They invested in the land, industrial plants, and slaves and managed all the intimate details of production through their agents. Initially, the labor force comprised of a mixture of free men from Europe, few local serfs or peasants, and slaves captured in various wars some of which were between Christians and Muslims.

In a classic essay entitled "Africa Remembered," Koelle (1963) notes that it could have been possible to attract voluntary migrants as was the case when Germans migrated to the east to open new lands during the same period. But this solution was never tried partly because the institution of slavery that had survived earlier in the Roman empire offered cheaper means of labor supply. In eastern Mediterranean, the need to concentrate people for economic reasons was enhanced by the already established Mediterranean slave trade. Elsewhere, especially in Europe and the Americas, slaves, Christians and Muslims alike, were regularly bought, sold and transported from one part of the Mediterranean basin to another. In fact, both Christians and Muslims themselves believed that it was legal to enslave prisoners of the rival faith, and thus this practice became a dominant source of labor supply. Legal or not, there were many accounts of Christian slaves in Christian lands and Muslim slaves in Muslim countries and as such the sale of slaves from one religion to another was widespread.

In addition to the established slave institutions within the Mediterranean basin itself, Koelle (1963) argued that there were two other important sources of slave trade. He notes that the earliest of these was the slave markets in the ports along the northern and eastern coat of the Black Sea. These markets were opened to Latin Christians with the fall of Byzantine Constantinople in 1204, and continued as the leading source of slaves for the whole Mediterranean basin until about the middle of the fourteenth century.

From a historical perspective, the option to import labor from elsewhere had grave and far-reaching consequences for the African continent and its people in particular, and on human race relations in general. Consequently, a second major external source of slaves was no doubt the sub-Saharan Africa. Part of the West African slave trade was directed toward exporting the slaves to North Africa though most of it was internal. Toward the end of the nineteenth century, the long distance trade in slaves within West Africa had been well established as a definite and powerful economic base. As Mungo Park (1816) wrote, "the price of a prisoner of war close to his homeland was low, so he is better off escaping; yet the farther off he is away from home, the more difficult his escape." Thus, slave prices varied significantly with the distance from the base of capture, and often they were sold from one dealer to another until they were eventually exported. By the early fourteenth century, African slaves were beginning to flourish in

Europe; first through captures across Mediterranean warfare and later by purchases from North Africa.

Meanwhile, the sugar plantation as an economic institution had grown far beyond its places of origin. Plantations were noticeable in Italy, Spain, Portugal, and various ancient European cities of the time. In addition, with the early capitalists coming from trading cities of northern Italy and southern Germany, the management of these new complex organizations quickly took an international dimension. Managers and technicians were also attracted from the established plantations to direct the creation of new ones. All along, they took with them the institutions to which they were accustomed, including slavery. The laborers were chattels (personally owned) and were forced to work long hours under intense supervision. Eventually, they were subjected to nothing more than rural workers with little or no control over their lives. They were also kept away from the rest of the society with no possibility for upward mobility. This practice, according to James Buckingham (1842), marked the beginning of an ugly chapter in human history.

Slavery in the Antebellum South

As Kenneth Stamp (1956) remarked, in the life of the Southern slave, the crucial fact was that slavery was above all labor systems. In the south, wherever the slave master lived, and regardless of the number of slaves he owned, it was his bondsmen's productive capacity that he valued most. The great majority of slaves worked from morning to night on farms and plantations cultivating cotton, tobacco, rice, sugar, and food crops. In judging the day-to-day relationships between the slave masters and the slaves, Stamp (1956) argued that slavery was essentially a paternalistic institution. How much paternalism was there and what was its true nature? Stamp insists that some slaves aroused paternalistic impulses in their owners. In Stamp's words, "there was the kind and faithful old nurse" who watched over her master in his infancy, the body servant who cared for him during sickness and anticipated all his wants, and then there was the "faithful and devoted" field hand who earned his regard by implicit obedience to all his commands (Stamp, 1956).

Furthermore, Stanley Elkins' (1968) analysis of her life in Louisiana plantation exemplified yet another account of the daily life of the slaves in the antebellum South. According to Elkins, visitors were often surprised to see the social intimacy that existed between the masters and slaves in certain situations. From such close association, a slave master might develop a deep affection for his slaves. At a glance, these rare accounts were fact of real life out of which the false idea of racial harmony in the south originated. In fact, some supporters of slave ownership often used these fewer accounts to justify and/or generalize slavery and human bondage as a paternalistic and patriarchal institution. But in reality, many of the best examples of paternalism came from small businesses where absentee landlordism was rare, where overseers were seldom employed and where contacts between the masters and slaves were numerous.

In these rare instances, discipline tended to be less severe and less rigid. But the fact of the matter, however, is that only a minority of the slaves lived in conditions so small that the masters were more or less constantly in close association with them. Plantation paternalism was, in most cases, in essence a form of leisure class indulgence of family domestics. For example, in the slave master's household, there often were more slaves than were necessary for the labor required of them and many were kept for luxury. Since the "domestics" were continually in the presence of their masters, mistresses and their guests, they were usually treated fairly well in contrast to the plantation slaves. Frances Kemble's (1838) accounts of a Georgian plantation exemplified the extent of the paternalistic nature of southern plantation slavery. Kemble recalled that a planter whimsically selected a slave or two for special pets. He pampered them, consulted them with mock gravity about larger matters, and permitted them to be impertinent about small household issues.

In some instances, the masters allowed their favorite slaves to occasionally carry their familiarity. This kind of paternalism which often arose from the master's genuine love, gave the slaves privileges and some degree of comfort but made them something less than human. As Kemble (1838) pointed out, the most generous master, so long as he was determined to be a master, could be paternal only toward a "fawning dependent; because slavery, by its nature could never be a relationship between equals." In reality, paternalism in southern slave plantations is analogous to a relationship between a parent and his child. Thus, the slave with less confidence in himself, less pride in his manhood, who stood before his master with hat in hand, and head slightly bent, was the one best suited to receive the favors and affection of a patriarch. The system was at best, a process of childlike race whereby the masters saw their "Negroes" as irresponsible children who needed guidance and supervision, and as well as paternal love. From this standpoint, it was typical of an indulgent master not to take his slaves seriously, but to look upon them as comic figures, such that even the most sensitive master called the slave men "boys" and the women "girls," until in their old age he made them honorary "aunties and uncles."

Clearly, to enjoy the bounty of a paternalistic master, a slave, whether domestic or not had to give up all claims to respect and the independence associated with adulthood. To some extent, the antebellum south had a class structure based upon property ownership. Inherent in this class structure was a caste system which separated those whose appearance allowed them to claim pure White ancestry from those whose appearance indicated as of black or Negro ancestry. Members of the White or Caucasian caste, regardless of wealth or education, considered themselves naturally superior to Negroes and therefore were entitled to all rights and privileges. They also maintained a high degree of case solidarity to ensure that the Negroes were "kept in their place." This in effect, was responsible for the sociological rise of white supremacy in the United States. The slaves reportedly were caste-conscious too, and showed remarkable loyalty toward one another. Although the slaves were generally loyal to their caste, they, like the whites, had their own class structure. As Davis (1943) remarked, the slave masters helped to create a social hierarchy among the slaves by giving them specialized tasks for the sake of economic efficiency, and by isolating domestic slaves from field slaves as a control technique (Pinkney, 1992; and Blackwell, 1991).

Nonetheless, the stratification of slave society also resulted from the internal forces amongst the slaves themselves, perhaps, due to the natural inclination to gain some recognition as potential human beings. For the slaves, human aspiration was more important and in fact, crucial for their daily survival in the plantations. Each slave cherished whatever amount of respect he could get.

The Slave Family in the Antebellum South

In Africa, the Negroes were accustomed to a strictly regulated family life and coherent moral codes. But, in the plantation, the break up of their social organization and family life destroyed the traditional sanctions which had enabled them to respect their established customs and traditions. Under bondage, the African slaves found that whites organized into families with greater degrees of social and economic importance, but regulated by different laws. In the plantations, the slaves were more or less encouraged to live as families and to accept white standards of morality. The most obvious differences between white and black family structures is evidenced in legal code upon which the families rested.

As Winston Coleman (1940) recalled, in every state, white marriages were recognized as civil contracts which imposed obligations on both parties and penalties for their violation. Slave marriages on the other hand, had no such recognition in the state codes. Instead slave marriages were regulated by whatever rules the slave owners deemed appropriate. In some instances, the masters randomly assigned husbands to women who had reached the "breeding age," but ordinarily, the slaves were allowed to pick their own mates but with permission. On the plantations, most slave owners refused to allow the slaves to marry outside the home and would in fact buy additional slaves when sexes were out of balance. Similarly, it was not unusual for slave husbands and wives to belong to different masters, respectively. In this instance, when a slave wished to marry the slave of another owner, a sale would have to be made to unite them. The slave family had no greater importance as an economic unit. Parents and children might spend some spare hours together in their garden living quarters, but unlike the whites, slaves worked most of their time in groups that had no family relationship. On the plantations where the husbands were neither the head of the household nor the provider, if a wife or the child was beaten by the overseers (as often the case was), he would stand by in helpless humiliation, demoralization and defeat.

So, in an age of patriarchal families, the important function of male slaves within the family structure was simply to procreate. Indeed, a typical slave family was headed by a female, such that the female role was far more important than that of the males. The husband was at best, his wife's assistant, her companion, and sex mate. As Milton Emerson (1841) rightly stated, with the absence of legal marriages, the families' minor social and economic significance, and the father's limited role, it was not surprising then to find that slave families were highly unstable. Lacking at both outside and internal pressures of the day, the slaves were also exposed to the threat of forced separation through sales. In fact, Emerson recalled that preachers united slave couples in wedlock by adding "until death or distance do you part."

Thus, slave masters could not promise that his debt would not force sales or guarantee that his death would not cause divisions. Some of the problems that troubled slave families, had nothing to do with slavery, rather they were tragically human problems which have always affected marital tranquility. One such domestic problem involved a slave whose wife did not return his devotion. However, other kinds of family tragedies were uniquely a part of life in bondage. A typical example was the scene that transpired when an overseer tied and whipped a slave mother in the presence of her children. The frightened children pelted the overseer with stones, and one of them ran up and bit him in the leg. The atmosphere was filled with the cry of the mother and her children.

The Social Consequences of Slavery

Allen Weinstein (1968) once wrote that if there is anything peculiar about plantation slavery, it is the extraordinary rigidity that fastened itself upon virtually every aspect of American lives. In essence, the legal codes, commonly called Black codes, the plantation etiquette, and the racial assumptions that defined the social and individual status of the slaves were well grounded in strict control such that even the most gifted black man could not fully realize himself as an autonomous individual. He could not be free, have rights and opportunity, or self-actualize. Slavery in America was, at best, an institutionalized economic, political, intellectual, moral and psychological warfare against the people of color. Unfortunately, a society that prided itself on a "pragmatic" spirit in dealing with so many of its social problems, proved unwilling to face the moral and human problem of slavery. In fact, prior to the time before the American Civil War, even the most enlightened men such as Jefferson and Abraham Lincoln, despite their dislike for slavery, found it quite impossible to envision a state in which free blacks and whites might live side by side in the spirit of legal, political and economic equality and social harmony.

Considering how fiercely the south defended slavery during the Civil War, one is tempted to think that defeat on the battlefield was not enough to accept the ugly chapters of the American slave era. The Emancipation Proclamation Act of 1863, for all it was worth was nothing short of a double standard and piecemeal at best. African Americans are still subjected to all forms of institutional discrimination and racial bigotry. The social, psychological, and cultural effects of slavery can never be underestimated. Although the civil rights movements of the 1960s exposed the ugly side of American institutional racism, much is yet to be done to deconstructively assimilate African Americans within the mainstream of American society. Worse still, mainstream culture has continued its policy of miseducation, propaganda and tokenism.

Throughout the five centuries of slavery, this pervasive and chattel institution affected the Africans and their continent negatively. The institution of slavery and slave trade undermined Africa's domestic economic, moral and social development. This form of underdevelopment frustrated Africa's potential by linking it to an inferior relationship with the Western capitalist economy. The continent's perception of itself as inferior treatment contributed to its being developmentally and invariably arrested. This form of "stunted" development aborted its economic and technological evolution (Northrup, 1994).

African Consciousness: The Global Idea

Recent scholarly activity, the communication network industry, and news media networks are some of the most active means through which knowledge about Africans at large, in other words, Africans and the African Diaspora, has been and is being revealed. While the knowledge itself could be very scanty, less rigorous, and simply unsystematized, the sources of that knowledge are, perhaps; inadequate for providing more credible scientific evidence that is instrumental to arriving at more valid conclusions. In some cases, good studies have been done by eminent professional scholars and scientists. In other cases, the field of African and African-American studies awaits luminary minds to illuminate it with prolific and profound wisdom. One of the approaches which will assist scholars in the creative discovery and revolutionary analysis may be grounded in interdisciplinary scientific scholarship. Taken seriously, the approach is more likely than otherwise, to produce good results in terms of prolific scientific theories and knowledge whose triadic dialectic may challenge the worth of Africanist scholarship. The triadic dialectical concerns understanding and interpreting change by using European, African and American intellectual universes.

Consciousness is an individual's or community's perpetual awareness of the existing reality of life. Perceptual consciousness is diametrically opposed to mental subconsciousness (*New Webster's Dictionary and Thesaurus,* 1992) [though both may be used synergistically]. Philosophically, consciousness is the corpus of "self knowledge acquired by virtue of the mind's capacity" to perceptually reflect upon itself introspectively. In other words, the mind is active, alert, and alive rather than being emotionally and conceptually anaesthetized (Flew, 1984, pp. 72-73). Introspectively speaking, making the subject the object of his/her own awareness may appear to be scientifically controversial, but increasingly less contradictory. Introspectively, cognition is the mind's ability to utilize past and present schemas, chunking, ideas that are forms of memory, creativity, invention or insight that is retrieved, compoundedly reproduced as problem solutions. Solutions may be viewed as negative or positive (Posner, 1989).

Scientific, philosophical and religious ideas of human consciousness are originally either African or Middle Eastern and may have been borrowed, modified, plagiarized, fabricated and contextualized in new Western and Eastern environments for the enrichment of other civilizations (Sagini, 1996). For example, for illustrative purposes let us use the example of *Mexico Vs. United States of America*. If Mexico becomes a superpower during the end of the 3rd millenium and at the beginning of the 4th millenium, Mexican scholars, scientists, and the political and bureaucratic elite will be tempted to deny, for intrinsic and other reasons, that the United States never became a superpower during the twentieth and twenty-first centuries of the Christian era. As a superpower, Mexico will use its values (i.e., political, cultural, technological, economic, military and scientific preeminence) to try to dominate and influence the world—our planet. Perhaps the Mexican system of government, religious values, science, astronomy, medicine, theology, philosophy, law and the arts will be used by Mexican elite universities to spread knowledge, skills, wisdom and culture. Through imperial conquest of interaction with other cultures, diffusion of Mexican influence will be felt. At that time, categories of ancient, medieval and modern history, derived from European and Mexican experience, will apply awkwardly at best to the histories of China, India, Africa, Arabs and other parts of the Western hemisphere. Why would Mexican intellectual elite and scientists be tempted to deny that the United States was not a superpower that had a great constitution, magnanimous political institutions, a sense of freedom unequaled to none, a robust economic, military and political establishment, a liberal immigration policy that continually enabled the incoming scholars, students, scientists, entrepreneurs, refugees and others to be politically and culturally socialized for citizenship and political participation?

To answer this question, we can say that Mexico would want to preserve its unique place, identity and leadership in the world. In other words, as a world leader, its scholars and scientists who would be proud of their international empire, which they own, rule, extol, used to civilize and rationalize, will for intrinsic reasons, say that during the twentieth and twenty-first centuries, the influence of the Untied States was small in the world. The wars the Untied States had against foreign countries were minor clashes that humiliated it in the Middle East, Korea, Vietnam and during the First and Second World Wars. These were not really wars, but minor clashes and skirmishes. American historic isolationism prevented it from getting deeply involved in the colonization and civilization of the world. Moreover, its internal diversity and multicultural issues were too fragile and conflictual to allow it to be more forcefully involved in world affairs. Therefore, in essence, America has not made any significant contributions to world civilizations. Even, the only seven people manned satellite (The Challenger) that exploded and killed everyone was technologically inferior to land on the moon or on any planet of our galactic system.

This example of Mexico versus the U.S. is a fictional but intellectual historical analogy that portrays the deconstructive debates between the Eurocentric and Afrocentric scholarship in respect to African contributions to world civilizations, and how those contributions and interactions with other cultures have either reinforced or enriched the complexity of the consciousness nexus. For instance:

> Legions of scholars have examined the effects of cross-cultural interactions in modern times while exploring themes such as long-distance trade, exchanges of plants, animals, and diseases, transfer of technology, imperial and colonial ventures, missionary campaigns, the transatlantic slave trade, and the development of global capitalism which have reaffirmed the contributions and interactions (Bentley, 1996, pp. 751-752).

The previous quotation is an authoritative affirmation of the contributions and interactions in question. Quite apart from the imposition of foreign rule and taxes on conquered peoples, imperial expansion also was associated with the establishment of commercial and diplomatic relations between distant peoples, as well as the spread of cultural traditions. The economic or commercial value of *exotic commodities* served as "symbols of power, status, and authority" (p. 753). The ability to "display them, consume them, or bestow them on others was crucial for the establishment and maintenance of political and social structures" (p. 753).

For instance, between 4,300 and 4,000 BCE, to improve their transportation technology, the Egyptians, like their Chinese and Mesopotamian counterparts, made innovations in the construction of tools, weapons and the domesticated horse. These resources were used for colonization and imperial expansion. Their deities were also borrowed. For instance, the Egyptian Zeus was borrowed by Greece. Egyptians constructed sailing ships that enabled them to "ply the waters of the Persian Gulf, Arabian Sea, Red Sea, and the Mediterranean Sea" (p. 756). During the same time wheeled carts and wagons were invented and used in Mesopotamia, Ukraine and Southern Russia. Egyptians adopted "art motifs, boat designs, mud-brick construction and the writing of hieroglyphics" (p. 757). Migration promoted the diffusion of horse domestication and bronze metallurgy both of which influenced the development of states and societies from China to Egypt. Egypt also acquired bronze technology which the ruling elite used for the manufacture of weaponry. The search for the relatively rare deposits of copper and tin ores stimulated trade with neighboring peoples, as well as military campaigns designed to establish control over the deposits. This situation parallels contemporary American influence in South Africa, especially during the Cold War, due to the strategic minerals that are used for making fighter aircraft engines (Wyk and Manton, 1988).

In his new paradigm for teaching, research, and theory construction, Sagini's (1996) *The African and African-American University: A Historical and Sociological Analysis*, deconstructively argues, among other things, that the spirit of African intellectual, scientific and irrational classicalism are the reinforcers of both modern and post-modern empirical rationalism. Our ability to study, know and store such knowledge in medicine, astronomy, mathematics, religion, philosophy, and science helps us to understand and appreciate not only the diffusion and fusion of these disciplines, but the contributions and emancipatory character of African preclassical people and their education.

Africa is the cradle of human civilization because archeological evidence shows that the first homo sapiens lived in Eastern and Southern Africa between 2.5 and 4 million years ago. In addition, the earliest preindustrial civilization which invented urban life, domesticated plants and animals, and invented fire and ironwork technology was African in origin. Further, recent scientific evidence based on "mitochondrial DNA support a compelling case for an African origin" of the human species in spite of the fact that a "preponderance of scientific evidence is still inadequate" (Fagan, 1996, p. 11). If the human race has an African origin in its blood, then the spirit of African consciousness is not only human, but it is also global in its genetic originality and physical and biochemical universality.

Ronald Segal (1995) who authored *The Black Diaspora* which has existed for over the last 500 years, has used a journalistic but sharp and penetrating analysis to describe the life, struggles, and contributions of the African Diaspora both in Africa and elsewhere in the Western hemisphere. Segal shows that Africans were forcefully, deceptively, and unintentionally captured and taken into the unknown lands that are

Organizational Behavior

called Jamaica, Saint Domingue, North America, Brazil, Cuba, Britain, Canada, Haiti, Guyana, Suriname, Barbados and Trinidad. His analysis shows that about 10 million Africans may have arrived on these exotic Western shores. Within the 350 years of slavery and slave trade, over 100 million of them may have perished in their procurement and transportation through the middle passage. The author shows that through the contributions of the lot of slavery and slave trade, huge profits were made by the merchants, manufacturers, investors, and planters all of whom relied on the racist, exploitative, and oppressive ideology that was religiously, politically and legally rationalized to ward off the fear of the master's economic dependence and ecological vulnerability.

Through their sojourn in life, slaves were not reactionless or insensitive objects of exploitation and humiliation by the mercantile, imperial, feudal and capitalist systems of private property and ownership. In contradistinction, they were rational, reactive and revolutionary individuals whose resistance against oppression in terms of attempts to escape, arson, and the Jacobin revolution (in Haiti), guerrilla warfare against Jamaican and West Indian Maroons, and the 250 slave revolts in the U.S. (Pinkney, 1991) are heroic reflections of their struggle for emancipation, freedom, humanity and diversity. In the long run, the forces of darkness that colonized, enslaved and oppressed them were overthrown through revolutionary and militant activity of the Civil Wars, civil rights, and the pre-colonial independence revolutionary movements.

In these distant and exotic lands, the diasporization and rediasporization of the African Diaspora is by no means indistinguishable. Their lot in terms of poverty, ghettoiazation, slums, lack of suitable amenities, lack of medical and nutritional affluence, the prevalence of ignorance, illness, and lack of means for total emancipatory education and liberalization permeate(d) the social structures and organizational institutions that have helped to institutionalize societal values that are used for their accommodationistic, assimilatory and exclusionary stratification within and without the larger society. Given the reality of their political, economic and social marginalization, these Black, cross-cultural and multicultural communities have become creative enough in order to search for solutions to their common and comparatively variant problems. While the solutions to their urgent social and economic problems may be sought in the fields of expressive and sonorous music, visual and physical arts, linguistic pidgins and Creoles, athletics, religion and the professions, the instrumentation and articulation of the solutions to problems has been and is being carried out by the diasporic intellectual who is the natural and authentic product and conscience of the diasporic community through whom its consciousness is constructed, reconstructed, raised, and articulatively popularized for consumption, change and affirmation by the community (Martin, 1995; Grant, 1996).

The preindependence and postindependence diasporic intellectual is a socially powerful evolutionary and revolutionary critic and incubator of African consciousness and the ideological base that frees it from the womb of Pan-Africanism. This womb gives birth to the spirit, or consciousness, or the living soul. The soul is expressed in values, desires, historiographic romance, historic diaspora, and continental and transcontinental new world traditions and achievements (Kramer, 1997). The historicity and authenticity of African consciousness may be viewed as a form of nationalist sentimentalism, or as irrationalism and religious inspiration which is rationalized through continental and extracontinental traditions by the diasporic and continental intellectual elites. Others may see it as a form of identity rooted in abstract ideological reality. Truly, African consciousness is celebrated in unique and strange ways in order to:

> Appropriate religious traditions as they developed their sacred symbols (flags), sacred texts (constitutions, declarations of independence), sacred figures (founding fathers, virtuous heroes), evil figures (traitors or heretical subversives), sacred places (national monuments, cemeteries), public rituals (national holidays and parades), sense of mission (responsibility to promote national ideals), mobilizing crusades (conflicts with those who oppose the nation's mission), and sense of sacrifice (the nation has been saved by the blood of those who died, so that it might live) (Kramer, 1997, p. 534).

If intellectual elites try to politicize their consciousness by appealing to narrow and shallow elements of nationalistic consciousness comparable to those of the pre-World War II German intellectuals, it might lead their communities to breed fanaticism, intolerance, violence and deadly war. African consciousness is not "naturally pure" because its evolutionary development has been influenced by both the internal and external forces. Internal forces are of African origin and external forces are global and extracontinental. Its synergistic eclecticism is not a uselessly evolving and immaterial illusion, but rather, a class and color consciousness or living spirit which persistently yearns for independence, liberation, civil rights, human rights, development, the goodness of cultural diversity and political unity. African consciousness is diametrically opposed to colonization, oppression, and alienation of individual and of the Pan-African communities. Like nationalism, African consciousness originated or originates in economic, cultural, social, political, religious, linguistic and literary contexts of human interaction, motivation and action. Such contextual spheres are not devoid of the discourse of color, gender, class, sexuality and ethnicity (Kramer, 1997).

More than two and one-half millennia ago, Achimedes said that, "To every action there is an equal and opposite reaction." Clearly, the force which makes things to act causes other things to respond or react proportionately. The forces which course African people to migrate intra-continentally and intercontinentally are many and complex. Of the many forces this chapter highlights, the most salient ones comprise of problems associated with depeasantization, political, economic and ethnic nature, and colonial legacy and human rights abuses. The complex interplay of these forces upon each other and the intensity, extensiveness, duration of such an interplay creates a climate of despair, anxiety, and hopelessness. The longer these forces negatively wallow the human spirit, psyche, and physique, the more they become an unpalatable vicious-cycle that pathologically and consistently evokes a crisis-consciousness mentality. To extricate themselves from these kinds of conditions, the learned, the physically and economically able, and the lumpen proletariats are forced to make partially informed decisions to migrate across political environment and culture. Internal forces of immigration are intraterritorial (within a territory or country). These forces of migration, due to their ecological complexity, may interpretively contradict the structural terrain of migration. The external ones tend to greatly exacerbate the intensity, size, volume, and international effects of migration. Specifically, the extraction of the brain-drain from their cultural and environmental roots may not only have reflected its negative continental side effects, but, the influences of their being uprooted from their national and cultural roots may have become global in character. Further analysis, nature, and complexity of these forces in Africa is instructive.

Depeasantization

On the global scale, studies on the peasantry have been carried on in Europe (1500-1900). Mexico (1910), Russia (1905-1917), China (1921-1949), Vietnam (1945-1975), Algeria (1959) and Cuba (1958) (Araghi, 1995). Given this global view of analyzing the peasantry, global theories which explain the lot of the peasantry and its ideological social forces are being analytically refracted on the pleasantries of the Third World nations. Although the Third World literature on the peasantry is scanty and less sophisticated in its theoretical and ideological underpinnings of peasantry life, a factor that is attributable to low levels of technology and the infrastructure of production, consumption and distribution, these low levels of technology, infrastructure and distributive production do not stimulate high demand and competition. Higher demand on the part of peasant productivity would tend to change the technology and infrastructure of production including the attraction and production of scholarly literature.

In 1950, 29% of the total world population and 16% of the Third World peoples were urbanized. Projections indicate that by the year 2000, nearly half of the world population and the 41% of the Third World peoples will live in cities. Comparatively speaking, 70% of Latin Americans and Middle Easterners live in cities (UN, 1988; 1990). In addition, the history of Western European peasantry, collectivized Russian peasantries and the peasantries of other communist states has shown a high degree of urbanization too. Viewed in this global perspective, it can be argued that depeasantization or deruralization has been, up until recently, and perhaps will continue to be, a phenomenal global process. Depeasantization tends to depopulate rural areas and massively tends to overurbanize towns and cities. One of the major external forces that has continued to massively deruralize populations for urban concentrations has been the inevitable expansion of capitalism. The mission of capitalism is to urbanize, modernize, rationalize, and civilize. On the contrary, the mission of peasantization or ruralization is not only simplicity and rural undifferentiatedness (*gemeinschaft*), but also reflections of primitive, traditional, peripheral and moribund (Max Weber, E. Durkheim) living. Unlike differentiated, complex, industrial, urban (*gessellschaft*) and capitalistic environment, the economic underdevelopment of the Third World has not been "rooted out" or destroyed by the relations of the capitalistic production. Therefore, the apparent indestructibility of rural peasantism, has, up and until this century and probably until the next century, left the "agrarian question" unresolved. In other words, capitalism and urbanization have yet to learn to change the rural countryside in order to advance its civilization.

The unresolvedness of the "peasant question," it might be argued, is still resilient largely because of the peasantry's functional role. Functionally, the peasant sector produces cheap labor for urban communities that have experienced capitalistic modes of production. In return, urban areas provide the rural sector with goods and specialized services. By doing that, rural conditions make it possible for the needs of capitalism to be met. Given the dichotomous and functionally interdependent relations between urban and rural settings, scholars use the terms "sectoral disarticulation" and contradictory "functional dualism" (Rey, 1975; Meillassoux, 1981; Araghi, 1973; Wolpe, 1972) to describe not only the interdependent nature of the rural-urban settings, but also the unique resilience of "rural indestructibility" by capitalism.

Teleologically, and contrary to *gemeinschaft* and *gessellschaft* theories, recent studies on the peasantry indicate that they are essentially differentiated as owners and wage earners. Their lot makes them to resist capitalistic expansiveness. They will hardly "disappear" from the scene regardless of the expansionary forces of capitalism. In other niches they contribute to the permanence of their indestructiveness. Unlike capitalists, peasants persistently produce in order to live rather than make a profit.

The dominant ideological currents that animate the peasantry and related movements in Africa include globalism, internationalism, decolonization, communism and anticommunism, modernity and postmodernism, and perhaps, Christianity versus Islam, and the East-West controversy. During the Cold War, these ideological currents animated Third World Africans to perceive political, economic and social reality through East-West confrontation for global domination and the control of the wares of market. Such hegemonic ambitions of the Superpowers were the inherent sources of conflict that resulted in nationalist, ethnic, colonial and interstate rivalry that produced clashes and consequently resulted in massive population movements across national and cultural boundaries. Generally speaking, women dominate short-distance rural to rural migrations. Men are predominantly involved in international and internal rural-urban migrations.

For Asia, Africa, Latin America, Europe, N. America and Canada, evidence indicates that "for each intercensal period, the ratio of the rate of rural out-migration to the rate of rural natural population increase (times 100) reflects a rough estimate of the rate of deruralization" (Araghi, 1995, p. 350). Given the global environment, the contradictions of capitalist development in the south, "Contrary to Leninist expectations, were manifested as a strong tendency towards deruralization as opposed to capital accumulation in the country side" (p. 354). The "rural push factors" are the urban centers of capital accumulation and population density associated with high level in-migration and natural increase. Contrary to this view, the "global pull factors" include the brain-drain, the refugee factor and to the lesser extent, commerce.

In brief, between 1945 and 1973, the processes of peasantization and depeasantization were responsible for the relative, rather than the absolute decline of the pleasantries especially in Africa. The teleological and changing character of capitalistic history influenced a fast-paced deruralization process in the Third World. Third World peasants, migrants, and refugees became city dwellers, urban wage workers, wage earners, and the brain drain.

Modernization, Economics, and Politics – The Ethnic Factors

Ethnicity is an ethnonationalistic identity through which people practice politics and life in general in the context of one's common language, religion, race and culture. In such a situation, intergroup problems become pathologies or expressions of anxiety, hostility, and estrangement directed at other groups. When a politically stronger, ethnic group becomes ethnonationalistic and exclusionary as Nazi German, Idi Amin's Uganda, Apartheid South Africa, Serbian-Bosnia conflict in former Yugoslavia and more recently, the Hutu-Tutsi tribal conflict in Rwanda, it disrupts and destabilizes society. The ethnonationalist group cultivates negative ethos for formally, informally, and militantly confronting those they regard as enemies. Such ethos strengthen ideologically and enable them to use their past sufferings and future threats from outsiders to cement their own relationships. Emotionally, the ethos reflect inner frustrations that are expressed as "grief, fear ... animosity, anger and contempt" (Rothschild and Growth, 1995, p. 69). Having cemented their relationships, ethnonationalists use majoritarian or minoritarian ideologies for development and advancement of their own sense of identity and unity. Also, they help their followers to learn a new version of interpretive history through which they ritualistically observe, and continuously recall not only the oppression, persecution, exploitation, and repression, but, through which they can also celebrate struggles, victories, and martyrdom. The ethnonationalist group creates a worldview of "otherness" at which they cast their "hostility, malevolence, suspicion, and mistrust" (p. 71). The existing climate reveals a consciousness of great antagonistic manifestations.

In the case of Ethiopia, Eritrea and to some extent Rwanda, the creation of colonial boundaries whose fixation created these modern states has never been legally and politically accepted by certain groups within these nation states. This is viewed as a deprivation. In addition, rapid, discontinuous, and disruptive change occurs in the organization, structure, and values of society. This often includes "rapid and traumatic urbanization; the displacement of old industries by new ones; technological and cultural innovations bringing old and new social elements into conflict; break up in traditional linkages and associations" (p. 73). The conflict is viewed to be further generated by loss of sense of territorial, social and psychological boundaries. Such a loss may not only be the source of the outbreak of communal versus nation state violence and tension, but the situation may also create a hostile climate that warrants massive political migration of refugees across national and cultural boundaries. The fact that the struggle to make new boundaries for positive political action is a common thing that reminds us against relying on the assumption that the nation state is inevitable. Given that assumption, political development may not necessarily lead to modernity. Ethnicity and the conflicts associated with it may be viewed as confusion that arises from conflicting claims for maintaining tradition and modernity. There may lie, in visionary terms, the seeds for future political innovation and prosperity.

Economically, Third World peoples especially in Africa fight against inequitable regional allocation of resources, "loss of jobs and livelihood; inflation; stagnant or declining living standards; burdensome taxes, debts, other economic obligations; displacement of" local "industries by foreign ones and equivalent-market place changes" (p. 74). For instance, when Nigeria suffered from these problems seventeen years ago, she expelled one and a half million Ghanaians in order to create job opportunity for Nigerian citizens. Within less than five years, these rejectees had either gone back to different regions of Nigeria or other West African nations, particularly Cote d'Ivoire, Libya, Liberia, Gambia, Western Europe and U.S.A. (Peil, 1995; and Osaghae, 1995). Some of the well qualified Ghanaians migrated as refugees and work with international organizations like "ECA, ADB, FAO, ILO, UN, UNCTAD, WHO, NGOs, etc." (p. 351). In general between 10% and 20% of Ghanaians live and work in other countries. Many of them are excellent scientists, scholars, doctors and businessmen, ministers and the lumpen proletariats.

Politically, state institutions are so fragile that they function ineffectively because they lack legitimacy. Their lack of effectiveness and legitimacy makes them incapable of mediating the struggles that exist between competing groups. As a result, these lacks distance them from realizing claims of modernity and constructive political and economic development. Such societies which have weak political institutions have no ability "to curb the excess of personal and parochial" desires; "unable to channel participation along predetermined lines, the overloaded state becomes isolated and aloof from society, unable to structure the relations between these interests and itself" (Rothschild 1995, p. 74). Other political factors of the state versus society that intensify and help to magnify intergroup contradictions include the "displacement of one regime by another; the violent creation of new states, and the changes in frontiers and jurisdictions of political bodies that create new and untested relationships among groups and individuals" (p. 74). These disruptive and destabilizing problems are not only collectively and psychologically provocative and displacing, but, they also make individual persons lose jobs, status, prestige and property. These individuals fear "an uncertain future and the less tangible, but psychologically quite real, needs for massive readjustments in terms of new values, outlooks, and orientations." They constantly look for new model personalities since the collapse of universal collectivization left them no model for emulation. In such a context, ethnicity erupts into hostility and enmity. Enemy stereotypes are directed at minorities and majorities alike. Anxiety and stress are "channeled towards scapegoat objects" (p. 75). Such descriptive behavior may not be scientifically observable and objectified though it could be exaggerated. When ethnic people are viewed as "aliens," they become the outlet for "anguish, despair, confusion and fear" (p. 75). If an atmosphere of ethnic hysteria crupts, violence, terrorism, aggression and even interethnic war can break up as the recent Liberian and Somalian experience has shown. These happenings cause people to move across their national and cultural frontiers.

Depeasantization, war, famine, economic and political insecurity, the rapid tempo for modernization and the abuse of human rights are the major forces of migration in Africa. In countries like Rwanda, Somalia and Liberia where the states virtually collapsed during the 1990s, and where, at a certain point in time, it was impossible to enforce security and stability, the movement of refugees was increasingly voluminous and outbound. In other states like Kenya and Zambia where mechanisms for rationalizing the future of democratization are still fragile, political actors have virtually disempowered the masses and alienated the peasantry (Schraeder, 1995).

Weiner (1995) has produced a comprehensive and multifaceted analysis of the migration crisis and has helped to shade light to clarify some critical and theoretical issues that are central to national and international politics of migration. Among the issues that obtain are citizenship, the resistance of sovereignty and the impact of the global economy. In both moral and philosophically attuned ethical notions, anyone would support the migration of expertise, migrants, and refugees. Given this aspect of humanitarian understanding, Western liberal democratic nations that advocate fundamental rights of people to emigrate also continue to guard the "gates of entry to heaven" whose social and economic policies are exclusionary, and marginalizing. Though these nations construct these self-protective policies for fear of "invasion", such a form of irrationality, xenophobia, and paranoia are based on false notions that assert that the global economy and infrastructure are extremely powerful forces of international migration. In reality, receiving states are powerless to handle and control the "fleets of emigrees." While governments, with the exception of failed states, have a sovereign right to control who penetrates their borders, one of the problems these governments may have could be their struggle to define their meaning of "identity and purpose" of emigrees. As they struggle to define the meaning and purpose of various types of emigrants, they discover that they are faced with challenges of multiculturalism and limitations of equal opportunity, welfare, and affirmative action policies. These issues are not only neo-Marxian in their orientation, but, the tempo and political power with which they resonate when articulated possesses revolutionary power that translates into effective and managerially paralyzing populist political niches.

Conclusion

African consciousness is not the invention of Africa. It is not the savage mind idea that excites and entertains the classical anthropological Eurcentric mind. It is not the dynamic Black ideologies of mysticism, religion, sensuality, Ujamaa, Harambee, Marxism, negritude, conscientism, communism, Islam and traditionalism (Mudimbe, 1988). Unfortunately, while some of the above mentioned ideas may singly or collectively assume an element of African consciousness, they do not definitely define and rationalize it. Afrocentricity is the ideologically refined African centered world view. It is a viable tool for decolonizing and liberating the infinitively limited mind. What then is African consciousness? African consciousness is a theory of Blackness. This theory is Africanism rather than Africology or Afrocentricity. Like nationalism, devoid of its irrational manifestations, it tells us who we are, where we are, where we have come from, where we are going, and what we want to be. African consciousness rationally or intuitively tells us when we need to do certain things and when we do not have to. For instance, it tells us when, why, and how to celebrate the past and the present in order to provide predictive continuity for the future. In this case, we celebrate a dead past in the present. In other words, we vivify or memorialize it. By so doing, we make a dead past alive not only for sentimental and emotional reasons, but also for establishing a link with a memorable, inspiring, or glorious past which is a model of our identity, uniqueness and experience. At this juncture, the past speaks to us in what looks like real thoughts, dreams, or symbols that may be imaginary, yet are real. In doing so, the African spirit is kept alive in terms of historical consciousness, adaptability and resilience. This resilient and adaptable element of the African consciousness is not static by any means. Instead, it changes with contextual, historical, political, economic and cultural forces of stability, diffusion, interaction, and disequilibrium. Since these forces are at work all the time, their singular and synergistic influence tends to perpetuate the historical continuity of African consciousness in its evolutionary adaptability and change in space over time. Therefore, this makes it a dynamic and living spirit that permeates the universe. The universality of African consciousness is ontologically explanatory, scientifically verifiable and humanistically expressive and instrumental.

This documentary analysis of the forces of migration in Africa, first and foremost, and elsewhere, secondarily, has been done with the use of classical, Marxist, and contemporary theoretical underpinnings in the social sciences. The relevance of using classical and Marxist or neo-Marxist theoretical ideas to analyze contemporary or current problems on the African scene is, based on the analytically global and intellectual universe, quite interesting. On the one hand, it is interesting because the internal and external forces of migration were theoretically, in one way or the other, animated by the Eurocentric, imperial, and pragmatic implementation of the theories in question. On the other hand, these economic, political, and global forces of migration in Africa and elsewhere may be viewed to be "factors of organizational instability and destabilization" of African countries and their institutions. Therefore, broadly speaking, the forces behind migration should be viewed in the context of, and as elements of, a wider national, regional, and international complexity and character. These forces of instability and destabilization may also be viewed to be agencies of change that positively or negatively help transform the structure and operation of the family, city, school or college, the church, the government, the state, the unions, the professions and society in general. The chronicity, sporadic violence, and ruthlessness associated with the change in question underscores the managerial and leadership capabilities of

Third World countries which opt for the laws of the jungle rather than using reason, logic, tolerance, and dialogue to solve their most urgent problems.

For instance, Adepoju has shown that a combination of political and economic mismanagement has sparked off and sustained the emigration of skilled professionals. The deteriorating working conditions of professionals and the poor working environment are rooted in large part in the foreign exchange shortages in recent years that have made it difficult and expensive to buy needed facilities and equipment. Practically, university research grants have "fizzled out." Professionals are not satisfied with the jobs they do. They are not effectively recognized or rewarded for their efforts, expertise, and contributions. As a result of such negative treatment by their employers, the professionals have intensified the exodus elsewhere. Out of frustration, the more competitive professionals have temporarily or permanently migrated to the West where their qualifications and skills are in effective demand and international in character. Even unskilled labor has been lured by higher pay to immigrate westwards in spite of the irregularity and untenurability of the work environment. In some cases, the devaluation of national currencies in the Third World nations has reinforced this westward migratory tendency regardless of the low level of wages available to unskilled workers from the South.

Finally, though the international community and Third World governments have tried to establish institutional, scientific, and programmatic mechanisms for retaining professionals in Third World countries, and although this retention strategy is aimed at strengthening the communicative competence of the researchers, scientists, educators, and their institutions, the rhetoricity of these kinds of overtures are, out of necessity, undermined by respective organizations and governments that set the rules for such retention and containment. As a result, migration trends of Africans from the South to the North are likely to continue indefinitely.

Some people migrate for reasons not discussed in this chapter, such as looking for a lost dream, visiting friends and relatives, following others blindly, being a dependent of an immigrant, and so on. Whatever the forces behind African migration are, the morphology of the forces in question is complex and difficult to comprehend fully. Further research on the subject, particularly of anthropological and sociological nature, could provide some instructive insights. Irrespective of the motives for migration, the circumstances through which involuntary and voluntary immigrants have rediscovered each other in a new playing field is interesting, meaningful and far reaching.

References

Adas, M. 1989. *Machines as the Measure of Men: Science, Technology, and Ideologies.* Ithaca, N.Y.: Cornell University Press.

Aidoo, A. 1993. Africa: Democracy without human rights? *Human Rights Quarterly* 15: 703-715.

Ajayi, J.F. 1971. *The History of West Africa.* London: Longman Group Publishers.

Allen, W., and G.O. Frank. 1968. *American Negro Slavery: A Modern Reader.* New York: Oxford University Press.

Ansah, J.F. 1991. New approaches by bankers could bring surge of funds for African universities. *The Chronicle of Higher Education* June 5: A28-A30.

Araghi, F.A. 1995. Global depeasantization, 1945-1990. *The Sociological Quarterly* 36, 2: 337-368.

Arrighi, G. 1973. Labor supplies in historical perspective: A study of the proletarianization of the African peasantry in Rhodesia. In *Essays of the Political Economy of Africa.* eds. J.S. Saul and G. Arrighi. New York: Monthly Review Press.

Baker, J., and T.A. Aina, eds. 1995. *The Migration Experience in Africa.* GOTAB, Sweden: Nordiska Afrikainstitutet.

Baker, J., and P.O. Penderson, eds. 1992. *The Rural Urban Interface in Africa: Expansion and Adaptation.* Upsaala: The Scandinavian Institute of African Studies.

Bently, J.H. 1996. Cross-Cultural Interaction and periodization in world history. *American Historical Review:* 749-770.

Bernal, M. 1987. *Black Athena: The Afroasiatic Roots of Classical Civilization, Volume I.* New Brunswick, N.J.: Rutgers University Press.

Buckingham, J.S. 1842. *The Slave States of America.* New York: Oxford University Press.

Carney, M. 1995. Theoretical and practical contributions of Afrocentricity to Pan-Africanism. *21st Century Afro Review* 1, 2: 48-72.

Cliff, T. 1997. Cinemas of the black diaspora: Diversity, dependence, and oppositionality. *Cineaste,* 22, 4: 66-67, epub@oclc.org

Coleman, W. 1940. *Slavery Time in Kentucky.* Chapel Hill: University of North Carolina Press.

Crush, J., A. Jeeves, and D. Yuldeman. 1991. *South Africa's Labor Empire: A History of Black Migrancy to the Gold Mines.* Boulder, Colorado and Oxford: Westview Press.

Davis, E.A. 1943. *Plantation Life in the Florida Parishes of Louisiana.* New York: AMS Press.

Desrochers, R.E. 1997. Not face away. The narrative of Venture Smith, art African-American in the early republic. *The Journal of American History,* 8, 1: 40-66.

Diop, C.A. 1955. *The African Origin Civilization: Myth or Reality.* Chicago, IL: Lawrence Hill Books.

Durkheim, E. 1893. *The Division of Labor in Society.* Glencoe: Free Press, 1960.

Elkins, S.M. 1968. *Slavery: A Problem in American Institutional and Intellectual Life.* Chicago: University of Chicago Press.

Emerson, M. 1841. In the journal of Milton Emerson. Durham, N.C.: Duke University Library.

Fagan, B.M. 1966 *The Oxford Companion to Archaeology.* New York: Oxford University Press.

Freeman, M. 1994. The philosophical foundations of human rights. *Human Rights Quarterly* 16: 491-514.

Gonzalez, A. 1992. Higher education brain drain and overseas employment in the Philippines: Towards a differentiated set of solutions. *Higher Education* 23: 21-31.

Grant, F. 1996. You can go home again, you just can't stay. Stuart Hall and the Caribbean diaspora. *Research in African Literatures,* 27, 4: 28-48: 987-988, epub@oclc.org.

Head, J. 1995. Migrant mine labor from Mozambique: Employment prospects and policy options in the 1990s. *Journal of Contemporary African Studies* 13, 1: 91-120.

Jalali, R., and S.M. Lipset. 1992-93. Racial and ethnic conflicts: A global perspective. *Political Science Quarterly* 107, 4: 585-606.

Joseph, M.C. 1996. Historical narratives and the meaning of nationalism. *Journal of the History of Ideas* 58, 3: 525-545.

Kemble, F. 1838. *Journal of a residence on a Georgian Plantation in 1838-1839.* New York: Vintage Publishers.

Koelle, S.W. 1968. *African Remembered: Narratives by West Africans for the Era of the Slave Trade.* Madison: University of Wisconsin.

Kramer, L. 1997. Historical narratives and the meaning and the meaning of nationalism. *Journal of the History of Ideas,* 58, 3: 525-545.

Lenin, V.I. 1899. *The Development of Capitalism in Russia.* Moscow: Foreign Language Publishing House, 1960.

Mahmud, S.S. 1993. The state and human rights in Africa in the 1990s: Perspectives and prospects. *Human Rights Quarterly* 15: 485-495.

Manning, P. 1996. The problem of interactions in world history. *American Historical Review:* 771-782.

Marx, K. 1859. *A Contribution to the Critique of Political Economy.* London: Lawrence and Wishart, 1971.

McDonald, K.A. 1996. Standing room only? Book explores arguments, but doesn't take sides. *The Chronicle of Higher Education* February 9: A10, A11 and A17.

Mellassoux, C. 1981. *Maidens, Meal and Money: Capitalism and the Democratic Community.* Cambridge: Cambridge University Press.

Mudimbe, V.Y. 1988. *The Invention of Africa: Gnosis, Philosophy, and the Order of Knowledge.* Bloomington, ID: Indiana University Press.

Mundende, D.C. 1989. The brain drain and developing countries. In *The Impact of International Migration on Developing Countries,* ed. R.T. Appleyard, 183-195. Paris: Organization for Economic Cooperation and Development.

Niarchos, C.N. 1995. Women, war and rape: Challenges facing the international tribunal for the former Yugoslavia. *Human Rights Quarterly* 17, 4: 649-690.

Northrup, D., ed. 1994. *The Atlantic Slave Trade.* Lexington, MA: D.C. Heath and Company.

Odhiambo, T. 1993. *UNESCO World Science Report.* Paris: UNESCO.

Ohaegbulam, F.U. 1995. New world blacks and the emergence of African nationalism. *21st Century Afro Review,* 1, 3: 1-33.

Osaghae, E.E. 1995. The Origini Uprising: Oil politics, minority agitation and the future of the Nigerian State. *African Affairs: The Journal of the Royal African Society* 94: 376, 345-344.

Pacey, A. 1990. *Technology World Civilization: A Thousand-Year History.* Cambridge, MA: MIT Press.

Park, M. 1816. *Travels in the Interior Districts of Africa.* London: John Murray Publishers, Inc.

Pedersen, P.B. 1990. Social and psychological factors of brain drain and reentry among international students: A survey of the topic. *McGill Journal of Education* 25, 2: 229-243.

Peil, M. 1995. Ghanaians abroad. *African Affairs: The Journal of the Royal African Society* 94,376: 345-367.

Peters, E. 1996. Afrocentricity: Problems of logic, method and nomenclature. *21st Century Afro Review* 2, 1:1-44.

Pinkney, A. 1993. *Black Experience.* Englewood Cliffs, N.J.: Prentice Hall.

Posner, M.I. 1989. *Foundations of Cognitive Science.* Cambridge, MA: The MIT Press.

Redford, D.B. 1992. *Egypt, Canaan and Israel in Ancient Times.* Princeton, N.J.: Princeton University Press.

Rey, P.P. 1975. The lineage mode of production. *Critique of Anthropology* 3: 17-79.

Rothschild, D., and A.J. Growth. 1995. Pathological dimensions of domestic and international ethnicity. *Political Science Quarterly* 110, 1: 69-82.

Sadri, A. 1992. *Max Weber's Sociology of Intellectuals.* New York: Oxford University Press.

Sagini, M.M. 1997. African consciousness: The global idea. Paper presented at the MAAAS Regional Conference, at the University of Oklahoma, Summer.

Sagini, M.M. 1996. *The African and the African-American University: An Historical and Sociological Analysis.* Lanham, MD: The University Press of America.

Schraeder, P.J. 1995. Review essays: Understanding the "Third Wave" of democratization in Africa. *The Journal of Politics* 57, 4: 1160-1168.

Segal, R. 1995. *The Black Diaspora.* New York: Farrar, Strauss and Giroux.

Stamp, K.M. 1956. *The Peculiar Institution: Slavery in the Ante-Bellum South.* New York: Random House Inc.

Toews, J.E. 1991. Historically psychoanalysis: Freud in his time and our time. *The Journal of Modern History* 63, 3: 504-545.

United Nations. 1990. *World Population Monitoring 1989. Special Report: The Population Situation in Less Developed Countries.* New York: UN Publications.

United Nations. 1988. *World Population Prospects.* New York: UN Publications.

Verlinden, C. 1953. Les origines coloniales de la civilization Atlantique. *Journal of World History,* 5, 2: 230-355.

Weber, M. 1903-1917 1949. *The Methodology of Social Sciences.* Glencoe: Free Press.

Weiner, M. 1995. *The Global Migration Crisis: Challenges to States and Human Rights.* New York: Harper Collins College Publishers.

Welch, C.E. Jr. 1991. The African Commission on Human Rights: A five-year report and assessment. *The Journal of Modern African Studies* 29, 4: 43-61.

Wolpe, H. 1972. Capitalism and cheap labor power in South Africa: From segregation to apartheid. *Economy and Society* 1, 4: 425-456.

Wyk, K.V., and V.B. Manton. 1988. The debate on South Africa's strategic minerals revised. *Comparative Strategy,* 7, 2: 159-172.

Chapter 19

Conclusion — A Comparative and Deconstructive Critique: The New Paradigm for the Third Millennium

To a large extent, the modern organization is an evolutionary product of industrial and postindustrial era. Industrial organizational modernization took place between 1760 and 1950s. For almost two hundred years, the evolutionary development of industrial organizations was characterized by immense scientific and technological breakthroughs in the areas of "agriculture, medicine, communications, transportation, energy, chemicals, electronics" and other areas (Shrivastava, 1995, p. 119). Within these two hundred years, the tempo of scientific and technological progress was more highly pronounced during the latter century. The inherent byproduct of massification of industrial production is risk. The proponents of the theories of industrial modernization and its effects are Karl Marx, Habermas and Parsons. These utopian evolutionists downplay organizational effects, discontinuities and crises in the ecological zone. These eminent and scholarly theoreticians use "concepts of development of means of production, communicative rationality...structural differentiation and functional integration as mechanisms behind the exceptional evolutionary economic and social transformation" (p. 119). This was the period of "big is the best and only way." The industrial revolution was viewed as a form of rational progress (Habermas, 1989; Parsons, 1982; Halpern and Stern, 1998; and Zey, 1998).

In their institutional form, these organizations, particularly those in the public sector, were made up of regulative, normative and cognitive elements that were harnessed to secure stability and meaning. The same organizations tended to respond to institutional pressures not only through compliance, but by crafty "avoidance, defiance, manipulation" and creative resistance (Scott, 1998, p. 1048).

Modern organizational postindustrialism is 40 years old particularly in Western industrialized societies. The economic, political and social characteristics of this era include but are not limited to the following conditions: "(a) much of the economic production occurs in service and high-technology sectors; (b) there is increasing globalization of finance, production, labor, and product markets; (c) economic growth is confronted with ecological limits; and (d) there is a movement toward democratization of markets and politics" (Shrivastava, 1995, p. 119; Bell, 1975; and Giddens, 1990). A number of scholars of whom Beck (1992a), Douglas and Wildarsky (1992), and Lash (1993) have credibly argued that the side effects of the evolutionary transformation of organizations from the industrial to the postindustrial state has made them and their communities to become ecocentrically risky. By the term evolutionary I do not mean the Darwinian biological processes of variation, selection and retention, but evolutionary notion connotes changes which evolve from adaptive and dynamic problem solving capacity of organizations. The knowledge base for adaptive organizational creativity and problem solving does not rest with the organization per se, it is a product of creative individuals within the organization (Baum and Singh, 1994).

To What Extent is Risk a Problem?

Risk is destructive and complex exposure to loss, injury, danger and uncertainty. The realm of social science disciplines has analyzed the concept of risk in a variety of ways. First, psychologists define risk in terms of perceptual and psychological loss that can be measured psychometrically (Slovic, 1989). Second, economists view risk in terms of uncertainty because of the potential for economic gains and losses. Uncertainty can be measured with the use of models of statistical probability. Third, in a volatile climate of financial uncertainty, analysts view risk to be associated with "market risks, inflation risk, liquidity risk, credit risk, interest rate risk, currency risk, structural risk, reinvestment risk, and prepayment risk" (Shrivastava, 1995, p. 120 and Bernstein, 1992). Fourth, sociologists understand that risks are social processes and established ways of handling hazards (Krimsky and Golding, 1992; Perrow, 1984; and Short and Clarke, 1992). For academic institutions, risk may be associated with uncertainty concerning funding formulas and budget deficits, interinstitutional competition for faculty, students' reform and over expansion, and funds for research and development—problems that face most private institutions (Mingle and Associates, 1981).

Sociologically, risk as it applies in this chapter, is a "systematic way of dealing with hazards and insecurities" that have been brought about by modernizational processes of industrial and postindustrial organizations (Shrivastava, 1995, p. 120). Risk is a product of modernization risks that are concomitant elements in the struggle for the production of industrial wealth. Modernization processes which try to satisfy human needs with the use of technological production and productivity create new wealth. "Exponential growth in the productive forces unleashes hazards, potential threats and risks...excessive production of hazards and ecologically unsustainable consumption of natural resources are the root source of modern risks" (p. 120).

During classical industrial society, i.e., 100 years ago, "the logic of risk wealth production dominated the logic of risk production" (p. 120). At that time, risks were not only minor side effects, but they also were inevitable externalities of the production processes. During the last 40 years of postindustrial society, the relationship has changed because the logic of risk production and distribution has become dominant in all processes of social change. "Just as production and distribution of wealth (social welfare) were central organizing concepts in the classical industrial society, risk is the central organizing concept of the postindustrial society" (p. 120). This society is "the risk society" in which "the productive forces have left their innocence in the reflexivity of modernization processes" (Beck, 1992a, pp. 12-13). Increasing and ceaseless production and accumulation of wealth tends to reinforce risk potential and potential for risk.

Risks influence systematic and irreversible harm on humans and the natural environment. Linguistically, risks can be defined as causative agents. Knowledge about their existence can be realistically "changed, modified, magnified, channeled and dramatized" to enhance their definition and social construction (Clarke, 1989). Although risk can be defined scientifically, "scientific rationality is no longer an adequate arbiter of risk disputes" (p. 20). The dialectical relationship between corporations and the public synergistically produces scientific interpretations that are reflective of their respective political interests. In other words risk knowledgeability and expertise is associated with great political power. Also, since risk politicizes scientific knowledge, it is capable of casting doubt on social and scientific rationalities (Nelkin, 1979).

Risks are not accidents of historical periodicity. They characterize every era and civilization. They may be viewed as acts of God or nature (earthquakes, plagues, pestilence, diseases, famines, droughts, etc.). Attribution on these risks lay without the province of society. Contrary to such naturally and mythically induced risks, modern risks are attributed to a lack of internal mechanisms for controlling problems that are the inevitable products of their productive creativity. As a result of such a lack, people depend on "political, economic, social and organizational" decisions to resolve the risks. In other words, "risks are not caused by people's ignorance of solutions; they are caused by unintended and unforeseen effects of the solutions themselves" (Shrivastava, 1995, p. 121). In other words, the source of danger is inventive scientific and technological knowledge rather than managerial or organizational ignorance (Beck, 1992a)

Contrary to ancient risks of societal antiquity,

> Modern risks are rooted in ecologically destructive industrialization and are global, pervasive, long-term, imperceptible, incalculable, and often unknown. Radio activity and chemical contamination or exemplars of such risks. Risks emanating from Chernobyl nuclear accident were geographically pervasive, temporally transgenerational, crossed national boundaries, and remain incalculable. Ecological degradation contradicts the interests that advance industrialization, and it has differential impacts on people. Differential distribution of risks puts people in different social risk positions. Risks cross-economic class, gender, ethnic, generational and national boundaries. Risk positions exacerbate inequalities based on these variables, but wealth or power does not provide complete protection from modernization risks (Shrivastava, 1995, p. 121).

The risks adversely affect those who produce them without discrimination. In other words, since these risks transcend their traditional boundaries, their harmful effects are classless, raceless, nationless and genderless. The risks do not discriminate without merciless indiscrimination (Clarke, 1989; and Luhmann, 1990).

The science of producing risk, spreading or diffusing risk and commercializing it is inherent in capitalistic and socialistic modes of production through which human needs are not only articulated, but, the satisfaction of those needs is an element of societal self-edification and self-referencing. "Modernization, in seeking economic growth, inadvertently but systematically unleashes risks and hazards. Once created, such risks can expand and evolve independently of economic gains" (p. 121).

Risk has proliferated and its influence has become a global problem in terms of "population explosion, industrial pollution, environmental degradation and lack of institutional capacity for risk management" (p. 121). For instance, the world population has increased from 2.8 billion to 5.65 billion during the last 40 years (Getis, Getis, and Fellmann, 1998). In the next 40 years, it will double and reach 11.3 billion. Such an uncontrollable expansion becomes a risky ecological burden on the earth's ecosystems particularly when their natural resources are depleted (Ehrlich and Ehrlich, 1991). Furthermore, over 50% of the world's fish resources have been depleted in 50 years. Over 42,000 square miles of wildlife—tropical and rain forest are destroyed annually. Industrial agriculture contributes to soil degradation in terms of dehumusification, erosion, destruction of natural habitats and pollution and reduction of water table supply systems. Above all, the annual desertification of 26,000 square miles of productive land is a further risk in terms of human incapability to manage nature's bounty for his or her own long-term survival. To make matters worse, the rates of consumption growth in world reserve oil, natural gas, coal and minerals are likely to be depleted within a single century if these natural resources are not consumed with caution. The current population needs 3 to 15% annual increase in world production of goods and services in order to create a viable and balanced momentum for ecological sustainability (Clark, 1989; Daly, 1977; McNeill, 1989; and *World Commission on Environment and Development*, 1987).

The risks of industrial pollution to human health have diffused to become "urban air pollution, smog, global warming, ozone depletion, acid rain, toxic waste sites, nuclear hazards, obsolete weapons arsenals, industrial accidents and hazardous products" (Shrivastava, 1995, p. 122). For example, the United States alone has more than "30,000 documented uncontrolled toxic waste sites" which increase at the rate of 2,000 to 3000" annually (p. 122; Carson, 1962).

The pollution and mismanagement of the environment and organizations particularly in the "weapons policy" area seemed to have been built on "convoluted logic." For instance, Charles Bandy has argued in *The Age of Paradox* that both the two rival twentieth century superpowers manufactured more and more weapons of mass destruction but these missiles with multiple warheads did not only lead to less and less security, but the management of these weapons became more and more numerically unmanageable. Their management became less and less secure as knowledge of their production increased and the wisdom of handling them became more and more obsolete. In managerial leadership terms, "wisdom is the capacity to endure despair, and to endure despair means to face and to bear the hopelessness" (Sievers, 1993, p. 265).

The organizations of the military industrial complex were so hopelessly addicted to power, lust and greed that the admission of such a situation became paradoxical. These organizations demand the leadership of ethical, moral and spiritual quality which would save civilization from the madness of nuclear accidents and a potentially dangerous path toward nuclear winter (Bandy, 1994). In addition, industrial and postindustrial corporations and governments need to be actively involved in continuous organizational restructuring as an adaptive and dynamic experience. Adaptive restructuring should be externally induced and based on an active market for corporate control. However emphasis should be placed on the need for and effectiveness of voluntary restructuring which is internally based (Donaldson, 1994). Such restructuring, it must be made clear, has winners and losers. As a whole, voluntary restructuring is a form of strategic change, and an effective and workable internal governance system.

Corporations and governments accumulate risks without adequate remedies. It will take up to $150 billion a year to clean up this "mess." Proliferation of environmental and technological risk is self-policed, it is unmanageable, accidents escalate continually (Perrow, 1984) and the situation is worse outside the U.S. "Technoenvironmental" risks have caused people to experience skepticism and "increased dependency on obscure and inaccessible social institutions and actors. NIMBY (not in my backyard) grassroots movement has evolved in the U.S. to resist the activities of corporate and regulatory agencies. NIMBY resists the development of hazardous industrial and urban development projects in U.S. communities (Couch and Kroll-Smith, 1991; Goldstein and Shorr, 1991; Krimsky and Golding, 1992). Chernobyl-Russian, Exxon Valdez-U.S. and Bhopal-India, are industrial accidents whose incidence has provoked global consciousness about the danger of technoenvironmental risks and the essence of effective regulatory efforts (Mitroff and Pauchant, 1990; and Smith, 1992).

Given the traditional management paradigm in which technoenvironmental risks have undermined the entire reservoir of managerial wisdom, "it is not sufficient to manage corporations to optimize production variables, such as profits, productivity, jobs, and growth. Corporations must manage risk variables, such as product harm, pollution, waste, resources, technological hazards, and worker and public safety" (Shrivastava, 1995, p. 123).

There are four eras of corporate environmentalism in which regulatory, normative, mimetic and cognitive measures were taken to regulate environmental risk. First, industrial environmentalism (1960-1970) focused on internal cognitive and mimetic institutions. Second, regulatory environmentalism (1970-1982) focused on compliance of regulatory and coercive institutions with the law. Third, environmentalism (1982-1988) as social responsibility focused on pollution prevention and waste reduction caused by external industry associations and voluntary or normative institutions. Finally, strategic environmentalism (1988-1993) focused on top management and board integration of environmental strategies that are proactive (cognitive and mimetic institutions). While industry and nonprofit associations became the driving forces of environmentalism, social responsibility, investors, insurance companies and competitors were influential in strategic environmentalism (Osterman, 1996).

The ecological system which technoenvironmental risks have severely impaired is not addressed as one of the mature goals of management theory and practice. It is, however, one of the many sociotechnical problems, which challenge the vitality, and viability of the corporate sector. Other problems that are less ecosystemic include but are not limited to "race and gender discrimination, business ethics and fraud, corporate philanthropy, minority concerns, community welfare, and stakeholder demands (Shrivastava, 1995, p. 124; Carroll, 1979; and Preston, 1985). Some of these problems can be solved if ethical and moral conduct of organizations were reinforced (Etzioni, 1988).

How Organizations Solve Problems: Think Tanks

Public organizations recruit idea brokers who are the think tanks or the policy elite. These elitist intellectuals hold advanced degrees in astrophysics, engineering or the social sciences. The think tanks are consultative scientific experts whose advice on solving technical social problems is based on contextualizable policy research. The Evolution of the think tank movement started during the progressive era when it addressed child and family issues. Frederick Taylor's gospel of scientific management and efficiency characterized the progressive era with the use of scientific authority in solving budgetary and planning problems (Smith, 1991) in public agencies and institutions. Later, the confluence of business interests and philanthropy with those of the academic social scientists worked for the New York Bureau of Municipal Research. Subsequently, the Bureau became known as the Brookings Institution in 1927.

President Wilson used the advise of scholars and businessmen to organize the domestic front during World War I. Although he was an academic himself, he was not comfortable with experts even when he took some to Versailles to witness the signing of the armistice. Roosevelt used "the Brains Trust" in formulating the New Deal philosophy. The Brains Trust included economists and scholars from Harvard University including John Maynard Keynes whose ideas he valued greatly. These scholars assisted him in constructing a strong economy which also became a welfare or liberal society. The Brookings scholars who are ideologically conservative did not like to work in the FDR's administration.

During the Cold War and immediately after the Second World War, RAND (Research and Development) was created to replace government contracts particularly in the defense industry. Both RAND and Hudson Institute became involved by "thinking the unthinkable" concerning the nuclear war. Their affiliate scholars were bound by top secret security classifications. These professional institutions became resourceful and contributed to game theory, systems theory and the planning, programming and budgeting (PPBS) model of bureaucratic management in terms of policy formulation.

As RAND idea brokers and researchers became more sensitive to and specialized in Cold War and Vietnam era matters, the Brookings Institution got involved in Public policy analysis in areas of social programs during the Kennedy and Johnson administrations. The Kennedy administration is credited for hiring the brightest and most effective minds in America to deal with domestic and foreign policy agenda. These 1960s think tanks rendered their services to both the university and the political establishment.

The policy research institutes are about 100 years old. Some of these institutes are the partisan advocacy think tanks such as the Heritage Foundation and the American Enterprise Institute. The evolution of these institutes developed with their being funded by the ideologically conservative New Right. Their goal is to become a source for building a structure for intellectual infrastructure comparable to the variant intellectual elite of the liberal establishment. Smith (1991) has not only described how policy research institutions evolved and served society, but, he has also shown the relationship between power and knowledge in terms of the extent to which specialists are used to generate evaluative public policy in a democratic society. In other words, social science expertise, at least for 100 years, has been used to solve the problems of modern industrial society in order to accommodate and legitimize the classical and traditional efficiency of mechanistic Taylorism and bureaucratic rationality.

Though these institutions have become highly specialized, secretive in their analytical traditions and more public relations oriented, they have become apathetic to their scholastic roots. As a result, historians, political scientists, public administrators and journalists who use their ideas may not solve problems effectively. Consequently, there are risks, crises, and doubt in public and corporate organizations which deal with the maintenance of structures rather than the efficient and effective execution of humanistic, emancipatory and managerial processes in private and public organizations. These organizations have four main limitations.

Organizational Limitations and Challenges

First, most organizations were constructed during the industrial era. The traditional management paradigm is narrow and shallow rather than broad and deeply anchored in its existential reality. For instance, traditionally, management viewed the organization environment to be consisted of economic, political, social, and technological elements. Its economic aspects rationalized the viability of markets, industrialists, competitors and regulatory influences. This traditional definition of the management paradigm ignored the natural environment of which the biosphere, hydrosphere, heliosphere and the ecosystem are paramount. In other words, the organizational environment should not only constitute the "economic, social, technological, and political elements, but also biological, geological and atmospheric ones" (Shrivastava, 1995, p. 125). Of these, the business environment comprises of "(a) the ecology of the planet earth; (b) the world economic, social, and political order; and the immediate market, technological, and sociopolitical context of organizations" (Shrivastava, 1995, p. 125' Davis, 1991; Emery and Trist, 1965; Fahey and Narayanan, 1984, and Stead and Stead, 1992). Only few organizations have started to use this expanded concept of new management paradigm because most of them still see organizational environments to be in "abstract, disembodied, and ahistorical" (Shrivastava, 1995, p. 125) that need to be procured, exploited and unbundled. This is a denatured conception of the environment.

Second, the production/consumption role or biases are organizational assumptions rooted in traditional management paradigm, which reinforce environmental degradation in Western and global industrialism. This consumption-production bias of organizational functionalism assumes that business organizations are neutral, rational and technologically based systems of production which provide service to stakeholders. Business, educational, and scholarly activities are used to improve organizational productivity and efficiency. The emphasis placed on production is destructive because management ignores the damaging influences of unrestricted production which becomes the sources of "externalities" such as "environmental pollution, toxic products and wastes, and technological and occupational hazards and risks" (p. 125). In addition, the promotion of the concept of consumerist society by the traditional management school has contributed to the problems emanating from unrestrained consumption. More than $120 billion are used for advertising at the detriment of environmental degradation and abuse of public health (Commoner, 1990; Rao, 1998). Rao argues that organizational forms are cultural objects that are formed by existing institutional, entrepreneurial and professional interests that are politically enshrined. Organizational forms that are not ascendant have lost their cultural frames because they do not enjoy political, professional and entrepreneurial support. Since they have lost the frames, they can exit, migrate or join the ascendant ones. In this case, their boundaries and cultural contents are formed by politics (Rao, 1988).

Third, traditional management paradigm has a bias toward financial risks. Financial risk, which is dominant in business studies, is associated with financial and product markets. Financial risk is assessed and managed in respect to economic performance. Managers also "manage product—market risks that involve uncertainty about product demand caused by changing economic conditions, consumer preferences, market demographics, competitive pressures, and regulatory changes" (Shrivastava, 1995, p. 126). The organizational management ignores risks particularly those which are connected with "technology, its location, its waste products, and its impact on the natural environment. This mindset ignores the numerous ecological, technological and health risks" (p. 126) which radiate from industrial hazards.

Fourth, traditional management paradigm treats the environment anthropocentrically. Its ideology stresses the "separateness, uniqueness, primacy, and superiority of the human species" (p. 126). This understanding makes it legitimate for humans to unbundle the environment exploitatively and carelessly. Nature can be preserved if its preservation strengthens human interest. The purpose of preserving it is to create potential for its future maximum and amoral exploitation regardless of the preconditions to the contrary. Such an attitude is deeply rooted in classical economic theory of property rights and free market, a notion which disregards the protection of natural resources (Daly and Cobb, 1989).

Traditionally, organizations have lost their "souls" because they have contributed to risk, crisis and despair. At their innermost "souls," they reveal "shadows, disorderliness, and meaninglessness because they have marginalized multicultural (global) ethical and ecological concerns for the purpose of achieving unachievable goals – excellence (Pauchant, 1998). Even when these organizations downsize to control costs, such downsizing is productively ungainful rather than profitable (Harris, 1998).

The Need for New Management Paradigms: Critical and Radical Humanism

The traditional management paradigm of classical industrialism has lost its causes. The paradigm is "anti-biosphere, unecosystem" and a health risk which physically, psychologically and economically alienates the natural environment, employees and workers from itself. Since mainstream management theories suffer from a paucity of theoretical and paradigmatic assumptions concerning newly emerging and dynamic organizational paradigms for postindustrial organizations, it is the purpose of this book to offer elegant and conclusive observations on a new theoretical model that is desirable for the visionary, emancipatory and "humanistically" rooted global and postindustrial organizations. As a result, management theorists, practitioners, and bureaucrats should integrate such a concept in order to better understand how to replace traditional and Taylorist functionalism with the emerging radical, neoMarxist and humanistic and structural tradition. The new management paradigm will ... "transform the passive-obedient Taylorist employee into an active-cooperative one" (Aktouf, 1992, p. 407). By doing so, organizational management and research agencies need to adopt such a global view of humanity in order to legitimately give employees and workers sizeable control over their working environments. In the "new world order," technology will be viewed as a physical and structural medium of communicative practices through which organization members actively participate to advance liberal, radical and neofeminist agenda for the purpose of transforming organizational communication in order to overcome the inefficient ineffectiveness of traditional and patriarchal structures, practices and processes that unnaturally and severely alienate and subordinate women and other organizational "outsiders" (Kovacic, 1998).

The new organizational paradigm will be used by theoretical and practical organizational management to integrate economic, social, rational and cognitive powers in order to interpret the historical and professional context of organizational operations. These leaders need to realistically analyze the demographic composition of their organizations, identify their diverse and homogeneous strengths and weaknesses, use their strengths for influencing organizational change and institutional advancement, and establish viable and credible systems of control that provide incentive systems for strengthening and monitoring surveillance, socialization, and the role of organizational culture in enhancing organizational vitality. These mechanisms are commonly used by excellent organizations for exercising power and influence for ratifying the bargaining power of the same organizations. Above all, organizations should be physically and sociologically designed to concentrate not on what they do, but rather on the practices and processes of how they do it (London, 1998).

While Japan and the Pacific Rim countries have made great strides in the improvement of their postindustrial management models which are rooted in strong economic, political, cultural and technological traditions, Western management models of productivity and industrial efficiency have become socially, morally, economically and technologically inferior and risk or crisis prone. They are obsessed with short-term profits, myopic negligence and outright recklessness in both the private and public sectors (Brown, 1990; Cans, 1990; Dumont, 1988, Etzioni, 1989; Lovelock, 1979; Mintzberg, 1989; Morgan, 1986; and Pestel, 1988). Such a state of affairs requires management scholars and practitioners to think and act radically by implementing "a dialectico-conflictual vision" (Aktouf, 1992, p. 408) comparable to that of the historical Marxist tradition which will challenge and replace the risky elements of "consensual functionalism" (p. 408). Though prominent management and organization scholars including Crozier (1989), Mintzberg (1989), and Peters and Waterman (1982) have advocated a systematic and thorough reassessment of the classical, traditional and industrial Western management models, these scholars have not changed the fundamental ideological assumptions upon which the traditional management practices are based. This static philosophical perspective which clings to the past, calls for management thinkers and practitioners to search for excellence in the radical humanistic tradition of "self-actualization, ... cohesiveness, ... commitment, ... mobilization" (Aktouf, 1992, p. 408). Humanism is radical because it is a departure from past ineffective management traditions. Its humanism centers "attention and debate on the 'person', his or her deeds, sense of self, and pivotal role in all organized activities" (p. 408).

Reformist Managerial Debates on Humanism

Since the 1970s, there has been an attempt carried by prolific scholars in management circles, to deconstructively criticize the traditional management model of "utilitarian functionalism and neoclassical economic thought (Burrell and Morgan, 1979; Caille, 1989; Etzioni, 1989; and Perrow, 1986). These debates have evolved as a result of Japan's economic pre-eminence and dominant role in world markets (Lee, 1980; Ouchi, 1981; Pascale and Athos, 1981; and Peters and Waterman, 1982). The corporate culture of traditional management paradigms is under attack as the Japanese Keiretsu explained in *In Search of Excellence* by Peters and Waterman (1982) and in *Theory Z* by Ouchi (1981). This type of literature shows how the "manager was asked to become a hero, a creator of myths and values, a catalyst for the constellation of symbols to mobilize an enthusiastic industrial workforce galvanized for productivity and unflagging" performance (Shrivastava, 1992, p. 409; and Peters and Austin, 1985). In addition, Japan is known for employing "total quality ... quality circles, zero stock systems and zero faults of just-in-time" manufacturing (Shrivastava, 1992, p. 409); Crosby, 1979; and Duncan, 1974). Repetitively, certain terms like team spirit, shared values, common project and quality circles have been articulated to radicalize managerial thinking and practices (Archier and Serieyx, 1988; DePree, 1989; and Scherkenbach, 1988). Grafted into these commonly used terms is the interest expressed in terms of managerial styles such as "cohesiveness, complicity, initiative, and creativity" at the three levels of organizational management. Evidence indicates that these debates emphasize the practice of "common values, teamspirit, initiative, collaboration, equity, quality, morality and honesty" (Shrivastava, 1992, p. 409).

Up until the end of the 1970s, Taylorism and Fordism of the traditional and classical management philosophy still maximized production targets with speed. Firms gained control of the product and range of products which were used for flooding the market. Managers used theories for harnessing production techniques and faster instruments of production in plants. Firm employees and workers executed orders diligently and obediently. The excellent employee was the "right person at the right place" (p. 409). He executed plans that were developed by contracted, paid and intelligent thinkers, management analysts and planners. The role of managers and theorists was to motivate and mobilize employees to deal with specialization of labor, technical division of tasks and cost effectiveness. These concerns made work less attractive and more dull and meaningless. For example, Henry Ford remarked that hundreds of tasks were suitable for the mentally and physically challenged. His engineers harnessed the assembly line for the Model T in which "a portion of a man would be paid a portion of salary" (Toffler, 1980, p. 71 and Shrivastva, 1992, 1992, p. 410).

Like the Japanese, the Germans' and Swedes' who believe in excellence, production objectives are no longer purposed to produce products " faster and faster and at the lowest cost, but it is to produce them qualitatively, creatively and reliably. In other words, the concept of efficiency is no longer tenable. It is under attack. All employees must be active and intelligent workers. But champions are heros and skunkworkers whose bold and maverick behavior are reflections of the passion for excellence" (Peters, 1987).

The Western management style that is rooted in classical, industrial and patriarchal managerial traditions is characterized by "economism, shortsightedness, utilitarianism, and mechanistic technicism" (Shrivastava, 1995; Aktouf, 1992, p. 411; Etzioni, 1989; Minc, 1990; and Mintzberg, 1989). The management style is authoritarian rather than humanistic, emancipatory and empowerment-driven. Its authoritarianism is imposed on the organization by the organizational leaders. Its successive waves of scientism, instead of the scientific tradition, have unstrategically invaded the fields of "Taylorism, behavioral sciences, decision making, management information systems, office systems and robotics" (Aktouf, 1992, p. 411). To chart new directions for managerial practice requires a system that socializes employees to belong to, to excel in and to serve the firm with cooperation, distinction, intellect and commitment.

This traditional, classical and Taylorist model of management style treats the worker and the employee as an appendage or "instrument of paradigm, as some sort of 'needs-driven mechanism,' as a rational and avid maximizer of profits, as a resource to be exploited and monitored, as cost to be controlled and minimized" (p. 411). To reverse this pessimistic attitude toward the employee who is the anchor and link pin of productivity, he/she should be seen not as a passive cog, but as an active, and potentially productive and frontline agent of organizational rationality, productivity and creativity. Given this understanding, the worker-employee does not then, deserve to be exploited and alienated, but rather, to be liberated, respected, and empowered in terms of autonomy, and "sharing of power, of management and decision-making rights, and of rights over means, profits, and so forth" (p. 412).

The relations of production under the traditional industrial model, are dialectical because they are rooted in historical materialism and exploitative classcism of Marxist intellectual and economic philosophy. This is seen in relation to how the worker is treated for his surplus labor which has surplus value (profits). These relations need to be changed symbolically in order to make corporate culture appealing to and supportive of the worker-employee without whose efforts no corporation will exist. The corporation then, should share profits, power, property and decision-making. Such actions will make the employee to feel that he belongs to the corporate culture where he is a "living" and "breathing ambassador for his or her firm" (p. 412).

Traditional management paradigms do not allow managers to give employees the freedom to exercise discretionary power because the former will lose power to authorize, control, command, govern and limit the influence they do not cherish. As a result, the employee who is viewed as resourceful human capital will find it difficult to be given power, control over profits and division of labor or specialization. In other words, emancipatory and radical humanism which attempts to disempower management through employee or worker liberation is viewed with distaste and skepticism. This traditional management paradigm is resistant to the new culture of synergy and collaboration which is characteristic of "convergence, closeness, and sharing" (p. 412).

What is Radical Humanism?

The scholarly and philosophically embedded scientific works of Marx, Freud, Evans-Pritchard, Sartre and to some extent Maslow have tried to answer "humankind's" quest for radical and emancipatory humanism. This radical departure from dogmatic authoritarian, and culturally established classical and industrial conventions is a challenge to the "only best way" assumptions of theoretical and managerial practices of the past. First, humanism is an intellectual, historical and philosophically established tradition of human destiny, 'self-consciousness' and emancipatory vocations. Its essence is to liberate humanity from the yoke of historical materialism, diachrony and structures of oppression, industrial and organizational dehumanization, organizational and cultural slavery by using right judgment, free will and self-actualization rather than predestination and myopic forms of patronage. In other words, and as Fromm (1961) has demonstrated, humanism is the concern for and articulation of the human-centered principles of integrity, development, dignity, liberty and involved participation through which his or her actions and capacities help to determine his/her place in history.

Second, in human history, it is known that by nature, humankind is a social and 'political animal' who lives in society that is community oriented. By living among others, humankind's relationships with others is used to help them reflect on their identity in terms of personality structure, selfworth, self-consciousness and economic and spiritual rationality. Regardless of his community status, historical technological and economic conditions caused humans to shift their preindustrial management and theoretical paradigm from organic to mechanical or mechanistic, or from Oikos to bureaucracy, or from one class to another. The change from one class or management system to another is a form of positive development in terms of the trajectory of human social evolution and organizational, corporate, and temporal advancement. In other words, the next evolutionary stage of the postindustrial society is its graduation from the patriarchal, mechanistic and narrow functionalistic management paradigm of the traditional and classical industrialism to the new model of humanistic, emancipatory, ecocentric and global paradigm.

Third, Karl Marx and other lesser writers on how the worker or employee is dehumanized and alienated by work in the work place, have contributed prolifically on the two subjects—dehumanization and alienation. Marx's works especially *Capital, The Manuscripts* (1844), *Misery of Philosophy* (1847), *Work, Salary and Capital* (1949), *Grundisse* (1857-1858), and *Contributions to the Critique of Political Economy* (1859-1861) are an excellent and original exposition on the place of the worker, conditions of service and the worker's evolutionary transition in the sea of historical (dialectical) materialism. The other writers on the subject of dehumanization and alienation of the worker-employee include but are not limited to Calvez (1970), Gramsci (1971), Heilbroner (1970, 1980), Kolakowski (1968), and Lucaks (1971). These writers have shown that human labor and the results of that labor are alienated from workers who produce the labor and its results (Kolakowski, 1987). An alienated worker is dehumanized. The worker is destroyed or dehumanized in the following way:

> The heart of the process of dehumanizing 'man' is alienation through work. "In this" primordial "process, the workers alienate themselves by selling their capacity for work (and their work, which would be a creative act) while contributing to the development and consolidation of forces (merchandise, profits, capital) which are exterior, foreign, and, in the final analysis, hostile to them and, thus, even more 'dehumanizing.' The finality pursued is no longer the person and what is most human in him or her (e.g., satisfaction of needs through utility value) but the 'unlimited growth of exchange value' (Aktouf, 1992, p. 414).

This quote is a reflection that the worker's consciousness of himself is alienated by social, economic and political structures whose goal of production is crisis and contradiction-prone and therefore criticizable for dehumanization and alienation. In other words, "the alienated person is neither different, nor cut off from the 'proletarian' caught up in production relations that are structurally, materially, and historically determined and dialectically inscribed in a spiral of contradictions" (p. 415).

Fourth, the human being (worker) is treated as an object rather than the subject. Sartre (1948, 1966, and 1976) argues that the worker or employee is treated with bad 'faith' which reinforces the "false consciousness" and "alienation" discussed earlier. According to Evans-Pritchard human beings are viewed mechanistically as disalienated organisms or strategic "termites" which exist to be anthropocentrically manipulated. Since they are not subjects, they are objects not ruled by "reasons, feelings and choices" (p. 415) rather than 'causes.' They are forced, other-determined, or alienated, objectified, reified and instruments of "disalienation" (p. 415).

Radical humanism is rationalized by critical theorists who advocate the initiation of emancipatory managerial and organizational practices. Emancipation as a concept evolved with the Frankfurt school advanced by critical theorists who like Foucault, are proponents of poststructuralism. These theorists argue that emancipation is the process through which people become "freed from repressive social and ideological conditions, in particular those that place socially unnecessary restrictions upon the development and articulation of human consciousness. The intent of critical theory is to facilitate clarification of the essence of human need and opportunity to be autonomous, free, reflective and expressive in personal and social life (Alversson and Willmott, 1992, p. 432).

Critical and humanistically emancipatory theorists who believe in the Enlightenment tradition advocate the changing of institutions, e.g., the "divine-right of kings, the church, feudal bondage and prejudiced and superstitious ideas" (p. 435) because of their repressive underpinnings. The theorists assert that social science can and should contribute to the liberation of people from unnecessary "restrictive traditions, ideologies, assumptions, power relations, identity formations...that inhibit or distort opportunities for autonomy, clarification of genuine needs and wants, and thus greater and lasting satisfaction" (p. 435; Fay, 1987; Fromm, 1976; Habermas, 1971, 1984; Horkheimer and Ardono, 1947; and Marcuse, 1964).

Postmodernism

Emancipatory and critical humanism are elements of post-modernism. The former is Marxist and historically dialectical, the latter is normatively deconstructive and in line with feminist patriarchy and antihegemonic stability. Semantically, post-modernism is different from postmodernism. Post-modernism is the period which succeeded modernity. The unhyphenated post-modernism is the theoretical tradition which originated with the deconstructive French poststructuralists such as Derrida, Foucault, Deleuze, Guattari and Lyotard (Bergquist, 1993).

Weberian bureaucratic hierarchy is associated with modernism rather than post-modernism. The post-modern management paradigm advocates "flatter hierarchies, decentralized decision making, greater capacity for tolerance for ambiguity, permeable internal and external boundaries, empowerment of employees, capacity for renewal, self-organizing units, and self-integrating coordination mechanisms. Leadership in these new organizations seems to reflect a shift from maintaining rational control to leadership without control" (Daft and Lewin, 1993, p. ii).

The post-modern organizational paradigm cannot be rationalized by traditional organization theory which is rooted in mechanistic Taylorism, Sino-Russian autarchy, Weberian bureaucratic hierarchy, Spencerian structuralism, Marxist historical materialism, Darwinian evolutionism, or the Japanese Keiretsu. The post-modern organization will be relatively structureless but processually oriented. It views the idea of stability as a situation which suppresses the process for the purpose of achieving uncontrollable control.

Post-modernism is rooted in tragic or existential instability by which humans are burdened. Philosophers such as Thales view the existential self to be unstable, indeterminate and unintegrated in (plans and interests) with the rest of the community or society. As a result, this leads to humility, limitation and ephemerality of human endeavor. Viewed from the political perspective, post-modernistic ideology, in its emancipatory rhetoric, sees that modernist ideology maintained and extended the power of a small elite to oppress them. This elite used its ideology of expression and established order that marginalized other groups. Other groups were disfavored parts of the greater self. For instance, the elitist political and ideological rhetoric marginalized "women, people of color and gays" by silencing them (*Academy of Management Review,* 1995, p. 216). In other words, modernist ideology "served to maintain and extend the power of a small, repressive elite" (p. 216). The post-modern period "is marked by the subversion and overthrow of the hegemony of modernist ideology and bureaucracy and the emergence of the voices and spontaneous expression of the previously suppressed" (p. 216). The "tools" for overthrowing the oppressors are democracy, globalism, multiculturalism intellectual synergy and calculated computation.

In other words, post-modernism wants to liberate the unfreed. Modernist organizations are too big and sluggish to compete with smaller ideologically vibrant and younger organizations. The ideology of bigness and obsession with certainty and control created problems the new organizations need to deal with (Bergquist, 1993). Post-modern organizations seek radical and irreversible change.

Premodern life organizations maintained the distinction between "organizational mission and boundary" (*Academy of Management and Review*, 1995, p. 217). For instance,

> ... both the mission and the boundary of the organization, especially the boundaries between working life and family life, were vague. This vagueness occurred because organizations directly served both the needs of the persons involved in them and the communities with which they transacted. Modern organizations, by contrast became entities that had needs in their own right to which individuals had to subordinate their own sense of purpose. These organizations came to be defined by their boundaries, by determinations of who and what was inside them, and they lost what sense of mission was derivable from the lives of their participants or the inhabitants of their environment" (p. 217).

Unlike premodernism which maintained the differences between the mission of the organization and the organizations boundary, modern organizations kept that difference vague subordinating individuality for the success of the organization's mission. However, post-modern organizations are responsive by competing in a world whose boundaries between organizations and the environment is also vague. "They want to define themselves not by who their employees are and what is in them, but by a clear sense of mission, of what they are doing" (p. 217). This is called strategic planning and organizational policy.

Like premodern organizational life then, post-modern organizations have become "an expression of human purpose, mission and community processes that highlight the importance of the question of social responsibility" – accountability (p. 217). Bergquist shows, in this analysis, that what is chaotic in one level of analysis is good common sense in another. Organization leaders in these situations, should try to make sense out of chaotic randomness. Such leaders should be spiritually courageous rather than being technically practical. Such leaders bring community, spirituality and courage in the sea of irrationality, immaturity and irresponsibility where "organizational structure is replaced by spontaneous networking and random conversation" (p. 218). Central to this commentary is the idea that there is no elite and dominant control in the post-modern order because it has been replaced by freedom. Loyalty to self is more important than being loyal to the organization. Such loyalty should not be used selfishly, unresponsibly. It should be used ecocentrically.

The purpose of this critique is to use critical, emancipatory and post-modern humanism to assess traditional, modern and post-modern organizations. Traditional organizational management paradigms have been theoretically discredited by leftist and post-modern theoretical, critical, and emancipatory thought. Traditional management paradigm is rooted in conservative, radical and liberal socioeconomic and ethical philosophy rather than on neodialectical historicism. Since traditional management paradigms have lost their "salinity" and become relatively dysfunctional, archaic, and repressive, the purpose of this chapter and certainly the entire volume is to assist in constructing a model whose vision is ecocentrically and globally sustainable. This paradigm is an ambitious project which should be modeled on by all organizations of all kinds in the democratic and authoritarian nations. This model is not only experimental and incomplete, but it also helps to chart a new trajectory upon which human civilization and its institutional and organizational forms of productivity, distribution, service and consumption should be based.

Traditional management paradigm will be difficult and slow to change in both Western and global communities where industrial ecosystems will, due to differential technological and cultural influences, tend to slow down technocultural and ecocentric management systems which reinforce "interorganizational relations and internal organizational elements. Industrial ecosystems provide a vision of organizational populations and interorganizational relations that are compatible with bioregional natural systems" (Shrivastava, 1995, p. 127). Ecocentric and global management in contrast, "seeks ecologically sustainable organizational designs, practices and paradigmatic models.

If the ecocentric idea of organizational populations and inter and intra organizational relations can be based on ecological interdependence and the mini and macroecological performance of organizational communities, then the industrial ecosystem, which is a network of connected interdependent organisms and their environments that give and take resources from each other" will survive (p. 127) and be sustained. For instance, in a marine ecosystem, large fish eat small ones. Small fish feed on insects. Insects live on weeds and plankton. The "products of natural photosynthesis and waste fishes and insects serve as nourishment of weeds, plankton, and fish habitats" (p. 128). This example of self reliance is self-sufficient, environmentally safe and healthy and naturally regulated and dynamically balanced ecosystem—hence sustainability.

If the industrial ecosystems of the postindustrial society emulate the ecosystemic notion, interorganizational networks will join resources to minimize environmental degradation. In other words, industrial ecosystems should be designed to use each other's waste or byproducts and cooperate to share in order to minimize the wasteful use of natural resources (Allenby, 1993). Cooperation to facilitate local, regional, national and international (global) industrial ecosystems can sound complex and remote because of its ambitious and complex nature. However, if biolocally or bioregionally efficient and effective ecosystems will be desirably affordable for their resources, energy, markets, waste and pollution control they should be initiated on a gradual and rationally calculated and almost riskless pace (Frosch and Gallapoulos, 1992).

Focusing on organizations as elements of industrial ecosystems logically implies that basic reforms in their operational scope, strategies or missions, cost structures, location, theoretical insight and management practices need to occur. Creatable bioregional or biolocal organizations will require a new standard for product development, financing, entrepreneurship and infrastructure services (Shrivastava, 1995). The biolocal or bioregional ecosystem will be naturally rather than cybernetically self-regulated. Its energy and resource use and conservation will be more environmentally friendly and economically tenable than those of the traditional and industrial systems. The use of scientific knowledge to solve ecosystemic and postindustrial problems will demand the use of "many interdependent best ways" rather than the "one best way." In addition, "large-scale adoption of the industrial ecosystem model for restructuring interorganizational relations will require new economic and industrial regulations, new industrial infrastructure services, new roles for markets ... new markets for ecologically sound products" (p. 129). Theoretically a new discipline of industrial relations whose forces and relations of production will be different than those of the traditional industrial paradigm, will emerge (Allenby, 1993; Costanza, 1992; Naess, 1987; and the *World Commission on Environment and Development,* 1987).

The Mission of Postindustrial Management Paradigm (Global Ecocentricism)

The need for risk reduction, waste elimination, elimination of environmental pollution and maintenance of workplace safety and welfare are major concerns the old traditional and industrial management paradigm has failed to deal with. That failure has not only put human civilization on a wrong course of development, but it has increasingly demonstrated that if it is left unchecked, the finite depletion of the natural resources from the environment will in the long-run, cease us to be. Given this kind of scenario, a new management paradigm is imperatively required for the promotion of positive aspects of socioeconomic and post-modern and postindustrial relations. That model is the global ecocentric paradigm whose dynamic values have been compared with those of the traditional management paradigm of the old industrial order (see Table 19.1).

The new paradigm is expected to harmoniously function ecocentrically to promote the productive integration of the natural and nonnatural relationships of the ecosystem. To initiate and operationally rationalize the postindustrial ecosystem paradigm will involve the restructuring of "organizational goals, values, products, and production systems as well as organization, environment, and business functions" (Shrivastava, 1995, p. 130). As shown, Table 19.1 is a synthesis of the comparative values of the industrial management paradigm compared with the projected, postindustrial and ecosystem based management paradigm. The values are an antagonistic and dychotomous pair of the two paradigms none of which is purely devoid of the influences of the other.

Table 19.1. Traditional (Modern) versus Post-Modern (Millennial) Paradigm

Traditional Management Paradigm	21st Century Management Paradigm
Organizational Goals Economic development, profit, Shareholder wealth, mission	Sustainability, quality, stakeholder welfare
Organizational Values Anthropocentric, rationality and packaged knowledge, patriarchal values	Biocentric, ecocentric, global, intuitive awareness, humankind values including trust, honesty, courage, and synergy
Organizational Products Designed for specific function, style and price, packaged waste	Environmentally friendly designs
Production System Energy and resource intensive, technical efficiency	Low energy and resource use, environmental efficiency
Organization Hierarchical structure, top-down decision centralized high- income differentials	Relatively hierarchical structure, authority, participatory decision-making, decentralization of authority, medium to low income differentials
Organizational Environment Domination over nature, environment managed as infinite resource, pollution, waste are externalities	Harmony with and from nature, resources regarded as finite, pollution/waste risk and elimination and risk reduction management
Aim of Business Functions Marketing for increasing consumption, money making for short-term profit maximization, accounting is conveniently cost-reduction based, human resource management aims at increasing labor productivity	Marketing for consumer education, finance (money) aims at long-term sustainable growth, accounting focuses on environmental costs, human resource management aims at making work meaningful and the workplace safe and healthy
Organizational Theory and Ideology One best way-mechanistic and organismic orientation	Many theories-each suited for specific designs, functions and purposes
Organizational Personnel Relatively specialized, especially in public and profit-making arena	Will require highly specialized personnel to minimize or eliminate risk, waste especially in profit-making organizations
Organizational Problem Solving Use of structured problem-solving strategies	Use problem-solving processes

The postindustrial and ecosystem paradigm targets the creation of sustainable economic development and the improvement of quality life for stakeholders all over the world. The paradigm is a proposed and elegant model characterized by ecocentric and relatively informed postpatriarchal values that freely challenge the dominance of archaic and socioeconomically unhealthy systems of values particularly those which were dominant in traditional industrial order. Though the postindustrial paradigm places emphasis on intuition and understanding, these values should be used in the light of, rather than instead of scientific rationality. If they are not, then feminist patriarchy will just be as harmful as masculine patriarchy of the traditional industrial order.

The action consequences of ecocentric management are logically and derivatively connected with organizational aspects such as the mission, inputs, throughputs, and outputs. In terms of mission, the corporate mission of the traditional industrial order was narrow, nationally based rather than globally and ecocentrically oriented, and tactically short-ranged rather than strategically long-ranged. Their main marketing goal was to satisfy the demands of domestic stakeholders, both investors and customers and government agencies and local communities (David, 1989). Other than their interest in financial profits, ecocentrically managed corporations will harmoniously maximize their activities with the natural environment. The natural environment is considered to be a stakeholder in both the domestic and global arena. The missions of ecocentrically managed corporations will integrate the natural environment in their policy agenda (Campbell and Young, 1991). The alliance of the organization's strategies, structure, systems, processes and theoretical insight will be understood as a widely shared vision both within the ecosystems and the ecocentric and global environment. To be effective, ecocentrically managed corporations should lessen the use of "virgin materials and nonrenewable forms of energy, eliminate emissions, effluents and accidents and reduce the life-cycle cost of products and services" (Shrivastava, 1995, p. 131).

In relation to inputs, ecocentric management should not allow "uncontrollable organizational use of inputs in the form of natural resources and energy" (p. 132). The principle of sustainable use of natural resources should be maintained. "Sustainable use means pacing the exploitation of renewable resources in such a way that they can regenerate themselves through natural processes" (p. 132). The grounds for this argument is the realization that the earth's resources are finitely scarce and limited. The use of virgin materials and nonrenewable forms of energy can be minimized through the use of conservation techniques, recycling and renewable materials and energy and replenishment." For instance, the use of solar architectural design, energy-efficient fixtures, conservation programs and wind energy plants are examples of resource and energy conservation measures. Some parts of Holland and Scotland use wind energy.

The throughput system is the production processes that have traditionally been associated with environmental risks, occupational and public health risks, and waste. Ecocentric management is interested in the elimination of emissions, effluents and workplace hazards, risks and accidents. The aim of the production process is to attain "a zero discharge goal and a zero risk goal" (p. 132). Effort is focused on the virtual removal of waste. This is a preventive rather than controlling measure. The Dow Chemical ethylene plant in Fort Saskatchewan, Canada, is a classic example. In this plant, only 10 gallons per minute are used instead of 360 gallons per minute. This cost-saving strategy generates revenue and is cost-effective. The other two companies using it include 3M company's Pollution Prevention Pays Program (3P) and Water Reduction Always Pays Program (WRAP). For instance, "3M saved nearly $500 million and prevented 500,000 tons of pollution between 1975 and 1989" (p. 132). The function of the 3P program is to "eliminate or reduce pollution, save energy, or materials and resources, ..., demonstrate technological innovation, and ... save money" (p. 132).

The results of organizational throughputs is its outputs. Outputs consist of products and waste. Therefore, product choice and design have significant implications for the natural environment. For instance,

> Products that lack durability or are difficult to repair place greater demand on the resource base of new materials and energy products that are difficult or expensive to reuse or recycle result in unnecessary costs for waste and disposal. Ecocentric management seeks to minimize the life-cycle cost of its products and services. Life-cycle costs attach a monetary figure to energy impact of a product, i.e., disposal costs, legal fees, liability for product harm, loss of environmental quality, ... product-development decisions have been based not only on projected cash flow, but also on the projected future costs associated with each product design (p. 133).

Postindustrial managerial leadership tends to ecocentrically view organizational waste as both a business opportunity and as environmental risk. As a result, the designed waste management strategies include but are not limited to waste reduction, reuse, and landfilled. Both cost reduction and safe disposal of hazardous waste is great. The use of systems theory for managing ecocentricism is strategically and methodologically sound. However, at a later stage of ecocentricism's evolutionary advancement, other theoretical and methodological systems which address the particularity rather than the universality of ecocentric management may be used.

This conclusive chapter is a sharp critique of organizational theory and the industrial (modern) management paradigm whose philosophical, ideological and empirical values are rampantly infused with those of postindustrial and post-modern paradigms. The paramount theme of modernizational postindustrialism is the multiplicity of technological and environmental risks and crises. These externalities are caused by corporate and public agencies that use traditional methods of industrial production, distribution and consumption. One of the weaknesses of the traditional industrial paradigm is its incapacity to effectively respond to the demands of the risk society by being amelioratively ecocentric. The ecocentric and global management paradigm advances an ecologically centered conception of interorganizational relations and strategic rectification by being bioregionally and ecologically sustainable. Given this scenario which predates ecological interdependence, ecocentric management attempts to sustainably decrease environmental impact of organizational mission, inputs, and throughputs.

If the post-modern management and organizational paradigm employs benign and radically humanistic neo-Marxism for emancipatory an critical embourgeoisment, then the obedient and alienated Taylorist employee will be liberated to unleash energy for superior productivity, innovation, competitiveness, and cooperation.

The veracity, validity and reliability of postindustrial management paradigm will metaphorically be sustained by its "base, the engine, the consciousness and the superstructure" (Table 19.2). The base is the ecosystem because it acts as the supporting foundation or underlying concept upon which the observed logic and premise from which all reasoning concerning the ecocentric model emanates. The harmonious and balanced evolution of the ecosystem is governed by the laws of nature upon which the ecocentric paradigm is being paralleled. The engine of postindustrial ecocentricism are the processes of organizational leadership, organizational communication, organizational decision-making, organizational technology, organizational motivation, organizational control, organizational change, and organizational chaos and instability. The synergistic fusion of these processes produce energy for propelling the "engine" to relate itself to the base in dynamic, adaptive and productive ways.

Table 19.2. The Metaphor of Organizational Behavior

Base	Structure	Elements
	Ecosystem	The interactive, symbiotic and productive relationship between the living and nonliving environment
Engine		
	Processes	Organizational leadership, communication, decision-making, technology, motivation, control, change and instability
Consciousness		
	Theories	The rational system, the open system, the behavioral system, the ecocentric paradigm
Superstructure		
	Culture and the Disciplines	Diversity, culture, the social sciences, the behavioral sciences, scientific and technological knowledge

For the "engine" to revolve smoothly on the "base", it must be governed by its evolutionary "consciousness." The evolutionary consciousness of the "engine" whose base is deeply rooted in the ecosystem is the theoretical gamut from which the management philosophical ideology and tradition receives its attitudes, opinions and sensitivities for planning reenergizing, redirecting, and redesigning for organizational, individual, and groups of shareholders and stakeholders. And last but not least, the fourth attribute whose consciousness is energized by the engineered base is the "superstructure." The superstructure is a structure built on another structure. In other words, the issues of organizational diversity, organizational culture and the analytical use of the behavioral and social science disciplines collectively form the superstructure which rests on "a consciously engineered base" to enhance organizational and ecocentric sustainability. In other words, the consciously engineered base is harmoniously rationalized by the multifaceted, solvent, and mechanomorphic superstructure.

Within the American context, and perhaps in other contexts as well, organizational theory which is the managerial and philosophical organizational ideology (consciousness) is influenced by the dynamics of American cultural nationalism. For instance, and in some cases except in the least observed phenomena, American cultural nationalism is ideologically and hegemonically rather than critically or intellectually constructed. It is racially and economically exclusive. In principle, it asserts its Enlightenment ideological canons in terms of individualism, populism, egalitarianism, liberty and laissez-faire. Its belief in genetic neutrality as opposed to the other two contradictory positions demands that other groups within the mainstream culture, conform to their standards. When such expectations for conformity are rejected by racial, national and religious minorities, these various national groups organize themselves into collectivities or groups whose structures of gender, race, and class, are organized and structured by the elitist order within each category. Such ideological behavior is sanitized to influence key organizational and managerial perspectives in most institutions of society especially in the school, the church, the university, the congress, military units, and the corporate sector, all of which are led by the elite.

Modern organization theory is theoretically deeply rooted in the behavioral and social sciences disciplines. Its evolutionary development depends on the use of scientific methodology whose investigatory techniques help to generate data for analysis, explanation, prediction and control. In its entirety, organization theory concerns organizational behavior. Organizational behavior is the behavior of organizations that is rooted in socioeconomic and political history, local, regional, national and global synergy and heterogeneous cultural and technological traditions. These organizational traditions are complex and perennially mechanomorphic experiences of the ecologically determined rationale of organizational structures. In their classical evolution (1850-1920) under the old management paradigm, they "transcended ideologies, defined political structures, ignored moral dictums, overturned social orders, and unraveled the fabric of tradition" (Klein, 1998). In America in particular, they uniquely formalized American values in ways that have been instrumental for the emergence of a new center for the diverse social order and the consumer economy.

Traditionally, the world view of organizations sees them as economic and legal entities that are created by groups of people with common goals. Organizational engineers or promoters invest their own resources for the realization of the organization's mission. These organizations are systems of production whose goal is to serve the interests of stakeholders rather than shareholders. The organizations operate in a dynamically economic, social and political environment where they rationalize and actualize the diversity of their interests. In this milieu, organizational theorists tend to examine the contingent match within and among organizational structure, size, environment, technology, resources and design processes. On the one hand, strategic management theorists who analytically rather than synthetically tend to align organizational resources with environmental demands in order to reach objectives by optimizing investor returns—define organizations by using the mission to achieve objectives. On the other hand, organizational behavior and human resource management theorists concentrate on the uses and functions of organizational personnel.

Scholars who use cultural theories of the organization examine organizational values, belief, assumptions, norms and mores in order to conceptualize that organizational ideas as cultural constructs. In miniature, though these scholarly theorists, who rigorously and intelligently analyze organizations ignore the ecological impact on the organizations, they demonstrate that behavior is inseparable from people's culture. The ecological environment which is largely internal and external to organizational rationality, consensus, and consensual functionalism is ecoculturally more deterministic than otherwise.

Based on traditional organizational paradigm, classical theory, human relations theory and contingency theory help to explain further that organizational behavior can be analyzed, explained, predicted and controlled multitheoretically. By doing so, their functions, structures and processes are distilled. For instance, the classical theory of division of work, delegation of authority, chain of command and span of control was the "parent theory" from which both the human relations and the contingency theories were distilled.

The essence of these economic, legal, and cultural organizations that are ecocentrically, ideologically and hegemonically constructed is to maintain and perpetuate the economic stability thesis. These organizations have empirically established moral and ethical codes. They use professionally specialized, technical, legal and bureaucratic rationality whose ideology of structuralism, functionalism and consensus illogically tends to, for dialectical and culturally embedded mainstream reasons, marginalize Marxist, feminist and humanist emancipatory values and practices. The latter theoretical models are marginalized and considered irrelevant by theorists of the traditional management paradigm for their holier-than-thou attitude, poststructural negativism, nonuniversal essentialism, potential for generating conflict, and rigorous and apparently archaic and elitist but leftist intellectual elements of the critical and radical humanist tradition. Though some ideals of critical humanism may be rhetorically and intellectually noble, their utopian and strong leftist theoretical and practical underpinnings renders them empirically invalid during a post-Cold War era that is dominated by conservative, liberal and organizationally established theoretical models of the traditional management paradigm. However, if the humanist theoretical tradition can show that some of the nobility of its ideals could be adopted by the modern organizations to create the impetus for dialogue aimed at liberating employee efforts, motivation, morale, commitment and creative and superior elements such as the ones that are found in Keiretsu, then traditional management and theoretical models of the conservative and liberal establishment should be wisely advised to "take the risks" and learn to incorporate the best elements of organizational theory and management from the left. After all, no man or woman is an island in the "modern village" of our global economy. If fairness can be restored into "laws and principles of capitalism, historically and culturally anchored gender stereotypes, and the domination of professional and managerial ideologies" (Alvesson and Willmott, 1992, p. 449) of oppression, then the humanist tradition which liberated society from its myopic and unscientific feudal past and the negative elements of religious and cultural dogma, for the liberation of the human spirit, would have served its cause well.

Between the Neolithic Period (8,000 BC) and the 14th century, A.D., scientific and technological advancements were used to view human organizations and their progress in organismic terms. Every living thing including humankind was viewed as an organism. Knowledge, life, science and technology were dominated by religious orthodoxy, dogmatic and authoritarian regimes and the practice and emulation of tradition rather than innovation. Organizational forms and institutional life were antiquated unscientific and archaic. Any innovations available took centuries or millennia to diffuse and be adapted for change.

With dawn of the 15th century, elements of modernity emerged. The modern period spans to the 19th century. This period was enlightened by the mathematical and scientific and economic works of Isaac Newton, Rene Discartes, Karl Marx, Adam Smith, Lenin, and Charles Darwin. Their scientific, economic and political ideas became popular in mathematics, economics, physics, chemistry, biology and industrial technology. Knowledge, religion and culture were not only influential and theoretically and empirically empowered with these scientific breakthroughs, but the scientific knowledge became the intellectual property that was technologically instrumental for the evolution of modern industrial and professional organizations. Mechanistic Taylorism, rationality and sociological functionalism were the dominant theoretical paradigms of the age.

The 20th century was enlightened by the scientific theories of quantum physics and the theory of relativity. These theories view organizational and institutional life to be dynamic and interrelated experience in which there are no absolutes. Since there are no absolutes, post-modern human relations, organizational humanism, diversity and organizational culture are bounded by rationality in decision making and organizational operations. Existing problems can be solved through experimentation, research and development, consulting and counseling services of experts and specialists. The solutions to problems require organizations to be managerial in terms of participatory management, use of networks and high-technology to process information, theories and assumptions in order to discover and solve existing and systemic problems of the post-structural, post-modern, and post-industrial world. This indicates that though modern organizations and their management theories, structures and practices are elaborate, highly specialized, equipped and complex systems, their origin is deeply rooted in past evolutionary development, characterized by historical traditions of scientific, literary, and ascientific nature.

Within this evolutionary and historico-scientific tradition, the cumulative effects of premodern, modern and post-modern management theory and practice have gradually evolved to the current state of advancement. In the light of this thought, the ecocentric management paradigm could have critical implications for management theory and practice. In this new paradigm, corporate leaders are likely to experience a variety of strategic, tactical and operational concerns. For instance, there is difficulty as to how they will redesign and triangulate their business portfolios in order to reach "ecological limitations and bottlenecks." What will be the human resources needs of the ecosystem-based organization? How will ecological costs change the financial structure of investment projects and firm or corporate competitiveness? What will be the market potential for ecosystem and ecofriendly technologies? These are questions to be answered by future researchers, planners, engineers, scientists and bureaucratic and corporate elite. These elites will deal with markets that are characterized by six types of capitalism. First, there is the corporatist countries of northern Europe. Second, there are countries where unionism is decentralized and its power is declining particularly in the U.S. and the U.K. Third, there are countries with strong syndicalist traditions especially France, Italy and Euro-Latin American countries. Fourth, the East Asian block particularly Japan, Taiwan, and Korea where government and employers (corporations) are the main actors because their unions are relatively weak and decentralized (Jacoby, 1997). Fifth, the Chinese economy, which is the third largest in the world, is a form of state-driven and autocratic corporatism in which unions, if there are any, have no influence. The sixth is the Third World in which purchasing power is dominated by the authoritarian political and economic elite who are externally regulated by the World Bank, IMF and the NGOs; workers have no place in decision making of any kind.

The new management paradigm of the postindustrial and global society will practically and theoretically challenge the vestiges of traditional management theory and practice. That challenge will be a concern with how managers will triangulate the business environment in order to strategize, redesign, abandon theoretical anthropocentricism, for its functionalism and organismic inferiority, application of ecocentricism, to deal with ecobiospheric externalities, to rationalize new organizational missions (both constructive and destructive) and how to make operational, accounting, marketing, finance, administration and human resource management, both in the profit-making and nonprofit making sectors, more ecocentric.

In other words, according to Lawler (1997), the new organization, which is metaphorically viewed as a hologram, will be a socially constructed entity that is characterized by purpose, cultures, practices and people and comparable to this book's four-legged metaphor of the base, engine, consciousness and superstructure.

During the 1990s, the Third Industrial Revolution called the Information Age was born "from the womb of failed traditional industrialism" which is still alive but weak. The characteristics of this revolution are:

1. Global interconnectedness through electronics and communications.
2. Technological innovation and diffusion.
3. Speedy, dramatic and radically unpredictable inventiveness.
4. Change seems to take place in geometric rather than arithmetic progressions and configurations.
5. New knowledge has become critical, deterministic and valuable.

6.   Globally-based industrial restructuring.
7.   Potential for the evolution of a new "wild" center of economic, geopolitical, scientifically-oriented and strategico-technologically induced dominance.

In other words, we are living in a turbulent, risky and unpredictable environment where each organization can design strategies for its own competitive advantage; involvement is the only source of effective control; every employee should be valued in order to add desirable value; lateral rather than vertical processes are the source of organizational effectiveness; organizations are designed to become ecocentrically product and customer-centered rather than capitalistically structured and profit-centered; and finally, where culturally rooted and effective leadership which motivates people, uses technology and encourages the use of participatory decision-making and integrates chaotic theory with constructive change to eliminate pathologically and technically regressive situations. In other words, effective leaders manage "strategy, people, rewards, structure, processes" (Lawler, 1997, p. 180) in the light of the organization's mission.

Implications for Private, Public and Nonprofit and Academic Organizations

The post-communist world has become freer, more relatively democratized and autonomously ethnicized. A new world order has emerged from the ruins of old one which was dominated by two superpowers (U.S. and USSR) and which used the traditional management paradigm. This new world order is being forged to reflect a high degree of regional competitiveness in terms of (NAFTA, WTO, APEC, EU, OPEC, and the less organized, technologically challenged and socioeconomically poor nations of the Third World). All these regional powers competitively converge on the global idea for geopolitical and economic supremacy and technological suzerainty. They are rivals which conduct turbulent trade and diplomatic wars to offset each other from the dominance in world markets or compromise to accept each other's regionally perceived hegemonic controversy. The centripetal rather than the centrifugal dynamics of global regionalism are the magnetic forces which spirally continue to propel regionalism for diffusion and infusion into the global idea. The same forces rather than military or ideological overtones, are and will be the fulcrum for globally based regional coexistence and equilibrial global balance of power.

Zhao (1997) has analyzed theories of regionalism and regime formation in Asia between the Opium War (1842) and now. The analysis was constructed to observe periodic changes in the regional balance of power. Having used a close reading of East Asian history and international relations, he sensitively generalized that the West destroyed Chinese suzerainty in the region, and forcefully influenced Japanese modernization and economic imperialism in the last 55 years. Within the same period, China has used its ancient Confucian philosophy, the state-centric authoritarianism and Mao-centric revolutionary rhetoric for urbanized villagization and managerially state-centric capitalistic industrialization. Such measures have helped China to liberate itself economically culturally and environmentally. While China and Japan have regionally emerged as stable and rising economic powers, the United States, which lacks understanding, in terms of cultural, contextual, and neorealist aspirations of Easterners, has become the suffering looser. The competitive dynamic which governs the three world giants is what Zhao calls the power competition.

Within this analytical arena, Katzenstein and Shiraishi (1997) have systematically observed East Asian regionalism. They argue that the evolution of informal network structures are so typically regionalized and regionalistic that they lack satisfactory Western explanations that are made clear by "rational choice, realist nor functionalist" theoretical models. Both Katzenstein and Shiraishi conclude that by asserting that the mode of East Asian cooperative regionalism can be explained by using an historico-institutionalist paradigm rather than the Weberian, Marxist, or Eurocentric models. It is conceptualized that Japan could if she would, influence Asia to accept open regionalism as the new formula for the region's competition in the global arena. This formula will be consistent with U.S. norms and continuous geostrategic involvement. Such a strategy for continuous engagement is based on intellectually analyzed historical perceptions of Japan's pre-War and post-War ideological visions of regionalism in Asia. Conclusively, evidence suggests that a new Asianist and establishmentarian ideology has been existing in Japan since the 1970s. The ideological vision expresses itself within Japanese liberal framework. Like its pre-1940 ideological proponents, it seeks to utilize intellectual elitism to help Japan in constructing and rationalizing Japan-based regional hegemonic stability. Inevitably, the Asiatic hegemonic stability thesis tends to provoke the U.S. whose ethnocentric construction of Japanese-Asian "otherness" creates spasmodic and continuous economic conflict which the ideology revaberatively sustains.

Though the United States' ascendant penetration in the capitalist world is deeply rooted, its viability will be challenged by a relatively independent but rising Sinocentric East Asian system which has regained some influence in Taiwan, Korea and Japan. Given this scenario, this triangular relationship will be moderated by Japan whose position and behavior is critically important in determining the unknowable predictions of the impending and monstrous calculus. Though corporate elite has reduced the influence of bureaucratic power in Japan and elsewhere in the region largely due to the fact that the state coordinates economic penetration, this coordination has not worked well in the last 12 years. However, networked Japanese state-centric and business entrepreneurs have effectively extended the same network of informal structures overseas in order to promote and coordinate the realization of export-oriented strategies in Southeast Asia.

Shiraishi (1997) has demonstrated that Japanese cartoonist imagery shown in literature, TV, movies and video games are evidences of Japan's growth in cultural, political and economic leadership whose methodology of production needs to be emulated. However, U.S. hegemonic influence and Japan's economic "omnipresence" are being challenged by the proliferation of the vibrant and expanding Chinese domestic trade in the Asiatic region as a political economy. The evolution of China's domestic and regional politico-economic influence is the springboard for its global enterprise and politico-strategic reintegration.

Other scholars have asserted that Japan is secure as it continually relies on U.S. hegemony. However, Japanese have shown a strong interest in having their own independent security system which is complementary to and exclusive of the current U.S.-Japan strategic alliance. Due to the need for the promotion of inclusive multilateralism and regional economic and security concerns, Japanese weak and timid rather than bold and aggressive domestic leadership is unable to generate definite and insolvent strategic vision. Just like other regions, East Asia is determined by a variety of historical, institutional (organizational), cultural, technological and internationally established structural forces. Within these forces, Japan has built itself an asymmetrical and market-driven infrastructure for maritime economic interdependence within the region. In this arena, U.S. politico-military and economic structures and the Chinese trade networks overlap those of Japan with which they parallel. This market-driven and politico-economically coordinated and integrated East Asia is the result of interesting synergistic factors whose fusion has produced what you see. Such is the politico-economic and global climate in which twenty-first century organizations will be expected to function. The European German-based eternal contradiction tends to undermine its potential which the U.S. always tries to enhance.

Implications for Private Organizations

In order to survive in this turbulent and risk-driven environment, twenty-first century private organizations must strive to achieve strategic flexibility (Hitt, Keats and DeMarie, 1998) necessary for more powerful competition in a "new economic terrain." Since about one-third of the U.S. corporate labor force is unskilled and on part-time, temporary or on contract (Pfeffer, 1994) the corporations should initiate an aggressive and global policy of campaigning to recruit intelligent, skilled and trainable labor force. On the average, U.S. firms use $1,800 annually for training and development of 8% of the new employees. "British firms invest approximately $5,000 annually for training one employee. German firms invest $7,500 per employee annually. European firms train 20% of all the new employees while the same training is given to 74% of all new Japanese employees (Useem, 1996). Given this reality, U.S. corporations and firms should make knowledge and skills training a basic ingredient of their planning schemes (Singh, 1995). The firms should establish cooperative and compatible partnership for sharing capital and risk in an ecocentric and global environment. Evidence indicates that strategic and cooperative partnership is difficult to maintain at the international level due to incompatibility. As a result, about 60% of strategic and cooperative alliances fail annually (Dacin et al., 1997). This requires firms to have visionary and effective leaders. Such leaders should create multiethnic and multicultural management teams. Visionary leaders will place emphasis on the employment of better management skills which require nonlinear learning and thinking (Jackofsky, 1989). To compete in the new competitive landscape will require management leaders who have vision and courage for disrupting the equilibriated status quo in order to redesign, adapt, reposition and strengthen the corporation.

Implications for Academic Organizations

Colleges and universities are likely to initiate programs where machines that "learn, diagnose, adapt, reconfigure, and recreate themselves" (Hitt, 1998, p. 220) will be a major learning strategy. Such machines will be driven by the human touch or sound rather than by the Windows or Netscape Navigator. The machines will be more user friendly, accessible, and convenient for ecological sustainability. These "intelligent systems will eliminate the boundary that exists between training and performance. For instance, people will be online without stopping and virtual reality will come to the classrooms (Flynn, 1997). Machines will replace some of the teachers' tasks.

Most research that has been done in the past is based on disciplinary orientation. Currently, emphasis is shifting towards multidisciplinary thinking. This approach is used at Santa Fe Institute. Multidisciplinary thinking will be a more effective tool for studying the evolution, operation and adaptation of organizations particularly where complex, chaotic, and dramatic organizational changes take place. Research effort will collaboratively be conducted by global academics, scholars and scientists. Complex situations, concerns and pathologies will be analyzed through nonlinear thinking strategies which will require the utilization of sophisticated research designs.

Given the fact that the United States is increasingly becoming more and more interdependent rather than dominant due to stiff competition for resources from other regions of the world, and from each state and within each state in the union, some schools especially in business and other fields will close down. More schools will be opened up globally and some of those schools will have more power and prestige than many schools in the U.S. Other global centers of academic excellence will attract bright and eminent scientific scholars and scientists because of their economic power, funding ability and ample opportunity. This diffusion of top faculty talent, some of whom will be found in less prestigious institutions, will be one of the major characteristics of the New Millenium (Cannella and Paetzold, 1994). The numbers, sizes and quality of schools external to North America, especially in Asia and Latin America will grow (Arnst and Browder, 1997). In its entirety, the nature of management education and other scientific disciplines will become global for the purpose of maintaining an ecocentrically sustainable environment. Given the tempo of development of business schools outside the U.S., North America will not be the center of business education in the world. The center will be somewhere else in the globe.

Currently, there are 1,400 corporate universities in the U.S. and many more will proliferate. Public funding for higher education will continue to decrease as other priorities consume more money. New technology will be used to market global distance education. A small number of

U.S. business schools have become globally entrepreneurial. Since tenure will be an issue for controversy on U.S. campuses, elitist scholars and researchers will hardly be contained on the U.S. campuses.

In this kind of competitive and challenging environment, universities must do four things for their own survival. First, every university needs to plan strategically and realistically in order to become part of the world in which we live, move and have our being. U.S. institutions of higher learning should eliminate their "phobia about otherness" by learning to become scholarly and scientific communities solving locally and globally based problems of their interdependent communities, nations, and peoples. American scholars and scientists should join scholarly and scientific research based bodies with their counterparts in other countries and universities for the purpose of scholarly and scientific exchange of knowledge. Some business schools and organizations have established similar links with Asiatic and Hispanico-Iberian institutions.

Second, excellent institutions of higher learning should promote research and use it for effective teaching and community service. They should use the results of the research to formulate policy, initiate processes rather than shortcuts through which problems are solved and use global but relevant strategies to solve local problems when local solutions to problems are insolvent. Continuous learning, research production and involvement in community affairs are the correct springboard strategies for enhancing innovative and adaptive change. These institutions should use basic and applied research, create new knowledge and use it for community and organizational empowerment.

Third, academic organizations should evaluate and see whether the services they provide are effective in fulfilling their members' needs. They should encourage them to continuously use technology. Finally, academic institutions should plan strategically in order to compete effectively. They should pursue cooperative research strategies, and alliances that are mutually beneficial. Above all, for organizations to succeed in carrying out their unique missions, they will be expected to be ecocentric, flexible, and horizontal rather than vertical, focused rather than muddling through, externally networked rather than narrowly and internally dynamic, and become nonlinear in order to challenge ineffective management and operational traditions of paradoxical disequilibria.

This book has been constructed by drawing from a rich variety of theoretical models and intellectual traditions. In doing that, its construction transcends the narrowness of ideological and theoretical confinements by which they are narrowly boxed in certain intellectual traditions. For instance, the United States uses population ecology, the British use structuralism, the French concentrate on using post-modernism and deconstruction while longitudinal case studies are popular with the Scandinavian intellectual traditions. Scholars should not undermine the notion that contradictory intellectual traditions, unless they are juxtaposed to evolve new theories, should enhance consistency. Using these traditions for analysis of social problems, issues and trends is risky. Risk, as it was discussed earlier, like control, is "integral to technological innovation and constitutes the paradox of postindustrialization" (Nelson and Cooperman, 1998, p. 583).

References

Adler, N.J., and D. Izraeli. 1994. *Competitive Frontiers: Women Managers in a Global Economy.* Cambridge, MA: Blackwell

Aktouf, O. 1992. Management and theories of organizations in the 1990s: Toward a critical radical humanism. *Academy of Management Review* 17, 3: 407-431.

Allenby, B.R. 1993. *Industrial Ecology.* New York: Prentice Hall.

Alvesson, M., and H. Willmott. 1992. On the idea of emancipation in management and organizational studies. *Academy of Management Review* 17, 3: 432-464.

Anderson, J. 1999. Factories have history of dodging EPA. *Edmond Evening Sun,* March 14: 6A.

Archier, G., and H. Serieyx. 1984. *L'enterprise du 3e Type (The Corporation of the 3rd Kind).* Paris: Seuil.

Bandy, C. 1994. *The Age of Paradox.* Boston: Harvard Business School Press.

Beck, U. 1992a. *Risk Society: Towards a New Modernity.* Newbury Park, CA: Sage.

Bell, D. 1975. *The Coming of Post-Industrial Society.* New York: Basic Books.

Bernstein, P.L. 1992. *Capital Issues: The Impossible Origins of Modern Wall Street.* New York: Free Press.

Berquist, W. 1993. *The Post-modern Organization: Mastering the Art of Irreversible Change.* San Francisco: Jossey-Bass.

Boje, D.M., and R.F. Dennehy. 1993. *Managing in the Post-modern World: America's Revolution Against Exploitation.* Dubuque, IA.: Kendall Hunt.

Brown, L.R. 1990. *State of the World 1990.* Washington, D.C.: Worldwatch Institute.

Buell, L. 1995. *The Environmental Imagination: Thoureau, Nature Writing and the Formation of American Culture.* Cambridge, MA: Harvard University Press.

Burrell, G., and G. Morgan. 1979. *Sociological Paradigms and Organizational Analysis.* London: Heinemann Educational Books.

Caille, A. 1989. *Critique de la Raison Utilitaire, Manifeste du MAUSS (A Critical Look at Utilitarian Intelligence—The MAUSS Manifesto).* Paris: La Decouverte.

Calvez, J.Y. 1970. *La Pensee de Karl Marx (The Thinking of Karl Marx).* Paris: Seuil.

Campbell, A., and S. Young. 1991. Creating a sense of mission. *Long-Range Planning* 24: 10-20.

Cannella, A.A., and R.L. Paetzold. 1994. Pfeffer's barriers to the advance of organizational science: A rejoinder. *Academy of Management Review 19*: 331-341.

Cans, R. 1990. *Le Monde Pouberlle (The World as a Garbage Can).* Paris: First.

Carroll, A.B. 1979. A three-dimensional conceptual model of corporate social performance. *Academy of Management Review* 4: 497-505.

Carson, R. 1962. *Silent Spring.* Greenwich, CT.: Fawcett.

Clark, M. 1989. *Ariadne's Thread.* New York: St. Martin's Press.

Clarke, L. 1989. *Acceptable Risk. Making Decisions in a Toxic Environment.* Berkeley: University of California Press.

Commoner, B. 1990. *Making Peace with the Planet.* New York: Pantheon Books.

Costanza, R. 1992. *Ecological Economics.* New York: Columbia University Press.

Couch, S., and S. Kroll-Smith. 1991. *Communities at Risk.* New York: Peter Lang.

Crosby, P.B. 1979. *Quality Is Free.* New York: McGraw-Hill.

Crozier, M. 1989. *L'enterprise a l'ecoute (The Listening Cooperation).* Paris: InterEditions.

Dacin, M.T., et al. 1997. Selecting partners for successful international alliances: Examination of U.S. and Korean firms. *Journal of World Business* 32: 3-16.

Daly, H.E. 1977. *Steady State Economics.* San Francisco: Freeman.

Daly, H., and J. Cobb. 1989. *For the Common Good.* New York: Beacon Press.

David, F. 1989. How companies define their mission. *Long-Range Planning* 22: 15-24.

Davis, J. 1991. *Greening Business.* Oxford, England: Basil Blackwell.

Deng, Y. 1997. *Promoting Asian-Pacific Economic Cooperation: Perspectives from East Asia.* New York: St. Martins.

Donaldson, G. 1994. *Corporate Restructuring: Managing the Change Process from within.* Boston: Harvard Business School Press.

Douglas, M., and A. Wildavsky. 1982. *Risk and Culture.* Berkeley: University of California Press.

Dumont, R. 1988. *Un Monde Intolerable. Le Liberalisme en Question (An Intolerable World: A New Look at Liberalism).* Paris: Seuil.

Duncan, A.J. 1974. *Quality Control and Industrial Statistics.* Homewood, IL: Irwin.

Ehrlich, P., and A. Ehrlich. 1991. *The Population Explosion.* New York: Touchstone.

Etzioni, A. 1989. *The Moral Dimension: Toward a New Economics.* New York: Free Press.

Etzioni, A. 1988. *The Moral Dimension.* New York: Free Press.

Evans-Pritchard, E.E. 1950. *Social Anthropology.* London: Cohen and West.

Fagenson, E.A, ed. 1993. *Women in Management: Trends, Issues, and Challenges in Managerial Diversity.* Newbury Park, CA: Sage.

Fay, B. 1987. *Critical Social Science.* Cambridge, England: Polity Press.

Fletcher, B.R. 1990. *Organization Transformation Theorists and Practitioners: Profiles and Themes.* New York: Praeger.

Flynn, J. 1997. British Telecom: Notes from the ant colony. *BusinessWeek,* June 23: 108.

Fromm, E. 1976. *To Have or To Be?* New York: Harper and Brothers.

Frosch, R.A., and N.E. Gallapoulos. 1992. Towards an industrial ecology. In *The Treatment and Handling of Waste,* ed. A.D. Bradshaw. London: Chapman.

Getis, A., J. Getis, and J.D. Fellman. 1998. *Introduction to Geography.* Boston: McGraw-Hill.

Giddens, A. 1990. *The Consequences of Modernity.* Stanford, CA: Stanford University Press.

Goldstein, R.L., and J.K. Shorr. 1991. *Demanding Democracy after Three Mile Island.* Gainsville: University of Florida Press.

Gramsci, A. 1979. *Selections from the Prison Notebooks.* New York: International Publishers.

Habermas, J. 1989. *A Theory of Communicative Action.* Boston: Beacon Press.

Habermas, J. 1984. *The Theory of Communicative Action.* Vol. 1. Boston: Beacon Press.

Habermas, J. 1971. *Toward a Rational Society.* London: Heinemann.

Harris, D.H. 1998. *Organizational Linkages: Understanding the Productivity Paradox.* Washington, D.C.: National Academy Press.

Heale, M.J. 1997. The revolting American elites: Christopher Lasch and his enemies. *Journal of American Studies* 31, 1: 103-114.

Heibroner, R. 1980. *Marxism For and Against.* New York: Grove Press.

Heibroner, R. 1970. *The Worldly Philosophers.* New York: Washington Square Press.

Heyel, C., ed. 1982. *The Encyclopedia of Management.* New York: The Free Press.

Hitt, M.A. 1998. Twenty first-century organizations: Business firms, business schools, and the academy. *Academy of Management Review* 23, 2: 218-224.

Hitt, M.A., B.W. Keats, and S.M. Marie. 1998. Navigating in the new competitive landscape: building strategic flexibility and competitive advantage in the 21st century. *Academy of Management Executive.*

Hoffman, A. 1997. *From Heresy to Dogma: An Institutional History of Corporate Environmentalism.* San Francisco: New Lexington Press.

Horkheimer, M., and T. Ardono. 1947. *The Dialectics of Enlightenment.* London: Verso.

Jacoby, M. 1997. *The Workers of Nations.* New York: Oxford University Press.

Katzestein, P.J., and T. Shiraishi. 1997. *Network Power: Japan and Asia.* Ithaca, N.Y.: Cornell University Press.

Klein, M. 1998. The flowering of the Third America: The making of an organizational society, 1850-1920. *Journal of American History.*

Kolakowski, L. 1987. *Histoire du Marxisme (A History of Marxism). Vol. 1.* Paris: Fayard.

Kolakowski, L. 1968. *Toward a Marxist Humanism.* New York: Grove Press.

Kovacic, B. 1998. *New Approaches to Organizational Communication.* Albany: State University of New York Press.

Krimsky, S., and D. Golding. 1992. *Social Theories of Risk.* Westport, CT: Praeger.

Lash, S. 1993. Reflexive modernization: The aesthetic dimension. *Theory, Culture and Society* 10, 1: 1-23.

Lawler, III, E.E. 1997. *From the Ground Up: Six Principles for Building the New Logic Corporation.* San Francisco: Jossey Bass.

Lee, J.A. 1980. *The Gold and the Garbage in Management Theories and Prescriptions.* Athens: Ohio University Press.

London, M. 1998. *Career Barriers: How People Experience Overcome and Avoid Failure.* Mahwah, N.J.: Lawrence Erlbaum Associates.

Lovelock, J.F. 1979. *Gaia, a New Look at Life on Earth.* New York: Norton.

Lucaks, G. 1971. *History and Class-Consciousness.* Cambridge, MA.: Cambridge University of Press.

Luhmann, N. 1990. Technology, environment, and social risk: A systems perspective. *Industrial Crisis Quarterly* 4, 3: 223-232.

Marcuse, H. 1964. *One-Dimensional Man.* Boston: Beacon Press.

McNeill, J. 1989. Strategies for sustainable economic development. *Scientific American,* September: 155-165.

Miller, D., et al. 1996. The evolution of strategic simplicity: Exploring two models of organizational adaptation. *Journal of Management* 22, 6: 863-887.

Minc, A. 1990. *L'argent Fou (Mad Money).* Paris: Grasset.

Mingle, J.R., and Associates. 1989. *Challenges of Retrenchment.* San Francisco: Jossey-Bass Publishers.

Mintzberg, H. 1994. *The Rise and Fall of Strategic Planning: Reconceiving Roles for Planning, Plans, Planners.* New York: The Free Press.

Minztberg, H. 1989. *Inside of Our Strange World of Organizations.* New York: Free Press.

Mitroff, I.I., and T. Pauchant 1990. *We're So Big and Powerful Nothing Bad Can Happen to Us.* New York: Birch Lane Press.

Morgan, G. 1986. *Images of Organizations.* Beverly Hills, CA: Sage.

Naess, A. 1987. *Ecology, Community and Lifestyle: Ecosophy.* Cambridge, England: Cambridge University Press.

Nelkin, D. 1979. *Controversy: Politics of Technical Decisions.* Newbury Park, CA: Sage.

Nelson, J.I., and D. Cooperman. 1998. Out of utopia: The paradox of postindustrialization. *The Sociological Quarterly,* 39, 4: 583.

Nye, J.S. 1998. Finding ways to improve the public's trust in government. *The Chronicle of Higher Education,* January 16: B6-B7.

Osterman, P. 1996. *Broken Ladders: Managerial Careers in the New Economy.* New York: Oxford University Press.

Ouchi, W.G. 1981. *Theory Z: How American Business Can Meet the Japanese Challenge. Reading, MA: Addison-Wesley.*

Parsons, T. 1982. *On Institutions and Social Evolution.* Chicago: University of Chicago Press.

Pauchant, T.C. 1998. *In Search of Meaning: Managing for the Health of Organizations, Our Communities and the Natural World.* San Francisco: Jossey-Bass Publishers.

Perrow, C. 1984. *Normal Accidents: Living with High Risk Technologies.* New York: Basic Books.

Pestel, E. 1988. *L'homme et la Croissance, Rapport au Club de Rome (Man and Growth: Report to the Club of Rome).* Paris: Economica.

Peters, T. 1987. *Thriving on Chaos.* San Francisco: Knopf.

Peters, T., and N. Austin. 1985. *A Passion of Excellence.* New York: McGraw-Hill.

Peters, T., and R. Waterman. 1982. *In Search of Excellence.* New York: Harper and Row.

Pfeffer, J. 1994. Competitive advantage through people. *California Management Review* 36, Winter: 9-28.

Prasad, P., A.J. Elmes, and A. Prasad. 1997. Managing the organizational melting pot: Dilemmas of workforce diversity. Thousand Oaks, CA: Sage.

Preston, L., ed. 1985. *Research in Corporate Social Performance.* Greenwich, CT: JAI Press.

Rao, H. 1998. Caveat emptor: The construction of nonprofit consumer watchdog organizations. *American Journal of Sociology* 103, 4: 912-961.

Roy, W.G. 1997. *Socializing Capital. The Rise of the Large Industrial Corporation in America.* Princeton, N.J.: Princeton University Press.

Sartre, J.P. 1976. *Critique of Dialectical Reason. Vol 1.* London: New Left Books.

Sartre, J.P. 1966. *Being and Nothingness.* New York: Washington Square Press.

Sartre, J.P. 1948. *Existentialism and Humanism.* London: Methuen.

Schoenberger, E. 1997. *The Cultural Crisis of the Firm.* Cambridge, MA: Basil Blackwell.

Scott, R.W. 1981. *Organizations: Rational, Natural and Open Systems.* Englewood Cliffs, N.J.: Prentice Hall.

Short, J.F., and L. Clarke. 1992. *Organizations, Uncertainties and Risk.* Boulder, CO: Westview.

Shrivastava, P. 1995. Ecocentric management for a risk society. *Academy of Management Review* 20, 1: 118-137.

Sievers, B. 1993. *Work, Death and Life Itself: Essays on Management and Organization.* Berlin-New York: de Gruyter.

Singh, K. 1995. The impact of technological complexity and interfirm cooperation on business survival. *Academy of Management Best Papers Proceedings:* 67-71.

Slovic, P. 1987. Perception of risk. *Science* 236: 280-285.

Smith, D. 1992. *Business and the Environment.* London: Chapman.

Smith, J.A. 1991. *The Idea Brokers: Think Tanks and the Rise of the New Policy.* New York: Free Press/Macmillan.

Toffler, A. 1980. *The Third Wave.* New York: William Morrow.

Useem, M. 1996. Corporate education and training. In *The American Corporation Today, ed.* C. Kaysen, 292-326. Oxford, England: Oxford University Press.

World Commission on Environment and Development. 1987. *Our Common Future.* New York: Oxford University Press.

Young, O.R. 1997. *Global Governance: Drawing Insights from the Environmental Experience.* Cambridge, MA: MIT Press.

Zhao, S. 1997. *Power Competition in East Asia.* New York: St. Martin's Press.

Author Index

Subject Index

570, 572-573, 575-576, 597, 603, 605, 608, 629, 640-642, 652, 654, 670

group cohesiveness 54, 92

group membership 54, 92, 259

hakimiyya 64

heartless 74

hegemony 63, 282, 318, 331, 570, 581, 665, 681

heritage 53, 64, 223, 433

Herzberg's two-factor theory 456-459

hicrarchy 14, 30, 37, 40, 53, 84, 93, 122, 181-182, 185-186, 192, 208-209, 224-225, 252, 256, 258-260, 300-301, 346, 395, 426-427, 442, 452-453, 455-459, 461, 474, 481, 483, 485, 487, 494, 500, 537, 561-562, 625, 664

hierarchy of needs 453, 457-458, 461

high-technology politics and standards 427-429

hijrah 66

holocaust 74

Holy Bible 71

homeostasis 98, 127

homogeneity 54, 59, 62, 100, 250, 253, 279-280, 300

homophily 231-236, 239

human relations 3-4, 6, 8, 22, 83, 87, 90, 93-95, 105-106, 112, 209, 297, 306, 336, 370-370-371, 433, 515, 647, 675, 677

humanism 6, 14, 22, 83, 87, 94-95, 112, 129, 209, 542, 657-664, 666, 676-677

humanistic 3, 8-9, 13, 96, 105-106, 208, 280, 286, 288,

333, 487, 490, 500, 580, 655, 657, 659-660, 662, 664, 672, 675

hypodermic needle 343, 345

idealism 89

ideology 50, 52, 66, 101, 193, 228, 270-271, 323, 327, 331-332, 335-336, 357, 399, 437, 441, 564, 577, 592, 596, 622, 656, 665, 669, 673-675, 680-681

ignorance 21, 63, 89, 257, 260, 399, 410, 632, 650

IMF 207, 575, 576, 678

imitation 47, 49

impersonality 34

importation 49

industrialization 2, 43, 45-46, 50, 101, 252, 650, 680

inferiority 54, 678

informal organization(s) 8, 11, 83, 91-92, 95, 128

inhumanity 63

insecurity 50, 243, 270, 639

institutionalism 201, 203

institutionalization 97, 101, 205, 523, 568, 581

institution(s) 8-9, 43, 48, 51, 55-56, 66, 68, 74, 98, 109, 135, 187, 219, 221, 247, 251-252, 272-273, 277, 279-280, 282-283, 286, 312, 316, 321, 328-334, 336, 358, 363, 367, 378, 390, 396-397, 424, 429, 434, 437, 442, 488, 490, 501, 505, 516, 520, 534, 563, 567, 575-576, 579-581, 620-624, 627, 629, 632, 638, 641-642, 649, 652-656, 664, 674, 683-684

Author Biographical Sketch

Dr. Meshack M. Sagini distinctively passed the Cambridge Ordinary and Advanced level (diploma) examinations in 1966 and 1968, respectively. He also studied at the University of East Africa Dar-es-Salaam for two years, Middle East College in Beirut, Lebanon, for two years, Newbold College, England, for one year, and University of the West Indies for another year and received a B.Ed. (Honors) in History and a minor in Education. In 1982, he received a Masters degree in higher education management from Andrews University in Michigan. In 1987, he was awarded a Ph.D. in college and university administration from Michigan State University after submitting his doctoral dissertation on strategic planning and management. In 1997, Dr. Sagini completed a postdoctorate course in management and public policy from Oklahoma State University.

Professionally, Dr. Sagini is an educator with twenty years' experience in the teaching profession. Initially he worked as a teacher in elementary and high schools in Kenya during the late nineteen-sixties and early nineteen-seventies. He also served as a deputy high school principal for three years at Nyanchwa in Kisii, Kenya. In 1979/80 academic year, Dr. Sagini became a lecturer in the College of Education at the University College of the West Indies, Jamaica. At the same time, he intermittently worked as a sales manager for a Norwegian corporation (Norskbokforlaget) for eight summers (1976-83). Before the completion of his doctorate from Michigan State University, Dr. Sagini worked in the University as a Swahili language tutor for three years and as Graduate Administrative Assistant for one year. Between 1989 and 1991, he served as an assistant professor of

Social Science and Organizational Psychology at Lansing Community College in Michigan. Since 1991, he has worked a Langston University as Assistant and Associate Professor of History, Political Science, and Management Studies.

Since 1999, Dr. Sagini has actively participated in public policy research and analysis. He has published several articles in professional journals and two books. His first book, *The African and the African-American University: A Historical and Sociological Analysis,* was published in 1996. This book was written while Dr. Sagini was an adjunct associate professor at the University of Oklahoma (1994 and 1995). The present volume, *Organizational Behavior,* is his second book.

Dr. Sagini has traveled extensively by visiting four continents (he has not been to Australasia and Oceania). He has been awarded a variety of honors, the best of which was given in the summer of 1997 by the American Political Science Association (APSA) for excellence n teaching. He is a member of several professional organizations including the American Political Science Association, Oklahoma Political Science Association, Oklahoma League of Political Scientists, Mid-America Alliance for African Studies, Association for International Development, African Professionals Association, and Langston University National Alumni Association. Above all, Professor Sagini is an interdisciplinary scholar who writes proposals for funding, presents scholarly papers in professional organizations and teaches with power, interest, and excitement.